THE ARCHITECTURE OF DEMOCRACY

OXFORD STUDIES IN DEMOCRATIZATION

Series Editor: Laurence Whitehead

. . . .

Oxford Studies in Democratization is a series for scholars and students of comparative politics and related disciplines. Volumes will concentrate on the comparative study of the democratization processes that accompanies the decline and termination of the cold war. The geographical focus of the series will primarily be Latin America, the Caribbean, Southern and Eastern Europe, and relevant experiences in Africa and Asia.

OTHER BOOKS IN THE SERIES

The Architecture of Democracy

Constitutional Design, Conflict Management, and Democracy

. . . .

Edited by
ANDREW REYNOLDS

OXFORD
UNIVERSITY PRESS

OXFORD
UNIVERSITY PRESS

Great Clarendon Street, Oxford OX2 6DP

Oxford University Press is a department of the University of Oxford.
It furthers the University's objective of excellence in research, scholarship,
and education by publishing worldwide in

Oxford New York

Auckland Bangkok Buenos Aires Cape Town Chennai
Dar es Salaam Delhi Hong Kong Istanbul Karachi Kolkata
Kuala Lumpur Madrid Melbourne Mexico City Mumbai Nairobi
São Paulo Shanghai Singapore Taipei Tokyo Toronto
and an associated company in Berlin

Oxford is a registered trade mark of Oxford University Press
in the UK and in certain other countries

Published in the United States
by Oxford University Press Inc., New York

British Library Cataloguing in Publication Data

Data available

Library of Congress Cataloging in Publication Data

The architecture of democracy: constitutional design, conflict management, and
democracy/edited by Andrew Reynolds.
p. cm.—(Oxford studies in democratization)
Includes bibliographical references and index.
1. Democracy. 2. Democratization. 3. Comparative government.
I. Reynolds, Andrew, 1967– II. Series.
JC421 .A73 2002 321.8—dc21 2001052058

ISBN 0–19–924645–9
ISBN 0–19–924646–7 (Pbk.)

1 3 5 7 9 10 8 6 4 2

Typeset by Hope Services (Abingdon) Ltd.
Printed in Great Britain by
Biddles Ltd., Guildford & King's Lynn

eight feet

Front row (left to right): Ashutosh Varshney (Notre Dame), Brendan O'Leary (London School of Economics), Fran Hagopian (Notre Dame), René Antonio Mayorga (CEBEM), Bolivia), Bernard Grofman (UC Irvine), Andrew Reynolds (Notre Dame), Carina Perelli (United Nations Electoral Assistance Department), John Carey (Washington University, St Louis), Steven Levitsky (Harvard).

Second row: Olga Shvetsova (Washington University, St Louis), Timothy Frye (Ohio State), Nigel Roberts (Victoria University of Wellington), Rotimi Suburu (Woodrow Wilson Center), Brij Lal (Australian National University), Cheryl Saunders (University of Melbourne), Giovanni Sartori (Columbia), David Stuligross (Michigan).

Third row: Tony Messina (Notre Dame), Vincent Maphai (President's Review Commission, South Africa), Alfred Stepan (Columbia), Bereket Selassie (UNC Chapel Hill), Robert Johansen (Notre Dame), Rein Taagepera (UC Irvine), José Antonio Cheibub (Yale).

Fourth row: Scott Mainwaring (Notre Dame), Arend Lijphart (UC San Diego), Pippa Norris (Harvard), Jørgen Elklit (Aarhus, Denmark), Richard Soudriette (International Foundation for Election Systems), Donald Horowitz (Duke), Ruth Lapidoth (Hebrew University, Jerusalem), Juan Linz (Yale), John Packer (OSCE High Commission on Minorities).

Back row: Fred Riggs (Hawaii), William Liddle (Ohio State), Steven Solnick (Columbia), Michael Coppedge (Notre Dame), Dieter Nohlen (University of Heidelberg, Germany).

Photograph by Tom Weis

Preface

This book was born out of an enjoyable gathering of over 100 academics and practitioners in the electoral and constitutional field at the University of Notre Dame in December 1999. That conference was in turn the spin-off of a personal wish I had had a few years earlier. Since 1991 I had spent most of my professional life immersed in the study of elections and constitutions in emerging democracies. After the dramatic growth of that field, which came along with the third wave of democratization, I wanted to set up a group photograph of the most influential and articulate protagonists in the discipline: my own mentors, and the scholars who had actually penned the books which I had spent so much time poring over. I also wanted to gather together the new wave of scholars in the field who were doing both cutting-edge quantitative work and sophisticated social science studies of the relationships between institutional design and democratic endurance. The photograph, which appears on page vi and is the real reason for this book, doesn't include everyone I had hoped for. Robert Dahl and Matthew Shugart were unavoidably occupied, Larry Diamond was—unusually—travelling, and Notre Dame's own Guillermo O'Donnell was being honoured at the inauguration of the new Argentinian president: a more than reasonable excuse. But what is remarkable about the photograph—and the conference itself—is how many of the icons of the field were on the stage. Arend Lijphart and Donald Horowitz were mischievously set up as the two opposing team captains and played their roles with grace and aplomb. Alongside them Giovanni Sartori, Juan Linz, Al Stepan, Dieter Nohlen, Bernie Grofman, Rein Taagepera, and Scott Mainwaring brought a huge weight of innovative inquiry and practical experience to the proceedings. Brendan O'Leary, Pippa Norris, Brij Lal, Cheryl Saunders, Nigel Roberts, René Antonio Mayorga, Vincent Maphai, Bereket Selassie, Jørgen Elklit, Bill Liddle, and Ruth Lapidoth came from far and wide, representing the collected wisdom of five continents. Then there were the Young Turks: the East European troika of Shvetsova, Solnick, and Frye; the Latin American foursome of Carey, Coppedge, Chiebub, and Levitsky; and the 'rest of the world' team of Varshney, Suberu, and Stuligross. Finally, we were joined by representatives of the practitioners who work with elections and the design of institutions on a day-to-day basis in the reality of emerging democracies: Carina Perelli, head of the United Nations' Electoral Assistance Division; Richard Soudriette, director of the International Foundation for Election Systems; John Packer, legal adviser to the OSCE's High Commissioner on Minorities; and Peter Manikas, senior executive at the National Democratic Institute.

The weekend was a great success, and I believe the chapters presented in this book capture not only the spirit of enthusiasm for new avenues of investigation prevalent at the conference but the feeling that constitutional design can, if appropriately considered, be a lever of great good for very troubled societies. It may also be worth noting an interesting anthropological phenomenon from the conference. Participants were compelled to endure a 'Reynolds Quiz Night' which covered subjects both trivial and obscure. It was fascinating to see how academics turn into very different animals when a competitive test of their breadth is on the table and how alliances forged in battle cross traditional boundaries. Lijphart, Sartori, and Stepan were as one gathering together a huge team around them—Norris, O'Leary, Solnick among them—attempting, without shame, to crush all comers. This they did, but not without the serendipity of Lijphart's mother being born in Paramaribo— thus giving them the capital of Suriname. Grofman and Elklit took a bolder path leading a team of only three. Their honour only managed to achieve the position of dead last in the final rankings which didn't stop them spending a fair part of the rest of the conference trying to prove with mathematical voting models that technically they had actually won the quiz.

However, I digress. The Constitutional Design 2000 conference and this resulting book would not have become a reality without the support of Julius Ihonvbere of the Ford Foundation and grant makers at the United States Institute of Peace; along with Notre Dame supporters, Seamus Deane of the Keough Institute for Irish Studies, Bob Wegs of the Nanovic Institute for European Studies, the Henkles fund for visiting scholars, and the Institute for Scholarship in the Liberal Arts. But perhaps the greatest debt goes to Scott Mainwaring, director of the Kellogg Institute at the University of Notre Dame, who believed in this protect from the beginning and made that belief manifest through consistent support, advice, and backing. There are few institutes which could have pulled off such an exercise so successfully and it is testament to Scott Mainwaring that Kellogg continues to develop as one of the pre-eminent centres of international studies in the world today. If this work does little else, it will at least allow the undergraduate and graduate students of the future to actually put faces to the names of writers they are assigned: indeed, some of them look less intimidating when you see them in person.

Andrew Reynolds
March 2001

.

·················

Contents

·················

....

List of Figures

....

List of Tables

Contributors

Andrew Reynolds is Assistant Professor in the Department of Political Science at the University of North Carolina, Chapel Hill. He received his MA from the University of Cape Town and his Ph.D. from the University of California, San Diego. Reynolds has worked for the United Nations, the International Institute for Democracy and Electoral Assistance (IDEA), and the Organization for Security and Cooperation in Europe (OSCE) and has served as a consultant on issues of electoral and constitutional design for Angola, Burma, Fiji, Guyana, Indonesia, Jordan, Liberia, Northern Ireland, Sierra Leone, South Africa, and Zimbabwe. His interest in Africa has concentrated on democratization and electoral politics, political consequences of electoral systems, and political theory of representation, for which he has received research awards from the US Institute of Peace, National Science Foundation, and Institute on Global Conflict. Among his publications are *Electoral Systems and Democratization in Southern Africa* (1999); *Election '99 South Africa: From Mandela to Mbeki* (1999); and *Elections and Conflict Management in Africa* (1998), co-edited with T. Sisk.

Katharine Belmont is a Ph.D. candidate in the Department of Government and International Affairs at the University of Notre Dame. Her interests include ethnic conflict, the politics of nationalism, and democratization in plural societies. She is currently working on her dissertation comparing nationalism, democratic development, and problems of ethnic conflict in Malaysia and Sri Lanka.

José Antonio Cheibub is Assistant Professor of Political Science at Yale University. He is co-author of *Democracy and Development: Political Institutions and Material Well-Being in the World, 1950–1990* (2000). He has published in several edited volumes and in journals including *World Politics*, *Comparative Political Studies*, *Politics and Society*, *The Journal of Democracy* and *Studies in Comparative International Development*. Cheibub is currently working on a project about the political and economic performance of presidential and parliamentary regimes, and on another about the relationship among economic performance, elections, and alternation in power in democratic regimes.

Larry Diamond is a Senior Fellow at the Hoover Institution and a professor by courtesy of political science and sociology at Stanford University. He is also co-editor of the *Journal of Democracy* and co-director of the National Endowment for Democracy's International Forum for Democratic Studies in Washington, DC. Diamond is the author of *Developing Democracy: Toward Consolidation* (1999), *Promoting Democracy in the 1990s* (1995), and *Class, Ethnicity and Democracy in Nigeria* (1988). His recent co-edited books include *The Global Divergence of Democracies* (2001), *Democratization in Africa* (1999), and *The Self-Restraining State: Power and Accountability in New Democracies* (1999). Diamond's current research examines the comparative dynamics of democratic consolidation in developing countries and post-communist states; democratic consolidation in Taiwan; and public opinion in East Asian democracies.

Timothy Frye is Assistant Professor of Political Science at Ohio State University. He has contributed chapters to several edited volumes and published in *Comparative Political Studies*, *The American Economic Review*, and *Post-Soviet Affairs* and is the author of *Brokers and Bureaucrats: Building Market Institutions in Russia* (2001). His research has been supported by grants from the Social Science Research Council, the Institute for the Study of World Politics, the Kosciuszko Foundation, Columbia University, and the University of Rochester. He received his Ph.D. from Columbia University in 1997.

Yash Pal Ghai is the Sir Y. K. Pao Professor of Law at the University of Hong Kong. After degrees at Oxford and Harvard he was admitted as a Barrister to the Middle Temple in 1962. Since that time he has taught constitutional law in Africa, the United States, and the United Kingdom. He is the editor of *2000 Autonomy and Ethnicity: Negotiating Claims in Multi-ethnic States* (2000), *The Hong Kong Bill of Rights: A Comparative Perspective* (1993) and *Put our World to Rights: Towards a Human Rights Policy for the Commonwealth* (1991). Ghai is the co-author of *The Law, Politics and Administration of Decentralisation in Papua New Guinea* (1993).

Donald L. Horowitz is James B. Duke Professor of Law and Political Science at Duke University. He has published extensively on legal institutions and on ethnic relations, most recently in *The Deadly Ethnic Riot* (2001) and in earlier works, such as *Ethnic Groups in Conflict* (1985 and 2000) and *A Democratic South Africa?*

Constitutional Engineering in a Divided Society (1991). He has served widely as a consultant on topics related to state structure, electoral systems, and constitutional design. Horowitz has received fellowships from the National Science Foundation, Woodrow Wilson Center, Council on Foreign Relations, Rockefeller Foundation, Social Science Research Council, Guggenheim, the National Humanities Center, and the Carnegie Corporation, and has been a visiting fellow at Cambridge University, the University of Chicago Law School, Bellagio Study Center (Italy), the University of Canterbury School of Law (New Zealand), the London School of Economics, and the University of Malaya (Malaysia). Among other honours, his book *A Democratic South Africa?* received the APSA's Ralph J. Bunche Award for the best book on ethnic and cultural pluralism. In 1993 he was elected a Fellow of the American Academy of Arts and Sciences.

Brij V. Lal is Professor of History and Director of the Centre for the Contemporary Pacific at The Australian National University, having previously taught Pacific and world history at the universities of the South Pacific, Papua New Guinea, and Hawaii. He was a member of the Fiji Constitution Review Commission whose report formed the basis of the 1997 multiracial constitution. A Fellow of the Australian Humanities Academy, he was appointed an Officer of the Order of Fiji for his distinguished contribution to the public life of Fiji. In 2000, the Fiji Millennium Committee chose him as one of 70 people who had shaped the course of 20th century Fiji, citing him as the 'most distinguished Fiji-born academic of his generation'. Among Lal's many books are *Broken Waves: A History of the Fiji Islands in the 20th century* (1992), *Another Way: The Politics of Constitutional Reform in Post-coup Fiji* (1998), and *Chalo Jahaji: On a Journey of Indenture through Fiji* (2000). He is currently editing the Fiji volume for the *British Documents on the End of Empire* series.

R. William Liddle is Professor of Political Science at Ohio State University and a specialist on south-east Asian, particularly Indonesian, politics. Recent scholarly publications include *Leadership and Culture in Indonesian Politics* (1996); 'The Islamic Turn in Indonesia', *The Journal of Asian Studies* (August 1996); 'Coercion, Co-optation, and the Management of Ethnic Relations in Indonesia', in Michael Brown and Sumit Ganguly (eds), *Government Policies and Ethnic Relations in Asia and the Pacific* (1997); 'Indonesia's Unexpected Failure of Leadership', in A. Schwarz and J. Paris (eds), *The Politics of Post-Suharto Indonesia*

(1999); and 'Indonesia's Democratic Opening', *Government and Opposition* (1999). His Indonesian-language writings have been collected in *Islam, Politik, dan Modernisasi* (1997). He is currently conducting a major survey of voting behavior in the 1999 Indonesian parliamentary election.

Arend Lijphart is Research Professor Emeritus of Political Science at the University of California, San Diego. He has taught at the University of Leiden in the Netherlands and at the University of California, Berkeley, and has held visiting and research appointments at Harvard University, the Institute of Advanced Studies of the Australian National University in Canberra, the Netherlands Institute for Advanced Study in Wassenaar, Nuffield College (Oxford), the Science Center Berlin, the Rajiv Gandhi Institute for Contemporary Studies in New Delhi, the Institute for Advanced Studies in Vienna, and the Universities of Canterbury and Auckland in New Zealand. He has been a Guggenheim Fellow and a German Marshall Fund Fellow. He is the author of more than 20 books; the best-known are *Democracy in Plural Societies* (1977 *Democracies* (1984), *Power-Sharing in South Africa* (1985), *Parliamentary versus Presidential Government* (1992), *Electoral Systems and Party Systems* (1994), and *Patterns of Democracy* (1999). He was the founding editor of the *European Journal of Political Research* and he has served on the editorial boards of several other professional journals such as *American Political Science Review*, *The British Journal of Political Science*, *Comparative Political Studies*, *Electoral Studies*, and *The Journal of Democracy*. Lijphart has served as president of the American Political Science Association and vice-president of the International Studies Association. He is a member of the American Academy of Arts and Sciences, the British Academy, and the Netherlands Academy of Sciences.

Scott Mainwaring is Director of the Kellogg Institute for International Studies and Eugene Conley Professor of Government. His latest books are *Rethinking Party Systems in the Third Wave of Democratization: The Case of Brazil* (1999); *Presidentialism and Democracy in Latin America* (1997); and *Building Democratic Institutions: Party Systems in Latin America* (1995, coedited).

Pippa Norris is Associate Director of the Shorenstein Center on the Press, Politics, and Public Policy and she teaches at Harvard University's John F. Kennedy School of Government. Her research compares political behaviour. She has published more than two dozen books and the most recent include *Comparing Democracies 2* (2002), *Digital Divide: Information Poverty, Civic Engagement and the Internet Worldwide* (2001), *Britain Votes 2001* (2001), *A Virtuous Circle* (1999), *On Message* (1999), and *Critical Elections* (1999). Her current research has focused on a new book, *Count Every Voice: Political Participation Worldwide* (Cambridge University Press, 2002). Norris co-edits *The Harvard International Journal of Press/Politics* and has served on the Council of the American Political Science Association, the Executive of the International Political Science Association, and the Political Science Association of the UK.

Brendan O'Leary is Professor of Political Science and Head of the Department of Government at the London School of Economics and Political Science. In 2001–2 he will be Visiting Professor of Political Science at the University of Pennsylvania. He is the author, co-author, or co-editor of twelve books, including *The Asiatic Mode of Production* (1989), *The Politics of Ethnic Conflict Regulation* (1993), *Explaining Northern Ireland* (1995), and *Right-Sizing the State* (2001). With John McGarry he wrote *Policing Northern Ireland: Proposals for a New Start* (1999) which had a significant impact on the deliberations of the Patten Commission on police reform. Since 1988 he has been a constitutional adviser to Irish, British, and American politicians and public officials working on the Irish peace process, and in recent years he has worked for the European Union and the United Nations on and constitutional initiatives in Somalia, and for the UK's Department of International Development in Kwa-Zulu Natal. O'Leary is currently co-authoring an intellectual biography of the late Ernest Gellner.

Bereket Habte Selassie is William. E. Leuchtenbug Professor of African Studies and Law at the University of North Carolina, Chapel Hill. He was the Chair of the Constitutional Commission of his native Eritrea and adviser to the Constitutional Commission of Nigeria. He has written extensively on law and politics, including; *The Executive in African Governments* (1974), *Conflict and Intervention in the Horn of Africa* (1980), and *Eritrea and the United Nations* (1989). He has just completed *Constitution Making in Eritrea*, which is due to be published in 2001.

Olga Shvetsova is Assistant Professor of Political Science and Research Assistant Professor of Political Economy at Washington University in St. Louis. She received her Ph.D. in Social Sciences from the California Institute of Technology in 1995 and has conducted research at the University of California, Irvine. Shvetsova was a faculty associate on a National Science Foundation grant to study electoral and party systems and bargaining. Recent publications include articles in *Electoral Studies, Communist and Post-Communist Studies, Constitutional Political Economy, Law and Society Review*, and *The Journal of Democracy*.

Steven L. Solnick is Associate Professor of Political Science and Program Coordinator for Russian Studies at Columbia's Harriman Institute. He is the author of *Stealing the State: Control and Collapse in Soviet Institutions* (1998), as well as numerous articles on Soviet and post-Soviet affairs. Solnick received his Ph.D. in 1993 from Harvard University. He has been a National Fellow at the Hoover Institution at Stanford University, a Research Fellow at the Kennan Institute in Washington, DC, a Fulbright Scholar at Moscow State University, and a Marshall Scholar at Oxford University. He is currently researching political dynamics between the central and regional administrations of the Russian Federation and is incorporating that research into a book on the origins, structure, and stability of federal states and other territorial polities.

David Stuligross is South Asia editor at the journal *Asian Survey* and South Asian Nuclear Dialogue coordinator at the Nautilus Institute. He was awarded a Ph.D. in May 2001 by the University of California, Berkeley, for a dissertation titled 'A Piece of Land to Call One's Own: Multicultural Federalism and Institutional Innovation in India'. Recently published articles include 'Federalism and Development in Northeast India', *Alternatives* (Fall 1999), and 'Elections and Governance in India', *Current History* (December 1999).

Rotimi T. Suberu is a Senior Lecturer in Political Science at the University of Ibadan, Nigeria, where he received his Ph.D. in 1990. Professor Suberu has been a fellow in the Jennings Randolph Program of the United States Institute of Peace and is currently a fellow in the International Studies Division of the Woodrow Wilson Center in Washington, DC. Suberu is the author of *Ethnic Minority Conflicts and Governance in Nigeria* (1996), *Public Policies and National Unity in Nigeria* (1999), and *Conflict and Federalism in Nigeria* (forthcoming), and he is a contributing co-editor of *Federalism and Political Restructuring in Nigeria* (1998).

Rein Taagepera is Professor Emeritus in the School of Social Sciences, University of California, Irvine, and Professor Emeritus of Political Science of Tartu University (Estonia). He received a Ph.D.

in Solid State Physics from the University of Delaware, followed by a Masters degree in International Relations. At Tartu University he was founding dean of the School of Social Sciences. Professor Taagepera has published over 80 research articles and numerous books. Books in English include *The Finno-Ugric Republics and the Russian State* (1999); *Estonia: Return to Independence* (1993); *Seats and Votes: The Effects and Determinants of Electoral Systems* (1989) with M. Shugart; *The Baltic States: Years of Dependence 1940–1990* (1993) with R. Misiunas; and *Softening without Liberalization in the Soviet Union: The Case of Jüri Kukk* (1984). During Estonia's liberation struggle (1988–1992) Taagepera gave public speeches, made televised appearances, and wrote over 100 articles for the press on democratization issues. In 1990 he was elected to the Estonian Congress, in 1991 elected by the Congress to the Estonian Constitutional Assembly, and in 1992 received 23 per cent of votes in Estonian presidential elections.

Ashutosh Varshney is Associate Professor of Political Science and Director of the Center, Center for South Asian Studies, at the University of Michigan. He is a former associate professor of government at Harvard and Columbia Universities. He obtained his Ph.D. in political science from the Massachusetts Institute of Technology under Myron Weiner's direction. He has written extensively on democracy, political economy, and ethnic conflict. His publications include *Ethnic Conflict and Civic Life: Hindus and Muslims in India* (2000), *India in the Era of Economic Reforms* (1999), co-edited with Jeffrey Sachs; *Democracy, Development and the Countryside: Urban-Rural Struggles in India* (1995); and *Beyond Urban Bias* (1993).

Introduction

Institutional Design, Conflict Management, and Democracy

Katharine Belmont, Scott Mainwaring,
and Andrew Reynolds

During the 1990s, macro institutional rules, the clay for constitutional designers, have become key in the efforts to expand democracy and reduce violent conflicts in divided societies, that is, societies with sharp ethnic, religious, national, and/or linguistic cleavages. Scholarship on the interrelationship among institutional design, conflict management, and democratic development has burgeoned. Eminent scholars such as Robert A. Dahl, Donald Horowitz, Arend Lijphart, Juan J. Linz, Dieter Nohlen, Giovanni Sartori, and Alfred Stepan have posited that political institutions affect the prospects for democratic endurance. These scholars have differed widely, however, as to their prescriptions for which institutions best foster democracy in divided societies. Although this volume does not purport to resolve the issue of which institutions are most propitious, it provides an overview of the debate on institutional design and conflict management in divided societies and offers new perspectives on this subject.

In December 1999 pioneers of the discipline reviewed the state of democratic design at the conference *Constitutional Design 2000* held under the auspices of the Kellogg Institute at the University of Notre Dame. The chapters in this book, with the exception of Yash Ghai's, are based on papers presented at that meeting. Along with representatives of the international policy-making and diplomatic communities, participants explored which political institutions can help process conflict through democratic means. This book addresses the following questions:

- How have political institutions acted as levers of conflict management in divided societies in the twentieth century?

- Can constitutions of divided or plural societies be engineered to help bring about intercommunal accommodation and strengthened democracy?
- How do political institutions affect the trajectory of democratization in divided societies?

The challenge of further expanding democracy in the contemporary world rests significantly on divided societies. Therefore, the challenge of expanding democracy globally cannot be separated from that of managing conflict democratically in plural societies.

Our rationale for focusing on institutional rules as a way of managing conflict democratically in divided societies is threefold. First, in the short term, structural, cultural, and international factors that affect the prospects for building a stable democracy cannot be changed profoundly. With rapid economic growth, poverty can be alleviated significantly in a decade or a generation, but not in a few years. In any case, rapid economic growth does not automatically transform values in a way that mitigates religious, national, or ethnic conflicts, which often prove more intractable than class conflict in the face of economic growth. Authoritarian political heritages and cultures may give rise to more democratic values, but this process usually takes a substantial time. International factors that support democracy may change in a relatively short time period, but democratic actors in a divided society undergoing a process of democratization can hardly set about changing the international environment in the short term. In contrast, political institutions can be altered to increase the likelihood of managing conflict democratically. Thus, to the extent that democrats can proactively take steps to improve the prospects for democracy, institutional design is one of their key tools.

Second, democracy can be sustained even in countries that face daunting structural and cultural obstacles: poverty, inequality, and deep ethnic, national, or religious divisions. Structural and cultural factors help shape prospects for democracy, but a healthy dose of optimism regarding the potential for democracy under even adverse conditions has emerged. If in earlier periods of the twentieth century democracy was generally limited to a couple dozen countries that enjoyed auspicious social, economic, and cultural conditions (Dahl 1971; Lijphart 1984), after the beginning of the 'third wave of democratization' (Huntington 1991) in 1974, and especially after the collapse of the Soviet empire beginning 1989, many countries with less propitious conditions have embarked on democratic—or at least semi-democratic—experiments (Diamond 2000). This situation poses the question of how best to foster democracy under these more difficult conditions. Institutional engineering is one possibility.

Third, it is probably in divided societies that institutional arrangements have the greatest impact. In societies that do not have profound ethnic, religious, or national cleavages, institutional choices are probably less relevant for democratic stability because they do not readily skew the political system to favour or adversely affect different groups. In contrast, in divided societies institutional design can systematically favour or disadvantage ethnic, national, and religious groups. To provide but one example, a first-past-the-post electoral system may systematically and profoundly disadvantage even large minority groups, especially those that are geographically dispersed. Under these conditions, building loyalty to the system is likely to prove more difficult.

This book is predicated on the idea that institutional design makes a difference in how effectively political leaders are able to manage conflict democratically in divided societies. We make little effort in this volume to address the important question of how much political institutions matter relative to structural, international, or cultural factors or to the quality of democratic leadership. Assessing the importance of political institutions relative to other factors is an engaging issue, but it falls outside the domain of this project.

We share the belief of most contributors to this volume that political institutions significantly shape the logic and outcomes of democratic politics (Thelen and Stenmo 1992). Moreover, we share the viewpoint that some political institutions are more likely than others to successfully facilitate conflict management in divided societies. Nevertheless, two caveats are in order.

First, although this volume emphasizes how political institutions can be designed to help facilitate conflict management in divided societies, some political conflicts are intractable in the short term. It would gravely misread the message of this book to conclude that institutional design is a panacea that could enable all countries to establish thriving democracies.

Second, we do not to prescribe a uniform institutional design that should be applied in all divided societies. The purpose of this book is not to prosyletize. We believe that some mechanisms of power sharing, hence some institutions to promote what Lijphart (1984; 1999) called 'consensus democracy', are important in most divided societies. But the 'best' way of achieving power sharing may vary across cases. For example, in principle we favour parliamentary over presidential systems, but in cases of undisciplined parties, a reasonable case can be made for semi-presidential or presidential systems (Sartori 1997; Shugart and Carey 1992). A decentralized federal system has powerful advantages in a territorially large and diverse divided society, but the drawbacks of federalism may outweigh the advantages in smaller and less divided societies. Rather than resolving what specific institutions are best in divided societies, this book is intended to sharpen an existing debate about that issue.

Seeing Constitutional Design as a Matrix of Institutions

A considerable amount of work has been done in recent decades on the relationship between *specific* political institutions, conflict management, and democracy. For example, a decades-old debate has addressed whether proportional representation—or other electoral systems that facilitate multipartism—or single-member plurality districts are more conducive to democracy. Similarly, since the 1980s the merits and perils of presidentialism have received renewed attention.

Although good scholarship on specific institutions is also invaluable, this book is predicated on the belief that it is useful to analyze political institutions as a holistic package. Political institutions interact in complex ways; such interactions are not fully recognized by studies that address more specific and delimited themes. For example, the fear that presidentialism may produce highly majoritarian results, meaning that the winner of the presidential election thoroughly dominates the political system (Linz 1994), is attenuated when legislatures are powerful, when the state is federal, and when the electoral system encourages a dispersion of legislative seats (Mainwaring and Shugart 1997b). With such institutional arrangements, there are many 'veto players' (Tsebelis 1995), and presidents need to constantly negotiate their preferences. Conversely, the fear that presidentialism may foster deadlock diminishes—albeit potentially at a high cost in terms of democratic accountability—when the legislature is weak, the state is unitary, and the electoral system encourages limited dispersion of legislative seats. Under these conditions, presidents typically encounter little effective opposition.

The book has three parts. Part I presents arguments by two seminal figures in the field—Donald Horowitz and Arend Lijphart—about the relationship between political institutions and democracy in divided societies. Part II examines specific institutions and their impact on democracy in divided societies: presidentialism and parliamentarism, electoral systems, and federalism and decentralized systems. Part III offers six key country studies.

Part I: Institutional Design in Divided Societies: An Overview

Because of our desire to focus on institutional combinations, the book begins with synthetic chapters by two seminal thinkers in the field of institutional design and conflict management: Donald Horowitz and Arend Lijphart. In Chapter 1 Donald Horowitz examines the relevance of integrative and consociational theories to current debates. He pushes the debate beyond the traditional question of what is the best design for divided societies to ask how designs are implemented in practice, noting that the nuances of the process of constitution-making often frustrate attempts to implement any unified theory of institutional design. Thus his chapter challenges scholars to address the obstacles and consequences of design processes as well as institutional outcomes.

In Chapter 2 Arend Lijphart returns to familiar themes of consociational theory and examines its characteristics and relevance in light of twentieth-century evidence. He maintains that executive power-sharing and group autonomy are the best options for divided societies and suggests that consociational theory continues to provide answers to many of the substantive debates in the constitutional design literature.

In Chapter 3 Olga Shvetstova analyzes the transitional development of the countries of east and central Europe in the ten years following the fall of communism in that part of the world. She focuses on the effects of majoritarian and power-sharing institutions on party-system formation in the transitional phase to assess how such institutions influence long-term chances for democratic consolidation. She concludes that the focus of design should not necessarily be on long-term consequences of institutions but instead on institutions' expected ability to promote or inhibit short-term processes of coalition making within a transitional party system.

Part II: Presidentialism, Federalism and Decentralization, and Electoral Systems

After beginning with these architectonic debates about institutional design and conflict management in divided societies, the book examines three more specific institutions—but in the context of part of the overall institutional structure. These three institutions are among the most important that affect democratic conflict management in divided societies.

Executive type: Is a given system of government presidential or parliamentary?

Recent debates over constitutional design in fledgling democracies have often highlighted parliamentary democracy as preferable to presidentialism (for example, Linz and Valenzuela 1994). Critics of presidentialism have claimed that this system of government fosters zero-sum competition, easily promotes deadlock between the executive and the legislative branches, and encourages personalist leadership (Linz and Valenzuela 1994). The scholarly opinion in favour of parliamentarism, however, has not been reflected in practice; nearly all new democracies have had elected presidents with varying degrees of political power (Shugart and Carey 1992; Lijphart 1992; Mainwaring and Shugart 1997a). Some scholars have attempted to move beyond the straight dichotomy between presidentialism and parliamentarism (Duverger 1980; Shugart and Carey 1992; Sartori 1997). In the 1990s a few scholars (Horowitz 1991) advocated presidentialism, and others pointed to some advantages it offers (Mainwaring and Shugart 1997b; Shugart and Carey 1992), leading to a new turn in the debate. For the most part, the literature on presidentialism and parliamentarism has not addressed the question of conflict management in divided societies,[1] which is central to our concerns.

A related concern revolves around different forms of parliamentarism. The debate over whether it is better to entrench coalition power-sharing governments of national unity or allow for single-party administration has been contentious. Some scholars see oversize unity cabinets as an essential part of transitional power-sharing arrangements in a divided society (Lijphart 1977; Sisk 1996; Reynolds 1999a, b), while others have seen mandated governments of national unity as detrimental to the evolution of 'normal' politics within a new democracy (Jung and Shapiro 1995; Maphai 1996).

In this volume, Timothy Frye (Chapter 4) and José Antonio Cheibub (Chapter 5) address the debate about presidentialism and parliamentarism. Timothy Frye examines how some presidents in post-communist countries have been able to expand their powers while others have not. He offers an explanation that stresses the

---

[1] Lijphart (1994) and Linz (1994) are exceptions: both advocate parliamentarism.

need to examine economic development along with political developments in post-communist countries. He concludes that the dual transformation weakens institutions and creates a patron-client relationship between individual politicians and 'economic winners' while frustrating the development of strong institutions.

In Chapter 5, José Antonio Cheibub asks if the institutional explanations of democratic instability in Latin America, primarily focused on the weaknesses of presidentialism, stand up to empirical investigation. He finds that neither divided government nor deadlock negatively affects the longevity of presidential regimes. While acknowledging that there may be reasons why presidential regimes are less desirable than parliamentary ones, he rejects the traditional assumptions of divided government, deadlock, and the dangers of the separation of powers as reasons for preferring parliamentarism.

The constitutional nature of the state: What are the advantages and disadvantages of federal and unitary political systems for managing conflict democratically in divided societies? What are the benefits and drawbacks of symmetrical and asymmetrical federations?

When communal groups are geographically concentrated within the nation-state, some type of federalism or decentralization is often promoted as the key to reassuring minorities that they will have some political influence. Federalism or decentralization enables religious, national, and ethnic groups that are a minority at the national level to have significant input or even to govern at the local or State level. For this reason, federalism has advantages in divided societies. Some of these advantages can be reproduced through decentralization in formally unitary systems. On the other hand, Linz (1997) and Stepan (1997), among others, have also pointed to some drawbacks to federalism. Federal arrangements, both symmetrical—in which different sub-national governments have roughly similar powers—and asymmetrical—in which some units of the federation have more autonomy and authority—have also been discussed by Horowitz (1985) and Ghai (2000c).

Two chapters address the relationship between decentralization, federalism, and conflict management in divided societies. In Chapter 6, Yash Ghai notes that three important constitutional mechanisms for the inclusion of minority voices—autonomy, inclusive representation, and power sharing—in their asymmetry can be seen as compromising the form of the classical liberal state.

Nevertheless, Ghai traces the trend away from uniformity in institutional structures and highlights the power of such innovative mechanisms for conflict management.

In Chapter 7, Steven Solnick examines the process of bargaining between central and regional powers in states in transition. His analysis suggests that even when an optimal constitutional design is on the agenda, participants in the transition process may be unable to agree on it *ex ante* and/or unable to enforce it *ex post*.

Electoral systems: what are the advantages and disadvantages of different electoral systems for managing conflict under democracy?

Electoral systems have long been recognized as one of the most important institutional mechanisms because they structure the arena of political competition. They offer incentives for political actors to behave in certain ways by rewarding them with electoral success. They can reward particular types of behaviour and place constraints on others (Sartori 1997; Lijphart 1977; 1984; Horowitz 1991; Reynolds 1993; 1999a; Reilly 1997). Electoral systems also affect the number of parties that win seats, the degree of proportionality between seats and votes, and the type of representation (Taagepera and Shugart 1989; Lijphart 1994a; Cox 1997). By shaping the number of parties in a party system, electoral rules affect whether a democracy is toward the majoritarian or consensus end of Lijphart's (1984; 1999) famous continuum; in a majoritarian democracy, the winners take all, whereas a consensus democracy has strong mechanisms of power sharing. Thus electoral systems are one of the chief levers of constitutional engineering in mitigating conflict within divided societies.

From Lewis (1965) to Reynolds (1999a), the weight of literature has posited that majoritarian—winner-takes-all—electoral systems are particularly inappropriate for divided societies because they typically under-represent minorities and generate zero-sum competitions. However, Horowitz (1991), Sartori (1997), and Reilly (1997) have questioned this conventional wisdom arguing that under certain demographic conditions multi-ethnic coalition can by encouraged by more majoritarian electoral systems.

In this volume, Pippa Norris (Chapter 8) and Rein Taagepera (Chapter 9) address the relationship between the electoral system and conflict management in divided societies. Pippa Norris uses survey data from the second release of the Comparative Study of Electoral Systems (CSES) to, among other things, assess the consociational claim that proportional representation party-list systems produce greater minority ethnic group satisfaction than do straight majoritarian systems. She finds this to be unconfirmed by the initial data.

In Chapter 9 Rein Taagapera questions the very possibility of defining electoral systems. He recommends that scholars and advisers should keep electoral rules simple and that countries in transition should maintain an electoral system for at least three cycles before making any changes.

Part III: Country Studies

Part III includes six case studies of divided societies that have gone through, or are going through, important processes of constitutional design and engineering. These country studies illuminate how political institutions have shaped conflict management in specific efforts to build democracy. They share with Part I an effort to see political institutions as an interactive combination rather than focusing on specific institutions.

The book as a whole, and Part III in particular, focuses mainly on countries that meet three conditions. First and foremost, we selected divided—or plural—societies that offer interesting lessons in terms of constitutional design. Second, most of these countries are new democracies, although Part III includes a case study of India as an example of a mainly successful older democracy that has endured despite deep ethnic, religious, and linguistic cleavages. Finally, most are also poor or intermediate-income countries because of our decision to concentrate on more recent democracies. We have, however, included a chapter on Ireland, which despite having attained a high standard of living in recent decades remains one of the world's most fascinating and troubling cases of conflict management in the context of deep religious and national conflicts.

In Chapter 10 Brij Lal outlines the process of the Constitutional Review Commission in Fiji and credits the inclusive nature of the Commission with the wide understanding and eventual acceptance by a broad support base for Fiji's dramatic institutional changes. In Chapter 11 Brendan O'Leary describes developing institutions in Northern Ireland as a blend of consociational and integrative majoritarian theory. He argues that timing more than altruism or statesmanship explains the capacity for agreement. In Chapter 12 Bereket Selassie, like Lal, stresses the importance of public inclusion in the decision-making process. He outlines a long process of civic education and public discussion in Eritrea preceding constitutional change and

stresses the importance of public ownership of institutional change
in producing stable outcomes.

The fourth most populous nation in the world, Indonesia has
recently joined the fold of countries struggling to build democracy in
the context of a divided society. In Chapter 13 William Liddle examines three stages of the recent crisis in Indonesia: the challenge to
Suharto, the regime legitimacy crisis following Suharto's resignation, and the challenge of electing a new president after the June
1999 general election, and concludes that the resolution of each crisis moved Indonesia one step closer to democratization. Though
many factors played a role in resolving each crisis phase, Liddle
shows how the acceptance and use of the 1945 constitution allowed
Indonesian elites to maintain a familiar set of rules during a time
of great turmoil. He notes that the elite's use of this constitution
served two ends, one intended, the other unintended: reduction of
uncertainty through institutionalized guarantees, and the elite and
popular acceptance of a strong, central executive.

Africa's most populous country, Nigeria is a fascinating case in
which institutional design might help preserve democracy in the
face of complex ethnic cleavages. In Chapter 14 Rotimi Suberu and
Larry Diamond discuss the Nigerian experience in terms of its
vertical and horizontal federal systems, formal and informal strategies for national integration and ethnic accommodation, and
autonomous institutions of political restraint. They find that
balanced systems of federalism and both formal and informal
measures for national integration can help to contain the threats to
institutional stability posed in multi-ethnic, developing states.
They conclude that the distortion or decline of federalism, the transgression of basic democratic processes, and general underdevelopment of institutions inflamed the fissures of a plural society, and
precipitated the disintegration of Nigeria's multi-ethnic state.

Our book would have a noticeable gap without a chapter on India,
which has long defied conventional wisdom regarding the difficulty
of building democracy in a deeply divided society, and originally—
that is, in the decades after 1947—a very poor one. Notwithstanding
shortcomings and ongoing tensions, Indian democracy in many
respects stands out as a remarkable success story in enabling different religious, linguistic, and national groups to manage conflict
in generally peaceful ways. In Chapter 15 David Stuligross and
Ashutosh Varshney describe the development of India's multi-
ethnic democracy and conclude that political institutions have
played a major role in effectively managing inter-ethnic violence.
They stress the importance of the federation of linguistic States in

providing a sense of security for culturally differentiated groups but also point out the necessity of the link languages of English and Hindi for allowing a multi-level pattern of identities to emerge.

I

....

Institutional Design in Divided Societies:
An Overview

....

Constitutional Design:
Proposals Versus Processes

Donald L. Horowitz

Constitution-making has become an international and comparative exercise in a way that it rarely was in the century before 1989. 'International' in the sense that the involvement of experts and practitioners across state boundaries has been welcomed, indeed encouraged, to the point at which a new democracy that excluded foreigners entirely from its constitutional process might stamp itself as decidedly insular, even somewhat suspect. 'Comparative' in the sense that there have been attempts to learn from the experience of states and societies that are similarly situated. In 1978, during the extended session of an elected Nigerian Constituent Assembly that reviewed and rewrote the product of an expert Constitution Drafting Committee, there was great demand for information about the United States constitution (see Horowitz 1979). The US embassy was only too happy to supply copies of the *Federalist Papers*, for which there was then a great thirst. But Nigerian comparative curiosity did not extend much beyond the United States. The situation is changed now. The experience of what are seen as the world's most successful democracies is still sought, but so, to some extent, is the experience of states that have faced what are viewed as comparable problems. If the answers remain elusive, the questions have become far more sophisticated.

I do not want to exaggerate the increase in the diffusion of constitutional innovation across international boundaries. This is, after all, a process that began more than two centuries ago. The framers of the United States constitution were, of course, students of ancient republics. In the nineteenth century, Latin American states were

I am pleased to record my gratitude to the United States Institute of Peace and the Harry Frank Guggenheim Foundation, both of which have supported my ongoing research project on constitutional design for divided societies.

much influenced by constitutional models deriving from the United States. In Europe, proportional representation spread across state boundaries. There are many other examples of borrowed political institutions, including the diffusion of judicial review, mainly in the post-World War II period. Much, though not all, institutional borrowing before 1989, however, was confined to borrower and lender states within the same cultural zone. The heyday of European nationalism, from roughly the mid-nineteenth to the mid-twentieth century, was a period in which state boundaries were, to a considerable degree, impervious to international institutional learning. The making of constitutions was regarded as an intimate act, for which sovereign shades should be drawn.

By contrast, the post-1989 period has been a time of constitutional liberation. In this period, democracy has been marketed aggressively as a product that ought to be available to everyone. Even if purchases of off-the-shelf varieties are a bit dangerous and tailor-made versions are preferred, the implication is that those with less experience can profit from consulting those with more. Western governments have been forthcoming with assistance—although some, fearing being held responsible for the results, were slow off the mark; a spate of non-governmental organizations has sprung up to meet the demand and to create it where it was slow to arise; the United Nations and other international organizations have responded; and professional bodies such as the American Bar Association have assembled cadres of provision merchants, lawyers, and judges eager to dispense ready-made constitutional clauses on request. If the nineteenth was the century of Christian missionaries, the twenty-first may become the century of constitutional missionaries.

In spite of all this cross-boundary involvement and in some ways because of it, constitutions that have been *designed*, as opposed to merely constructed, are difficult to find. The sheer proliferation of participants makes it less, rather than more, likely that a design, with its consistent and interlocking parts, will be produced at the outset and adopted at the conclusion. I shall return to a fuller discussion of impediments to realizing designed constitutions soon enough. Suffice it to say here that the results since 1989 do not suggest the triumph of constitutional design or even of comparative learning, however great the efforts have been. A study of new east European electoral systems, for example, concludes that their framers consulted foreign models and then proceeded to adopt an array of idiosyncratic hybrids (Elster, Offe, and Preuss 1998: 80). A similar study of sub-Saharan African electoral-system change finds a good deal of change, often, surprisingly enough, change involving borrowing across colonial traditions but, again, no particular pattern, just a variety of purely local adaptations (Albaugh 1999). If constitutional design were thought, reasonably enough, to produce some standard solutions, locally modified, to recurrent problems, more discernible patterns than these would be visible. New democracies, like older democracies, seem inclined toward adopting hybridized, sometimes inconsistent, institutions. In the electoral field, a more general tendency toward hybrid systems is visible from Italy to Israel to Japan. This is a tendency that reflects a desire to graft one institution on to another rather than to design an ensemble of institutions.[1] Perhaps counter-intuitively, homogeneity of outcome is not the hallmark of the more intense international contact of the current period.

Despite international consultations, many countries produce constitutions that are more or less impervious to whatever international wisdom has been purveyed or, for that matter, to what a careful examination of comparative experience might reveal. In spite of abundant experience, in Africa and elsewhere, showing the futility of prohibiting the formation of ethnically-based political parties, Bulgaria, a state with large Turkish and Pamak minorities, adopted such a prohibition. (When the lawfulness of the Movement for Rights and Freedoms, universally known as a Turkish party, was litigated, Bulgaria was saved from the counterproductive consequences of its action by a judicial determination that what everyone knew to be true was nonetheless false [Ganev 1997].) The majority of states, urged to adopt constitutional designs of one kind or another, have proved to be most conservative. I shall explore the sources of some of this conservatism shortly.

None of this should this be surprising. Even that most theoretically informed, deliberate group of men who assembled in Philadelphia in 1787 to reform the Articles of Confederation and who are credited with having produced a brilliant constitutional design actually improvised at every step. They abandoned reform for reconstruction. They composed their bicameral legislature to resolve an impasse between small states and large. The supremacy

[1] Although I shall speak here of 'constitutional' design, I mean to include fundamental political institutions, such as electoral systems, the regulation of political parties, and devolution, whether or not these matters are embraced formally in the constitution, as sometimes they are and sometimes they are not. In Indonesia, for instance, new laws on all these subjects were adopted in 1999, while the 1945 constitution, sacrosanct as it was, was left unchanged for the time being. The adoption of these laws was meant to be, and certainly was, a constitutional act.

of federal authority over the states was the unintended consequence of a dispute over a different issue (Farrand 1913: 120). The institution of judicial review was omitted from the document, was assumed to be inherent in it by some (Farrand 1913: 156–7), and was probably not contemplated by others. The presidency, truly an original contribution to government, was the result of a *coup* against the majority of the constitutional convention by partisans of a strong executive operating in two committees of the convention; most delegates were wary of executive power, believing that parliament was the palladium of liberty (see Horowitz 1987: 10–11; Thach 1969: 118). The framers of 1787 could justify the design that emerged, but they could hardly claim to have planned the result.

If it is true that designs are not generally adopted, that does not render constitutional design an unimportant subject. It is a naive view of the relation of ideas to institutions that concludes that ideas are unimportant merely because institutions do not reflect them fully or quickly. The difficult path of democracy itself, from 1680 to 1789 to 1989, makes this clear enough. Ideas are contested by other ideas, ideas are met with a variety of non-ideational barriers, and even ideas that survive these tests must go further: they must be put in adoptable forms, they must be legitimized by opinion leaders and opinion-leading states, and they must be seen to be in the interests of those who must approve their adoption before they find their way into institutions. In the case of constitutional design, the battle of ideas is not over, non-ideational obstacles are strong, it is still early days in terms of constitutional iterations, the interests affected by adoption are not uniform, and retrogression is possible after adoption. In the remainder of this paper, I shall expand on some of these themes, with particular reference to constitutional design for societies severely divided by ascriptive groups, whether the lines of division are said to be national, ethnic, racial, or religious.[2]

---

[2] By 'severely divided societies' I mean those in which ethnic-group identities have a high degree of salience, exceeding that accorded to alternative identities—including supra-ethnic, territorial, ideological, and class-based alternatives—and in which levels of antipathy between ethnic groups are high. This definition leaves open the institutional manifestations of severe divisions and so allows us to evaluate the effects of constitutional designs on institutions exacerbating or mitigating conflict. Compare the broadly similar definition of Nordlinger (1972: 9).

The Contest of Ideas

If there is a subject called constitutional design, then there must be alternative constitutional *designs*. Assuredly there are, but even now most constitutional drafters and reformers are, at best, only vaguely informed by anything resembling an articulate theory of their enterprise. Most act on the basis of inchoate and partially worked-out ideas, such as the notion that assuring legislative representation for minorities is the crucial step in inter-group accommodation: a notion that has animated many judicial and legislative determinations under the Voting Rights Act in the United States. Politicians have their own ideas, and these are not so easily dislodged, even with the growth of constitutional design and various sub-fields, such as electoral-system design, as matters for experts. Individual politicians can still make their influence felt, even in very large countries.[3] Before we even reach the contest of explicitly stated theories, we need to recognize the more significant, albeit often subliminal, contest between explicit theories and the more influential, implicit theories espoused by practitioners. The inarticulate theories call out for study. As of now, we lack a theory of their theories.

We also lack a consensus emerging from the articulate theories, whether these relate to electoral systems, presidential or parliamentary structure, or the costs and benefits of centralized or devolved power. Lack of consensus is the first obstacle.

No treatment of the contest of ideas can avoid an encounter with consociational democracy. There is much to admire in the efforts of Arend Lijphart in behalf of managing inter-group conflict, most notably his realism about group divisions (they are not to be wished away) and his optimism (they do not need to produce civil war). Yet Lijphart, in his contribution to this volume, is right to identify me as a dissenter from the consociational approach, although, as I shall point out, completely wrong to identify me as an opponent of either power-sharing or territorial devolution. I want to move on to a brief statement of a more promising approach and to a fuller treatment of the gap between constitutional design and the constitutions that actually emerge from processes of constitutional innovation, but I need first to state why I think consociational theory is not a fruitful path for constitutional designers.

---

[3] I am thinking here of the singular part played by Viktor Shaynis, a parliamentarian, in designing the Russian electoral system.

To avoid restating objections to consociationalism that I have advanced in several previous publications (Horowitz 1985: 568–76; 1991: 137–45, 167–71; 1997: 439–40; 2000: 256–9), I shall resort to a list of the main objections.

1. The consociational approach is motivationally inadequate. Lijphart (1977: 53, 165) identifies statesmanship as the reason elites will form a cartel across group lines to resolve inter-ethnic differences. In his view, leaders are motivated by a desire to avert the danger of mutual destruction. But why should majority-group leaders, with 60 per cent support, and the ability to gain all of political power in a majoritarian democracy, be so self-abnegating as to give some of it away to minority-group leaders? There may be instances of this sort of generosity, in the face of the attractiveness of a less-than-maximal coalition (see Riker 1962: 32–3), but the motive of avoiding ultimate mutual destruction is based on a time horizon longer than that employed by most political leaders, who, in any case, are apt to think that retaining control for themselves is the best way to avoid disaster. On this point, Lijphart (chapter 3) now contends that the motive is not statesmanship but the desire to enter into a coalition. This, of course, does not account for the motives of leaders of majorities, who do not need coalitions, much less the all-inclusive or grand coalitions that Lijphart (1977) specifies as a central element of the consociational prescription.[4] The failure to make the elementary distinction between the different incentives of majorities and minorities, to which I shall return, is crucial. Even states that start out multipolar, with several ethnic groups, can become bipolar and bifurcated—witness the growth of northern versus southern groups in many African states—thus obviating the need for a coalition across group lines for the group that is slightly larger. In general, bipolar states, with a majority and a minority, are the more seriously conflicted. A theory of conflict reduction that cannot cope with hard cases is of limited utility.[5]

[4] Lijphart sometimes includes and sometimes omits the grand-coalition requirement. The tendency to shift ground about the indispensable requisites of the theory is one of the main reasons why consociationalism attracts such strong criticism (see, for example, Dixon 1997; Halpern 1986).

In the actual experience of constitutional innovators, there are some examples of motivation to accept consociational arrangements, but these are idiosyncratic and cannot be assumed to be widely distributed. Motivation always needs to be treated as an issue, not a given.

[5] The claim that the bipolar (60–40) problem is rare (which Lijphart made in an earlier version of the paper published in this volume) cannot be sustained. In many developing countries, bipolar alignments emerge as a result of the amalgamation of group identities.

2. To the extent that the imputed motive is still statesmanship rather than self-interest, the assumption that elites in divided societies are likely to be more tolerant of other ethnic groups or less inclined to pursue advantage for their own group is extremely dubious. Studies of ethnocentrism show educated elites in some countries to be less ethnocentric than their followers, in others more, in some others neither less nor more, and in still others more with respect to some groups and less or the same with respect to other groups (see Horowitz 1997: 457 n.31; 1991: 140–1 nn. 44–50). It is very risky to count on statesmanship (see Reilly and Reynolds 1999: 13).

3. When leaders compromise across ethnic lines in the face of severe divisions, there is usually a high price to pay. Counter-elites arise who make an issue of the compromise, referring to it as a sell-out. Consociational theory assumes the existence of 'group leaders', but, even when groups begin with a single set of leaders, compromise across group lines is likely to show those leaders to be merely party leaders opposed by leaders of other parties seeking the support of the same group. The centrifugal competition for group allegiance is an enormous constraint on compromise across group lines, and it renders the grand coalition, under conditions of free elections, a contradiction in terms. Not one of the four developing countries cited by Lijphart (1977) as consociational—Lebanon, Malaysia, Surinam, and the Netherlands Antilles—had a grand coalition. Each had an inter-ethnic coalition of some parties, opposed by other parties representing the same groups. Some of the four also violated other core conditions of consociational theory, such as proportionality in allocations, proportionality in executive participation, and cultural autonomy, but were claimed for the theory nonetheless. For reasons I shall enumerate later, it is not amiss to refer to consociational *elements* or consociational *practices*, but consociational regimes in the developing world are, to be generous about it, few and far between.[6]

---

[6] The tendency to shift the goal posts and to claim countries for the theory is palpable. Whenever a divided society seems to be more or less democratic and more or less lacking in the most severe forms of conflict, the reason must be that it is consociational. India, the leading example of adversary democracy in Asia— and adversary democracy is the form of democracy to which consociationalism is juxtaposed as an alternative—is said to be consociational (Lijphart 1996). If South Africa settles its differences peacefully and electorally, even if it lacks central elements of consociationalism, such as minority vetoes, then South Africa must be consociational (Lijphart 1994*b*).

To be perfectly clear at the outset, it is not possible to identify states that have adopted an incentives approach—or any other coherent, conflict-reducing approach— across the board either. The difficulty of adopting constitutional designs *in toto* is precisely the point of this chapter.

Consociational theory exaggerates the latitude enjoyed by leaders in ethnically divided societies where free elections prevail.

4. If the grand coalition, proportional resource allocations and shares of executive power, and the minority veto all encounter the motivational problem mentioned earlier, cultural autonomy encounters a different problem. Presumably, groups are to find satisfaction—and power—in the ability to manage their own affairs, and that will contribute to stable democracy (Lijphart 1977: 42; this volume, chapter 3). But those who work on the sources of conflict in ethnically-divided societies know there is more to it than that. Cultural matters, such as the designation of official languages and official religions, and educational issues, such as languages of instruction, the content of curricula, and the official recognition of degrees from various educational streams associated with various ethnic groups, are habitually divisive issues in severely divided societies. These issues go straight to the heart of the conflict in three of its most important respects. To accord equal recognition to all cultures, religions, and languages is to concede equal ownership of the state, contrary to what groups are very often willing to concede (see Wimmer 1997). To accord equal recognition is also to concede another core issue: the issue of group superiority, which is contested by reference to disputes over cultural superiority and primacy. To accord equal recognition is, finally, to concede the issue of the identity of who will get ahead, which otherwise would be regulated by limitations on languages and educational streams associated with competitors. In short, cultural autonomy, with its implication of equality, is the product of the reduction of inter-ethnic conflict, not an ingredient of a conflict-regulating prescription at the threshold.

5. Lijphart fails to make a critical distinction between pre-electoral and post-electoral coalitions. The coalitions recommended by consociational theory are post-electoral coalitions, which no doubt entail compromise over the division of cabinet portfolios, but typically not compromise over divisive inter-ethnic issues. A better analysis of Lebanon and Malaysia during their most accommodative periods would have put the emphasis on the need of candidates, parties, and coalitions to attract votes across group lines, rather than on post-electoral compromise. In those cases and others, pre-electoral coalitions across group lines required compromise on ethnic issues. The combination of list-system proportional representation and political parties based on ethnic-group support does nothing to foster compromise on ethnic issues. The zero-sum relation of party lists to each other translates into a zero-sum electoral competition between ethnic groups (see Horowitz 1991: 167–76).

These criticisms suggest that when consociational arrangements are adopted a conflict is probably already on the wane, and they also point the way towards alternative power-sharing prescriptions. Certainly, to conflate consociation with all of power-sharing is completely unwarranted.[7] Again, in setting out the outlines of an alternative perspective, I shall not be comprehensive, because I am as much concerned with the under-explored fate of constitutional designs as I am with the designs themselves.

Several points follow from what has already been said. If it is true that inter-group conflict involves a conflict for control and ownership of the state, for group superiority, and for group success, all measured in relative terms, then compromise will be difficult to achieve. The divisive issues are not easy to compromise. No single formula will assure the reduction of conflict. Progress will be, in most cases, incremental and, in many of these, reversible. When electorates are alert to ethnic issues, as they typically are, exhortations to leaders to compromise are likely to be futile in the absence of rewards for compromise. Attention needs to be devoted, therefore, to maximizing incentives for accommodative behaviour. For elected politicians, those incentives are likely to be found in the electoral system. Electoral systems that reward inter-ethnic accommodation can be identified and can be made to work more or less as intended (see Reilly 1997; see also International Crisis Group 1998; 1999). Where electoral rewards are present, they can provide the motivation ethnic leaders otherwise lack, they can operate even in the presence of ethnocentrism, and they can offset electoral losses that leaders anticipate as a result of making concessions to other groups. Where these rewards are present, they typically operate by means of vote-pooling arrangements: the exchange of votes by ethnically-based parties that, because of the electoral system, are marginally dependent for victory on the votes of groups other than their own and that, to secure those votes, must behave moderately on the issues in conflict. The electoral rewards provided to a moderate middle compensate for the threat posed by opposition from those who can benefit from the aversion of some group members to inter-ethnic compromise.

Where vote pooling takes place, as it did in Lebanon and Malaysia, it promotes pre-electoral coalitions, coalitions that need to compromise in order to attract voters across group lines but that may be

[7] Others have also pointed out that the appropriation of the term 'power-sharing' to refer exclusively to the consociational approach is confusing and conceptually constricting (see, for example, Dixon 1997: 23, 32).

opposed by ethnic parties on the flanks. A recent instance in which a vote-pooling electoral system was used successfully to induce the formation of a multi-ethnic coalition that won the election was the alternative vote (AV), adopted in the 1997 Fijian constitution. The electoral incentives in Fiji were weak, but they had a powerful effect.[8] A severely divided society, Fiji elected a thoroughly multi-ethnic government, led by its first-ever Indian prime minister (see Lal 1999). A year later, that government was overthrown, but not because the incentives did not work.

Incentives, then, are the key to accommodation in difficult conditions, but the difficult conditions imply that the incentives approach will not be attractive to everyone or attractive at all times. Some times are more propitious than others, and the problem of motives does not disappear by invoking the incentives approach. The incentives approach has had no more success in securing full-blown acceptance than has any other. Now the question becomes who will opt for this approach, when, and why. This is a problem I shall turn to shortly. First, however, I need to flesh out a few more implications.

If political leaders are likely to be more willing to compromise under some electoral systems than under others, it follows that the electoral system is the central feature of the incentives approach to accommodation. Indeed, differing electoral logics can create differing ethnic outcomes, reversing even favourable and unfavourable starting points, an argument I have made in a comparison of Sri Lanka, which began with a relatively easy ethnic problem, and Malaysia, which began with a very difficult one (Horowitz 1989*a*).

Vote pooling is the major, but not the only, goal of the incentives approach. As the difficulty of reconciling majorities to non-majoritarian institutions suggests, multipolar fluidity makes inter-ethnic accommodation easier, since, by definition, it lacks a majority. The presence of many groups, no one of which can lay claim to majority status, in Tanzania and India is conducive to the mitigation of conflict. But group identities can change: as I mentioned earlier, a large number of groups can consolidate into a smaller number, and the formal institutional structure can facilitate the change from multipolar fluidity to bipolar opposition. Where multipolarity prevails, another purpose of the electoral system is to preserve it against consolidating tendencies. Among others, the Lebanese system did this for a long time. By acknowledging

---

[8] By way of disclosure, I should report that I served as a consultant to the Fijian Constitution Review Commission that recommended the AV system (see FCRC 1996). Arend Lijphart was also consulted by the Commission.

the plasticity of group identities, which consociational theory completely neglects, the incentives approach can prevent the crystallization of identities and the emergence of more severe conflict.

It is not usually recognized, however, that territory can act in aid of or in lieu of electoral mechanisms for such purposes. Territory can partition groups off from each other and direct their political ambitions at one level of government rather than another. Federalism, and especially the proliferation of federal units, or regional autonomy can act in effect as an electoral reform and can preserve multipolar fluidity. There is very good evidence of this in the case of the proliferation of Nigerian federal units.

Federalism and regional autonomy have other conflict-reducing functions as well. If the units are homogeneous, they may foster intra-group competition, at the expense of an exclusive focus on inter-group competition. If the units are heterogeneous, they may provide an experience in political socialization for politicians of different groups who become habituated to dealing with each other at lower levels before they need to do so at the centre.

Does devolution lead to secession, as central-level politicians so often fear? The intervening variables here are timing and the ties woven with the centre. Early, generous devolution, coupled with carefully crafted connections of the regional population with the centre, is likely to avert rather than produce separatism. Late, grudging devolution, coupled with a view at the centre that members of a group residing in the autonomous territory should henceforth look exclusively to the regional unit for their satisfaction, is far more likely to encourage departure from the state. Hesitation about devolution creates a self-fulfilling prophecy. Because of hesitation, devolution often comes too late.

The incentives approach is as difficult as, or more difficult than, the consociational to adopt, but, once adopted, it has an important advantage. Consociation is certainly easier to understand: one size fits all. But, even if adopted, consociation is far from self-executing, because compromise is not likely to be rewarded by the electorate. The matter will not be left in elite hands. By contrast, politicians who benefit from electoral incentives to moderation have continuing reason to try to reap those rewards, whatever their beliefs and whatever their inclination to toleration and statesmanship. Politicians who are merely exhorted to behave moderately may be left with mere exhortations.

Structural Sources of Constitutional Conservatism

Once we move past arguments about the best constitutional course for divided societies, hubris should subside and humility should return quickly. There is ample reason, after all, to be humble. Why is it so easy to point out how few, if any, states have adopted completely one prescription or another? Because adoptions are likely to be partial at best. The processes of constitution-making are uncongenial to the creation of a set of institutions that derive from any single theory. Beyond that, there are systematic biases of constitutional actors that favour and disfavour particular approaches. And there are variations in the positions and interests of ethnic groups participating in and affected by constitutional processes. For all of these reasons, the result is far more likely to be the adoption of a mix containing elements drawn from several approaches than of a document embodying a consistent perspective and method.

This is inadequately mapped terrain, so the best I can do is to sketch some of the constraints.[9] Perhaps I can begin by illustrating hybrid outcomes, using an example I referred to earlier: Fiji.

Fiji is a severely divided society with a population that is, very roughly, half Fijians, two-fifths Indians, and one-tenth other minorities. After a military regime promulgated a quite exclusionary, pro-Fijian constitution in 1990, the regime promised a review of that constitution, to take place several years later. A Constitution Review Commission was duly appointed. In 1996, the commission reported (FCRC 1996). Based on its view of the benefits of the vote-pooling approach, it recommended an AV electoral system and the creation of as many heterogeneous constituencies as possible, so that ethnic parties would have incentives to make arrangements with other ethnic parties across group lines to secure the 50 per cent plus one that AV requires for victory.[10] Fiji, however, has a history of ethnically reserved seats and communal rolls, that is, the electorate for each seat is limited to voters of the group for whose candidates the seat is reserved. The commission was unable to abolish these seats altogether, so it retained 25 of them in a proposed house of 70, leaving 45 open seats. The Fijian parliament more than

---

[9] For an altogether different set of constraints, see Reilly and Reynolds (1999: 10–19).

[10] For the powerful incentives AV creates for voters to cross party lines—and, by inference, in an ethnically divided society, to cross ethnic lines—see Sartori (1997: 5–6). Lijphart (this volume, chapter 3) mistakenly equates the incentives of AV to those of the majority, two-round runoff system.

reversed these numbers: it enacted a constitution specifying 46 reserved seats and only 25 open seats. It also adopted a proposal requiring that any party securing at least 10 per cent of the seats be invited to be represented proportionately in the cabinet, but without a veto. The British convention of majority confidence was explicitly retained.

Here, then, was a hybrid constitution, drawing inspiration from the incentives approach, the consociational approach, and the majoritarian approach (for a fuller treatment, see Horowitz 2000). What I want to argue here is that such mixed outcomes are more likely than not, and I want to enumerate some of the reasons.

The first is that there is an asymmetry of preferences. It should come as no surprise that representatives of the Indian minority, weary of leading the parliamentary opposition, proposed the provision for inclusion in the Fijian cabinet. (Ironically, however, one Indian party did so well that it became the largest party in the coalition that won the election and so did not need the provision, while the other Indian party did so poorly it could not take advantage of the provision.) The consociational approach involves guarantees, and minorities are more likely to favour minority guarantees. Majorities, however, favour majority rule. While, in this case, Fijians conceded a single consociational *feature*, they certainly did not concede a consociational *approach*. Nor did they concede the full thrust of the incentives approach so clearly preferred by the commission. Rather, they watered it down.

This asymmetry of preferences is systematic; it derives from the exigencies of minority and majority position. But position is not the only source of mixed outcomes.

Two other sources are a multiplicity of participants and a multiplicity of objectives. Theorists often think—correctly, in my view— that the dangers of ethnic conflict are so great that a nearly single-minded focus on its amelioration is warranted in the design of institutions. Others, however, have additional objectives. The more others there are, the greater is the chance that competing objectives will intrude and need to be accommodated. An example from Bosnia will make the point. While a three-member international committee worked for many months devising and testing an electoral system to mitigate Bosnia's ethnic conflicts, an internal drafting committee and some other members of the international community, although also concerned about ethnic conflict, were equally concerned about the responsiveness of legislative candidates to constituents—a classic concern of the electoral-system literature. This led to a quite different electoral proposal. This, in Bosnia, a state in which there is serious apprehension of renewed ethnic warfare if the international community should depart.

Now there are undoubtedly ways to narrow the composition of participants playing a part in such deliberations, but some of the most likely ways may not be productive. It is tempting to think that some form of *diktat* would surely produce more consistency. The only problem then would be to convince the author of the diktat of the soundness of one theory or another. These days, however, any diktat that emerges is likely to emanate from international actors. While these often have a view of the benighted condition of the troubled territories needing their help, a jaundiced view that might be conducive to imposing some strong medicine on their wards, international actors are exceedingly unlikely to speak with a single voice or, if they can find any responsible voices in the target territories, to speak with any voice at all. The possibility of a diktat that comes with international involvement carries with it the proliferation, rather than the reduction, of participants. (Never mind whether a diktat can produce a legitimate constitutional design: it certainly did in some ex-colonies.)

What I have already said about Fiji and Bosnia also implies that the invocation of expertise or the detachment of outsiders, such as the distinguished chair of the Fijian commission (a Maori who had served as governor-general and previously as archbishop of New Zealand), will yield a consistent product in the end. The recommendations of experts and outsiders can be rejected and modified as inconsistent with local conditions or simply as inconsistent with the preferences of local actors.

If there are many actors, constitutional processes are likely to entail bargaining. By definition, bargaining involves the exchange of preferences, and that exchange is inimical to the realization of a single constitutional design.

There are times when there is a discernibly different process at work, when a sober contemplation of unpleasant experience produces a determination to depart from the institutions producing that experience. Those propitious times needs to be specified more precisely than they have been thus far. As I said earlier, the very problems that make constitutional innovation necessary generally impede acceptance of constitutional departures. And so a focus on exceptional times, hospitable to innovations, is well warranted.

At some such times, the past has been so unpleasant and the future is so uncertain that the ethnic groups' sense of their own future interests becomes elusive. In Nigeria in 1978, groups found it impossible to foresee the pattern of ethnic political advantage and disadvantage. Faced with the veil of ignorance, they set out to choose institutions they could live with regardless of future position. Among these were a separately elected president, so that control of parliament by a single ethnic group would not be sufficient to exclude the rest. The president was to be chosen by a vote-pooling formula involving plurality plus geographic distribution—as territory was a rough proxy for ethnicity. Unfortunately, the Nigerian framers did not opt for conciliatory electoral systems for legislative office, and so one set of institutions worked against others. Propitious moments may produce a suspension of interest asymmetry, but they do not necessarily produce adequate innovations. Epiphanies do not compensate for all the defects of the human condition, such as failures of information, foresight, and thoroughness.

To a considerable degree, the list of obstacles to constitutional innovation recapitulates the standard impediments to policy change. This, I want to suggest, is a useful function, since tidy constitutional designs have generally been propounded without regard to untidy processes of adoption. In the terms familiar to the literature on agenda setting (for example, Kingdon 1984; cf. Horowitz 1989*b*), constitutional prescriptions are solutions awaiting problems, but in this case the problem whose serendipitous occurrence produces a new receptivity to pre-existing solutions is likely to be a human catastrophe, such as a civil war or a hurting stalemate (see Zartman 1991). Neither of these will necessarily assure the adoption of any prescription in its totality. In many such dire cases, there is likely to be a sense that any compromise is better than no agreement. This is an outcome that is highly likely to be encouraged by outside mediators. In short, the existence of a design does not repeal the laws of policy-making or negotiation.

One structural condition is certainly conducive to constitutional innovation in the service of conflict reduction: monopoly position within one's own ethnic group. Lijphart (1977: 25) refers to 'a grand coalition of the political leaders of all significant segments of the plural society'. Most of the time, however, it is difficult to identify a single set that can be called the political leaders of each group. Groups usually have more than one set contesting for leadership, and this, as I have argued, is a major constraint on inter-group compromise. Where, however, a single set of leaders is as yet unchallenged, it has, for the moment, leeway to compromise that it would not otherwise enjoy. The Malaysian compromises of the 1950s go back to this fortuitous structural condition. Once the compromises were made, however, counter-elites arose within each group to challenge them. These alternative, ethnically more exclusionary leaders hemmed in the compromising coalition partners, limiting their latitude, and also drove the coalition partners together, since their majority increasingly depended on their ability to pool votes with each other. Without monopoly position at the outset, it is unlikely that the initial compromises could have been made.

In spite of all these obstacles, including lack of monopoly, one recent agreement stands out by its exceptional character: the largely consociational agreement reached in Northern Ireland on Good Friday, 1998. The agreement is not perfectly consociational, and its early implementation involved some deviations from strict proportionality. Yet, on the whole, the consociational coherence of the document stands out. Even more remarkable are the maximal commitments to inter-group accommodation made by the signatories. In a separate paper, based on interviews in Belfast and London (Horowitz 2002), I show that the Northern Ireland agreement was made possible by a concatenation of exceptional circumstances that suspended nearly all the obstacles I have identified here.

The one obstacle not overcome at Belfast—intra-group competition—particularly on the unionist side, threatened to preclude agreement in the first instance and then delayed implementation of the agreement for a year. The principal constraint on David Trimble, leader of the Ulster Unionist Party, was opposition not only from outside the UUP, from Ian Paisley's Democratic Unionist Party, but also from inside his own caucus. The two are related. The existence of the DUP, criticizing compromise from the Protestant flank, leads members of the UUP to depart from the compromises, lest the exclusive appeal of the DUP draw support away. If the agreement does not collapse completely, the same risk may materialize on the Catholic side. Should there be a shortfall of delivery on the maximal commitments of the agreement, the main beneficiaries of which are on the Catholic side, Catholic moderates of the Social Democratic and Labour Party stand to suffer at the hands of Sinn Féin, which is likely to outflank them on such issues.

The actual workings of a regime of this sort are, therefore, made quite precarious by intra-ethnic divisions. In particular, when parties of the middle cannot count on electoral support from their partners in compromise, in order to offset losses incurred within their group as a result of the compromises, they will proceed haltingly at best, and they may be caught in centrifugal processes initiated by their intra-group competitors. That is a strong reason why intra-group monopoly is best at the outset (though it will not last); it is also a reason why vote-pooling mechanisms are exceedingly helpful. And it is also a reason why there can be no guarantees of success for any prescription or mix of prescriptions: compare Reynolds (1999*b*: 5).

Which Models, Which Histories? Sources of Bias

The process of constitutional choice is fraught with the prospect of bias and distortion. Two of the more prominent sources of skewed choice concern the relative attractiveness of alternative constitutional models across states and the interpretation of constitutional experience within states. The pitfalls, therefore, are inappropriate comparison and misinterpreted history.

In cross-state comparisons, there are, in turn, at least four sources of difficulty. The first is a preference for the best or most successful cases. The second is a preference for source countries of colonial, cultural, or regional affinity. The third is a preference for single outstanding examples, at the expense of a run of dissonant examples. The fourth is a preference of international actors for home-country institutions.

As Nigerians looked to the United States in 1978, so, too, have many countries aimed to resemble Switzerland rather than Nigeria, even though their problems may have resembled Nigeria's more than Switzerland's. Success attracts admirers, although success may imply an easier problem that may have made possible the adoption of institutions that are held, in retrospect, to be responsible for the success. Severely divided societies need to look to other severely divided societies that have made some progress in reducing conflict, rather than to societies that are less severely divided, especially if the reduction of divisions in the less divided countries can causally be attributed to political institutions that antedate the onset of democracy.

Anglophone countries in Africa and elsewhere generally express an affinity for British institutions; Francophone countries, for French institutions, such as the presidency with two-round elections. Post-colonial conditions can and do change, but powerful networks, habits, and pressures can retard the change. The same goes for the English-speaking world's general, albeit imperfect, allergy to list-system proportional representation and comparable aversions to other systems in other cultural zones. Inter-regional boundaries also constitute powerful impediments to constitutional borrowing. Bosnia's and Northern Ireland's cleavages may be similar in structure and in severity to those of some Asian and African countries, but in neither have constitutional designers been inclined to look east or south for models. There is not yet completely free trade in constitutional innovation.

A more subtle source of difficulty derives from a different selection bias. Those with an interest in a specific innovation may focus on a single attractive case, to the neglect of the range of relevant outcomes. Take the case of Tatarstan, which in the early 1990s aimed to secure a specially favourable, asymmetric federal arrangement with Moscow. Policy-makers in Kazan focused on a model far from home: the relationship between Puerto Rico and the United States, which, not surprisingly, seemed remarkably favourable to the peripheral territory. They neglected the relevance of several other cases in which asymmetrical federal arrangements, conceded when necessary for the centre to forge the association, were diminished or revoked when the centre was in a position to do so: Cameroon, Ethiopia-Eritrea, Peninsular Malaysia-Borneo Malaysia. This is, of course, an instance of the bias toward success and perhaps also of a geographical-cultural bias. It is also, however, something more subtle: a bias toward the more visible and against the less visible, the same bias that has made South Africa conspicuous in debates in Northern Ireland (Guelke 1999).

Finally, there is a nearly imperceptible but, in some cases, palpably important source of skewing among international actors: the bias of international bureaucrats toward home-country institutions. To the extent that so-called failed states become wards of international actors, those states may find themselves subject to the democratic forms and processes of the leading custodian states. Hence, for example, reports of American military authorities who conduct ad hoc judicial proceedings along home-country lines in Kosovo. The same is undoubtedly true in constitutional design. There is also a subset of home-country bias: a preference for the institutions of a state in which decision-makers have studied. Indonesian decision-makers, educated in the United States, had a preference for plurality elections in single-member constituencies and for electoral commissions that included representatives of the contesting political parties. The latter innovation made for great delay and doubt about the count in the 1999 general elections, as an unwieldy commission sought to cope with objections from officials of literally scores of parties.[11]

People bring with them what they know and what they are habituated to. How all this plays out is unclear in a multinational occupation or in the increasingly common situation in which advice is

---

[11] I am grateful to Ben Reilly for calling the source of this difficulty to me.

taken from several sources, but competing home-country biases are unlikely simply to cancel each other out. The biases may, however, interact in peculiar ways with adoptions based on other biases. In the early 1990s, Nepal opted for first-past-the-post elections, because it wished to emulate the experience of its powerful neighbour, India. It also wished to discourage party fragmentation. Consequently, on the recommendation of a German adviser, Nepal adopted a 3 per cent threshold; but, of course, such a threshold sits uneasily with single-member constituencies in which the threshold for victory is already determined to be a plurality virtually certain to exceed 3 per cent. Nepalese decision-makers, therefore, decided that a party securing less than 3 per cent of the vote would be ineligible to run candidates in the *next* election—a rule that also proved attractive for the same reasons, but without the German adviser, in Indonesia in 1999.[12]

Examples of this sort raise the more general question of interaction effects. If hybrid institutions are produced by asymmetrical preferences, processes of exchange, and multiple-source biases, it becomes more difficult to predict the incentives they create (see Shvetsova 1999).

Model biases are an instance of reference-group behaviour (Turner 1956). Those who search for models, personal or institutional, do not cast a net indiscriminately. They emulate or borrow selectively from donors thought to be appropriate sources of values or ways of conducting business. This is an old, but under-appreciated, story in the transference of legal systems across boundaries (see, for example, Watson 1985: 23). In the quest for the best institutions, students of the subject have neglected the subterranean screening that takes place in processes of constitutional adoption.

The study of the subject does not end with model bias. There is also historical bias to contend with. Although state decision-makers may learn something from the experience of other states, they inevitably have already learned something from their own historical experience. This they will bring to the table, whether or not they are conscious of it. Again, the American presidency is a good example. The nature of this office was uncertain until the end of the 1787 convention, because there was differential experience among the delegates. Many delegates, recalling the imperiousness of the British Crown, wanted a weak executive. Many others, who had recently witnessed what they saw as unbridled legislative domination and popular

---

[12] I am indebted to Jørgen Elklit for the Nepalese example, but the interpretation is my responsibility.

revolt, culminating in Shays' Rebellion, feared populist legislative supremacy. A third group, ultimately decisive, came from the few states that had had strong executives during the Articles of Confederation period. Their experience proved decisive, as they captured the crucial committees that resolved the issues (Thach 1969). One set of delegates was focused on Britain, a second on developments in some states, a third on developments in others. Each thought its slice of history definitive.

It is, however, not experience alone that is decisive, but how experience is filtered and interpreted, how some events are remembered and others are forgotten, and how transcendent moments in the past are invoked to make them relevant to present problems (Fentress and Wickham 1992: 127–37). As Nigerians associated their catastrophic conflicts with the easy capture of parliament and so looked favourably on a separation of powers, others may associate past problems with dictatorial presidents, and that may lead them in a parliamentary direction (see Horowitz 1990). There is an emerging literature on the role of historical memory in fostering conflict (see, for example, Posen 1993), but none yet on its impact in discriminating among institutional designs.

Yet memory weighs on policy-makers, and memory is subject to bias. Those who adopted the institutions agreed for Northern Ireland on Good Friday 1998 believed that everything else had been tried; in the process, they arguably misinterpreted Northern Ireland's previous failures, especially the failure of the so-called power-sharing government of 1973–4 (see Horowitz 2002). In Indonesia, drafters of the electoral and political parties laws enacted in 1999 were much concerned to avoid the danger of a fragmented parliament, and they drafted strong provisions to prevent regional or ethnic parties from securing a parliamentary foothold. In doing so, they were moved by what they saw as the deadlock of the 1955 parliament, the only freely-elected parliament in Indonesia's history. It is natural, perhaps, that the drafters should have looked for lessons to the only pertinent previous elections. Nevertheless, the degree of fragmentation in the 1955 parliament was not unmanageable. The admittedly non-electoral experience of 1965, when bifurcation and polarization overtook the Indonesian state, with truly disastrous consequences, was at least equally relevant but utterly neglected by the drafters (Horowitz 1999). In the short run, the drafters were right, as fragmentation has outweighed polarization as a problem, both in and out of parliament, but the cleavage between secular nationalists and Muslims can hardly be said to have been bridged permanently, any more than the cleavage between the armed forces and the communists was in 1965. The prevention of polarization may yet be an important purpose of constitutional design in Indonesia.

Lessons that policy-makers draw are almost always partial, and the sources of skewing in one case will certainly not be identical to those in another (cf. Jervis 1976: 218–20, 274–5; John Anderson 1990: 239–42). If there is, for the moment, peace but none the less pessimism, as in Bosnia, there will be great risk aversion, and experience will be interpreted to make only small changes possible. But the full repertoire of recipes for hospitality to innovation in one direction or another has yet to be uncovered. The combination of model bias and historical bias in individual countries opens the way to a great many permutations of institutions rather than anything resembling homogeneity. Designers who propound one-size-fits-all prescriptions will be especially disappointed.

Constitutional Spillage

It is one thing to prescribe and quite another to take the medicine. I have been emphasizing here the slip between the constitutional cup and the adoptive lip: the spillage rates are great, but our knowledge of them is thus far so primitive that we can only regard spillage as being close to random in its incidence and configuration.

There is the further problem of retrogression. Designs have effects on the distribution of power, and those who gain power as a result may wish to alter the design to favour themselves. Of course, it is possible to build in safeguards or tripwires that make alterations difficult or set off alarms when attempts are made. But the looser the design and the easier the adoption, the easier the alteration as well. Slippage is not complete at the moment of adoption.

Certain electoral systems, for example, depend for their continued efficacy on constituency boundaries. Electoral results can be changed without changing the electoral system itself, by altering those boundaries. The integrity of the design, therefore, will depend on the integrity of the boundary delimitation process. In Malaysia, where vote pooling was the fortuitous product of an unusual pattern of intra-ethnic party monopoly, inter-ethnic party competition, and demographic imbalances (see Horowitz 1985: 398–404), rather than constitutional design, the emergence of a strong Malay party in the ruling coalition produced changes in electoral boundaries that made Chinese voters less important (Lim 1997). As Chinese votes became less important to the coalition, Chinese political influence declined. Yet, in spite of the new boundaries, when Malays became more divided, marginal Chinese votes for Malay candidates became more valuable again, and this was reflected in ethnic policy and electoral appeals, most recently in the 1999 elections. The revival of Chinese influence, I cannot resist emphasizing, points to the utility of vote-pooling incentives as a source of accommodation, even in the face of retrogression.

Everything I have said thus far is intended to highlight the unlikelihood that constitutional designs can or will be adopted or, if adopted, retained in anything resembling their original form. I have assumed that this shortfall is as dangerous to divided societies as shortfalls in construction are to buildings designed by architects. But, of course, this assumption is really a conceit. Although some constitutional designers see the adoption of designs as an elite matter, this cannot really be the case (see Tsebelis 1990: 12). There are attentive voters, and most constitutional reformers contemplate facing election. If designs were really adopted in unmodified form, their democratic legitimacy might be at risk. The hash that is made of designs in the process of adoption may make conflict reduction much more difficult than it might be, but there may be some compensating advantages. A messy process of adoption, replete with design-destroying reciprocity, may give rise at least to a sense of local ownership of the product,[13] even if the institutions fall short of what is required to mitigate conflict.

Many states will inevitably make do with what they have or what they acquire in fits and starts: inherited institutions, patched-together institutions, partial adoptions, and strange hybrids. Their conflicts may continue, perhaps intermittently; they may change course, as they have in Nigeria (Suberu 1993: 42–4); or they may abate. In the most fortuitous cases—Thailand and Taiwan conspicuous among them—ethnic cleavages may decline greatly in salience as a by-product of other political changes. Political institutions, the sort embodied in constitutions, are very powerful determinants of the course of conflict, but fortunately they are not the only ones.

---

[13] It is, of course, easy to exaggerate the lack of legitimacy enjoyed by imported or imposed institutions. Counter-evidence can be supplied by reference to the healthy status of the MacArthur Constitution in Japan or of a number of constitutions imposed by colonial powers. They are many ways to indigenize, and so claim ownership, of external models, short of rejecting or radically reconfiguring them.

The Wave of Power-Sharing Democracy

Arend Lijphart

The assignment that I was given by the editor of this volume was not to write yet another treatise on consociational or power-sharing democracy, but to prepare an introductory overview of the general topic of 'Constitutional Design in the Third Wave'. This is not an easy task for me. For three reasons, I cannot help but look at this question through the prism of consociational theory. First, this volume is about more than just constitutional design; it also focuses on the specific design ingredients of conflict management and democracy. Second, I have been 'Mr Consociation'—as the late Stein Rokkan referred to me on several occasions—for a long time, and I still believe that consociational democracy is not only the optimal form of democracy for deeply divided societies but also, for the most deeply divided countries, the only feasible solution.

Third, what has happened in the 1990s is that ethnic divisions have replaced the cold war as the world's most serious source of violent conflict. This phenomenon has clashed with the third wave of democratization. In fact, this third wave, which started with the democratic revolution in Portugal in 1974 (Huntington 1991), culminated in the early 1990s with the demise of the Soviet Union, but ran into trouble by the mid-1990s. Larry Diamond (1996: 28) calls attention to 'the increasing shallowness of democratization in the latter part of the third wave' as demonstrated by 'the continued growth of electoral democracy, but stagnation of liberal democracy'; and mere 'electoral' or 'illiberal' democracy is, of course, not really a democratic form of government at all. In another ten years, when we shall be at the end of the first decade of the twenty-first century, we may well decide in retrospect that the third wave of democratization ended in the mid-1990s and that a third reverse wave started at about the same time. If this is indeed the case, I would place a major portion of the blame on the problem of ethnic conflict and on the inability of constitutional designers to deal constructively with this problem.

Fortunately, I believe that I can combine the objective of providing an introductory overview with my strong predisposition toward consociational theory by arguing that consociational theory, when broadly defined in terms of the key elements of executive power-sharing—grand coalition—and group autonomy, is a very comprehensive theory that, first, commands widespread support among the experts, and, second, has a broad substantive range that includes the main topics discussed in the next seven chapters: the debate between majoritarianism and power-sharing, the parliamentarism versus presidentialism debate, the questions of decentralization, federalism, and autonomy, and the design of electoral systems. I shall return to the relationship between consociational theory and these four subject matters later in this chapter. I shall also return later to the controversial matter of how narrowly or broadly the basic consociational concepts have been and should be defined, because I am very much aware that some of my critics have accused me of insufficient precision in this respect.

Points of Agreement among the Experts

I believe that most experts on divided societies and constitutional engineering are in broad agreement on several points. First, they agree that deep ethnic and other societal divisions pose a grave problem for democracy and that *ceteris paribus* it is more difficult to establish and maintain democracy in divided than in homogeneous societies. This proposition can be traced back to John Stuart Mill's (1861: 230) assertion that democracy is 'next to impossible in a country made up of different nationalities'—that is, in a multi-ethnic society—and completely impossible in linguistically divided countries, where the people 'read and speak different languages'. Mill puts this in stronger terms than today's experts do, but the general thrust of the argument has remained the same. Second, the experts agree that the problem of ethnic and other deep divisions is greater in countries that are not yet democratic or not fully democratic than in the well-established democracies. This also means that such deep divisions present a major obstacle to further democratization in the twenty-first century. On these two points, I cannot think of any expert who disagrees, and agreement appears to be universal or near-universal.

The third point of broad but not universal agreement—for instance, Donald L. Horowitz is a partial dissenter—is that the two key ingredients for successful democracy in divided societies are the sharing of executive power and group autonomy. These are what I have called the two 'primary characteristics' of consociational democracy (Lijphart 1995a: 859). Power-sharing means the participation of the representatives of all significant groups in political decision-making, especially at the executive level; group autonomy means that these groups have authority to run their own internal affairs, especially in the areas of education and culture.

Agreement on the central role of these two characteristics extends far beyond the consociational school. A good example is Ted Robert Gurr's book *Minorities at Risk*, which is, as the subtitle accurately reflects, a truly 'global view of ethnopolitical conflicts'. Gurr clearly does not take his inspiration from consociational theory and, in fact, he barely mentions it. Instead, he pursues a relentlessly inductive strategy which is so full of detailed operational definitions and explanations that I doubt that many readers reach the two concluding chapters that make up the final tenth of the text. This is very unfortunate because these final chapters contain a series of significant conclusions about the possibilities of settling ethnic conflicts. The overall evidence shows (1) that such conflicts are by no means intractable; (2) that they can usually be accommodated by 'some combination of the policies and institutions of *autonomy* and *power-sharing*'; and (3) that democracies have an especially good record of ethnic accommodation (Gurr 1993: 290–2, emphasis added). In order to distinguish the more general recommendation of power-sharing and autonomy, as in Gurr's book, from the consociational model, I shall refer to the former as the sharing/autonomy prescription.

If there is such strong agreement on the sharing/autonomy prescription, while consociational theory has been under attack by scores of critics—including the all-out assaults by Brian Barry (1975a, b), M. C. P. M. van Schendelen (1984), Ian Lustick (1997), and Matthijs Bogaards (2000)—wouldn't it be better to simply forget about the consociational literature and all the controversy it has generated and concentrate instead on the two key concepts of power-sharing and autonomy that we can agree on? This is a legitimate question but I think that the answer should be 'no'. For one thing, consociational theory recommends two additional ingredients that can strengthen executive power-sharing and autonomy: the 'secondary characteristics' of proportionality and mutual veto. For another, power-sharing and autonomy as well as proportionality and the veto can assume many different forms, and useful guidelines concerning the relative advantages and disadvantages of these institutional forms can be found in the consociational literature.

Moreover, it is not necessary for consociational theory to surrender
to its critics, because almost all of the criticisms are unjustified or
exaggerated.

Critiques of Power-Sharing and Autonomy

It is neither necessary nor helpful in this chapter to discuss all of
the objections that have been raised against consociational theory.
For a host of relatively minor bones of contention, I can simply refer
to my book on South Africa, in which I devote an entire chapter to a
comprehensive and systematic response to my critics (Lijphart
1985: 83–117). However, I think that I should summarize the six
most important criticisms and my responses to them, especially
because these criticisms also apply to the sharing/autonomy prescription on which, as I have just argued, there is broad agreement
and approval. Three of the criticisms focus on alleged deficiencies of
executive power-sharing: (1) that it is not sufficiently democratic;
(2) that it cannot work in practice; and (3) that a key explanation for
its failure is that it does not contain incentives for moderate behaviour. Two critiques target alleged problems of giving autonomy to
ethnic groups: (4) that especially regional autonomy is a slippery
slope that is likely to lead to secession and partition; and (5) that it
strengthens rather than weakens the cohesion and distinctiveness
of ethnic groups and, as a result, increases conflict between them.
The sixth objection is that both elements of the sharing/autonomy
prescription as well as the other elements of the consociational
model are based on European or Western experiences and are foreign and unsuitable for multi-ethnic societies in other parts of the
world.[1]

1. When executive power-sharing takes the form of a grand-
coalition cabinet, that is, a coalition of all of the major parties, it
conflicts with the view that a strong opposition is 'the sine qua non
of contemporary democracy' and that the opposition's prime purpose is 'to become the government' (Lawson 1993: 192–3). It also
fails the 'turnover' and 'two-turnover' tests that are frequently used
for determining whether a democracy has become stable and consolidated; for instance, according to Huntington's (1991: 266–7)
two-turnover test, 'a democracy may be viewed as consolidated if
the party or group that takes power in the initial election at the

---

[1] See also my discussion of these criticisms in *The Encyclopedia of Democracy*
from which the following paragraphs liberally borrow (Lijphart 1995a: 858–61).

time of transition [to democracy] loses a subsequent election and turns over power to those election winners, and if those election winners then peacefully turn over power to the winners of a later election'. My response to the opposition and turnover criteria is that they are narrowly based on one conception of democracy, the majoritarian conception, which does not exhaust the range of democratic possibilities.

A related criticism faults the compromises negotiated, often behind close doors, by the leaders of the various groups. Moreover, power-sharing systems often use list forms of proportional representation (PR), in which party leaders have a great deal of influence on the composition of the lists and hence on who can get elected. These observations are not wrong, but it is wrong to imply a stark contrast with majoritarian democracy. For instance, in the United Kingdom, the flagship of majoritarian democracy, all important decisions are typically prepared by bureaucrats, adopted in the cabinet in complete secrecy, and, after being announced, hardly ever changed under parliamentary or public pressure. And, in spite of Britain's plurality electoral system, party leaders are usually able to reserve safe seats for themselves, just as party leaders in list PR systems usually have safe places at the top of the list. Elite domination does not vary a great deal among democracies. The difference between majority rule and power-sharing is not whether leaders do or do not predominate but whether they tend to be adversarial or cooperative.

2. When power is broadly shared, the critics argue, it will be difficult or even impossible to make decisions; the result is immobilism, deadlock, and, in the end, democratic breakdown. The critics have also placed great emphasis on the failure of power-sharing democracy in two of its major examples—in Cyprus in 1963 and in Lebanon in 1975—as well as the British government's difficulties in solving the Northern Ireland problem by power-sharing, until 1999. However, there are also clear cases where power-sharing has worked successfully in ethnically divided countries—Switzerland since 1943, Belgium since 1970, Lebanon from 1943 to 1975, Malaysia from 1955 to 1969, Suriname from 1958 to 1973, and the Netherlands Antilles from 1950 to 1985—as well as in three countries with deep religious-ideological cleavages—Austria from 1945 to 1966, the Netherlands from 1917 to 1967, and Luxembourg during the same period of about half a century. In addition, there are three more countries which I also regard as power-sharing cases but that are more controversial: Colombia from 1958 to 1974, India ever since 1947, and South Africa since 1994. Czecho-Slovakia was a

power-sharing democracy from 1989 until its amicable partition in 1993. During 1999, two new power-sharing systems were set up: in Fiji—where, however, it collapsed in 2000—and in Northern Ireland.[2]

Moreover, when the failures of power-sharing in Cyprus and Lebanon, in 1963 and 1975 respectively, are analysed more closely, they actually demonstrate the strength and promise of power-sharing instead of its weakness. In the Lebanese case, first of all, the outbreak of the civil war in 1975 should not obscure the fact that power-sharing worked quite well in this severely divided country from 1943 to 1975. Second, a major part of the blame for the collapse of power-sharing belongs not to internal problems caused by the power-sharing system itself but to Lebanon's precarious position in the international arena of the Middle East and, in particular, to repeated Palestinian, Syrian, and Israeli interventions. In this sense, the civil war that broke out in 1975 was not an ordinary civil war but an international conflict fought on Lebanese soil. Third, it must be admitted that Lebanon's power-sharing system had some weak spots. The Christian sects continued to have greater representation and influence in the government in spite of the fact that the Muslims had gradually become the majority of the population, and the most powerful political office, the presidency, was permanently assigned to the Maronite Christians. But the Lebanese themselves have recognized these problems and have tried to solve them. The 1989 Taif Accord changed the 6:5 ratio for parliamentary elections favouring the Christians to equal parliamentary representation for Christians and Muslims, and it also roughly equalized the powers of the Maronite president and the Sunni Muslim prime minister.

The most important lesson of the Lebanese case is that power-sharing needed to be repaired and improved rather than replaced. In the eyes of most Lebanese and knowledgeable foreign observers, a switch to a majoritarian form of democracy has not been regarded

---

[2] According to my definition, provided above, of grand coalition, or executive power-sharing, as the participation of representatives of all significant groups in political decision-making, all of these examples—including the developing countries India, South Africa, Lebanon, Malaysia, Colombia, Suriname, the Netherlands Antilles, and Fiji—are clearly characterized by grand coalitions as well as most of the other elements of power-sharing with only minor exceptions. One mistake that many critics make is not to distinguish between power-sharing as an ideal type and power-sharing as an empirical category; they argue that few or no power-sharing systems exist because few or no examples of 100 per cent pure and perfect power-sharing can be found.

as a realistic option. It is even more significant that the same conclusion applies to Cyprus, where admittedly power-sharing never worked well. Instituted in the 1960 constitution, it was ended by the 1963 civil war, and it appeared to be permanently doomed by the Turkish invasion in 1974 and the subsequent de facto partition of the island into a Greek Cypriot southern state and a Turkish Cypriot northern state. Nevertheless, since 1985, UN Secretary-General Javier Pérez de Cuéllar and his two successors have made several proposals for a unified Cyprus that strikingly resemble the basic power-sharing features of the 1960 constitution. Their efforts demonstrate their recognition of the fact that power-sharing, although it may not succeed, represents the optimal chance for a successful solution. Similarly, the British government's failure until 1999 to have its power-sharing proposals for Northern Ireland accepted and implemented never budged it from its basic conviction that power-sharing was the only possible and acceptable solution there.

3. A special reason why executive power-sharing is likely or even bound to fail has been advanced by Donald L. Horowitz. He argues that its fatal flaw is that lacks incentives for compromise. In multiparty situations with ethnically based parties, 'the mere need to form a coalition will not produce compromise. The incentive to compromise, and not merely the incentive to coalesce, is the key to accommodation'. Without incentives to compromise, the only coalitions that will be formed are 'coalitions of convenience that will dissolve' (Horowitz 1991: 171, 175). Coalescence and compromise are indeed analytically distinct, and there are plenty of examples, cited by Horowitz, of coalitions that have been unable to compromise and that, as a result, have fallen apart. But there are also many contrary examples and, logically, the desire to coalesce does imply a need to compromise.

A general and uncontroversial assumption in political science is that political parties want to gain power. Based on this assumption, a further basic premise underlying virtually all coalition theories ever since the pioneering work of William H. Riker (1962) is that, in multiparty systems, parties will want to enter and remain in coalition cabinets. Only more recently have a few coalition theorists, notably Kaare Strom (1990), pointed out that under special conditions parties may prefer not to join governing coalitions; for instance, parties may prefer to stay in the opposition if they believe that this will enhance their electoral fortunes and hence their ability to enter future cabinet coalitions in a stronger position, and they may also be satisfied with a formal opposition role if influential legislative committees give them the opportunity to have a major say in government policy without being in the government themselves—especially if the government is a relatively weak minority government. But these are the exceptions, and the more usual inclination of parties is to want to be included in cabinets. Because the only way for ethnic or any other parties not just to enter but also to stay in the cabinet is to reach compromises with their coalition partners, they have a very strong incentive to compromise—political power!—instead of no such incentive, as Horowitz mistakenly argues. This does not mean, of course, that political power as a short-term objective is the only incentive for politicians: it is far too cynical, as well as unrealistic, to argue that constructive statesmanship, based on enlightened and long-term self-interest and even some altruism, cannot play a significant role too.[3]

4. Some critics have argued that autonomy, when groups are geographically concentrated and when autonomy takes the form of a federal or strongly decentralized system, is dangerous because the groups involved are unlikely to be satisfied with it and will press for outright secession. For instance, Eric A. Nordlinger excludes federalism from his recommended set of conflict-regulating practices in divided societies because it may result in the breakup of the state: 'The combination of territorially distinctive segments and federalism's grant of partial autonomy sometimes provides additional impetus to demands for greater autonomy', and, when these demands are refused, 'secession and civil war may follow' (Nordlinger 1972: 32). One answer to this argument is that it is hard to imagine that the imposition of a unitary and centralized democratic system would be able to prevent secession if the basic ingredient of separatist sentiment would be strong. More important, however, is that the empirical evidence does not support Nordlinger's fears. On the basis of his worldwide comparative analysis, Gurr's conclusion is as follows: 'Neither in theory nor in practice is there anything inherent in autonomy agreements that leads to future civil war or disintegration of the state. The recent historical record shows that, on balance, autonomy agreements can be an effective means for managing regional conflicts' (Gurr 1993: 300–1).

---

[3] Minorities obviously have stronger incentives than majorities to enter coalition governments. That is why I have emphasized that the first of nine conditions that favour power-sharing is an all-minority situation, that is, the absence of a majority group (Lijphart 1995a: 859).

5. Another alleged weakness of group autonomy, even if it is not on a territorial basis, is that it may encourage ethnic conflict by explicitly recognizing the legitimacy of ethnic groups and by making them stronger, more cohesive, and more distinctive. However, the existence of strong and autonomous ethnic groups does not necessarily translate into serious conflict among them. On the contrary, the strengthened ethnic groups are designed to play a constructive role in conflict resolution. Gurr's conclusion on this matter is again well worth quoting. In his final chapter, he raises the question: 'What is the functional place of communal groups in the global system of states?' He answers that the optimal approach is 'the positive-sum coexistence of ethnic groups and plural states', which means 'both *recognizing* and *strengthening* communal groups within the existing state system' (Gurr 1993: 323, emphasis added).

6. Because power-sharing, autonomy, and other aspects of the consociational model have been studied more extensively in the European cases and by European scholars, it is sometimes alleged to be a European or Western model that is foreign and unsuitable for multi-ethnic societies in other parts of the world. This criticism is clearly erroneous because it ignores such major examples as Lebanon, Malaysia, and Colombia, where power-sharing and autonomy were developed by indigenous leaders without external influence or assistance. It is also worth pointing out that Sir Arthur Lewis, whose *Politics in West Africa* (1965) can be regarded as the first modern treatise on consociational theory, was not a European or a student of European politics but a native of the Caribbean island of St Lucia and a black scholar whose interest was in African politics. Finally, numerous non-Western scholars and political leaders have emphasized that majority rule violates their native traditions of trying to arrive at consensus through lengthy deliberations—traditions that correspond closely to the power-sharing idea. For instance, Lewis (1965: 86) himself states that, in Africa, 'the tribe has made its decisions by discussion, in much the way that coalitions function; this kind of democratic procedure is at the heart of the original institutions of the people'. Another example is Philippine statesman and scholar Raul S. Manglapus's emphasis not only on the strong democratic traditions that he finds in non-Western countries generally but also on the fact that these traditions are power-sharing rather than majoritarian traditions: 'the common characteristic [is] the element of consensus as opposed to adversarial decisions' (Manglapus 1987: 69).

Problems of Definition and Measurement

My above defence of the sharing/autonomy prescription and the consociational model do not mean that I believe consociational theory to be flawless. An especially valid and serious criticism is that its key concepts have been very hard to define and measure precisely. I have come to the conclusion, however, that this is an insoluble problem and that we shall simply have to live with concepts that have very important theoretical and policy significance but that cannot be measured precisely. In the late 1970s and early 1980s, I made a major effort to operationalize and quantify degrees of executive power-sharing, degrees of federalism and decentralization, degrees of proportionality, degrees of minority veto power, and so on. This led to the development of the concept of consensus democracy, of which every aspect can be expressed in quantitative terms, and which is clearly related to the concept of consociational democracy—but which is just as clearly not the same as consociational democracy (Lijphart 1984; 1999). Let me add that the many critics who have pointed to the problems of definition and measurement have not been able to propose constructive solutions either.

Is the lack of precision in consociational theory acceptable or does it involve too much 'conceptual stretching' (see Sartori 1970)? Lustick (1997) argues that so much stretching has happened that the entire enterprise has become meaningless. The substantive problem is that the basic characteristics of consociational democracy are inherently stretchable: they can assume a large number of different institutional forms.[4] For instance, the most straightforward form of executive power-sharing is that of a grand coalition cabinet of ethnic parties in a parliamentary system, as in Malaysia and South Africa. Another possibility is a grand coalition in cabinets, defined not in partisan terms but more broadly in terms of the representation of linguistic or other groups in a pre-determined ratio, such as the equal representation of Dutch-speakers and French-speakers in Belgian cabinets. During the period of the Congress Party's dominance in India, cabinets were one-party cabinets, but close to proportional shares of ministerships were given to the different linguistic groups, States, and regions of the country

---

[4] In view of the great variety of forms that the four elements of power-sharing can assume, it is difficult to understand how Horowitz can call power-sharing a 'one size fits all' solution.

as well as to the Muslim minority of about 12 per cent of the population and the even smaller Sikh minority of roughly 2 per cent.

The above examples are all parliamentary systems, but grand coalitions can also occur in non-parliamentary systems. In the Swiss separation-of-powers system, the executive is constituted in such a way that all major religious and linguistic groups as well as the four largest political parties are given representation. In presidential systems of government, a grand coalition is more difficult, but not impossible, to arrange: the top governmental offices—such as the presidency, prime ministership, and assembly speakership in Lebanon, and the presidency and vice-presidency in Cyprus—may be allocated to specified ethnic or religious groups. In the 1958–74 Colombian system, executive power-sharing was in part achieved sequentially: it was agreed that Liberal and Conservative presidents would alternate in office.

Can all of these formal and informal rules and practices be subsumed under the one concept of executive power-sharing? My feeling is that they have enough of a common core to justify it. Conceptual stretching is an error to be avoided—but so is conceptual rigidity and conceptual timidity.

Practical Guidelines Derived from Consociational Theory

As indicated in the introductory section of this chapter, I believe that consociational theory has considerable practical utility in that it provides specific guidelines and recommendations for the design of power-sharing, autonomy, and other consociational institutions. All of the consociational principles can assume a great variety of institutional forms, but these forms do not serve the basic purpose of ethnic accommodation equally well: some can be recommended, while others should be warned against. I shall discuss these guidelines under the four headings that correspond to the four topics analyzed in the next several chapters.

1. *The power-sharing versus majoritarian debate.* The first warning is, very obviously, against attempts to establish a pure majoritarian system with a one-party cabinet, a party system with two dominant parties, and a plurality system of voting. However, somewhat less obviously, the warning also extends to Horowitz's vote-pooling recommendations, which he regards as alternatives to majoritarianism, but which from a consociational perspective do not differ a great deal from majority-rule democracy. His key vote-pooling proposal is the alternative vote in single-member districts.

To give a hypothetical example, if there are three candidates, *A*, *B*, and *C*, supported by 45 per cent, 40 per cent, and 15 per cent of the voters respectively, *A* and *B* will have to bid for the second preferences of *C*'s supporters in order to win—which will, according to Horowitz, reward moderation. The problem is that precisely the same argument can be used in favour of the plurality method. In the same example, but under plurality rules, many of *C*'s supporters will not want to waste their votes on *C*'s hopeless candidacy, or may not even be able to vote for *C* at all because *C* has wisely decided not to pursue a hopeless candidacy. Here, too, *A* and *B* will have to appeal to *C*'s supporters in order to win.

The alternative vote resembles the majority-run-off method—also often called the double-ballot or second-ballot system—even more closely. In the same hypothetical example, *C* is now eliminated in the first round, and *A* and *B* have to compete for the votes of *C*'s supporters in the run-off. The alternative vote accomplishes in one round of voting what requires two ballots in the majority-run-off system. The incentives for moderation are exactly the same. The majority-run-off method was commonly used in Western Europe for parliamentary elections until the beginning of the twentieth century. In most cases, it was replaced with proportional representation, and the main reason for this change, as noted by Rokkan (1970: 157), was the unsatisfactory operation of the majority-run-off in linguistically and religiously divided societies and the need to provide for minority representation. This historical evidence throws additional doubt on the value of the alternative vote for the management of ethnic conflict. Both the logic and the practical effect of the alternative vote are clearly majoritarian.[5]

The debate on this subject between Horowitz, myself, and others (see, for instance, Sisk 1996) has been mainly on the relative advantages and disadvantages of vote-pooling versus power-sharing. A different and at least equally important question is: which of the alternatives is more likely to be chosen in a negotiated transition to democracy?[6] It is hard to imagine that in a situation where one or more relatively small minorities face a majority or several large groups, the minorities will be willing to accept a system that does not offer them the chance to be represented by their own leaders but

---

[5] Although all three methods are majoritarian, the alternative vote is preferable to plurality because it selects a majority instead of a mere plurality winner, and it is preferable to the majority-run-off because it picks the majority winner more accurately as well as in just one round of voting.

[6] I owe this insight to Jennifer N. Collins, a Ph.D. candidate in political science at the University of California, San Diego.

merely by the more moderate leaders of majority or the larger groups. In the case of Northern Ireland, for instance, it is highly unlikely that Protestant rule, with the proviso that the more moderate Protestants would be in charge, would ever be acceptable to the Catholic minority. The only situation where the alternative vote may be freely agreed on is that of a divided society with groups of roughly equal size, such as the two ethnic groups in Fiji; this kind of situation is very rare, however.[7]

2. *The presidential-parliamentary debate*. The choice between these alternatives is an easy one from the consociational point of view: parliamentary government is clearly superior. One reason is the majoritarian nature of presidential elections. As Juan Linz (1994: 18) states, 'perhaps the most important implication of presidentialism is that it introduces a strong element of zero-sum game into democratic politics with rules that tend toward a "winner-take-all" outcome'. Moreover, it is much more difficult to form grand coalitions of the representatives of all significant groups in a presidential than in a parliamentary system. The difference between these systems is usually defined in terms of two criteria: in parliamentary systems, the executive is selected by the legislature and is dependent on legislative confidence, whereas, in presidential systems, the executive is elected, directly or indirectly, by the voters and is not dependent on the confidence of the legislature. An equally important third difference is that the executive in a parliamentary system is a collegial body—the cabinet—whereas the president is a one-person executive with a presidential cabinet consisting of advisers to the president instead of co-decision-makers. The collegial nature of the cabinet in a parliamentary system is obviously a much more favourable setting for forming a broad power-sharing executive.

The recommendation against presidential government also applies to the various 'diluted' forms of presidentialism; even if some sharing of executive power is introduced, the zero-sum nature of presidential elections does not change because there can be only one winner. Parliamentarism remains the better option. In semi-presidential systems, there can be considerable power-sharing

---

[7] Moreover, the alternative vote played a very small part in bringing about the Fijian power-sharing government in 1999. The much more important factor was that the leaders of the two main ethnic groups had become convinced that future governments should include representatives of both groups, as shown by their decision to put mandatory power-sharing—for any party with more than 10 per cent of the seats in the House of Representatives—in the new constitution.

between president, prime minister, and cabinet, but it is also possible for the president to be even more powerful than in most pure presidential systems. In France, the best-known example of semi-presidentialism, the president usually exercises predominant power, and the 1962–74 and 1981–86 periods can even be labelled 'hyperpresidential' phases (Keeler and Schain 1997: 95–7). Horowitz (1991: 205–14) favours a president elected by the alternative vote or a similar vote-pooling method, but in other respects his president does not differ from presidents in pure presidential systems.

Much the same applies to the Colombian presidency in the 1958–74 period in spite of alternation between the two main parties and parity in the cabinet; a prime minister and a cabinet in a parliamentary system would have been a better way to institute power-sharing. Finally, in the Lebanese case—not a pure case of presidentialism because the president is elected by the legislature—considerable executive power-sharing is achieved by the rule that the president be a Maronite and the prime minister a Sunni, and that the cabinet be composed according to a roughly proportional sectarian formula; moreover, the prime minister's powers were increased to approximately the same level as the president's powers in 1989. However, the presidency is still widely regarded as the most important and prestigious office, and there can be only one president.

The Lebanese and Colombian systems have the additional drawback that they are systems in which the constituent groups are predetermined, that is, a system that explicitly names the population groups that will act as the principal partners in power-sharing: the religious sects in Lebanon and the two traditional parties in Colombia. It is preferable to allow the groups to identify and define themselves. Pre-determination is inevitably discriminatory: in favour of the groups that are included, and against groups, especially smaller groups, that are not recognized. Pre-determination also entails the assignment of individuals to the specified groups, which may be controversial, offensive, or even completely unacceptable to many citizens. It also means that there is no place for individuals or groups who reject the premise that society should be organized on an ethnic or communal basis. Finally, in systems of pre-determination, there is a strong tendency to rigidly fix shares of representation on a permanent basis, such as the 6:5 Christian-Muslim ratio in pre-Taif Lebanon and the 7:3 Greek-Turkish ratio in the cabinet according to the 1960 constitution of Cyprus. In contrast, self-determination can be entirely non-discriminatory, neutral, and flexible.

The distinction between pre-determination and self-determination also applies to cabinets in parliamentary systems, and *ceteris paribus* self-determination is to be preferred. An example of pre-determined groups are the Dutch-speakers and French-speakers who, according to the Belgian constitution, should participate in the cabinet in a 1:1 ratio. A good illustration of self-determination is the provisional 1994 constitution of South Africa, which gave any party, whether ethnic or not, with a minimum of 5 per cent of the seats in parliament the right to participate in the cabinet on a proportional basis.

3. *Decentralization, federalism, and autonomy.* According to consociational theory, federalism offers an excellent opportunity for group autonomy if the groups are geographically concentrated. The logic of this recommendation entails that the federal boundaries coincide as much as possible with the ethnic or other group boundaries, as in India, Switzerland, and Belgium. It contrasts with Seymour Martin Lipset's proposition that federalism should 'cross-cut the social structure'; Lipset (1963: 81) specifically recommends against federalism that divides a country 'between different ethnic, religious, or linguistic areas, as it does in India and Canada. Democracy needs cleavage within linguistic or religious groups, not between them'. Furthermore, in order to be able to make the federal dividing lines coincide as much as possible with the ethnic boundaries, consociational theory recommends a federalism with relatively many and relatively small constituent units.

When groups are dispersed geographically, autonomy can be instituted on a non-territorial basis. Here, too, a distinction can be made between pre-determined and self-determined forms. Belgian federalism is partly non-territorial—for the approximately 15 per cent of the population who live in Brussels—and it is a pre-determined system in that people are classified as French-speakers or Dutch-speakers. A good model of non-territorial autonomy on a self-determined basis is the Dutch system of educational autonomy adopted in 1917: all schools, public and private, were to receive equal financial support from the state in proportion to their enrolment. Although the new law was primarily designed to accommodate the main religious groups and their religious schools, it was formulated in neutral language and allowed any group to establish and run schools as long as basic educational standards would be observed. As a result, it has also been taken advantage of by small secular groups interested in particular educational philosophies to establish, for instance, Montessori schools.

In my work on consensus democracy, which, as noted earlier, can be regarded as an extension of consociational theory, I have found that the degree of federalism and decentralization is strongly related to four other institutional characteristics: the degree of bicameralism—with two houses that have equal power and are differently constituted as the strongest form—the degree of strong and active judicial review, the degree of constitutional rigidity, and the degree of independence of the central bank (Lijphart 1999: 243–6). These are important elements of institutional design, and high degrees of all of them offer additional safeguards for minority interests and autonomy.

Their statistical relationships with the degree of federalism and decentralization and with each other are strong and linear, but we should be careful not to conclude that 'more' is necessarily 'better'. Two legislative chambers with equal powers and different compositions present special problems in parliamentary systems, because it may be difficult to form cabinets that have the confidence of both chambers, as the 1975 Australian constitutional crisis illustrates (Lijphart 1984: 102–3). In the upper house of federal bicameral systems, small States are often over-represented; this can work very well, but as over-representation increases, equality of individual representation suffers. Rigid constitutions that are difficult to amend, strong judicial review, and independent central banks have obvious advantages, but this does not mean that the most extreme forms—rigid and virtually unamendable constitutions, the most interventionist high courts, and central banks that are completely independent of executives and legislatures—are to be recommended.

4. *Electoral system design in new democracies.* Proportionality is a general principle of consociational democracy that applies not only to the electoral system but also to the composition of the public service and to the allocation of public funds—as in the example of Dutch education mentioned above. As far as the electoral system is concerned, the proportionality principle dictates some form of proportional representation (PR). PR is clearly preferable to majoritarian methods like plurality, the majority-run-off, and the alternative vote. It is also preferable to semi-PR because, as the latter's label indicates, it is only partly proportional. And it is superior to systems that try to achieve proportionality without the benefit of straightforward PR, such as the Lebanese system in which, in each district, candidates have to be elected according to a pre-determined sectarian ratio, for instance, two Maronites, one Sunni, and one Druze in a four-member district. It has all of the disadvantages of pre-determination discussed earlier.

With regard to the specific form of PR, three further recommendations can be derived from consociational theory. In order to encourage the formation of cohesive and disciplined parties with strong leaders, it is wise to give party organizations the preponderant power over nominations. Therefore, (1) list PR is preferable to the single transferable vote, and (2) list PR with closed or almost closed lists is preferable to open-list PR. In addition, (3) in order to obtain full or close to full proportionality, it is wise not to introduce high electoral thresholds. The electoral thresholds in PR systems range from no formal threshold in South Africa and the very low 0.67 per cent threshold in the Netherlands to the 5 per cent threshold in Germany and New Zealand. The appropriate threshold depends on the particular minorities and their respective sizes in a given country, but my inclination would be to recommend a threshold not exceeding about 3 per cent.

Electoral laws may have unintended consequences, especially when the electoral rules are complex, but my work on consensus democracy shows that the degree of electoral proportionality is strongly related to the degree of multipartism, which in turn is closely related to the type of cabinets formed in parliamentary systems and to executive-legislative relations. For instance, the 1996 and 1999 elections under the new PR system in New Zealand immediately produced a shift from a two-party system with a majority party to a multiparty system with no party winning a majority of the seats, coalition and minority cabinets instead of the previous one-party majority cabinets, and cabinets that are less predominant over the legislature than before (Lijphart 1999: 25–7, 243–7). However, with regard to multipartism, too, 'more' is not necessarily 'better'. The well-established democracies tend to have effective numbers of parties below six—roughly in line with Sartori's wise counsel against extreme party pluralism with six or more significant parties, that is, parties strong enough to have coalition or blackmail potential (Lijphart 1999: 76–7; Sartori 1976: 131–45).[8]

A final distinction with regard to all of the above issues of constitutional design is between formal and informal rules. Should consociational rules be laid down in formal documents or rely on merely informal and unwritten agreements and understandings among the

---

[8] The electoral and party systems are further related to the type of interest group system. Countries with plurality elections and two-party systems tend to have pluralist interest group systems with free-for-all competition among groups. Countries with PR and multipartism tend to have coordinated and 'corporatist' interest group systems aimed at compromise and concertation (Lijphart 1999: 171–84). The latter can be recommended as a useful complement to power-sharing arrangements in ethnically divided societies.

leaders of the main groups? My reading of the evidence is that informal rules generally work better because they are more flexible—but perhaps also because they reflect a higher level of trust among groups and group leaders. When sufficient mutual trust is lacking and inter-group relations are highly contentious, there is probably no alternative to formal constitutional and legal rules to govern power-sharing and autonomy in deeply divided societies.

Institutions and Coalition Building in Post-Communist Transitions

Olga Shvetsova

In the ten years of the post-communist transitions, the countries of the east-central European region passed through several cycles of elections and government, generating new evidence of the influence of formal political institutions on transitional political dynamics. This essay specifically addresses the transitional development of their party systems as a function of institutional choices. Focusing on party systems, we identify the process of coalition formation as the transmission mechanism by which institutions at this stage influence political consolidation. Transitional political consequences of formal democratic procedures are, in turn, best perceived through the impact that they have on coalition-building.

From a designer's point of view, most of the institutions' work is done in transitions and consists of moving the political system in a direction of a consolidated democracy of a particular desirable shape by forming a stable pattern of expectations about the political interactions (O'Donnell 1994). Once transitions are over and the consolidated stage is achieved, formal institutions start acting more in a supportive, 'holding', capacity rather than a system-shaping one. While different systems of formal rules end up 'supporting' different consolidated systems, by overlooking the earlier, active stage of their work we miss important information and, among other things, fail to identify the rules that do not direct the political system to a consolidated state, as well as those that fall early and are replaced by non-democratic alternatives. In other words, even if the ultimate objective of constitutional design is to achieve a specific 'stable' shape of a political system commonly associated with a particular general set of formal institutions, whether this objective can be reached by applying those institutions will depend on their transitional performance. The latter, in turn, can be potentially driven

by the details of rules, peculiarities of societies, and complex interactive effects that institutional research on mature systems does
not detect.

Addressing the use of institutions in directing the process of party
system formation, we necessarily focus on how formal rules direct
the change in political behaviour. At the transitional stage, in contrast with the consolidated environment, players make decisions
about how they will *change* their strategies. In fact, these decisions
supply some of the instability of expectations about the nature of
transitional political interactions. Decisions whether to coalesce, or
split, or continue as a distinctive political organization made by
political elites are at the base of the transitional evolution of party
systems. Evidence from the post-communist region indicates that
these decisions are influenced by institutions; moreover, different
institutional variables affect them interactively. In a political system at a consolidated stage, choices of this kind become rare, while
political expectations stabilize. Thus, institutional influence on
behavioural change is no longer easily observable. Past institutional effects, however, remain embedded in equilibrium patterns of
political competition and multipartism which can be viewed as end-
points of the process of party system formation.

This chapter addresses the transitional influence of combinations
of majoritarian and power-sharing institutions, suggesting that
their interactive effect may undermine or weaken the incentives for
party-building that each of them separately can provide.

Coalition-building as the Main Mechanism of Party System Development

The notion of parties and, therefore, party systems remains elusive
during transitions. If we view as parties entities that enter electoral
contests and receive votes at the polls, we would be struck by how
many of them there are in transitional elections. Also, electoral contestants on a typical proportional-representational (PR) ballot can
range from what Duverger (1954) would characterize as mass parties obtaining at times a plurality vote nationwide, as is the case
with some successors of former regime parties, to organizations that
rely exclusively on the appeal of a highly visible leader, to numerous minuscule special issues 'parties'. If that approach does not get
us sufficiently close to Sartori's (1976) notion of an 'atomized' party
system, we could take a closer look at the PR ballots and notice that
most entries on those ballots are themselves alliances of something

smaller, each alliance member in turn calling itself a party.[1] Adding to all that the propensity of transitional parties to experience organizational splits, we may also have to recognize that some of these proto-parties consist of even smaller factions or latent parties. If, furthermore, we move to electoral mechanisms that either completely rely on or partially incorporate single-member districts (SMDs), a definition of parties as separate electoral entities would lead us to include in this category independent candidates who contest and win those races in huge numbers.[2]

All of these entities receive some votes in elections, although the vote shares of many of them are negligible. Some of them receive parliamentary seats. This, however, does not imply that what we would identify as parties if we look at parliaments is equivalent to electoral parties receiving representation. Many electoral formations which in fact are alliances break up as soon as their mission of obtaining seats for their members is fulfilled. Parliaments are also a good place for the 'latent' parties to break away from their host electoral organizations. On the other hand, independent MPs may either form their own parliamentary factions or join the delegations of elected parties. By looking at parliaments, especially in the early years of transitions, we would discover party systems substantially different from those that we see in either preceding or subsequent elections.[3]

It probably should not be surprising that during the time when parties and party systems are forming, any operationalizable notion of a party would include entities that, in relation to either previous or following stages in the political process are, in fact, coalitions. In the same light, the elite side of the process of party formation in transitions is a story of forming and breaking coalitions.[4] The mechanism through which formal institutions enable a particular party system to form by the time the transition is over is their ability to

[1] Thus, 18 contestants were on the ballot in the 1994 Slovakia election. These, however, included a total of 31 parties grouped into various coalitions (Wolchik 1997: 228). Similarly, the 1995 Estonian election was contested by 9 parties and 8 coalitions, while the latter included 21 more independent parties.

[2] In Russia, despite the fact that dozens of parties contested the elections both on the PR ballot and in SMDs, in 1993, more than 60 per cent of district seats were won by independent candidates. In 1995, this number exceeded 30 per cent.

[3] In Slovakia in 1994, for example, seven electoral lists obtained parliamentary seats. But once in parliament, they quickly fragmented into 16 political parties and groupings (Olson 1998).

[4] Kitschelt *et al.* (1999), analysing the party systems development in eastern Europe, describe electoral parties as lasting coalitions of politicians who pool resources in electoral campaigns.

promote a desirable type of coalition formation in the course of the transition and to ensure the stability and organizational unity of the resulting coalitions—that is, parties.

Institutional influences on coalition formation in post-communist transitions are characterized by the multiplicity of institutional contexts where the same basic decision of the involved proto-parties— that is, whether to cooperate or fight each other electorally—may lead to different and, sometimes, opposite implications. As a consequence, the effect of any given institution on strategic coalition formation may be muted or even completely reversed by the effects of other institutions. At times, the institutions' combined effects may appear completely counterintuitive as they can lead to participants' strategies which are sub-optimal in any single institutional context.

When alternative rules apply together in real time, as is the case in the mixed electoral systems or when parliamentary and presidential elections are held concurrently, we can expect players' choices of strategies for cooperation to accommodate the demands of all such institutional contexts at once. Poorly compatible institutions used at different stages of the electoral cycle may pull the development of the party system in opposite directions, institutions at one stage undoing the work of institutions at other stages. Finally, rules that we expect to promote political consolidation may have the predicted effect, but induce merely tactical coalescing, with alliances being viewed by participants even prior to their creation as opportunistic and easily reversible.[5] Evidence from the region, in particular, supports the hypothesis that majoritarian mechanisms, when used to supplement power-sharing institutions, can slow or disrupt cooperative processes among party elites and slow down the development of party systems.

Combined Influence of Multiple Institutional Incentives on Coalition Formation

We might expect a party strategy to be selected to best fit the combined requirements of all institutionally structured situations.[6]

[5] A widespread practice of forging temporary electoral alliances explicitly for the purpose of passing electoral thresholds recently prompted a number of countries to introduce legal restrictions on such alliance-building. Thus, Estonia in 1998 modified its electoral law to prohibit electoral alliances, forcing several parties to terminate the electoral coalitions they had formed for the previous election in 1995.

[6] This statement should apply in equal measure to transitional as well as developed party systems. What is different between the two, though, is the range of

A decision to campaign as a separate party rather than joining an electoral alliance affects all the electoral contests in which the party participates. And because goals generated by different races are assessed jointly when a party strategy is formulated, the observed institutional influence may differ from what one could expect in any given race.

To illustrate how objectives of parties in different races can stand in conflict with each other, consider a problem of two—out of possibly many—'new' pro-reform parties which are strongly motivated to create a workable political alliance being confronted in elections by the unified anti-reform—that is, communist—opposition. The choice that the new parties face is whether to compete against each other or to cooperate during the campaign. The same decision applies in both institutional contexts, one based on power-sharing and the other on majoritarian rules.[7] Under reasonable hypothetical payoffs in the two institutional environments, not only can alternative incentives generate opposite patterns of cooperation in equilibrium, but in combination they may undermine incentives for cooperation that each of them separately could offer.

In the institutional context of power-sharing, such as, for example, a highly proportional electoral system, if the two proto-parties decide to cooperate in forming an alliance, a coalition, or even a new party, payoffs to each of them are maximal. They retain their initial support and possibly attract an additional following by sending a signal of expected electoral strength and policy cohesiveness. Besides, if there are qualifications in the electoral mechanism that need to be met, such as an electoral threshold, cooperation not only makes it easier to succeed, but is sometimes necessary for success. Parties that cooperate do not waste any votes by falling below the threshold; so acting together gives them more seats per vote and a stronger presence in the parliament.

If, on the other hand, one of the parties acts cooperatively while the other competes against it, electoral losses to the cooperating player diminish the payoffs to both parties; for example, their potential combined weight in the parliament declines. It would, thus; be irrational for either of them to compete against a potentially cooperative partner. In the case of power-sharing institutions,

strategic choices, which in transitions are more numerous and far-reaching and include such things as the very existence and the independent identity of a party.

[7] We may expect this assumption to hold if the two rules are used in the same election or in two separate elections held concurrently. But even in the case of separate non-concurrent elections, there will be some strategic spillovers where the goals of a later race would affect the behaviour in the earlier one.

the two ideologically compatible parties in some degree 'share' in each other's success.[8]

However, it is reasonable to expect that if one of the two insists on contesting the election separately, the best response for the other is to compete against it in return. When the two parties contest elections separately, their chances of electoral success are reduced, as are their expected payoffs compared with the 'cooperative' situation. Based on such a payoff structure, there are two pure strategy Nash equilibria in the game in Fig. 3.1: one where both players offer cooperation, and one where both players decide to act non-cooperatively. The first seems very likely to prevail as it Pareto-dominates the other.

Party II

		To cooperate	To contest
Party I	To cooperate	6,6	2,5
	To contest	5,2	4,4

FIGURE 3.1: *Incentives and choices in a power-sharing mechanism*

Meanwhile, in the majoritarian context, the strategic situation is similar to the Game of Chicken (Fig. 3.2). There are no increasing returns to scale here; that is, the combined benefit to the parties does not increase when both cooperate as compared with the situation where one cooperates and the other competes—between them, the two parties win the seat as long as they do not run against each other. The inducement for cooperation is produced by the fear of losing the race to the opposition if the vote is fragmented. Because of the cost of internal competition, for both to contest the election is not an equilibrium, but neither is full cooperation. Each player wants the other to yield and prefers to reserve the fixed and non-divisible reward of a single majoritarian office for himself. In other words, if one player decides to cooperate, the other one will compete, and before any election alliance could be formed, parties would need

---

[8] This payoff structure can be described as increasing returns to scale. Kitschelt *et al.* (1999), in particular, argue that the players' electoral payoff from running under a single label is greater than the combined payoffs they would receive if they ran individually. The gains from cooperation come from economies of scale in devising the electoral campaign and in turning out the vote.

to agree whose candidate will represent it. Both equilibria of this game are situations where one party joins the other as a junior partner or withdraws from the race, and, to determine who should make a sacrifice, the parties must resolve the coordination problem.

		Party II	
		To cooperate	To contest
Party I	To cooperate	6,6	4,8
	To contest	8,4	3,3

FIGURE 3.2: *Participants' incentives in the majoritarian context*

Equilibrium predictions for power-sharing and majoritarian games reflect the conventional wisdom that, when cooperation and coordination are beneficial, participants would find ways to avoid mutually destructive competition. In each of the institutional settings, we expect ideologically similar parties to succeed in doing this, in one way or another. But given that choices with regard to cooperation are made in an institutional context which combines institutional settings, actual strategic decisions will reflect the combination of institutional incentives, as in Fig. 3.3.

		Party II	
		To cooperate	To contest
Party I	To cooperate	6,6	2a+4(1–a), 5a+8(1–a)
	To contest	5a+8(1–a), 2a+4(1–a)	4a+3(1–a), 4a+3(1–a)

Parameters a and (1–a) indicate the relative weights that parties assign in their utility functions to the rewards that they receive in each of the two institutional contexts.

FIGURE 3.3: *Synthetic payoffs to politicians*

As a result, we have a game with new strategic properties not matching those induced by either of the two partial institutionally defined contests. In particular, for a fairly broad range of weights a and $(1-(a)$—specifically, for $\frac{1}{3} < a < \frac{2}{3}$ the two proto-parties find themselves locked in a strategic situation of the Prisoner's Dilemma type, where non-cooperation is the only outcome that can be sustained. Generally, as the utility weights on the rewards from the two institutional contexts shift—as rewards from participating in the game organized on the power-sharing principles become dominated by the majoritarian rewards—the predicted competitive behaviour of proto-parties changes from willingness to join forces to the non-cooperative Prisoner's Dilemma-like readiness to compete against each other, and, finally, to the situation when one of them consents to give way in competition (see Fig. 3.4).

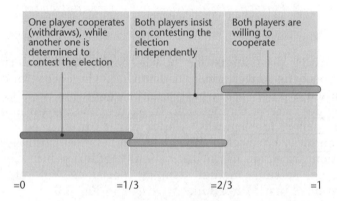

FIGURE 3.4: *Equilibria induced by the combination of power-sharing and majoritarian institutional contexts*

In order to be able to derive hypotheses about the role of specific institutional variables and their combinations in motivating or inhibiting coalitional processes, it is important to note is that the weights a and $(1-(a)$ and the payoffs in the two original games are themselves variables subject to the influence of formal institutions. Institutional choices that affect these parameters should, in the model, affect the extent of participants' willingness to act cooperatively.

Several observations follow from this brief game-theoretic illustration.

1. The more restrictive the qualifications such as threshold requirements on the power-sharing mechanisms, the greater, other things being equal, are the incentives to cooperate in the power-sharing game and, as a consequence, the synthetic game.
2. The greater the extent of proportionality in the power-sharing mechanisms—for example, the greater the magnitude of PR districts—the lower are the payoffs to coalescing in the power-sharing game.
3. The more the party weighs the rewards obtained in the majoritarian institutional context $(1-(a)$ in its utility function, the more the synthetic game resembles the Game of Chicken with the resulting coordination problem.[9] For some combination of power-sharing and majoritarian electoral goals of a party, the game structured by a combination of institutional incentives actually becomes a Prisoner's Dilemma with a unique non-coalitional equilibrium.
4. At the post-electoral stage, the stronger the majoritarian office of the president and the lower the political pressure to form sustainable parliamentary coalitions for the purpose of government, the lower are the payoffs of cooperation in the power-sharing institutional context.
5. The more initially fragmented the support for coalition-bound parties, the greater, other things equal, would be the advantages of forming alliances.

This list can be extended. Its main purpose, however, is merely to indicate that while individual institutional variables influence coalition-building at the formative stage of party-system development, they do so in a way mediated by the entire constitutional system, the full institutional and societal context. In this light, we turn in the next section to the analysis of the impact of specific combinations of power-sharing and majoritarian institutions on coalitional processes in post-communist transitions.

---

[9] The relevant weights depend on a party's organizational choices, duration of its existence, and the nature of the majoritarian institution in question: for example, on the proportion of seats filled in SMD if it is a mixed electoral system, or on its electoral reliance on the appeal of a dominant personality in the case of a presidential election.

Institutional Performance in Complex Institutional Contexts

Mixed electoral systems

Mixed electoral systems combine in a single election two different seat-allocation mechanisms: PR and SMDs. In the 1990s, such systems became popular among institution-makers and were adopted in countries as different as Italy, Japan, Taiwan, Venezuela, Mexico, Senegal, Hungary, Macedonia, Lithuania, Russia, Ukraine, and Kazakhstan. In most cases, the adoption of the mixed electoral system was a result of political bargaining and compromise between parties and politicians who favoured pure PR and those who preferred majoritarian elections. Strong and ruling parties and parties with popular candidates tended to like the majoritarian approach, hoping to benefit disproportionately in the seat allocation, while smaller parties tended to support PR as a system which allowed them a better chance of representation. Such plain calculations led to compromise solutions, with bargaining and controversy often centring on the respective numbers of seats to be allocated though PR and SMD.

Overall, by the end of the twentieth century, no fewer than 30 countries with about one-fifth of the world's population had employed mixed systems (Massicotte and Blais 1999). More than a half of all post-communist countries were a part of this group.[10] There are two ways to combine PR and SMD ballots in one election. One is the approach adopted by Germany, Italy, and, alone among the post-communist states, Hungary. Countries in this group connect the two seat allocations in such a way that, despite the presence of SMD races, the final partisan composition of the parliament reflects parties' vote shares very closely.[11] The other approach, dominant in the post-communist region, is to treat the two ballots separately, so that the number of seats that a party obtains from one has no influence on the number of seats it obtains from the other. It is in this latter case that power-sharing and majoritarian incentives become mechanically combined in the electoral system

[10] In addition, in the late 1990s, several post-communist countries—for example, Slovenia and Moldova—debated electoral reform proposals that would have moved them from their current PR towards mixed systems.

[11] It may reflect parties' vote shares in the proportional ballot only, as in Germany, or in both ballots together, as in Hungary and Italy. The latter systems produce somewhat less perfectly proportional results.

and must be weighed separately in parties' utility functions when they make decisions regarding their competitive strategies. Electoral practitioners generally assume that the effects of the two systems will balance each other, combining the best of both proportionality and majoritarianism: the representativeness of PR with the advantages of strong local ties between voters and legislators fostered by plurality elections.

Scholars frequently assume that this type of mixed electoral system will produce electoral outcomes similar to those under pure PR, but with less fragmented party competition because parties will join broader electoral coalitions in order to succeed in the SMD part of the election. That is, the PR ballot produces national party organizations which will serve as catalysts for coalition-building in majoritarian districts, while the need for coalitions among *parties* to avoid SMD over-nomination will eventually serve to reduce PR-induced multipartism. However, evidence from the post-communist transitional sample reveals a different pattern. Countries with mixed electoral systems experience more fragmented party competition than those with pure PR. The effective number of parties competing in the last elections of the 1990s was on average 5.4 in post-communist countries with pure PR electoral systems and 8.1 in countries where mixed systems were used. Though the number of parties on the PR ballot tends to be high, an even greater number together with independent candidates may contest SMDs.[12] Countries that combine PR and SMDs consistently witness many more parties being admitted to parliament through small territorial races than through party lists (Table 3.1).

From the point of view of institutions promoting or inhibiting coalition formation, this seemingly counterintuitive effect of adding majoritarian races to proportional elections is easy to reconcile with the theoretical argument in the previous section. The legal thresholds associated with PR may compel the smallest parties to form coalitions or to join larger parties (Moraski and Loewenberg 1999), but SMDs serve to weaken those incentives. There is no nationwide minimum vote required for a party or a candidate to be eligible for SMD seats. A victory in a district directly translates into a seat in the parliament. While small politically close parties competing in the same district undermine each other's chances, instead of joining they should try to coordinate on one of the equilibria where one of

---

[12] For example, in Macedonia in 1998, 17 electoral lists contested the 35 available PR seats. The 85 SMD seats, meanwhile, were contested by 29 political parties.

TABLE 3.1: *Parties admitted to parliaments by PR and SMD ballots in countries with mixed electoral systems, 1990–1999*

Country	Election year	Number of parties registered for PR	Parties with PR seats	Parties with SMD seats
Armenia	1995	20	5	7
Bulgaria	1990	26	4	6
Croatia	1995	14	5	8
Georgia	1995	53	3	11
Hungary	1990	45	6	7
Hungary	1994	19	6	8
Hungary	1998	32	5	6
Lithuania	1992	17	5	14
Lithuania	1996	28	5	14
Russia	1993	13	8	11
Russia	1995	43	4	23
Ukraine	1998	30	8	25

Sources: Successive volumes of *Electoral Studies* and *European Journal of Political Research*; Rose, Munro, and Mackie (1998); Filippov *et al.* (1999); Shvetsova (1999).

them withdraws. If they succeed in doing that, both may fail in PR but one or both may get into the parliament through the SMD. Thus, more parties may get representation in SMDs and therefore decide to take part in elections in general than can reasonably expect to win seats through PR.

Parties' failure to reach agreement in transitional mixed systems implies greater multipartism in those systems. For the last elections of the 1990s, Table 3.2 reports the comparison of average numbers of such indicators of multipartism as the number of parties on the ballot and the number of parties with over 1 per cent of the popular vote, electoral fragmentation measured as the effective number of parties, and the percentage of vote loss, in elections by pure PR compared with those in mixed electoral systems. All indicators are consistently higher in mixed systems. Table 3.3, moreover, shows that mixing majoritarian and PR districts statistically significantly contributes to both multipartism and fragmentation.

Combination of parliamentary and presidential electoral incentives

In an emerging party system, a party and its politicians weigh the relative attractiveness of different electoral and political objectives

TABLE 3.2: *A comparison of average measures of multipartism, electoral fragmentation, and absolute vote loss in the last elections in the 1990s for mixed and purely proportional electoral systems*

	Number of parties registered for the PR ballot	Number of parties with at least 1% of the the total vote	Effective number of parties	Average combined vote given to parties that failed to pass thresholds
Pure PR systems (n = 10)	23.7	9.8	5.4	12.0
Mixed electoral systems (n = 7)	28.7	14.3	8.1	31.2

TABLE 3.3: *Influence of the combined use of majoritarian and proportional districts on electoral fragmentation and multipartism in post-communist elections, 1990–1999[a]*

	Number of parties with at least 1% of the vote	Effective number of parties
Intercept	11.25 (18.7)[b]	6.39 (13.9)
Mixed electoral system[c]	2.75 (2.2)	2.18 (2.3)
Number of observations	31.0	31.0
R^2	0.14	0.15

[a] First—'founding'—elections in each country are excluded from the sample. Hungarian elections are coded as conducted by PR.
[b] *t-statistics* is in parentheses.
[c] This is a dummy variable which equals 1 for mixed and 0 for pure PR electoral systems.

while the institutionally determined means of attaining those objectives might be in conflict with each other. A party can simultaneously hope to succeed in the bid for the presidency, and in receiving a ministerial portfolio, and in ensuring for itself safe parliamentary representation. Applied to the institutional combination of a parliamentary and a presidential elections, the theoretical argument above suggests that the prospect of running for the presidency may prevent parties from joining forces with ideologically similar partners, whereas the strength and certainty of their parliamentary

representation would have improved if they did.[13] Meanwhile,
opportunities for parliamentary representation created by PR
would prevent the exit of some political contestants from competition, which the pressures of the presidential race alone may have
compelled them to do.

Presidential incentives that inhibit coalition-building among
parties are not necessarily limited to those created by the immediately forthcoming presidential race. Though the number of
registered candidates in the early post-communist presidential
elections was large—for example, 21 in the 1991 Bulgarian election,
17 in the 1995 Polish election, and 11, out of 78, who succeeded in
gathering 1,000,000 valid constituent signatures each in the
Russian 1996 election—it did not reflect all those who could have
feasibly entertained future presidential ambitions and accordingly
structured their party-building decisions. If one recalls that many
political leaders in post-communist countries in the beginning of
the 1990s were in their late thirties or early forties, it becomes clear
that these people could reasonably count on participating in future
presidential elections and invest in their political capital accordingly. In fact, some Russian politicians already in 1996 had
announced their intentions to run for the presidency in 2000, 2004,
and as late as 2008. In view of such long-term presidential ambitions it may actually be harmful to be a part of either the government or the major opposition, as that implies some responsibility
for the deterioration of living standards and the stress accompanying the economic reforms.

On the side of the electorates, the punishment of parties that
choose to compete against their natural allies is also far from immediate and well-targeted. Duverger's (1954) original argument was,
indeed, based on the rationality of voters, not politicians. As party
systems mature, it is the voters' side that applies the crucial pressure to them, ultimately reducing multipartism through the so-
called 'psychological effect'. But theories advanced to explain the
psychological effect assume that voters can anticipate each others'
electoral response to any set of choices that politicians can offer on
the ballot, and can switch to vote strategically for the strongest
acceptable candidate. This assumption may be reasonable in the

---

[13] The weight of presidential goals in parties' utility functions at early stages of
transitions may have been further enhanced by the fact that many members of new
parties were non-professional politicians—scientists, journalist, writers, lawyers—
who themselves may have had little desire to pursue political careers in the parliament but were ready to support their leaders as presidential candidates and to
accept the 'presidential' objectives of their parties.

context of a continuing system, with either past elections or pre-election polls serving as good predictors of the outcome of the future vote, but it makes these theories largely inapplicable to the transitional context where neither previous elections—if there were any—nor public opinion polls provide reliable predictions. In fact, the discrepancy between the polls taken only weeks apart can be very significant.[14] Thus, at the transitional stage, electoral uncertainty greatly reduces the pressure of the psychological effect.

Several country-specific examples below illustrate the strategic link between presidential electoral aspirations and the failure of parties not only to coalesce but even to sustain the integrity of initial political organizations. While in any single case alternative explanations could be advanced for the failure of small parties to cooperate, the cross-country comparisons that follow show the systematic statistically significant impact of the institution of elected presidency as a variable that contributes to sustained fragmentation in parliamentary elections.

Poland

The first few years in the history of the new Polish party system can be written from the perspective of politicians' presidential ambitions. It was the antagonistic nature of the presidential campaign of 1990 that cracked Solidarity's unity and led to serious conflicts among Solidarity leaders, effectively preventing the possibility of the reunification of the movement. In the subsequent 1991 parliamentary election, in place of Solidarity there were dozens of parties, though most of them were still appealing to the entire society in their programmes. There was not much improvement by the time of the next—parliamentary— election in 1993. Arguably, the parties of the centre-right—for example, Centre Alliance (PC), Solidarity, Coalition for the Republic (KDR)—and the Solidarity wing of the agrarian movement had no ideological reason to run separately, yet they competed, in essence, for the same constituencies, and did not unite exclusively because of their leaders' personal ambitions (Jasiewiecz 1994). This cost them representation. Meanwhile, had they combined forces, their estimated payoff would have been between 40 and 50 seats in the *Sejm*, the parliament's lower house.

---

[14] For the discussion of the reasons why public opinion in post-communist transitions was so volatile and difficult to measure, see Shlapentokh (1994); Rose (1995); White (1995).

In a similar way, the Centre Alliance, led by Jaroslaw Kaczynski, and Olszewski's Movement for the Republic failed to form a pact in 1993 despite their close positions on policies and even attempts at negotiations. Both parties failed to pass the parliamentary threshold, but both leaders, Kaczynski and Olszewski, were nominated as presidential candidates in 1995.[15] Another right-of-centre party, the Union of Real Politics (UPR), also ran on its own and failed in the parliamentary election, but its leader, Korwin-Mikke, was nominated as a presidential candidate.

Attempts at forging an alliance for the 1995 presidential race in Poland failed because the participants disagreed over who would head such an alliance. Fourteen right-of-centre political groups and parties conducted 'primaries' in July of 1995 and by a secret ballot voted to nominate the president of the Polish Bank, Hanna Gronkewicz-Waltz, as their joint candidate. But groups supporting Olszewski, the former prime minister,[16] and the right-wing extremist Moczulski dissented from the majority decision and nominated candidates separately. In the end, almost all major parties attempted to nominate candidates in 1995. The 17 candidates who actually ran for the presidency were those who, in addition to being nominated, managed to collect the required 100,000 signatures each and thus were registered for the ballot.

Romania

In Romania, the close timing of local, presidential, and parliamentary elections in 1992 initially forced political parties to form broader coalitions. Observers noted, however, that the campaign was remarkably unfocused until the end, making it difficult to distinguish one party from another (Shafir 1992). Most political organizations addressed voters in generic, consensual terms, avoiding distinctions that could alienate important segments of the electorate. Most coalitions crumbled as elections with higher stakes approached. The National Liberal Party (PNL) formed an alliance with the Democratic Convention, itself an alliance of 18 political parties and formations, before the 1992 local election, but decided to run independently for parliament, failing as a result to pass the 3 per cent threshold. Right before the split, though, the PNL leader Campeanu stated his strong disagreement with the plans of a

---

[15] Kaczynski was nominated even though before the presidential campaign the Centre Alliance, in agreement with other right-wing parties, planned to support Adam Strzembosz as a united presidential candidate (Brown 1994).

[16] Jan Olszewski received 6.86 per cent of the vote.

leader of another influential party within the Convention to run for the presidential office.

Like the PNL, the Party of Civic Alliance (PAC) disagreed with the Convention leadership over the presidential candidate in 1992, and was thereafter constantly contemplating leaving the alliance. In August 1994, a PAC declaration stated that Constantinescu, who headed the Convention and was its designated presidential candidate, intended to marginalize the PAC because of his fear that the PAC leader Manolescu would challenge him for presidency; however, the declaration continued, Manolescu had no such intentions. Despite the absence of such intentions, in 1995 the PAC was the first CDR member to rebel against Constantinescu's leadership when he prepared to run for a second term as chairman of the Convention and as its presidential candidate (Shafir 1995). Later, the Party of Civic Alliance, the Social Democratic Party (PSDR), the Liberal Party '93 (LP '93), and the National Liberal Party-Democratic Convention (PNL-CD) all refused to support Constantinescu's candidacy. The leader of PNL-CD tried to challenge Constantinescu in the race to become the united opposition's presidential candidate. The PAC, PSDR, and LP '93 left the Democratic Convention in March 1995, after refusing to sign the protocol which stipulated a joint parliamentary list and support for a single presidential candidate. Observers note that the continuous problems with unification of the pro-democracy parties such as the PNL-CD, LP '93, PAC, and PNL were connected to the personal ambitions of their leaders, several of whom entertained their own hopes of running for presidency.

Cross-country evidence

Despite their majoritarian nature, direct presidential elections so far have played a fragmenting role in the post-communist party systems. Specifically, the effect of the institutional combination of presidential races and parliamentary electoral competition was to inhibit coalition formation and to promote fragmentation and multipartism beyond what parliamentary electoral institutions alone would have led us to expect. This effect occurs regardless of the scope of the real prerogatives of the presidential office and is attributable to the combined impact of the parliamentary and presidential electoral incentives on parties' choice of strategies. Table 3.4 compares the average measures of multipartism, electoral fragmentation, and vote loss among the countries that combine the use of PR in their parliamentary elections with electing presidents either by their parliaments or directly. All these measures are strongly and positively affected by the use of the majoritarian mechanism of direct presidential elections. At the regional level, elections of presidents during transitions are statistically associated with greater electoral fragmentation, measured as the effective number of parties in parliamentary races. In addition, elected presidency leads to more crowded ballots in terms of the number of registered parties and increases electoral multipartism measured as the number of vote-getting parties in parliamentary elections.

TABLE 3.4: *A comparison of average measures of multipartism, electoral fragmentation, and absolute vote loss between elections in political systems that use PR in parliamentary elections and elect presidents by parliaments versus those that elect presidents directly*

	Number of parties registered for the PR ballot	Number of parties with at least 1% of the total vote	Effective number of parties	Average combined vote given to parties that failed to pass thresholds
No direct presidential elections (n = 13)	18.8 (15.4)[a]	10.7 (9.2)	6.0 (5.7)	13.8 (9.9)
Direct presidential elections (n = 18)	37.3 (30.1)	12.7 (12.7)	7.5 (6.9)	22.9 (24.7)

[a] The averages for the last elections of the 1990s are in parentheses.

Table 3.5 presents estimated coefficients on parliamentary and presidential institutional variables for the full set of elections for the first ten years of post-communist transitions. Both electoral multipartism and electoral fragmentation are statistically significantly affected by the presidential variable, even when controlled for the magnitudes of electoral districts, thresholds, and the use of an adjustment district into the parliamentary electoral rules.

To further support the hypothesis that majoritarian institutions of SMD and of elected presidency in combination with parliamentary PR push parties to adopt non-cooperative strategies and to gamble on the hopes of attracting voters away from each other, Table 3.6 shows that parties are more numerous and voters in parliamentary elections 'waste' votes more often in countries with one or both majoritarian features.

TABLE 3.5: *Influence of the combined use of presidential elections and proportional representation on electoral fragmentation and multipartism in post-communist elections, 1990–1999*[a]

	Number of parties with at least 1% of the vote	Effective number of parties
Intercept	7.97 (5.3)[b]	4.16 (3.5)
Elected presidency[c]	2.33 (2.2)	1.78 (2.2)
Binding district magnitude[d]	0.18 (2.1)	0.12 (1.8)
Number of observations	31.0	31.0
R^2	0.23	0.2

[a] First—'founding'—elections in each country are excluded from the sample.
[b] *t-statistics* is in parentheses.
[c] This is a dummy variable which equals 1 for systems with and 0 for systems without elected presidents.
[d] Binding district magnitude is equal to the average magnitude of the PR electoral district or the inverse of a threshold for representation, whichever is the smaller (Filippov *et al.* 1999).

Constraints on Institutions' Ability to Influence Coalition Formation and Party Development

Theoretical discussion in this chapter and the evidence it offers of consolidating or fragmenting influence of particular institutions and institutional combinations was based on an important premise. It was assumed that proto-parties—political elites in elections—experienced few limitations as to the kind of alliance or party where they could invite their voters to follow them. This assumption was necessary to ensure that coalitions that we or the institutional designer may want to stimulate can feasibly be formed. On the other hand, it was also assumed that numerous politically independent potential members of such coalitions could be available to make the strategic decisions of whether or not to cooperate with each other. Without them, there would be no players in the political system to follow our institutional lead. But the very existence of these independent proto-parties is based on their ability to divide and sub-divide the vote, at least in the early elections. This means that enough uncertainty should be present in a political system at this stage regarding who can hope to attract electoral support, and by what means. If such uncertainty about the future direction of political mobilization is absent, if the electorate is effectively divided by some other, pre-existing factors unrelated to the fine details of electoral institutions and procedures, transitions

TABLE 3.6: *Influence of majoritarian features in combination with the power-sharing approach to parliamentary elections:*

(1) on multipartism in parliamentary elections (average number of parties with at least 1 per cent of the popular vote)

	Presidents elected by parliaments	Direct presidential elections
Pure PR parliamentary electoral systems	10.7	11.9
Mixed parliamentary electoral systems	n/a	14.0

(2) on electoral fragmentation (average effective number of parties)

	Presidents elected by parliaments	Direct presidential elections
Pure PR parliamentary electoral systems	6.0	6.9
Mixed parliamentary electoral systems	n/a	8.6

(3) on wasted votes (average percentage of vote given in PR to parties without PR representation)

	Presidents elected by parliaments	Direct presidential elections
Pure PR parliamentary electoral systems	13.8	16.4
Mixed parliamentary electoral systems	n/a	33.1

would not start with the proliferation of proto-parties (or would pass that stage in a blink of an eye) proto-parties would not be induced to adopt competitive strategies of the kind envisioned by the designer, and the strategic influence of formal electoral institutions may turn out to be very insignificant.

The distinction between transitions—if such a stage is found in the life of a given political system—and mature systems is itself theoretically connected to the nature of institutional performance. Transitions, simply put, correspond to the 'out-of-equilibrium' (Kitschelt 1992) condition of a political system, while in an established democracy the political system is in an 'equilibrium' state. Alternatively, to avoid the terminological ambiguity involved in the systemic use of the notion of an equilibrium, we could differentiate established democracies—or, similarly, established non-democracies —from transitions as stationary as compared with the non-stationary stages in a political system's development.

Removal of transitional non-stationarity in the behaviour of political players in a controlled way, under the pressures applied by the formal rules of the game introduced by a designer, is what allows the political system to assume the expected shape by the time it reaches its mature state. If formal institutional provisions remain the same through both stages in the political system's development, the difference must lie in the behaviour of political players: in the way they act in response to the given formal rules. While formal rules translate expressed preferences into general outcomes acting as 'brutal facts of politics' and supplying basic constraints on political interactions, players' reactions to such constraints during transitions change from one cycle of decision-making to another, reflecting the changes in their expectations about the way the game would be played. Eventual stabilization of players' expectations is equivalent to the reduction of uncertainty in the political process and corresponds to the development of new informal institutions which would be compatible, in one way or another, with the enacted formal rules.

From this it logically follows that the success of democratic institutional design requires the presence of a transitional stage during which the strategies of players are subject to change in response to institutional inducements. There must, therefore, be enough flexibility in the strategies that elites can adopt: flexibility based on the ability of numerous players to divide and subdivide the electorate, which requires the non-existence of an obvious and fail-safe mobilization strategy: that is, requires the presence of uncertainty in the electoral system. Otherwise, institutional tools cannot induce any significant change in political behaviour and are thus useless in shaping or reshaping political systems.

In the sample of transitional elections considered in this chapter, players' strategies continued to change from one election to another. Table 3.7 reports vote volatility by country and election, indicating the extent of this change in strategies. Because much of this generally high electoral volatility is attributable to the change in the set of competitors and to coalescing or breaking alliances among them, the change in elite strategies is an important contributor to the overall change in electoral behaviour. Moreover, these changing strategies of players appear to be leading the party systems in question to a more consolidated state, as fragmentation in them exhibits some decline over time (Table 3.8).

TABLE 3.7: *Aggregate electoral volatility in terms of PR votes (percentage of votes changing hands),[a] 1990–1999*

	Between the first and second elections	Between the second and third elections	Between the third and fourth elections
Bulgaria	20.3	22.7	45.2
Czech	67.3	28.7	17.5
Estonia	54.0	49.3	–
Hungary	27.8	32.7	–
Latvia	62.8	50.0	–
Lithuania	41.6	–	–
Poland	34.5	54.6	–
Romania	80.9	31.0	–
Russia	52.4	–	–
Slovakia	33.7	35.5	48.8
Slovenia	44.2	31.6	–

[a] Calculated as the sum of absolute values of % changes for all participants divided by two.

TABLE 3.8: *Electoral fragmentation on the PR ballot (effective number of parties), 1990–1999*

	2nd election	3rd election	4th election
Bulgaria	4.19	3.85	3.0
Czech	7.29	5.33	0.72
Estonia	8.73	5.93	6.87
Hungary	5.49	4.6	–
Georgia	11.98	–	–
Kazakhstan	5.87	–	–
Latvia	9.61	7.0	–
Lithuania	7.92	–	–
Macedonia	5.04	–	–
Moldova	5.7	–	–
Poland	12.49	9.79	4.6
Romania	6.93	6.06	–
Russia	10.98	–	–
Slovakia	5.36	5.81	5.3
Slovenia	8.36	6.32	–
Ukraine	10.0	–	–
Average	7.87	6.08	4.9

Uncertainty, and the associated cooperation and coordination problems encountered by political actors, is not an exclusive feature of new democracies. Nor does it necessarily exist in every new democracy. Old democracies may see enough uncertainty brought about by either external shocks or by the internal crises of the political system to enable them to conduct meaningful institutional reforms. Meanwhile, some newly democratizing countries may not respond to attempts to institutionally re-coordinate their political processes because specific mobilizational strategies are certain to produce outcomes exactly as expected. Theoretically, the problem of coordination can be solved through change of rules, communication, or the emergence of a focal point (Schelling 1960). Therefore, where some commonly available information in a political system can serve as a focal point, the problem of coordination would be instantly solved. Thus, the problem of coordination may be non-existent from the very beginning of the attempts to democratize: if, for example, salient ethnic cleavages are available for use in political mobilization and make political outcomes and even the choice of the formal rules predictable. Because there are very few feasible coalitions that can form in such circumstances, the ability of institutions to direct coalition formation is, clearly, impaired. Thus, the ability of a designer to foster 'desirable' political outcomes through institutional choices is undermined, even if we assume for the moment that meaningful institutional design can take place in such an environment. This is why post-communist countries characterized by low-uncertainty initial political environments—that is, Bosnia, Croatia, and Serbia—were excluded from the above discussion of institutional impact on political outcomes.

Conclusion

I argued above that, because new political systems are in a 'non-equilibrium' state and uncertainty about future electoral developments is high, electoral cooperation and coalescing among emergent parties is simultaneously affected in a significant way by all major parameters of electoral and constitutional systems. Systems of enacted rules enable and direct the process of political coalition building. Looking at the actual effect of several institutional factors, we can say that their impact often differs from what could be expected from majoritarian versus power-sharing institutions on the basis of the experience of old democracies. The main argument of this chapter is that the focus of design should be not on projected long-term consequences of formal political institutions as they are known from the studies of mature democracies, but on institutions'

expected ability to promote or inhibit the initial process of formation of coalitions of a desirable sort among political players found in
a specific country of interest, as well as their ability to do so on a
permanent basis rather than through repetitive alliance-building
and breaking with every new electoral cycle.

II

Presidentialism, Federalism and Decentralization, and Electoral Systems

Presidents, Parliaments, and Democracy: Insights from the Post-Communist World

Timothy Frye

Introduction

In countries undergoing regime change, are presidential or parliamentary systems more likely to lead to democracy? Some of the best-known figures in political science have sought to answer this question, but many theoretical insights and empirical findings remain contested (Linz 1994; Horowitz 1996; Lijphart 1994*a*; Shugart and Carey 1992; Linz and Stepan 1996; Przeworski *et al.* 2000). Indeed, one gets the sense that the original combatants have settled in for a long period of trench warfare. The strategies of frontal assaults and claims of rapid advance that mark the initial debates have given way to far more cautious attempts to merely hold ground captured earlier in the campaign. If early on the advocates made strong cases against presidentialism or parliamentarianism, they now spend much of their time qualifying, refining, and defining scope conditions for their theories.

Existing literature on the merits of presidential and parliamentary forms of government has tended to take one of two approaches. Some scholars have examined the qualities of particular kinds of political institutions to deduce the potential effects of these types of institutions on democracy (Linz and Valenzuala 1994). For example, relying on the fixed terms of presidential regimes, they argue that these systems are more rigid than parliamentary systems, and are therefore more prone to democratic breakdown. These scholars tend to illustrate their arguments with insights generated from deep

I thank John Carey, Martin Raiser, Kira Sanbonmatsu, and Kuba Zielinski for insightful comments and help with the data. I also thank the organizers of Constitution 2000 for inviting me to take part in this project. In particular, I thank Andrew Reynolds for his patience. All errors are my own.

knowledge of particular cases. This body of work has generated many hypotheses, but has yet to test them in a rigorous manner.

Other scholars have tested hypotheses quantitatively by examining the probability that countries with a certain institutional arrangement become or remain democracies. Relying primarily on large data sets, they seek to establish an association between the institutions—presidential and parliamentary—and outcome—democracy or not. For example, controlling for economic development and political culture, Gasiorowski and Power (1998) find that the type of political institutions has no significant impact on the likelihood that democracy will survive. These scholars have produced important findings, but have yet to specify the causal mechanisms that link institutions and outcomes.

A *slightly different approach*

This chapter takes a somewhat different approach. It examines how institutional features combine with other factors to exacerbate one particular threat to democracy: the expansion of presidential power. It identifies the conditions under which presidents in societies undergoing regime-change expand their formal powers. More specifically, it asks: why have some executives in competetive presidential systems in the region dramatically expanded their powers, while others have failed to do so? It finds that economic reforms that produce concentrated benefits lead the winners from reform to seek institutional change in the powers of the presidency.[1] It also finds countries with fragmented parliaments—those with a high number of independents—are also likely to experience an increase in the powers of the presidency. Finally, it finds that presidents in systems with a newly adopted constitution are no less likely to expand their powers than presidents in systems governed by revised versions of communist-era constitutions. Thus, adopting a post-communist constitution does not seem to constrain presidents seeking to expand their powers.

Having identified two factors that drive changes in presidential power, this chapter then tentatively examines how these changes in presidential power have affected the prospects for democracy. It finds that, on balance, these increases in presidential power have

---

[1] This finding should be seen as preliminary. Data on economic inequality from the last years of the second administration in Ukraine, Russia, and Moldova have not yet been published by the data source used here. Dropping these cases does not change the essence of the results. This finding may be subject to changes as more data become available. These results do not extend to pure parliamentary or highly autocratic systems in the region.

had negative consequences for democracy, although this is not true in all cases. These findings undercut arguments in favour of giving presidents expanded powers early in the transition in hopes that these leaders can serve as guardians of democracy during a period of extraordinary politics (Holmes 1995).

The approach adopted here differs from preceding work on the relationship between political institutions and democracy in two ways. First, it breaks the process by which institutions mediate outcomes into discrete elements. It identifies the conditions under which presidents expand their formal powers and then examines the impact of these expansions of power on prospects for democracy. Thus, it charts a middle road between large C 'N' quantitative studies that often have difficulty identifying causal mechanisms that drive the process of democratization and small 'n' case studies that often have difficulty making general claims about relationships between institutions and outcomes.

Second, it examines the interaction of economic and political reforms: an interaction that has been greatly neglected in the debate over the merits of presidential and parliamentary systems.[2] By identifying how specific coalitions form and change institutional arrangements, it begins to build a more solid foundation upon which to examine the effects of institutions on democracy.

A roadmap

The chapter proceeds in five parts. First, I begin by recounting the main theoretical and empirical points in the debate over the merits of presidential and parliamentary systems for democracy. Second, I identify several obstacles to progress in this debate. Third, I examine how economic reform and the adoption of a new constitution influence changes in presidential power. In this analysis, I address two criticisms of this literature made in the preceding section: the lack of attention to causal mechanisms and to the interaction of economic and political reform in many studies. Fourth, I tentatively examine how these expansions of presidential power have altered democratic governance. I conclude by drawing lessons from this debate for our understanding of constitutional design.

---

[2] Haggard and Kaufman (1995) and Hellman (1998) are exceptions.

Presidentialism and Parliamentarism

Advocates of parliamentarism

The most recent round of debate over the merits of presidential and parliamentary forms of government can be traced to Linz's seminal essay originally circulated in 1984 and published most definitively almost a decade later (Linz 1994). Linz praised the parliamentary form of government as more likely to promote democracy for at least four reasons. In his view, a parliamentary government has a single source of governing authority and thereby avoids the 'dual democratic legitimacy' that is inherent in presidential systems. In the latter, both the executive and the assembly can claim to be the legitimate authority of the citizenry, and this competition can lead to spirals of conflict.

Parliamentary systems are also said to be more flexible than presidential systems because the latter have fixed terms. In a parliamentary system, the prime minister has to maintain support in the assembly or lose her position. For this reason a parliamentary government is far less likely to succumb to immobilism due to a lame duck executive. For this same reason it is less likely to fall victim to weak support in the assembly for extended periods, as it is claimed often happens in presidential systems.

This school also notes that parliamentary forms of government increase the likelihood that the executive has a wealth of political experience because potential prime ministers have to work their way through the party ranks before assuming office. Through the direct vote, presidential systems encourage outsiders with little political experience to run and lower the barriers to their success. This can lead to the election of 'dark horse' executives with little experience and strong incentives to rule outside of the existing institutional rules.

Linz refrains from making a deterministic argument about the effects of presidential and parliamentary institutions for democracy. He notes only that 'the odds seem to favor' parliamentary institutions and that other factors may be more important than the kinds of institution governing the transition (Linz 1994: 70).

To support the argument, Linz and other advocates of parliamentarism point to the difficulty of building democracies in presidential systems in Latin America and Africa in the 1960s and 1970s.[3] Their

---

[3] Indeed, many of the arguments made in the Linz and Valenzuala (1994) volume are against presidential systems rather than in favour of parliamentary institutions.

arguments find some empirical support in a large 'n' quantitative study by Stepan and Skach (1993) that focused on countries that achieved independence after World War II. Excluding the OECD countries from their analysis, they found that of the 36 countries in the post-war world that chose presidential systems at independence, none was continuously democratic between 1980 and 1989. In contrast, 15 of the 41 countries that chose a parliamentary system at the time of independence were democracies at all times between 1980 and 1989. These findings were seen as support for the argument that parliamentary systems promote democratic consolidation.[4]

Sceptics of parliamentarism

Proponents of parliamentary forms of government seem to have had the better of the argument in the early 1990s, but work by Shugart and Carey (1992) among others began to question the supposed 'perils of presidentialism' (Mainwaring and Shugart 1997a). While not seeking to deride parliamentary forms of government, these authors noted that presidential forms of government are far more diverse than typically depicted. In their view presidential forms of government are often as different from each other as they are from parliamentary forms of government.

Moreover, Horowitz criticized Linz for taking a 'mechanistic' view of presidential systems and attributing all failures of democracy to presidentialism when other culprits were likely to have been responsible. Commenting on Linz's dismissive treatment of successful presidential democracies, Horowitz (1996: 145) noted, 'political success, has so to speak, many parents; political failure only one: presidentialism'.

The sceptics of parliamentarism also noted that presidential systems have some significant advantages over parliamentary forms of government. In their view, presidential systems can be more accountable than parliamentary governments. In the former, it is far more difficult for executives to avoid responsibility for failed policy by hiding behind coalition partners. Thus, it is easier to identify the politicians responsible for policy choices in a presidential system.

---

[4] However, as Power and Gasiorowsky (1997) noted, 10 of the 15 successful non-OECD parliamentary democracies in the study have populations smaller than 100,000 and 14 of the 15 are former British Colonies. This suggests that the study might have benefited from more control variables and that the relationships identified in the article may be spurious. See Power and Gasiorowski (1997) and Gasiorowski and Power (1998) for a critique.

Moreover, because presidents are elected directly, voters can sanction them for misbehaviour far more easily than they can sanction a prime minister who is elected indirectly.

According to Mainwaring and Shugart (1997*a*: 37) presidential forms of government can also reduce political conflict because the assembly is elected independently of the executive. Because the tenures of the executive and the assembly are not tied in a presidential system, legislators can consider bills based on their merits rather than on their effect on the fate of the prime minister and the government. In their view, the mutual independence of the parliament and the executive can make political conflict more manageable.

Empirically, the sceptics of parliamentarism point to democratic breakdowns in the parliamentary governments of inter-war Europe to bolster their argument. They also question the strength of quantitative studies that support parliamentarism by noting that these studies sometimes include micro-states that tend to be parliamentary. Because small country size has been shown to be conducive to democracy, they question the importance of parliamentary government for democratic consolidation in these settings.

Moreover, they claimed that such studies typically suffer from 'selection bias and hence, spurious correlation' (Mainwaring and Shugart 1997*a*: 19). They argue that because parliamentary systems were more common than presidential systems in societies with background conditions conducive to democracy—for example, small, wealthy populations—it is difficult to analyze the independent impact of parliamentarism on democratic stability and consolidation. They add that since Latin American countries are dominated by presidential regimes and have background conditions that are not conducive to democracy, selection bias may be a real danger in quantitative studies that lack proper controls.

Just as the sceptics of parliamentary forms of government began to make some inroads, Przeworski *et al.* (2000) provide evidence in favour of a parliamentary form of government. Using data from both OECD and non-OECD countries during 1950–90, they find that parliamentary governments have a higher rate of survival as democracies than presidential forms of government. An impressive data set and considerable methodological sophistication make their work a significant advance.

Others studies that focus on the developing world produce somewhat different results. Power and Gasiorowski (1997) suggest that debates over presidential and parliamentary systems for the consolidation of democracy have missed the forest for the trees. In their study of 56 transitions to democracy in non-OECD countries, they find no significant difference in the rate at which presidential and parliamentary regimes survive as democracies. In other work, Gasiorowoski and Power (1998) find that institutional factors, such as presidentialism and parliamentarism, are far less important than structural factors, such as the level of economic development, for the survival of democratic governments.

Cheibub (1999) supports the preceding argument by seeking to identify causal mechanisms that underlie the supposed greater fragility of presidential governments. In a study of presidential democratizing countries outside of the OECD, he finds that divided governments in presidential systems do not tend to lead to gridlock and breakdown. This work finds that if presidential governments are more prone to breakdown, then it is not due to gridlock between the executive and legislative branches.

Obstacles to Progress

More than a decade of theoretical and empirical debates have yet to resolve conclusively the fundamental question asked in the title of Linz' 1984 manuscript: 'Presidential or Parliamentary Democracy: Does it Make a Difference?' This work identifies several obstacles that continue to inhibit progress in this area.

First, the literature has suffered from inattention to causal mechanisms.[5] The literature includes a laundry list of potential causal mechanisms that may shape prospects for building democracy. For example, presidential systems are said to promote 'dual democratic legitimacy', rigidity, a 'winner take all' approach to politics, and easy access for outsiders who may have little experience in government. In cases of the failure of presidential governments, we often do not know which of these potential causal mechanisms are at work and/or which have the greatest causal impact.[6]

---

[5] Other obstacles to progress also exist. For example, scholars have often misunderstood the nature of the endogeneity problem in this literature. In other words, countries that are likely to choose a particular institutional arrangement may also be likely to succeed or fail to become democracies for reasons unrelated to the choice of institutions. For example, it is easier to argue that Kazakhstan has a presidential system because it is not a democracy than to argue that Kazakhstan is not democracy because it has a presidential system.

[6] More broadly, the literature would benefit from closer attention to the actual operation of presidential and parliamentary systems in transition environments. Are presidential systems in the transitional societies more rigid? Do parliamentary

This shortcoming is significant because scholars continue to debate how institutional arrangements actually shape the prospects for democracy. Scholars may agree that presidential systems are more rigid than parliamentary systems, but disagree over whether rigidity promotes, inhibits, or has no effect on democracy. Rigidity may lead actors to take more extreme positions that inhibit compromise. On the other hand, rigidity may encourage all actors to take a longer-term perspective and thereby promote cooperation among rival political groups who control competing branches of government. It would be helpful to identify conditions under which rigidity promotes or inhibits democratic consolidation.

Second, the literature has often neglected to examine how institutional design interacts with other variables, such as social structure. Scholars such as Power and Gasiorowski (1997) have only recently begun to analyze the relative impact of institutions in comparison with other factors that promote or inhibit democratic consolidation. They find that social structure is far more important for democracy than is the choice of presidential or parliamentary regimes. This finding suggests the potential marginality of institutional design.

Third, the literature often fails to examine how institutions interact with other tasks facing politicians during periods of transition. For example, some scholars argue that strong presidents insulated from social forces have important advantages for conducting economic reform, while recognizing that these features may be less conducive to promoting democracy (Haggard and Kaufman 1995). Political institutions may have different impacts in cases where economic reform is high or low on the political agenda. This suggests a potential trade-off between the promotion of economic reform and the consolidation of democracy. Because choosing political institutions and conducting economic reform both have important distributive consequences, we likely need to examine the interaction of these processes.

Post-Communist Presidential Democratizing Countries

This chapter begins to address these shortcomings in the debate over the merits of presidential and parliamentary systems for

systems in transitional societies promote responsible oppositions? Does parliamentarism undercut economic reform? By posing more tractable questions about how presidential and parliamentary systems work in transitional societies, we can begin to take steps that may eventually lead us to learn whether presidential or parliamentary systems are better for building stable democracies.

democracy. It examines changes in presidential power in democratizing post-communist countries that have presidential forms of government. In these countries presidents have been directly elected in at least one competitive election and have a fixed term of office. Countries included in the analysis are Armenia, Belarus, Croatia, Georgia, Kyrgyzstan, Lithuania, Moldova, Poland, Romania, Russia, and Ukraine. Most countries have experienced two presidential administrations. The important consideration is that all countries in this set at some point in the transition had a directly elected president who came to office in at least one relatively free election. (I exclude pure parliamentary and highly autocratic systems. The dynamics of presidential power are likely very different in these settings.) This part of the chapter presents a preliminary explanation for expansions of presidential powers across administrations. Why have some presidents managed to dramatically increase their powers, while others have not?

Measuring presidential powers is difficult (Lucky 1994; McGregor 1994). Formal powers are easier to measure than informal powers, but capture only part of the powers of the office. A president's informal powers, including his or her moral or personal authority, can sometimes offset weak formal powers. Informal powers are especially important during a transition when institutions are weak and in flux (Jowitt 1992; O'Neill 1997). Formal powers are an important measure in their own right. First, the formal powers of the presidency in most post-communist countries generally accord with the conventional wisdom about actual powers held by the president (Frye 1997). The nasty authoritarian governments tend to have nasty authoritarian constitutions. Second, formal powers often have important policy outcomes. Hellman (1997) finds that the formal powers of the presidency have had a significant impact on economic reform across countries.

Third, the supporters and opponents of increased presidential powers often devote great resources to achieving their preferred outcome. The prospect of changes in the formal powers of the presidency has led to mass petition drives to conduct referendums on the issue, significantly altered political coalitions, and evoked calls by political elites for changes of regime-type. Perhaps the best evidence of the importance of formal rules is the great resources devoted to change the formal powers of the presidency across a wide variety of cases. Changes in the formal powers of the presidency often mark critical junctures in the political history of a country and these changes often have lasting impacts.

This chapter uses a version of the Shugart and Carey (1992) scale of presidential power that has been slightly modified by Frye,

Hellman, and Tucker (2000) and Frye and Commander (1999) to fit the post-communist cases.[7] Other scales also register these increases in presidential power (McGregor 1994).

Taking a brief look at the data, we find that presidential powers have been expanded in 9 of 23 presidential administrations in the countries under study. In 8 of these 9 cases the increases have been dramatic. For example, Ukraine increased the powers of its presidency from 8 to 13 in 1995, while the power of the Croatian presidency has remained constant at a score of 9 throughout the post-communist period. Russia, Lithuania, and Moldova began the transformation with similar levels of presidential power: a 6 according to our scale. Over time, Russia adopted a very powerful presidency and Moldova raised, then lowered the powers of its presidency, while Lithuania left the powers of its presidency unchanged. Figure 4.1 depicts changes in presidential power over time in the countries under study.

Towards an explanation

This section examines two factors that may promote increases in the institutional power of the presidency, including economic reform outcomes and the degree of fragmentation of the parliament. First, the distributional consequences of economic reform produce political coalitions that under some conditions may have the incentive and the means to pursue institutional change in the powers of the presidency. More specifically, economic reforms that produce concentrated

---

[7] Modifications as follows:

Dismissal Government
4 = unrestricted
3* = only restricted in case of PM
2 = restricted by any body (including PM or parliament)
1 = if must propose alternative minister/cabinet

Decree Powers
4 = unlimited (to defend the Constitution and its laws)
3* = for limited time
2 = subject to *ex post* approval
1 = only negative powers

Referenda, Same Add:
1* = needs parliamentary approval

Appointing Government, Same add:
2* = President appoints PM, and then appoint

*measure added according to Frye, Hellman, and Tucker scale.

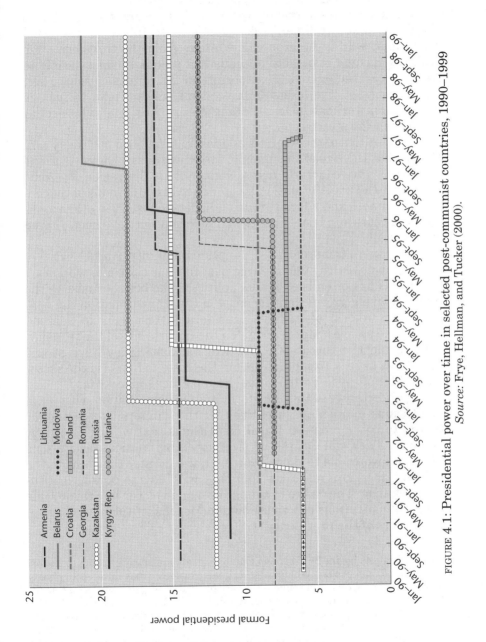

FIGURE 4.1: Presidential power over time in selected post-communist countries, 1990–1999
Source: Frye, Hellman, and Tucker (2000).

winners who seek to increase their influence over policy may have the political side-effect of increasing presidential powers.

Economic reforms create winners and losers (Haggard and Kaufman 1995; Hellman 1998; Milanovich 1998). In the post-communist world, the economic winners from the transformation typically include managers of industrial plants, businesspeople in the financial sector, and the exporters in the natural resource sector. In contrast, the losers from economic reform tend to include pensioners, workers in loss-making enterprises, and white-collar workers in the state sector.

The identities of the winners and losers have been relatively consistent, but the size of the gains to the winners and the costs to the losers has varied greatly across countries in the region. In some countries, the transformation has produced small groups of concentrated winners and a large group of dispersed losers. In other countries the costs and benefits of the transformation have been shared more equally.

The winners from reform in the post-communist world have typically grown wealthy due in large part to their close ties with state agents. As has often been noted, politics is the best business in the region. Having grown wealthy early in the transformation the winners from reform often have considerable resources to demand favourable policies. Moreover, given the uncertainty of the transformation and the threat of a political backlash, they have strong incentives to seek to capture part of the state to increase the security of their often 'ill-gotten gains' from political opponents.

The uncertainty of the transformation in combination with weak institutions may create incentives for the winners from economic reform to try to create political institutions that will protect their property. They can do this by strengthening political institutions that are favourable to them. Moreover, the greater the gains to the winners, the more resources that they will have to pursue institutional change. The desire to change economic power into favourable political institutions can spark demand for institutional changes in the powers of the presidency.[8]

---

[8] The analysis begins by assuming that presidents are always looking to expand their institutional powers. Whatever other goals presidents may have—policy goals, retaining office, or raising revenue—it is very likely that they will see increasing the formal powers of the office as a means to these ends. This assumption finds some empirical support from an unlikely source. On several occasions, Vaclav Havel, the consummate anti-politician, has championed greater powers for the Czech presidency (Elster, Offe, and Preuss 1998). Yet post-communist presidents face a variety of political and economic constraints that may prevent them from doing so.

A coalition with the winners from economic reform can also be attractive for a sitting president. The winners from economic reform can provide campaign financing, friendly coverage in the media, and private benefits to the executive in exchange for more secure property rights. In some cases, the winners from economic reform can also provide votes. Industrial managers in the post-communist world have been known to pressure workers to vote for their preferred candidates. Similarly, governors in regions benefiting from the current policy may ally with the incumbent to maintain their privileged position. These governors can deliver votes and tax revenue: valuable resources for an incumbent politician. We might expect to find that countries with a high concentration of economic winners from the transformation experience large increases in presidential power.

Presidents facing parliaments with a high number of independent deputies may also be well-positioned to expand their powers. A large number of independent deputies may make it more difficult for the parliament to defend its collective interests against a president bent on expanding his power. Deputies within a parliament face a collective action problem. All members of the parliament may have a collective interest in defending the powers of their institution, but each prefers that other deputies expend the resources needed to protect it. Where many deputies do not belong to political parties, it may be more difficult to engage in a concerted defence of the institution. Parties often have many means to discipline members that are not effective when used against non-party members.

Moreover, where the president can offer private benefits to individual deputies, the executive can use splits among party members and independents to divide and conquer the opposition within the parliament. Thus, a large number of independent deputies may make it more difficult to organize a defence against a president seeking to expand his powers.

A third factor may also affect the prospects for an expansion of presidential power. Newly adopted post-communist constitutions may raise the costs of changing the powers of the presidency and thereby affect expansions of presidential power. Changing new constitutions may be more politically costly for incumbents than changing the revised versions of communist-era constitutions or sub-constitutional documents, like a law on the presidency. Post-communist constitutions likely have greater legitimacy than earlier constitutions or laws on the presidency that were passed in a handful of countries. Moreover, altering a post-communist constitution may present a clear signal to foreign governments and investors of political unrest.

As is often the case, it is difficult to determine the independent impact of formal constitutions in this study because the ability to adopt a post-communist constitution may reflect underlying processes that influence the probability of changes in presidential power. For example, social cleavages may influence the adoption of a new constitution and the degree of change in presidential power. Recognizing this difficulty, this chapter takes the first step of examining whether the presence of a new post-communist constitution shapes the probability of a change in presidential power.[9] According to the logic cited above, we might expect to find that countries that have adopted post-communist constitutions experience lower levels of change in the powers of the presidency.

Analysis

To measure the concentration of the gains to the winners, I use the rate of change in the Gini coefficient during a particular presidential administration. The Gini coefficient (which measures the extent to which the distribution of earnings in a society deviates from equality) is derived from the cumulative distribution of earnings across the population, ranked by per capita incomes. It is defined as 'one-half of the mean difference between any two observations in the earnings distribution divided by average earnings' (EBRD: 1999: 18).[10] A perfectly equal society has a measure of zero. The rate of change in earnings inequality measures the concentration of the benefits delivered to the winners at the expense of the losers during the period of reform.

This measure varies dramatically across countries. In no cases in this survey, and in only one case in the entire post-communist world—Slovenia—does the level of income inequality fall in any given year. The average rate of change in the Gini coefficient during a presidential administration in the countries under study is 25 per cent. During Yeltsin's first term in Russia, the Gini coefficient increased by 48 per cent and represented the tremendous gains made by a small group of concentrated winners.[11] In Kwasniewski's Poland, the Gini coefficient has increased by only 7 per cent. Such large changes in social structure over such a short period of time are rare.

[9] See Riker (1990) for a sceptical view of the impact of formal constitutions on outcomes.

[10] Data on economic inequality from Flemming and Micklewright (1999). Some years are missing. For Croatia, the measure is based on monthly income; for all other countries, it is based on monthly earnings. Some data also from European Bank for Reconstruction and Development Office of the Chief Economist for 1998.

[11] This figure reaches 75% if it measured from 1989 rather than 1991.

To measure the effect of fragmentation on the probability of an increase in presidential power, I use the number of deputies elected as independents. The number of independents is weighted by months when parliamentary and presidential elections are staggered. The average number of independents in the post-communist parliaments under study is 15.5 per cent.

To assess the impact of a new constitution on expansions of presidential power, I include a dummy variable that takes the value of 1 if a new post-communist constitution is in place when a new administration comes to office, and 0 if a new administration comes to office under a revised version of the communist-era constitution. In most cases, this distinction is clear, but some cases require a brief explanation. For example, I count Poland's interim 'small constitution' of 1992 as a new constitution because it represents agreement among the major actors in the political system on the basic rules of the political game. In addition, in some cases, like Ukraine under Kuchma, a new constitution is passed that enshrines new presidential powers after the president takes office. I count these cases as a 0, because Kuchma expanded his powers while being governed by a revised Soviet-era constitution.

I also include several control variables in the analysis. I control for some differences in the initial conditions facing these countries. For example, it is often argued that countries of the former Soviet Union (FSU) face greater obstacles on the path of democratization than do the countries of Eastern Europe. These greater obstacles may encourage calls to centralize power in the executive. I also try to control for the initial level (Level) of presidential power that an incumbent possesses. This initial level of presidential power may influence the incentive and ability of executives to seek more power. For example, presidents who begin the term with many powers may find it easier to expand their formal powers still further. Table 4.1 presents the raw data used for this analysis.

Results

To measure the impact of concentrated winners from economic reform and a post-communist constitution, I conduct a probit analysis (Table 4.2) on changes in presidential power during each presidential administration. This method allows us to make statements about the probability of particular events. The dependent variable takes the value of 0 if the presidential powers do not change during an administration, and 1 if they increase.

TABLE 4.1: *Presidential power: an overview*

Country	Start of the term	Size of increase	Initial presidential power	Number of independents	Change in Gini coefficient
Armenia 1	10.91	2.50	14.50	35.0	0.47
Armenia 2	9.96	0.00	16.00	0.5	0.19
Belarus 1	7.94	4.00	18.00	38.0	0.20
Croatia 1	8.92	0.00	9.00	3.6	0.02
Croatia 2	6.97	0.00	9.00	3.7	n/a
Georgia 1	10.92	5.00	8.00	37.0	0.46
Georgia 2	11.95	0.00	13.00	16.0	0.13
Kyrgyzstan 1	10.90	4.00	11.00	20.0	0.22
Kyrgyzstan 2	12.95	3.00	15.00	67.0	0.35
Lithuania 1	2.93	0.00	6.00	7.0	0.01
Lithuania 2	1.98	0.00	6.00	1.0	0.29
Moldova 1	12.91	3.00	6.00	1.0	0.56
Moldova 2	12.96	0.00	9.00	1.0	0.03
Poland 1	0.07	0.00	6.00	1.0	0.15
Paland 2	12.90	1.00	6.00	3.5	0.24
Poland 3	11.95	0.00	7.00	1.0	0.07
Romania 1	5.90	0.00	6.00	2.8	0.11
Romania 2	9.92	0.00	6.00	3.8	0.11
Romania 3	11.96	0.00	6.00	4.8	0.39
Russia 1	6.91	9.00	6.00	15.0	0.48
Russia 2	7.96	0.00	15.00	20.0	0.04
Ukraine 1	12.91	0.00	8.00	0.0	0.46
Ukraine 2	6.94	5.00	13.00	58.0	0.14
Average		1.66	9.98	15.49	0.23

Model 1 suggests that both the degree of change in the Gini coefficient and the number of independents are significantly correlated with changes in presidential power. The greater the changes in the Gini coefficient, and the higher the number of independents, the more likely is an increase in presidential power. Model 2 finds that changes in inequality remain significant controlling for differences in initial conditions between eastern European and former Soviet states (FSU).[12] The number of independents falls just at the 0.10 level of significance (0.103) in this model. Model 3 finds that

---

[12] Countries of the FSU face greater economic and political obstacles to democracy at the start of the transformation than do countries in Eastern Europe. FSU states receive a score a 1, and others receive a score of 0.

TABLE 4.2: *Accounting for changes in presidential power*

	Model 1	Model 2	Model 3	Model 4
Gini change	7.06[b]	8.58[b]	6.82[a]	7.50[a]
	(3.41)	(4.17)	(3.69)	(4.30)
Independents	0.11[b]	0.16[a]	0.30[a]	0.13
	(0.06)	(0.09)	(0.18)	(0.08)
FSU		−1.05		
		(1.21)		
Level of presidential power			−0.56	
			(0.45)	
Constitution				−1.50
				(1.12)
Constant	−3.34[b]	−3.47[b]	0.13	−2.85[a]
	(1.39)	(1.58)	(2.5)	(1.75)
N	22	22	22	22
LR chi2(2)	19.78	20.63	22.31	21.99
Prob>Chi-square	0.0001	0.0001	0.0001	0.0001
Prob>Chi-square	0.0001	0.0001	0.0001	0.0001

[a] Significant at the 0.10 level.
[b] Significant at the 0.05 level.

both variables of interest retain their significance controlling for the initial level (Level) of powers held by the president.[13]

Model 4 finds that post-communist constitutions do not seem to constrain increases in executive power.[14] Countries with post-communist constitutions are just as likely to experience an increase in presidential powers as countries operating with revised soviet-era constitutions, controlling for changes in the Gini coefficient and the number of independent deputies. Thus, this analysis finds that increases in economic inequality and a high number of independents in the parliament are associated with increases in presidential power.

These results are consistent with the theory presented above. However, the analysis does not explain the direction of causation. Increases in presidential power may lead to changes in economic

[13] (FSU) and (Level) are correlated at the 0.51 level and are thus not included in the same regression.

[14] Unreported analyses find that GDP per capita, incumbency, and levels of income inequality also do not affect the results. The results are weaker but still significant if Russia 1991–6 is dropped from the analysis. I note this analysis to alleviate fears that the Russia case alone is driving the results.

inequality rather than the other way around. The largest changes in the Gini coefficient, however, typically occur prior to the increases in presidential power. Most changes in presidential power happen in the second half of the presidential term. On average, executives that manage to increase their powers do so 29 months after the start of a term.

Similarly, it may be the case that strong presidents lead to a high of number of independent deputies rather than vice versa. Data on the number of independents are taken from elections prior to the increase in presidential power so there are good grounds to believe that the causal arrow runs from the number of independent deputies to increases in presidential power rather than in the opposite direction.

In addition, a brief glance at some cases supports the plausibility of the model. In Russia, a coalition of ex-bureaucrats, industrial managers from the export sector, and governors from regions benefiting from reform were President Yeltsin's strongest supporters in struggles to expand and preserve his extraordinary presidential powers. In Ukraine, the winners from reform—managers in the industrial lobby—backed Kuchma's call for expanded powers in 1995 against opposition from the losers of reform—managers in the agricultural lobby. Kuchma, a former industrial manager himself, has maintained close ties to other industrial managers, and this group has been a net gainer from reform in Ukraine.

In contrast, the level of income inequality generated through economic reform in Poland has been relatively small and the main parties agreed to a 'Little Constitution' in 1992. President Walesa repeatedly tried to significantly increase his power during his tenure as president, but failed to do so.

Explaining why some presidents have dramatically increased their powers while others have not is a difficult task. Several caveats to the cross-country analysis are in order. First, the analysis relies on a small number of cases. Given that the data set consists of only 23 observations, caution is prudent. (This concern is especially important given the properties of probit analysis.) Second, there is a non-trivial amount of measurement error. Data on income inequality are generally difficult to collect under most circumstances and in the post-communist cases these difficulties are only magnified. The economic inequality data are probably the most accurate available, and are most likely biased against the argument made here. For example, the incentives to under-report wages are lower than the incentives to over-report wages. This would suggest that the high figures of earnings inequality are understated.

Links to Democracy

Having identified two factors that seem to contribute to the expansion of presidential power, this chapter now turns to the impact of these changes in presidential power on democracy in the countries under study. Expansions of presidential power are not always the death knell of democratization, but they do seem to have had negative consequences for the expansion of political and civil rights in some cases. Most of the countries in this set that have experienced increases in presidential power—Moldova, Kyrgyzstan, Russia, Ukraine, Armenia, Georgia—are stuck in the 'partly free' category, according to Freedom House. In contrast, Romania, Lithuania, and Poland experienced no increases in presidential power and no backsliding in their Freedom House scores of political and civil rights. These three countries have advanced to the 'free' category.

Table 4.3 provides more direct evidence. It presents the average Freedom House Score during each presidential administration and the change in the Freedom House Score during each administration. Freedom House publishes an annual index of political and civil rights. Each of these types of rights is scored on a scale of 1 to 7, with lower scores indicating countries with more rights. Table 4.3 presents the average sum of these two types of rights, with higher scores indicating more autocratic governments. It suggests that countries with increases in presidential power tend to have more autocratic governments as measured by Freedom House.

Table 4.4 indicates that administrations that have experienced increases in presidential power have become more autocratic by 1.44 points on the combined political and civil rights scale as calculated by Freedom House following an increase in presidential power. In contrast, countries that did not experience an increase in presidential power became more democratic by 1.0 point according to this same scale.

Changes in presidential power have been followed by less democratic Freedom House scores in Kyrgyzstan, Belarus, Russia, and Armenia. Indeed, Belarus has reverted to the 'not free' category (Freedom House 1998). In Kyrgyzstan, President Akaev increased his formal powers and received more autocratic scores from Freedom House during both of his terms. In 1994, following the adoption of a new constitution that included expanded presidential powers, Akaev pressured the courts to close newspapers critical of his administration (Anderson 1999: 55). He later led a public campaign that pressured deputies to give up their seats and dissolve parliament. This

TABLE 4.3: *Expansions of presidential power and democracy*

Country	Start of the term	Size of increase in presidential power	Annual Average Freedom House score C2–14	Change in Freedom House score during the term
Armenia 1	10.91	2.50	7.80	−2.0
Armenia 2	9.96	0.00	8.70	−1.0
Belarus 1	7.94	4.00	11.50	4.0
Croatia 1	8.92	0.00	7.80	−0.2
Croatia 2	6.97	0.00	8.00	0.0
Georgia 1	10.92	5.00	7.80	−2.2
Georgia 2	11.95	0.00	7.30	−2.0
Kyrgyzstan 1	10.90	4.00	7.50	−1.0
Kyrgyzstan 2	12.95	3.00	8.70	2.0
Lithuania 1	2.93	0.00	3.00	−2.0
Lithuania 2	1.98	0.00	3.00	0.0
Moldova 1	12.91	3.00	9.00	−2.0
Moldova 2	12.96	0.00	6.70	−2.0
Poland 1	12.90	1.00	4.00	0.0
Poland 2	11.95	0.00	3.00	−1.0
Romania 1	5.90	0.00	10.50	−1.0
Romania 2	9.92	0.00	7.50	−3.0
Romania 3	11.96	0.00	4.30	−3.0
Russia 1	6.91	9.00	6.80	1.0
Russia 2	7.96	0.00	7.00	1.0
Ukraine 1	12.91	0.00	6.70	1.0
Ukraine 2	6.94	5.00	7.00	0.0
Average		1.66	6.98	−0.61

TABLE 4.4: *The consequences of expanded presidential power*

	Start of the term	Size of increase in presidential power	Change in Freedom House Scores after increase in presidential power
Armenia 1	10.91	2.50	1.0
Belarus 1	7.94	4.00	4.0
Georgia 1	10.92	5.00	1.0
Kyrgyzstan 1	10.90	4.00	2.0
Kyrgyzstan 2	12.95	3.00	2.0
Moldova 1	12.91	3.00	0.5
Poland 1	12.90	1.00	0.0
Russia 1	6.91	9.00	1.0
Ukraine 2	6.94	5.00	0.0
Average		4.56	1.44

move led to pre-term parliamentary elections using electoral rules much more favourable to the president. After his pre-term election in December 1995, Akaev immediately called for greater powers, including the right to appoint judges at all levels and to name and dismiss ministers without the approval of parliament. Relying on an alliance of governors from prosperous regions, the state-controlled media, and his base supporters in southern Kyrgyzstan, Akaev obtained these changes to the constitution as election-weary voters granted the presidency increased powers in a referendum in February 1996 (Huskey 1997: 259).

Increased presidential power does not seem to have improved political and civil rights in Kyrgyzstan. Freedom House scores reveal increasing authoritarianism under Akaev's rule. In each of his two terms the combined Freedom House scores became more autocratic by 2 points.

In Belarus, following a relatively free and fair presidential election in 1994, President Lukashenka used his expanded powers to undermine democracy. Less than a year after winning election, Lukashenka used special military forces under his command to disperse political opponents at a rally staged by the Belarussian Popular Front. He proceeded to sabotage parliamentary elections by taking steps to suppress turnout and prevent a majority of deputies from gaining the necessary 50 per cent of the vote in their district needed to gain a seat (Mihailisko 1997). He enshrined his powers in a new constitution in 1996. In recent years, Lukashenka has only become more autocratic, even imprisoning some of his political opponents. Belarus under Lukashenka has seen a greater increase in autocracy than any other government in the region, according to Freedom House.

In contrast, Ukraine dramatically increased the powers of the presidency during Kuchma's first term, but experienced no decline in its level of democracy as measured by Freedom House. Poland experienced a slight increase in the powers of the presidency in the Little Constitution of 1992, and saw movement toward greater democracy. In Russia, President Yeltsin significantly expanded his powers after the bombardment of parliament in October 1993, and Freedom House scores remained constant for five years before increasing by one point following the second military conflict in Chechnya. Thus, there is not always a direct tie between expansions of presidential power and increased levels of autocracy. The link between expansions of presidential power and the quality of democracy should, however, be made with some caution because many confounding factors exist in these cases. Personal factors, foreign aid, and social cleavages may also intrude on these outcomes in individual cases.

Implications and Conclusion

Despite strong arguments made by some of the most prominent scholars in the field, the debate over the merits of presidential and parliamentary institutions for countries in transition remains unresolved. It is possible that no relationship exists between institutional arrangements and that this literature is a dead end. However, it may be premature to make this assessment. An alternative route is to examine shortcomings in the existing literature, such as a lack of attention to causal mechanisms and to economic reform, and seek to address them.

This chapter aimed to ground the debate in two ways. First, rather than seeking to establish a correlation between institutions and outcomes, it sought to examine the process by which institutional arrangements shape outcomes. It traced the rise of a coalition in support of expanded presidential power that is rooted in a reaction to the weakness of the post-communist state. Seeking to increase the security of their property rights, the winners from economic reform have allied with presidents to push for increased executive powers.

Second, it examined how institutions interact with other processes under way in countries undergoing transition. Rather than ignoring how economic reform interacts with institutions to shape the prospects for democracy, it placed this interaction of economics and politics centre-stage. It examined how concentrations of wealth created through economic reform have led to increases in presidential power in a range of post-communist countries.

Having established the roots of expansions of presidential power, this chapter then found that these increases in presidential power have often been accompanied by reductions in civil and political rights in the post-communist world. While countries that experienced no increases in presidential power generally became more democratic, countries that increased their presidential powers generally became less democratic.

Three lessons emerge from the analysis for constitutional designers. First, they should recognize the limits of our knowledge. Much effort has been expended to trace the impact of presidential and parliamentary systems, but the debate continues. We still have much work to do to identify the conditions under which either of these systems is more conducive to democracy. Moreover, advisers should also recognize that scholars continue to search for the conditions under which institutions have a significant impact on democracy in transitional societies. In short, a bit of humility is in order.

Second, advisers should understand the importance of favouring electoral laws that do not lead to a large number of independent deputies. This suggests using closed-list proportional representation and avoiding first-past-the-post electoral rules when possible. In addition, constitutional designers need not rush into a post-communist constitution in hopes of constraining executive power. The analysis provided here suggests that executives ruling in countries with and without new constitutions expand their powers at roughly the same rate.

Third, the cases emphasize the importance of context. Advisers engaged in constitutional design should recognize that building democracy is not the only task facing politicians. They also often face daunting economic problems that demand attention and may alter the effects of institutions on political outcomes. In a setting of massive redistribution of wealth in countries undergoing transformation, the impact of institutions may be different from that in settings where economic redistribution is less pronounced. Thus constitutional designers should recognize how the political and economic tasks facing politicians interact.

5

Presidentialism and Democratic Performance

José Antonio Cheibub

Introduction

Of the 133 transitions to and from democracy that occurred in the world between 1946 and 1996, 59 took place in Latin America.[1] Early theorizing on the causes of political instability in the region has tended to focus on structural variables—the degree of dependency, the level of inequality, poverty, and so on—which supposedly created conditions that were conducive to the demise of democratic regimes. Recent research has moved away from this focus on economic and social conditions and has concentrated instead on the impact of institutional features on the survival and operation of democracy in Latin America. Stimulated by the formulations first advanced by Juan Linz,[2] the breakdown of democratic regimes and the alleged 'crisis of governability' of new democracies have been attributed to presidentialism, which, in combination with permissive electoral systems and weakly institutionalized political parties, produce divided governments, deadlocks, institutional paralysis, and, ultimately, the breakdown of democratic institutions.

Yet Latin American democracies, all of which are presidential, survive in many countries, even as governments implement policies

Research for this work was supported in part by grants from the University of Pennsylvania Research Foundation and the Christopher H. Browne Center for International Politics at the University of Pennsylvania. I thank Amel Ahmed and Dan Miodownik for valuable research assistance. I also thank Argelina Figueiredo, Fernando Limongi, Scott Mainwaring, and Adam Przeworski for comments on earlier drafts.

[1] This represents 44.4% of all transitions, concentrated in 23 countries. The remaining 74 transitions were spread among the other 166 countries. These numbers come from Alvarez *et al.* and the author's update.

[2] See also Linz (1990*a*, *b*).

aimed at radically restructuring their economies. This fact suggests that we need to take another look at arguments that attribute to presidentialism a causal impact on regime instability in Latin America, or at least that we need to reconsider the causal mechanisms that are allegedly responsible for presidentialism's relatively poor performance.

The purpose of this chapter is to do so by examining empirically the factors that, according to the prevailing view, should account for variation in the performance of presidential regimes. The goal is to probe whether the factors usually identified as the reasons for presidentialism's (poor) political and economic performance are capable of explaining, as they should if they were indeed important, observed variation in the outcomes produced by presidential regimes. Here I am primarily concerned with two outcomes: the survival of presidential regimes and the accountability of presidents and their parties to economic outcomes. There are several other aspects of performance that are potentially interesting but which are not examined here.

The analysis presented below is based on data for all presidential and mixed regimes between 1946 and 1996. Due to variation in the availability of data, particularly of economic data, many analyses are based on slightly different samples, covering a shorter period of time and/or a smaller set of countries. Although my primary concern is with pure presidential regimes, mixed systems are also considered in order to assess whether their presence modifies what is found for pure presidential regimes. It can be anticipated here that, despite some significant institutional features regarding presidential veto and term limits, the inclusion of mixed systems does not modify any of the findings about pure presidential regimes. The Annex contains a brief discussion of the criteria utilized to classify the regimes, a list of the countries included in the data set, and the definition of other variables used in the analysis.

The chapter is organized as follows. The next section assesses the extent to which presidential regimes are characterized by divided government and examines the impact of partisan and electoral variables on the incidence of divided government. The following section does the same for 'deadlock' situations. Next, the impact of divided governments and deadlock on the survival of presidential regimes is examined, followed by an analysis of their impact on the accountability of presidents with respect to economic outcomes. In the conclusion I situate the findings in the context of the debate about the merits of presidentialism relative to parliamentarism, and suggest ways in which research on this issue could be advanced.

Divided Government in Presidential Regimes

Conventional wisdom concerning presidential regimes suggests that they are prone to deadlocks between executives and legislatures, which would explain their high degree of instability and relatively poor economic performance. The absence of mechanisms for the resolution of conflicts between the president and congress within the existing constitutional framework generates incentives for actors to search for extra-constitutional means of resolving their differences. At the same time, by frequently generating situations in which decisions cannot be made, it prevents governments from dealing with important economic issues. Thus, executive-legislative relations in presidential regimes are thought to be characterized by conflict and deadlock, with important repercussions for both the survival of the regime and its economic performance.

Studies of the performance of presidential regimes tend to *postulate* the negative consequences of divided governments and deadlock for the performance of presidents and presidential regimes, and then proceed to study the conditions that are more likely to produce divided government and deadlock.[3] Valuable as they are in helping understand the institutional conditions that are more likely to produce presidents with legislative majorities—the type of electoral system, the number of parties, and the electoral cycle are the most important variables identified in this literature—these studies offer little evidence to the effect that divided government and deadlock are frequent in presidential regimes, or that these regimes' performance is indeed affected by the alleged pervasiveness of divided governments and deadlock. Demonstrating, for instance, that proportional representation systems, multipartism, or non-concurrent elections are more likely to produce presidents who lack a legislative majority is not, however, sufficient empirical grounds to conclude either that proportional systems, multipartism, or non-concurrent elections are bad for the performance of presidential regimes, or that the divided governments these factors are likely to produce are bad for the performance of presidential regimes. Electoral systems, party systems, and electoral cycles may indeed affect the president's legislative support and produce divided governments. Whether they induce deadlock, or affect performance, however, is another question.

[3] For examples, see Jones (1995*a*), Mainwaring (1993), Carey (1993) and Mainwaring and Shugart (1997*b*).

In this section I examine the incidence of divided government and deadlock in presidential democracies. Governments are divided when the party of the president does not control a majority of seats in the legislature—or, in bicameral systems, when it does not control a majority of seats in at least one of the chambers.[4] Divided government is a frequent occurrence in presidential regimes: in about 61 per cent of the years the party of the president did not control a majority of seats in congress. This rate is lower if we only consider pure presidential regimes—58 per cent—particularly in unicameral systems—48 per cent. Still, almost half of the years in these systems were of divided government.

As suggested by Mainwaring (1993) and others, the president's legislative support is associated with the number of political parties. The frequency with which the party of the president does not hold a majority in congress increases markedly with the number of effective parties: in pure presidential regimes it goes from 38.67 per cent of the years when there are no more than two effective parties, to 41.01 per cent when there are two to three effective parties, to 89.43 per cent when there are three to four effective parties, to 90.38 per cent when there are four to five effective parties, to 98.11 per cent when there are more than five effective parties (Table 5.1).

TABLE 5.1: *Frequency of divided government in presidential regimes by the number of effective political parties*

Number of effective parties (EP)	% Divided government	
	Mixed and presidential	Pure presidential
EP≤2	38.07	38.67
2<EP≤3	42.72	41.01
3<EP≤4	90.00	89.43
4<EP≤5	94.12	90.38
EP>5	98.92	98.11
All	61.38	58.08

[4] Contrary to Shugart (1995), I do not distinguish between the situations in which the minority president faces a unified opposition from the situations in which there is no majority. Although not politically irrelevant, these situations are not empirically important: they are a direct function of the number of political parties and the fact that they are not distinguished in the analysis does not affect any of the results to be presented below.

The timing of presidential and congressional elections also seems to affect the likelihood of divided government. Table 5.2 shows that unified governments are more frequent when presidential and congressional elections coincide—54.22 per cent—than when they do not coincide—60.26 per cent—or are held alternately concurrently and non-concurrently—65.57 per cent. Note, however, that, contrary to expectations (Shugart 1995; Jones 1995a) this is not due to the fact that the number of parties is larger when presidential and legislative elections do not coincide. As we can see in Table 5.3, the frequency with which we observe two-party systems is higher when presidential and congressional elections are not concurrent. At the same time, systems with two to four parties are more frequent when elections coincide than when they do not coincide. As a matter of fact, when presidential and legislative elections are not simultaneous, either because they are never held at the same time or because they alternate, the frequency of cases first decreases and then increases as the number of parties increases. Thus, even though the timing of presidential and legislative elections matters for the occurrence of divided governments in presidential regimes, the reason why it does needs to be further investigated.[5]

TABLE 5.2: *Frequency of divided government in presidential regimes by the timing of presidential and congressional elections*

Presidential and congressional elections	% Divided government	
	Mixed and presidential	Pure presidential
Non-concurrent	67.26	60.26
Alternate	65.57	65.57
Concurrent	55.31	54.22
All	61.01	57.68

[5] This analysis employs a crude measure of electoral cycle. Cox (1997: 210), for example, provides a more refined measure of proximity of presidential and legislative elections, which would allow us to gauge with more precision the impact of electoral cycle on presidential majorities and the number of parties. The measure employed here, however, is sufficient to establish that, as expected, the timing of electoral and presidential elections is related to the frequency with which presidential parties control a majority of seats in congress. This is all that is needed in the context of this analysis.

Table 5.3: *Timing of presidential and congressional elections by the number of effective parties (EP)*[a]

	non-concurrent		alternate		concurrent	
	mixed and pres.	pure pres.	mixed and pres.	pure pres.	mixed and pres.	pure pres.
$EP \leq 2$	36.76	23.67	33.82	40.80	29.41	35.50
$2 < EP \leq 3$	32.15	22.87	8.85	10.24	59.00	66.89
$3 < EP \leq 4$	50.75	23.32	3.02	4.51	46.23	69.17
$4 < EP \leq 5$	74.28	58.11	4.29	8.11	21.43	33.78
$EP > 5$	70.63	63.16	9.79	14.74	29.47	22.11

[a] Entries are the proportion of year in each category.

Finally, divided government is more frequent when legislative elections are held under proportional representation systems (Table 5.4).

TABLE 5.4: *Frequency of divided government in presidential regimes by electoral system regulating legislative elections*

Electoral system	Mixed and presidential	Pure presidential
Majority-plurality	51.72	47.55
Pure proportional	64.64	59.36
Mixed	64.10	80.00
Pure proportional + mixed	64.61	60.40
Total	61.71	57.52

It seems, thus, that, as suggested by comparative analyses of presidentialism, proportional representation, multipartism, the timing of presidential and congressional elections, and divided government are all interconnected in presidential democracies. Note, however, that the arguments go beyond ascertaining this relationship. It is not only that presidents do not control a majority of seats in congress under some conditions, but that, when they do not, deadlock and stalemate are likely to characterize executive-legislative relations, thus affecting the regime's performance. So the issue at stake is whether, as claimed by Linz and others, presidential regimes are likely to produce stalemate.

Deadlock in Presidential Regimes

In the comparative literature, it is often assumed that whenever the presidency and congress are controlled by different parties deadlock will occur. This, however, is not entirely accurate. Whereas unified governments are obviously unlikely to generate deadlock between the executive and the legislature, divided governments will not necessarily lead to deadlock between the two branches: when the opposition controls enough votes to override presidential vetoes the government is divided; yet, since the bills preferred by the opposition are likely to become law, there will be no deadlock. Thus, before we proceed, we need to be able to identify empirically the conditions under which deadlock situations are likely to exist.

Assume a situation in which there are two parties, the party of the president and the opposition. P is the share of seats held by the party of the president and O is the share of seats held by the opposition. Legislation is passed by votes of at least M members of congress and, in the case of bicameral systems, bills have to be approved in both houses. Under these conditions we can distinguish the situation in which the party of the president controls a majority of seats in congress, and hence congress passes bills that are the ones preferred by the president, from the situation in which the party of the president does not control a majority of seats in congress. When this is the case, congress approves bills that are not the ones preferred by the president, either because it reflects the preferences of the opposition, or because it reflects some compromise that had to be struck between the houses in bicameral systems so that the bill could be approved. In these situations, if constitutionally allowed, the president vetoes the bill. Presidential vetoes can be overridden by at least V members of congress. Thus, $0 < M < V < 100$.

This set-up defines four possible situations in terms of executive-legislative relations:

(1) $P < (100 - V)$ and $O \geq V$
(2) $(100 - V) \leq P < M$ and $M \leq O < V$
(3) $M \leq P < V$ and $(100 - V) \leq O < M$
(4) $P \geq V$ and $O < (100 - V)$

Under (1), congress passes bills preferred by the opposition and these bills are likely to become law: even if the president vetoes the bill, the opposition has the votes to override the presidential veto. In these cases we can say that the opposition 'rules'. Under (3) and (4), congress passes bills preferred by the president, the president signs the bills, and they become law. In these cases we can say that the president 'rules'. It is only under (2) that deadlock can occur: congress passes bills preferred by the opposition, the president vetoes these bills, and the opposition does not have enough votes to override the presidential veto. There is a stalemate between congress and the president, and, as suggested by several commentators, there is no constitutional solution to this stalemate. This is the situation that should make presidential regimes the most vulnerable since both the president and the opposition would have an incentive to seek extra-constitutional solutions to the stalemate.

Thus, in general, conditions for deadlock are present only if the president is likely to veto a bill and the opposition does not have enough votes to override the presidential veto. We need, therefore, to assess the frequency of these situations in presidential regimes. Empirically, these situations depend on five factors:

(1) On the distribution of seats in congress or, more specifically, on the share of seats held by the party of the president (P);
(2) on whether the president has veto power;
(3) on the type of congressional majority necessary to override the presidential veto—the location of V with respect to M;
(4) on whether the system is unicameral or bicameral; and
(5) on whether in bicameral systems veto override is by a vote in each chamber separately or in a joint session of both chambers.

Table 5.5 presents the distribution of cases (country-years) of both presidential and mixed systems according to the four institutional factors listed above. Note, to begin with, that there is only a handful of cases in which the president has no veto powers: 4.7 per cent and 5.5 per cent in presidential and mixed systems, respectively. The bulk of these cases come from Switzerland, but they also include the Congo 1992–6, Croatia 1991–6, Kyrgyzstan 1991–2, Peru 1956–61 and 1963–7, Romania 1990–6, Russia 1991–2, South Africa 1994–6, Sri Lanka 1989–96, Suriname 1988–9 and 1991–6, and Uganda 1980–4. At the same time, only Cyprus grants veto powers to the president without allowing congress to override it: all 38 cases in this category come from this country. The bulk of the cases in pure presidential regimes—81.7 per cent—are those in which the president has veto powers and congress can override the presidential veto by a super-majority, either of two-thirds— the most common situation—or of three-fourths. In 8.4 per cent of the cases although presidents can veto legislation, veto override can be achieved with the same majority that passed the legislation in the first place. These situations are also common in mixed systems—39.4 per cent—although the most frequent situation in these systems is the one in which disagreement between congress and the president regarding legislation is decided either by a constitutional court or by referendum—42.8 per cent.

Now, in some of the situations represented in Table 5.5 deadlock between the president and congress will not occur, regardless of the share of seats the party of the president controls in congress. This is obviously true for the cases in which the president has no veto powers, congress cannot override the presidential veto, or disagreements between the president and congress are resolved by referendum: if presidents cannot veto legislation, whoever controls a majority of seats in congress 'rules'; if presidents can veto legislation but congress cannot override the presidential veto, the president has the final world and no impasse emerges; if disagreements are referred to a third party, deadlock will not occur. Deadlock will not occur either

Table 5.5: *Distribution of cases (country-years) by the number of chambers, presidential veto, and conditions for veto override:*

(1) Pure presidential systems (n = 727)				
	Unicameral		Bicameral	
	Veto	No veto	Veto	No veto
1. No override	38	–	0	–
2. Absolute majority	34	–	27	–
2A. Separate chambers	–	–	18	–
2B. Joint chambers	–	–	9	–
3. 2/3 majority	214	–	335	–
3A. Separate chambers	–	–	251	–
3B. Joint chambers	–	–	84	–
4. 3/4 majority	0	–	45	–
4A. Separate chambers	–	–	4	–
4B. Joint chambers	–	–	4	
5. Third party or referendum	–	–	–	–
TOTAL	286	23	407	11

(2) Mixed systems (n = 236)				
	Unicameral		Bicameral	
	Veto	No veto	Veto	No veto
1. No override	0	–	0	–
2. Absolute majority	83	–	10	–
2A. Separate chambers	–	–	5	–
2B. Joint chambers	–	–	5	–
3. 2/3 majority	29	–	0	–
3A. Separate chambers	–	–	0	–
3B. Joint chambers	–	–	0	–
4. 3/4 majority	0	–	0	–
4A. Separate chambers	–	–	0	–
4B. Joint chambers	–	–	0	–
5. Third party or referendum	56	–	45	–
TOTAL	168	8	55	5

in unicameral systems in which presidential veto can be overridden by an absolute majority in congress. In these cases, to use the symbols defined above, $V=M$, thus defining a situation that is functionally similar to the situations in which presidents cannot veto legislative bills. In these cases, whoever controls the congress, whether the president or the opposition, 'rules'. If the president's party does not hold a majority in congress, the same majority that approved a bill in the first place may override the presidential veto. Together these situations—that is, the situations in which the distribution of seats in congress does not affect the conditions for deadlock—represent a small share of the cases of pure presidential regimes observed since 1946: 14.58 per cent. In mixed regimes, however, they are more frequent; they constitute 83.47 per cent of the cases, largely due to the frequency with which impasses between the president and congress are resolved by a third party.

The remaining cases are more complex and deadlock may or may not emerge, depending on the share of seats controlled by the party of the president and, in bicameral systems, on whether veto override requires a separate vote in each house or a joint vote in both houses.

- When veto override is by a majority vote in each of the houses of a bicameral system—line 2A in Table 5.5—deadlock will emerge if the party of the president controls a majority of seats in only one of the houses. In these cases, the president will veto the legislation but the opposition, lacking control in one of the houses, will not be able to override the presidential veto.
- When veto override is by a majority vote in a joint session of both houses, deadlock will emerge only if, lacking control in one of the houses, the party of the president also holds less than 50 per cent of the seats in the joint congress. In this case, the president will veto the legislation, and the opposition will lack enough votes to override the veto. However, if the party of the president holds more than 50 per cent of the seats in a joint meeting of both houses, deadlock will not emerge, even if it does not control a majority in one of the houses.
- When veto override is by a two-thirds majority in a unicameral system, deadlock will occur only if the party of the president controls more than 33.3 per cent but no more than 50 per cent of the seats.
- When veto override requires a two-thirds majority and the system is bicameral, deadlock situations will depend both on the share of seats held by the party of the president and on whether the vote is to be taken in each chamber or in a joint session of both chambers. Table 5.6 illustrates the possible scenarios when the vote is to be taken in each chamber separately. Here, deadlock may be pervasive; it is unlikely to occur only if the opposition holds more than two-thirds of the seats in both houses, or the party of the president holds more than 50 per cent of the seats in both houses. All the other cells in Table 5.6 represent situations in which deadlock is likely to occur.

- If the system is bicameral and veto override is at two-thirds in a joint session of both houses, deadlock conditions will exist if the party of the president does not control a majority in either house but controls more than 33.3 per cent of the votes in the joint congress. In these cases, the president will veto legislation, but the opposition will not control enough votes in the joint congress to override the presidential veto.
- Finally, in the cases in which veto override requires a three-fourths majority, deadlock conditions are analogous to the cases in which the requirement is a two-thirds majority, except that the cut-off points change from 33.3 per cent to 25 per cent.

TABLE 5.6: *Possible scenarios regarding executive-legislative relations in a bicameral setting with a two-thirds veto override requirement to be voted separately in each chamber*

% of seats held by the party of the president in the:			
Lower house:	0–33.3	33.3–50	>50
Upper house:			
0–33.3	Possible veto; Opposition overrides lower house	Possible veto; Opposition cannot override in the lower house	Possible veto; Opposition cannot override in the
33.3–50	Possible veto; Opposition cannot override in the upper house	Possible veto; Opposition cannot override in either house	Possible veto; Opposition cannot override in either house
>50	Possible veto; Opposition cannot override in the upper house	Possible veto; Opposition cannot override in either house	No veto

These are thus the situations in which deadlock can emerge in presidential regimes. They depend on the constitutional provisions regarding presidential veto and its override, the number of legislative chambers, and the distribution of seats in congress. The variable DEADLOCK was created to indicate these cases. It is coded 1 for all the cases in which deadlock or stalemate between the president and congress is likely to occur, as specified above, and 0 for the cases in which it is not likely to occur, either because the president 'rules' or because the opposition 'rules'.

We are now in a position to assess more precisely the relationship between divided government and deadlock. If we consider both pure

José Antonio Cheibub

presidential and mixed regimes we find that, when governments are divided, conditions for deadlock are as likely to be present as they are to be absent. If we consider only pure presidential regimes, conditions for deadlock are more likely—61.50 per cent of the cases—although by no means certain. Thus, we cannot assume that deadlock is necessarily induced by divided government.

Table 5.7 also allows us to examine the impact of electoral and partisan variables on the occurrence of deadlock. As we can see, the number of effective parties, the coincidence of presidential and legislative elections, and the electoral system have no systematic impact on the probability that deadlock will occur. Thus, whereas the probability that presidential governments will be divided increases with the number of effective parties, with non-concurrent presidential and legislative elections, and with legislative elections held on the basis of proportional representation, this does not mean that the probability of deadlock will also increase. Again, divided government is not synonymous with deadlock situations, and hence the factors that induce one do not necessarily induce the other.

TABLE 5.7: *Frequency of deadlock situations in presidential regimes by divided government, number of effective parties, electoral system, and timing of elections*

	% Deadlock situations	
	Mixed and presidential	Pure presidential
All	24.56	32.03
Divided government	49.48	61.50
Number of effective parties (EP):		
EP≤2	31.69	37.91
2<EP≤3	28.44	32.85
3<EP≤4	29.47	41.60
4<EP≤5	20.29	32.88
EP<5	3.85	6.10
Electoral system:		
Majority-plurality	27.78	37.16
Proportional	23.22	29.67
Proportional + mixed	22.56	29.23
Timing of legislative and presidential elections:		
Non-concurrent	8.33	15.79
Alternate	54.10	54.10
Concurrent	32.51	33.85

There are two possible objections to the way deadlock situations are being identified in this analysis. The first has to do with multipartism. Returning to the four possibilities for executive-legislative relations defined above, we can see that multipartism does not affect situations (3) and (4): if the president's party controls more than M, congress will pass bills that the president will sign into law, regardless of the number of parties that are in the opposition. However, with multipartism, it becomes difficult to assess situations (1) and (2), that is, those cases in which $P<M$. Here, O is likely to contain a subgroup of parties (O_p) that may support the president. Whether a stalemate will occur depends, of course, on the size of O_p, which cannot be assessed with the available information.[6] Thus, in general, under multiparty regimes stalemate could also occur under situation (1), which above was defined as a situation in which the opposition 'rules', characterized by the absence of deadlock. This, however, would be of little consequence for the results presented so far, and for the results to be presented below. If we were to define multipartism by the presence of more than two effective parties and were to consider nothing but the share of seats held by the party of the president, the number of deadlock situations would increase by 150 in unicameral systems and 84 in bicameral systems. However, we know that deadlock situations also depend on the constitutional provisions regarding the presidential veto and the conditions for its override. Taking this into consideration reduces the number of additional cases of deadlock to only 58, bringing the incidence of deadlock situations in presidential regimes from 24.55 per cent of the time to 30.55 per cent. Substantively, this means that even if we were to abandon the assumption that parties different from the party of the president are in the opposition, deadlock situations in presidential regimes would occur in less than one-third of the time and would be unrelated to the occurrence of

---

[6] Comparative data on the partisan basis of presidential governments are scarce, partly because the dominant view of presidentialism implies that coalition governments are unlikely in these regimes and, when they exist, they are precarious if not absolutely meaningless. A few analysts, like Mainwaring and Shugart (1997*b*) for example, have attempted to assess the partisan composition of presidential governments by measuring the legislative seats held by the parties that participated in the coalition that supported the president at the elections. However, they recognize the limitation of this measure to indicate the size of the coalition of parties that support the president in congress, ultimately concluding that the share of seats held by the party of the president is a better measure of the president's legislative support (Mainwaring and Shugart (1997*b*): 403). To my knowledge, only very recently have some analysts focused their attention on governing coalitions in presidential regimes. See Dehesa (1997), Amorin Neto (1998), Foweraker (1998), and Altman-Olin (1999).

divided government, as well as the electoral and partisan variables that induce the emergence of divided government.

The other objection to the way deadlock has been defined here has to do with party discipline. The measurement of deadlock situations adopted in this analysis assumes disciplined parties. With undisciplined parties the whole exercise unravels since the idea that there is such a thing as 'the party of the president' or 'the opposition' simply does not make sense: party labels do not predict anything about how members of congress will behave.

Assessing the degree of party discipline comparatively is quite complex and here I would like to argue that the assumption of party discipline is at least as plausible and analytically useful as the alternatives, which consist of either inferring discipline from electoral and partisan legislation or postulating that the constitutional design of presidential regimes is compatible with only very minimal degrees of party discipline.

The most common way to deal with the issue of party discipline comparatively is to classify countries in terms of the permissiveness of their electoral and party legislation: party discipline is considered to be low in systems where the legislation is more permissive from the point of view of the individual candidate: that is, where the electoral and party legislation do not provide the party leadership with mechanisms to control their rank and file. The problem with this approach is that party discipline is a behavioural concept and, for this reason, cannot be inferred from electoral and partisan legislation: what matters is whether party labels are good predictors of how members of congress will vote.[7] And we know that party labels can be very good predictors of congressional behaviour even in situations of highly permissive electoral and partisan legislation. As Limongi and Figueiredo and Figueiredo (1995) and Limongi (2000) have shown, Brazil, arguably the presidential system with the most permissive party legislation, has considerably high levels of party discipline. Classificatory schemes based on electoral legislation, therefore, are not a good way to assess the degree of party discipline of a system.

As for the second alternative, the issue is whether we have reasons to expect party discipline to be weaker under presidential regimes than under other constitutional designs. Part of the case about the difficulties faced by presidential regimes is made on the

[7] Mainwaring and Shugart (1997*b*), for instance, base the 'party discipline component' of their index of president's partisan powers on three aspects of party and electoral legislation: selection of candidates, the order in which candidates are elected, and the way votes are counted for candidates and their parties.

grounds, sometimes implicit, that party discipline in parliamentary regimes is inherently higher. There are two reasons why this is so. First, governments in parliamentary regimes depend on their party's capacity to enforce discipline and pass legislation in order to exist; there is, so to speak, a 'majoritarian imperative' in parliamentary regimes that is absent in presidential regimes. Second, individual members of parliament have an incentive to vote the party line in order to avoid bringing the government down and risk losing their seats.

In my view, however, these arguments excessively simplify the operation of parliamentary regimes, assuming that governments always have to hold a majority of seats in parliament and that the consequence of government dissolution is invariably an early election. Neither, however, is true. Strom (1999) was probably the first to point out that minority governments in parliamentary regimes are not an anomaly, but rather a frequent occurrence that can be explained in terms of the goals of political actors. Indeed, according to his and other counts, about one-third of governments in parliamentary regimes are formed even if they control less than 50 per cent of the seats. My own counting (Cheibub, 1998), based on data for 21 industrialized parliamentary regimes between 1946 and 1995, shows a similar proportion of cases. During this time, 31 per cent of the elections in these countries produced minority governments: more frequently in proportional representation systems—38 per cent—than in majority-plurality systems—13 per cent. At the same time, in 24 per cent of all the years in these countries governments held less than 50 per cent of the seats: again much more frequently in proportional representation systems than in majority-plurality systems—30 per cent against 7 per cent of the time. Thus, not only are governments in parliamentary regimes frequently formed with less than a majority of seats; they are not, as Strom has forcefully demonstrated, accidents or pathologies of some political systems.[8]

The relevance of this observation for a study about presidential regimes is that it demonstrates that the 'majoritarian imperative' is not really an imperative. The frequency and rationality of minority governments violate what Strom (1990: 7), again, calls 'the expectation that [in parliamentary regimes] executive and legislative coalitions are identical'. A significant share of prime ministers have to build coalitions around specific issues, much in the way presidents

---

[8] See also Laver and Schofield (1998) for a discussion of minority governments in European parliamentary regimes and for an argument for the inappropriateness of the 'majoritarian imperative' for the analysis of these systems.

do. There is nothing that suggests that these coalitions have to be of disciplined parties, or parties taken to be disciplined by the lesser degree of permissiveness of the existing electoral and party legislation.

As for the argument about early elections, the calculus of the individual legislator under parliamentarism cannot be entirely connected with the risk of election for the simple reason that early election is not the necessary consequence, or even the most frequent consequence, of a government dissolution. My data on 21 industrialized parliamentary democracies from 1946 to 1995 (Cheibub, 1998) show that 163 out of 291 (56 per cent) prime ministers observed during this period changed without an election taking place; that the party controlling the premiership changed 62 out of 162 times (38 per cent) again without an election taking place; that the partisan composition of the government—a 'weak' notion of alternation in power—changed 125 out of 274 times (46 per cent) without elections; and that the major party in the government—a 'strong' notion of alternation—changed 24 out of 101 times (24 per cent) with no elections. And note that these figures somewhat underestimate the frequency of government dissolution without elections since they consider only the cases in which a change in the composition of the government occurred; cases in which the government is formally dissolved but the same prime minister or parties form a new government are not counted.

The frequency of government changes in the middle of the electoral term obviously vary with the type of electoral system, the number of parties, and the type of government, that is, coalition or single party ; but the bottom line is that elections are far from being the necessary outcome of government dissolution in parliamentary regimes. What these observations imply, in my view, is that as much as parliamentarism is not sufficient for us to infer the incentives of individual members of parliament to vote along party lines and support the government, presidentialism per se is not sufficient for us to infer the behaviour of presidents in building coalitions and the incentives of parties and individual members of congress to participate in them. We need to know more about how presidents build coalitions and how these coalitions are kept together. Meanwhile the best that can be done is to assume that presidents command the support of those members of congress that belong to their own party.

To summarize, thus, we find that, although frequent, divided government is not the overwhelming condition of presidential regimes. As suggested in the literature, divided government is associated with proportional representation systems, with multipartism, and with systems in which presidential and legislative elections do not coincide. Deadlock situations, however, or situations that are potentially conducive to a stalemate between congress and the president are not inherent to divided governments, and do not depend on the number of parties, on the timing of presidential and congressional elections, or on the type of electoral system regulating congressional elections. This conclusion, however, is based on a more imprecise measurement since it assumes both that presidents govern only with the support of their own parties and that parties are disciplined.

Divided Government, Deadlock, and the Survival of Presidential Regimes

Do divided governments and the stalemate they are supposed to generate affect the performance of presidential regimes? There are several arguments suggesting that, through a variety of roads, they do. To begin with, to the extent that divided governments and deadlock spell government paralysis, they are likely to produce relatively bad economic and social outcomes which, in turn, may produce instability and undermine the legitimacy of the regime itself. If this does not directly lead to a change of regime, it is likely to lead to at least a change of government, implying a relatively high rate of leadership turnover which, in turn, may affect the survival of the regime as a whole. Divided government and deadlock also provide incentives for dissatisfied actors to search for extra-constitutional solutions to the paralysis they supposedly induce. This is so because there is no constitutional principle that can be invoked as a way out of paralysis. Finally, accountability, allegedly one of the high points of presidential regimes when compared with parliamentary regimes,[9] is negatively affected by divided government and deadlock.

How are these expectations supported by the data? In this section I examine the survival of presidential regimes as a function of divided government and deadlock situations. In the next section I will examine the impact of these variables on accountability of presidents and their parties with respect to economic outcomes.

As indicated in Table 5.8, between 1946 and 1996 there were 91 presidential regimes—including mixed—of which 42 'died', that is, changed into a non-presidential type of political regime, and 49

---

[9] Shugart and Carey (1992), but see Cheibub and Przeworski (1999).

were in place as of December 1996. The vast majority of the presidential regimes that 'died' became dictatorships; only Bangladesh in 1991 changed the constitutional framework of its democratic regime, abandoning a mixed system for a pure parliamentary regime.[10]

TABLE 5.8: *Distribution of spells of presidential regimes (pure and mixed), presidents, and presidential parties by mode of exit and average duration*[a]

Mode of Exit	Regime	Presidents	Party
In place as of 31 December 1996	49 (20.02)	49 (3.49)	49 (5.67)
Death (natural, accidents, suicides)	–	11 (3.27)	5 (4.80)
Assassination	–	3 (3.00)	–
Constitutional: elections	–	129 (5.05)	89 (6.31)
Constitutional: not elections	1	19 (3.05)	13 (5.77)
Non-constitutional: overthrown	30 (7.50)	30 (3.83)	30 (4.43)
Non-constitutional: consolidation	11 (10.27)	11 (4.09)	11 (4.55)
All less in place as of 31 December 1996	42 (8.16)	203 (4.51)	148 (5.70)
All	91 (14.55)	252 (4.31)	197 (5.70)

[a] Age in years in parentheses.

Table 5.9 presents the transition probabilities of presidential regimes as a function of divided government, deadlock situations, the electoral systems for congressional elections, the timing of presidential and legislative elections, and the number of effective political parties. If the arguments about divided government and deadlock are correct, presidential democracies should face higher risks of dying when the presidency and congress are controlled by different parties, when conditions for deadlock between the president and the congress are present, when presidential and legislative elections do not coincide, when the electoral system is proportional, and when the number of parties is large. Yet, with the qualified exception of multipartism, to be discussed below, none of this is true. Presidential regimes are as likely to die when governments are divided as when governments are unified. The difference between deadlock and non-deadlock situations is small and in

[10] In general, democratic regimes are very resilient in their form of government. The only other changes occurred in Brazil in 1961—from pure presidential to mixed—and 1963—back to pure presidential—which in this data set does not appear as a change, and in France with the inauguration of the Fifth Republic in 1958, when a mixed system replaced the parliamentary regime of the Fourth Republic.

favour of the former: whereas one in every 23 presidential regimes dies when there is no deadlock, one in every 28 regimes dies when there is deadlock. The difference in transition probabilities between plurality and proportional systems is also negligible. Concurrent elections do reduce the chances that a presidential regime will die. This effect, however, does not survive statistical analysis.[11]

TABLE 5.9: *Transition probabilities by various political and institutional conditions*

	Pure presidential	Presidential and mixed
Unified governments	0.0427	0.0444
Divided governments	0.0470	0.0426
No deadlock conditions	0.0430	0.0342
Deadlock conditions	0.0348	0.0336
Number of effective parties (EP)		
EP#2	0.0592	0.0637
2<EP#3	0.0239	0.0206
3<EP#4	0.0752	0.0502
4<EP#5	0.0541	0.0357
EP>5	0.0105	0.0140
EP≤3.5	0.0383	0.0362
2<EP≤3.5	0.0283	0.0231
3.5<EP≤5	0.0748	0.0488
EP>5	0.0105	0.0140
Electoral System:		
Plurality	0.0427	0.0426
Proportional	0.0391	0.0316
Proportional + mixed	0.0371	0.0297
Timing of legislative and presidential elections:		
Non-concurrent	0.0506	0.0337
Alternate	0.0504	0.0503
Concurrent	0.0376	0.0386

The story with the number of political parties is somewhat more complex. It is not, contrary to Mainwaring (1998) and Jones (1995), multipartism per se that affects the survival of presidential regimes. In presidential democracies high risks are associated with

[11] When a duration model is estimated we see that the impact of the timing of elections on the survival of presidential regimes is not statistically different from zero.

situations of very low pluralism, or situations conducive to moderate pluralism, which as Sartori suggested, are the ones in which there are between 2 and 5 relevant political parties. Presidential democracies with more than 5 effective parties, the cases that tend to be conducive to 'polarized pluralism' in Sartori's typology, have an expected life considerably higher than the presidential democracies with less than 5 effective parties: 95 years against 21.[12]

Why should moderate pluralism affect the survival of presidential democracies so strongly? One possibility would be that, somehow, moderate pluralism reduces the share of seats controlled by the president thus making stalemate more frequent and making it more difficult for presidents to govern. This seems to be partly confirmed by the data. If we consider unicameral and bicameral systems separately and, in the latter, the support for the president in the lower and the upper houses, we find that the share of seats held by the party of the president reaches one of the lowest points when the number of effective parties is around 3.5 and 4.5, after which the support for the president increases. Note, however, that the share of seats held by the party of the president falls sharply when there are more than 5 effective parties, even though the hazard rates in these cases are, as we have seen before, the lowest. Note also that 3.5 effective parties does not represent the point at which presidents cease controlling a majority of seats in congress. According to Table 5.10, this happens when the number of effective parties is 2.5. Thus, the higher hazard rates of systems with a moderate number of political parties cannot be entirely accounted for by the fact that the party of the president does not control enough seats in congress.

One alternative explanation would have to do not so much with the share of seats controlled by the party of the president but rather with the distribution of strength of the three largest parties as indicated by the number of seats they hold. What may be difficult for presidential regimes—and for that matter any democratic regime—is the existence of three political forces of relatively equal strength, each of which is attempting to implement its own programme either alone or in alternating coalitions. Pluralism, in such

---

[12] The way the data are grouped does make some difference. For instance, if we use 3.5 as the cut-off point, we find that, indeed, one in 32 presidential democracies dies when there are fewer than 3.5 effective parties and one in 13 dies when there are more than 3.5 parties. There is, however, too much aggregation in this number as we find, for example, that the hazard rate of presidential democracies is even higher when the number of effective parties is between 3.5 and 5, falling drastically when the number of parties is greater than 5.

TABLE 5.10: *Average share of seats held by the party of the president in congress by the number of effective parties (EP)*

EP	Unicameral		Bicameral (lower)		Bicamera (upper)	
	Mixed and pres	Pure pres.	Mixed and pres.	Pure pres.	Mixed and pres	Pure pres.
$-1<EP\#1.5$	63.15	84.25	76.83	79.42	75.13	76.59
$1.5<EP\#2$	68.78	67.15	53.30	52.99	55.51	56.52
$2<EP\#2.5$	55.23	56.83	52.76	51.95	56.37	56.02
$2.5<EP\#3$	46.11	47.99	44.04	43.69	49.01	49.01
$3<EP\#3.5$	37.64	38.57	40.85	41.50	49.83	46.85
$3.5<EP\#4$	30.75	30.75	34.00	33.54	40.28	42.20
$4<EP\#4.5$	32.56	34.66	34.59	26.81	25.39	25.14
$4.5<EP\#5$	27.64	45.44	54.12	59.66	48.60	49.97
$EP>5$	22.49	22.29	49.32	57.28	23.39	16.42

cases, will be moderate, with the number of effective parties hoovering between 3 and 4. More importantly, compromises may be difficult as they would be inherently unstable: agreements among any two parties could be undermined by counter-offers from the third one.

Although not conclusively, the available data suggest that this hypothesis at least makes sense. Table 5.11 summarizes a couple of traits of party systems in presidential regimes. The goal is to present

TABLE 5.11: *Party system characteristics by number of effective parties (EP)*

EP	Mixed and presidential		Pure presidential	
	Party struct. I	Party struct. II	Party struct. I	Party struct. II
$1<EP\#1.5$	92.06	1.17	91.98	1.16
$1.5<EP\#2$	95.12	1.47	97.09	1.50
$2<EP\#2.5$	92.97	1.69	93.99	1.73
$2.5<EP\#3$	90.92	1.92	91.31	1.93
$3<EP\#3.5$	87.58	2.12	87.84	2.10
$3.5<EP\#4$	79.40	2.16	79.09	2.22
$4<EP\#4.5$	78.79	2.09	75.58	2.11
$4.5<EP\#5$	73.49	2.43	74.30	2.48
$EP>5$	61.88	2.41	60.90	2.46
$EP>5$ (less LGSTP<30)	63.57	1.78	66.34	1.81

measures that could help characterize the distribution of party strength without, of course, being correlated with the number of effective parties. 'Party Structure 1' is simply the sum of seats held by the three largest parties in congress, while 'Party Structure 2' is this sum weighted by the share of seats of the largest party. This last measure is an index of equiproportionality among the three largest parties, at least in the range of cases in which the largest party gets more than 30 per cent of the votes: in this range, the closer this number is to one, the more concentrated the distribution of strength among the three largest parties is; the closer it is to three, the more evenly divided are the seats held by the three largest parties. As we can see in the table, the three largest parties are likely to hold an equal share of seats in moderate and strong pluralism—number of effective parties > 3.5—than in weak pluralism. The closest the distribution of seats among the three largest parties gets to being equal is when the number of effective parties is between 4 and 5. Note that the figure for strong pluralism is contaminated by the large number of cases in which the largest party holds less than 30 per cent of the seats. If we exclude these cases, we find that the index for 'Party Structure II' drops from 2.46 to 1.81, almost identical to the average value for weak pluralism. In moderate pluralism, however, the average is 2.12, suggesting that, in comparison with the other situations, moderate pluralism is likely to be characterized by three strong political parties.

Statistical analysis strongly confirms the findings suggested by the descriptive transition probabilities of Table 5.9. Divided government is found to have no statistically significant effect when a model of survival of presidential democracies is estimated. This remains true even after controlling for the type of electoral system, by the electoral cycle, by the number of effective parties, by the level of economic development as indicated by real per capita income, by the presidential systems of Latin America, and by the presence of the United States in the sample. The same is true with deadlock situations: survival models reveal no statistically significant effect on the probability that presidential regimes will continue in place.[13] Thus, the expectations generated by the comparative literature

[13] These effects are robust to model specification: they do not change if hazard rates are modelled as being constant, monotonically increasing or decreasing, or changing directions; it is also robust to sample heterogeneity. Note, in addition, that these results, contrary to the figures presented in Table 5.9, do take into consideration the fact that a number of regimes were still in place when observations ended. Coefficients are omitted due to space considerations. They can be obtained from the author on request.

regarding the survival prospects of presidential regimes under divided government and conditions of deadlock are refuted by both descriptive and statistical evidence.

To conclude, we can say that part of the effects of institutional factors on presidentialism commonly postulated in the comparative literature can be observed empirically: the electoral system, the timing of elections, and the number of parties affect, as expected, the legislative strength of presidents and the likelihood that we will observe divided governments. These governments are more frequent in proportional representation systems, when presidential and legislative elections do not coincide, and when the number of parties is large. The conclusion drawn from the existence of these effects, however, is not warranted by the data: neither the type of electoral system nor the timing of presidential and legislative elections has any impact on the survival of presidential regimes; the number of parties, in turn, matters for the survival of presidentialism, but not in the way postulated in the literature—what matters is not multipartism per se but whether pluralism is moderate—and probably not for the reasons postulated—moderate pluralism affects survival of presidentialism not because of its effect on the president's legislative support, but most likely because of the distribution of strength among the three largest parties. Most importantly, none of these factors affects the likelihood of deadlock situations which, contrary to all expectations, does not have a negative effect on the survival of presidential regimes. It seems, thus, that there must be other mechanisms operating in presidential regimes that allow them to survive under conditions that presumably make them doomed.

Divided Government, Deadlock, and Accountability in Presidential Regimes

Even if the regime is not affected by the political conditions under which it exists, presidents could be affected by them. One way in which this could occur is that presidents may be more or less accountable with respect to economic outcomes depending on the kind of support they may have in congress.

Governments are 'accountable' if citizens can discern whether governments are acting in their best interest and sanction them appropriately, so that those incumbents who satisfy citizens remain in office and those who do not lose it. In general presidential regimes are considered to be more accountable than parliamentary regimes on the grounds that they allow for more clarity of responsibility.[14] Under divided government and deadlock, however, this is not true; in these cases, it is more difficult for voters to identify and punish those responsible for the policies implemented, or not implemented, by the government and hence to hold governments accountable.

As defined here, governments are accountable if the probability that they survive in office is sensitive to government performance: otherwise they are not accountable. Specifically, accountability can be characterized by the derivative of 'hazard rate' with regard to the outcomes that were generated during some number of past years, where the hazard rate is the conditional probability that, having been in office for some duration $t=0,1,2, \ldots$ incumbents lose office at $(t+dt)$, $d+\rightarrow0$. Presidents are accountable with respect to economic outcomes if their hazard rate increases, and the probability of surviving in office falls, when economic performance declines.

Note that here the primary question is not about the impact of economic performance on the survival of presidents in office. Neither is it about the impact of divided government and deadlock on the survival of presidents.[15] Since the interest here is on the impact of divided government and deadlock on accountability of presidents, the question is about the impact these variables have on the relationship between economic performance and the survival of presidents in office. To the extent that divided governments and deadlock situations blur responsibilities and make accountability more difficult, we should observe a stronger impact of economic performance on the survival of presidents once they are controlled for.

Before we proceed, there is one point that needs to be made. In a way the question of electoral accountability of presidents makes no sense given a feature common in presidential regimes. In order for elections to induce accountability, voters should be able to punish governments when they perform badly *and* to reward governments when they perform well. Yet this last condition is absent in the vast

[14] See Powell (1989) for a discussion of the relationship between 'clarity of responsibility' and accountability, and Powell and Whitten and Whitten (1993) and Palmer (1996) for an analysis of the relationship between 'clarity of responsibility' and accountability in parliamentary democracies. For an argument about the superiority of presidentialism on the grounds of accountability see Shugart and Carey (1992). See, however, Cheibub and Przeworski (1999) for contrary evidence concerning presidentialism and Cheibub (1998) for contrary evidence concerning 'clarity of responsibility'.

[15] Both questions are interesting in themselves and something will be said about the second one below.

majority of presidential regimes. Only 18 per cent of the presidents in pure presidential regimes were in systems with no restrictions on re-election; another 18 per cent were in systems where they could be re-elected once. If we exclude those who were already serving their second term—as well as Switzerland, where the presidency is collective—we find that only 28.3 per cent of all presidents could have been re-elected. To think of accountability of presidents, therefore, is problematic since a vast majority of them could not face the electorate due to constitutional term limits.

Terms limits, therefore, need to be taken into account in order to examine the impact of divided government and deadlock on accountability of presidents. Since in the majority of cases presidents will have to leave office regardless of their performance, it will not be surprising if we find that economic performance has no impact on their survival in office.[16]

There are two ways to take care of the problem of term limits in studying accountability under presidentialism. First, we can treat the presidents that are constitutionally barred from re-election as cases of 'censoring', in the sense that we cease to observe them for reasons that are exogenous to the process that we want to investigate—other 'censored' cases are presidents that remained in office after 31 December 1996, and presidents who died of natural causes while in office. In this case the term limit issue is resolved statistically, with no substantive meaning. Second, we can use the survival of presidential parties in office, and not of presidents, to analyze accountability in presidential regimes. Since it is individuals and not political parties that are barred from re-election, voters can, if they wish, keep parties indefinitely in office. The downside of this solution is that presidents are assumed to care about having a member of their own party succeed them in the same way that they care about being re-elected. But whether this assumption is true may depend on the specific type of term limit stipulated by the constitution. When presidents have to wait one term to run again their best strategy could be to be succeeded by a weak member of the opposition.

Table 5.12 presents the coefficients for the impact of divided government, deadlock, and several economic variables—GDP growth,

---

[16] Note, incidentally, that this is a plausible explanation for the difference in performance observed between presidential and parliamentary regimes by Przeworski *et al.* (1996). The relatively poor record of presidential regimes could be due to the fact that presidents, apart from personal idiosyncrasies, have no incentives to perform well.

José Antonio Cheibub

per capita growth, inflation, and growth of private consumption—
on the survival of presidents and presidential parties in office. Due
to data availability, the results are based on different samples, the
size of which is indicated in the table.

TABLE 5.12: *Effect of divided government, deadlock, and economic conditions on the survival of presidents and presidential parties in office[a]*

Presidents	Controlling for:		
Type of sample (N)	Alone	Divided government	Deadlock
Divided government (664)	0.2767439 0.0779	–	–
Deadlock (718)	0.3131824 0.0686	–	–
Inflation (548)	0.0003360 0.7906	0.0000218 0.8609	0.0000406 0.7527
Per capita growth (320)	0.0017170 0.9832	0.0003556 0.9674	0.0000603 0.9929
GDP growth (476)	−0.0130600 0.3721	−0.0150031 0.4865	0.0127234 0.3255
Consumption (418)	−0.0030024 0.7864	−0.00171722 0.8884	0.0018875 0.8801
Presidential parties	Controlling for:		
Type of sample (N)	Alone	Divided government	Deadlock
Divided government (664)	−0.2366619 0.0252	–	–
Deadlock (718)	−0.1902367 0.1883	–	–
Inflation (548)	−0.000469 0.6088	−0.0000239 0.6657	−0.0000546 0.5157
Per capita growth (320)	−0.0011261 0.9295	0.0001295 0.9785	−0.0004897 0.9562
GDP growth (476)	−0.0153365 0.3894	0.00459801 0.7305	0.0083779 0.6128
Consumption (418)	−0.0038281 0.7830	0.00501239 0.6078	0.0032676 0.8204

[a] Dependent variable is the log of age (in years) of presidential administrations and the log of duration (in years) of presidential parties in office. For each variable, the first row is the estimated coefficient of a Weibull survival model, the second is z = coefficient/standard error, and the third is $P[|Z|z]$.

The results regarding the relationship between economic performance and survival are unambiguous: the chances that presidents stay in office are not affected by economic performance, even if we take into consideration the fact that many of them are constitutionally prevented from seeking re-election. This finding is robust: nothing changes if we control for level of economic development as indicated by real per capita GDP, for the presence of the United States, or of Latin American countries, or of some ex-Soviet republics in the sample.[17] It does not change either if, instead of considering current economic conditions, we consider economic conditions in the previous year. Most importantly, controlling for the cases of divided government or those in which deadlock situations exist makes no difference: presidents go on, with their chances of remaining in office unaffected by economic conditions their countries experience. The same is true of the parties of presidents, suggesting either that the lack of accountability with respect to economic outcomes we observe among presidents is not entirely due to the popularity of term limits in these regimes, or that the goals of presidents and their parties do not always coincide.

The real surprise in Table 5.12 is the positive effect of divided government and deadlock on the survival of presidents. This effect, again, is robust to all sorts of controls and alternative estimations, suggesting that they are indeed real. I will leave the examination of the reasons behind this finding for future work. For now what matters is that, again, contrary to much of what is implied in the comparative literature, accountability of presidents and their parties is not affected by their lack of legislative majority or by deadlock situations.

To summarize, we find that the probability that presidents, and their parties, survive in office is hardly affected by current economic performance, even if we control for situations that should, at least in principle, make it harder for voters to punish the incumbent electorally. From the point of view of this work what matters to retain is that presidents who do not control a majority of seats in the legislature or who are facing deadlock situations are not any less likely to survive in office, or any less accountable in the sense defined here, than their colleagues who face a better legislative environment.

---

[17] Switzerland during the whole period and Uruguay from 1952 to 1966 are excluded from this analysis because of their collective executives.

Conclusion

In the comparative literature, divided government and deadlock have been singled out, implicitly or explicitly, as the reasons for the relatively poor performance of presidential regimes when compared with parliamentary regimes. Indeed, we do know that parliamentary democracies tend to last considerably longer than presidential democracies: the probability that a presidential system would die during any particular year between 1950 and 1990 was 0.0477; the probability that a parliamentary system would die was 0.0138. Although apparently small, these probabilities translate into expected lives equal to 73 years for parliamentarism and 21 years for presidentialism. We also know that this difference between parliamentarism and presidentialism is not due to the wealth of countries in which these institutions were observed, to their economic performance, or to the social conditions under which they emerged. Neither is it due to any of the political conditions under which they functioned.[18]

The findings reported in this work reaffirm this last point. If it were the paralysis generated by divided government and deadlock that explained the relatively poor performance of presidentialism when compared with parliamentarism, we should find that the survival of the regime, of the president, or of both, would be threatened when a president faces a congress in which he or she does not control a majority, or when a deadlock between the president and congress may emerge. Yet what we find is that these circumstances generally make no difference to the survival of presidential regimes or of presidents in office. When they do make a difference, it is in the opposite direction. The comparative literature is correct in relating electoral and party variables to the likelihood of divided government: characteristics of the electoral and party systems do affect the level of support for the president in congress and hence the likelihood of divided governments. However, neither divided government nor the factors that make it more likely to occur affect the probability that deadlock situations will occur. And, most importantly, neither divided government nor deadlock affect negatively the longevity of presidential regimes or the survival in office of presidents and their parties.

[18] These figures come from Przeworski *et al.* (2000) Note, however, that Power and Gasiorowski (1997), using a sample of developing countries and measures of performance that are somewhat arbitrary, find that there is no difference between the two regimes.

I would like to conclude by offering two possible explanations for the variation in performance among presidential regimes and, ultimately, for the differences in performance between presidential and parliamentary regimes. These are preliminary hypotheses that contain some normative implications but which still require empirical validation.

The first explanation has to do with the fact that presidents rarely change because they are defeated in elections. Most of them leave office because they are required to do so by constitutionally imposed term limits. Recall that over 70 per cent of the changes of presidents observed between 1946 and 1996 were necessitated by term limits: voters could not re-elect the incumbent even if they had wanted to. In turn, whenever incumbent presidents could run and did, a large proportion of them won re-election. Among 22 presidents who faced re-election without impending term limits between 1950 and 1990, only 14 were not re-elected, and of those only six can be counted as real defeats by incumbents.[19] Hence, given that incumbents won in 8 and lost in 6 elections, their odds of being re-elected were 1.3 to 1. Just for reference, the odds of re-election for prime ministers during the same period was 0.66 to 1 (Cheibub and Przeworski 1999).

It appears, therefore, that presidentialism gives an excessive advantage to the incumbents when they are legally permitted to run for re-election and, in order to prevent the incumbents from exploiting this advantage, it obliges them to leave office whether or not voters want them to stay. What may thus happen is that either incumbent presidents use their advantage to stay in office despite voters' dissatisfaction with their performance, or they are legally forced to leave office despite their high degree of support. In either case, there is a temptation to proceed in an extra-legal way: either some groups of civilians turn to the military to throw the president out of office, or the president, counting on his support in the population, illegally retains office. The latter was clearly the case with Ferdinand Marcos in 1971 and may have been the case with Alberto Fujimori in 1992. Moreover, by removing the possibility of electoral

---

[19] In the Dominican Republic in 1978, when Joaquín Balaguer lost to Antonio Guzmán Fernández; in Nicaragua in 1990, when Daniel Ortega Saavedra lost to Violeta Chamorro; in the US in 1977, when Gerald Ford lost to Jimmy Carter and 1981, when Carter lost to Ronald Reagan; and in the Philippines in 1953, when Elpidio Quirino lost to Ramon Magsaysay, as well as in 1961, when Carlos Garcia lost to Diosdado Macapagal. In all the other cases the incumbent, for various reasons, did not run. These include, for example, Lyndon Johnson in 1969 in the US, Salvador Jorge Blanco in 1986 in the Dominican Republic, Nereu Ramos in Brazil in 1956, Hector Campora in Argentina in 1973.

rewards, term limits may also remove the president's incentive to perform well.

Unfortunately, analysis of this issue is hindered by the very dearth of cases of presidents who are not constitutionally barred from re-election. But what matters here is that term limits are not an inherent feature of presidentialism. It may be true that presidents, if left unencumbered, may use their office for their own electoral advantage. And it is also true that such behaviour, at least its excesses, should be inhibited. Constitutional term limits, however, may be just too blunt an instrument and one that imposes too high a price. There may be other instruments that accomplish similar goals of limiting presidential electoral advantage without generating incentives for extra-legal action or interfering with the operation of accountability mechanisms. Examples include strict regulation of campaign finance and procedures, public funding of campaigns, free access to media, and the strengthening of agencies that oversee campaigns. These are devices that will limit the ability of presidents to use the office for undue electoral advantage and yet will not remove their incentives to perform well with an eye to being re-elected.

The second possible explanation for variation in the performance of presidential regimes may be located in a set of variables that have received very little attention in comparative research. Consider that the main indicator of presidential legislative support used in this work—the share of seats held by the party of the president—is limited in terms of the information it conveys about the president's actual capacity to obtain support in congress. Presidents everywhere do form governing coalitions, parties do merge with one another, and legislators do change parties in the middle of the term. Moreover, presidents do have legislative powers, and legislatures do operate according to rules and procedures, both of which affect these actors' ability to approve their preferred legislation. Thus, the share of seats obtained by the party of the president at elections, a function of electoral and partisan variables, is far from being sufficient for conveying the entire picture regarding the degree of legislative support the president can count on. What this suggests is that, if presidential regimes fail, they do not fail because the president does not control enough seats to impose, so to speak, his or her own policy agenda. As we have seen, whether the president controls or does not control congress makes no difference for the survival of the regime. What may matter is the presence or the absence of some of the factors just mentioned above which allow presidents with very little legislative support to work with congress, or prevent presidents with a majority of seats in congress to have legislation passed. It is to these variables—particularly the ones that regulate the internal workings of congress and the relations between the executive and the legislative—that we should shift our attention in order to understand the performance of presidential regimes. This, however, raises again, but now at a different level, the issue of the trade-off between 'representation' and 'governability', so central in the debate about presidentialism and parliamentarism.

Much of the discussion about presidentialism has implicitly assumed the existence of a trade-off between representation and governability. This is what is behind several defences of parliamentarism and their suggestion that presidential regimes perform better when representation is more restricted: when voters are faced with fewer choices, presidential majorities are more likely to be produced, and the regime will have a better performance (see, for examples, Mainwaring (1997); Stepan and Skach (1993); Lamounier (1994).

This way of reasoning, however, is problematic. As and Limongi and Figueiredo (1995) and Figueiredo and Limongi (2000) and have shown with their study of Brazil, government performance cannot be accounted for by an exclusive focus on electoral and partisan variables: the post-1988 governments in Brazil have performed reasonably well, at least in terms of being able to implement the president's legislative agenda, in spite of the fact that the electoral and partisan legislation are among the most permissive in the world. The explanation they offer also involves limits to representation: the ability of recent Brazilian presidents to approve their legislative agenda and the existence of highly disciplined parties in Congress are the product of mechanisms that essentially make the preferences of individual legislators irrelevant: these are the power the president has to control the legislative agenda and the power congressional party leaders have to control the way information flows to individual legislators. These are institutional features that limit representation and in this sense are non-democratic: they enhance 'governability' at the expense of 'representativeness'.

It seems, therefore, that there are at least two ways in which representation and governability can be traded off. One of them limits representation by limiting the variety of views that can enter the political process: restrictive electoral and party legislation reduces the number of parties and increases the likelihood that governments will obtain substantial legislative support, thus enhancing 'governability'; the other is permissive at the level of the variety of views that can enter the political process, but limits the role that individual representatives have in deliberation and decision-making. In the first model, the one that informs most of the discussions about presidentialism and parliamentarism, the price to be paid is the limitation of the number of interests that find their way into the political system; in the second model, a large number of interests are allowed to enter the political system, but they are less effective in terms of decision-making. Both systems may work and this is probably why we do not find, statistically, that the share of seats held by the party of the president affects the regime's performance. But the question remains as to whether these systems are ultimately equivalent in the effectiveness with which interests are represented in the political process.

Even though presidential regimes seem to be more frail than parliamentary regimes, we do not really know why. The reasons that are usually highlighted in the comparative literature—divided government and deadlock—could not account for the differences we observe since they do not affect presidential regimes in the way suggested by this literature. Most importantly, the separation of powers that defines presidentialism is not invariably associated with conflict, divided governments, and 'deadlock'. If there are reasons why we may want to have a presidential system—and I believe that there may be some—then the issue becomes one of finding the institutional mechanisms that can correct some of its excesses without pre-empting its operation.

Annex

Criteria for regime classification

This chapter uses a subset of a data set that classifies political regimes for 189 countries between 1946 and 1996. Countries were first classified as democracies and dictatorships for each year during this period according to rules spelled out in detail in Przeworski *et al.* (2000). The cases of democracy were further classified as parliamentary, mixed, or presidential. These types of democracy are defined as follows. Systems in which governments must enjoy the confidence of the legislature are 'parliamentary'; systems in which they serve at the authority of the elected president are 'presidential'; systems in which governments respond to both legislative assemblies and elected presidents are 'mixed'.[20]

[20] This criterion coincides almost perfectly with the mode of selection of the government: by legislatures in parliamentary systems, by voters—directly or indirectly—in presidential systems. For a review of the differences, see Lijphart (1992).

In parliamentary systems the legislative assembly can dismiss the government, while under presidential systems it cannot.[21] Some institutional arrangements, however, do not fit either pure type: they are 'premier-presidential', 'semi-presidential', or 'mixed', according to different terminologies. In such systems, the president is elected for a fixed term and has some executive powers but governments serve at the discretion of the parliament. These 'mixed' systems are not homogeneous: most lean closer to parliamentarism in so far as the government is responsible to the legislature; others, notably Portugal between 1976 and 1981, grant the president the power to appoint and/or dismiss governments.

The primary focus of the chapter is on pure presidential regimes. Many analyses are also performed on a sample including the mixed systems in order to assess whether their presence modifies what is found for pure presidential regimes. In spite of significant institutional differences between the two systems regarding term limits and presidential veto, which significantly affect the occurrence of deadlock, the inclusion of mixed systems does not modify any of the findings reported for presidential regimes.

Cases of pure presidentialism

Argentina, 1946–55	Colombia, 1946–96
Argentina, 1958–62	Congo, 1960–2
Argentina, 1963–66	Costa Rica, 1949–96
Argentina, 1973–6	Cyprus, 1960–96
Argentina,1983–96	Djibouti, 1977–82
Armenia, 1992–6	Dominican Republic, 1966–96
Bangladesh,1986–91	Ecuador, 1948–63
Benin, 1991–6	Ecuador, 1979–96
Bolivia,1979–80	El Salvador, 1984–96
Bolivia,1982–96	Gabon, 1960–7
Brazil,1946–64	Ghana, 1979–81
Brazil,1979–96	Guatemala, 1986–96
Cameroon, 1960–3	Guatemala, 1946–54
Chile, 1946–73	Guatemala, 1958–63
Chile, 1990–6	Guatemala, 1966–82

---

[21] The Chilean 1891–1925 democracy does not fit this classification. While it was popularly called 'parliamentary', this is a misnomer. The Chilean lower house frequently censured individual ministers but could not and did not remove the government or the chief executive, the president. In parliamentary systems, except for some early rare cases, the responsibility of the government is collective.

Guyana, 1992–6
Honduras, 1957–63
Honduras, 1971–2
Honduras, 1982–96
Kyrgyzstan, 1991–6
Malawi, 1994–6
Namibia, 1990–6
Nicaragua, 1984–96
Nigeria, 1979–83
Panama, 1949–51
Panama, 1952–68
Panama, 1989–96
Peru, 1946–8
Peru, 1956–62
Peru, 1963–8
Peru, 1980–92
Philippines, 1946–72

Philippines, 1986–96
Russia, 1991–6
Rwanda, 1962–5
Sierra Leone, 1996
South Korea, 1963–72
South Korea, 1988–96
Suriname, 1988–90
Suriname, 1991–6
Switzerland, 1946–96
Uganda, 1980–5
Ukraine, 1991–6
United States, 1946–96
Uruguay, 1947–73
Uruguay, 1985–96
Venezuela, 1946–8
Venezuela, 1959–96
Zambia, 1991–6

Cases of mixed regime

Albania, 1992–6
Central African Republic,
   1993–6
Comoro Islands, 1990–5
Congo, 1992–6
Croatia, 1991–6
Finland, 1946–96
France, 1958–96
Haiti, 1991–2
Haiti, 1993–6
Iceland, 1946–96
Lithuania, 1991–6

Madagascar, 1993–6
Mali, 1992–6
Mongolia, 1992–6
Niger, 1993–5
Pakistan, 1972–7
Poland, 1989–96
Portugal, 1976–96
Romania, 1990–6
São Tomé o Príncipe, 1991–6
Somalia, 1960–9
South Africa, 1994–6
Sri Lanka, 1989–96

Variables used in the analysis

Political variables

AGEP: Number of years the party of the president has been in power.
AGEPR: Number of years the president has been in power.
AGER: Number of years the political regime (as coded by REG) has
   been in place.
BICAMER: Dummy variable coded 1 when the system is bicameral,
   0 otherwise.

COINCIDE: Variable coded 0 when presidential and legislative elections do not coincide; 1 when they alternate (coincide and do not coincide); 2 when they always coincide.

DEADLOCK: Coded 1 when conditions for deadlock between the executive and the legislative exists; 0 otherwise. The coding of this variable takes into consideration the constitutional provisions regarding presidential veto and its override by the legislature, the number of chambers, and the share of seats controlled by the party of the president in each chamber. The coding procedure is discussed in detail in the body of the chapter.

DIVIDED: Coded 1 when the party of the president does not control more than 50% of the seats in the legislature in a unicameral system; or when it does not control more than 50% of the seats in at least one of the chambers in a bicameral system; 0 otherwise.

EFFPARTY: Number of effective political parties, defined as $1/(1-F)$, where F = Party Fractionalization Index.

ENTRYPR: Mode of entry in power (president), coded 0 if non-constitutional entry; 1 if constitutional entry resulting from elections; 2 if constitutional entry not resulting from elections (nomination by parties, interim presidents, etc).

EXITPR: Mode of exit from power (president), coded 0 if president is still in power by December 1996; 1 if by death; 2 if by assassination while in office; 3 if constitutional exit due to elections; 4 if constitutional exit not due to elections; 5 if non-constitutional due to coups; 6 if non-constitutional due to consolidation of incumbent power.

LGSTPS: Share of seats held by the largest party in the lower house.

OVERRIDE: Constitutional provision for legislative override of presidential veto, coded 0 if no override; 1 absolute majority; 2 if 3/5 majority; 3 if 2/3 majority; 4 if 3/4 majority; 5 if decision is by constitutional court or referendum.

PARTYH: Dummy variable coded 1 when there is a change of presidential party, 0 otherwise.

PLOWER: Share of seats held by the party of the president in the lower house.

PRESH: Dummy variable coded 1 when there is a change of president, 0 otherwise.

PROP: Variable coded 0 when legislative elections are held under a plurality system; 1 when they are held under a proportional representation system; 2 when they are mixed, whether because they adopt different formulas when there are multiple tiers or because they use different formulas in different parts of the country.

PTLTYPE: Presidential constitutional term limit, coded 0 if no constitutional restriction; 1 if president has to wait one term for re-election; 2 if president has to wait two terms for re-election; 3 if president can only serve a maximum of two terms; 4 if president can only serve a maximum of three terms; 5 if no re-election is ever allowed.

REGTRANS: Dummy variable coded 1 for the year before a regime transition (to dictatorship) took place, 0 otherwise. Note that it codes the year before the transition occurs. Hence, correlates of regime transition are lagged with respect to the transition.

TERMLIM: Dummy variable coded 1 when the current president is constitutionally prevented from seeking re-election, 0 otherwise.

VETO: Dummy variable coded 1 when the president is constitutionally allowed to partially or totally veto legislation; 0 otherwise.

Economic variables

G87: GDP per capita, PPP, growth (annual %). Growth of GDP per capita based on purchasing power parity (PPP).

GDPNL87G: GDP growth (annual %). Annual percentage growth rate of GDP at market prices based on constant 1987 local currency.

INFCPIG: Inflation, consumer prices (annual % change).

VCONSPCG: Private consumption per capita growth (annual %).

The coding of presidential regimes was based on Przeworski *et al.* (2000) and updated by the author. Information on distribution of legislative seats, constitutions, and electoral systems was taken from Banks (1993, 1997); Nohlen (1993); Morrison, Mitchell, and Paden (1989); Bratton and Van de Walle (1996); Jones (1995*b*; 1997); Kurian (1998); Blaustein and Flanz (1971); Carey, Amorin Neto, and Shugart (1997); and Peaslee (1970). A number of more specific sources were also consulted: Choe (1997); Lande (1989); McGuire (1995); Banlaoi and Carlos (1996); and Carlos and Banlaoi (1996). In addition, the following web sites were consulted: 'Constitution Finder' (http://www.urich.edu/~jpjones/confinder/const.htm); 'Elections Around the World' (http://www.agora.stm.it/elections/elections.htm); 'Parline Database' (http://www.ipu.org/parline-e/parlinesearch/asp).Economic data was extracted from World Bank (1997).

Constitutional Asymmetries: Communal Representation, Federalism, and Cultural Autonomy

Yash Pal Ghai

The New Constitutionalism?

It has been argued that the modern state, with its lineage of the market oriented and homogenising regime, built on the principle of individualism and equal citizenship, is inherently incapable of dealing with ethnic and social diversity that characterizes most countries. Constitutionalism associated with the modern state was concerned at first with limits on power and the rule of law, to which were later added democracy and human rights. It is argued that constitutionalism is not primarily concerned with the relations of groups to the state, or relations between groups.

Noting different communities or groups who are seeking constitutional recognition of their cultural or social specificity—immigrants, women, indigenous peoples, religious or linguistic minorities—James Tully concludes that what they seek is participation in existing institutions of the dominant society, but in ways that recognise and affirm, rather than exclude, assimilate, and denigrate, their culturally diverse ways of thinking, speaking, and acting. He says that what they share is a longing for self-rule: to rule themselves in accordance with their customs and ways (Tully 1995: 4). The modern constitution is based on the assumption of a homogenous culture, but in practice it was designed to exclude or assimilate other cultures and thus deny diversity (Tully 1995: 58).

He argues that a constitutional order, which should seek to provide a framework for the resolution of issues that touch on the concerns of the state and its various communities, cannot be just if it thwarts diverse cultural aspirations for self-government (Tully 1995: 6). Symmetries of power, institutions, and laws which define the modern state are inconsistent with the diversity of forms of self-government that Tully considers necessary for a just order in multi-ethnic states. The necessity of a constitution which is based on mutual recognition of diversity is reinforced by the consideration that there is no escape from multi-ethnic states as the alternative of over 1,500 'nation states' is not feasible. Such a constitution should be 'a form of accommodation' of cultural diversity, of inter-cultural dialogue in which the culturally diverse sovereign citizens of contemporary societies negotiate agreements on their forms of association over time (Tully 1995: 30).

A similar approach is taken by Bikhu Parekh, who argues that the theory of the modern liberal state presupposes a culturally homogenous society and becomes a source of disorder, injustice, and violence when applied to culturally heterogeneous societies. He identifies various institutional and structural features of the modern state that impose uniformity and ignore diversity. The organizing principle is state sovereignty, which justifies the cen-tralization of power and displaces local and group sites of power. This sovereignty operates on a territorial basis, with hard bound-aries. Rules for the exercise of this sovereignty are biased towards majoritarianism, stifling the voices of minorities. Much of his crit-icism is encapsulated in his view of sovereignty as 'a rationalised *system of authority*, is *unitary* and *impersonal* in nature, is the *source* of all legal authority exercised within the state, is not *legally* bound by the traditions, customs and principles of morality, and is not subject to a higher internal or external authority' (Parekh 1997: 183). People relate to the state through the concept of citizenship, based rigidly on equal rights and obligations of all persons, premised on loyalty to the state, and acknowledging no distinctions of culture or tradition. Citizens have rights but these are rights of individuals, based on an abstract and uniform view of the human person. The state operates through the medium of the law, but it is the law created by the state, rather than pre-existing bodies of customs or local law. The state favours the uniformity of structures and seeks to achieve the homogenization of culture and ideology, propagating them as universal values. The domain of the state is the public space, with an ever-shrinking area of private space, which alone allows some expression of cultural diversity.

The specificity of this system, despite its claims of universality, is demonstrated by both Tully and Parekh by contrast with pre-modern polities. These polities cherished cultural diversity. It was no function of the state to impose moral or religious order, much less to impose conformity. The public sphere was narrow and the private extensive, allowing ample space for diverse cultural and religious traditions. Nor did the centre aim towards a tight or detailed regulation of society, but was content with a large measure of decentralization, frequently based on cultural communities. It accepted pre-existing bodies of customs and laws. There were multiple layers of authority and borders were porous, adding to the flexibility of the polity. Similar accounts of the diversity and flexibility of pre-modern or pre-colonial polities have been presented by other authors (for example, Kaviraj 1997; Tambiah 1992).

It is not my purpose to engage directly with this thesis—except to remark that it exaggerates the uniformity in the modern state and the flexibility and diversity in the pre-modern. Pre-modern China's experience, where the centralization of authority and the confucianization of the emperor's subjects were vigorously pursued, seems inconsistent with the picture sketched by Tully and Parekh. Several modern states have different categories of residents, there are differential spatial distributions of power, and religious and cultural affiliations are recognized for many public purposes. Many multi-ethnic states recognise diversity through a variety of devices, including differential citizenship rights as in Israel (Peled 1992), Malaysia, and Fiji. Even 'modern states' like the US, Canada, Australia, and the Nordic countries had less than a uniform system of laws, citizenship, or institutions when they dealt with indigenous communities. If Lijphart (1977) is right about the prevalence of consociationalism in several parts of Europe, then also the monopoly of the centralized modern state is questionable. Several recent instruments and recommendations of the Organisation of Security and Cooperation in Europe and the Council of Europe seek to promote linguistic and religious diversity: decentralization, cultural councils, special voting rolls, language rights, and so forth. The general international law has come to recognize various categories of collectivities, such as minorities and indigenous people, with varying group rights. Even the regime of human rights, castigated for its obsession with the individual, has increasingly recognized group entitlements (Ghai 2000a). There is considerable flexibility in the design of states, such as Bosnia-Herzegovina—perhaps in response to the kinds of criticisms levelled at the modern state by Tully and Parekh.

Nor is recognition of diversity always a virtue. The colonial state was par excellence a state of diversity and discrimination, deeply acknowledged, indeed entrenched, in constitutional and legal systems. The organization of the apartheid regime in South Africa which 'gloried' in racial and cultural diversity used these distinctions to build its edifice of oppression. Jewish control over Israel is maintained through various legal institutions and distinctions which discriminate against Arabs or fragment the political community. More benignly, the essential principle for the organization of the political, social, and economic system of colonial Fiji was race: legislative representation and participation in the executive was allocated racially; indigenous Fijians had their own system of administration and the right to review legislative proposals before they reached the legislature, and there were several institutions to safeguard Fijian customs and laws. The division of labour was also structured along racial lines. Many features of the colonial system survived into the independence period, not always with positive effects on racial harmony. The separation of the political and economic organization of indigenous peoples in the US, Canada, Australia, and much of Latin America had the effect, as was the intention, of marginalizing them.

However, it is not my contention that the political recognition of diversity is always fragmenting or oppressive. Special regimes for communities based on sensitivity to their vulnerabilities, or the recognition of the centrality of cultures to them, or of past injustices, have contributed to justice as well as improvement in inter-ethnic relations. Whether the political recognition of diversity is fair or beneficial depends on the context, the preferences and aspirations of the various communities, and the forms that political recognition takes. Moreover, support for it depends on differing theories of ethnicity. What I do in this chapter, in order to make a preliminary assessment of potential of political recognition to ameliorate or aggravate ethnic tensions, is to examine three principal devices: communal representation, asymmetrical federalism, and cultural autonomy.

Communal Representation

It is only in recent years that consideration has been given to the adaptation of electoral systems to minority representation. Two widely different approaches have been advanced. The first focuses on ensuring representation of a minority by members of the minority, ideally proportional to their size of the population, either through electoral systems which will facilitate this or, if necessary, by a system of separate representation. The second approach is less concerned with direct minority representation than it is with its political integration. There is not always a clear distinction between the two approaches, for some methods which may be used for direct minority representation are compatible with its integration, such as proportional representation. In practice the distinction between systems which do and do not provide for separate minority representation is greater.

It is generally accepted that most traditional electoral systems, which constitute the most numerous of the world's electoral systems, are not conducive to minority representation. Sometimes the plurality—'first–past–the–post'—system can yield minority representation if a minority is concentrated in a constituency. If minorities are politically well integrated with the majority, their members may well be elected in such a system, as with the Jewish community in Britain. Majoritarian systems are even less favourable to minorities, for a candidate needs to secure at least 51 per cent of the votes to win. Proportional representation (PR) systems, which aim at relating the number of representatives to the votes cast for particular candidates or parties, are more favourable to minorities. Sometimes these traditional systems are adjusted to favour minorities: in the southern States of the US, constituencies may be gerrymandered to create a black majority. In many countries constituencies are to be drawn to reflect 'community of interests', which in some instances, as in colonial Mauritius, were taken to ensure adequate representation of two major communities, Hindus and the General Population (de Silva 1998: 77–8). In Nepal, which like the US has plurality voting, parties are required to nominate at least 5 per cent of candidates from among women. In Poland and Spain, which follow the PR system, a minority party does not need to cross any threshold in order to win seats. However, these adaptations have not resulted in significant representation of minorities, prompting consideration of systems for separate and guaranteed representation of minorities—typical forms of electoral asymmetry

The pre-occupation with minority representation in recent years, particularly as part of complex constitutional schemes for the governance of multi-ethnic territories, has led to provisions in many of them for separate representation for ethnic groups, particularly for minorities—called here 'communal representation'—as in Bosnia-Herzegovina, Hungary, Romania, Slovenia, Croatia, and Finland. Communal representation was the corner-stone of British colonial system, but at independence most former colonies abolished this system of separate representation, the outstanding exceptions being Cyprus and Fiji. It is also to be found in China—

where minorities are deliberately over-represented—New Zealand, and Samoa. The revival of communal representation calls for an assessment, which I do by examining a number of experiences.

Cyprus

From the very start of representative politics in Cyprus, Britain introduced communal representation. Such was the bitterness between the dominant Greek community and the minority Turkish community, fuelled no doubt by their 'kin states', that independence could be secured only through an intricate constitution built around far-reaching consociational principles. De Smith (1964: 285) commented that the constitution was 'weighed down by checks and balances, procedural and substantive safeguards, guarantees and prohibitions. Communalism has run riot in harness with constitutionalism'. The Greek—including Maronites—and the Turkish communities were treated as separate entities, and the entire system of representation, government, administration, and social services was based on proportionality, with Greeks counting for 70 per cent and Turks 30 per cent of the population. This entailed a slight overrepresentation of Turks. The House of Representatives consisted of 50 members, of which 35 were Greek and 15 Turks, elected on a communal basis. The president of the House had to be a Greek, the vice-president a Turk. In addition to the full House, there were also communal chambers of Greeks and Turks members respectively, which had wide law-making powers in educational, religious, and personal affairs, and other matters delegated to them by the House. The president of Cyprus had to be a Greek, elected by Greek voters, and the vice-president a Turk who was elected by the Turks, each with his own special powers. Ministerial posts were also divided among the two communities; Greek ministers were appointed—and removed—by the president; the vice-president performed similar functions in relation to Turkish ministers. As is well known, the system produced extreme rigidity; it was resented by the Greeks for giving disproportionate powers to Turks, and Turks resented the permanent dominant position of the Greeks. The Greeks wanted to change the constitution; the Turks boycotted arrangements agreed at independence, over which, it should be stated, the decisive influence has been of metropolitan powers. Cypriot politics were also complicated by political and military interventions by Greece and Turkey, which eventually spelled the end of the republic as described above.

India

The Indian National Congress which led India to independence was opposed to ethnic electoral rolls and representation which the British had introduced in 1909. It would have been willing to contemplate them after independence if Pakistan had not been carved out of the subcontinent as the homeland for Muslims; separate rolls had been devised primarily to secure representation for Muslims. Austin (1972: 144) says that the 'members of the Constituent Assembly had one predominant aim when framing the Legislative provisions of the Constitution: to create a basis for the social and political unity of the country'. He summarizes the situation at independence as follows: '. . . not only did the provinces lack even a semblance of popular government . . . but the small electorate that existed was itself thoroughly fragmented . . . split into no less than thirteen communal and functional compartments for whose representatives seats were reserved in the various parliamentary bodies'. Similar distinctions were applied in the indirectly central legislature. Austin (1972: 144–5) concludes: 'Quite evidently, the members of the Constituent Assembly could not pursue the goals of national unity and stability by perpetuating a system of government that accentuated existing cleavages in Indian society and tended to create new ones.'

The Constituent Assembly did agree to one form of special representation, for scheduled castes and tribes, as part of the package of affirmative policies for these communities. Seats are reserved for each of these communities in proportion to their share of the population in both the lower house at the national level and in the States (Arts 330 and 332 respectively of the Indian Constitution).[1] The scheduled castes constitute about 15 per cent of the population, and the scheduled tribes 7 per cent, so that they enjoy significant guaranteed representation in the lower houses. The law also provides for smaller election deposits for candidates from scheduled castes and tribes.

All registered voters may vote in constituencies in which seats are reserved for scheduled castes or scheduled tribes, so that only members of these groups may be candidates; but there is no similar restrictions on voters. The Delimitation Commission, an independent body, determines in which constituencies seats will be reserved for them. Constituencies are first formed on the basis of the normal criteria of contiguity, communications, absence of natural barriers,

---

[1] The following account draws heavily on Galanter (1984).

and cultural and ethnic homogeneity. The Commission then ear-
marks constituencies for scheduled castes and tribes based on the
concentration of their population. Since tribes still live in particular
areas, these constituencies contain a high proportion of their population, more than 50 per cent in more than half constituencies so
reserved, so that the bulk of scheduled tribes—about 70 per cent—
would live in such constituencies. As scheduled castes are more dispersed than the tribes, constituencies reserved for them have to be
spread through the country, and to be located, as far as possible, in
constituencies in which 'the proportion of their population to the
total is comparatively large'.[2] Thus constituencies with reserved
seats for scheduled castes contain proportionately fewer of them
than is the case with scheduled tribes. The largest contain about 30
per cent.

There is considerable opposition from other communities to the
designation of the constituencies in which they live as reserved constituencies, as it deprives their members of the right to the seat.
Galanter (1984: 48) says that, on the whole, constituencies reserved
for the scheduled castes 'tend to be political backwaters—slightly
less urban, with less newspaper circulation and a slightly greater
percentage of agricultural labourers'. Scheduled tribe constituencies tend to be more isolated and less urban than general constituencies, given their habitat.

The effect of the reservations is to ensure the representation of
these two communities who are otherwise politically and economically marginalized. This is particularly important for the scheduled castes since they are dispersed throughout the country, and
nowhere in a majority. Given that over 20 per cent of seats are held
by the members of these communities, all major parties have an
interest in promoting candidates from them. The candidates have
likewise an incentive to project their appeal beyond their own communities, particularly in the scheduled caste constituencies, where
their own community would be in the minority. This has helped to
integrate them into the constitutional and political system, but this
result has perhaps been achieved at the expense of abandoning particular advocacy of the claims of their own community. The present
system replaced an earlier one in which several constituencies had
two seats, one reserved for the scheduled castes, for which they
alone could vote, in addition to their vote for the other seat. In this
way they controlled the election of one seat in such constituencies,
a possibility which is remote under the current arrangements.

[2] Delimitation Act 1972, sec. 9(1)(c).

Nevertheless, there are parties which are based predominantly on their support, particularly at the State level (Mendelsohn and Vicziany 1994), where their members have achieved high office. Reservations have given the two communities considerable political influence. It has facilitated their entry into the government and their lobbying has been crucial for the maintenance and improvement of other affirmative action policies, which for the most part are authorized but not mandatory; some of these are discussed in the section on economic and social rights below.

Bosnia-Herzegovina

The Federation of Bosnia-Herzegovina is composed of two Entities: Bosnia and Srpska. Most powers are vested in the Entities, the federation being left largely with those powers which are necessary to constitute and exercise external aspects of state sovereignty. The constitution is built around the concept of ethnic communities as separate corporate bodies. Arrangements for representation and power-sharing take the communities as building blocks, carrying forward the proposition stated in the preamble of the Constitution that Bosniacs, Croats, and Serbs are 'constituent peoples' of Bosnia and Herzegovina, 'others' and 'citizens' being mentioned only in passing. Zoran (Pajić 1999: 38) implies, critically, that this makes these three communities, rather than the people as a whole, the source and bearers of sovereignty.

The parliamentary assembly consists of five Croats and five Bosniacs from Bosnia and five Serbs from Srpska; they are elected by voters of their own communities (Art. 4). Nine of them constitute a quorum, so long as there are at least three from each community. The House of Representatives is constituted on the same principle and in similar proportions. The result of these arrangements is that politics are entirely communal, and almost perforce all political parties are ethnically based. Parties get together in parliament or government only after the elections. The system creates incentives for parties and their leaders to intensify appeals to narrow ethnic interests, linked to their kinfolk in other states, which does little for the unity of the country. In the 1996 elections, the most extreme ethnic party in each community won, leaving their leaders the impossible task of finding a common purpose. Recent local government elections show some erosion of support for nationalist as opposed to multi-ethnic parties, but hopes that this trend would also be reflected in the national elections have been disappointed.

Fiji

One of the most difficult questions that the leaders of the different ethnic communities had to resolve at independence in 1970 was the electoral system. Since independence Fiji has experienced three different electoral systems, and is about to design a fourth. The 1970 constitution was based on the separation of races. Its centrepiece was the electoral system dominated by communal seats and communal voting. Although there was provision for national seats, their structure was still based on a racial allocation of seats, while the logic of communal seats prevailed over the logic of national seats which was intended to provide a basis for non-racial politics. There were 52 members, 27 elected on communal franchise: 12 by indigenous Fijians, 2 by Indo-Fijians, and 3 by General Electors, principally Europeans and their part-descendants and Chinese. Twenty-five 'national seats' were allocated communally—10 each to indigenous Fijians and Indo-Fijians and 5 to the General Electors— but as all the voters in the country voted for them the system came to known as 'cross voting'. Every voter had three votes in the contests for national seats, each to be cast for members of different ethnic groups. This formula gave a slight over-representation to indigenous Fijians and to the General Electors, who had traditionally allied themselves with the indigenous Fijians. The rationale of national seats was to politically integrate ethnic groups, promote inter-ethnic parties, and prepare the transition to complete common roll. However, the logic of the system was dictated by the communal rather than the national seats.

Political parties were organized essentially on ethnic lines in order to compete for communal seats. There was one dominant party for each of the communities. While the need to contest national seats compelled each of the major parties to extend its appeal beyond the community it principally represented, for the most part this was not successful: each party was content to field a few candidates from other ethnic groups. National seats were decided principally by communal votes; thus, indigenous Fijian candidates sponsored by the dominantly Indo-Fijian National Federation Party were successful in areas dominated by Indo-Fijians as a result of Indo-Fijian votes, and so on. This was possible because of the concentration of the two major communities in different constituencies. Consequently, national seats won by candidates who relied on the votes of the other sponsoring community had little support in their own community, while those who relied on votes from their own communities had little support in other communities. In this way cross-voting seats became an extension of communal seats.

The Alliance Party—the dominant party of indigenous Fijians—was a partial exception to this trend. It attracted a significant percentage of Indo-Fijian votes, especially for the cross-voting seats, in which it often achieved over 20 per cent of the vote. By contrast, the National Federation Party commonly gained less than 5 per cent of indigenous Fijian votes. However, the Alliance Party had to maintain its support among indigenous Fijians if it was to remain a serious political contender, especially as militant indigenous Fijian parties were bidding for the support of its principal electorate. The logic of the system compelled the Alliance Party to progressively champion exclusively indigenous Fijian interests. The disregard by it of Indo-Fijian interests gradually led to the attrition of its Indo-Fijian support, so that by 1997 it had lost most of it and the parties had settled back to relying on their old ethnic constituencies.

The 1990 constitution, adopted by the military government following the 1987 coups, abolished the national seats. It not only removed any vestiges of cross-voting, completing the separation of ethnic groups—and making politics almost totally racial—but also aimed to ensure the permanent and undisputed rule of indigenous Fijians. It gave a disproportionately large representation to them in both houses of parliament, in the House of Representatives 37 out of 70 seats being reserved for them. In addition it provided that a prime minister had always to be an indigenous Fijian. It also dispensed with the rather awkward, residual agenda of the 1970 constitution that the ultimate aim was the development of a multiracial Fiji. The sidelining in this way of the Indo-Fijians had the predictable effect of releasing factionalism within the Fijian community that had been largely contained under the more balanced allocation of communal seats in the 1970 constitution.

The 1997 constitution, overthrown in May 2000 but reinstated by a decision of the Court of Appeal in March 2001, largely abandoned that approach, but it continued with significant reliance on communal representation. It provided for 25 open seats in the House of Representatives, out of a total of 71, which were open to candidates of any ethnic group and for which all voters resident in the constituency could vote, and 46 communal seats—to be voted communally—divided between the ethnic communities. The voting for these, as for communal seats, was by the alternative vote (AV) system. While in communal seats this method of voting served principally the purpose of ensuring that the winning candidate enjoyed clear majority support, its purpose in open seats was to provide incentives for political parties to cooperate across racial frontiers. Under the AV system, a voter has to declare his or her preference among all the candidates. Since a winning candidate has to have an absolute majority, the second and subsequent preferences of a voter can be crucial in determining the result, for if no candidate obtains an absolute majority after the count of first preferences, the second—or subsequent—preferences of those who voted for candidates who come bottom of the poll on first count have to be taken into account. This method thus opens up possibilities of arrangements between political parties for the trade-off of the second and subsequent preferences of their supporters. The trade-off can of course take place between parties of the same ethnic group, but, since it may be assumed that they would in fact be in competition in constituencies where the members of that ethnic group predominate, the trade between political parties of different racial groups makes better political sense. The logic of the system might well have led to multiracial parties, as was the expectation of the Reeves Commission which recommended it. Additionally, it was expected that candidates with moderate views would have an advantage over those espousing extreme views, as they would have a chance of capturing more second preferences (FCRC 1996: 9.150–2 and 10.31–109; see also Horowitz 1997*b* who advised the Commission on the electoral system). The result would be either a coalition government or, better still, government by a party with multiracial membership.

The results of the first general election seemed to have vindicated some of the assumptions of the Reeves Commission. Two broad coalitions of communal parties were formed and contested the elections. However, it was not only moderate parties with conciliatory policies that tended to trade preferences, as the Reeves Commission had envisaged. In fact, the more ethnically conciliatory coalition lost the election. In particular it seems that a basic assumption of the new system was not borne out by the results. The assumption is that, if a party is extremist, it may get a significant proportion of first preferences, but that that the more moderate parties would get the second and subsequent preferences. Doubts about this assumption in a multi-ethnic state were expressed before the adoption of the system (Ghai 1997). As an acute observer of the results has commented:

> Where racial polarization is particularly sharp, it is easy to envisage a situation where a majority of ethnic group's first preferences are picked by the militant flank party, which also attracts, at the second, third or

subsequent count, the preference votes from eliminated more moderate parties representing the same ethnic group. Here the AV system could serve, not as a vehicle for inter-ethnic compromise, but as a means of cohering a politically fragmented ethnic group around an extremist position. (Fraenkel 2001:15)

Few first preferences in open seats were cast across ethnic divides, but some transfer did take place through second and subsequent preferences—although it is widely believed that this resulted from voters' ignorance of the voting procedures. A major party with predominant Indo-Fijian support failed to secure a single seat, although its share of the communal vote was over 32 per cent. It does not seem therefore that the electoral system led to cross-ethnic voting on any scale, nor to any proportionality, but the logic of open seats on the AV system did lead to multi-ethnic coalitions (Prasad 2000). Unfortunately, it is not possible to make a reliable assessment of this interesting system, for it was tried only once, when knowledge of its operations and of electoral strategies to exploit the system was limited. But the experience may reflect limits of electoral designs and the ability of voters, particularly in rural areas, to handle elaborate voting systems.

Assessment

Where both the majority and minorities are agreed that minorities should be represented separately, there may be no objection to communal electorates. There may indeed be cases of minorities which are so small, or where politics are so communalized, that the only realistic prospect of representation is through a communal roll. But the case studies examined here raise doubts whether separate representation in general is desirable. A particularly acute observer of constitutional politics, Stanley de Smith, concluded that communal representation 'tends to magnify existing communal differences, in as much as communities are stirred to fuller self-consciousness and electoral campaigns are dominated by appeals to communal prejudices; and new communities discover themselves as further claims to separate representation are lodged' (de Smith 1964: 118). It is exceedingly hard to establish national parties, necessary for political integration, when voting is communal. Religious, particularly Hindu-Muslim, conflict in British India is often attributed to the introduction of separate representation for Muslims in 1906.

Communal forms of representation often irritate and provoke majority groups, although this is not in itself a reason for not adopting them. Members of minorities have fewer prospects of high office if they rely on their own separate parties and representation than if they were members of national parties—unless there are provisions for power sharing. Communal representation also tends to obscure social and economic interests that sections of different communities have in common. Moreover, leaders and parties of the majority party have little incentive to woo electors of minorities or to design policies to suit them. Within the community itself, the interests of the wealthy elite tend to dominate. Commenting on the consequences of communal representation in Lebanon, which applied it for 40 years from the early 1940s, Rabinovich (1985: 26) claims that Parliament reflected the 'web of relationships among the traditional foci of power . . . in upholding the principles of confessionalism and playing down the notions of nation and class, the Lebanese political system acquired an archaic complexion, and from the mid-1960s, it found itself challenged by the political attitudes prevailing in most of the outside world'. On the other hand, the Indian post-independence experience shows that arrangements for the representation of scheduled castes has integrated them politically with other Indians while giving them special influence on national policies. Therefore, when it is desirable or necessary to give special representation to an ethnic group, preference should be given to integrating it within the general electoral system, such as mandatory nomination of a minimum number of minority candidates.

The largely negative record of communal representation strengthens the case for electoral systems designed to integrate different communities, creating incentives for political parties to broaden their appeal in order to attract votes from all communities, so that representatives have a broad base of support. The aim, therefore, is not so much to ensure direct minority representation but to ensure that those who are elected are likely to enjoy the support of minorities and thus be moderate in their policies. The rules for the election of the Nigerian president under the 1982 constitution were based on this approach, which has recently been used in Kenyan presidential elections. The AV system in Fiji's 1997 constitution was adopted for the same reason, whose success might have been greater if communal representation had been eliminated or reduced. Singapore provides an example of a system which both secures minority representation and integrates communities. A number of constituencies, called the Group Representative Constituencies (GRC), return either three or four members. A political party which wants to contest in these constituencies has to present a slate of three or four candidates, of which at least one must be from a minority. Electors vote for the slate rather than individual candidates. This system is justified on the basis that it secures the election of some minority candidates, although its opponents criticized it as an attempt by the government to stifle opposition parties who would have difficulty in securing enough qualified candidates given the constraints under which opposition parties operate. It is certainly the case that so far all GRC seats have been won by the ruling party (Thio Li-am 1997: 107–8). In order to encourage the political integration of Maori, in 1993 New Zealand altered its system of representation for them by giving them the option to vote on a separate electorate or common roll—the more Maoris opted for the common roll, separate representation would be correspondingly reduced. A substantial number of Maori opted for the common roll, and the community secured higher representation than in the past.

Territorial Autonomy

Territorial autonomy is a device to allow ethnic or other groups claiming a distinct identity to exercise direct control over affairs of special concern to them while allowing the larger entity to exercise those powers which cover common interests. Autonomy has become the most sought-after and resisted device for conflict management. However, autonomy is controversial, and many conflicts themselves are about the demand of autonomy and resistance to them. At other times autonomy seems to offer a way out of conflict or the transformation of the conflict. The promise to consider or negotiate autonomy has been used successfully to bring truce among warring parties. Autonomy has sometimes secured a breathing space as an interim or even ambiguous expedient while longer-term solutions are explored and negotiated. Autonomy has been used to separate as well as to bring people together. In recent years it has been seen as a panacea for cultural diversity, and as, under the influence of identity politics, the realization of the extreme heterogeneity of states dawns on us, autonomy seems to provide the path to maintaining unity of a kind while conceding claims of self-government.

Autonomy has several features which distinguish it from the model of the modern state described by Tully and Parekh. It is multi-layered, state sovereignty is divided, there are many sites of power and authority—qualifying majoritarianism—there is explicit or implicit recognition of cultural or ethnic diversity, and there are various asymmetrical features, even in classical federations. However, not all federations are hospitable to this degree of diversity; there has been considerable resistance to multi-ethnic federations and asymmetry. Federations in liberal societies, it has been argued, are meant to reflect principles of equality—symmetry—and common values (Glazer 1977). Moreover, the diverse arrangements for territorial autonomy have begun to distinguish one state from another, so that the model criticized by Tully and Parekh is becoming less 'universal'. Federal systems where one or more regions are vested with special powers not granted to other provinces are known as 'asymmetrical' (Stevens 1977; Watts 1994; Agranoff 1994; Boase 1994; Brown-John 1994).

The best known form of autonomy is federalism, where all regions enjoy equal powers and have an identical relationship to the central government. Traditionally, federalism has not been used as a way to solve problems of ethnic diversity, except for Switzerland and Canada. Classical federalism, where all regions have equal powers, may not be sufficiently sensitive to the peculiar cultural and other needs of a particular community, and it is not surprising that Swiss and Canadian federations have various asymmetrical features, as have more recent multi-ethnic federations, such as India, Spain, Russia, and Malaysia. The federal model may be unnecessary if the need is to accommodate only one or two minority groups. In these situations, special powers may be devolved only to a part of the country where the minority constitutes a majority; these powers are exercised by regional institutions. Normally very significant powers are devolved and the region, unlike in a federation, plays relatively little role in national government and institutions. This kind of autonomy is some times referred to as regional autonomy (Heintze 1998: 10–11) or federacy (Stevens 1977; Elazar 1987: 7). Examples of autonomous regions include Åland Islands (Finland), South Tyrol (Italy), Kosovo (the former Yugoslavia), the Cordilleras and Mindanao (the Philippines), Puerto Rico (US), Zanzibar (Tanzania), Hong Kong and Macao (China), Greenland and Faroes (Denmark), New Caledonia (France), and Scotland (UK). By its nature, this kind of regional autonomy is asymmetrical

A special instance of spatial organization of government is 'reserves', which were first used by European settlers in the Americas to isolate and dominate indigenous peoples, and were subsequently adopted in Australia, Africa, and parts of Asia. The apartheid policy of Bantustans was a modern version. However, in recent years the aspirations and historical claims of indigenous peoples have been recognized through the transformation of reserves into self-governing areas, particularly in Canada and the Philippines, although the extent to which they can opt out of national laws, which may be necessary for the preservation of their political and cultural practices, is variable.

A new but uneven element in the spatial organization of government is the emergence of international regional organizations in which national sovereignty has been traded for a share in participation and decision-making in these organizations. Common policies over larger and larger matters are determined by the regional organization, so that a measure of control of the affairs of a national region has been transferred from national to supranational authority. The consequences are that the diminution of the salience of national sovereignty opens up possibilities of new arrangements between the state and its regions, the state feeling less threatened by regions in a multi-layered structure of policy-making and administration and the region being more willing to accept the national sovereignty which may be the key to its participation in the wider arrangements. This trend is most developed in the European Union, with its developing concept of the Europe of Regions (Bullain 1998), which is helping to moderate tensions between states and border regions previously intent on secession, as in Spain and Belgium and which has facilitated the interesting spatial arrangements for policy, administration, and consultation in the two parts of Ireland, each under separate sovereignty, which underlie the new peace settlement. Attempts to provide for unified Nordic arrangements for the Saami people, including a substantial element of autonomy, regardless of the sovereignty they live under, are another instance of similar kind (Hannum 1990: 256–62).

The Distinctiveness of Ethnically Based Autonomies

Ethnically based federations or regional autonomies have different structures and orientations from federations like Australia or the United States. Naturally, ethnic federations emphasize diversity and multiplicity of values. Such federations are more likely to be the result of devolution or disaggregation, as in Canada, India, Spain, Papua New Guinea, and Ethiopia. Because they start with a centralized structure and because there is unease about the political implications of devolution, national powers tend to be dominant, including, not infrequently, the power to suspend regional governments. It is worth noting that Indian federation emerged at a time when state building through central management and homogenization was the dominant paradigm; concessions to ethnicity were reluctant and grudging. Because, ideally, a region is supposed to provide ethnic or cultural homogeneity, the size of regions is likely to be uneven and agreement on boundaries hard. There is also likely to be more emphasis on self-rule than shared rule, particularly with regional autonomy. But, at the same time, there is likely to be greater regional representation at the federal level. Watts (2000: 45) says that 'in both Canada and Switzerland the "representational syndrome" whereby different linguistic, religious and geographical groups are carefully represented within each of the federal policy making bodies, including the federal executive, is very marked'. Klug's (2000) account of South Africa establishes the same point, indeed, even more so since the principal form of 'autonomy' is not the exercise by regions of power in the regions but participation at the centre. In Ethiopia, a crucial role is ascribed to the House of Federation, composed of regional representatives, where relations between regions and the federation and between the regions themselves are mediated and resolved.

The division of powers is likely to be more focused on cultural matters, like education, religion and arts; and the normal tensions of federalism, like fiscal redistribution or regional influence, take on an ethnic dimension and become aggravated. Distinctions between the private and public spheres may be less sharp than in other types of federations. Inter-regional mobility is likely to be contentious. The party structure may be different as there may be no great connection between national parties and regional parties. National parties often lack viable affiliates in particular localities; relations between centre and region depend significantly on this 'asymmetry'. As G. Smith (1995: 9) notes, 'such enduring asymmetry can be symptomatic of inter-communal tensions and lead to pressures not only for greater autonomy but also for secession from federation'.

But, most of all, the major factor which distinguishes ethnic autonomy from classical federations is its asymmetrical features. Just as in liberal theory all individuals must be equally treated, so must regions in a federation. This approach is not very constructive when autonomy is used to acknowledge and manage ethnic differences. Asymmetry acknowledges the unevenness of diversities and opens up additional possibilities of awarding recognition to specific groups with special needs or capacities, such as indigenous peoples whose traditional culture is central to their way of life, or a minority linguistic group. Examples of asymmetry abound; China has at least four types of autonomy—economic zones, metropolitan cities, ethnic minorities, and special administrative regions—responding to different imperatives (Ghai 2000*d*). So has India, with its 'standard provinces', special arrangements for Kashmir, and provinces in the north-east, tribal areas, and union territories, each enjoying a distinct relationship with the centre.

Asymmetry arises in various ways. Regional autonomy is by definition asymmetrical. Sometimes it is the result of a constitutional provision enabling regions to negotiate separately with the centre for autonomy and establishing a menu of which powers may be devolved—Spain, Papua New Guinea, Russia. Regions may make different use of concurrent powers. Regions may be endowed with the power to determine their own structures for the exercise of autonomy, leading to differences in constitutional arrangements. National laws may apply differentially for other reasons, the outstanding example being the 'notwithstanding' clause in Canada which enables a province to opt out of most provisions of the Charter of Rights under prescribed conditions, and another provision which limits the application of the charter in aboriginal areas by virtue of the supremacy of treaties between indigenous groups and the Crown. Asymmetry can also be used as a general technique for opting out of a scheme, or for a phased entry to full membership, as has happened frequently with the European Union. Other forms of asymmetry include special representation for a region at the centre—Quebec's entitlements to seats in the Senate and the Supreme Court—or special voting power given to the region at the centre, such as double voting or vetoes. Residents of a region may have special rights, at least in the region, that are not available to other citizens, as in the concept of permanent resident of the Hong Kong Special Administrative Region. The questions of the feasibility of negotiating and sustaining asymmetry are therefore fundamental to the design and operation of ethnic autonomy. The validity of the Russian federation depends on the acceptance and successful operation of autonomy: 88 units have differing relationships with Moscow.

These developments regarding federalism and autonomy have helped political leaders to devise arrangements for forms of self-government to suit varying circumstances and contingencies. In addition there are variations in detailed arrangements within each category, such as in the division of powers between different layers of government, structures of government, the relationship between these structures at different levels, and the distribution of financial and other resources. While this flexibility is important in the negotiation process and facilitates compromises, there is the danger that it may lead to complex arrangements and systems, producing a lack of cohesion and problems of governability. When negotiations enter a difficult phase, there is the temptation to device some fancy scheme which may produce a temporary consensus which is hard to operationalize: thus there is a conflict between immediate and long-term interests. Federal or autonomy arrangements are inherently hard to operate, requiring both great administrative capacity and political skills, and the embroidery on classical systems that tough negotiations may lead to would undermine long-term prospects of settlement by their sheer weight or complexity. A good example of this experience is the regional arrangements in Kenya's independence constitution (Ghai and McAuslan 1970), Papua New Guinea's system of provincial government established in 1976 (Ghai and Regan 1993), and even Spain's autonomous communities (Conversi 2000). Lack of resources is likely to negate large parts of Ethiopia's complex and complicated constitution of 1994, as Paul (2000) argues.

Perhaps it is not surprising that asymmetry has also become controversial; concerns about it have, for example, prevented a satisfactory resolution of Canada's constitutional problems. It is in Canada that the issue has been most extensively debated, in political as well as academic circles. Canadian scholars have argued that differences over asymmetry may be the undoing of ethnic or multinational federations; Milne (1994: 159) notes an 'overwhelming' hostility towards proposals for asymmetry in Canada (see also Kymlicka 1998*a*, *b*). There is resentment in India at the privileged position of Kashmir (Kashyap 1990), although it has not emerged as a major political issue, perhaps because of Indo-Pakistani conflict over Kashmir. It is said that President Habibie offered independence to East Timor because he was afraid that the UN proposals of autonomy would set a precedent for other provinces of Indonesia, and that it would be politically difficult to restrict the high degree of substantive and institutional autonomy to East Timor.

One objection to asymmetry is that it is administratively and politically difficult to manage. The centre has to deal with regions with varying degrees of devolution and different institutional structures. This can pose problems in states as well developed as Spain; it can be a nightmare in states with less efficient bureaucracies or with politicians not given to compromise, as in Papua New Guinea and Ethiopia. A consultancy firm which advised Papua New Guinea on the implementation of decentralization, expected to be asymmetrical under negotiated constitutional provisions, recommended the equal devolution of powers to all provinces, regardless of their capacity or willingness to assume these powers. If this proposal avoided one bureaucratic nightmare, it created another:

poorly equipped provinces struggling to carry out new responsibilities which they neither understood nor wanted. The result was continuing domination by central bureaucrats and a not inconsiderable degree of inefficiency (Ghai and Regan 1992).

But the political problems with asymmetry are even more decisive. I have already referred to the difficulty of conceding autonomy on a purely ethnic basis. The difficulty is greater if only one or two groups are to enjoy autonomy. If the national government is inclined to support autonomy, it may have to generalize the conditions for granting it. In Papua New Guinea in 1976, negotiations for autonomy were conducted between the national government and the representatives of Bougainville. The assumption was that the arrangements under negotiation were for Bougainville only; and, in fact, Bougainville leaders insisted that only their province was to be entitled to them, to recognize their distinctiveness. However, the government realized that parliamentary support for these arrangements could not be guaranteed unless all provinces were given similar options. Similar developments took place in Spain, where all provinces or groupings of provinces were given roughly the same options as the 'historic territories'. Increasingly, Spain takes on the appearance of a federation, and a symmetrical federation at that. The devolution to provincial councils in Sri Lanka followed a similar trajectory, diluting the special claims of Tamils to autonomy. In Britain, following autonomies for Scotland and Wales, there is agitation for English regions. The tendency towards symmetry is, however, not universal. Sometimes there may be recognition of the historical claims of a community or the clear distinctiveness, and vulnerability, of a culture—as of Greenland, Faroes, Åland, Corsica, and the Cordilleras. A community may desire a greater measure of national integration than asymmetry would permit: the Swedish-speaking community on the Finnish mainland rejected the offer of an Åland-type of autonomy.

Asymmetry is particularly controversial when the region benefiting from it wants equal or even superior representation in central institutions. Logically, the region should not participate in decisions at the national level on areas which are within its autonomy, for then it would be making decisions for other regions, especially when the votes of its representatives hold the balance. When there is substantial asymmetrical autonomy, the moral or political right of the representatives of that region to count towards a parliamentary majority, thus determining the formation of the central government group, can be questioned. Claims might be made by the rest of the country that representatives from that region should be excluded from holding ministries whose portfolios cover areas within asymmetrical autonomy or, indeed, that the number of ministries given to them should be severely restricted. If there is equal representation for the autonomous region, other provinces will resent it; if the representation is less favourable, the region will tend to look inwards, political parties will tend to become regional, and the region's integration with the state will weaken.

The conversion of asymmetry into symmetry would not necessarily be against the interests of the original claimants of autonomy. They would cease to be the object of envy and resentment. A greater number of beneficiaries would produce a more balanced state. It would also increase the capacity of regions to negotiate with the centre and extract higher benefits. But, for many groups, the exact amount of devolved power is less important than that they alone should enjoy some special powers as a way to mark their status. If the powers they have are generalized, they increase their own demands for more, not only leading to a higher level of general devolution than is desirable or desired but also pushing the special groups towards confederal solutions. They regard asymmetry as a proper recognition of their 'distinct society' status. This conflict, rather than bureaucratic problems of managing diversity, is the real problem besetting asymmetry. Kymlikca (1998*a*, *b*) points to a number of provisions about asymmetry that make it unsustainable. If a group insists on asymmetry and others do not concede it, the stalemate may result in attempts at secession. On the other hand, the concession of asymmetry merely encourages the demand for further powers and emboldens the group, having already won and operating with a large measure of autonomy, to go to the logical next step: separate statehood.

The future feasibility and viability of multi-ethnic autonomy thus depends greatly on how asymmetry is negotiated. While the utility of asymmetry may be acknowledged, political and bureaucratic difficulties may limit its application. On the other hand, it must be noted that, outside Canada, the difficulties are more theoretical than practical. The Indian experience and that of other federations show that groups claiming or enjoying autonomy do not see themselves as nations alienated from others. They are strongly bonded to the wider nation and their representatives through regional or national parties, and play a full part in national institutions. But equally one must not underestimate the ability of politicians to erect these theoretical difficulties into real barriers to asymmetrical autonomy.

Cultural Autonomy

A major limitation of territorial devolution of power, its restriction to circumstances where there is a regional concentration of an ethnic group, can be overcome by 'corporate or cultural autonomy' whereby an ethnic group, dispersed geographically, is given forms of collective rights. There are different forms and uses of corporate autonomy. Rights or entitlements protected under such autonomy can be personal, cultural, or political. They can be entrenched or subject to the overriding authority of the government. They normally consist of positive and substantive rights and entitlements, but they can be negative, such as a veto. They form the basis of the communal organization of politics and policies and of the collective protection of their rights. The Cyprus constitution of 1970 was an example of expansive corporate autonomy, while the current constitution of Bosnia-Herzegovina combines more traditional federalism with corporate shares in power and communal vetoes.

Cultural autonomy was a significant feature of old and modern empires. Modern examples include provisions in the constitutions or laws of Estonia, Hungary, Slovenia, and the Russian federation, which countries provide for the establishment of councils for national minorities that assume responsibility for the education and cultural affairs of the minorities (Eide 1998: 256–9). In principle, a council can be set up if a majority of the community desire it, as expressed in votes. Once established, its decisions bind members of the community throughout the state, except that a member can opt in or out of membership—the important principle of self-identification is maintained. Within the areas in relation to which powers are vested in it, the council's regulations prevail over those of the state. The council has the power to levy a tax on its members and also receives subsidies from the state. It has authority over the language, education, and culture of the minority. The principal objective of the system is the maintenance or strengthening of the identity of the minority, based on language and culture. The objective is to take culture out of 'politics', and leave other matters to the national political process, in which minorities may or may not have a special status through representation. It is too early to evaluate their experience as the few councils established so far, often under external pressure, have existed for only a short period. However, it would seem that the distinction between culture and politics may be too simplistic, especially today when the survival of culture is closely connected to the availability of resources and to national policy in several areas.

More central reliance on group autonomy through cultural councils is found in the developing constitutional dispensation of Belgium. In 1970 separate councils were established for Dutch, French, and German language speakers with competence over aspects of cultural and educational matters; their competence was considerably extended in the 1980s (Peeters 1994; Murphy 1995). In some new constitutions group autonomy is related to, or is part of a package of, federal or other devices for protection of ethnic communities, frequently in consociational arrangements, such as in Belgium, Bosnia-Herzogovina, and Fiji.

Cultural autonomy can take the form of the application to the members of a community of its personal or religious laws, covering marriage and family, and occasionally land, particularly for tribal communities (see Ghai 1998: 52–9); for an historical account of its use in Europe, see Eide 1998). The application of personal laws, and thus the preservation of customary law or practices, is considered important for maintaining the identity of the community. When India tried, during the drafting of its constitution, to mandate a common civil code for all of the country, some Muslim leaders objected. The supporters of a common code argued that common laws were essential for national unity. The opponents argued that it amounted to the oppression of minorities and the loss of their communal identity. The result was that the constitution merely set a common code as an objective of state policy, and it is now a well-established convention that the *shariah* will continue to apply to Muslims so long as they desire it.

The scope of the application of personal laws, quite extensive during the colonial period in Africa and Asia, is now diminishing under the pressure of modernization, although it is being reinforced in some countries committed to a more fundamentalist view of their religion. However, one place where regimes of personal laws still apply with full vigour is Israel, where each of the major religions has its own laws on personal matters (Edelman 1994, on which the following account is principally based). Israel has civil courts, military courts, and courts of 14 recognised religious communities. The principal and exclusive jurisdiction of religious courts is over matters relating to marriage and divorce, there being no civil marriage or divorce in Israel. These courts also resolve other personal and private-law issues. Since legislative authority over these matters is rarely exercised, courts have a profound effect on shaping the country's political culture, involving rights of women, contacts between members of different communities, and more generally the lives of Israelis. For the Jews, most matters of personal law fall exclusively within the rabbinical courts, while Muslims are subject to the jurisdiction of *shariah* courts applying the *shariah*. Although linked to and supported by the state, these courts are administered independently of the state. For the Muslims the presence of *shariah* courts has reinforced their sense of community and the values they want to live by, and helped in the social reproduction of the community—an important factor for a minority, many of whom live under foreign occupation. These conclusions corroborate an argument for cultural autonomy, namely, that it 'supports political stability by providing non-dominant (and unassimilable) groups with mechanisms that enable them to minimise the effects of their inferior position in the larger society' (Jacobsohn 1993: 30).

But the separate regime of Muslim law has isolated Arabs from the mainstream of Israeli politics. For the Jews, the rabbinical courts have been deeply divisive, symbolizing the fundamental schism between orthodox and secular Jews. In both instances the courts give the clergy, committed to the preservation of orthodoxy, a specially privileged position. The law is slow to change in these circumstances, and can lag well behind social attitudes and social realities. In contrast to civil courts, which have sought to promote a democratic political culture based upon the rule of law, religious courts and personal regimes of laws have sharpened distinctions among Israel's communities, and retarded social relations among them and the development of a unifying political culture. Edelman (1994: 119) concludes that religious courts have emphasized group identity and solidarity at the expense of a unifying political culture: 'Yet without a shared political culture and the concomitant sense of a shared national identity, the prospects for a sustained, peaceful national existence are not bright'. This view is not endorsed by Jacobsohn (1993: 37), who says that studies of Jewish public opinion in Israel reveal that shared ethnicity and a shared set of religious symbols are much more important than a shared set of values in providing unity for Israeli society. 'Thus, the subordination of cultural aspects to individual liberties on the basis of the assertion that the latter are "principles" has less justification in a polity where cultural imperatives may legitimately demand principled consideration.'

One of the major problems with cultural/religious/legal autonomy of this kind is that it puts certain sections of the relevant community at a disadvantage. Edelman (1994) shows how both Jewish and Muslim women come off worse in their respective autonomous courts. In India, Muslim women are unable to benefit from the more liberal legal regime that has applied to other Indian women after the reforms of the 1960s. One aspect of their disadvantage was illustrated in 1985 by the famous *Shah Banu* case,[3] where the Supreme Court held that the maintenance that a Muslim divorced woman could claim from her former husband was to be determined under the general national law, which provided a higher amount than she would get under the *shariah*. This decision provoked a violent reaction from a section of the Muslim community, which considered that its identity was thrown in jeopardy. The government gave way to pressure from the Muslim clergy and other sections of the Muslim community and legislatively overruled the decision. The rise of Hindu nationalism is often ascribed to this 'capitulation' by the government to Muslim minority demands. In Canada the application of the customary law of Indian bands has also disadvantaged women; the UN Human Rights Committee has held invalid the law which deprived an Indian woman of her land and other community rights if she married an outsider, men who marry outside the community not incurring a similar liability.[4] In South Africa, demands by traditional leaders for the continuation of customary laws were resisted by African women because of the discriminations against them, such as in relation to custody and inheritance. The South African solution was to provide for the application of customary law but subject to the Bill of Rights. The Canadian government is negotiating a similar solution for the band laws.

Finally, I examine the system of cultural and administrative autonomy that the British established for indigenous Fijians in the late nineteenth century and which was subsequently entrenched in the independence and later constitutions. British policy was directed at the preservation of indigenous Fijians' social and economic structure, in view of the destruction of indigenous communities in the South Pacific. It was to be done principally through the preservation of communal responsibility, ownership, and hierarchy. At the same time Britain aimed to exploit the resources of the country, leading to the development of market and modern economic relations. It met the need for labour by recruiting indentured labour from India, and the need for land by very limited alienation of land, leaving most of it under customary ownership. It was therefore necessary both to preserve the Fijian traditional system and to insulate it from external influences. For this purpose a separate system of

[3] (1985) 2 Sup. Ct. Cases 556.
[4] *Sandra Lovelace v. Canada* (Report of the Human Rights Committee. GAOR. Thirty-sixth session, Supplement No. 40 (A/36/50), 166–75.

native Fijian administration was established. It consisted of a Council of Chiefs, which was largely advisory to the governor, and a Fijian Affairs Board, consisting of senior bureaucrats and, later, indigenous members of the legislature, which had the power to review legislative bills, particularly for their impact on Fijians, before their introduction in the legislature, and to make regulations for the social and economic life of Fijians. The Council of Chiefs also used to nominate Fijian members of the legislature while representatives of other groups were elected. There were provincial and district councils with jurisdiction over only indigenous Fijians, in which a key role was created for chiefs. Fijian courts were set up to administer customary law and regulations of the Board and the Council. Later legislation provided for a special administrative body to deal with customary land, particularly leases to outsiders.

The Fijian administration could also be seen as a system of indirect rule. This is manifested in the key role played by colonial officials in it and the ways in which chiefs were bolstered and land system administered, sometimes contrary to customary ways. Furthermore, the system of Fijian administration was regulated and supervised by the Ministry of Fijian Affairs—as is still the case. There is not much doubt that these policies had the effect of protecting indigenous Fijians from exploitation and the destruction of their cultures and institutions, even though aspects of these were reconstructed by the colonial authorities.

But after independence the Fijian administration was used less for indirect rule than for maintaining the authority of the chiefs and the cohesion of the community. The Council of Chiefs acquired greater political authority, although its legal powers remained unaltered, and the provincial administration became a device to develop Fijian consensus, particularly on matters regarding relations with the Indo-Fijians. It became increasingly a system which, from a communal base, affected and shaped the policies of the state, representing a reversal of the original purpose: it came to dominate the state rather than being an adjunct to it. But because it is a communal system, it is discriminatory and exclusionary. The Council of Chiefs has been mobilized by Fijian politicians wanting indigenous political hegemony; it attempted to legitimize all the *coups d'état* through its support. At the same time Fijian administration has prevented the full integration of indigenous people in the modern economy—it is the absence of a fair role for them in the economy which has been a cause of resentment and sometimes the justification for the *coups*. Moreover, the separate system has retarded fair and amicable inter-ethnic relations and a more integrated political system. Its original rationale no longer applies, particularly as market relations increasingly dominate life in Fiji and large numbers of indigenous Fijians have moved to urban areas. The ability of Fijian administration to bring cohesion to the indigenous Fijians has been seriously eroded, as many of the values it sought to promote have little resonance with the ordinary Fijians, who see it principally as a means to bolster chiefly privileges.

Conclusion

The cases studied here show that no simple judgement on the utility or justice of the political recognition of ethnic diversity is possible. Separate legislative representation has sometimes been worthwhile, as the Indian example shows; but mostly it has been harmful. Asymmetrical federalism has great capacity to respond to the varying circumstances and needs of ethnic groups. But it is hard to negotiate and sometimes hard to operate. Cultural autonomy can give a beleaguered community a sense of identity and moral cohesion, and assist in preserving its traditions. But as with other asymmetrical devices, it can cause injustice to both the members of the autonomous community and those outside it. All three can produce resentment and conflict.

Each of these devices has supporters and opponents. Even if it were agreed that one of them was the preferred approach, it may be hard to generalize about the usefulness of particular modalities. The choice between these options may depend, in many situations, less on their inherent merits than on circumstances and constraints. The objective circumstances as well as the aspirations of minorities vary from place to place and from time to time. For example, the size of the minority is a material factor: a substantial and economically well-off minority might not require special rules for legislative representation, but a small minority might. Moreover, in the former case special rules might be resented or mistrusted by the majority, but not necessarily in the latter case.

The choice of approach and modalities would depend on the ultimate goals that the state and minorities have set themselves. The problem arises when there is no consensus either between the majority and the minority or within either group. A section of a minority may want to preserve its social structure and culture at all costs; another may wish to escape the constraints or even the oppression of the community and seek its identity in a cosmopolitan culture. The choice would also depend on the balance between individual and communal rights. Nor are particular solutions valid for all times; they may need to be reviewed as the socio-economic and demographic situation changes. It is worthwhile to caution against reifying temporary or fluid identities, which are so much a mark of contemporary times. There is a danger of enforcing spurious claims of primordialism and promoting competition for resources along ethnic lines, thereby aggravating ethnic tensions. Separate representation and institutions tend to lead to ethnic manipulation or extremism. Many proposals for diversity which have being made in recent years are untried; and, even when tried, it is too early to assess their success. Many of them are concerned excessively with conflict management, and perhaps not sufficiently focused on long-term objectives.

Nevertheless, these studies highlight some aspects of the constitutional recognition of diversity that pertain to policy on this matter. Several examples of legal recognition of cultural diversity were imposed rather than sought by minority groups—for example, apartheid structures, or divide-and-rule mechanisms used by colonial authorities. Historically, diversity arrangements have been connected with discrimination and domination. Often, if culture or religion is constitutionally recognised, it is the culture of the majority, resulting in the domination of the culture of others—Sri Lanka, Malaysia. Separate cultural systems are also a way of privileging some members of a community, such as traditional elites—usually male—or the wealthy, over others. For similar reasons, emphasis and efforts that go into developing separate systems for separate cultures mean that urgent social problems, whether of a community or of all the people, may be neglected.

Cultural rights may also put at risk human rights. The literature on group rights has highlighted how the rights of both certain members of the cultural community and outsiders may be infringed in this way. While it is true that human rights may themselves be culture-specific, the fact is that modern human rights are for the large part negotiated norms to which different traditions have contributed, and they do represent the aspirations of many people around the globe. Rules for cultural autonomy should be sensitive to the needs of individuals for more cosmopolitan identities, and, on the principle of self-identification, provide a reasonable basis for 'exit'. Nor should rules for cultural autonomy overlook the contingency and dynamic of cultures. Cultural autonomy tends towards conservatism and conservation at a time of rapid social and technological change when many of its assumptions are being undermined.

Constitutional recognition of cultures tends to sharpen differences between communities. Many schemes for recognition have been controversial and divisive. Progress towards a fair and integrative constitution in Fiji in the 1990s was obstructed by the entrenchment of 'diversity' from the past; indeed, the entrenchment of Fijian administration ran counter to the integrative aspirations of other parts of the constitution and of many people. Cultures should be recognized in a way that builds bridges and increases mutual understanding and appreciation of cultures; we need more inter-cultural than multicultural enterprises. Instead of a multiplicity of laws, we should work together for a genuine integration of laws, drawing together what is valuable in each culture. We ignore the implications of such recognition for inter-ethnic relations at our peril.

Federalism and State-Building: Post-Communist and Post-Colonial Perspectives

Steven L. Solnick

Introduction

Many observers have noted parallels between the collapse of the communist system and earlier episodes of large-scale decolonization (see for example Barkey and Von Hagen 1997; Dawisha and Parrott 1997). One similarity has received relatively little attention, however. The largest post-communist states, just as the largest post-imperial units in earlier epochs, faced the daunting challenge of using drastically weakened central government resources to create new institutions that could integrate territorially fragmented polities. In almost all such cases, the institutions of the successor states emerged in large part, though not exclusively, out of bargaining between central and regionally-based elites.

This chapter examines the process of bargaining over the creation of new rules and institutions after radical regime transitions. The analysis addresses the limited but important class of cases where a weakened central authority—whether constituted by the provinces or established as a legacy of imperial administration—must win the support or acquiescence of a minimal coalition of territorial actors in order to remain in power. In other words, the central government in these cases faces an acute challenge of *state-building* after transition.

While there are many mechanisms at work that together determine institutional design, this chapter focuses on the relationship

The author is grateful to Dawn Brancati and Leslie Powell for research support. This chapter is based on research funded in part by the National Council for Eurasian and East European Research (NCEEER) and the Smith Richardson Foundation.

between two variables. On the one hand, the chapter seeks to explain variation in the outcomes of the state-building process along a continuum from state disintegration, through confederation and federation, to a unitary state. An important distinction will be drawn between two *types* of federal states: those in which all provinces are subject to the same laws and rules, here labelled 'universal', and those in which certain provinces or provincial blocs enjoy special privileges, either de jure or de facto: here labelled 'exploitative'.

The chapter hypothesizes that these different outcomes can be explained in large part by the specific nature of the bargaining process or, more precisely, by the *mode* of bargaining. In political systems in which the centre is able to bargain bilaterally with provinces and can exploit information asymmetries, the centre will be able to coopt pivotal provinces while exploiting the divisions among provinces. This would lead us to expect an asymmetric system with a predatory centre. On the other hand, systems in which groups of territories are able to bargain together effectively as blocs may see certain territories winning concessions from the centre without offering central authorities much in the way of a *quid pro quo*. The analysis, therefore, traces the link between provincial coordination, modes of transitional bargaining, and the resulting configuration of state institutions.

The chapter proceeds as follows. The next section develops a framework for analyzing the bargaining between central and provincial elites during the state-building period following a radical transition. It focuses on the structure and mode of bargaining, and utilizes game-theoretic reasoning to suggest how different bargaining dynamics should lead to different state-building outcomes. The chapter does not develop a formal model of the bargaining situation; rather, it draws on standard game theoretic insights—regarding collective action among bargainers, imperfect information, and problems of bargain enforcement—to illuminate the specific constraints on centre-regional bargaining interactions. It also presents a logic for using multiple cases to 'test' the bargaining model with data varying over time and space.

The third section looks at post-communist state-building in Russia, and explores whether collective and bilateral bargaining by Russia's regions helps explain the peculiar asymmetrical and unstable outcome we see after ten years of transition. The fourth section suggests how a comparative approach might be put into practice by sketching the outlines of other cases that began in a situation similar to Russia's but developed quite differently: post-colonial state-building in contemporary Ukraine, and the consolidation of the Indian state in the years surrounding 1947. This section also suggests other cases that could help validate the model, including the preservation of Brazil as a single state in the nineteenth century and the emergence of a strong central government in the United States. The chapter concludes with a brief recapitulation of the main arguments and implications for further research.

State-building and Federal Institutions

Conceptual preliminaries

Before considering a simple model of centre-provincial bargaining, some definitions are in order. 'Transitional state-building', as considered in this chapter, is a distinct category from the cases of evolutionary state-building that are the focus of much of the classic state-building literature (Spruyt 1994; Tilly 1990). While many analyses of evolutionary state-building also consider negotiations between central and peripheral elites over long periods of time (Barkey 1994; Given 1990; Thomson 1994), the challenge presented to central governments after transitions is more acute. In these cases, newly constituted central governments must simultaneously consolidate their power and establish the domestic and international legitimacy of the new states.[1] Thus, in transitional state-building cases, new central governments must simultaneously exercise sovereignty in the international community while consolidating sovereignty on the domestic stage.[2]

Decolonization represents the paradigmatic case of such transitional state-building, since new states are created that must simultaneously consolidate power domestically while asserting their sovereignty on the international stage. From this perspective, then, the formerly Soviet states also faced transitional state-building challenges, since the collapse of the Soviet Union represented, in very real terms, the end of an empire. Even Russia, though the former imperial metropolis, confronted a similar challenge, since its

---

[1] For a work that bridges these two literatures, see Spruyt (1998).

[2] For a discussion of different aspects of sovereignty, see Krasner (1999: 9–25). The distinction I aim to draw here is between asserting the supremacy of domestic authority structures within the borders of the state claimed by the central government, and claiming the role of legal representative of the state in international arenas.

political organization and institutions were fused with the imperial structures of the Communist Party and had little legitimacy outside that context. The post-communist states of eastern and central Europe, by contrast, faced less acute challenges, since their international legal sovereignty had been accepted all along.

One final but critical feature of transitional state-building is that the successor government, by virtue of its incomplete domestic consolidation of power, cannot unilaterally impose its policies on provinces in the face of universal opposition. In other words, as least some consent must be secured from provincial leaders, though as I note below the nature of this consent and the size of a potential veto coalition may vary by issue area.

On most issues, however, the federal government can survive without the *universal* support of the constituent parts of the federal union. All it requires, minimally, is a tacit coalition of compliant provinces. As Hardin (1989) has noted with respect to constitutions more generally, once a sufficient number of constituents have accepted a set of institutional rules, these rules emerge as the most viable solution to the coordination problem of institutional design. In other words, the choice is no longer between these rules and *other* rules, but between these rules and *no* rules (Hardin 1989). Similarly, once the federal government has assembled a supportive coalition allowing it to collect revenue and create public goods, regions not belonging to that coalition have little choice but to accept the emerging rules provided the benefits of belonging to the union continue to outweigh the costs of leaving it. This remains true even if provinces outside the dominant coalition pay a disproportionately high share of the costs of federal public goods or enjoy a disproportionately low share of its benefits.

As an institutional configuration, 'federalism' is defined here in the traditional sense used by political economists and comparativists (Riker 1964; 1975; Weingast 1995): a compound political system in which each level of government has at least one area of jurisdiction over which it is guaranteed a final say. In the context of such transitional state-building, federalism must be viewed not as an exogenously determined institutional parameter but rather as an endogenous response to the challenge of integrating provincial units into the new state. In other words, for the bargaining situations considered here, federal structures might well be the institutional starting point and therefore, from one perspective, could represent the 'reversion point' of the bargaining process; but alternative paths of development are viable outcomes of the bargaining as well. Thus, the objective of the analysis is not simply to explain *why* a federal or other outcome emerged from the transitional situation, but why *alternative* institutional structures did not emerge.

'Institutions' in this analysis refer not simply to formal structures of government but also to the 'compliance procedures, and standard operating practices' that structure the relationship between political actors.[3] This distinction is particularly important in evaluating the differences among federal systems. In this discussion, I am primarily interested in two variations on the federal theme. In 'asymmetric' federal systems, different rules apply to different constituent units of the federation. These differences may be constitutionally enshrined, such as the special status enjoyed by the historic regions in Spain, or they may depend on the discretion of the central government. By contrast, in 'symmetric' federations all constituent units face the same set of rules in their relations with the centre and each other.[4]

These asymmetries of outcomes are not to be confused with the heterogeneity of the territorial units. In all compound political systems constituent units will vary in population, resource endowments, geographical location—proximity to borders and so forth—and other parameters that can translate into bargaining power. One critical question to be considered here is whether this distribution of structural resources translates directly into institutional privileges in the transitional period and beyond.

In the simple bargaining framework presented here, the central government and provincial governments are modelled as single actors. Naturally, a more sophisticated framework would consider the impact of divisions within the central and provincial government and how these factions at different levels might be interrelated. To a first order of approximation, however, presenting the central government as the 'president' and the regional governments as 'governors' permits some leverage on the bargaining dynamics. This stylization of the bargaining situation also corresponds with the empirical fat that in most transitional polities democratic processes that would produce divided representation at the centre or regions are relatively underdeveloped.[5]

---

[3] This is consistent with Peter Hall's (1986: 18) use of the term.

[4] This does not imply a formal equality of regions. That is, certain regions may receive far more from the centre in fiscal transfers than others, which is inevitable in a redistributive federation—which most are. In addition, some regions may be overrepresented in political institutions (Stepan 1999).

[5] To be more precise, in the cases considered here, neither Ukraine nor Russia had universally elected provincial leaders after independence, and the Indian Princely States were non-democratic.

Centre-periphery dynamics can be portrayed as an ongoing and simultaneous bargaining problem between the president and each of the governors. Two primary *constitutional* issues are at stake in these negotiations:[6]

(1) Which policy questions are to be decided at which level of government?
(2) How are inter-governmental disputes—centre-region and region-region—to be resolved?

For the purposes of this discussion, I will assume that a third key constitutional question—which territories are to join the federal union—has been provisionally resolved. In other words, the analysis focuses on institutional origins given an initial roster of constituent units rather than on the creation of the federal union per se. In most cases, the initial roster of territorial units and the very existence of an administrative centre is the legacy of the *ancien régime*. The analysis thus segregates the issue of *partition*—which played a crucial role in the evolution of both India and Russia, if we consider the Soviet breakup as a de facto partition—as one to be treated separately.[7]

Bargaining mechanisms

William Riker (1964) famously referred to federalism as a 'bargain' between provincial and central elites to provide a defence against a perceived external or internal threat. Riker's analysis of cases beyond the United States had relatively little to say about the process of bargaining, however, and almost nothing systematic to say about federal bargaining. More recently, certain scholars have attempted to explicitly model the bargaining that leads to the creation of federal institutions,[8] but these models assume that differences among the provinces play little or no role in determining the

---

[6] Inman and Rubinfeld (1997) define federal constitutions with a different set of parameters: 'assignment' of policy jurisdictions—analogous to (1) in this discussion—and 'representation' of territorial units in the central government. In this analysis, I begin by treating the central government as autonomous. For a consideration of the consequences of allowing regional units to constitute the central government see Stepan (1997).

[7] The question of which units sit at the bargaining table—a function of history, geography, institutional legacies, resource endowments, and pure contingency—is beyond the scope of this chapter, but is considered separately in a monograph in preparation.

[8] Bednar (1998); Figueiredo and Weingast (1997); Ordeshook and Shvetsova (1996); Treisman (1999a).

bargaining outcome.[9] In the framework presented here, by contrast, the heterogeneity of provincial units determines whether and how provinces bargain collectively with the centre, and this, in turn, determines whether the centre can exploit rivalries among provinces to recentralize power during the transition.

The bargaining game is straightforward; while I will not analyze it formally in this chapter, it may clarify the exposition if I utilize a few symbolic tools to describe the basic dynamics. Consider a president P bargaining with n provincial governors (G_i; $i = 1 \ldots n$). We will assume that the president and governors are independent actors.[10] For the purposes of this simple game we can represent the division of power between the president and each governor by a single parameter x_i representing, in stylized form, a bundle of grants of jurisdictional control: tax collection, personnel appointment, judicial autonomy, control over specific policy areas, and so forth.[11] As a first approximation, we might assume that each governor seeks to maximize x_i, that is, maximize provincial autonomy, while the president in a state-building period seeks to minimize it; a straightforward variant would be to assign each governor her own ideal point based on the structural characteristics of her province.[12]

The bargaining proceeds as follows. At time t, the president proposes a division of authority between the national and sub-national levels: X_t, a vector consisting of $x_{i,t}$, for $i = 1 \ldots n$. Each governor then accepts or rejects the presidential 'offer'. Communication among the

---

[9] An important exception is Bednar (1999), who does model asymmetries among federation units. Weingast (1997:262) notes in passing that heterogeneity among subjects in a polity could be one factor that leads to exploitative, asymmetrical outcomes, but his analysis concentrates on homogenous actors and on the factors leading to symmetrical outcomes.

[10] Naturally, a more refined model would recognize that presidents can designate governors in some prefectural systems, while most democratic federations employ mechanisms of territorial representation that makes the federal government, at least in part, a creature constituted by the provinces.

[11] For simplicity we can think of x ranging from 1 (complete autonomy) to 0 (complete subordination). A simpler representation, consistent with some political economy models of federalism, might be to interpret x simply as 1 minus the per capita tax rate for each province. In a more sophisticated rendering, x_i could be represented explicitly as a bundle of k separate positions on specific policy areas.

[12] In a more elaborate game in which different policy areas are treated separately rather than aggregated into a single parameter x, we might assign each governor a weighting representing the priorities accorded to specific policy areas. A governor of an ethnic region might assign greater weight to cultural autonomy, for instance, than to fiscal control. Alternatively, we might introduce two 'types' of governors, with different preferences for autonomy, based on the structural characteristics of their States.

governors is permitted, but one governor will not necessarily know the content of offers made to other governors. The president then examines the responses of governors, and the game repeats with a new presidential offer, X_{t-1}. In equilibrium, $X_t = X_{t-1}$. The scheme is depicted in Fig. 7.1.

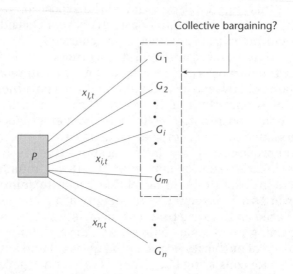

FIGURE 7.1: *Bargaining 'moves'*

In almost all cases, rejection of the presidential offer by isolated governors will not threaten the survival of the larger state. Faced with defiance by a single province, the president can make a more attractive offer, ignore the provincial defiance, or attempt to punish the defiant province. For their part, individual provinces have two structural characteristics that combine to determine the outcome. First, we can think of bargaining 'strength' as the capacity to hold out longest without agreement. This quality can be interpreted as the capacity to withstand punishments from the president for a protracted period. We might also evaluate an actor's 'strength' as deriving from her indispensability to a minimum winning coalition.[13] This notion manifests itself here as the cost *to the president* of governing without the cooperation of a particular governor. A governor

---

[13] This operationalization of power is implicit in many of the 'power indices' developed in coalition analysis. For a discussion see Brams (1990: Ch. 8).

has *veto power* if her rejection of X_t makes it impossible for P to govern in subsequent rounds.[14]

In any bargaining situation, actors who bargain collectively increase their influence. We can, therefore, distinguish between bargaining situations in which a coalition of governors acts as a single bargaining unit with veto power, and other situations in which no single provincial bargaining unit—governor or binding coalition of governors—can exercise a veto.[15] Where provinces are 'atomized', the president can bargain bilaterally with all governors simultaneously, ultimately tailoring x_i individually for each region to secure adequate support to govern. When provinces are 'unionized',[16] the president may be forced to accede to the demands of a bloc of governors, especially if the bargaining bloc is sufficiently large that the president is unable to successfully govern in the face of its defiance.[17]

A special case of unionized bargaining occurs when all governors belong to a single bargaining 'union'. This approximates the idealized situation portrayed in models of symmetrical, democratic federations in which all provinces abide by the same rules and therefore collectively police transgressions by the central government (Weingast 1997). Under the bargaining scenario outlined here, however, collective action among governors is not an all-or-nothing proposition but could conceivably link just a subset of provinces.

How are collective bargaining units—or unions—formed, and how do we know whether they have veto power? The formation of such units depends on a number of factors:[18] (1) coordination

[14] We might formally capture the notions of 'indispensability' and 'tenacity' by introducing the discount rates of central and provincial leaders.

[15] Treisman (1999*a*) captures a similar dynamic by modeling the 'assurance game' between subnational leaders seeking to withhold taxes from the central government.

[16] The analogy with labour bargaining is quite suggestive for capturing the dynamics of bargaining among non-homogenous units that may or may not act collectively. For an extended discussion, see Elster (1989: Ch. 4).

[17] There may be one or more 'unionized' bloc of governors. In the ante-bellum United States, for instance, both the north and south could be portrayed as coordinated blocs with veto power over the centre.

[18] The basic intuition of collective action among 'subjects' of a federation is entirely consistent with Weingast's (1993; 1995; 1997) discussion of the factors conducive to deterring transgression by a predatory sovereign through coordinated resistance among citizens, even when transgressions would favour one citizen at the expense of another. Weingast's analysis stresses the importance of coordination mechanisms to ensure that all citizens agree on what constitutes a transgression. The analysis presented here goes beyond Weingast's—which is relatively silent on the structure of bargaining—by introducing the possibility of heterogeneity among citizens.

mechanisms—trigger strategies—to ensure that all governors in a bloc will aid each other in the event of a presidential transgression against their rights and privileges and also to ensure that no governor seeks his own bilateral deal with the centre; (2) the nature of collective goods produced and distributed by the centre—collective action is easier to enforce when these goods are club goods rather than purely private or purely public; (3) relative bargaining strength among provinces, defined as ability to withstand a presidential sanction—which may depend greatly on a common provincial feature, such as natural resource endowments, or degree of industrialization, or simply geographic proximity; and (4) information symmetries and asymmetries among the governors, which makes a coordination mechanism more or less feasible to implement.[19] Beyond listing them, I will not dwell here on a theoretical discussion of factors conducive to or obstructive collective action among provincial leaders.[20] For the purposes of this chapter, it is relatively straightforward to recognize collective versus bilateral bargaining, and to trace the rise and fall of efforts at collective bargaining by all or some governors.

Determining whether a governors' bloc or even a single governor may have veto power over the president poses a thornier challenge. Given the fluid nature of political institutions during periods of transitional state-building, it is not always obvious how coalitions are formed and how they 'vote'. For different issues, blocs and 'votes' may be manifested differently. For states in which a parliamentary tradition and rule of law is fairly strong—as was the case in most of the former British colonies—we might look at debates and voting behaviour in national—and constitutional—assemblies to provide a road map of provincial collective action. However, in some transitional states, the very heart of the constitutional debate is the scope of issues to be decided by the national legislature. In these cases, we must look not only at whether certain blocs prevailed in a vote in parliament or a constitutional assembly but also at whether the outcome of this vote actually affected the behaviour of the president and governors.[21]

---

[19] In a more refined version of the game, coordination among governors would also depend critically on preference compatibility, defined as their weightings (w) across k separate policy areas that constitute the presidential offer of X_t.

[20] For a more detailed discussion of the sources of collective action among provinces, see Solnick (1998).

[21] To complicate matters even further, some provinces or provincial blocs may exert veto power over only a limited domain of issues. Coastal regions, for instance, may be able to interrupt the collection of tariff revenues and threaten a key source of federal revenues. If these revenues flow largely to provincial rather than central

As noted above, collective bargaining among governors is easier to sustain in an open information environment.[22] An 'open' or 'symmetrical' information environment is defined here as one in which each governor knows the terms of all other governors' deals with the centre. A closed, or asymmetrical, information environment is one in which each governor knows the terms of only her own deal with the centre. The president, naturally, knows all deals in either case; however, he may be unsure about the durability of collective action among governors.

We can expect members of a bargaining coalition to successfully punish 'union-busting' provinces only if they have common information on suspected defections from the bargaining bloc. Absent assurances that such information will be readily obtained, the bargaining unit may fail to form in the first place.[23] Conversely, any bilateral deals with individual governors risk catalyzing an opposing coalition of governors demanding symmetrical treatment unless the details remain obscure. Any universal coalition of governors, that is, a binding commitment by all governors to demand symmetrical treatment for all provinces, would appear to be unsustainable in an environment of asymmetric information.

The informational symmetry of the transitional bargaining environment is determined in large part by the characteristics of transitional political institutions. Bargaining within legislatures or a constitutional assembly, for instance, is relatively transparent, as all provincial leaders will at least be aware of the terms being offered to other provinces.[24] Bilateral negotiations conducted

coffers, however, the leverage of the 'coastal' bloc over the central government on non-tariff matters will be minimal, since any revenue interruption would merely be self-defeating. This example demonstrates a fundamental feature of transitional state-building: the state institutions being created during the transition will also help determine the relative influence of the provinces in the post-transition period. Consequently, we should expect the power imbalances among regions witnessed at the transitional moment to exhibit strong lock-in tendencies.

[22] The models developed by Bednar (1998; 1999) also incorporate information asymmetries, where incomplete information about compliance rates across subjects of the federations complicates the construction of a trigger strategy to punish shirking.

[23] The *ex ante* failure of institutions as a result of a lack of guarantees of *ex post* contracts enforcement is a central theme of the new institutional economics Oliver Williamson (1985).

[24] Note that this conception of symmetric information during the bargaining process is distinct from the concept of transparency of the process *to non-participants*. The latter sense of transparency can also have a dramatic impact on constitutional negotiations—see, for instance, Schiemann (1999)—and open negotiations are certainly more likely to produce symmetric information among participants than closed negotiations. But my use of the concept here is more limited.

seriatim behind closed doors represent the other extreme, in which the president can offer ad hoc deals with individual governors whose terms are not known to the remaining governors. Such secret deals are more difficult to enforce, of course, but this is largely because, as noted above, individual provinces bargaining on their own are usually powerless to overturn central transgressions without the assistance of other provincial leaders. Somewhere in the middle of the spectrum lies coalition talks with political parties that are regionally based. In these cases, the *fact* of a special deal may be impossible to conceal, but the *terms* of that deal may not be revealed in full.

Figure 7.2 pulls together the basic insights that emerge from the bargaining framework to suggest how provincial coordination and symmetry of information combine to shape the outcome of transitional state-building. The vertical dimension represents the degree of collective action among the provincial actors (governors) and whether any coalitions have formed that could act as veto blocs. When provinces are atomized, the bargaining mode is essentially bilateral; when provinces are 'unionized', there is collective action among at least one group of governors—or, as a special case, among all of them—that the president cannot safely ignore.

	Asymmetric information	Symmetric information
Unionized provinces	Exploitative asymmetry	Constitutional norms
Atomized provinces	Predatory centre	Unstable?

FIGURE 7.2: *Transitional state-building*

When some or all of the governors bargain collectively and information is asymmetric, we would expect to see the central government appeasing the strong governor's bloc at the expense of the weaker, non-organized provinces. In effect, the sectional bloc in this case 'captures' the federal centre. The resulting equilibrium offers each province in the veto bloc more autonomy than remaining provinces. I label this 'exploitative asymmetry' to suggest the exploitation of uncoordinated provinces by the privileged bloc.[25]

If information is symmetric, however, the 'non-unionized' regions will be forced either to ratify the privileges accorded to the sectional bloc or to seek to join the privileged bloc, making it universal. In either event, the result will resemble a federal system in which provincial leaders collectively police the central government, ensuring that any attempt by the centre renege on its earlier offer—that is, to exploit—will trigger a coordinated response from all provincial elites.[26] I label this 'constitutional norms' to suggest the coordination among regions enforces a symmetric or asymmetric—constitutional or quasi-constitutional—equilibrium that is ratified by all.

When governors bargain independently and bilaterally, however, the centre has much greater room for manipulation and exploitation. Where information is asymmetric, the centre can select different provinces against which to transgress on different turns, counting on the lack of coordination among provinces to make resistance manageable. While this may at times resemble the exploitative asymmetry noted above, I label it here a case of a 'predatory centre' to connote the added discretion in the hands of the president. While this system may retain the institutional trappings of federalism, that federalism would essentially be degenerate, as it offers no *guarantees* of areas of protected jurisdictional autonomy. The result is a bargaining analogue of cycling in a legislature in which an agenda-setter can propose a series of measures that disadvantage particular minority coalitions in turn, never reaching an equilibrium.

Finally, in cases where bargaining is bilateral but information is open it is difficult to perceive what a stable outcome might look like. Any proposed constitutional deal that privileges a minority group of regions will produce the coordinated resistance of the exploited minority, for whom the asymmetric offer serves as a trigger. Any deal that privileges a majority of provinces is likely to trigger threats of withdrawal from non-privileged regions, who will see no assurance of winning such privileges for themselves in the future. Most likely, the privileged provinces will recognize their common interest and organize to lock in the privileges won bilaterally, transforming the situation into one of exploitative asymmetry.

[25] Such a system might be an asymmetric federation or it may be a hybrid, with the 'exploited' provinces under central rule and the 'privileged' provinces essentially enjoying federated status.

[26] This outcome of universal coordination is similar to the Pareto-optimal outcome of Weingast's (1997) transgression game.

As this last example suggests, much of the dynamic of transitional bargaining over state-building can be interpreted as a struggle by provincial and national elites to determine which quadrant of Fig. 7.2 will represent the actual bargaining environment. Geographical, structural, or historical differences among provinces, for instance, may make collective action and transparency among sets of provinces more or less likely. Different institutional innovations introduced by the federal centre may also facilitate or impede sub-national coordination. The framework therefore offers a lens for understanding how the struggle to shape the transitional *environment* can translate directly into different *outcomes* of the process of state-building after radical transitions.

Empirical implications of the model

The analysis presented here does not aspire to be a general theory of territorial bargaining. It does, however, aspire to provide insights that extend beyond a single case. The class of transitions considered here—state-building after radical transitions in states with territorially-defined polities—is fairly small and each instance represents an event of world-historical significance. There can be no theory applying to all these cases that can claim to encompass all the causal forces at work shaping final outcomes.

Instead, the 'test' of such models is whether they are useful in explaining the outcomes of specific cases.[27] But here the very concept of 'explanation' needs elaboration. An explanation is compelling if it (1) suggests linkages between aspects of the empirical record not previously seen as connected, and therefore suggests new areas of empirical investigation, and (2) convincingly explains why, at critical junctions, certain paths were chosen *and other available paths were not*.

Russia is the focus of the next section. The framework developed above leads us to ask a series of questions about the nature of central-provincial bargaining in Russia between 1990 and 2000, as the newly constituted Russian government sought to take over from the Soviet government and simultaneously halt the momentum of disintegration that had produced the Soviet collapse. Specifically, I will examine Russian federal bargaining to see whether the ebb and

---

[27] This approach is broadly consistent with recent work on 'social mechanisms' (Hedström and Swedberg 1998). In Elster's terms, the move from covering law to social mechanisms is akin to the shift from claiming that 'If A, then always B' to 'If A, then sometimes B' (Elster 1998: 49).

flow of provincial autonomy on the whole, and the patterns of privileged regions in particular, are linked with the emergence or failure of collective action among Russian regions. Does bilateralism help the centre and more powerful regions, and do weaker regions seek coalitions? In addition, I will explore how the institutions that structured centre-periphery bargaining in Russia affected the flow of information about specific bilateral deals, and whether they in turn favoured the emergence of certain forms of provincial coordination.

To further test the robustness of this explanation, two other cases will be more briefly interrogated in a subsequent section. Both of these cases feature weakened central governments bargaining with territorially organized elites after a radical transition, and each offers a slight twist on the Russian situation. In the case of Ukraine, the challenge is to explain why a state that began with a similar internal structure to Russia's and sharply drawn territorial identities rejected a federal organization of the state. In the case of India, the challenge is to explain why over 550 Princely States—which enjoyed far greater autonomy from the new Indian government than did Russia's 'autonomous republics'—were so readily absorbed into the new Indian state by the end of the 1940s. The point of including these contrasting cases is not to offer the bargaining model here as a general theory of transitional state-building, but rather to further probe the plausibility of the bargaining model and strengthen the causal inferences drawn from the Russian case.

I turn now to Russia.

Russia: From Collective Bargaining to Bilateralism and Back Again

Since the late Gorbachev era, relations between Yeltsin's administration and Russia's 89 regional administrations have been characterized by extensive and protracted negotiations. Central and provincial leaders have bargained over division of budgetary funds, natural resources, policy jurisdictions, personnel appointments, and other questions of fiscal and policy competence. This period can be divided into three distinct phases, marked by degrees of subnational coordination.

1990–4: collective bargaining

The Soviet Union was a multi-ethnic federation in which major ethnic groups were associated with particular national 'homelands'. At the top of this hierarchy were the 15 Union Republics, like Ukraine, Kazakhstan, or the Russian Federation (RSFSR); each of these became independent after 1991. The Union Republics were themselves composed of some 20 autonomous republics, 18 autonomous *oblasts/krais*, and 120 territorial-administrative *oblasts* or *krais*.

In June 1990, the Russian Federation's newly elected legislature followed the lead of the Caucasian and Baltic republics and declared Russia to be 'sovereign'. The most important implication of this declaration was that Russia's laws were to take precedence over Soviet laws, and that Russia was to control the disposition of natural resources on her territory. This action was quickly mimicked by the 16 autonomous republics within the borders of the Russian Federation (Fig. 7.3), eager to seize the opportunity to gain greater control over their own affairs. Russian President Boris Yeltsin encouraged them, reluctant to provide Soviet President Mikhail Gorbachev with any precedent for recentralization; in August 1990, he famously told the leaders of the republics to 'take as much autonomy as you can swallow'.[28] By early 1991, all 16 republics had passed their own 'sovereignty declarations'.

The sovereignty declarations of the autonomous republics represented an attempt to upgrade their status *within* a federal structure rather than any bid to *leave* a federal structure.[29] We should not, therefore, interpret subsequent conflict between regions and the centre as threatening the territorial integrity of Russia. Instead the struggle was over the distribution of powers between the federal and regional governments, and especially the distribution of resources.

In the waning months of the Soviet Union, the autonomous republics were able to goad the Russian and Soviet governments into a high-stakes bidding war. In 1990, for instance, Yeltsin promised the government of Sakha/Yakutia, home to most of the Soviet Union's diamonds, that it could keep a share of its diamonds

[28] TASS (1990). Yeltsin initially directed the comment to oil-rich Tatarstan, whose sovereignty declaration did not acknowledge its membership in the Russian Federation. Yeltsin's remark was repeated, and more widely cited, in an interview with *Komsomol'skaia pravda* (1991).

[29] In particular, the autonomous republics sought to be represented as equals alongside the Union Republics in negotiations for a new *Soviet* Federation Treaty, then being proposed by Gorbachev (Filippov and Shvetsova 1999).

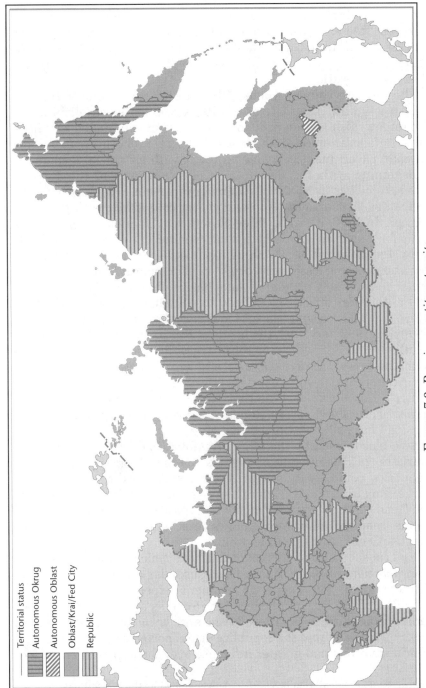

FIGURE 7.3: *Russia: constituent units*

Source: author, based on Russian Constitution

for independent sale. In addition, eleven regions sought and received 'free enterprise zone' status, offering tax and regulatory concessions (Filippov and Shvetsova 1999). Tatarstan, for its part, began negotiating a bilateral 'treaty' to clarify its powers with the Russian Federation.

The abortive coup of August 1991 put an abrupt end to the bidding free-for-all. The December 1991 agreements establishing the Commonwealth of Independent States effectively ended any hope for a confederation retaining a Soviet centre. From this point on, the Russian government bargained directly with provincial leaders.

Beginning with the declarations of sovereignty of the Russia's ethnic republics in 1990, the federal government in Moscow pursued a strategy that amounted to bargaining collectively with groups of regions. In 1992, it signed three 'Federation Treaties' to serve as the basis for a new Russian constitution. Similar but distinct documents were signed with Russia's ethnic republics—augmented to 20 by the elevation of some lesser territories—predominantly Russian *oblasts/krais*, and sparsely populated autonomous *okrugs*. In doing this, federal authorities effectively defined three major groupings of regions which it would recognize in subsequent collective bargaining.

During 1992 and 1993, the heads of Russia's ethnic republics met regularly and defined a coherent bargaining bloc in their relations with the federal centre. *Oblasts* and *krais* were unable to match their coherence, despite abortive efforts to define analogous *oblast*-centred 'republics', such as the Urals Republic led by Sverdlovsk *oblast* or the Far Eastern Republic led by Primorskii *krai*. Unlike these ad hoc collaborations based on geographic proximity, the collective bloc formed by the ethnic republics had readily identifiable markers of membership: regions defined constitutionally as 'republics' could easily recognize their stake in the success of the bargaining unit. Their leaders met regularly in a formal 'Council of the Heads of the Republics', and when Moscow granted a concession to one 'republic' all other republics could and did claim it as their constitutional entitlement as well.

As a consequence or this coordination, ethnic republics retained a disproportionate share of both fiscal subsidies and policy autonomy through 1993. Per capita government expenditures for the 20 republics of the Russian Federation taken as a whole exceeded per capita expenditures in the *oblasts* and *krais* by 37 per cent in 1992.[30] Officials from the republics also reported that their regional administrations had greater influence over the appointment of fed-

---

[30] This calculation is based on data compiled by the World Bank.

eral officials at the branch level than that enjoyed by the governors of *oblasts* and *krais*.[31]

This catalogue of privileges enjoyed by the republics can be misleading, however. Fiscal data were often ambiguous or misleading, especially when annualized figures failed to distinguish between transfer payments made in January and identical payments made in December, despite the corrosive effect of the high inflation rates being experienced at the time.[32] Many of the jurisdictional privileges enjoyed by republics were based on the discretion of the central government, and the lion's share of those benefits went to three republics: Tatarstan, Bashkortostan, and Sakha. Nevertheless, governors of the 58 non-ethnic regions, which comprised 85 per cent of the population of Russia, complained publicly and consistently that they were short-changed as a group in the federal bargain. As one observer wrote in 1992, 'Twenty three million Russian subjects will live in a federation and another 124 will live in a unitary state' (Glezer 1992).

1994–8: Bilateralism

After the ethnic republics failed to collectively support Yeltsin in his showdown with the Russian parliament in 1993, the centre moved to dismantle their structural advantages. It did so by attacking the unifying principle of their bargaining unit—their common stake in securing collective privileges.

Beginning with the 1994 bilateral 'treaty' with Tatarstan, the Kremlin began distributing resources and autonomy to regions based on individual rather than collective deals. Beginning first with selected republics, and then extending the practice in 1996 to

[31] This finding emerged from a survey of regional officials conducted jointly by the author and William Smirnov of the Institute for State and Law of the Russian Academy of Sciences and Vladimir Komarovskii of the Russian Academy of State Service. They are not responsible for the conclusions presented here. The surveys of 229 officials from 70 'subjects' of the federation were taken in the spring of 1996 and spring of 1997. Officials were asked to respond retrospectively about relations between their provinces and the federal government.

[32] There are other problems with a focus on inter-budgetary transfers, which remained the most widely analyzed indicator of centre-periphery bargaining. Among other things, the measure fails to distinguish between, say, an oil-rich region that gets to market all of its oil independently on the world market and a neighbouring poor region whose social welfare programmes are being underfunded by the federal centre. The most sophisticated analyses of these data—for example, Treisman (1999*b*)—attempt to control for such indicators of need and tax capacity, but such distinctions are generally lost in the governors' own tallies of 'donor' and 'dependent' regions. See Lavrov (1996; 1997).

selected *oblasts* and *krais*, the federal government began defining its relations with specific regions through direct bilateral negotiations. As a consequence, it was able to restrict the privileges enjoyed by some republics without incurring the ire of other republics fearing their privileges were also at stake. Thus, in 1997, the Kremlin was able to restructure Sakha's highly lucrative diamond marketing concession without encountering any protests of solidarity from other resource-rich regions. Similarly, the Kremlin was able to prosecute its bloody war against Chechnya without encountering united protests from other Islamic republics. In instances like these, it was clear than regions were conceiving and structuring their relations with federal officials bilaterally rather than collectively. By June 1998, more than half of the 89 constituent units of the Russian federation had signed bilateral 'treaties' with the federal government.

As more provinces structured their relations with the centre bilaterally, however, the centre gradually gained greater latitude to roll back certain privileges granted in earlier bargaining rounds. Bilateral treaties were accompanied by packets of agreements between federal and provincial 'ministries', key provisions of which were published only after long delays, if at all.[33] Consistent with the expectations generated by a model of a predatory centre, outlined above, given non-transparent, atomized bargaining, the centre faced few effective constraints on its opportunism. Thus, by mid-1998 the republic of Tatarstan was complaining that federal authorities were refusing to renew an agreement on inter-budgetary relations that had accompanied its 1994 bilateral treaty, and were seeking to renegotiate terms more favourable to the centre. At the same time, Tatar leaders complained, federal compliance with provisions of the treaty ceding policy autonomy to the Tatar government was erratic at best.

Yeltsin also practiced bilateral, ad hoc distribution of fiscal benefits, though these were much more difficult to track. During the 1996 presidential campaign, Yeltsin's trips to regional capitals were occasionally accompanied by the conclusion of a bilateral treaty, but were almost always accompanied by new federal investments and a rush to retire the federal governments debts to workers, pensioners, and enterprises in the province (Treisman 1998; 1999). While intergovernmental transfers after 1994 were determined by a transparent formula intended to equalize economic conditions across the federation, fiscal flows *within* the federal budget were not

---

[33] In particular, key appendices to agreements on inter-budgetary relations outlining specific tax sharing rates were generally unpublished.

regionally tallied (Lavrov 1996). Furthermore, the federal budget itself was of little use in tracking actual fiscal flows because most budget articles were only partially funded by the deficit-strapped federal government, and the final decisions on which regions would receive the money owed to them were made on an ad hoc basis.[34]

While Yeltsin increasingly relied on bilateral contacts after 1994 to structure bargaining with Russia's provincial leaders, his December 1993 constitution created an institution that undermined this strategy by facilitating greater transparency about federal relations and providing a mechanism for universal coordination among provincial leaders. The Yeltsin constitution created a bicameral legislature, with an upper house—the Federation Council—composed of two representatives from each of Russia's 89 regions. While these representatives were elected in dual-mandate districts in 1993, from 1996 the heads of the regional legislative and executive branches were simply appointed ex officio. Thus, after 1996, the Federation Council became the ideal incubator for a 'governors' union'.

The Federation Council has played a peripheral role since 1996, however. Upon closer examination, the reasons for this appear entirely consistent with the bargaining analysis presented above. As the Council's members all hold full-time elected positions in their home provinces, sessions are relatively brief—one or two days—and infrequent—monthly on average. Voting in the Council is generally done by closed ballot, and the votes are not recorded. Between 1996 and 1999 only six roll-call votes were taken in the Federation Council.[35] These events offered little indication of which regions might be colluding with the centre at the expense of others.

Furthermore, some of the most powerful regional leaders tend to keep strikingly low profiles during debates within the Council.[36] In

[34] In November 1999, a St Petersburg assemblyman successfully sued the federal government for allowing the Ministry of Finance to be guided by a 'secret budget' that bore little relationship to the annual budget law. As one analyst described it, 'There is always a shortage of money and the Finance Ministry often decides who will get priority and who will not get anything . . . This is really a major factor in political games' (Borisova 1999).

[35] Of these six, only one was central to Yeltsin's economic or political reform package, namely, the February 1998 vote narrowly upholding Yeltsin's veto of a new land code that prohibited the purchase and sale of real estate. The other votes, on such topics as the indexing pensions, the 'trophy art' law, an all-Union protest action, and Ukrainian Friendship Treaty were either more symbolic than substantive or lopsided votes.

[36] A study of Federation Council debates is being undertaken by the author jointly with Nikolai Petrov of the Carnegie Moscow Centre. For some preliminary observations on patterns of participation in Council debates, see Petrov (1999).

particular, governors from some of the regions that received the earliest bilateral treaties almost never speak on the floor of the Russian 'senate'.[37] The evidence suggests that at least some of the governors of regions enjoying privileged access to federal resources have little incentive to invest in institutions designed to distribute those public goods more equitably.

Centre-periphery relations after 1998

Beginning in 1998, the Kremlin's reliance on bilateral bargaining with the regions became increasingly costly. At the same time, a new and more threatening model of regional collaboration emerged, raising anew the possibility that a bloc of regions could emerge to constrain the opportunism and predation of the centre. By the spring of 1998, the central government was already losing access to the policy levers it needed to maintain a strategy of bilateral bargaining with regions.

One important element of the bilateral treaty packages signed with regions was a separate protocol of federal properties transferred to regional control. By early 1998, the federal government had already divested the most valuable properties in the its portfolio. In addition, regions were accepting shares in regional enterprises to settle regional tax debts, and were using this mechanism to accumulate far more valuable enterprises than the centre could offer.

In addition, the fiscal crunch already created by the debt crisis of early 1998 limited the centre's capacity to offer fiscal benefits through bilateral deals. As the debt crisis deepened, the centre came under pressure from international lenders—especially the IMF—to discontinue all non-cash transactions that crowded out cash contributions to the federal budget. Consequently, the centre lost the option of allowing regions and regional enterprises to settle debts through mutual offsets, barter, or wechsel schemes. With growing pressure from international institutions to re-monetarize the tax and budget system, central discretion over doling out fiscal benefits shrank dramatically.

Finally, the Treasury system (*kaznacheistvo*) put in place by 1998 further standardized the budgetary system across the federation and curtailed the centre's opportunities to offer rewards through

---

[37] This list of low-participation members includes the leaders of Bashkortostan, Saratov, Sverdlovsk, and Primorskii *krais*. The president of Tatarstan and the mayor of Moscow, on the other hand, are reasonably active speakers.

bilateral horse-trading. The impact of these reforms should not be overstated, however, as a large share—as great as 50 per cent by Russian estimates—of federal expenditures continued to flow through extra-budgetary channels.

As the federal centre was losing its ability to reward bilateral bargaining partners, it was also watching regional leaders grow more assertive in their willingness to defy the Kremlin. In early 1999, the Federation Council resisted Yeltsin's pressure to accept the resignation of Prosecutor General Yurii Skuratov. This act of defiance, while immaterial to Skuratov's fate, represented a rare instance of regional defiance uniting regional leaders across the political and territorial map.

More troubling to the Kremlin has been the emergence of 'governors' blocs' as players in the 1999 parliamentary election. While still just loose alliances with overlapping memberships, parties like Golos Rossiia and Vsia Rossiia amount to regional blocs defined not by inherited constitutional status, like the heads of republics, or accidents of contiguity, like Urals or Far Eastern associations. Instead, these new unions of governors represent political alliances specifically aimed at influencing the post-Yeltsin succession. Indeed, the most durable of these, Vsia Rossiia, was co-founded by Tatarstan's president, still bitter over federal intransigence in renewing budgetary provisions of its 1994 agreement.[38]

A regional alliance fashioned as a political party, united by a common political goal rather than mercenary self-interest, could prove less susceptible to manipulation by the Kremlin than earlier provincial coalitions. Yeltsin's response to this new regional threat has been dramatic, as consolidation of Vsia Rossiia's alliance with Moscow Mayor Yurii Luzhkov precipitated the dismissal of Prime Minister Sergei Stepashin. In the wake of his dismissal, federal officials moved swiftly to organize their own 'counter-movement', labelled Yedinstvo (Unity). Previous efforts to create a provincial bloc from above—the party-building effort surrounding Viktor Chernomyrdin's Nash Dom Rossiia (Our Home Is Russia)— revealed the difficulties in sustaining such a centre-forged bloc for longer than a single electoral cycle.

At the end of the summer of 1999, then, Russia appeared poised to once again shift the parameters of the centre-provincial bargaining

[38] Vsia Rossiia forged an electoral alliance with Otechestvo, another regional bloc led by Moscow mayor Yurii Luzhkov. The new party, known by its acronym *OVR*, recruited former Prime Minister Yevgenii Primakov to lead it into the in the December 1999 Duma elections, where it polled a disappointing 13% of the party-list vote.

environment. For the first time since the Soviet collapse, a grass roots provincial 'union' stood a chance of gaining power, after which we might have expected to see a realignment of patterns of regional exploitation, and a return to the earlier contours of exploitative asymmetry. In the event, however, the sudden surge in popularity enjoyed by Prime Minister Vladimir Putin in the wake of his renewal of the war in Chechnya produced a crisis in the ranks of the governors. As a victory by Putin in the 2000 presidential elections began to look more realistic, and as rising oil prices refilled federal coffers, governors feared that active membership in an opposition bloc could leave them excluded from future federal benefits. By the beginning of 2000, governors were abandoning the moribund Vsia Rossiia alliance and climbing aboard the Yedinstvo bandwagon. Remarkably, what looked like a crisis for the centre seemed to transform itself during the 1999–2000 electoral season into a new round of federal recentralization.

Alternative Post-colonial Perspectives: Ukraine, India, and Others

The account of Russian federal evolution presented above uses a simple bargaining model to reveal several insights into the Russian case: the importance of inter-provincial coordination in establishing constraints on federal autonomy; strategies employed by the centre to promote bilateralism, or at least to combat the emergence of 'like-minded' unions of provinces; and the importance of the structure of federal institutions for promoting or impeding inter-regional coordination.

The stylized narrative presented above cannot tell us much about 'off the path' behaviour. For that, we must look at other cases, whose bargaining problems bore some fundamental resemblance to Russia's, but which differed in one or more key aspects. The capsule presentations that follow are not meant to be definitive accounts of the cases invoked, but are meant rather to provide an additional indicator of the plausibility and usefulness of the bargaining framework developed here. More importantly, perhaps, by recasting these cases in the same bargaining framework, new questions about the emergence of these earlier political systems should emerge to drive further research.

Ukraine: the federal road not taken

Within the Soviet system, the union republic of Ukraine was organized analogously to the Russian Federation. Ukraine at the end of Soviet rule consisted of 25 *oblasts*, relieving it of the burden of constitutional asymmetries that confronted Russia at the moment of transition. In many ways, however, Ukraine represented a more divided polity than Russia as a consequence of its tumultuous history in the twentieth century (Fig. 7.4). The Western provinces of Ukraine had been divided during the inter-war period among Romania (Bukovina), Czechoslovakia (Transcarpathia), and Poland (Galicia, Volhynia, and other territories). These provinces were not incorporated into Soviet Ukraine until 1944, and during the period of their separation from eastern Ukraine were subjected to a range of different political and religious systems with lasting effects to the present day. The influence of the Catholic Church in eastern Ukraine, for instance, is probably greater than in any of the post-Soviet states outside the Baltics.

In addition to these different historical trajectories within Ukraine, the Ukrainian state in 1991 also contained the Crimean peninsula. Crimea was home to the Soviet Black Sea Fleet, and its largely Russian population had been governed as an autonomous republic within the Russian republic until the expulsion and deportation of the Tatar ethnic group in 1944. It was subsequently transferred to the Ukrainian republic by Nikita Khrushchev—himself a former head of the Ukrainian Communist Party—in 1954.

Thus, at the moment of independence, Ukraine was 'a territorial space inhabited by people who were not yet a nation administered by bureaucrats who did not yet comprise a state' (Motyl and Krawchenko 1997: 258). More crucially for the project of state-building, the territorial space of the new Ukrainian state was potentially fragmented: a 'European' east, a 'Russified' west, including the coal-rich Donbass, and restive Crimea in the South. Why has Ukraine emerged far more unitary in its state structure than Russia?

To begin to answer this question, it is useful to deploy the bargaining framework outlined above. In essence, President Kravchuk's first 'offer' to regional elites was to constitute Ukraine purely as a unitary state. Initially, this faced resistance from Crimea, where activists pressed for a referendum on re-association with Russia, and independent local elections. Kravchuk responded with an offer to transfer extensive autonomy to Crimea, granting it the status of an autonomous republic within Ukraine (Solchanyk

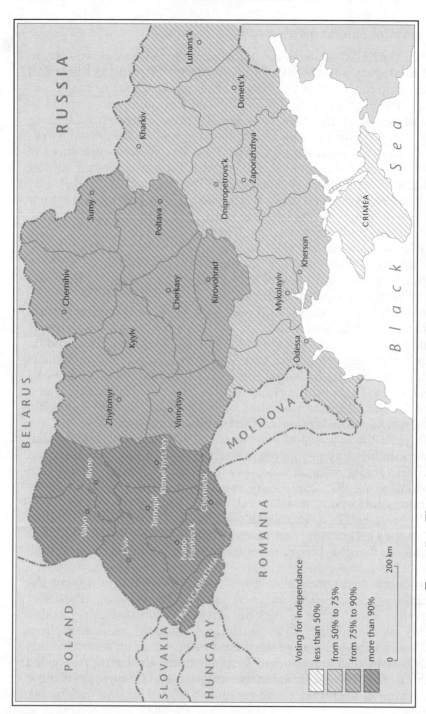

FIGURE 7.4: *The variation in the vote for Ukraine independence (December 1991)*
Source: Khmelko and Wilson (1998: 63).

1994). Over the course of negotiations, however, Kravchuk backtracked on some of the central provisions of his initial offer, and the Crimean parliament responded in June 1992 by declaring independence, subject to an August referendum. Over the next two months, Ukrainian and Crimean authorities engaged in a tense stand-off over the degree of autonomy to be granted to Crimea, with both sides ultimately accepting an ambiguous compromise that defused the current crisis.

In 1995, Ukraine permitted presidential elections to be held in Crimea, and they were won by a pro-Russian separatist, Yuri Meshkov. In August of that year, Crimea's capital, Sevastopol, declared itself to be a Russian city, finally provoking a response from the Ukrainian *Rada*. In September, newly elected Ukrainian President Leonid Kuchma stripped Meshkov of many of his powers, and appointed a pro-Kiev premier to run the Crimean government. After Crimean legislators failed to bring their laws into conformity with Ukrainian law, the Crimea was placed under direct rule from Kiev on 17 March 1996. The brief experiment with autonomy was summarily ended, Meshkov was fired, and the Crimean 'constitution' passed in 1992 was annulled.

The extinguishing of the autonomy movement on the Crimean peninsula removed a significant roadblock to the passage of a new Ukrainian constitution in May 1996. That constitution eschews any references to federalism, declaring instead that the territorial structure of Ukraine is 'based on the principles of unity and indivisibility of the state territory' (Art. 132). Nevertheless, the constitution does devote a full chapter (Ch. 10) to the 'Autonomous Republic of Crimea'. Unlike the republics in the Russian Federation, however, the autonomy of the Crimean government is sharply curtailed and there is no pretence of sovereignty attached to the status.[39]

Why were Crimean separatists unable to forge some sort of coordinated bargaining position with representatives of other provinces and force the Ukrainian government to propose a less centralized and unitary state structure? Even a cursory examination of the bargaining environment in post-Soviet Ukraine suggests several reasons.

---

[39] For instance, the prime minister of the Crimean government is appointed by the Crimean legislature 'with the consent of the President of Ukraine' (Art. 136). In addition, in areas of jurisdictional authority, the Crimean government is reduced essentially to an implementing branch for decisions taken in Ukraine. All quotations from the Ukrainian constitution are from the official translation on Ukraine's parliamentary web site (http://www.rada.kiev.ua/const/conengl.htm).

First, Crimean separatism, rather than serving as a catalyst for provincial coordination against the centre, instead served to trigger provincial opposition to Crimean separatism. Looming behind all discussions of Crimean autonomy rose the shadow of the Russian Federation. As Motyl and Krawchenko (1997: 260) note, '[Crimea's] successful secession would still depend far more on Russia's willingness to absorb it—and thereby set a precedent for its won dismemberment—than on Ukraine's incapacity to prevent it'.

Russia, while not eager to absorb Crimea, did little to allay fears of Ukrainian elites that it sought to limit Ukraine's newly-won sovereignty. On 9 July 1992, even as the Crimean parliament was voting to indefinitely postpone its independence referendum, the Russian parliament voted to declare the 1954 transfer of Crimea to Ukraine to be 'without force of law' (Solchanyk 1994: 52). The decision was quickly denounced by Yeltsin, but it came against a backdrop of Russian intransigence over the division of the Black Sea Fleet, based in Sevastopol. Even more troubling to Ukrainian elites, Russian authorities occasionally expressed 'concern' of the rights of Russian-speaking minorities in the eastern parts of Ukraine. Given the fact that voters in every province of Ukraine, east and west, had overwhelmingly supported the 1991 referendum on Ukrainian independence, it was clearly important to draw the line between supporting a federal system within Ukraine and surrendering integral parts of the new state back to Russia.[40] The Russian role in Crimea and the Donbass made it impossible for elites in the west, where independence was particularly popular, to coordinate with activists in the south or east.

Nevertheless, several groups in Donbass and Transcarpathia began in 1991 to agitate for a federal solution in Ukraine. These rumblings at the grass roots failed to be reflected in any coordination at the level of regional leaders. In part, unlike Russia, Ukraine lacked the institutional stratification that could facilitate inter-provincial coordination on demands for devolution. With the exception of the Crimea, which coordinated more with Russian officials than neighbouring Ukrainian leaders, there was no provincial hierarchy to defend. Even the unicameral legislature deprived regional elites of a provincial chamber where federal bargains might be struck.

Instead, lines of communication remained highly centralized, and the Ukrainian president controlled most key channels of information.

---

[40] The independence referendum also carried in Crimea, where it received a narrow majority.

In a unitary system of government, presidential discretion vis-à-vis regional policy is greatly enhanced. Ad hoc privileges, fiscal and otherwise, were easy enough to distribute in Ukraine's unreformed economic and political system.[41] Unable to bargain collectively with the centre, and unable to comprehensively track the flow of fiscal and other policy benefits, regional leaders could offer little resistance to the predations of the centre.

There is, however, an alternative explanation of the Ukrainian outcome. Successive presidents may have cultivated their respective 'machines' based in specific regions. In this case, the Ukrainian case would emerge as one in which information about centre-provincial bargaining remained asymmetric, but the centre colluded with a cluster of regional elites rather than playing on the threat of dismemberment to keep them atomized. In this case, we would expect to see a consistent pattern of privileged regions enjoying the fruits of redistribution from the remaining provinces. Further research into the political economy of post-independence Ukraine could help clarify which scenario better captures the dynamic of centre-periphery bargaining that has produced a constitutional structure with little power devolved to the provincial level.

India: the weakness of the Princely States

After the First World War, as Britain began to move toward greater home rule in India, the subcontinent represented an even more fragmented and asymmetrically organized polity than either Russia or Ukraine (Fig. 7.5).[42] The British provinces of India were directly ruled by the Crown. However, they coexisted alongside more than 500 Indian States—or Princely States—whose maharajas, darbars, chiefs and princes enjoyed substantial sovereignty in return for acknowledging the 'paramountcy' of British rule. These States comprised just under half the territory of pre-partition India, and just under a quarter of its population.

---

[41] For instance, as noted in the Russian case, during periods of hyperinflation as experience in Ukraine, the *timing* of transfer payments is as critical as the *amount* of such payments. In addition, Ukraine, like Russia, suffered from a massive non-payments crisis. Under such circumstances, the right to accept tax payments in kind rather than in cash can be extremely valuable.

[42] The account here of the Indian States is elliptic at best, and drawn from a more detailed treatment in a monograph currently being written. I rely heavily here on three excellent accounts of the Indian States and the new Indian state: Copland (1997), Phadnis (1968), and Menon (1956).

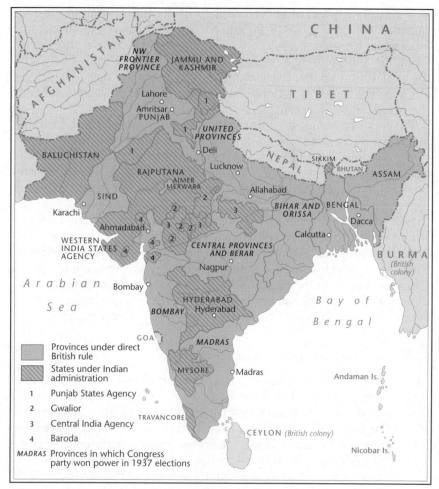

FIGURE 7.5: *Administrative structure of India in the 1930s*
Source: O'Brien (1999: 248).

The States' rulers fashioned their powers and relationship with the Crown purely bilaterally, and until the second decade of the twentieth century the British colonial authorities went out of their way to discourage communication and coordination among the States and their rulers. While the Crown ceased its policy of absorbing the Indian States as a reward to loyal princes after the mutiny of 1857, it was fairly efficient at the sort of bilateral co-option one would expect to find when the lesser bargainers were atomized and the bargaining was not open: that is, information was highly asymmetric.

In the wake of First World War, however, the nationalist movement among the Hindu population in the British provinces began to gather steam. One response by colonial authorities was to fashion the princes into a more cohesive political force, to serve in essence as a counterweight to the restive provinces. By 1921, the British government had presided over the creation of a new consultative body, the Chamber of Princes, intended to be the first step toward integrating the princes into a malleable, loyal, but powerful political force. As one contemporary put it, the princes had gone from onlookers to 'steady goalkeepers in the great Indian game' (Copland 1997: 44). Put within the bargaining framework, the British, confronted by an increasingly 'unionized' India, thanks to the work of the Congress, sought to create their own Princely 'union'.

Assembling the princes into a single body was far from simple. Large, medium, and small States began with radically different deals with the Crown, and with substantially different powers to bargain without the help of the other princes.[43] Consequently, large States like Hyderabad and Mysore were distinctly unenthusiastic about the creation of the Council, preferring instead to rely on their direct ties with the British viceroy. At the other extreme, 327 of the smallest States had no representation at all in the Chamber, while 127 small States were represented by just 12 deputies.

The Chamber of Princes was, it turned out, the first step in what became Britain's plan for federation in India. The federal plan was developed in the early 1930s, and envisioned a federation under British dominion, consisting of British India on the one hand and the States on the other. This asymmetric union of States and provinces, reminiscent in many ways of the basic asymmetrical scheme found in Russia, became the heart of the British India Act of 1935.

The new federation was conditional, however, on its acceptance by States containing at least half the population of the States as a whole, and commanding at least half the seats in the proposed Upper Chamber. The struggle to win accession of individual States went on until 1939 before it was abandoned with the onset of war. Ultimately, the several of the largest States, particularly Hyderabad and Bikaner, resisted the plan because they felt it did not offer sufficient imperial guarantees of their sovereignty. The British struggled to refashion the terms of the offer to win the approval of a bare majority, and as they struggled to sell the princes on the idea that federation offered 'the

[43] While the Chamber was a deliberative rather than bargaining assembly, my assumption here, consistent with the model presented earlier, is that *any* effective collective body makes collective bargaining more feasible by simplifying *ex ante* coordination problems and *ex post* enforcement.

most efficacious, if not the only, means of defending themselves' in the face of the developing 'threat' from Congress' (from British India Office records cited in Copland 1997: 176). But before any counter-proposals could be considered, Britain was at war, and the plan for federation was shelved.

As it turned out, the failure of the British to win the approval of the princes for the proposed federation—itself largely a failure of collective action among the princes—doomed the princes less than a decade later.[44] The collapse of the federation plan meant that the Princely States on the eve on Indian independence were still atomized—in sharp contrast to the Russian republics at the moment of the Soviet collapse. Any impetus to band together after the war seems to have been lost on the princes themselves, who apparently surveyed the post-war domestic horizon and saw no immediate threat to their survival (Copland 1997: 226–7). This left them vulnerable to being isolated and neutralized by India's new leaders over a remarkably brief period.

One of the first, and strongest, divisions to emerge among the princes was between large and small States, as it became increasingly clear that the post-colonial Indian Union would accommodate only States with relatively large populations. Many smaller States scrambled to find regional unions in games of musical chairs that left many rulers with no place to sit. Then, rather than exploit the widening rift between the Hindu Congress and the Muslim League, the princes allowed themselves to be drawn into this divisive struggle as well.[45] Finally, the ruler of Bhopal made an ill-prepared bid to persuade the States' representatives to boycott the 1947 Constituent Assembly. When a delegation of nationalist princes broke ranks and met separately with Nehru, any hopes that the princes could transform solidarity into a set of credible guarantees to preserve their monarchical order essentially vanished. Nehru's deputies worked with the outgoing viceroy, Mountbatten, to secure the accession of the princes individually to the new Indian state. And then, lacking the coordination they required to enforce these bilateral deals, they watched almost helplessly as the new Indian government integrated their territories into the new body politic.[46]

---

[44] Copland (1997: 279) comes to a similar conclusion: 'The princes missed a golden opportunity to entrench themselves constitutionally by accepting the offer made to them in 1939 to join the all-India federation'.

[45] This was a particularly acute problem in States, like Bhopal, where Muslims ruled over non-Muslim populations.

[46] Of course, some States, like Hyderabad, were less helpless than others. See Menon (1956: 314–89).

Other post-colonial cases

The record of imperial endings presents a wealth of other cases of transitional state-building in which weakened central governments bargained with territorial elites. Cast within this bargaining framework and contrasted with other cases, fresh questions emerge from these cases. While I lack the space here to provide any real detail on additional cases, I would like to suggest how some of these other cases might be framed.

In South America, Portuguese and Spanish empires developed side by side. Yet, when the European powers were expelled, Brazil remained a single country while the Spanish colonies were transformed into 17 different countries. This striking outcome invites a close examination of the bargaining among provincial elites in these two imperial outposts.[47] Within Brazil, later in the nineteenth century, a lasting asymmetrical pattern was established in which the federal government was essentially captured by two rich southern provinces, Minas Gerias and Sao Paulo. This 'politics of the governors' is puzzling given the bargaining framework developed here, since it poses the question of the why federal government was unable to exploit the differences among these two key alliance partners and the vast territories of the north to gain greater leverage for itself.

The early American Union, by contrast, offers an example of a weak central government that was able to exploit differences among the strongest provinces. Conflicts among States over western land claims led to the passage of the land ordinances that culminated in the Northwest Ordinance. As the larger States abandoned their claims to the west, the central government simultaneously gained the power to define *new* States. In addition, simmering border conflict between neighbours, and lingering tensions between large and small States, paved the way for the radically strengthened central government constituted in 1787—a government that could save the States from themselves.[48]

[47] For a useful overview of this puzzle, see Jose M. Carvalho (1982). The most common explanation for this divergent outcome points to the transfer of the Portuguese crown to Brazil in 1807 and the impact of that experience on the forging of a more unified elite in Brazil. Carvalho adds to this the impact of the Portuguese system of centralized colonial education on forging a more unified elite. A useful extension of this analysis, therefore, would be to trace the effect of elite fragmentation of homogeneity on the bargaining dynamics between centre and provinces.

[48] On early American border conflicts and the western land cessions, see Onuf (1983). The centrality of the Northwest Ordinance is echoed by North (1990).

Conclusion

This chapter has not attempted to offer prescriptions for constitutional 'design'. Instead, it has sought to portray how state structures after radical transitions may be determined more by the characteristics of the transitional environment than by any deliberate blueprint. By implication, the analysis suggests that, even when an optimal constitutional design can be articulated, participants may be unable to agree on it *ex ante* or enforce it *ex post*.

In the Russian case, for instance, differences in the status of provinces at the moment of transition created a natural 'bargaining unit' that successfully defended group privileges for several years. At the same time, this association was largely an accident of history rather than common interest, and ultimately fell victim to the central government's 'divide and rule' co-option strategies. When fewer resources were available to fuel this bilateral bargaining approach, the centre confronted more cohesive bargaining coalitions.[49]

In the Ukrainian and Indian cases, by contrast, federal solutions that could have preserved special privileges of historically distinct regions were not realized, in large part because of the incapacity of sub-national units to overcome obstacles to collective action and to mitigate information asymmetries. Without passing judgement over whether the resulting outcomes were 'better' or 'worse' for the states in question, the analysis demonstrates the importance of studying not just the bargains between the central and provincial elites but the bargaining among them as well.

In short, this chapter offers a perspective on constitutional design that complements the normative and positive arguments elsewhere in this volume. As bargaining theory makes clear, even when all actors in a negotiation desire an agreement, sometimes reaching that agreement may prove impossible. Analysts and practitioners may argue at length over the potential benefits and weaknesses of competing constitutional designs. However, the cases of transitional state-building considered here suggest that the set of *desirable*

---

[49] The poor showing of governors' blocs in the December 1999 presidential elections—leading to the virtual collapse of the Otechestvo-Vsia Rossiia coalition—suggests that the divergences of interest among regional leaders may be persistent and divisive. By contrast, the rush of regional elites to join the Kremlin-sponsored Yedinstvo movement in the wake of Yeltsin's resignation on 31 December 1999 provides powerful evidence that the threat of regional bargaining coalitions has been surmounted, at least for the 1999–2000 electoral cycle.

institutional models may be quite different from the set of *attainable* institutional equilibria.

Theorists of constitutional design, therefore, must consider not only whether a particular institutional design is attractive for a given polity but also whether the transitional environment makes it likely that the given design would be adopted. It is one thing to design a shining city on a hill; it requires a different—and complementary—analysis to find a hill that people will be able to climb.

Ballots Not Bullets:
Testing Consociational Theories of Ethnic Conflict, Electoral Systems, and Democratization

Pippa Norris

Some of the most difficult issues facing established and new democracies concern the management of ethnic conflict. The familiar litany of problems ranges from the inclusion of diverse racial groups in South Africa and Namibia to long-standing tensions between Catholic and Protestant communities in Northern Ireland, violence in the Basque region, the Palestine and the Balkans, and the dramatic eruption of bloody wars in Rwanda, Kashmir, and East Timor. Ethnic identities can be best understood as social constructs with deep cultural and psychological roots based on national, cultural-linguistic, racial, or religious backgrounds.[1] They provide an affective sense of belonging and are socially defined in terms of their meaning for the actors, representing ties of blood, soil, faith, and community. Agencies concerned with the peaceful amelioration of such antagonisms have increasingly turned towards 'constitutional engineering' or 'institutional design' to achieve these ends. The aim has been to develop rules of the game structuring political competition so that actors have in-built incentives to accommodate the interests of different cultural groups, leading to conflict management, ethnic cooperation, and long-term political stability.

I would like to thank Andy Reynolds, Jorgen Elklit, and Ben Reilly for many helpful comments concerning an earlier draft of this chapter and Phil Shively and the CSES team for release of the data-set.

[1] There is a large literature on the concepts of ethnic and national identity, and ethnic conflict. See, for example, B. Anderson (1996), Billig (1995), Gellner (1983), Brown *et al.* (1997), and Taras and Ganguly (1998).

One of the most influential accounts in the literature has been provided by the theory of 'consociational' or 'consensus' democracy developed by Arend Lijphart, which suggests that nations can maintain stable governments despite being deeply divided into distinct ethnic, linguistic, religious, or cultural communities.[2] Consociational systems are characterized by institutions facilitating cooperation and compromise among political leaders, maximizing the number of 'winners' in the system, so that separate communities can peacefully coexist within the common borders of a single nation-state. Electoral systems represent perhaps the most powerful instrument available for institutional engineering, with far-reaching consequences for party systems, the composition of legislatures, and the durability of democratic arrangements (Lijphart and Waisman 1996). Majoritarian electoral systems, like first past the post, systematically exaggerate the parliamentary lead for the party in first place with the aim of securing a decisive outcome and government accountability, thereby excluding smaller parties from the division of spoils. In contrast, proportional electoral systems lower the hurdles for smaller parties, maximizing their inclusion into the legislature and ultimately into coalition governments. Consociational theories suggest that proportional electoral systems are more likely to facilitate accommodation between diverse ethnic groups, making them more suitable for new democracies struggling to achieve legitimacy and stability in plural societies.

These are important claims that, if true, have significant consequences for agencies seeking to promote democratic development and peacekeeping. To explore the evidence for these arguments, the first section of this chapter summarizes the key assumptions in consociational theories of democracy and outlines the central propositions examined in this study. The second section describes the data, research design, and methods. Evidence is drawn from the current release of the 1996–8 Comparative Study of Electoral Systems (CSES),[3] based upon national election surveys in a dozen nations at

---

[2] Lijphart and Grofman (1984), Lijphart (1984; 1986; 1991*a*, *b*; 1994*a*; 1995*b*; 1999).

[3] I am most grateful to the Comparative Study of Electoral Systems (CSES), based at the Center for Political Studies, University of Michigan, Ann Arbor, for release of this data-set, and all the collaborators who made this possible, including in particular the directors of the 1997 British Election Study. It should be noted that more nations will eventually be incorporated into this data-set so this analysis remains preliminary. Details of the data-set, questionnaire, research design, and collaborators are available at http://www.umich.edu/~nes/cses.

different levels of democratic and socio-economic development. The study compares three nations with majoritarian electoral systems—the United States, Britain, and Australia; three using 'mixed' or parallel electoral systems—Taiwan, Ukraine, and Lithuania; and six countries with proportional representation (PR) systems—Poland, Romania, the Czech Republic, Spain, New Zealand, and Israel. The study compares political attitudes and behaviour among a diverse range of ethnic minorities such as the Russian-speaking population living in Ukraine, residents in the Catalan, Galician, and Basque regions in Spain, African-Americans in the United States, the Arab/Muslim populations in Israel, the Scots and Welsh in Britain, the Hungarian minority in Romania, the mainland Chinese in Taiwan, and the Maoris in New Zealand. The framework contains relatively homogeneous nations such as Poland and Britain as well as plural societies like Israel and Ukraine. Some countries like Australia are long-established democracies, others like Spain consolidated within recent decades, while others like Ukraine remain in the transitional stage, characterized by unstable and fragmented opposition parties, ineffective legislatures, and limited checks on the executive.

The third section defines and analyzes the major ethnic cleavages in each of these societies and tests the central propositions about the effects of electoral systems on differences in minority-majority support. The results of the analysis suggest that there is no simple relationship between the type of electoral system and majority-minority differences in political support. In particular, the study finds no evidence for the proposition that PR party-list systems are directly associated with higher levels of support for the political system among ethnic minorities. The conclusion considers broader issues of effective electoral designs and conflict mediation through constitutional engineering, summarizes the key findings in the chapter, and discusses the implications.

Theoretical Framework

Ever since seminal work by Maurice Duverger (1954/1964) and by Douglas Rae (1971), a rich literature has developed typologies of electoral systems and analyzed their consequences. The most common approach has compared established democracies in the postwar period to identify the impact of electoral institutions upon the political system, such as for the proportionality of votes to seats, levels of party competition, executive stability, the social composition of legislatures, and voter turn-out.[4] During the 1990s the research agenda dramatically expanded in scope and reach. Newer work has extended the comparative framework to a broader universe of democracies worldwide,[5] analyzed the wider impact of electoral institutions upon the public policy-making process (Lijphart 1999: Chs 15, 16), and examining the dynamics of system change in established democracies like Britain, New Zealand, Israel, Italy, and Japan.[6]

There is a consensus in this literature that no 'perfect' bespoke electoral system fits every democracy. Instead, arrangements have to be tailored to each particular context; and choices involve trade-offs. Debates about electoral systems in established and in newer democracies, while emphasizing different concerns, share certain common features. The mechanical questions concern what designs lead to what consequences under what conditions. Underlying these arguments are contested visions about the fundamental principles of representative democracy.[7] Advocates of majoritarian systems argue that the 'winner's bonus' for the leading party produces strong yet accountable single-party government, and single-member districts strengthen effective links between voters and their representatives that promote local constituency service. In contrast, proponents of proportional systems suggest that PR produces a fairer translation of votes into seats, the election of more women into office, and greater voter participation (see for example Reynolds and Reilly 1997).

The central issue examined here derives from Arend Lijphart's theory of consociational democracy, in particular the claim that PR systems are more effective at engendering support for the political system among ethnic minorities. The core argument is that, in

---

[4] See, for example, Lakeman (1974); Nohlen (1996); Bogdanor and Butler (1983); Grofman and Lijphart (1986); Taagepera and Shugart (1989); Nohlen (1996); Reeve and Ware (1992); Norris (1997*a*); Farrell (1997); Cox (1997); Katz (1997); Reynolds and Reilly (1997).

[5] For post-communist nations see Simon (1997); Ishiyama (1997); Pammett and DeBardeleben (1998); Shvetsova (1999); Kitschelt *et al.* (1999). For Latin America see Jones (1994; 1995*a*); Soberg and Carey (1992); Mainwaring and Scully (1995). For Asia see Hsieh (1997). For Africa see Mozaffar (1997); Vengroff (1994); Jung and Shapiro (1995); Reynolds (1993; 1995). There are also numerous studies documenting the outcome of particular elections in particular countries in successive issues of *Electoral Studies, Representation: Journal of Representative Democracy*, and the *Journal of Democracy*.

[6] On electoral reform, for Britain see Jenkins (1998); Norris (1995). For New Zealand see Boston *et al.* (1996); Vowles *et al.* (1998). For Israel see Hazan (1996*a*). For Japan see Hideo (1998); Sakamoto (1999).

[7] See, for example, the discussion of democratic theory in Katz (1997) and Norris (1997*b*).

contrast to majoritarian electoral systems, PR (1) produces a more proportional outcome; (2) this facilitates the entry of smaller parties into parliament; (3) this includes the election of ethnic minority parties; and in turn (4) this produces greater diffuse support for the political system among ethnic minority populations (see Fig. 8.1). Although the theory is widely influential, the existing evidence for some of these claims is limited and remains controversial.

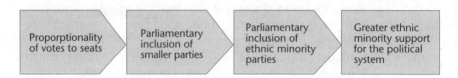

FIGURE 8.1: *Effects of proportional representation*

Proportionality

The first claim is that *majoritarian electoral systems are less proportional in translating votes into seats.* This proposition has received widespread support in the literature (see, for example, Cox 1997; Katz 1997. For example, using the Gallagher index, Lijphart found that in elections during 1945–96 in 36 democracies the average electoral disproportionality ranged from 1.30 (the Netherlands) to 8.15 (Spain) under PR systems, and from 9.26 (Australia) to 21.08 (France) in majoritarian-plurality systems (Lijphart 1999: Table 8.2). Lijphart concludes that disproportionality is affected mainly by a combination of district magnitude—the number of members elected per district—and the 'effective threshold'—that is, the minimum level of votes which a party needs in order to gain seats.[8]

The inclusion of smaller parties

The second claim is that more proportional electoral systems *lower the barriers for the parliamentary representation of any political minority,* whatever their background or ideological persuasion, if groups seek to mobilize and contest elections.

[8] Lijphart (1994a). Other secondary factors influencing this process include the basic electoral formula translating votes into seats, whether majoritarian, mixed, or proportional; the assembly size, that is, the total number of seats in a legislature; linked lists or apparentement provisions; the ballot structure; malapportionment—the size and distribution of the electorate within each constituency; and the difference between parliamentary and presidential systems.

The relationship between electoral systems and party systems has generated an extensive literature, following in the long tradition established by Duverger's Law (Duverger 1964: 252). Although the association between electoral systems and multipartism is weaker than that between electoral systems and disproportionality, there is considerable evidence that more parties tend to be elected under PR than under majoritarian elections. Lijphart's comparison of 36 established democracies during 1945–96 found that the level of disproportionality in the electoral system was negatively related to the effective number of parties elected to the lower houses of parliament (r = −0.50 p.01) (Lijphart 1999: Fig. 8.2). Katz (1997: 144–60) concluded that PR is associated with greater party competition, including the election of a wider range of parties across the ideological spectrum. In an earlier study I found that in the most recent elections in the mid-1990s across 53 democracies, the effective number of parliamentary parties was 3.1 in majoritarian systems, 3.9 in mixed or semi-proportional systems, and 4.0 in proportional systems (Norris 1997a).

The inclusion of ethnic minority parties

The related claim is that by lowering the electoral barrier to smaller parties, PR *thereby increases the opportunities for any ethno-political minority to enter parliament if they want to organize as a party and run for office.* In plural societies with strong cleavages, consociational arrangements in general, and PR systems in particular, are believed to facilitate minority representation. As Lijphart (1999: 33) argues,

In the most deeply divided societies, like Northern Ireland, majority rule spells majority dictatorship and civil strife rather than democracy. What such societies need is a democratic regime that emphasizes consensus instead of opposition, that includes rather than excludes, and that tries to maximize the size of the ruling majority instead of being satisfied with a bare majority.

Yet the evidence for the relationship between the electoral system and ethnic representation is limited and controversial. Systematic comparative data on ethnic minorities is plagued by problems of operationalization and measurement, due to the diversity of ethno-national, ethno-religious, and ethno-linguistic cleavages in different countries. Rather than examining direct indicators, both Lijphart and Taagepeera argue that we can generalize from the proportion of women in elected office as a proxy indicator of minority

representation in general.[9] Reliable cross-national data on the
number of women in parliament worldwide is available from the
Inter-Parliamentary Union and many studies have established
greater female representation under PR party lists than under first-
past-the-post systems (Norris 1985; 2000; Rule 1994). But is it legitimate to generalize from this pattern to the representation of ethnic
minorities? In fact, there are many reasons why this may prove
misleading. Many ethnic minorities are clustered geographically,
allowing local gains in seats even within heterogeneous plural societies, whereas the ratio of males to female is usually fairly uniform
across different areas. The use of party quotas, reserved seats, or
other positive action strategies designed to promote opportunities
for women and ethnic minorities often differs considerably. And we
also know that, at least in Britain, women and ethnic-racial minorities face different types of discriminatory attitudes among selec-
tors and electors (Norris 1997c, d; Norris and Lovenduski 1995).
Given all these important considerations, and continuing debate in
the literature, we need more evidence to understand how majoritarian and proportional electoral systems affect the inclusion or
exclusion of different types of ethnic minority parties.

In addition, there remains considerable debate about how far we
can extend generalizations about the workings of electoral systems
in plural societies in established democracies to the resolution of
ethnic tensions in transitional and consolidating democracies.
Much existing research on consociational democracies is based on
the experience of Western political systems that, by virtue of their
very persistence, have come to a consensus about many of the basic
constitutional rules of the game and a democratic culture. The classic exemplars of plural societies are those such as the Netherlands,
Switzerland, and Belgium. But it may prove difficult to generalize
from the context of stable and affluent post-industrial societies,
with institutional arrangements and a liberal-democratic culture of
tolerance which evolved during the course of the twentieth century,
to the process of conflict-management in transitional democracies
struggling with the triple burden of socio-economic development,
the consolidation of the political system, and the global pressures of
the world market. Some of the older examples of consociational
democracies in developing societies, like Lebanon and Malaysia,
have had a mixed record of success.[10]

---

[9] Lijphart (1999: 280–2); see also Taagepera (1994), who adopts a similar strategy.

[10] The Gastil Index for these countries estimates that Malaysia can be classified
as Partly Free (4.5/7) and Lebanon as Not Free (5.5/7). See the Freedom House
Index of Freedom. http://www.freedomhouse.org.

The growing literature on new democracies remains divided on this issue. Sisk and Reynolds (1998) argue that PR systems have generally been most effective in mitigating ethnic conflict in culturally plural African societies by facilitating the inclusion of minorities in parliament and encouraging 'balanced' lists, but this process is contingent upon many factors, notably the degree to which ethnicity is politicized, the depth and intensity of ethnic conflict, the stage of democratization reached by a country, the territorial distribution and concentration of ethnic groups, and the use of positive action strategies in the selection and election process (see also Reilly and Reynolds 1999). Tsebelis (1990) suggests that, although useful in gaining agreement to a new constitution in the initial transition from authoritarian rule, in the longer term proportional arrangements may serve to reinforce and perpetuate rigid segregation along narrow ethnic-cultural, religious, and linguistic cleavages rather than promoting a few major catch-all parties that gradually facilitate group cooperation within parties. Barkan (1998) argues that the cases of Namibia and South Africa show that parties representing ethnic minorities are not necessarily penalized by majoritarian systems. Taagepera (1998) warns of the dangers of PR producing extreme multipartism and fragmentation, which may promote instability in new democracies. Since much of this work is based on country-specific case studies it remains hard to say how far we can generalize more widely, for example whether power-sharing arrangements in the new South Africa would work if transplanted to Angolan or Nigerian soil, let alone exported further afield to Ukraine or the Balkans. The unintended consequences of electoral reforms, evident even in the cases of relatively similar postindustrial societies such as Italy, Japan, Israel, and New Zealand, illustrate how constitutional engineering remains more art than science (Norris 1995).

The impact on specific and diffuse support for the political system

The last, and perhaps the most controversial and important, claim of consociational theory is that, by facilitating the inclusion of ethnic minority parties into parliament, *PR systems increase ethnic minority support for the political system*. Lijphart argues that political minorities are persistent electoral losers in majoritarian systems and excluded from representative institutions in successive contests, thereby reducing their faith in the fairness of the electoral outcome and eroding their diffuse support for the democratic system in general.

Especially in plural societies—societies that are sharply divided along religious, ideological, linguistic, cultural, ethnic, or racial lines into virtually
separate sub-societies with their own political parties, interest groups, and
media or communication—the flexibility necessary for majoritarian democracy is absent. Under these conditions, majority rule is not only undemocratic but also dangerous, because minorities that are continually denied
access to power will feel excluded and discriminated against and will lose
their allegiance to the regime. (Lijphart 1984: 22–3)

In contrast, under PR, because representatives from ethnic minority parties are incorporated within parliaments and coalition governments, consociational theory assumes that their supporters will
gradually come to feel that they have more of a say in the policy-
making process, so that minorities will become more satisfied with
the fairness of the outcomes of specific contests and more supportive at a diffuse level of the electoral system and the democratic
rules of the game. Under PR, minorities should display more positive attitudes towards the political system because no group that
can mobilize electoral support is systematically excluded from
elected office on a persistent basis. Political leaders will learn to
collaborate within parliaments through deliberation, negotiation,
and compromise—in short, through ballots not bullets—encouraging conciliation between their grass-roots supporters.

But there is little direct evidence about the impact of electoral
systems on cultural attitudes, such as satisfaction with democracy and support for the political system. Census data about the
electorate can be aggregated at district or regional level to analyze
ethnic minority voting patterns; for example, Horowitz (1991; 1993)
used this approach to examine the election results in Guyana,
Trinidad, Congo, Ghana, and India. Blais and Carty (1990) compared over 500 elections across 20 nations to demonstrate greater
voter participation in PR than in majoritarian electoral systems.
The main drawback with aggregate data is that we cannot establish
how minority groups felt about the available electoral choices or the
fairness of the electoral system (Mattes and Gouws 1999). If
the rules of the game mean that some groups are systematically
organized into politics and others are systematically organized out,
ideally we need to understand not just how groups voted but also
how they regard democracy and the political system.

Some light on this issue has been shed by a study by Anderson
and Guillory (1997) that compared satisfaction with democracy
among consensual and majoritarian political systems in eleven
European Union member states. They hypothesized (1) that system
support would be consistently influenced by whether people were

among the winners and losers in electoral contests, defined by whether the party they supported was returned to government; and (2) that this process would be mediated by the type of democracy. The study found that, in majoritarian democracies, winners expressed far higher satisfaction with democracy than losers, whereas consociational systems produced a narrower gap between winners and losers. This approach is valuable but it is confined to Western Europe, it does not allow us to distinguish many national-level factors that may co-vary with the political systems in these nations such as their historical culture and traditions, nor does it allow us to distinguish the impact of electoral systems per se from other institutional variables.

Expanding upon Anderson and Guillory, in an earlier study I examined the impact of electoral systems upon confidence in representative institutions by comparing a wider range of 25 established and new democracies, using the 1990–93 World Values Survey. Using regression models controlling for social background, levels of democratization, and socio-economic development, the study found that, contrary to expectation, institutional confidence was generally higher among respondents living in countries using majoritarian rather than PR electoral systems.[11] In an alternative approach, using a single-national 1993–6 panel study, Banducci, Donovan, and Karp (1999) tested whether the move from a majoritarian to a proportional electoral system in New Zealand produced more positive attitudes towards the political system among supporters of minor parties and the Maori population. The study found that, after participating in the first Mixed Member Proportional election, supporters of the minor parties displayed greater increases in political efficacy—they were significantly more likely to see their votes as counting and to see voting as important—than the rest of the electorate, although there was no parallel increase in political trust: 'The lack of change on the main measure of trust in government is particularly striking, suggesting that the roots of distrust in government lie in something other than the rules used to translates votes into seats' (Banducci, Donovan, and Karp 1999).

We can conclude that consociational theory makes strong claims for the virtues of PR in plural societies. Lijphart argues that consociational power-sharing arrangements, and particularly highly proportional PR electoral systems with low thresholds, are most

---

[11] Norris (1998*a*: Table 11.3). The social controls included age, gender, socio-economic status and education.

likely to include ethno-political minorities within legislatures and coalition governments, and thereby to promote support for democracy and cooperation between groups in states deeply divided by ethnic conflict. Yet this brief review of the literature suggests that the direct support for these claims remains limited. The most convincing and systematic evidence, demonstrated in successive studies, concerns the impact of electoral systems upon the proportionality of the outcome and upon the inclusion of smaller parties within parliaments. In turn, under certain conditions, the inclusion of smaller parties in PR systems may influence the electoral fortunes of ethnic minority parties. But it remains an open question whether the inclusion of ethnic minority representatives leads to greater diffuse or specific support for the political system among ethnic minorities under PR than majoritarian systems, such as stronger feelings of political efficacy, satisfaction with democracy, and trust in government. To go further we need surveys measuring support for the political system among members of different minority communities. In Israel, for example, does the Arab community feel that it can influence the Knesset? In Ukraine, does the Russian-speaking population regard the conduct of elections as free and fair? Do the Hungarian community and Roma—gypsy—groups living in Romania approve of the democratic performance of their political system? Are Basques and Catalans satisfied that their interests are represented through Spanish elections? It is to evidence about these matters that we now turn.

Testing Consociational Theories

To follow this strategy, this study draws on surveys of the electorate in twelve nations based on data from the second release of the Comparative Study of Electoral Systems (CSES).[12] The CSES uses a common module incorporated into cross-sectional post-election national surveys within each country, with, in total, 20,361 respondents, in elections that occurred during 1996–8.

Measuring political support and core hypotheses

What is the best way to measure the concept of 'support for the political system'? Elsewhere, building on the Eastonian framework, I have argued that this is essentially multidimensional and so

---

[12] See n. 3 above.

cannot be tapped reliably using single measures like, for example, political trust. This approach distinguishes between five levels of support ranging from the most abstract and diffuse level measured by support for the political community like the nation-state, down through support for democratic values, for the political regime, for political institutions, and for political actors. In this view, citizens can logically distinguish between levels: for example, trusting their local representative and yet having little confidence in parliament as an institution, or approving of democratic ideals but still criticizing the performance of their government, and so on (Norris 1998*b*).

Following this logic, four alternative indicators of political support were used for the analysis. Specific support was measured by perceptions of the *fairness of the electoral system*: the most direct evaluation of how well the election was seen to work. Responses to this could be expected to be coloured by the outcome of the specific campaign under analysis, for example, by the party that won office. Diffuse support, understood to indicate more general approval of the political system as a whole, was measured by general *satisfaction with the democratic process*. It would remain consistent to approve of the way the last election worked and still to remain dissatisfied with how democracy performed in general, or vice versa. The diffuse sense that citizens could influence the political process was tapped by measures of *political efficacy*. Lastly, *voting turn-out* was compared as a critical indicator of involvement in the specific election. Factor analysis, not reported here, revealed that these items fell into two principal dimensions: the 'approval' dimension meant that perceptions of the fairness of the electoral system were closely related to general satisfaction with democracy, while the 'participation' dimension meant that political efficacy was closely related to electoral turnout. Details of the items used in the analysis are listed under Table 8.4.

Survey evidence provides direct insights into political attitudes such as satisfaction with democracy or feelings of political efficacy, but at the same time it remains difficult to compare ethnic minorities directly across a diverse range of societies. Multiple factors can influence specific and diffuse levels of support for the political system, including perceptions of government performance, cultural values, and general levels of interpersonal trust and social capital, as well as the standard predictors of political attitudes at individual level, such as age, education, class, and gender (Norris 1998*a*). Even with suitable controls, given a limited range of countries it becomes impossible to isolate and disentangle the impact of the electoral system from all these other factors.

Yet what we can compare is the *relative* gap in majority-minority
political support within each nation. Given the existence of social
and political disparities within every democracy, in general we
would expect to find that ethnic minorities would prove more negative than majority populations; for example, that African-
Americans would be more cynical about the fairness of elections
than whites, that Catalans and Basques would be more critical of
the performance of Spanish democracy than other compatriots, that
Arabs would feel more powerless to influence Israeli politics than
the Jewish population, and so on. Therefore the first core hypothesis
is that within each country, *ethnic majorities will express greater
support than minorities for the political system.* Support can be
measured by attitudes towards the fairness of particular election
outcomes as well as more diffuse indicators such as satisfaction
with democracy, political efficacy, and voting turn-out. Focusing on
relative differences between groups within a country holds cross-
national variations constant.

Based on this process, as a second step we can then examine relative differences in political support among majority and minority
populations under different electoral systems. If consociational theories are correct in their assumption that ethnic minorities feel that
the political system is fairer and more inclusive of their interests
under proportional representation, then the second core hypothesis
is that *we would expect to find that relative majority-minority
differences would be smaller in countries with PR rather than
majoritarian electoral rules.* In contrast, if we find that the majority-minority gap in political support is as great under PR as under
majoritarian systems, this would favour the null hypothesis.

Classifying types of electoral systems

Electoral systems can be classified into four main types, each
including a number of sub-categories: *majoritarian* systems, including plurality, second ballot, and alternative voting systems; *semi-
proportional* systems such as the single transferable vote, the
cumulative vote, and the limited vote; *proportional representation*,
including open and closed party lists using largest remainders and
highest averages formula; and *mixed* systems, as in Taiwan and
Ukraine, combining majoritarian and proportional elements.[13]
Worldwide about half of all countries and territories use majori-

---

[13] For a discussion of 'mixed systems', see Massicotte and Blais (1999).

tarian electoral systems while one-third use proportional party lists, and the remainder are semi-proportional or mixed (see Table 8.1). As discussed earlier, the way these systems translate votes into seats varies according to a number of key dimensions; the most important concern district magnitude, ballot structures, effective thresholds, malapportionment, assembly size, and the use of open as opposed to closed lists. Within PR systems, for example, the combination of a national constituency and low minimum vote threshold allows the election of far more parties in Israel than in Poland, which has a high threshold and multiple constituencies. Moreover, electoral laws, broadly defined, regulate campaigns in numerous ways which fall outside the scope of this study, from the administration of voting facilities to the provision of political broadcasts, the rules of campaign funding, the drawing of constituency boundaries, the citizenship qualifications for the franchise, and the legal requirements for candidate nomination.

At present the CSES data-set compares elections to the lower house in 1996–8 in three majoritarian systems, including first past the post in the United States and Britain and the alternative vote in Australia. Six of the nations have PR based on party lists including Spain, Israel, Poland, Romania, New Zealand, and the Czech Republic. Three have mixed systems using different formulas, including Ukraine, Lithuania, and Taiwan. There are important differences in electoral systems within each category, summarized in Table 8.2, for example in the ballot structure of first past the post in Britain and the alternative vote in Australia, in the proportion of single-member districts and party-list members elected in mixed systems, as well as in level of electoral thresholds facing minor parties. The Annex briefly summarizes the electoral systems used in each country and the results in the specific elections under comparison. The comparative framework provides analysis of all the major categories of electoral system with the exception of semi-proportional systems.

Measuring the primary ethnic cleavage

'Ethnicity' is one of the most complex and elusive terms to define and measure clearly. As mentioned earlier, ethnic identities are understood in this study as social constructs with deep cultural and psychological roots based on linguistic, ethnic, racial, regional, or religious backgrounds. They provide an affective sense of belonging and are socially defined in terms of their meaning for the actors. In Bulmer's (1986) words:

Pippa Norris

TABLE 8.1: *Worldwide comparison of electoral systems, 1997–1998*

Type of system	All countries and territories		Established democracies		Free countries		Not free countries	
	N	%	N	%	N	%	N	%
Block vote	211	100	11	100	98	100	46	100
FPTP	70	33	11	31	35	36	17	37
List PR	67	32	15	42	39	40	10	22
2nd ballot	31	15	1	3	7	7	11	24
Parallel	20	9	1	3	5	5	5	11
Block vote	10	5	1	3	3	3	3	7
MMP	7	3	4	11	4	4	0	0
AV	2	1	1	3	2	2	0	0
SNTV	2	1	0	0	1	1	0	0
STV	2	1	2	6	2	2	0	0
Total	211	100	36	100	98	100	46	100

Notes: Established democracies as categorized by Arend Lijphart (1999). Lijphart includes all countries considered democratic now, and for the last 20 years, with a population of at least a quarter of a million people. 'Free' and 'Not free' classifications from Freedom House (1997). FPTP, first past the post; List PR, proportional representation; 2nd ballot; Parallel; Block Vote; MMP, mixed member proportional; AV, alternative vote; SNTV, Single non-transferable vote; STV, single transferable vote.

Source: http://www.aceproject.org/

TABLE 8.2: *Electoral systems for the lower house in selected countries under comparison*

	Year of election	Electoral system	Formula	Threshold %	Total N. of members	N. of SMD MPs	N. of List MPs	Total number of districts for lists	Voting-age population (VAP)	Average VAP per member	Prop.	ENPP	Max. years between elections
Majoritarian													
USA	1996	FPTP	Plurality	None	435	435			196,511,000	436,691	0.94	1.99	2
UK	1997	FPTP	Plurality	None	659	659			45,093,510	68,426	0.80	2.11	5
Australia	1996	AV	Majority	None	148	148			13,547,920	91,540	0.84	2.57	3
Mixed													
Taiwan	1996	SNTV+PR	LR-Hare	5	334	234/58	100	2	14,340,580	42,935	0.95	2.46	4
Ukraine	1998	FPTP+PR	LR-Hare	4	450	225	225	1	38,939,136	86,531	0.86	5.98	5
Lithuania	1998	2nd ballot+PR	LR-Hare	5	141	71	70	1	2,751,320	19,512	0.76	3.32	4
Proportional													
New Zealand	1996	FPTP+PR	St Laguë	5	120	65	55	1	2,571,840	21,432	0.96	3.78	4
Poland	1997	PR Lists	D'Hondt	7	460		460	52	27,901,720	60,656	0.82	2.95	4
Romania	1996	PR Lists	D'Hondt	3	343		343	42	16,737,320	48,796	0.82	3.37	4
Czech Rep	1996	PR Lists	LR-Droop	5	200		200	8	7,859,160	39,296	0.89	4.15	4
Spain	1996	PR Lists	D'Hondt	3	350		350	50	31,013,030	88,608	0.93	2.73	4
Israel	1996	PR Lists	D'Hondt	1.5	120		120	1	3,684,850	30,707	0.96	5.63	5

Notes: PR, proportional representation; FPTP, first past the post; AV, alternative vote; SMD, single member districts; List, party list; ENPP, effective number of political parties. For the measures of proportionality and ENPP, see Table 8.6. Note this classification distinguishes between NZ MMP where the outcome depends upon the proportion of votes cast in the party lists and mixed systems used in Taiwan, Ukraine, and Lithuania where the single member districts and party lists operate independently and in parallel.

Sources: Successive volumes of *Electoral Studies*; Richard Rose, Munro, and Mackie (1998): http://www.aceproject.org/

An 'ethnic group' is a collectivity within a larger society, having real or putative common ancestry, memories of a shared past, and a cultural focus on one or more symbolic elements which define the group's identity, such as kinship, religion, language, shared territory, nationality or physical appearance. Members of an ethnic group are conscious of belonging to the group.[14]

Table 8.3 shows the distribution of the ethnic minority populations in the countries under comparison. The ethno-national category classified respondents by their place of birth in all countries except Britain, Spain, and the Czech Republic, where this was measured by residency in regions with strong national identities like Scotland and Catalonia. The ethno-racial category in the US and Britain was based on racial self-identification. In the third category, the distribution of ethno-linguistic minorities was measured according to the language usually spoken at home.[15] The linguistic cleavage produced the strongest divisions in Ukraine, which was equally divided between Ukrainian-speaking and Russian-speaking households; Taiwan, where there were sizeable minorities speaking Chinese Mandarin and Chinese Hakka; and Israel, with its Arab population and Russian émigré groups, with Britain emerging as the most homogeneous population in its dominant language. Ethno-religious minorities were measured by the respondent's religious identity, with Australia, the Czech Republic, New Zealand, Britain, and the US the most heterogeneous, and Romania and Poland the most homogeneous, societies. It should be noted that this classification does not attempt to measure the strength of religiosity in the society or the 'distance' between religious faiths, for example, between Jewish and Muslim, both of which would increase the intensity of religious differences. The last category taps the centre-periphery cleavage classifying countries by the proportion in rural areas.

One consequence of their social construction is that the distinctions used to differentiate ethnic identities, and the political salience of ethnic cleavages, vary from one society to another. This greatly complicates the comparative analysis since we need to be sensitive to the particular conditions in each society, for example, the role of race in the United States, regional-national divisions in Britain and Spain, or the critical importance of religion in Israel.

[14] In contrast 'race', based on how members of society perceive group physical differences such as skin colour, can be regarded as a sub-set of broader ethnic identities.

[15] It is unfortunate that the merged National Election Study data do not appear to define the Hispanic population in the United States.

The relevant cleavages based on divisions of ethnic identity, race, language, region, or religion varied in the different countries under comparison. After examining the distribution of different social cleavages in the societies under comparison, as a first step to simplify the patterns under comparison it was decided to focus the analysis in this study upon groups selected as *the most politically salient majority-minority ethnic cleavage within each country* (see Table 8.4). For consistent comparison the aim was to identify the functionally equivalent groups across nations. Groups were selected based on the broader literature on ethnic cleavages in the electorate in each country and also based on scrutiny of the strongest cleavages predicting political support within each nation within the CSES data.

In three cases the primary ethnic cleavage was defined by language, namely, Mandarin Chinese- and Hakka-speaking minorities in Taiwan; the Russian-speaking versus Ukrainian-speaking populations in Ukraine; and the Hungarian-speaking population in Romania. In two cases it was defined by country of origin, namely, the Maori versus European populations in New Zealand and the Lithuanian versus Russian-Polish communities in Lithuania. In three cases the major cleavages was based on region, including the Basque, Galician, and Catalan minorities in Spain; the Bohemian versus Moravian communities in the Czech republic; and the Scots and Welsh versus the English in Britain. Racial identities were used in the United States to distinguish the white versus the African-American and Asian populations. In two nations, Poland and Australia, the main centre-periphery cleavage was based on rural versus non-rural populations. Lastly, religion proved the primary cleavage distinguishing the Arab versus Jewish populations in Israel. In some nations the cleavages were reinforcing, for example, the Hungarian population in Romania and the Arabs in Israel proved distinctive in terms of their country of origin, language, and religion. In some other nations there were two distinct and independent types of ethnic cleavages, for example, in Britain the main racial cleavage concerns the Asian and Afro-Caribbean minorities, estimated to be about 2.9 per cent of the electorate, and the centre-periphery cleavage dividing Scotland and Wales from England (see Table 8.3). The study excluded the separate scrutiny of single groups below 5 per cent of the population where there were too few cases for reliable analysis. Subsequent research will develop this further by comparing majority-minority differences across the full range of ethnic identities.

TABLE 8.3: *Major types of ethnic cleavages*

Ethno-national	% majority		%minority ethno-national groups							
Czech Rep (ii)	Czech	94.9	Moravian	1.8	Roma	1.2	Other	2.1		
Romania (ii)	Romanian	92.0	Hungarian	5.6	Roma (Gypsy)	1.4	Other	1.0		
Britain (i)	English	85.7	Scottish	9.1	Welsh	5.2				
Lithuania (ii)	Lithuanian	85.2	Russian	6.9	Pole	5.8	Other	2.1		
New Zeal. (ii)	NZ European	81.6	Maori	14.4	Asian	1.4	Other	2.6		
Spain (i)	Others	78.9	Catalans	15.8	Pais Vasco (Basque)	5.3				
Australia (ii)	Australian	77.8	European	16.6	Asian	3.0	Other	2.6		
Taiwan (ii)	Min Nan	75.2	Hakka	11.5	Mainlanders	12.5	Other	0.8		
Ukraine (ii)	Ukrainian	72.4	Russian	24.6	Other	3.0				
Czech Rep (i)	Bohemians	62.4	Moravians	37.6						
Israel (ii)	Jewish-Israeli	54.5	Jewish-European	20.1	Arab	14.2	Jewish-Asia	6.0	Jewish-Africa	4.5

Ethno-racial	% majority		% minority ethno-racial groups					
Britain	White	97.1	Indian/Asian	1.6	Other	1.3		
US	White	86.2	African-American	11.2	Asian	1.4	Other	1.2

Ethno-linguistic (iii)	% majority		% minority ethno-linguistic groups					
Britain	English	97.8	Other	2.2				
Romania	Romanian	93.6	Hungarian	5.0	Other	1.4		
New Zealand	English	84.9	Maori	9.1	Other	6.0		
Spain	Spanish	82.6	Catalan	10.6	Galician	5.4	Basque	1.4
Israel	Hebrew	73.6	Arabic	15.0	Russian	10.9		
Taiwan	Min Nan	67.3	Mandarin	28.1	Hakka	4.3		
Ukraine	Russian	50.4	Ukrainian	49.6				

Ethno-religious (iv)	% majority		% minority ethno-religious groups							
Poland	Catholic	97.1	Other	2.9						
Romania	Orthodox	89.1	Protestant	6.3	Other	1.7				
Israel	Jewish	87.0	Muslim	9.6	Christian	2.2				
Taiwan	Confucianism	71.4	Buddhism	8.4	None	8.6	Taoism	6.8	I-Kuan-Tao	1.8
Ukraine	Orthodox	67.4	None	25.8						
US	Protestant	55.5	Catholic	25.2	None	12.4	Jewish	1.9		
Britain	Protestant	54.9	None	32.0	Catholic	10.9				
New Zealand	Protestant	47.6	Catholic	13.3	None	26.3	Other	12.8		
Czech Rep	Catholic	45.3	None	46.7	Protestant	3.8				
Australia	Protestant	43.5	Catholic	28.6	None	15.8				

Centre-periphery (v)	% majority		% minority rural groups	
Australia	Urban	76	Rural	24
Poland	Urban	64	Rural	36

Notes: The figures represent the proportion of each group in the adult population (of voting age). Only groups over 1% are reported. Note that this survey was of the British electorate, not the UK, and therefore does not include respondents from Northern Ireland. (i) Based on place of birth. (ii) Based on standard regional classifications. (iii) Ethnic-linguistic cleavages are based on the main language spoken at home. (iv) Under religion, 'None' includes atheists and agnostics. (v) Urban includes small town, suburbs, or large town/city.

Source: Comparative Study of Electoral Systems 1996–98.

TABLE 8.4: *Indicators of majority-minority political support*

State	Major cleavage	Minority	Majority	Diff.	Sig.	Primary minority group	Elec sys.
Election fair		*% fair*	*% fair*				
Israel	Religion	52	15	30	**	Arabs/Muslims	PR
Spain	Region	92	79	12	*	Catalans, Galicians, Basques	PR
Czech Rep	Region	83	80	3		Moravians	PR
US	Racial	74	76	-1		Non-Whites	Maj
Britain	Region	79	81	-3	*	Scots/Welsh	Maj
Poland	Centre-periphery	70	73	-4	*	Rural	PR
Taiwan	Linguistic	58	64	-6	*	Mandarin/Hakka	Mixed
Ukraine	Linguistic	33	41	-8	*	Russians	Mixed
New Zealand	Ethnicity	71	80	-9	**	Maoris	PR
Romania	Linguistic	72	82	-10	*	Hungarians	PR
Lithuania	Ethnicity	39	58	-20	**	Russians/Poles	Mixed
Satisfaction with democracy		*% satisfied*	*% satisfied*				
Israel	Religion	58	53	5		Arabs/Muslims	PR
Lithuania	Ethnicity	34	35	-1		Russians/Poles	Mixed
Ukraine	Linguistic	9	10	-1		Russians	Mixed
Australia	Centre-periphery	72	80	-8	*	Rural	Maj
Britain	Region	69	78	-9	**	Scots/Welsh	Maj
Poland	Centre-periphery	57	66	-10	**	Rural	PR
New Zealand	Ethnicity	62	72	-10	**	Maoris	PR
US	Racial	72	82	-10	*	Non-Whites	Maj
Taiwan	Linguistic	40	51	-10	**	Mandarin/Hakka	Mixed
Spain	Region	48	64	-15	**	Catalans, Galacians, Basques	PR
Romania	Linguistic	28	45	-17	**	Hungarians	PR
Czech Rep	Region	42	62	-20	**	Moravians	PR

Political efficacy		% high	% high			
Taiwan	Linguistic	60	49	11 **	Mandarin/Hakka	Mixed
Ukraine	Linguistic	80	75	6 *	Russians	Mixed
Britain	Region	76	76	0	Scots/Welsh	Maj
Israel	Religion	15	17	−2	Arabs/Muslims	PR
Australia	Centre-periphery	67	70	−3	Rural	Maj
Czech Rep	Region	81	86	−5	Moravians	PR
US	Racial	64	72	−8	Non-Whites	Maj
Poland	Centre-periphery	69	76	−8	Rural	PR
New Zealand	Ethnicity	70	79	−9 **	Maoris	PR
Romania	Linguistic	61	71	−10 *	Hungarians	PR
Lithuania	Ethnicity	57	68	−11 *	Russians/Poles	Mixed
Spain	Region	59	71	−11 *	Catalans, Galicians, Basques	PR

Voting turnout (%)		% voted	% voted			
Romania	Linguistic	91	88	3	Hungarians	PR
Australia	Centre-periphery	95	95	0	Rural	Maj
Britain	Region	82	83	−1	Scots/Welsh	Maj
Taiwan	Linguistic	91	92	−2	Mandarin/Hakka	Mixed
Czech Rep	Region	86	90	−4	Moravians	PR
New Zealand	Ethnicity	92	96	−4 **	Maoris	PR
Ukraine	Linguistic	74	80	−7 **	Russians	Mixed
US	Racial	68	78	−10 **	Non-Whites	Maj
Spain	Centre-periphery	80	90	−11 **	Catalans, Galacians, Basques	PR
Poland	Rural	51	61	−10 **	Rural	PR
Israel	Religion	67	86	−18 **	Arabs/Muslims	PR

over /

Notes to Table 8.4: The difference represents the majority minus the minority. The significance of the difference between groups was tested with correlation coefficients. ** = p.01 * = p.05.

Fairness of election: *Q2. In some countries, people believe that their elections are conducted fairly. In other countries, people believe that their elections are conducted unfairly. Thinking of the last election in [country], where would you place it on this scale of one to five where ONE means that the last election was conducted fairly and FIVE means that the last election was conducted unfairly?* Percentage who believed election was fair (defined as categories 1 and 2).

Satisfaction with democracy: *Q1. 'On the whole, are you very satisfied, fairly satisfied, not very satisfied, or not at all satisfied with the way democracy works in [country]?'* The figures represent the percentage 'very' or 'fairly' satisfied.

Political efficacy: The 15-point political efficacy scale was constructed from the following items that were highly inter-correlated. 'High' efficacy was categorized as a total score of 8 or above.

Q11. (PLEASE SEE CARD 5) 'Some people say that members of [Congress / Parliament] know what ordinary people think. Others say that members of [Congress / Parliament] don't know much about what ordinary people think. Using the scale on this card, (where ONE means that the members of [Congress / Parliament] know what ordinary people think, and FIVE means that the members of [Congress / Parliament] don't know much about what ordinary people think), where would you place yourself?'

Q13. (PLEASE SEE CARD 6) 'Some people say it makes a difference who is in power. Others say that it doesn't make a difference who is in power. Using the scale on this card, (where ONE means that it makes a difference who is in power and FIVE means that it doesn't make a difference who is in power), where would you place yourself?'

Q14. (PLEASE SEE CARD 7) 'Some people say that no matter who people vote for, it won't make any difference to what happens. Others say that who people vote for can make a difference to what happens. Using the scale on this card, (where ONE means that voting won't make a difference to what happens and FIVE means that voting can make a difference), where would you place your-self?'

Turnout: The question measured whether the respondent cast a ballot in the election. Functionally equivalent but not identical items were used in each national election survey.

Source: Comparative Study of Electoral Systems 1996–8.

Analysis of Results

The first step in the analysis is to examine the relative difference between the majority and the minority populations in terms of the four alternative indicators of support for the political system. The results in Table 8.4 describe the percentage distribution of support, the percentage difference between majority and minority groups ranked by size, and the significance of the difference examined through simple correlations without any controls. Where the difference is in a positive direction, this indicates that the minority were more supportive than the majority. Where the difference is in a negative direction, this indicates the reverse. In most cases the results confirm the first hypotheses, namely, that where there were significant differences, the majority groups tended to prove consistently more positive towards the political system than minorities. In many cases the gap was substantively large, for example, there was far greater dissatisfaction with democracy among the Catalans, Galicians, and Basques in Spain, among the Hungarians in Romania, and among the Moravians in the Czech Republic. In five countries there was no significant difference in turn-out, but in six countries levels of voting turn-out were consistently lower for ethnic minorities such as among Arabs in Israel and the rural population in Poland. In only a few cases was there significant indication of greater political support among minority than majority populations, notably, assessments of electoral fairness in Israel and Spain, and also higher levels of political efficacy among minority populations in Taiwan and Ukraine. If we compare all types of political support, it is apparent that, compared with majority populations, minorities proved more positive on only 4 out of 47 indicators. In all the other cases either the gap was statistically insignificant or minorities proved more critical of the political system.

The second proposition was that the majority-minority gap would be related to the type of electoral system that operated in each country. Consociational theory suggests that ethnic minorities would prove most critical of the political system where they were systematically excluded from power due to a majoritarian electoral system. Yet the pattern established in Table 8.4 proves too complex to confirm this proposition. Evaluations of the fairness of elections can be regarded as the most direct support for the electoral system per se. On this indicator, it is apparent that the ethnic minority-majority gap is indeed reversed in Israel and Spain, both using PR.

Nevertheless, minorities under PR systems in Romania, New Zealand, and Poland proved far more negative than majorities by this measure.

In addition there was no consistent pattern across indicators. For example, when evaluating the performance of democracy in their country, understood as a more diffuse indicator of political support, minorities proved most critical in the PR nations of Spain, Romania, and the Czech Republic. Similarly, mixed patterns, unrelated to the type of electoral system, were evident in terms of the majority-minority gaps on political efficacy and voting turn-out. The analysis shows that there is no simple and clear-cut picture relating the type of electoral system directly to differences in majority-minority political support. The claims of consociational theory are not supported by this evidence, favouring the null hypothesis.

To examine this pattern further, a series of regression models was run in each country predicting levels of political support for majority-minority population, adding social controls for the age, education, and income of respondents. A positive coefficient indicates that the majority populations were more supportive than minority populations. Insignificant coefficients indicate no difference between majority and minorities. A negative coefficient indicates that the minorities were more supportive than the majority.

The results in Table 8.5 show few significant differences in minority political support in Australia, Britain, and the United States, all with majoritarian electoral systems. The only exceptions were the Scots and the Welsh, who proved slightly more critical of the fairness of the election and of British democracy, a pattern that could be explained at least in part by the heightened salience of the issue of devolution in the 1997 general election. In the countries using mixed electoral systems, the ethnic minority groups tended to be less satisfied with democracy and less convinced about the fairness of the election outcomes. Out of eleven regression models, majorities were more positive than minorities in six models, and the reverse pattern was evident in only two models.

Lastly, in the countries using PR, in the 24 separate regression models where there was a significant majority-minority difference, minorities were more critical of the political system in 14 cases, and the pattern was reversed only in two cases: perceptions of electoral fairness in Israel and Spain, noted earlier. Across all four indicators the Maori population proved consistently more critical of their political system, as did the Hungarian population in Romania, and a similar pattern was evident on three indicators for the Catalan and Basque populations in Spain. The evidence here fails to support the

TABLE 8.5: *Impact of majority-minority cleavage on political support, with social controls*

	Main cleavage		Electoral fairness Beta	Sig	Democratic satisfaction Beta	Sig	Political efficacy Beta	Sig	Voting turnout Beta	Sig
Australia	Centre periphery	Rural	N/A		0.035		0.005		−0.038	
Britain	Regional	Scots/Welsh	0.041	**	0.077	***	−0.012	***	0.000	
US	Racial	Non-White	−0.027		0.033		0.013		0.013	
Lithuania	Ethnic	Russian/Pole	0.133	***	0.027		0.060	*	N/A	
Taiwan	Linguistic	Mandarin/Hakka	−0.016		0.061	*	−0.061	*	0.005	
Ukraine	Linguistic	Russian	0.061	*	0.060	*	−0.057	*	0.088	**
CzechRep	Regional	Moravia	−0.003		0.110	***	0.012	***	0.007	
NZ	Racial	Maori	0.079	***	0.094	***	0.075	**	0.067	***
Israel	Religious	Muslim	−0.295	***	0.041		0.053	*	0.169	***
Poland	Centre-periphery	Rural	0.027		0.048		0.013		0.013	
Romania	Linguistic	Hungarian	0.077	***	0.095	***	0.040	*	0.092	**
Spain	Regional	Catalan/Basque	−0.068	**	0.071		0.091	***	0.123	***

Notes: These figures represent standardized regression coefficients for the effects of majority-minority membership of the main ethnic group within each country on the four indicators of support for the political system after controlling for age (years), gender (0 = female, 1 = male), standardized household income (5-point scale) and education (8-point scale). All models use OLS regression except for turnout that uses logistic regression. For the scaling of the dependent variables see the notes to Table 8.4. Significant positive coefficients indicate that majority populations are more supportive of the political system than minorities. Insignificant coefficients indicate that there is no difference between majority and minority populations. Negative coefficients indicate that the minority population is more supportive of the political system than majorities.

Source: Comparative Study of Electoral Systems 1996–8

consociational claims, which have to be regarded as unproven by this analysis.

Conclusions and Discussion

The issue of the most effective institutional design for managing ethnic tensions has risen in salience in the late twentieth century. The rules of the electoral system, for many decades accepted as stable and immutable, have become increasingly politicized. The wave of constitution-building following the surge of newer democracies in the early 1990s generated a series of negotiations about electoral laws that needed to be resolved before other constitutional issues could be settled. After the first elections, far from being settled, the consolidation process has frequently seen continued adjustments in electoral regulations, such as in threshold levels, the use of electoral formula, and the size of legislative bodies (Shvetsova 1999). More practical matters of electoral management have also risen in salience for national and international agencies, notably the issues of the prevention of electoral fraud, intimidation and corruption, voter registration, polling day administration, and ballot counting, campaign finance regulation, and 'free and fair' access to political broadcasting in transitional democracies.[16]

Major reforms in established democracies have also challenged the notion that electoral systems are stable. In most Western democracies, once the great debate about the universal franchise was resolved and the mass party system consolidated, electoral systems seemed, for the most part, settled and enduring features of the constitutional landscape. For example, Lijphart's (1994*a*) study of 25 established democracies from 1945 to 1990 found only one— France—had experienced a fundamental change from plurality to PR or vice versa. For an even longer comparison, Bartolini and Mair (1990: 154–5) noted only 14 unbroken transitions in Europe between 1885 and 1985, meaning a major shift in electoral rules between two democratic elections, excluding disruptions caused by wars, dictatorships, the establishment of a new state, or the reappearance of an old one. In Western countries the electoral rules of the game, within which political scientists could get on with analyzing individual-level voting behaviour, appeared settled and predictable. No longer. In the 1990s some established democracies experienced the most radical reforms to electoral systems for over a

---

[16] See, for example, the Ace project at http://www.idea.int.

century (Norris 1995). Out of the 21 countries originally identified by Lijphart (1984) in the mid-1970s as established post-war democracies, Israel, Japan, New Zealand, Britain, and Italy have all experienced major change from majoritarian to PR or vice versa, and more modest amendments have also been adopted in Austria, Portugal, and Switzerland (Katz 1997).

In the debate about constitutional choices there are divisions over the ultimate goals that electoral systems should fulfil as well as disagreements about how far different formulas can best achieve these goals. Proponents of majoritarian systems argue that links between citizens and their elected representatives are strongest in single-member districts, promoting accountability and constituency service through territorial representation, and that the decisive outcome produced by the 'exaggerative bonus' in the electoral systems promotes strong but accountable government. In contrast, proponents of proportional systems commonly respond that PR systems are fairer for minority groups, promoting inclusion and a reduction of ethnic conflict through social representation. As constitutional engineering has become increasingly popular in recent years, it has become even more important to analyze the evidence for these claims.

The strategy in this chapter has been to compare relative levels of satisfaction with the political system among majority-minority populations to determine whether the gap was reduced, or even reversed, under PR party-list systems, as consociational theory suggests. The findings indicate that there is a complex pattern at work here, and *the claim that PR party-list systems are directly associated with higher levels of political support among ethnic minorities is not confirmed by this study.*

Yet it could be argued that the model within this paper is perhaps too simple and there are a number of reasons why any relationship may be conditional and indirect. First, the *territorial distribution* of different ethnic minority groups varies considerably and, as Ordeshook and Shvetsova (1994; see also Horowitz 1991) suggest, geography has a considerable impact on the working of electoral systems. Some populations are clustered tightly in dense *networks* within particular geographic localities with distinct territorial boundaries, like the British Sikh and Bangladeshi communities in the centre of Bràdford, African-Americans living in inner-city Detroit, or the French-speaking population in Montreal. Some are living in *mosaics* where two or more groups are so intermingled within a territory that it is impossible to identify boundaries, such as in Northern Ireland, the South Tyrol, and the Balkans. Other *diasporas* are spread thinly over a wide area across the boundaries of many nation-states, notably the large Russian populations in the 'Near Abroad' such as in Ukraine and Lithuania, the Roma community in central Europe, and the Kurdish population in the Middle East (Budge, Newton *et al.* 1997: 106–7). The geographic dispersion or concentration of support is particularly important for the way votes get translated into seats in elections that require winning a plurality of votes within a particular single-member district, not across the region or whole nation. In British general elections, for example, Plaid Cymru can win seats roughly proportional to their share of the vote because of the heavy concentration of Welsh speakers in a few north coastal Wales constituencies, but, in contrast, the more dispersed Liberal Democratic supporters are heavily penalized by first past the post (Norris and Crewe 1994). African-Americans concentrated in inner city districts can get many more House seats than minorities widely dispersed across legislative districts (Rule and Zimmerman 1994). Territorial clustering allows homogeneous electoral districts representing different groups within heterogeneous societies.

Second, the way that the electoral system shapes ethnic representation can be expected to vary according to the *degree of politicization and mobilization* of ethnic populations into the political system, as well as the *type of cleavages*, whether based on ethnonational, cultural-linguistic, ethno-religious, or racial identities. Some groups represent little more than a formal census categorization which may have little resonance for the common identity of particular groups, like 'Asians' in America bringing together émigrés from diverse cultures in India, Korea, Vietnam, Indonesia, and China; others share a single predominant cleavage, like Hispanic groups in the United States with a common language but drawn from diverse national and political backgrounds; whereas still others like African-Americans are bound together by communities based on their common experience of racial and social inequalities, and a shared historical heritage. As Lijphart (1999: 58) points out, it is misleading to treat demographic classifications as equivalent to political divisions, for example to regard the Protestant-Catholic division in Northern Ireland as on a par to that in Switzerland. Some societies are sharply segmented organizationally into separate sub-cultures, where groups have distinct political organizations, educational facilities, and cultural associations, while others integrate groups into the mainstream culture. Within the countries in this study, certain minorities find organizational expression with parties such as the Hungarian Democratic Party in

Romania, the (Arab) National Democratic Alliance in Israel, the Catalan Nationalist Party in Spain, the Scottish Nationalist Party in Britain, Sinn Féin in Northern Ireland, or the pro-mainland unification New Party in Taiwan.[17] Yet other distinct ethnic groups forward their issue agendas as broader coalitions within mainstream parties, like African-Americans and Hispanics within the Democratic Party. Ethnicity is a particularly difficult concept to operationalize and measure, and single-dimension indicators based on the number and size of ethnic groups in different countries are unsatisfactory unless we can also gauge the geographic distribution and degree of politicization of these groups.[18] As with conceptions of class differentials, there is an important distinction between objective indicators of group membership, such as formal religious affiliations, and subjective consciousness of the political saliency of these group identities, such as religious debates over reproductive rights. Consociational theory assumes that ethno-political identities are given and proportional electoral systems therefore serve to mobilize ethnic parties into the political system. In fact, in the long term there is probably a more complex process of interaction at work whereby potential ethno-political identities are accommodated, but also mobilized and strengthened, by PR systems facilitating their organization and political expression.

Third, *majoritarian systems,* even if they discriminate systematically against smaller parties, *can still make special arrangements for minority representation.* These include the use of reserved seats, for example for scheduled castes and tribes in India, for Maori in New Zealand, and for the aboriginal community in Taiwan. Another option is the over-representation of certain districts or regions to increase the election of minority groups, such as the smaller size of the electoral quota in Scottish electoral districts and affirmative gerrymandering—or redistricting—for African-Americans, Latinos, and Asian Americans in the United States (Grofman and Davidson 1992; Amy 1993). The selection of parliamentary candidates can also be regulated by law or by internal party rules to ensure that minority candidates are chosen for single-member districts or for party lists, for example with the use of quotas or positive action strategies (Lovenduski and Norris 1993); Norris 1997*d*). Lijphart acknowledges that majoritarian electoral systems can make special provision for the inclusion of certain specified ethnic or religious

---

[17] For a comparison of regional parties and their electoral strength in European Union member states, see Hearl, Budge, and Pearson (1996).

[18] See, for example, the measure of the 'effective number of ethnic groups' used by Ordeshook and Shvetsova (1994). See also Amorim Neto and Cox (1997).

groups in parliament, but he argues that highly proportional electoral systems with low thresholds automatically minimize the barriers to office, which has the virtue of being seen as fairer than special provisions for special groups.

PR has the great additional advantage of enabling any minority, not just those specifically favoured by the electoral law, to be represented (as long as they attain a stipulated minimum level of electoral support). Compared with majoritarian systems, PR can be said to have the advantage of permitting representation by minorities that define themselves as groups wishing to have representation as minority parties. PR thus avoids any invidious choices in favour of certain minority groups and, as a consequence, against other minorities. (Lijphart 1994a: 140)

But the existence of alternative strategies implies that constitutional engineers could achieve minority parliamentary representation either through the choice of low-threshold PR systems or through majoritarian systems with deliberate recognition of predetermined minority groups. We need to take such special provisions into account in the analysis.

Lastly, *the electoral system, while important, remains only one component in consociational systems of democracy*. Other institutional arrangements can be expected to prove equally influential in shaping minority views of the political system, such as federal or decentralized designs for regional power-sharing, executive-legislative arrangements including single-party or multi-party coalitional governments, the adoption of parliamentary or presidential systems, and the division of powers between legislative houses, rigid constitutions protecting minority rights and subject to judicial review, and pluralist or corporatist interest-group systems. Nevertheless, consociational theory suggests that PR electoral systems combined with parliamentary government are the fundamental institutions from which many other arrangements flow.

Of course the evidence presented in this study remains limited, in terms of both the range of democracies included within the data-set and the way that ethnic minorities have been defined and operationalized. A broader comparison would increase confidence in the results. If there is a relationship, it may well be one that is more complex and indirect, depending upon intermediary conditions such as the geographical clustering of ethnic minority populations, their levels of politicization as a group, and the relationships between ethnic identities, party systems, and parliamentary representation. Special arrangements, like reserved seats for the aboriginal community in Taiwan or affirmative gerrymandering in the United

States, can overcome some of the barriers facing minority groups within majoritarian electoral systems. We need to take account of how far ethnic minorities see themselves as sharing a common identity with distinct political interests, and how far they believe these interests are represented by parties within the existing power structure. All these factors can be expected to act as intervening variables mediating the links between the electoral institutions and the way minorities perceive the political system. Understanding these issues is a major challenge before we can make any sweeping claims about electoral engineering; and we need to explore this further to understand under what conditions ethnic conflict can be managed most successfully by institutional designs. Nevertheless, given these important qualifications, the idea that more proportional electoral systems *directly* generate greater support for the political system among ethnic minority groups, as consociational theory claims, is not borne out by these results.

Annex: The Electoral Systems Under Comparison

Majoritarian systems

First past the post: The United States and UK   Plurality systems, otherwise known as 'first past the post' (FPTP), were used in the May 1997 British general election and the 1996 United States presidential and congressional elections.[19] The UK is divided into 659 single-member parliamentary constituencies where voters cast a single ballot and MPs are elected on a plurality of votes. In this system the party share of parliamentary seats, not their share of the popular vote, counts for the formation of government. Under FPTP, governments are commonly returned with less than a majority of votes; in 1997 the Labour Party was returned with almost two-thirds of the House of Commons, and a massive parliamentary majority of 179 out of 659 seats, based on 43.3 per cent of the UK vote. As the party in first place, Labour enjoyed a ratio of seats to votes of 1.47, whereas, in contrast, with 30.7 per cent of the vote, the Conservatives gained only 25 per cent of all seats, producing a seats-to-votes ratio of 0.81.

The winner's bonus was also particularly evident in American presidential elections; in 1996 Clinton was returned with 70.4 per

---

[19] For details of these elections see Norris (1997*e*); Evans and Norris (1999); Pomper (1997).

cent of the Electoral College vote based on 50.1 per cent of the popular vote. In 1996 the results for the 435-seat House of Representatives was highly proportional, however, because with two parties FPTP leads to a fairly even shares of votes and of seats. Important differences in the way the British and US systems operate include the number of parties contesting election, the size of the legislatures, the size of the electorate per district, and the maximum number of years between elections (see Table 8.2).

Alternative Vote: Australia The 1996 elections to the House of Representatives used the alternative vote, or 'preferential voting' as it is commonly termed in Australia.[20] This system was introduced for federal elections in 1919 and is now employed in all federal States except Tasmania, which uses the single transferable vote (STV). Australia is divided into 148 single-member constituencies and voters rank their preferences among candidate: 1, 2, 3, and so on. To win, candidates need an absolute majority of votes, not a mere plurality, in a constituency. If no candidate gets over 50 per cent after the first preferences are counted, then the least popular candidate is eliminated, and his or her votes are redistributed according to the second preferences amongst the other candidates. The process continues until an absolute majority for one candidate is secured. In the 1996 Australian elections there was a close call on the first preferences, with both the Australian Labor Party (ALP) and the Liberal-National coalition gaining 38.7 per cent of the vote. In the final preferences, however, the ALP won 46.4 per cent compared with 53.6 per cent for non-ALP candidates. Again, this process translates a close lead into a more decisive majority of seats for the leading party. This systematically discriminates against those at the bottom of the poll in order to promote effective government for the winner.

Proportional systems: Poland, Romania, Czech Republic, Spain, Israel, and New Zealand

Worldwide proportional electoral systems based on party lists in multi-member constituencies are used in 67 out of 211 countries, and in 5 of the countries under comparison.[21] Under party-list PR, parties nominate lists of candidates in multi-member constituencies.

---

[20] For details of the 1996 Australian election see Bean (1997); Bean *et al.* (1997).

[21] For details of these election see Rose, Munro, and Mackie (1998); Deletant and Saini-Davies (1998); Nachmias and Sened (1998); Hazan (1996*a*, *b*).

Voters cast their vote for the party lists and the seats in a constituency are allocated in proportion to the share of the party vote. There are considerable variations in how this is implemented in different countries including the use of open or closed lists of candidates, the formula for translating votes into seats, the level of the electoral threshold, and the size of the district.

Party lists can be open, as in Poland, where voters can express preferences for particular candidates within the list. In contrast, closed lists are used in Israel and Spain, where voters can select only the party, and parties decide the ranking of candidates within the lists, thus determining who enters parliament. In Israel the country is one constituency divided into 120 seats, but often lists are regional, as in the Czech Republic where 200 members are elected in total from 8 regional lists.

The mathematical formula translating votes into seats also varies among PR systems. The most widely used is the *d'Hondt* formula, employed in Poland, Romania, Spain, and Israel, which favours larger parties more than some other systems.[22] The *'pure'* *Saint-Laguë* method, used in New Zealand, is more proportional in its effects. An alternative is the *largest remainder* methods using a minimum quota that can be calculated in a number of ways. With the *Hare quota*, used for the list constituencies in Taiwan, Ukraine, and Lithuania, the total number of valid votes in each constituency is divided by the total number of seats to be allocated. The *Droop quota*, used in the Czech Republic, raises the divisor by the number of seats plus one, producing a slightly less proportional result.

Other important differences in the electoral systems under comparison within the PR category include the threshold that parties must pass to qualify for seats, ranging from the lowest threshold in Israel to up to 7 per cent of the vote in Poland. District magnitude—the mean number of seats per constituency—also varies from Israel, where all 120 members of the Knesset run in one nationwide constituency, to Spain, where the 350 members are elected in 50 list districts, each district electing on average 7 members. Generally, under PR systems the larger the district magnitude, the more proportional the outcome, and the lower the hurdles facing smaller parties.

In this study New Zealand is also classified as 'proportional' since the outcome depends upon the party-list share of the vote. The

---

[22] The d'Hondt formula is a variation on the *highest averages* method which requires the number of votes for each party to be divided successively by a series of divisors, and seats are allocated to parties that secure the highest resulting quotient, up to the total number of seats available.

Mixed Member Proportion (MMP) system used in New Zealand
gives elector's two votes, one for the district candidate and one for
the party list (see Boston *et al.* 1996; Vowles *et al.* 1998). As in
Germany, the list PR seats compensate for any disproportionality
produced by the single-member districts. In total 65 of the 120 members of the House of Representatives are elected in single-member
constituencies based on a simple plurality of votes in single-member
districts. The remainder are elected from closed national party lists.
Parties receiving less than 5 per cent of list votes fall below the minimal threshold to quality for any seats. All other parties are allocated seats based on the Sainte Laguë method, which ensures that
the total allocation of seats is highly proportional to the share of
votes cast for party lists. Smaller parties which received, say, 10 per
cent of the list vote but which did not win any single member seats
outright are topped up until they have 10 per cent of all the seats in
the House of Representatives. The 1996 New Zealand election saw
the entry of six parties into parliament and produced a National-
New Zealand First coalition government. Although defined as mixed
by Massicotte and Blais's (1999) criteria because the outcome
depends upon the party-list share of the vote, the New Zealand MMP
system can also be classified as PR (Lijphart 1999).

Mixed systems: Ukraine, Lithuania, and Taiwan

Lastly, the last three electoral systems under comparison vary substantially but Ukraine, Lithuania, and Taiwan can be classified as
'mixed' following the Reynolds/Lijphart classification, combining
two electoral systems used in parallel.[23]

Taiwan The system used for the March 1996 elections to the
National Assembly in Taiwan was composed of 334 seats, of which
234 were filled by the single non-transferable vote (STNV). Voters
cast a single vote in one of 58 multi-member districts, each with
5–10 seats. The votes of all candidates belonging to the same party
in all districts are aggregated into party votes and the list PR seats
are allocated among those parties meeting the 5 per cent threshold.
There are 80 PR list seats on a nationwide constituency and 20 PR
list seats reserved for the overseas Chinese community. Taiwan has
a three-party system, with the Nationalist Party (KMT) dominant
since 1945, the Democratic Progressive Party (DPP), founded in
1986, providing the main opposition, and the New Party (NP),

[23] It should be noted that Massicotte and Blais (1999) offer a different interpretation whereby New Zealand also falls into this category.

founded in 1993, with the smallest support. The major cleavage in Taiwanese party politics is the issue of national identity, dividing mainlanders who favour reunification with China from many native Taiwanese who favour independence. The NP is commonly considered most pro-unification and the DPP most pro-independence (Hsieh and Niou 1996; Grofman 1997).

Ukraine   The Ukrainian elections of 29 March 1998 were the second parliamentary contests held since Ukrainian independence. The elections used a parallel system whereby voters cast two ballots. Half the deputies were elected by FPTP in single-member districts and the remainder were elected from nationwide party lists, with a 4 per cent threshold. Unlike the system in New Zealand and Germany, the two systems operated separately so that many smaller parties were elected from the single-member districts. The 1998 elections were contested by 30 parties and party blocs, although only 10 of these groups could be said to have a clear programmatic profile and organizational base (Birch 1997; 1998; Birch and Wilson 1999). The Ukrainian result produced both an extremely fragmented and an unstable party system: 8 parties were elected through party lists and 17 won seats through the single-member districts, along with 116 Independents. The result produced the highest effective number of political parties (ENPP)—5.98—in the countries under comparison, and also a fairly disproportional ratio of votes to seats that benefited the larger parties. Ethnicity was reflected in the appeal of particular parties, including the Russophile Social Liberal Union, Party of Regional Revival, and the Soyuz (Union) Party, and also in the way that ethnic Russians were twice as likely to support the Communist Party as ethnic Ukrainians (Birch and Wilson 1999).

Lithuania   The single-chamber Seimas has 141 members elected for a four-year term. In the 1996 Seimas elections 71 members were elected in single-member districts by absolute majority with a second round run-off between the two leading candidates if there was no first-round majority. The remaining 70 members were elected by PR from closed party lists using the Largest Remainder-Hare formula, with a 5 per cent threshold for single parties and a 7 per cent threshold for party coalitions. As a result, 5 main parties entered parliament—14 parties in total—plus 4 independent candidates. Homeland Union on the right was the clear victor, doubling its share of seats and achieving an overall parliamentary majority, while the ex-communist Democratic Labour government lost seats and power (Krupavicius 1997; Rose, Munro, and Mackie 1998).

TABLE 8.6: *Results of elections to the lower house of parliament*

Date of election	Parties	ENPP	Prop	% vote	N. seats	% seats	Seats:
Majoritarian							
USA							
5 Nov 1996	Democrat			48.7	197	45.4	0.93
House of Reps	Republicans			48.6	236	54.4	**1.12**
	Other			2.7	1	0.2	0.07
	Total	1.99	.94	*100*	*435*	*100*	
UK							
1 May 1997	Labour			43.3	419	63.6	**1.47**
House of	Conservatives			30.7	165	25.0	0.81
Commons	Liberal Democrats			16.8	46	7.0	0.42
	Scottish National			2.0	6	0.9	0.45
	Plaid Cymru			0.5	4	0.6	**1.20**
	Other			6.8	19	2.9	0.42
	Total	2.11	80	*100*	*659*	*100*	
Australia							
2 Mar 1996	Liberal Party			39.0	76	51.3	**1.31**
House of Reps	Australian Labor Party			38.8	49	33.1	0.85
	National Party			8.2	18	12.1	**1.47**
	Australian Democrats			6.8	0	0	
	Others			7.7	5	3.4	0.44
	Total	2.57	84	*100*	*148*	*100*	
Mixed							
Taiwan							
23 Mar 1996	Nationalist Party (KMT)			49.7	183	54.8	**1.10**
National	Democratic Progressive Party						
Assembly	(DPP)			29.8	99	29.6	0.99
	New Party (NP)			13.7	46	13.8	**1.00**
	Other			6.8	6	1.8	0.26
	Total	2.46	95	*100*	*334*	*100*	

Ukraine — 29 Mar 1998 — Verkhovna Rada

Party	Votes (%)	Seats	Seats (%)	S/V ratio
Communist	20.7	122	27.1	**1.31**
Independents	25.8	116	25.7	0.99
Rukh	7.8	46	10.2	**1.31**
Socialist-rural	5.4	34	7.6	**1.36**
Popular Democrats	5.2	29	6.4	**1.23**
Hromada	3.9	23	5.1	**1.30**
Progressive Socialist	2.5	16	3.5	**1.40**
Greens	2.7	19	4.2	**1.55**
Social Democrats	2.7	17	3.8	**1.40**
Agrarians	3.6	8	1.8	0.50
National Front	2.5	5	1.1	0.44
Reforms and Order	2.2	3	0.6	0.27
Forward Ukraine	1.3	2	0.4	0.30
Christian Democrats	1.1	2	0.4	0.36
Party of Regional Revival	0.9	2	0.4	0.44
Razom	1.2	1	0.2	0.16
NEP	0.8	1	0.2	0.25
Fewer Words	0.3	1	0.2	0.66
Working Ukraine	1.7	1	0.2	0.11
Social Liberal Union	0.7	1	0.2	0.28
Soyuz	0.6	1	0.2	0.33
Total	*100*	*450*	*100*	
	5.98	*86*		

Lithuania — 20 Oct 1996 — Seimas

Party	Votes (%)	Seats	Seats (%)	S/V ratio
Homeland Union	31.3	70	51.1	**1.63**
Christian Democrats	10.4	16	11.7	**1.12**
Social Democrats	6.9	12	8.8	**1.27**
Center Movement	8.7	13	9.5	**1.09**
Democratic Labor	10.0	12	8.8	0.88
Lithuanian Poles	3.1	1	0.7	0.22
National Union	2.2	3	2.2	**1.00**
Freedom League	1.0	0	0	
Progress Movement	0.3	0	0	

TABLE 8.6: (cont.)

Date of election	Parties	ENPP	Prop	% vote	N. seats	% seats	Seats:
	Liberty Union			1.6	0	0	
	Christian Democrat Union			3.2	1	0.7	0.21
	Young Lithuania			4.0	1	0.7	0.18
	Women's Party			3.9	1	0.7	0.18
	National Minorities			2.6	0	0	
	Liberal Union			1.9	1	0.7	0.37
	Peasants' Party			1.7	1	0.7	0.42
	Russian Union			1.7	0	0	
	Prisoners and Deportees			1.6	1	0.7	0.43
	Economy Party			1.3	0	0	
	Others			2.5	4	2.9	**1.16**
	Total	*3.32*	*76*	*100*	*137*	*100*	
PR Lists							
New Zealand	12 Oct 1996 House of Representatives						
	National			33.8	44	36.6	**1.08**
	Labour			28.2	37	30.8	**1.09**
	New Zealand First			13.3	17	14.1	**1.06**
	Alliance			10.1	13	10.8	**1.07**
	ACT			6.1	8	6.6	**1.08**
	United			0.9	1	0.8	0.88
	Others			7.6			
	Total	*3.78*	*96*	*100*	*120*	*100*	
Poland	21 Sept 1997 Sejm						
	Electoral Action Solidarity/AWS			33.8	201	43.7	**1.29**
	Democratic Left Alliance			27.1	164	35.7	**1.31**
	Democratic/Freedom Union			13.4	60	13.0	0.97
				7.3	27	5.9	0.80

			Vote %	Seats	Seat %	Ratio
Polish Peasant Party			4.7	0	0	
Union of Labour			2.0	2	0.4	0.20
Realpolitik Union			5.6	6	1.3	0.23
Movement for Reconstruction of Poland			2.2			
National Pensioners' Party			1.6	0		
National Alliance of Pensioners			1.4	0		
National Christian Bloc			0.9	0		
Others				0		
Total	2.95	82	100	460	100	
Romania — 3 May 1996 Chamber of Deputies						
Democratic Convention of Romania			30.2	122	40.2	1.33
Democratic National Salvation Front			21.5	91	30.0	1.39
Social Democratic Union			12.9	53	17.5	1.36
Hungarian Democratic Union			6.6	25	8.3	1.25
Greater Romania Party			4.5	19	6.3	1.40
Romanian National Unity Party			4.4	18	5.9	1.34
Socialist Party			2.3			
Socialist Labor Party			2.1			
National Liberal Alliance			1.6			
Pensioners' Party			1.4			
Romanian Socialist Workers Party			1.7			
Total	3.37	82	100	303	100	

Table 8.6: (*cont.*)

	Date of election	Parties	ENPP	Prop	% vote	N. seats	% seats	Seats:
Czech Rep	31 May 1996 Sněmovna Poslancû		4.15	89		200	100	
		Civic Democratic Party			29.6	68	34.0	**1.15**
		Czech Social Democratic Party			26.4	61	30.5	**1.15**
		Christian and Democratic Union			8.1	18	9.0	**1.11**
		Civic Democratic Alliance			6.4	13	6.5	**1.01**
		Communist Party Bohemia & Moravia			10.3	22	11.0	**1.07**
		Association for the Republic			8.0	18	9.0	**1.12**
		Pensioners for Social Guarantees			3.1			
		Democratic Union			2.8			
		Free Democrats			2.0			
		Left Bloc Party			1.4			
		Independent Initiative			0.5			
		MNS			0.3			
		SDL			0.2			
		CMUS			0.5			
		CP			0.1			
		HSMSMNS			0.4			
		Total			*100*			
Spain	3 Mar 1996						*100*	
		Popular Party			38.7	156	44.5	**1.14**
		Spanish Socialist Workers' Party			37.6	141	40.2	**1.07**
		United Left			10.5	21	6.0	0.57
		Convergence and Union			4.6	16	4.5	0.97
		Basque Nationalist Party			1.3	5	1.4	**1.07**
		Canary Island Coalition			0.9	4	1.1	**1.22**

Country	Election	Party	Votes (%)	Seats	Seats (%)	ENPP	Index of Proportionality	Votes:seats ratio
		Nationalist Galician Bloc	0.9	2	0.6			0.66
		Popular Unity	0.7	2	0.6			0.85
		Catalan Republican Left	0.7	1	0.3			0.42
		Basque Solidarity	0.5	1	0.3			0.26
		Valencian Union	0.4	1	0.3			0.75
		Total	*100*	*350*	*100*	*2.73*	*93*	
Israel	29 May 1996 Knesset	Labor	26.8	34	28.3			**1.05**
		Likud-Gesher-Tzomet	25.1	32	26.6			**1.05**
		Shas	8.5	10	8.3			0.97
		National Religious	7.9	9	7.5			0.94
		Meretz	7.4	9	7.5			**1.01**
		Israel ba'Aliya	5.7	7	5.8			**1.01**
		Hadash	4.2	5	4.2			**1.00**
		United Torah Jewry	3.2	4	3.3			**1.03**
		Third Way	3.2	4	3.3			**1.03**
		Democratic Arab	2.9	4	3.3			**1.13**
		Moledet	2.4	2	1.6			0.66
		Others	2.7					
		Total	*100*	*120*	*100*	*5.63*	*96*	

Notes: The votes: seats ratio is calculated by dividing the proportion of seats into the proportion of votes for each party. ENPP is the effective number of parliamentary parties calculated following the method of Laakso and Taagepera (1979). The Index of Proportionality is calculated following as the difference between a party's share of the vote and its share of the total seats in Parliament, summed, divided by two and subtracted from 100. Theoretically it can range from 0 to 100. For details see Rose, Munro, and Mackie (1998).

Sources: Successive volumes of *Electoral Studies*; Rose, Munro, and Mackie (1998).

Designing Electoral Rules and Waiting for an Electoral System to Evolve

Rein Taagepera

One cannot design an electoral system. It's almost as chimerical as designing a party system. In systems theory, a system implies division of the world into external and internal. The system has some capacity to restore internal equilibrium when disturbed by external factors. An electoral system comes about in two phases. In a relatively short time the electoral rules are devised and adopted. Then, over many elections, politicians and voters learn how to use these rules within their socio-political context.

An electoral *system* emerges when the electoral rules have become embedded in a political culture where actors have acquired reasonable skills in handling the electoral rules for their enlightened self-interest. This includes most actors' long-term interest in preserving minimal stability. Such skills are based on experience. Hence electoral rules can become the containing carapace of an electoral system only when they have been used a fair number of times. If meanwhile the rules are altered, the evolution of a system is delayed.

On such a definition, developing an electoral system is part of developing a democracy rather than something established at the early stage of democratization. But some electoral rules must be specified very early in the game. One cannot design an electoral system, but one can devise more or less favourable starting points for a stable system to evolve.

Is this distinction between electoral rules and systems nitpicking? Not quite. By talking of design of electoral systems, when thinking of electoral laws, we raise exaggerated expectations. It's close to talking of designing a crime-free society when merely designing criminal laws. In the latter case, most people realize that laws, though needed, are not the entire story. In the case of electoral laws confusion is more likely. Excessive optimism about given electoral laws bringing certain results can quickly flip into excessive disillusionment when, for instance, single-member districts with the plurality rule (SMP) do not immediately produce a two-party constellation, as predicted by Duverger's rule.

Please note that I said 'party constellation', not 'party system'. I see little systematic in the kaleidoscopic party constellations in many new democracies. It takes many years and elections before something reasonably stable evolves, so that we can talk of a party system.

The same considerations apply to the main theme of this book: constitutional design. A functioning constitution consists of the written text, plus the layers of interpretations, precedents, and tradition added later on. The same written text may lead to different interpretations or may prove completely dysfunctional in some societies. Fortunately, the limits of the ability of constitutional design to revamp a polity are widely appreciated.

This chapter will address three issues. On what basis are electoral rules actually chosen in new democracies, and what are the consequences? On what basis should they ideally be designed? And in how much detail should the electoral rules be specified in constitutions? Regarding the two first questions—how electoral rules should be and actually are designed—I draw from two published articles (Taagepera 1997; 1998). The third question—the connection between electoral rules and constitutions—ties in with the central theme of this book. The second phase—waiting for a system to evolve—does not enter directly. Indirectly, however, the awareness of it colours the entire discussion.

How Electoral Rules Are Chosen and What the Consequences Are

How electoral rules actually are chosen

How are electoral rules chosen in new democracies? Often they are not designed in a harmonious way, as conjured by the word 'design'. All too frequently they are a patchwork of incongruous compromises. It may look hard-boiled realism to claim that the self-interest of the original decision-makers determines the choice. The trouble is that this claim is as non-falsifiable as 'Everything happens as God wills it'. Such statements retroactively explain every conceivable outcome and hence predict nothing specific. One's perception of one's self-interest is hard to specify even for oneself, much less for others. People decide what is in their interest on varied, conflicting, and often fleeting grounds.

The politician's self-interest cannot be defined solely as winning the next election. This goal can conflict with long-term interests, including preservation of stability. It can conflict with ideological preferences, including advice by foreign advisers belonging to the same philosophical strain. The force of habit and familiar examples from abroad also enter. Which of these will overshadow the others in defining 'self-interest'?

Moreover, the means used to achieve one's presumed self-interest can be misinformed and counterproductive. Assume that, for the old regimes in the Soviet-dominated area, winning the next election was overriding all other considerations. Such regimes often preferred keeping the Soviet electoral rules, which favour the largest party, not only by force of habit but also because they expected to be the largest party. It turned out to be a catastrophic misjudgement for them in many countries.

The predominant forces may stick to the rules inherited from the preceding political regime either by ignorance of alternatives or by trying to balance rationally the merits of the existing rules against the costs and risks of innovation. Thus most ex-British colonies adopted SMP without realizing that assembly size matters (Taagepera and Shugart 1989: 173–4; Lijphart 1990a; 1994a: 83–8). Under SMP, the effective number of parties tends to be appreciably larger in the large parliament of the UK than in the 15-seat assembly of a small island nation like the Seychelles. Instead of a healthy two-party system like in UK, the parliaments in small ex-British nations often ended up with an excessive largest-party representation and a completely decimated parliamentary opposition even when the votes were close to 50-50. Such was not the intent of the decision-makers, and in retrospect it hardly served their self-interest by any criteria.

Among the post-Soviet states, Ukraine maintained the Soviet two-round rule the longest, changing only in 1998 (Birch and Wilson 1999). This rule allows voting against all candidates and yet requires an absolute majority. What formally worked with Soviet one-candidate pseudo-elections led in multi-candidate elections to interminable repeat rounds. Indeed, some seats in Ukraine remained vacant until the next election. Maybe some clever politicians preferred such an outcome, but I suspect that most decision-makers were surprised.

The role of random events should not be underestimated. As Nigel Roberts (1987: 70) asks regarding New Zealand: 'What would have happened if David Lange had not made an inadvertent pledge during the 1987 election to hold a binding referendum on the question of electoral reform?' Except for this irretrievable slip of tongue, the ball may not have started rolling. If this could happen in stable New Zealand, then how often may it have happened in new democracies that the choice of the initial electoral rules was determined by who happened to be present at what meeting in what mood?

With 20-20 hindsight, one can always harness 'self-interest' to perfectly explain away this conglomeration of desire to win, yet follow tradition, avoid rethinking and gathering information, satisfy foreign ideological sponsors, and keep some idealism about future stability, combined with miscalculations and pure random chance.

Forgetting about the mushy notion of self-interest, what do we observe in actual new democracies? Unfortunately, there is a dearth of detailed English-language descriptions of how electoral systems historically emerged in various countries in recent times; the same applies to histories and analyses of constitutional assemblies and their equivalents. I have described the Estonian vagaries (Taagepera 1997; expanded in Grofman, Mikkel, and Taagepera 1999). On this basis, I proposed the following tentative sequence of attitudes, especially regarding input by political scientists.

Phase 0. This phase applies only to countries where the previous non-democratic regime conducted fake elections. The democratizing elites take the pre-existing electoral rules for granted. They see no cause for change and hence no need for outside advice or information.

Phase 1. The democratizing elites feel the need for new electoral rules, because none exist or the ones used for choiceless elections prove unworkable once choice is introduced. Unaware of the variety of electoral rules used by stable democracies, the elites try to reinvent the wheel, grasping at some simple formula that seems the only sensible one. If the variety of rules elsewhere is noticed, they are perceived as unfamiliar, complex, and unsuitable for one's own culture.

Phase 2. As homespun electoral rules backfire or more radical reformers replace the early ones, the multitude of options sinks in. Foreign advice is eagerly invited and sometimes overvalued. It may be followed more to the letter than the advisers intended it.

Phase 3. Knowledge of various electoral options increases, but confidence in having mastered it all grows even faster. As the united front of reformers fractionalizes, electoral rules become a political football. Emphasis is on perceived short-term goals, leading to counterproductive results when the relative strengths of groupings change. Foreign professional advice becomes undervalued, unless it agrees with one's momentary tastes. In some countries fractionalization and kaleidoscopic shifts in the party constellation bring popular disappointment with electoral rules and possibly democracy itself. Sub-optimal strategies by inexperienced actors in a fractionalized field may produce outcomes at variance with those in stable democracies using similar rules, further reducing the credibility of political science advice.

Phase 4. A more balanced use of political science advice develops, provided that democracy survives Phase 3, as local academics develop expertise in electoral rules, in tandem with growing practical experience.

In each of these phases it can be said that decision-makers follow their perception of self-interest: it's just that this perception changes. It is not clear to what extent the evolution of thought in other newly democratizing countries can be approximated by this Estonian-inspired scheme. A different scheme might work better, or it might turn out that no general pattern can be perceived.

How electoral rules matter and how they are evaluated in young democracies

The rules chosen at the beginning of democratization make a difference, but sometimes in unexpected directions, because of an unsettled political culture and party constellation. Compromises between various proposals all too often lead to complex rules, but complexity enhances unpredictability and the potential for getting the worst of both worlds.

A main decision concerns the balance between governability and the representation of minority views. Governability may be promoted by having only two major parties and one-party cabinets, which in turn often result from the SMP rule. Proportional representation (PR) of minority views, on the other hand, is best obtained when using a single nationwide district. One can have both if the political culture spontaneously develops only two parties, as was the case in post-war Austria, despite PR electoral rules. Another political culture may miss out on both accounts, as in present-day Russia, which has huge deviations from PR and yet a large number of parties.

Apart from the governability-representation balance, many other considerations enter, such as party cohesion and having a personal representative. In new democracies two aspects emerge more strongly than in the established ones. One is the legitimacy of electoral rules, or rather the perception of it. If, for whatever reason, right or wrong, these rules are perceived as illegitimate, then democracy is in trouble. The other aspect is the cost of elections, in both money and expertise. New democracies are often strapped for funds and skilled administrators, so that too many of these resources spent on the execution of elections may leave gaps elsewhere.

In their *Handbook of Electoral System Design*, Andrew Reynolds and Ben Reilly (1997) have presented a dispassionate overview of the various electoral systems and their components throughout the world. They list both the claimed advantages and shortcomings of the various approaches. They stress the issue of the cost of elections, in both money and the perception of legitimacy. Simple rules may be expected to keep the costs down, but what looks simple on the surface may involve costs elsewhere.

For instance, SMP might look like the simplest of all allocation rules, but the initial drawing of electoral boundaries is costly, and so is voter registration, because with SMP the outcome depends very much on *where* a given voter votes. Two-round rules double the cost of ballot papers, polling stations, and vote counting. There is also voter fatigue, plus disappointment, if a crowded first round leaves later only a choice between two poorly supported finalists. Multi-seat districts, on the other hand, may be costly in terms of voter education. Voter dissatisfaction may impair stability if too many ballots are spoiled because of ballot complexity or if the outcomes look mysterious because of a complicated allocation formula.

In an admittedly coarse count based on Reynolds and Reilly (1997: 119), the total cost handicap score of various rules is the following:

Two Rounds	10
Mixed Member Proportional	9
Parallel	8
STV and Alternative Vote	7
Block Vote	5
Single-Member Plurality	4
Single Non-Transferable Vote	4
List PR	2

Doubts about the legitimacy of election results can focus solely on the electoral rules and the political operators specifically held responsible for the purportedly unfair or inappropriate rules. But such doubts can also extend to the entire 'political class' or even democracy as such, risking the breakdown of democratization.

Understandably, there is an urge to evaluate the rules after the very first elections, but it might be too early. Political culture and party constellation are still in flux. The stable characteristics of the outputs of electoral rules cannot yet be measured because politicians and voters are still learning how to use these rules to their best advantage. There is a temptation to alter the electoral rules rather than wait for this learning process to take place. But if rules are continuously altered no such learning can ever occur.

A major criterion for whether electoral rules matter is whether inadequate rules have demonstrably led to collapse of democracy, or at least a severe crisis. Rarely have electoral rules been the only reason in the past, but they have contributed to crisis (see Taagepera 1998).

How Electoral Rules Should Be Designed

Ideally, electoral rules should be designed with enlightened self-interest in mind, making use of all the knowledge that political science can offer. Enlightened self-interest implies taking a long-range view. For instance, a large party cannot expect to remain large at all times, so it would be mistaken to promote rules that give a large seat bonus to the largest party, just on the basis of its present popularity. Making use of political science knowledge is a stickier proposition.

What do we know?

What do political scientists know that is worth transmitting to designers of electoral rules? We know quite a lot about past experience with electoral rules in democratic countries; see for example Lijphart and Grofman (1984), Grofman and Lijphart (1986), Sartori (1986), Shugart and Carey (1992), Lijphart (1994*a*), Rule and Zimmerman (1994), Nohlen (1996), and Cox (1997), to list just a few major works of the last 15 years. The question is how to extrapolate from it into future, and to other countries.

One way to proceed is by detailed empirical precedents. However, 40 years ago W. J. M. Mackenzie (1957: 54) maintained that 'The only thing that can be predicted with certainty about the export of elections is that an electoral *system* will not work in the same way in its new settings as in its old' (emphasis added). In my terminology, electoral systems cannot be exported: only electoral rules can. Export of electoral rules to different environments can be expected to lead to different electoral systems. In Harry Eckstein's (1966; 1998) terminology, if institutions are not sufficiently congruent with the existing political culture, they fail or yield unexpected results. This certainly applies to electoral laws.

But it is even worse than that. It is even risky to extrapolate from a country's past experience to the same country's future. According to Kavanagh (1992: 17), David Butler has pointed out how the so-called cube law of elections, after fitting British elections during the 1950s and 1960s, 'went sour' in the 1970s, shifting into a 'square rule' and then a power-index 1.5 relationship. This is getting close to the power index 1.0 of perfect PR. To the extent that a heavy impact of swing votes is a precondition for the workings of Duverger's law, this is a major change, and indeed the importance of third parties has increased in the UK without any change in the electoral rules.

At the level of recipes based on single country precedents, political scientists have little more to offer than historians or journalists, except for presenting a larger number of cautionary case studies. Any advice is likely to be as good as any other—or, rather, as ineffective. Fortunately, we have a little bit more than country portraits. We have comparative electoral studies, and there some fuzzy regularities emerge. Here are a few examples.

On average, increased district magnitude tends to reduce deviation from PR, unless overruled by other features of electoral rules. Increased magnitude may also go with increased number of parties, although the direction of causality is uncertain. With SMP the number of parties tends to increase slowly with assembly size, which itself tends to rise with the population represented. But deviations from these average trends are huge (cf. Taagepera and Shugart 1989; Lijphart 1994*a*), and how is one to figure out whether the given new democracy will be below or above the average trend?

There is a difference between empirically observed regularities and those based on rational models. All regularities observed in the covariation of two quantities depend on 'all other things being the same'. But if we do not know what makes *y* depend on *x*, how can we tell whether all other things remain the same? How could we predict whether the cube relationship would continue to hold in Britain if we did not know what caused it in the first place?

Rational models establish quantitative relationships that hold under specified conditions. When deviations occur, one sometimes may have to scrap the model, but often it suffices to pin down the conditions of applicability more stringently—which in itself represents an advance in knowledge. Thus, Boyle's law of ideal gases—

loi de Mariotte in French textbooks—started out as an empirical relationship between pressure, volume, and temperature, but later was explained in terms of a rational model of motion of molecules. The model, in turn, helps in introducing correction factors needed in the case of real gases.

One advantage of the rational model approach is that it narrows down the locus of discrepancy, if any occurs. The empirical cube relationship between the ratio of seats and the ratio of votes of two parties can be decomposed into a rationally supported power relationship, plus a rational explanation of what the power index should be (Taagepera and Shugart 1989: 157–88). The change Butler observes in Britain does not affect the power relation as such; it's just that the power index has shifted from 3 toward 1.5. The power index itself has been explained in terms of the number of voters and the number of seats available, subject to certain conditions. It tends to be close to 3 for parliamentary elections because most countries pick assembly sizes that approximate the cube root of their population: another regularity for which a rational model in terms of communication channels exists (Taagepera and Shugart 1989: 173–82). British population and assembly size have not changed significantly, so one would have to look into other factors which affect the seat-vote relationship: and this remains to be done.

Contrary to Butler, I have not lost my optimism regarding fundamental laws that govern electoral relationships. The reason is that I see a way out. As long as one deals with empirical relationships for which one has no rational explanation, one has no other option but disillusionment when the relationship fades. But when one has a rational model, one can decompose it into parts, pin down the locus of the discrepancy, and refine the model.

At the same time, I have no illusions about the momentous task still ahead of us before our knowledge reaches a widely applicable stage. Given the complexity of socio-political phenomena, electoral studies are about where astronomy was 400–500 years ago: lots of observations and little predictive ability.

Our present quantitative rational models may be as unsuitable as the attempts to fit the planetary trajectories with circular motions around epicentres of epicentres—or they may be the beginnings of fruitful models like Kepler's elliptic trajectories. Come to think of it, even epicentric attempts were useful. It would have been much worse to give up on looking for rational quantitative explanations in favour of mushily qualitative statements or purely empirical measurement. Rational models that fail force one to look for alternative models, while giving up on the search for rational explanations is an utter dead end.

What opportunity does all that leave for supposedly rational advice by neutral experts in electoral rules and systems? It is not up to the experts to decide on the motivational basis of the choice. They can only help avoid misconceived ways to reach the stated goals. They can ask 'What results do you want?' and then point out to what extent the rules under consideration may ensure or defeat the intended purpose. For instance, if low population imposes a small assembly and you still want to have single-party cabinets plus vigorous opposition, British-style, then you are not likely to get it with British-like M=1, because it might utterly decimate the opposition. Instead, you should consider low magnitude PR: say, M=3. Even then, Chile's experience with two-seat districts sounds a cautionary note.

In view of our modest grasp of the effects of electoral rules in stable democracies and even greater ignorance of their interaction with culture and learning processes in new democracies, it might seem that no advice can be given, apart from 'Pick anything and try to muddle through'. This is not quite so. Even recognition of ignorance is a positive step compared with cocksure application of pseudo-knowledge. Here are some very general suggestions, condensed from a published article (Taagepera 1998). Reynolds and Reilly (1997) have made some of the same points and offer further recommendations. In general, don't think of electoral rules as a panacea for all ills, but also don't underestimate their influence.

Keep the electoral rules simple

This is basic. Whatever we know about the impact of electoral rules applies mainly to simple systems. If simple rules produce undesirable outcomes in the given cultural context, we may at least know in retrospect what caused them, and then we can try incremental changes.

In the case of highly complex electoral rules, in contrast, any degree of rational predictability vanishes. If the seat allocation produces unwelcome surprises, incremental adjustment becomes impossible because one cannot even be sure which component of the rules was the major factor. Hence attempts at correction may make it worse.

Trying to obtain very specific outcomes by making new electoral rules complex assumes much better knowledge of the functioning of electoral rules—and their interaction with political culture—

than we presently have. It is all too easy to discard theory- and/or observation-based equations because they work only within a factor of two—and worse for new polities—and then fall for completely impressionistic voodoo.

Complexity increases the unpredictability of results and also makes elections costlier. On the other hand, one should also beware of apparent simplicity of rules that may hide complications elsewhere. Thus the simple SMP rule involves relatively high districting and voter registration costs. It has embroiled the United States in complex and interminable gerrymander and redistricting issues. When this entire package is considered, even Single Transferable Vote looks simple in comparison.

A further reason to start out with simple rules is that later corrections invariably go in the direction of further complexity. It is always easier to add to than subtract from existing laws and rules. When the electoral rules are complex to begin with, attempts to correct them may make them unmanageable—or can be seen as underhand by the voters.

Unfortunately, the reality during the selection of electoral rules often is that a recalcitrant player with some veto power agrees to go along with a simple electoral set-up only if some apparently tiny extra feature is added. Though looking innocuous, it may actually change the picture appreciably. The danger looms that some other player will offer a supposedly minor counter-correction—and the race towards complexity is on.

Make use of worldwide experience

Don't be afraid to innovate upon the electoral rules inherited from colonial rule or dictatorial sham elections. While innovating, don't think that your society is such a special case that it needs a unique set of rules. You'd most likely end up reinventing something that has been tried elsewhere and given up. On the other hand, don't expect either that rules borrowed from another single country would lead to the same outcomes in a different culture.

World experience includes not only that of different countries as packages but also the analytical results that cover the same features in many countries. They give some idea to what degree a change in input, such as district magnitude, affects an output, such as number of parties. And the scatter around these average trends also indicates to what degree a given feature may lead to different outcomes in various cultures.

Once chosen, keep the same rules for at least three elections

Don't think the first election outcomes are characteristic of the properties of the given electoral rules under your socio-political conditions. It takes several elections with the same electoral rules before their systematic effects stabilize. Parties and voters need time to learn how to use them to their best advantage. An electoral system consists of rules and skills in using these rules. If the rules are continuously altered, no stable electoral *system* can emerge.

Of course, no advice is absolute. There may be disastrous sets of rules to be given up in a hurry. But in nine cases out of ten, when electoral rules are altered it is done too early in two respects. First, the existing rules may not be so dysfunctional after all, once people learn to use them. Second, if you messed it up the first time, what guarantees that you now can do a better job rather than flipping from flaws discovered to flaws as yet unknown?

Consider incremental changes

When rules are altered so as to correct for specific flaws, avoid going overboard. Don't flip to a totally different set-up that may include new weak points. Fine-tuning may achieve the desired results more safely. Consider minor changes in district magnitude, legal threshold, and so forth.

Even so, apparently minor adjustments to correct one particular aspect may have unintended side effects elsewhere. Suppose for instance that one wishes to reduce intra-party competition for seats and reinforce the hand of party leaders by switching from open to closed lists. If this means that some personally popular politicians are placed low on the closed list, so that they have little chance to win, they may bolt the party and start a new one. The unintended result may be the proliferation of separate parties.

Sometimes the change needed may lie outside the electoral rules. Do parties strike election-time alliances but part ways once in the assembly? The gut response might be to set higher legal thresholds for alliances, but this may be hard to police and would complicate the electoral rules. In contrast, parliamentary rules that deny material benefits to parliamentary groupings that did not feature in elections may be self-policing.

Should Electoral Rules be Specified in the Constitution?

Some constitutions bypass electoral rules completely. Some others state them in great detail. Estonia's constitution of 1992 succeeds in having it both ways and thus offers a convenient starting point for discussing the relative advantages.

Estonia: the more it matters the briefer it gets

Estonia's constitution (Eesti 1992) stipulates essentially a parliamentary democracy where the prime minister and the cabinet must obtain and maintain the approval of the unicameral Riigikogu (state assembly). The president is a symbolic head of state whose veto on legislation can be overridden by a mere plurality in a repeat vote. The first president, whose second and final term ended in 2001, initially tried to increase his powers using some constitutional ambiguities, but did not succeed. Given this format, one might think that the constitution would devote appreciable space to parliamentary election rules and little to the presidential; but the reverse is the case.

The article on assembly elections (Art. 60) consists of eight sentences, a total of 77 words (in Estonian): 'Riigikogu has 101 members. Riigikogu members are elected in free elections *based on the principle of proportionality*. Elections are general, uniform and direct. Voting is secret' (emphasis added). The rest deals with age of candidacy—at least 21 years—normal duration—four years—and early elections, concluding: 'The Riigikogu election *procedure will be specified in the law on Riigikogu elections*' (emphasis added). Thus, adherence to the principle of PR is the only restriction Riigikogu faces in determining and modifying its own election rules. The rules actually chosen are pointlessly complex (see Grofman, Mikkel, and Taagepera 1999) but boil down to nationwide PR, subject to a faint largest-party seat bonus and a nationwide 5 per cent votes threshold for parties, with an escape clause for very strong individual candidates. The constitutionality of the 5 per cent threshold has been challenged— so far unsuccessfully—by those who interpret 'based on the principle of proportionality' to require as small a deviation from PR as possible. The constitution's vagueness on electoral rules allows Riigikogu to alter them—as it has done repeatedly at the margins—without going through the hassles of amending the constitution.

In contrast, the article on electing the figurehead president (Art. 79) consists of 17 sentences, a total of 200 words. It briefly specifies who has the right to nominate—at least one-fifth of Riigikogu members—who can run—aged 40 at least and Estonian citizen by birth—and who elects the president—at first glance, the Riigikogu—and here the fun starts.[1]

'A candidate is considered elected when receiving a two-thirds majority, out of all Riigikogu members.' This means at least 68 out of 101. If the first two rounds are inconclusive, the field is narrowed down to the two top candidates, but the two-thirds requirement still holds even in the third round. Given absences and abstentions, 68 votes is stratospheric. The two times the rule has been applied, in 1996 and 2001, the top candidate came nowhere close. The impossibly high hurdle was purposely pushed through the Constitutional Assembly by a blocking minority who thought they had more supporters in local assemblies and imagined this advantage would last for many electoral cycles.[2] Indeed, after an inconclusive third round in Riigikogu a locally dominated electoral college takes over. Art. 79 words it as follows: 'The electoral college consists of Riigikogu members and representatives of local self-government assemblies. Each local self-government assembly elects to the electoral college at least one representative, who must be an Estonian citizen.' This means several hundred local representatives, who swamp the Riigikogu members. The top two candidates from the third round in Riigikogu continue, but any 21 electoral college members can nominate new ones. 'The electoral college elects the President of the Republic by majority of the electoral college members who participate in the election.' If the first round doesn't produce a winner, the second round includes only the two top candidates from the first round.

So, unless the two candidates split the vote exactly 50-50, the second round in the electoral college is bound to reach a decision, right? Wrong. The wording in Art. 79—'majority of the electoral college members who participate in the election'—fails to exclude those who cast a blank or spoiled ballot. Indeed, in 1996 the top candidate, incumbent Lennart Meri, though markedly ahead of his competitor,

---

[1] Article 4 of the Law on the Implementation of the Constitution of the Republic of Estonia (Eesti 1992) made an exception for the very first election (1992). Bowing to popular demand, the first president since 1938 was to be elected by popular vote, provided a majority materialized in the first round. Failing this, the Parliament was to choose between the two top runners. The actual top candidate received 41.8% of the popular vote, thus falling short of the 50% threshold. The Parliament picked the runner-up, who had 29.5% of the popular vote.

[2] For a description of proceedings in Estonia's Constitutional Assembly, see Taagepera (1994). I was a member, but teaching obligations held me in California most of the time and especially during the end game.

only narrowly passed the hurdle due to the presence of many neutrals. The constitution does not specify what would happen after a second-round impasse in the electoral college; the possibility of such an outcome apparently was not perceived. In 1996 the predominant view in the press was that the choice would revert back to Riigikogu, still with the two-thirds hurdle, and so on ad infinitum . . .

Why did I pick these examples, apart from having been myself a (visibly ineffective) member of Estonia's Constitutional Assembly? These are textbook examples of both extremely short and quite lengthy ways to include electoral rules in a constitution. The fact that both occur in the same constitution, where the length of stipulation is inversely related to the importance of the election, emphasizes the lack of overall balanced design in the constitutional kitchen. What lessons are suggested?

I consider both Riigikogu electoral law and the presidential one as poorly designed. Both are excessively complex thanks to compromise upon compromise. The difference is that the electoral law for Riigikogu can be modified relatively easily, while the one for the president requires constitutional amendment.

The latter course is difficult—as changes in the constitution should be. Yet, once this particular amendment becomes popular, other constitutional amendments could be tacked on to the coattails of the presidential issue. This could put the entire constitution in jeopardy before it has time to test itself over several decades. Indeed, proposals to elect the figurehead president through direct popular elections had a field day in 1999. In sum, while being procedurally stable against change, the set-up is not stable from the viewpoint of perceived legitimacy; and this is a potentially explosive mix. Being embedded in the constitution certainly has not spared the presidential election procedure from criticism.

On the other hand, has the superficiality of the constitutional stipulations on Riigikogu elections left too much leeway to law-making by the Riigikogu incumbents? Electoral laws should have some stability. In principle, the Riigikogu could change electoral laws too fleetingly. This is counteracted, however, by the fact that the present incumbents obviously have profited from the existing rules. Many of them are quite reluctant to change a law that has served them well, personally.

By being more specific, has the article on presidential election at least left fewer loose ends than the utterly brief article on Riigikogu elections? As is often the case in politics, the more one explains, the more loose ends become exposed. The detailed stipulation of the steps for presidential election in the constitution fails to guard against the possibility of a deadlock: it only makes a solution more cumbersome than in the case of a simple law.[3]

Generalization

I very much believe that electoral rules are important. I also have made the case that they should not be changed too frequently. On both accounts, it would seem then that electoral rules should be included in the constitution. Yet the case study presented here suggests the contrary. Not all important things should be enshrined in the constitution. Principles belong in the constitution; instrumentalities are a different kettle of fish—and a very mixed kettle. Presidentialism versus parliamentarism, federalism versus unitarism, electoral rules, and so forth, all are instrumental to achieving stability, enjoyment of various goals, and satisfaction of principles such as those in the bill of rights. Which such instrumentalities belong in the constitution?

If the optimal settings for a given instrumental aspect are quite well determined, we might as well specify it in the constitution. At the other extreme, if we know very little about some other aspect, we might also need to enshrine some more or less arbitrary choice in the constitution so as to minimize further dissension. But if we know something, yet not enough, we are better off keeping this aspect out of the constitution, especially when our knowledge is rapidly expanding. Let us not freeze in something that the next stage of research findings may contradict.

The impact of electoral rules and their interaction with other socio-political factors so as to develop an electoral system: these are at such an intermediary stage between belief and knowledge. Therefore, I'd rather keep their details out of constitutions as much as possible.

---

[3] Another can of worms is contained in the requirement that electoral college members must be Estonian citizens. Given the clear non-eligibility of non-citizens to any elective office in the US, among many other countries, this requirement needs clarification. In contrast to the US, Estonia's constitution allows non-citizen permanent residents to participate in local elections (Art. 156). Given the purposeful Russian colonization during the Soviet occupation, at least a fifth of the residents have not yet satisfied citizenship requirements, which are of the same type as in the US. In some townships most of the voters are non-citizens. The latter indirectly determine a part of the electoral college composition. Given that Art. 56 reserves sovereignty—'highest state power'—to citizens, there is legal incongruity in non-citizens affecting the choice of the president. Thus, by going into too much detail on presidential election, the constitution has produced a conflict between the nationwide (Art. 56) and the local (Art. 156) levels.

General Conclusions

Stable electoral systems consist not only of electoral rules but also of the way these rules are used in the given democratic culture. This culture includes *informed* self-interest, meaning some concern for stability and tradition, and avoidance of gross miscalculations resulting from limited understanding of the effect of given electoral rules. Such experience comes with time. A stable electoral system consists of electoral rules that have withstood some test of the times.

Such time would be shortened if the local learning experience could be complemented by general scholarly knowledge about the properties of electoral rules and their interaction with other factors. To some extent every electoral system is *sui generis* because similar electoral rules are embedded in different historical and socio-political contexts. If this prevailed totally, then no advice to newly democratizing countries would be possible apart from the impressionistic, which varies from one adviser to the next. But this is not so. Some hard, transferable knowledge already exists to a limited degree.

Of course, we should be modest about our ability to predict the effect of electoral rules. Even for stable systems, one finds considerable variability of data and disagreement of opinion. Extension to newly democratizing countries must be even more cautious in view of their different and unstable political cultures. Recommending complex electoral formats, in particular, implies the pretence of knowing more than we do. Including electoral rules in constitutions could make it worse. Such inclusion should wait until theory is put on a much firmer basis than is presently the case. We have made a good start in this direction.

III

Country Studies

10

Constitutional Engineering in Post-Coup Fiji

Brij V. Lal

Ethnically divided societies such as Fiji present political theorists and constitutional engineers, not to mention their own citizens, with complex challenges of nation building. Divisions based on a combination of ethnicity, religion, custom, and language run deep. Social cleavages are often institutionalized, impeding unified political development. The search for shared common space is often overshadowed by deeply contested claims about the true character of the nation's soul. People invoke different historical metaphors and allude to different sets of cultural and historical experiences to validate their particular-and sometimes prior-considerations in the nation's affairs. Which symbols, rituals, ceremonies, and cultural practices get state recognition and support matter greatly; they go to the core of how people define themselves, and how they are perceived, within the wider polity.

This chapter describes the experience of devising a constitution for a small ethnically divided state in the South Pacific. The Republic of the Fiji Islands is a multi-ethnic state whose population in 1996 of 780,000 is divided between indigenous Fijians—51 per cent of the population—Indo-Fijians—43 per cent—and Others—6 per cent. It gained its independence from the United Kingdom in 1970 under a Westminster-style constitution which accommodated special Fijian interests and concerns through entrenched provisions within an overarching framework of parliamentary democracy. The assumptions and understandings which underpinned that order came under increasing challenge from the forces of social and economic change in the tumultuous years following independence (Taylor 1987). A military coup on 14 May 1987 removed from power a democratically elected government whose nominally non-racial ideology was seen to question the foundations of the post-colonial state and the range of vested social, political, and economic interests which sustained it, and installed a political order based on the principles of racial segregation akin in some important respects to the apartheid regime in South Africa. These principles found expression in the Fiji Constitution of 1990.

Origins of the Fiji Constitution Review Commission

The 1990 Constitution, decreed into existence by President Ratu Sir Penaia Ganilau five years after the military coups of 1987, with no popular participation in its formulation or its implementation, was assumed by its authors to be an interim document. Section 161 of the Constitution provided for its review at the end of seven years after the date of its promulgation, that is, before 25 July 1997. That the 1990 Constitution was a contentious document is beyond doubt. The Indo-Fijian community had rejected it and made its repeal, or at least review, the central plank in its election campaigns in 1992 and 1994 (see Lal 1993; 1995). Equally, on the Fijian side there was strong support for a document which was believed to entrench Fijian dominance in the political process. After the 1992 elections, which brought the Soqosoqo Vakavulewa ni Taukei (SVT) to power and Major General Sitiveni Rabuka to the prime minister's chair, the government and the opposition started discussions on the review of the constitution. A Joint Parliamentary Committee was set up to make recommendations on how the review process should be undertaken. After protracted discussions, the Joint Committee recommended, and both houses of parliament unanimously agreed in September 1993, that a Commission of Inquiry should be set up to review the Constitution. Parliament also unanimously approved the terms of reference for the Commission, but further progress was disrupted when the SVT government fell in November 1993. Early in 1994 the SVT returned to power with an increased majority and resumed discussion on constitutional review with the opposition parties. The most important unresolved issue was the membership of the Commission. Eventually, it was agreed that the Commission would consist of three persons: one appointed by the government, one by the opposition, and a chairperson to be an independent person from outside. The government nominated Tomasi Rayalu Vakatora, a former senior public servant, senator, minister, speaker of the house; the opposition nominated me, an academic specialist on Fiji history and politics; and both sides agreed on Sir Paul Reeves, former Anglican Archbishop and Governor-General of New Zealand, as chair. The three commissioners received their commission on 15 March 1995 and the two legal counsel assisting them—Alison Quentin-Baxter and Jon Apted—on 19 May. The Commission commenced its work in early June.

The terms of reference, themselves an historic achievement of consensus and compromise, considering the bitterness and hostility generated by the coups, required the Commission to recommend constitutional arrangements which would meet the present and future needs of the people of Fiji, and promote racial harmony, national unity, and the economic and social advancement of all communities. Those arrangements had to guarantee full protection and promotion of the rights, interests, and concerns of the indigenous Fijians and the people of Rotuma, have full regard for the rights, interests, and concerns of all ethnic groups in Fiji, and take into account internationally recognized principles and standards of individual and group rights. In accomplishing this task, the Commission was expected to have scrutinized the Constitution, facilitated the widest possible debate on the terms of the Constitution, and, after ascertaining the views of the people, suggest how the provisions of the 1990 Constitution could be improved upon to meet the needs of Fiji as a multi-ethnic and multicultural society. The terms of reference were wide-ranging, prompting some critics to wonder what they actually meant and whether they could be reconciled into a workable formula. These thoughts also crossed the Commission's mind, which devoted a great deal of time early on to analysing the text as well as the implications of the terms of reference (FCRC 1996: Ch. 3).

Unlike previous commissions of enquiry, such as the Street Commission of 1975 and others set up in the immediate aftermath of the coups,[1] the Reeves Commission, as it came to be known, was required to review the whole Constitution, not only the provisions relating to the electoral system and the composition of parliament. The review, then, was to be a fundamental, wide-ranging exercise, covering, besides the two critical areas just mentioned, the functioning of parliament, the relationship between the executive and the legislative branches, institutions of government and the mechanism for improving accountability and transparency in them, the administration of justice, citizenship, ethnic and social justice

---

[1] This chapter draws on three of my previous publications on the subject (Lal 1998; 1999a, b, c).

The Street Commission, named after its chairman Sir Harry Street, is in Fiji Parliamentary Paper 24/1975. Post-coup commissions of enquiry were led by Sir John Falvey in 1987 and by Paul Manueli in 1990.

issues, rights of communities and groups, the operation of local government bodies, public revenue and expenditure, emergency powers, and bill of rights, among others.

To accomplish the task, the Commission took an early decision regarding the modus operandi of its work: as far as possible, the process of consultation would be open, transparent, and inclusive. To ascertain the view of the people, and thus fulfilling one of the requirements of the terms of reference, the Commission decided to hold public hearings throughout the country to receive submissions. That exercise, exhausting and exhaustive, lasted from July to November 1995. More than 800 written and oral submissions were received from individual citizens, community, religious, cultural, and various interest groups, and all political parties. The over-whelming majority of the submissions were made in public, and are available to the public (FCRC 1996); but some individuals, for vari-ous reasons, chose to speak to the Commission in confidence, and these naturally form part of the closed record. The Commission also invited specific individuals, heads of statutory organizations, and others prominent in public life, to share their experiences and views privately. At the same time, the Commission commissioned papers from local and international researchers on a whole range of topics to deepen its knowledge of the local social and economic environ-ment and to better understand international conventions and con-stitutional arrangements for power-sharing in other jurisdictions. Three of them—Malaysia, Mauritius, and South Africa—the Commission visited to find out first-hand how they had resolved the problem of political representation in their multi-ethnic societies. While all these various sources of information were enormously helpful in facilitating an understanding of the task at hand, no one source was privileged over any other.

Fiji's Constitutional Arrangements

It is neither possible nor desirable to cover all the major areas dealt with in the Commission's report. For the purposes of this exercise, two sets of issues will be discussed. The first, and perhaps the more critical, concerns the election to and the composition of parliament. That question lay at the centre of the 'web' and was at the forefront of all the submissions. It was the one area of central disagreement between the major political parties and the two major communities. The second relates to the functioning of the institutions of govern-ment and issues of social justice and human rights.

From the outset, the Commission believed that, unless the systemic nature of Fiji's constitutional problem was clearly understood, there was little hope of devising constitutional arrangements which would not give rise to the same problems of ethnic rivalry in the future. From the evidence before it, the Commission concluded that it was Fiji's constitutional arrangements which had hampered the process of nation-building and impeded effective cooperation among the various communities in Fiji, which otherwise had shown a remarkable capacity for tolerance and respect for each other's cultural and religious traditions while sharing the values and interests they had in common. Fiji's constitutional problems, the Commission concluded, arose from four features of the country's constitutional arrangements (FCRC 1996: Ch. 2). Two were understandable responses to Fiji's multi-ethnic society: the principle that Fijian interests should be paramount and the communal system of representation in parliament. The other two reflected the Westminster system of government that Fiji inherited at the time of independence: the role of political parties and the principle that a government must command the support of a majority in parliament. All these four features underpinned both the 1970 and the 1990 constitutions.

The principle that Fijian interests should always remain paramount had been expressly enunciated by the colonial government since the early years of the twentieth century, partly reflecting genuine concern for the position of the indigenous Fijians, partly serving to deflect the Indo-Fijian demand for equal political representation, and partly serving as a tool to guide political change at a pace acceptable to the colonial state. None the less, the principle was widely accepted and became part of the political culture of Fiji. As Fiji moved towards self-government in the 1960s, the principle of political paramountcy became the focus of negotiations among the main political actors in the colony. The Fijian view was that the principle that their interests should be paramount could be secured only if Fijians had political paramountcy as well. As other communities already dominated the economy, Fijian leaders pointed out, it was only fair that Fijians should dominate in government. For their part, Indo-Fijian leaders agreed to the entrenched legislative protection of Fijian land ownership, culture, and separate system of administration, but did not see the paramountcy of Fijian interests as involving an ongoing commitment to secure the re-election of a predominantly Fijian government. If the democratic process provided for in the constitution gave them the opportunity, Indo-Fijian leaders saw no reason why they should not join other groups, including some Fijians, in electing a government in which they could participate. Differing interpretations of the meaning of Fijian paramountcy, then, were one contentious issue.

Another was the system of representation in parliament. From the very beginning, the electoral system in Fiji has been communal, the seats always allocated among the various ethnic communities. This arrangement grew out of the colonial government's view that, in an ethnically divided society, separate representation of different communities was natural and desirable. And the system enabled the government to keep the different ethnic groups apart as much as possible, thus accentuating its own role as an impartial and indispensable mediator of disputes among the communities. Until 1966, Fiji had only communal electoral rolls, with voters in each community electing members belonging to that community. Later, the communal rolls were complemented with cross-voting rolls, allowing members belonging to any community to be elected by all voters. This system also represented a compromise between the desire, shared by Fijians and Europeans, for communal representation from communal rolls and the Indo-Fijian commitment to the principle of a non-racial common roll. The compromise spawned more problems than it resolved.

The third feature of Fiji's political arrangement was that all its parties were essentially ethnic. The National Federation Party (NFP), formed in the aftermath of the 1960 strike in the sugar industry and based in the Indo-Fijian community, was able to attract only a handful of Fijian supporters over the years. The Alliance Party, formed in 1965 at the behest of Governor, Sir Derek Jakeway, was a Fijian- dominated party supported by the General Electors Association and the Indian Alliance. The Alliance was more multiracial, but at each successive election the ethnic basis of the two main parties was clear.

The final feature of Fiji's political arrangement was the Westminster system, whereby the prime minister is the leader of the party or combination of parties that can command majority support in the lower house. The cabinet is drawn exclusively from that party or coalition. Through its direction of the departments and other government agencies, the government of the day has effective control of policy. Because of its majority in parliament, it can secure the passage of its budget and other legislation. If the party in power is defeated at a general election, the control of government passes to the winning party.

The 1970 and 1990 Constitutions

These arrangements were reflected in both the 1970 and the 1990 constitutions. The 1970 Constitution, negotiated by the leaders of the two main political parties, the Alliance and the National Federation, was an 'interim solution'. The method of election had proved to be a major stumbling block in the negotiations leading to independence. Unable to break the impasse, the leaders agreed to defer the question of the electoral system to an independent commission. Meanwhile, the 1970 Constitution provided for a 52-seat House, of which 22 were to be Fijian, 22 Indian, and 8 General Electors, that is, those classified as neither Fijians nor Indians. Of the 44 Fijian and Indian members, 12 from each community were to be elected on the communal roll and 10 by cross-voting; 3 of the General Electors were to be elected from the communal roll and 5 from the national roll.

At the beginning, there were hopes for the development of multiracial politics. In the 1972 elections both the Alliance and the NFP made genuine attempts, although with limited success, to attract voters from all communities; but, as time went on, communal politics gained ascendancy. This was not surprising but a logical consequence of the constitutional arrangement in place in Fiji, which combined the Westminster system with communal representation. The communal system provided little incentive or opportunity for either voters or candidates to concern themselves with the problems of other communities. Communal sentiments were reinforced. It followed that those elected from the national, cross-voting seats, representing national constituencies, were not regarded as really legitimate representatives of their own community. And political parties, predominantly ethnic in character, focused their energy on the community whose interests they were formed to promote. The stress on communalism meant that those parties which were originally committed to multiracialism were inevitably driven back to promoting mainly or only the interests of the community from which historically they had derived their support.

From this follows the most serious problem of all: the role of ethnic parties in forming government. Because the political parties, responding to the communal system of representation, have each drawn their support mainly from a single community, government by one party is seen essentially as ethnic government. The defeat in a general election of the governing party by another party or coalition supported mainly by another ethnic group is seen as the defeat of one community by another. This is precisely what happened in Fiji. In 1987, when the Alliance was defeated by the National Federation Party-Fiji Labour Party coalition, many Fijians thought that their community was defeated, that they were deprived of the political ascendancy which they saw as essential to safeguarding their interests. Because they placed so much weight on political ascendancy, the Fijians were unwilling to accept the outcome of the election. Fijians saw the defeat of their party as a breach of the Indo-Fijians' tacit acceptance of the principle of Fijian political ascendancy, but the Indo-Fijians saw no inconsistency between their recognition of the principle of Fijian ascendancy, as they understood it, and seeking to form the government. The result of this mutual incomprehension was the military overthrow of the coalition government on 14 May 1987.

Yet the outcome of the 1987 election was entirely consistent with the principles of the 1970 constitutional arrangements. No constitution based on democratic principles can guarantee that a particular party will always remain in office. Nor can it guarantee that the party which wins a majority will always be one representing a particular ethnic community. The very essence of a democratic system is the ability of elections to change the government, to maintain their accountability and responsiveness to the people. The process of change, which is both natural and inevitable, has been evident in Fiji.

The 1990 Constitution reflected what Fijians believed to be the remedy for their political predicament. There were significant departures from the 1970 Constitution. The membership of the lower house was increased to 70, and there was no longer parity of representation between Fijians and Indo-Fijians. The 37 seats for the Fijians gave them an overall majority. Indo-Fijians were allocated 27 seats, and Rotumans, previously part of the Fijian electoral roll, were given one seat. The number of General Elector seats was reduced from 8 to 5, and the roll enlarged to include Pacific Island voters, who also were previously on the Fijian roll. The prime minister was to be a Fijian, and the president an appointee of the Great Council of Chiefs. All seats were to be filled by voting on communal rolls. There was no provision for cross-voting, so that no ethnic community could affect the selection of members to represent any community but its own. The upper house of 34 members consisted of 24 nominees of the Great Council of Chiefs, 1 of the Council of Rotuma, and 9 appointed by the president to represent the other communities. A number of positions were reserved for the indigenous communities, and affirmative action policies were prescribed to pay specific attention to their needs

The 1990 Constitution was a drastic response to what had been seen as a drastic situation. Its underlying assumption was that, if Fijians had more than half the seats in the House of Representatives, they would be able to maintain their hold on political power. An indigenous Fijian party winning all 37 seats would have the necessary majority to form a government. Splinter Fijian parties would submerge their difference and come together in the interests of the larger Fijian cause. And Rotumans and General Electors could be counted upon for their support. That was the hope, but in reality there was considerable divergence of interests across occupations and regions in Fijian society, created by the effects of the money economy which no amount of political engineering could hide. Even with the benefit of weighted representation, Fijians could not form government without the support of independent members and members of another party. Nor was the governing coalition able to maintain its own unity in all circumstances, most clearly seen in the defeat of the SVT-led coalition in November 1993.

The lesson was clear. First, the goal of permanent Fijian political unity was unrealistic and efforts to pursue it in the context of a rapidly changing environment had a high cost for Fijians themselves. Second, in the absence of unity, even a constitution as heavily weighted in favour of Fijians as the 1990 Constitution may not prevent a minority of Fijians from joining with an Indo-Fijian party or parties to form a government. And third, trying to keep a predominantly Fijian government in office in perpetuity may not be the best way of securing the ascendancy of Fijian interests. In short, the assumptions and understandings which underpinned the 1990 Constitution were proved by experience to be untenable. Fiji would need to chart a new course to move away from the cul-de-sac of communal politics and ethnic compartmentalization.

Charting a New Course

The Reeves Commission was convinced after listening to submissions that the people of Fiji wanted all communities to play some part in the cabinet and that voters should be able to cast votes for at least some candidates belonging to communities other than their own. They disagreed on the means of achieving that end and the pace of movement towards multi-ethnicity, but the broad goal was widely shared. The Commission agreed that progress towards the sharing of power among all communities was the only way to resolve some of Fiji's constitutional problems and the only way to attain racial harmony, national unity, and the social and economic advancement of all communities. Constitutional arrangements which promote the emergence of mufti-ethnic governments should be the primary goal. Such arrangements should protect the rights and interests of all citizens, particularly of the indigenous communities. And they should provide incentives for political parties to strive for the goal of mufti-ethnic cooperation and for the political process to move gradually but decisively away from the communal system of representation. The principle of Fijian paramountcy should be recognized, as in the past, in its protective role in securing effective Fijian participation in a multi-ethnic government, along with members of other communities, and in securing the fruits of affirmative programmes of social and ethnic justice based on a distribution of resources broadly acceptable to all. Fijian interests should not be subordinate to the interests of other communities. Ultimately, however, the best guarantee of the interests of all ethnic communities was a constitution that gave all political parties a strong inducement not to espouse policies that favoured the interests of one community over the interests of others. Instead, it should encourage them to see the important interests of each community as national interests which have to be met through the concerted efforts by all.

This goal of achieving an inclusive, democratic, open, and free multi-ethnic society is reflected in a number of the Commission's early recommendations. Fiji should be named The Republic of the Fiji Islands, which would give all Fiji citizens, if they wished, the opportunity of calling themselves by the common name of 'Fiji Islanders'. The Constitution should accord Fijian, Hindi, and English equal status and, wherever possible, services to the public should be available in all three languages. The Preamble should be broadly acceptable to all its citizens, touching upon the history of Fiji's multi-ethnic society and its shared beliefs and values. Perhaps most important, the values and principles which should be taken into account when forming governments should be stated in a Compact, an artefact of moral as distinct from legal force. These include respect for the rights of all individuals, communities, and groups, including those protecting the traditional ownership of Fijian land and the observation of lease arrangements between landlords and tenants; the right to freely practise religion, language, culture, and traditions; the right of the indigenous communities to governance through separate administrative systems; political freedom and full and equal citizenship rights for all; respect for the democratic process; fair and inclusive government and the need to negotiate in good faith to reach agreement to resolve differences and conflicts of interests; recognition of the principle of the ascendancy of Fijian interests as a protective principle to ensure that the interests of the Fijian community are not subordinated to the interests of other communities; and the need for affirmative action and social justice programmes to secure equality of access to opportunities, amenities, and services for the Fijian and Rotuman people, as well as other communities, and for all disadvantaged groups, to be based on an allocation of resources broadly acceptable to all ethnic communities (FCRC 1996: 82–4).

Institutions of Government

The values and principles set out above were given concrete constitutional form in the Commission's recommendations on the structure of government. They represent significant shifts from both the 1990 and the 1970 Constitutions. To begin with, the Commission recommended that not only should the Bose Levu Vakaturaga (BLV, Great Council of Chiefs) be recognized in the Constitution, as was the case in the 1990 Constitution, but that its composition, powers, and functions should be further specified. There was widespread support for this view, reflecting the respect which that institution is accorded for its pre-eminent role in Fijian affairs. Some Fijians wanted to return the BLV to its original status, restricting its membership predominantly to chiefs. The Commission regarded that view as impracticable and inconsistent with contemporary reality. It recommended that the BLV should consist of 20 members nominated by the three confederacies and 14 elected by the provinces, besides 5 ex-officio members comprising the president, the heads of the three confederacies, and the Minister for Fijian Affairs. The BLV should continue to be an advisory body, though with the important functions of nominating candidates for the office of president and exercising veto power over amendments to the entrenched legislation relating to Fijians, Rotumans, and the Rabi Island community, or any other legislation which the Attorney-General certifies as affecting Fijian land or customary rights. To exercise its functions impartially, the BLV should be independent not only from government but also from any political party. It should have its own secretariat and relative financial autonomy as well as electing its own chairperson. The Indo-Fijian community also wanted a body similar to the BLV for itself. The Commission recognized the need for such a body but felt that this was matter for the Indo-Fijian community to take up in the first instance.

It could be conferred statutory or constitutional status if it proved its utility as a representative body of Indo-Fijian opinion.

The Commission recommended the retention of the office of the president, largely with the same powers as the holder of the office of Governor-General in the Westminster tradition. This meant that executive power would rest with the cabinet, and the president would be bound to act on the advice of ministers. The ceremonial role of the presidency would be important, with the holder of the office expected to symbolize the unity of the nation, command the loyalty and respect of all the communities, and be seen to be impartial in the discharge of duties. There would be clearly spelt-out matters on which the president could act in his or her 'own deliberate judgement' but within the bounds of the conventions of the parliamentary system of government. Most submissions agreed that the president should continue to be an indigenous Fijian, an important symbolic recognition of Fijians as the indigenous people of the land, but they also suggested that this be balanced by the constitutional provision that there should be a vice-president who should be a non-Fijian. The president—and the vice-president, who would be the president's running mate as in the American system—would be elected without debate by the Electoral College comprising both houses of parliament from a list of between three and five names submitted to it by the BLV. There would be a President's Council of between 10 and 15 distinguished citizens of all ethnic communities and walks of life to provide the president with their well-informed, non-partisan views on issues of national importance, without in any way imposing constraints on the actions of the cabinet.

The Commission recommended the retention of the bicameral Westminster system which had been in existence in Fiji for nearly 30 years, but suggested important changes in both the composition of the two houses and the method of election. Both the houses should be elected. The Upper House, to be renamed Bose e Cake, should comprise 35 members, 2 each from the 14 Fijian provinces, 1 from Rotuma, and 6 appointed by the president on the advice of the Electoral Commission to represent communities and groups unrepresented in parliament, that is, religious and cultural groups, women, youth. Members of all communities have a very strong sense of territorial identity through both birth and residence as well as shared or complementary interests. Time and again the Commission was told by members of all communities belonging to a particular area that 'here, we all get on well together'. In the rural areas, most people were able to speak both Fijian and Hindi; indeed, in several places, some Indo-Fijians indicated to the Commission their desire to make their submissions in the Fijian dialect of the area. For these reasons, the Commission recommended that members representing the provinces in the Bose e Cake be elected by voters from all communities resident in the province, thus helping to strengthen the sense of common identification with the province and their economic, and some times social, interdependence. Provincial concerns would be articulated from a provincial rather than a narrow racial perspective. In terms of its powers and functions, the Bose e Cake would be similar to a house of review in the Westminster tradition.

The arrangements for electing members of the House of Representatives has attracted the greatest amount of attention nationally and internationally, understandably so as not only is it the main legislative organ of the country but also the party alignment of its members determines which party will form the government and which party leader will become prime minister. The Commission approached the delicate issue of the election and composition of the House with certain objectives in mind: the new arrangements should encourage the emergence of multi-ethnic governments, comply with international standards of equal suffrage, be based on a more open system of representation, and provide a gradual but decisive means of moving away from the present constitutional arrangements. Applying these criteria made it clear that the Fijian system of communal representation was anachronistic and generally contrary to international practice. A study of the voting systems of 150 of the world's 186 sovereign states by the International Parliamentary Union in 1993 (FCRC 1996: 291) showed that in only 25 states are some members elected or appointed to the legislature to represent particular groups, but in each case the number of special seats is very small in comparison with the size of the legislature. In Fiji, all the seats are elected on communal roll.

Many submissions supported the present arrangements and many Fijians wanted to see them even more heavily weighted in favour of the indigenous communities. Equally, there were many submissions from individuals and groups of all communities which wanted at least some seats to be filled by candidates elected by voters on a non-racial basis. Many advocated returning to the cross-voting seats under the 1970 Constitution, but that arrangement was fraught and only marginally successful in bringing about more conciliatory and less communally based politics, the community finding it hard to accept that members elected mainly by the votes of other communities really represented the community to which the seat belonged. Consistent with its view that the people of Fiji should make a gradual but decisive break from the present arrangements, the

Commission recommended a 70-seat lower house, to be called the Bose Lawa, made up of 45 seats elected from open constituencies, with no constitutional restrictions on the race of voters or candidates, and 25 from reserved seats allocated as follows: Fijians, including Pacific Islanders, 12; Indo-Fijians 10; General Electors 2; and Rotumans 1.

Communal representation is not in itself inconsistent with international standards, especially if it operates within the framework of individual choice and the principle of equal suffrage, but the Commission saw the reserved seats as a transitional measure to be discarded over the following decade or so. Hence any deviation from the principle of equality could be accommodated within the 'margin of appreciation' that international law allows to states in applying the international human rights standards. The allocation of reserved seats is broadly based on population figures, while taking account of historical and other factors that have affected the present and past allocations of communal seats. The point is that the allocation should be seen to be fair and acceptable.

The 25 reserved seats represent approximately 36 per cent of the total number of seats in the Bose Lawa and the open seats 64 per cent, the minimum necessary to allow them to act as a spur to the development of multi-ethnic politics. As a further incentive to the emergence of multi-ethnic governments, the Commission recommended that 45 open seats should be elected from 15 three-member constituencies, with their boundaries drawn in such away as to ensure that, as far as possible, and while taking into account traditional criteria such as geographical features, existing administrative and recognized traditional areas, means of communication, and mobility of population, the constituencies should be heterogeneous. That is, they should be composed of members of different communities, the object being to force political parties to appeal for votes for their candidates from communities other than the one in which they are based. The chances of a candidate or candidates of a community-based party succeeding will depend on the extent of support from other communities. The level of heterogeneity will naturally vary given the demography of Fiji—some places are predominantly Fijian and some predominantly Indo-Fijian—but the principle of multi-ethnicity should be borne in mind in designing constituency boundaries. The Commission took as the measure of heterogeneity the inclusion within the constituency of a mixed population ranging from a more or less equal balance between Fijians and Indo-Fijians to a proportion as high as 85–90 per cent of one community and 15–10 per cent of the other. The average distribution was 60 per cent of one community and 40 per cent of the other. The evidence before the Commission suggested that it was entirely possible to draw boundaries in Fiji in a way that achieved reasonable heterogeneity.

Along with open seats and heterogeneous constituencies, the electoral system can also play an important role in promoting multi-ethnic cooperation. Students of politics have long realized the crucial role electoral systems play in shaping the behaviour of political parties and the strategies they employ to win elections, and the incentives they provide in rewarding one outcome and punishing another. Fiji, like most ex-British colonies, inherited the British voting system at independence, namely, the plurality system known as first-past-the-post (FPP) under which the winning candidate is the one who gets the greatest number of votes. A logical system when the choice is between only two candidates, FPP is widely considered unfair and iniquitous where there are more than two candidates. It also denies voters expression of the possible range of preferences they may have. Because of the disadvantages of plurality systems, various modifications have been proposed over the years to ensure that a winning candidate gets an absolute majority of the votes cast, that is, more than 50 per cent, and several of these were mentioned to the Commission for its consideration.

Acknowledging the critical role the electoral system plays in determining political outcomes, the Commission identified and ranked a number of criteria against which to evaluate the various available options. These included, in order of importance, the encouragement of multi-ethnic government; recognition of the role of political parties; incentives for moderation and cooperation across ethnic lines; effective representation of constituents; effective voter participation; effective representation of minority and special interest groups; fairness between political parties; effective government; effective opposition; proven workability; and legitimacy. All electoral systems meet some of these criteria and some more than others. The single transferable vote (STV), which was recommended by the Street Commission in 1975, for example, mitigates against the winner-take-all outcome of the FPP and achieves better proportionality of seats to votes than FPP, but by requiring an extremely low threshold to get elected—in a three-member constituency, a successful candidate would need no more than 25 per cent—and by privileging the representation of community interests, it fails to meet the Commission's most important electoral criterion: the promotion of multi-ethnic governments. The list system of proportional representation allocates seats to parties in proportion to the number of votes cast for the party, and while it has considerable merit, its one weakness is that, by treating the whole country or major regions of a country as a single constituency, it fails to provide the important links between the voter and his or her member. It also provokes fears of small parties exercising disproportionate influence in the governance of the country.

In the Commission's view, the alternative vote (AV), also known as preferential vote, best met all the criteria it identified as being relevant. The AV is based on the same principle as second ballots but avoids the need for a second election at a later date. It is in effect a refinement of the FPP system in that it requires voters to rank candidates in their order of preference. To be elected, a candidate must have a majority of the votes cast, that is, at least 50 per cent plus 1. If no candidate reaches the threshold when first preferences are counted, then second and third preferences are counted and allocated. The process of elimination continues until one of the candidates has obtained the required quota. The AV provides incentives for vote pooling by requiring the winning candidate to obtain more than 50 per cent of the votes. In heterogeneous constituencies this threshold increases the need for the winning candidate to have multi-ethnic support. The system allows parties to trade preferences. Again, only moderate parties with conciliatory policies will agree to trade preferences and be able to persuade their supporters to honour the agreement. The system therefore encourages the emergence of such parties. Constituents are effectively represented at least in so far as candidates represent territorial constituencies, and citizens are given considerable opportunity to affect the outcome of the poll by expressing preferences among individual candidates. As a majoritarian, not a proportional, system, the AV is likely to encourage the emergence of a strong party or pre-election government. The Commission recommended that the AV system be used in multi-member constituencies, but there is nothing to stop its use in single-member constituencies.

As mentioned, the Commission recommended the retention of the Westminster system for Fiji. The people were familiar with its workings and conventions. None the less, its adversarial nature, pitting an 'Indian' opposition against a 'Fijian' government, elicited comment in the submissions. The Commission noted that, in Fiji, very often an opposition criticism of a government proposal, no matter how valid or rational, was portrayed as an Indian criticism of Fijian performance. People asked the Commission to suggest ways of minimizing the harmful effects of this aspect of the Westminster system so as to allow the House to use the talents of all its members to good advantage in a collaborative way. Fortunately, Commonwealth countries, including New Zealand, have devised such ways by setting up sector committees which permit all members of the lower house, except ministers or assistant ministers, and whether belonging to the government or the opposition, to take part in national decision-making. Sector committees are structured in such a way that all departments and other government agencies come within the supervision of some committee. The Commission recommended that, in addition to the existing standing committees, such as the Standing Select Committee on Sugar and the Public Accounts Committee, there should be five standing select committees, each dealing with one of the following sectors: economic services, social services, natural resources, foreign relations, and administrative services. These committees would systematically scrutinize all areas of government activity and consider bills referred to them by parliament. Their overall membership should reflect the balance of the parties in the house, with the chairperson and the deputy chairperson to come from opposite sides of the House.

All these various devices from the Compact, through the method of electing parliament from open heterogeneous constituencies using the alternative vote system, to the establishment of sector select committees are designed to achieve an open, representative, inclusive, and multi-ethnic government that protects the interests and addresses the concerns of all communities and groups within the overarching framework of a democratic system. That was the only way all the people of Fiji could aspire to realize for themselves and their children a prosperous and united future.

Issues of Governance and Accountability

While questions surrounding the election of parliament understandably occupy the centre stage in any constitutional review, there are other areas of considerable importance which impinge on the daily lives of the people that need attention. These include provisions relating to the acquisition and deprivation of citizenship, fundamental freedoms and bills of right, the independence and functioning of the judiciary, the enforcement of accountability in the performance of the public sector, and access to state services on a non-discriminatory basis. Often in these areas, the Commission was required not so much to formulate new proposals as to modernize or revise the existing ones in the light of new international conventions and practices which had been adopted over the last decade or so.

To illustrate, the 1990 Constitution already has a bill of rights, called fundamental rights and freedoms, adapted with few changes the one in the 1970 Constitution. But the independence bill of rights was in a form developed by Britain's Foreign and Commonwealth Office and included, with only slight variations, in the constitutions of most former British colonies. It naturally reflected British caution about including individual rights in a judicially enforceable constitution. Individual rights and freedoms were seen as already enshrined in common law. The emphasis was not on affirming their existence but on protecting them from unjustified interference by the state. The Commission recommended that, in keeping with modern trends, the Constitution should affirm rights and freedoms in positive terms, that these should be judicially enforceable, binding the legislative, executive, and judicial branches of government at all levels, and that they should not conflict with the international human rights standards but rather give effect to them where appropriate. It recommended the creation of a three-member Human Rights Commission to educate the public about the nature and purpose of the bill of rights, make recommendations to government about matters affecting compliance with human rights, and exercise any other functions conferred to it by legislation. The Commission adopted a similar approach to the issue of citizenship. Fiji's existing citizenship laws reflect the thinking of an earlier generation and were in some important respects not only archaic but also in breach of modern conventions. The independence constitution and its 1990 counterpart allowed non-citizen women automatic right to acquire Fiji citizenship upon marriage to a Fiji male citizen, but did not accord the same privilege to non-citizen husbands. Whatever the reason for that discrimination in the past, it was no longer acceptable. Nor did the earlier constitutions make specific reference to the rights of children. Most women's groups who made submissions were adamant that discrimination against women and children had to go, and the Commission agreed.

In the Westminster system, a vital corollary to the power of politically appointed ministers to direct government policy is the expectation that the administration of that policy will be carried out economically, efficiently, and effectively by politically neutral and impartial state services. Although the objectives of economy, efficiency, and effectiveness in state services have a long history in Fiji, they have never been expressly required in the constitution.

Because these objectives are so fundamental to the functioning of all state services, the Commission felt that they should be reflected in a constitutional provision. A related issue, to be considered alongside the ones mentioned above, was the 'fair treatment' of each community in the number and distribution of entry appointments. The 1970 Constitution directed the Public Service Commission to 'ensure that, so far as possible, each community in Fiji receives fair treatment in the number and distribution of offices to which candidates of that community are appointed on entry'. The 1990 Constitution obliges the government to ensure each level of each department comprises not less than 50 per cent of Fijians and Rotumans, and not less than 40 per cent of members of other communities. But this these quota has not been observed, nor, to be fair, is it possible to achieve at *every level* within *every department*.

Indo-Fijians complained of a significant reduction in their numbers in the state services, particularly at the senior levels. They expressed concern at falling Indo-Fijian representation in the police force and their almost total absence from the armed forces. Whatever the reason—occupational preferences, emigration—the Indo-Fijian complaint was well-founded. The Commission concluded that while efficiency, economy, and effectiveness should be the principal objectives in managing state services, some more appropriate account must be taken of the overall representation of different ethnic groups at all levels in all the various state services.

To that end, the Commission proposed a new general provision in the Constitution along the following lines. In recruiting and promoting members of all state services belonging to the executive branch of government, including the public service, the Fiji Police Force, and the Republic of Fiji Military Forces, and in the management of those services, the factors to be taken in to account must include the need (1) to ensure that government policies can be carried out effectively; (2) to achieve efficiency and economy in all the state's services; (3) to make appointments and promotions on the basis of merit; (4) to provide men and women and members of all ethnic groups with adequate opportunities for training and advancement; and (5) for the composition of each service, at all levels, broadly to reflect the ethnic composition of the population, taking into account, however, occupational preferences.

Closely related to the provision of state services is the issue of ethnic and social justice. Section 21 of the 1990 Constitution explicitly enjoined the government to introduce affirmative action programmes for the Fijian and Rotuman communities, which were perceived as lagging behind other communities in terms of their achievement in some sectors, notably education and commerce, and participation at the higher levels of the public service. These affirmative action policies have had an effect. In 1985, Fijians made up 46.4 per cent of established civil servants, Indo-Fijians 48 per cent, and General Electors and expatriates 5.6 per cent. The corresponding figures in October 1995 were Fijians 57.3 per cent, Indo-Fijians 38.6 per cent, and General Electors and expatriates 4.11 per cent. In 1995, of the 31 permanent secretaries, 22 were Fijians, 6 were Indo-Fijians and 3 General Electors. Indo-Fijians accepted the principle of affirmative action to redress imbalances in the public sector but wanted them to include disadvantaged members of all communities, not just the indigenous people. Their submission drew attention to growing poverty among sections of their people and their growing numbers in squatter settlements fringing towns and cities. The Commission agreed that the government needed to continue implementing policies and programmes to reduce inequalities between different ethnic communities, but, since there were areas in which other communities were also disadvantaged, social inequalities should not be neglected. It recommended a social justice and affirmative action programme for Rotumans and Fijians and other ethnic communities, for men as well as women, effective equality of access to education and training, land, and housing, participation in commerce, and all aspects of service of the state at all levels, and other opportunities, amenities, and services essential to an adequate standard of living. Furthermore, the programme should be authorised by an act, following parliamentary debate, which specified the goals of the programme and the identity of the persons or groups it was intended to benefit, the means by which those goals would be achieved, performance measures for achieving the efficacy of the programme, and the criteria for the selection of the members of the group entitled to participate in the programme. In short, to be effective, affirmative action policies should be transparent, properly debated, and carefully monitored.

Generally, for state services and institutions to be effective and impartial, they need to be subject to strict rules of accountability. The Commission received many submissions proposing constitutional provisions to prevent official corruption and achieving higher ethical standards on the part of those holding important offices of state. They were not accusations against ministers or state servants; they were about public confidence in Fiji's system of government and the integrity of its leaders. Existing statutes, regulations, and orders contain ethical standards and rules which apply to state servants and members and officers of statutory bodies, but the

Commission was convinced of the need to go further. It therefore proposed an 'integrity code' for the president, the vice-president, ministers, all members of parliament, and all constitutional office-holders which would require them not to place themselves in positions in which they had or could have a conflict of interest, compromise the fair exercise of their public or official functions and duties, use their offices for private gain, allow their integrity to be called into question, endanger or diminish respect for or confidence in the integrity of government, or demean their office or position. These principles should be enshrined in an act of parliament, which would make detailed and specific provisions to deal with the various kinds of conflicts of interest that arose in the context of Fiji's particular circumstances. The Commission also recommended the strengthening of the office of Ombudsman to investigate allegations of corruption or mismanagement of public office.

In an important and innovative recommendation, the Commission recommended the creation of a new Constitutional Offices Commission, which would recommend to the president the appointment of the Ombudsman and the Auditor-General and directly appoint the Solicitor-General, the Director of Public Prosecutions, the Secretary-General to Parliament, the Supervisor of Elections, and the Commissioner of Police.

A future constitution, the Commission felt, should be generally acceptable to all citizens; guarantee the rights of individuals and groups and promote the rule of law and the separation of powers; recognize the unique history and character of Fiji; encourage every community to regard the major concerns of other communities as national concerns; recognize the equal rights of all citizens; and protect the vital interests and concerns of the indigenous Fijian and Rotuman communities and all the other groups, within the inclusive and overarching framework of democracy.

Enacting the New Constitution

The Commission submitted its report to the President of the Republic of Fiji on 6 September 1996. Four days later the report was tabled in Parliament, and referred to a multi-party, multi-ethnic joint parliamentary select committee which was charged to 'consider and deliberate upon the Report of the Fiji Constitution Review Commission to secure the passage of such amendments and changes to the Constitution as may be agreed upon by and between the various parties and groups and/or as deemed necessary or desirable' (Fiji

Parliamentary Paper 17/1997). The committee, chaired by Major General Sitiveni Rabuka, the then prime minister and leader of the largest (Fijian) party in Parliament, met in its various subcommittees, concluding its deliberations on 13 May 1997. Following a long and emotional parliamentary debate, a new constitution was passed unanimously by Parliament, coming into effect a year after promulgation. In May 1999 the country held its general election under the new Constitution.

It is not possible, within the limits of space, to examine all the provisions of the new Constitution relating to power-sharing, nor is it possible to divine the mind of the parliamentary committee, for no records were kept of its deliberations. I have, however, provided the background to the negotiation elsewhere (Lal 1998). The committee adopted 577 of the Commission's 694 recommendations, amended 40, and rejected or made redundant 77. Overall, the committee embraced the basic thrust of the Commission's recommendations that the 'primary goal of Fiji's constitutional arrangements should be to encourage the emergence of multi-ethnic governments' (FCRC 1996: 673) but differed on the best method to achieve that goal. This is reflected in the Preamble of the new Constitution as well as in the Compact, which reassures all communities that their fundamental interests are properly protected and provides broad guideline to political leaders in the conduct of the nation's affairs.

The joint parliamentary committee agreed with the Commission on the need to remove all racial and gender discrimination in the new Constitution. To that end, the citizenship rights of foreign-born husbands and wives were equalized. The Constitution no longer requires the prime minister to be an ethnic Fijian. A comprehensive and justiciable bill of rights, incorporating the latest thinking on the protection of the rights and freedoms of the individual, was entrenched in Chapter 4 of the Constitution. So was the provision for a three-person Human Rights Commission whose task would include educating the public about the bill of rights and conventions on the elimination of discrimination. The constitutional independence of important state offices was guaranteed, including Ombudsman, Auditor-General, Director of Public Prosecutions, Secretary-General to Parliament, Commissioner of Police, and Governor of the Reserve Bank. And in recruitment and promotion the government was constitutionally required to observe the principles of efficiency and due economy, merit, and equal opportunity. The principle of proportionality among ethnic groups was recognized in the composition of the state services at all levels. So in matters of governance, the parliamentary committee adhered closely to the Commission's recommendations on the need to promote equity, fairness, economy, transparency, and accountability.

But on the composition of parliament the committee disagreed with the Commission. It recommended that both the president and the vice-president should be nominated by the Great Council of Chiefs in consultation with the prime minister instead of being elected by an electoral college of both houses of Parliament. In this respect, the Constitution retains the substance of the 1990 constitution. It also rejected the Commission's recommendations regarding the Senate, opting for a totally nominated body of 34 members, 14 appointed by the Great Council of Chiefs, 9 appointed by the prime minister, 8 by the leader of the opposition, and 1 on the advice of the Council of Rotuma. Why the committee *totally* rejected the Commission's recommendation is unclear, as it gave no reasons. Perhaps it feared rivalry between two elected houses, perhaps it was mindful of the expense involved, it wanted to retain the Westminster tradition of an upper house of review. But this is all speculation.

The parliamentary committee also rejected the Commission's proposal for the composition of the House of Representatives. It recommended that 46 of the 71 members be elected from reserved, that is, communal constituencies and 25 from open, non-racial seats. Of the 46 seats, 23 would be reserved for Fijians, 19 for Indo-Fijians, 3 for General Electors, and 1 for Rotuma. The three ethnic groups have the power of veto over the number of seats allocated to them, thus ensuring the maintenance of ethnic representation permanently rather than as a transitional measure. Further, all except 6 of the Fijian seats were to be contested from rural provinces, which creates its own problems, including fostering provincial loyalties at the expense of a national vision and breaching the principle of equal franchise. The retention of provincial boundaries will work to the detriment of Fijian unity and effective participation in national affairs.

The Commission took the view that power-sharing should be achieved through the electoral system and through multi-ethnic coalitions or political parties, convinced that political cooperation should flow from voluntary agreement, not constitutional requirement. But the parliamentary committee rejected this view. Some critics accused the Commission of having a doctrinaire opposition to all non-Westminster arrangements. Others thought its recommendations placed too heavy a burden on the electoral system to deliver an outcome broadly acceptable to the vast majority of the people. Yet others pointed to previous failed attempts to forge multiracial coalitions or political parties in Fiji and argued that, for all its risks, constitutionally mandated power-sharing between ethnically based political parties was a better alternative than the winner-take-all outcome produced by the Westminster system which, in Fiji's case, placed one ethnic group in power and another out of it. The committee was swayed by these arguments and recommended mandatory power-sharing. The prime minister determines the size of the cabinet, which would have to be multi-party. All parties with more than 10 per cent of seats in the House of Representatives would be entitled to be invited to join the cabinet in proportion to their numbers in the House. A party can, of course, decline to join the cabinet, in which case the prime minister is entitled to look to his or her own party or coalition for replacements, selecting ministers in consultation with the leaders of their parties.

The new 1997 Fiji Constitution is without doubt a great improvement on its two previous counterparts, but it is still full of compromises and contradictions. Its broad thrust is the encouragement of moderate multi-ethnic politics through the adoption of a new system of alternative voting and of a number of open, non-racial constituencies, the principle of proportionality in the pursuance of public policies, and through the values enshrined in the Compact. At the same time, two-thirds of the seats in the House of Representatives are contested on communal rolls which, as MacKenzie (1957: 35) observed nearly half a century ago, 'strengthen communal feeling, because in public debate appeals are made principally to the interest of each community, and within each community the more violent and selfish spokesmen of special interests outbid the moderate and public-spirited'. The electoral system intended to provide the space for pre-election political cooperation, yet the Constitution stipulates mandatory, post-election power-sharing. The Constitution enshrines values of equity and fairness, yet the way the constituency boundaries are drawn negates the fundamental principle of one vote one value. Fijians participate in national politics by utilizing the mechanism of traditional political institutions, causing conflict between traditional and modern patterns of behaviour.

Postscript

In 1999, Fiji went to the polls under the multiracial 1997 constitution (Lal 2000). Two major multiracial coalitions contested the elections: the People's Coalition comprising the Fijian Association Party, Party of National Unity, and the Fiji Labour Party, and the SVT-NFP coalition which also included the small United Generals Party. The Fiji Labour Party abused the spirit of the Alternative Vote by giving its preferences not to parties with a philosophy broadly similar to its own but to those which were opposed to the party posing the greatest threat to its electoral prospects, especially in the marginal seats. Hence, it put the National Federation Party last on its list of preferences. Sometimes, the parties Labour preferred to the NFP were vehemently opposed to its own policies. Labour won 37 of the 71 seats in the House of Representatives, the People's Coalition an astounding 58 seats. The NFP did not win a single seat, while the SVT did poorly among the Fijians, winning only 8. Mahendra Chaudhry, as the leader of the winning coalition, became prime minister.

A government of a fractious coalition with divergent interests and discordant voices produced its own problems. But far more important was the growing opposition to the government orchestrated by defeated politicians, some of whose own colleagues were in government. Chaudhry's confrontational, abrasive style became the focus of Fijian nationalists' anger. His hugely counterproductive tussle with the media made matters worse for the government. Small, isolated roadblocks and rallies gathered momentum with the passage of time, culminating in the George Speight-led hijacking of the government on 19 May 2000. Speight was the front man for an assortment of institutions and individuals aggrieved by the People's Coalition government: defeated politicians seeking revenge, those who had amassed enormous wealth during the Rabuka years in the 1990s, the unemployed and the unemployable, the human casualties of globalization.

Speight handed over power to the military after receiving an offer of immunity for his treasonous crime. For its part, the military abrogated the Constitution and installed an interim civilian administration. As one its first priorities the administration appointed a Fijian-dominated constitution review committee charged with the responsibility of entrenching indigenous Fijian political control: in effect, of reverting to the provisions of the 1990 constitution. Many Fijians believed that they had lost power because of the new constitution, in particular due to the Alternative Vote.

On 4 July, an Indo-Fijian refugee filed a summon in the High Court at Lautoka arguing that the attempted coup of 19 May was unsuccessful, that the declaration of emergency under the doctrine of necessity was unconstitutional, that the 1997 Constitution remained

in force, and the elected government was still the legitimate govern-
ment.[2] In his judgement delivered on 15 November, Justice Anthony
Gates upheld the continuing validity of Fiji's 1997 Constitution. The
interim administration challenged the ruling before the Fiji Court of
Appeal, now the highest court after the Chief Justice advised the
interim administration to abolish the Supreme Court. Chaired by
Sir Maurice Casey (New Zealand) Sir Ian Baker (NZ) Mari Kapi
(Papua New Guinea), Gordon Ward (Tonga) and Kenneth Handley
(Australia), the Court ruled that the 1997 Constitution had not been
abrogated and that the Parliament had not been dissolved.

The Court went further, comprehensively addressing the objections raised by the interim administration. The 1997 Constitution
was the product not of hurried but of extensive consultation. 'The
Commission report and the constitution that resulted from it
received almost universal acclaim', the Court ruled.[3] The Court
found 'erroneous' the claim that the electoral system was 'extra-
ordinarily complex, the results remarkably ambiguous and its
merit as a tool for promoting ethnic cooperation were highly questionable'. The final result, the victory of the People's Coalition,
would not have differed materially even under the first-past-the-
post system. It rejected the claim that the percentage of invalid
votes principally affected the indigenous Fijian votes. And finally,
the Court did not accept the interim administration's claim that the
1997 Constitution had diluted protection given to Fijian interests
and institutions under previous constitutions. 'Any perceived
attempt by the Government to change the law in relation to land or
to indigenous rights by stealth was impossible under the 1997 constitution and any suggestion that it needed to be replaced on that
ground cannot be substantiated.'

The Court of Appeal's landmark decision was accepted, albeit without much enthusiasm, by the interim administration, the military
forces, and the Great Council of Chiefs. That paved the way for a new
general election, under the electoral provisions of the 1997
Constitution, due in August 2001. The 1997 Constitution, the result
of the effort of so many over so many years, survived George Speight's
assault. But it will remain a piece of paper unless there is a united
will in the citizenry to make it work for the common good. In
Rousseau's words, the most important laws are those which are 'not
graven on tablets of marble or brass, but on the hearts of its citizens'.

---

[2] *Chandrika Prasad vs the Republic of the Fiji*. The judgement was published on
the Internet in several places. My copy is from ttp://www.pcgov.org.fj/docs_o/chan-
drikaprasad_ruling_gates.htm

[3] Judgement of the Fiji Court of Appeal, Cicl Appeal No.ABU0078/2000S, P.9.

11

The Belfast Agreement and the British-Irish Agreement: Consociation, Confederal Institutions, a Federacy, and a Peace Process

Brendan O'Leary

The multi-party and intergovernmental agreement reached in Belfast on 10 April 1998 and the subsequent treaty between the Irish and the UK governments, the British-Irish Agreement of 1999, jointly comprise an exemplary collective constitutional design for an ethno-nationally divided territory with rival claims to its sovereignty. The word 'design' is appropriate because the Belfast Agreement's makers knew they were effectively engaged in constitutional crafting, even if they disagreed over whether they were making a transitional, durable, or permanent settlement. Whether it will be fully implemented and institutionalized still remains uncertain. If it is, it will become an export model for conflict regulators, and is already acquiring this status even for unpromising places such as Kashmir (Bose 1999). If this continues it will make a nice counterpoint to the export of the Westminster constitutional model that served Northern Ireland ill (Madden 1980; O'Leary and McGarry 1996: Chs 3–5). If it is not implemented, partially implemented, or 'malimplemented', as at the time of writing, debates will

This chapter is an updated version of the paper presented at the 'Constitutional Design 2000' conference at Notre Dame. I must thank Bernard Grofman, Jorgen Elklit, Donald Horowitz, Arend Lijphart, Andrew Reynolds, Ben Reilly, Fred Riggs, Cheryl Saunders, Giovanni Sartori, and Al Stepan for very helpful comments. The paper draws freely upon prior and subsequently published work (O'Leary 1999*a*, *d*, *e*; 2001*a*, *b*, *c*) and the thanks given therein still stands, especially to John McGarry, Christopher McCrudden and Paul Mitchell. The Notre Dame conference itself prompted a joint paper with Bernard Grofman and Jorgen Elklit on the design of the executive that will be published elsewhere (O'Leary, Grofman, and Elklit 2001).

arise over whether there were critical design flaws. But notwithstanding serious difficulties in implementation, it represents the most comprehensive, ambitious, and successful attempt at constitutional conflict regulation of the last three decades.

The Name of the Agreement

Names matter in ethno-national conflicts and there is no unanimity on the title of this agreement. Under the description *The Agreement: Agreement Reached in the Multi-party Negotiations*[1] it was published, unaltered, as a dense 30-page text and distributed to all households before the referendum to endorse it in Northern Ireland in May 1998. Since then the UK government has officially styled it the 'Belfast Agreement' in its primary legislation, the Northern Ireland Act 1998, and in its parliamentary references. Its republican dissident critics call it the 'Stormont Agreement', advertizing their continuing rejection of the partition of Ireland executed by the Westminster Parliament in the Government of Ireland Act 1920, and their dislike of the final negotiating venue that once housed the hated Northern Ireland Parliament. But the text was negotiated in many other places: in Dublin, London, and Washington; in smaller cities, towns, and villages; and in airports, aeroplanes, and unofficial 'communications'. It was not signed by all of its makers in the final negotiations in Belfast; some had to await their parties' endorsements. Some know it just by its date: the 'April 10 1998 Agreement'. Its most popular name is the 'Good Friday Agreement' because the 'miracle' of its finalization occurred on the anniversary of Christ's crucifixion; but this name gives too much credit to Christianity, both as the key source of conflict and as a source of resolution.[2] It is perhaps most suitably called the 'British-Irish Agreement' (O'Leary 1999e), a designation that reflects an important fact, namely that it fulfils and, if implemented, supersedes its predecessor, the Anglo-Irish Agreement of 1985 (O'Leary and McGarry 1996: Ch. 6). But that name is now taken by the 1999 treaty which incorporates the Belfast text as an appendix. So I shall refer simply to 'the Agreement', where necessary distinguishing the Belfast text from the treaty.

[1] 'Government of the United Kingdom' is given as the author, but neither publisher nor place of publication is supplied.

[2] For the argument that the conflict in Northern Ireland is primarily ethnonational rather than religious see, *inter alia*, McGarry and O'Leary (1995a: Chs 5, 6; 1995b).

The Institutional Nature of the Agreement

The Agreement is internally consociational, a political arrangement that meets *all* of the criteria laid down by Lijphart:

(1) cross-community executive power-sharing;
(2) proportionality rules throughout the governmental and public sectors;
(3) community self-government—or autonomy—and equality in cultural life; and
(4) veto rights for minorities (Lijphart 1977).

A consociation is an association of communities: in this case British unionist, Irish nationalist, and 'others'. A consociation can be built without explicit theoretical guidance.[3] Most often consociations are the outcomes of bargains between the political leaders of ethnic or religious groups. This Agreement was the product of tacit and explicit consociational thought[4] and of 'pacting' by most of the leaders of the key ethno-national groups and their respective patron states.

But the Agreement is not just consociational, and departs from Lijphart's detailed prescriptions. It has important external dimensions; it was made with the leaders of national, and not just ethnic or religious, communities—unlike most previous consociations; and it is the first consociational settlement endorsed by a referendum that required concurrent majorities in jurisdictions in different states. To be formulaic: *the Agreement foresaw an internal consociation within overarching confederal and federalizing institutions; it has elements of co-sovereignty agreed between its patron states; it promises a novel model of 'double protection'; and it rests on a*

---

[3] Lijphart claims that consociational rules were invented by Dutch politicians in 1917, and by their Lebanese (1943), Austrian (1945), Malaysian (1955), Colombian (1958), Indian (in the 1960s), and South African (1993–4) counterparts later in the century. One does not have to agree with the citation of any of these cases to accept that politicians are capable of doing theory without theorists, see Lijphart (1990c: viii; 1996).

[4] Dr Mowlam, the UK Secretary of State for Northern Ireland in 1997–9, had an academic consociational heritage. Consociational thinking had an impact on the drafting of the Framework Documents of 1995 that prefigured the Agreement (O'Leary 1995), and the 'novel' executive formation in the Agreement, based on the d'Hondt rule, adapted coalition principles used elsewhere in Europe and in the European Parliament (O'Leary, Grofman, and Elklit 2001). Consociational thinking had had local resonance since the Sunningdale Agreement of 1973; the nationalist SDLP had been especially interested in power-sharing devices, and was the prime initiator of proposals in the internal negotiation (Strand One) of the Agreement.

*bargain derived from diametrically conflicting hopes about its likely
long-run outcome, but that may not destabilize it.*

The Internal Settlement: A Distinctive Consociation

The Agreement proposed and the 1998 Northern Ireland Act established a single-chamber Assembly and an Executive. The Assembly
and Executive have full legislative and executive competence for
economic development, education, health and social services, agriculture, environment, and finance, including the local civil service.
Through 'cross-community agreement'—defined below—the
Assembly may expand these competencies; and, again through such
agreement and with the consent of the UK Secretary of State for
Northern Ireland and the Westminster Parliament, it may legislate
for any currently non-devolved reserved function.[5] Within a traditional UK constitutional perspective, maximum feasible devolved
self-government[6] is therefore within the scope of the local decision-
makers: a convention may arise in which the Secretary of State and
Westminster 'rubber stamp' the legislative measures of the
Assembly.[7] Indeed, it is conceivable that most public policy in
Ireland, north and south, may eventually be made without direct
British ministerial involvement, though the British budgetary allo-
cation will be pivotal as long as Northern Ireland remains in the
UK.

Elected Assembly members (MLAs) must designate themselves
as 'nationalist', 'unionist', or 'other'. In this respect Lijphart's
injunctions in favour of 'self-determination rather than pre-
determination' are violated (Lijphart 1985; 1990*b*; 1993). After the
first Assembly was elected in June 1998 this requirement posed difficult questions for the Alliance Party of Northern Ireland (APNI)
and other 'cross-community' parties, such as the Northern Ireland

[5] The internal security functions of the state—policing and the courts—have not
been devolved, but they could be devolved in principle. I address the meaning of
'devolution' below.

[6] The Assembly may not legislate in contravention of the European Convention
on Human Rights or European Union law, modify a specific entrenched enactment,
discriminate on grounds of religious belief or political opinion, or 'deal with' an
excepted power except in an 'ancillary way'—which roughly means it may not enact
laws which modify UK statutes on excepted matters, such as the Crown.

[7] According to the UK's legislative enactment in the Northern Ireland Act 1998,
the Assembly can expand its autonomy only with regard to *reserved*, not *excepted*,
matters. Reserved matters, most importantly, include the criminal law, criminal
justice, and policing. Excepted matters include the Crown and the currency.

Women's Coalition (NIWC), who have both cultural Catholic and cultural Protestant leaders and voters. They determined that they were 'others', though they are free to change their classifications once in this Assembly, and, of course, in future Assemblies.

Through standard legislative majority rule the Assembly may pass 'normal laws' within its devolved competencies, though there is provision—the petition procedure—for 30 of the 108 Assembly members to trigger special procedures that require special majorities. But 'key decisions'—that is, the passage of controversial legislation, including the budget—automatically have these special procedures that require 'cross-community' support. Two rules have been designed for this purpose. The first is 'parallel consent', a majority that encompasses a strict concurrent majority of registered nationalists and unionists. It requires that a law be endorsed, among those present and voting, both by an overall majority of MLAs and by majorities of both its unionist and its nationalist members respectively. Table 11.1, which records the numbers in each bloc returned in the June 1998 election, shows that parallel consent with all members present currently requires the support of 22 nationalists and 30 unionists, as well as an overall majority in the Assembly. With all members present a majority of the Assembly is 55 members, so under parallel consent procedures laws may pass that are dependent upon the support of the 'others'—22 nationalists, 30 unionists, and 3 others enable the passage of a key decision. The rule does not automatically render the others unimportant.

The second rule is that of 'weighted majority'. It requires, among those present and voting, that to become law a measure must have the support of 60 per cent of members, currently 65 members when

TABLE 11.1: *The shares of blocs in the June 1998 elections to the Northern Ireland Assembly*

Bloc	First preference vote	Seats	
	%	No.	%
All nationalists	39.8	42	38.9
All others	9.4	8	7.3
All 'Yes' unionists	25.0	30	27.7
All 'No' unionists	25.5	28	25.9

Percentage figures for votes and seat shares rounded to one decimal place. 'Yes' unionists support the Agreement; 'No' unionists do not. The electoral system is the single transferable vote in six-member constituencies.

Source: O'Leary (1999*e*).

all members vote or 64 excluding the Presiding Officer, that is, the Speaker. But it also requires the support of 40 per cent of registered nationalist members and 40 per cent of unionist members: that is, in the current Assembly at least 17 nationalists and at least 24 unionists must consent. Presently all nationalists (42) and the minimum necessary number of unionists (24) have the combined support for any measure to pass in this way—without support from the 'others'. A combination of all the others (8) and the minimum number of nationalists (17) and the minimum number of unionists (24) cannot, by contrast, deliver a majority, let alone a weighted majority.

The outcome of the elections presented in Table 11.1 suggested that pro-Agreement unionist Assembly members (30) would be vulnerable to pressure from anti-Agreement unionists (28). Indeed, a member of the internally divided but formally pro-Agreement Ulster Unionist Party (UUP), Peter Weir, subsequently resigned his party's whip and must be counted as a 'No' unionist. This MLA has refused to be part of the unionist majority necessary to work the parallel consent rule. But this rebellion still left room for the Agreement to function. The UUP could deliver a workable portion of a cross-community majority under the weighted majority rule, even with six dissidents, providing David Trimble, its leader, could rely on the two pro-Agreement Progressive Unionist Party (PUP) Assembly members, and providing that he can live with support from Sinn Féin—a more uncomfortable prospect.[8]

The cross-community consent rules are central to the design of the internal consociation but are not entirely predictable. The UK legislation implies that the parallel consent procedure must be attempted first, followed by the weighted majority procedure, though the election of the premiers may only be effected by the parallel consent rule (see below). The operation of the rules depends not just on how parties register but also on their discipline within the Assembly. The lack of discipline of the UUP during 1998–2001 confirms this critical fact.

There is one 'supermajority' rule. The Assembly may, by a two-thirds resolution of its membership, call an extraordinary general election before its statutory four-year term expires. This was agreed by the parties, after the Agreement, in preference to a proposal that the UK Secretary of State should have the power to dissolve or

---

[8] There is one important exception to this possibility: the death or the resignation of either premier requires that both be replaced under the parallel consent rule, see below.

suspend the Assembly—a sign of the local parties' commitment to their self-government rather than accepting continuing arbitration from Westminster. Subsequently, to suspend the Assembly in February 2000, the Secretary of State for Northern Ireland, Peter Mandelson, had to pass new primary UK legislation through the Westminster parliament outside the remit of the Agreement— which is why Irish nationalists regarded the power of suspension as a breach of the Agreement, and indeed of the 1999 inter-governmental treaty (see below).

Executive power-sharing

The Agreement established an entirely novel Executive Committee, and at its head two quasi-presidential figures, a diarchy: a First Minister (FM) and a Deputy First Minister (DFM). Once elected the latter have presidential characteristics because it is almost impossible to depose them, provided they remain united as a team, until the next general election: the essence of presidentialism is an executive that cannot be destroyed by an assembly except through impeachment. The FM and DFM are elected together by the *parallel consent* procedure. This rule gives very strong incentives to unionists and nationalists to nominate a candidate for one of these positions that is acceptable to a majority of the other bloc's Assembly members. In the first elections for these posts, in *designate* form, pro-Agreement unionists in the UUP and the PUP voted solidly for the combination of David Trimble of the UUP and Seamus Mallon of the Social Democratic and Labour Party (SDLP). Naturally, so did the SDLP, which enjoyed a majority among registered nationalists. The 'No' unionists voted against this combination, while Sinn Féin abstained.

The rule ensures, though it does not officially require, that a unionist and a nationalist share the top two posts: it does not specify which must be First Minister. The Agreement and the Northern Ireland Act 1998 make clear that the two posts have identical symbolic and external representation functions. In the negotiations the SDLP conceded the difference in dignity in title between the positions but no differences in powers.[9] The sole difference is their titles: both preside over the Executive Committee of Ministers and have a role in coordinating its work.[10] This dual premiership critically

[9] Private information.
[10] Clause 15 (10) of the Northern Ireland Act 1998 enables the top two ministers to hold functional portfolios.

depends upon the cooperation of the two office-holders and upon the cooperation of their respective majorities—or pluralities under the weighted majority rule. In Art. 14(6) the Northern Ireland Act reinforced their interdependence by requiring that 'if either the First Minister or the deputy First Minister ceases to hold office, whether by resignation or otherwise, the other shall also cease to hold office'.

The formation of the rest of the Executive Committee, according to the procedure described below, did not proceed smoothly. Indeed, in the summer of 1999 Seamus Mallon resigned as Deputy First Minister (designate), complaining that the UUP was 'dishonouring' the Agreement and 'insulting its principles' by insisting upon decommissioning of paramilitaries' weapons before executive formation.[11] He did so to speed an intergovernmental review of the implementation of the Agreement. The question immediately arose: did Mallon's resignation automatically trigger Trimble's departure from office and require fresh elections to these positions within six weeks? The (Initial) Presiding Officer's answer to this question was that it did not, because the Assembly was not yet functioning under the Northern Ireland Act.[12] This answer was accepted. It implied, however, that if the review of the Agreement succeeded and the Agreement's institutions came into force, either that there would have to be fresh elections of the FM and DFM under the parallel consent rule or that Mallon's resignation would have to be rescinded. When the review succeeded and the Agreement came on line, the Assembly voted to nullify Mallon's resignation, thereby preventing a vote under the parallel consent rule that might have prevented Trimble's and Mallon's (re)installation in office—because the resignation of the UUP whip by Peter Weir would have left the pair one short of the required unionist majority.

This prime ministerial diarchy, forged in the heat of inter-party negotiations, is properly considered quasi-presidential because,

---

[11] See statement by the Deputy First Minister (Designate), Northern Ireland Assembly (1999: 325, 15 July).

[12] 'Members will recall that the First Minister (Designate) and the Deputy First Minister (Designate) were elected, and I use the common parlance, "on a slate", when we were in a post-devolution situation. That means that under the Northern Ireland Act, both positions would fall when one resigned, but the remaining individual would remain in a caretaker capacity for up to six weeks. Before the end of that period the Presiding Officer would call for a further election. However, we are still functioning under the Northern Ireland (Elections) Act for these purposes and, therefore, the position of the First Minister (designate), as I understand it—and you have simply asked me for an immediate view—is unchanged. It is possible that some Standing Order, or other arrangement, may already be on the way, but I have no knowledge of it' (Northern Ireland Assembly 1999: 326–7, 15 July).

unlike executive presidencies—and unlike most prime ministers—neither the FM nor the DFM formally appoints the other ministers to the Executive Committee. Instead, posts in the Executive Committee, or cabinet, are allocated to parties in proportion to their strength in the Assembly, according to the d'Hondt rule (O'Leary, Grofman and Elklit 2001; see the Annex below). The premiers do have implicit and explicit coordinating executive functions, as approved by the Shadow Assembly in February 1999 (Wilford 2001). To fulfil them, the Department of the First and Deputy First Ministers was created. It has an Economic Policy Unit and an Equality Unit, and is tasked with liaising with the other institutions of the Agreement, namely, the North-South Ministerial Council, the British-Irish Council, the Secretary of State on reserved and excepted UK powers, and EU/ international matters, and, of course, with cross-departmental coordination.

Posts in the rest of the Executive Committee are allocated to parties in proportion to their strength in the Assembly, according to the d'Hondt rule. The rule's consequences are fairly clear: any party that wins a significant share of seats and is willing to abide by the new institutional rules has a reasonable chance of access to the executive, a subtly inclusive form of Lijphart's 'grand coalition government'. It is a voluntary arrangement because parties are free to exclude themselves from the Executive Committee. No programme of government has to be negotiated in advance between the parties entitled to portfolios. The design in principle creates strong incentives for parties to take up their entitlements to ministries, because if they do not then the portfolios go either to their ethno-national rivals or to their rivals in their own bloc.[13] The d'Hondt allocation

---

[13] The rules of executive formation did not formally require any specific proportion of nationalists and unionists in either the dual premiership or the Executive Committee. But in the course of the crisis over executive formation in the summer of 1999, the UK Secretary of State, Dr Mowlam, introduced a new rule requiring that a well-formed executive consist of at least three designated nationalists and three designated unionists. On 15 July 1999, in a hand-written note to the Initial Presiding Officer, she introduced an additional Standing Order to the running of d'Hondt: 'On the completion of the procedure for the appointment of Ministers (designate) under this Standing Order, the persons appointed shall only continue to hold Ministerial office (designate) if they include at least 3 designated Nationalists and 3 designated Unionists.' This order, authorized under the Northern Ireland (Elections) Act 1998, in my view was the first breach of the letter of the Agreement by the UK government. Given that the parties had previously agreed that the executive should consist of ten ministers, in addition to the First and Deputy First Ministers, the standing order, in effect, gave a veto power to both the UUP and the SDLP over executive formation, because each party was entitled to three seats on the basis of its strength in seats. The standing order was introduced in a hurry to

procedure means that democratic parties get the absolute right to nominate ministers according to their respective strength in seats;[14] that is, no vote of confidence is required by the Assembly either for individual ministers or for the Executive Committee as a whole. Parties choose, in order of their strength, their preferred ministries—which leads to fascinating strategic decision-making (see Annex; O'Leary, Grofman, and Elklit 2001). An individual minister may be deposed from office by the Assembly under the cross-community rules, but the party that held the relevant ministry is entitled to appoint his or her successor from amongst its ranks.[15]

Crises over executive formation and maintenance have been the major signals that the Agreement might falter. Crisis over formation arose for political and constitutional reasons—politically because David Trimble insisted that the Irish Republican Army (IRA) deliver some decommissioning of its weapons before Sinn Féin members could take their seats in the Executive Committee: 'no government before guns' became his slogan. Otherwise, he would refuse to cooperate in the running of the d'Hondt procedure. Constitutionally—that is, under the text of the Agreement— Trimble had no warrant to exercise this veto.

1. No party was formally entitled to veto another party's membership of the Executive, though the Assembly as a whole, through cross-community consent, may deem a party unfit for office.

stop a running of the procedure for executive formation leading *either* to an all-nationalist executive, as actually transpired—given the decision of the UUP to fail to turn up to the Assembly when the process was triggered and the decision of the 'No' unionists not to take their ministerial entitlements—*or* to an executive in which there would have been no pro-Agreement unionists (Northern Ireland Assembly 1999: 317, 15 July). This panic measure, introduced for high-minded motives, subtly changed the executive incentive structures agreed by the SDLP and the UUP in the negotiation of the Agreement. It was consociational in spirit, but it was not negotiated by the parties, was not endorsed in the referendums, and encouraged moderates to over-bargain knowing that they could veto executive formation. Insecure 'moderates' as well as 'hardliners' can be troublesome agents in power-sharing systems. My perspective here is at odds with that of Donald Horowitz (personal conversations). The Standing Order no longer has force.

[14] A party as a whole may be excluded from a right to nominate if it is deemed by the Assembly, through cross-community consent procedures, to be in breach of the requirements of the Pledge of Office (see below). Efforts by unionist MLAs to have Sinn Féin so deemed have foundered because the moderate nationalists in the SDLP have not supported them.

[15] In the course of 2000 the anti-Agreement DUP decided to take advantage of this provision to rotate its MLAs through its two ministerial portfolios. Its critics observed that they did not, however, resign their entitlements to the two ministries.

2. The Agreement did not specify a starting date for decommissioning though it did require parties to use their best endeavours to achieve its completion within two years of the referendum, that is, by 22 May 2000.
3. Any 'natural' reading mandated executive formation as a necessary step in bringing all the Agreement's institutions 'on line'.

Trimble rested his flimsy case on a communication he had received from the UK prime minister on the morning the Agreement was made, indicating that it was Tony Blair's view that decommissioning 'should begin straight away'. Communications from UK premiers do not, of course, have the force of law—outside the ranks of New Labour—and the 'should' in Blair's text was in the subtle subjunctive mood rather than a mandatory reading of the text of the Agreement that had just been negotiated. Trimble's concern was to appease critics of the Agreement within his own party. His negotiating team had split, with one of his Westminster MPs walking out; a majority of his party's Westminster MPs opposed the Agreement; and his new Assembly party contained critics of aspects of the Agreement.

Trimble was initially facilitated in exercising his veto by the UK and Irish governments, which were sympathetic to his exposed position; and he took advantage of the fact that the SDLP did not make the formation of the rest of the executive a precondition of its support for the Trimble-Mallon ticket for FM and DFM. The SDLP wished to shore up Trimble's position. One provision in the Agreement gave Trimble further room for manoeuvre. The Agreement implied that there would be at least six other Ministers apart from the premiers, but that there could be 'up to' ten (Government of the United Kingdom (n.d. 1998: Strand One, paras 14 (explicitly) and 3 (implicitly))). The number of ministries was to be decided by MLAs through cross-community consent, and that gave Trimble the opportunity to delay executive formation. It would be December 1998 before the parties reached agreement on ten ministries, when the UUP finally abandoned its demand for seven rather than ten departmental ministries—with seven, unionists would have had an overall majority in the Executive Committee.[16]

Thereafter the bulk of 1999 saw protracted bargaining, including a failed running of the d'Hondt procedure to fill the executive in July, but no consensus on proceeding to formation. Seamus Mallon's resignation triggered a review of the Agreement, as permitted by its terms, under US Senator George Mitchell. In mid-November the

---

[16] For details of the ministries, see Table 11.4.

crisis looked as if, in principle, it would be resolved. The UUP accepted that executive formation would occur—with the IRA appointing an interlocutor to negotiate with the International Commission on Decommissioning—while actual arms decommissioning, consistent with the text of the Agreement, would not be required until after executive formation. In concluding his 'Review of the Agreement', and with the consent of the pro-Agreement parties, Senator Mitchell stated that 'Devolution should take effect, then the executive should meet, and then the paramilitary groups should appoint their authorised representatives, all on the same day, in that order'. This appeared an honourable resolution to what appeared a fundamental impasse. The d'Hondt procedure was followed, and Northern Ireland at last had its novel power-sharing Executive Committee—though the Ulster Unionist Council would later fatefully render problematic this settlement within the settlement.

The moment of suspension

To get the support of his party's more or less permanent electoral college, the Ulster Unionist Council, Trimble offered his party chairman a post-dated resignation letter, leaving his position as First Minister, to become operative if the IRA did not start decommissioning within a specified period: not one formally negotiated under the Mitchell Review. The IRA did not deliver on decommissioning, at least not in the way that Secretary of State Mandelson believed was required to stop Trimble making effective his resignation threat, though the IRA did appear to others to clarify that decommissioning would occur. In February 2000 Mandelson obtained from the UK Parliament emergency statutory powers to suspend the Assembly and Executive and did so at 5.00 p.m. on 11 February 2000. In doing so, he acted in classic Diceyan fashion, using the doctrine of parliamentary sovereignty to arrogate to himself the power of suspension—which had not been negotiated in the making of the Agreement or granted in its legislative enactment in the UK. The UK government's officials knew that suspension would breach the formal treaty incorporating the Agreement, because in the summer of 1999, when both governments contemplated a suspension mechanism, they proposed that the treaty that was about to be signed by the two governments, which incorporated the Belfast Agreement, should be amended to make it compatible with suspension. No such amendment was made.

The Secretary of State's justification for suspension was that it was necessary to save Trimble. His threat to resign would have become operative in an environment in which 'Yes' unionists no longer commanded an absolute majority of the registered unionists in the Assembly. Therefore, it was feared, Trimble could not have been resurrected as First Minister if he did resign. This reasoning was partial. The Assembly, by weighted majority, was entitled to pass any measure to amend its current rules for electing the dual premiers and to send this measure to Westminster for statutory ratification. It could, for instance, propose that when deadlocked under the parallel consent procedure the Assembly adopt the weighted majority procedure for electing the premiers. So there was a mechanism, within the terms and institutions of the Agreement, under which Trimble could have regained the position of First Minister. But, even if Mandelson's justification was utterly sincere,[17] the suspension was an unconstitutional and a partisan act. It was unconstitutional in Irish eyes because the suspensory power had not been endorsed with cross-community consent through the negotiation of the Agreement, or in the referendums, or in the UK's legislative enactment of the Agreement. It was partisan because neither the Agreement nor the Mitchell Review of the Agreement that took place in late 1999 required Sinn Féin to deliver decommissioning by the IRA because of a deadline set by the leader of the UUP. The then formally agreed deadline for decommissioning required all political parties to use their best endeavours to achieve full decommissioning by 22 May 2000.

One passage of the Agreement referred to procedures for review if difficulties arose across the range of institutions established on the entering into force of the international treaty, the British-Irish Agreement: 'If difficulties arise which require remedial action across the range of institutions, or otherwise require amendment of the British-Irish Agreement or relevant legislation, *the process of review will fall to the two Governments in consultation with the parties in the Assembly. Each Government will be responsible for action in its own jurisdiction*' (Government of the United Kingdom n.d., 1998; emphasis added). The italicized passages, read in conjunction with the whole Agreement, suggest that the UK government was obliged formally to consult the parties in the Assembly and the Irish government over obtaining any power of suspension, and that any remedial action required the joint support of the two governments, especially as regards their treaty. That each government would be 'responsible for action in its own jurisdiction' was not taken by the

---

[17] For a critical dissection see 'The Blame Game', Spotlight BBC Northern Ireland, produced by Justin O'Brien, reporter Andy Davies, 22 February 2000.

Irish side to mean that the Westminster parliament had unilateral discretion to alter, amend, suspend, or abolish the institutions of the Agreement. It merely meant that for agreed remedial action there would not be joint sovereignty but rather parallel legislative procedures.

The central purpose of the UK's assent, during the negotiation of the Agreement, to delete section 75 of the Government of Ireland Act 1920, and of the Irish state's assent to propose modifying Arts 2 and 3 of the Irish Constitution after a referendum, had been to show that both states were engaged in 'balanced' constitutional change, confirming that Northern Ireland's status as part of the UK or the Republic rested with its people alone, and that an exercise of Irish national self-determination had been organized. The UK's Diceyans, including Ulster Unionists, interpreted the UK's deletion of section 75 of the Government of Ireland Act as meaningless. In their eyes the UK Parliament's sovereignty remains intact in a given domain, even when it removes a statutory statement which says it remains intact! Irish negotiators regretted that they were not more careful: not for the first time the UK's 'constitution' has proved Ireland's British problem.

The suspension had at least three messages. First, it made plain that every aspect of the Agreement was vulnerable to Westminster's sovereignty. Its institutions, its confidence-building measures, its commissions, the promise that Irish unification will take place if there is majority consent for it in both parts of Ireland, are all revisable by the current UK Parliament, and any future Parliament, and Parliament's Secretaries of State, irrespective of international law or the solemn promises made by UK negotiators. By its actions the Westminster Parliament has affirmed that it regards its sovereignty as unconstrained by the Agreement. Had it sought and obtained the assent of the Northern Assembly—by cross-community consent—to its possession of the power of the suspension that would have been a different matter. It did not. Even if the Secretary of State's motives were entirely benign—and that has been questioned—his decision to obtain the power of suspension destroyed the assumptions of nearly a decade of negotiation.

Second, the suspension spelled out to some official Irish negotiators, and northern nationalists, the necessity in future negotiations of entrenching Northern Ireland's status as a 'federacy', perhaps in the same manner as the UK's courts are instructed to make European law supreme over law(s) made by the Westminster Parliament, through full domestic incorporation and entrenchment of the relevant treaty. A federacy, as Daniel Elazar (1987) clarified the concept, is an autonomous unit of government whose relationship with its host state is federal, even if the rest of the state is organized in a unitary fashion. A federal relationship exists when there are at least two units of government over the same territory and when neither can unilaterally alter the constitutional capacities of the other. It is my contention, supported by many in Irish officialdom, that the Agreement was intended to make Northern Ireland such a federacy, though not by that name, as long as it remained within the UK (see below). Northern Ireland's membership of the union was to be subject to the Agreement, not to the untrammelled sovereignty of Westminster; and change in the exercise or division of competencies would require due legal process in both the Assembly and Westminster. If Northern Ireland's status as such a federacy is not affirmed through a subsequent repeal of the Suspension Act 2000 then the Agreement cannot be constitutionalized consistently with Irish national self-determination. If Ireland's negotiators do not, in future, require the Westminster Parliament to repeal the Suspension Act and to declare that its sovereignty is circumscribed by the Agreement, then Northern Ireland's status merely as a devolved UK authority may be affirmed by the practice of the Irish state.

Third, unionists may one day rue the constitutional consequences of the suspension and the Suspension Act. What Westminster did on unionists' behalf it may take from them tomorrow—including membership of the Union. The Suspension Act means that in UK public law the Union does not rest on the consent of its component parts but rather upon Westminster's say so. Westminster, despite the referendums, is free, according to its constitutional norms, to modify the union in any way it likes: for example, through full-scale joint sovereignty over Northern Ireland with the Irish government or through expelling Northern Ireland from its jurisdiction.

Suspension did not completely save Trimble from the wrath of his party activists, 43 per cent of whom voted for a stalking horse to replace him, the Reverend Martin Smyth MP, a hardliner and former Grand Master of the Orange Lodge. Trimble remained leader but bound by a mandate for reformation of the Executive that neither the UK government nor republicans seemed likely to deliver. But in May 2000 negotiations between the pro-Agreement parties and the two governments produced a formula that appeared to break the deadlock. Republicans promised to deliver a 'confidence-building measure', which involved supervising international inspections of the IRA's arms dumps, the UK government promising to deliver fully on police reform (see below) and demilitarization, and the UUP and the UK government agreeing respectively to withdraw Trimble's resignation and to end the suspension. As we shall see, the salience of the suspensory power would recur.

Further consociational traits of the executive

The consociational criterion of cross-community executive power-sharing was clearly met in the Agreement, but there are special features of the new arrangements that differ from consociational experiments in Northern Ireland and elsewhere. Ministers take a 'Pledge of Office', not an 'Oath of Allegiance'. This cements what nationalists see as the binationalism at the heart of the Agreement: nationalist ministers do not have to swear an Oath of Allegiance to the Crown or the Union. The Pledge requires ministers to:

- discharge their duties in good faith;
- follow exclusively peaceful and democratic politics;
- participate in preparing a programme of government, and
- support and follow the decisions of the Executive Committee and the Assembly.

The duties of office include a requirement to serve all the people equally, to promote equality, and to prevent discrimination—which means, according to the UK's doctrine of ministerial responsibility, that civil servants will be bound to run their departments consistent with these obligations (McCrudden 1999a, b 2001). They include a requirement that the 'relevant Ministers' serve in the North-South Ministerial Council, a duty that, in conjunction with other clauses, was intended to prevent parties opposed to this aspect of the Agreement, such as the Democratic Unionist Party (DUP), from abusing their offices or taking offices in bad faith.

The UUP and the SDLP, in the negotiations over the Northern Ireland Act, agreed that junior ministers could be created. They are currently in place only in the Office of the FM and DFM, one from the UUP and one from the SDLP; more could be allocated places under the d'Hondt process, though they are not obliged to be appointed in this way.[18] Most of the leading members of the major parties, in consequence, 'win prizes' of one sort or another—something intended to assist the cementing of the Agreement and to provide incentives for a shift of posture on the part of ambitious anti-Agreement Assembly members. These incentives worked: the

[18] Section 19 of the Northern Ireland Act 1998 permits the First and Deputy First Ministers to determine, subject to Assembly approval, the number of junior ministers and the procedure for their appointment.

anti-Agreement DUP took its seats in the Executive and in the Assembly's Committees, and fought the 2001 Westminster general election not on a pledge to scrap the Agreement but to renegotiate it. It did, however, engage in ritualized protest. Taking advantage of the d'Hondt procedure, it decided to rotate its ministerial positions—which led its critics to accuse it of accumulating and distributing pension rights among its members while depriving its constituents of effective ministers.

This inclusive executive design, of course, means that the new Assembly has a rather small part of its membership free as an opposition for standard adversarial parliamentary debating in the classic Westminster mould, though the inter-party rhetorical engagement in the Assembly is sometimes difficult to reconcile with the fact that the four largest parties—the UUP, the SDLP, the DUP, and Sinn Féin—share the cabinet positions. The standard complaint of critics of consociation—that it weakens the effectiveness of parliamentary opposition—must surely be tempered in this case by the fact that the backbenchers from other parties in the government are likely to hold the relevant minister vigorously to account.

Evaluation of the Executive

How should we appraise the executive design that is at the heart of the Agreement? The special skill of the designers and negotiators was to create strong incentives for executive power-sharing and power-division, but without requiring parties to have any prior formal coalition agreement—other than the institutional agreement—and without requiring any party to renounce its long-run aspirations. The dual premiership was designed to tie moderate representatives of each bloc together and to give some drive towards overall policy coherence. It was intended to strengthen moderates and to give them significant steering powers over the rest of the executive. The d'Hondt mechanism, by contrast, ensures inclusivity and was carefully explained to the public as achieving precisely that;[19] it also saves on the transaction costs of bargaining over portfolios (see Annex). Distinctive coalitions can form around different issues within the Executive, permitting flexibility but inhibiting chaos—given the requirement that the budget be agreed by cross-community

---

[19] 'The purpose is to ensure confidence across the community . . . so that people know that their parties will, if they receive a sufficient mandate in the election, have the opportunity for their Members to become Ministers and play their part in the Executive Committee.' *House of Commons, Official Report*, 319 (18 November 1998), col. 1023.

consent. The Executive successfully agreed a budget and a programme of government through inter-ministerial bargaining during 2000–01: the DUP ministers agreed it though they then supported their colleagues in voting against in the Assembly! These creative incentives to keep parties in the executive despite strong disagreements means the Agreement differs positively from the Sunningdale power-sharing experiment of 1973 which sought to maintain traditional UK notions of collective cabinet responsibility.

What was not foreseen was that failure to timetable the formation of the rest of the Executive immediately after the election of the FM and DFM could precipitate a protracted crisis. Trimble availed himself of this loophole to prevent executive formation until November 1999. If the Agreement survives, amendments to the Northern Ireland Act 1998 could be adopted by the UK Parliament or by the Assembly that would be consistent with the Agreement to prevent any recurrence of this type of crisis. In future, candidates for FM and DFM could be obliged to state the number of executive portfolios that will be available, and the formation of the executive should be required immediately after their election. That would plug this particular constitutional hole. It may, however, be unnecessary. It is not likely that future candidates for FM and DFM will agree to be nominated without a firm agreement on the number of portfolios and the date of cabinet formation.

What was also not foreseen was that the dual premiership might prove the most brittle institution of all. Recall that it was separately negotiated by the two moderate parties as a carve-up in which they had very direct stakes. Other possibilities were excluded, such as filling the top positions by the d'Hondt rule or another allocation rule. And the posts were made tightly interdependent: the resignation or death of one triggers the other's formal departure from office, and requires fresh elections within six weeks. One consequence has been that all inter-communal tension has been transmitted through these posts. Mallon, as we have seen, deployed his resignation power before the executive was fully formed for the first time, and Trimble, as we have seen, deployed the resignation threat to precipitate suspension of the Agreement's institutions. As we shall see, he was to do so again in 2001, just before the Westminster general elections: a resignation that became operative on 1 July 2001 and that has opened a crisis yet to be resolved.

So the dual premiership has been a lightening rod for deep tensions at least as much as it has been a mechanism for joint coordination and creation of calm by moderate leaders. The relationship between the premiers progressively worsened after a promising beginning, and has recently culminated in Trimble giving Mallon two minutes notice of his intention to repeat his use of a post-dated resignation letter.[20]

Forms of proportionality

Consociational arrangements are built on principles of proportionality. The Agreement meets this test in four ways: in the d'Hondt procedure for executive formation discussed above; in the Assembly's committees; in the electoral system for the Assembly; and in recruitment and promotion policies within the public sector.

The Assembly's committees The Assembly has committees scrutinizing each of the departments headed by ministers. Committee Chairs and Deputy Chairs are allocated according to the d'Hondt rule. Committee composition is in proportion to the composition of the Assembly. Each committee must approve any proposed new law within its jurisdiction tabled by ministers, and indeed the committee can itself initiate legislative proposals. In consequence, a committee dominated by other parties may block the legislative initiatives of a dynamic minister, and it may initiate legislation not to that minister's liking—though the success of such proposals is subject to cross-community special procedures. So the committee system combines the two consociational principles of proportionality and veto rights. In the passage of the Northern Ireland Act 1998 the committees were explicitly prevented, by law, from being chaired or deputy-chaired by ministers or junior ministers, and are required, where feasible, to be organized in such a way that the Chair and Deputy Chair be from parties other than that of the relevant minister. This ensures the accountability of ministers at least to MLAs from other parties and inhibits full-scale party fiefdoms in any functional sector.

The Assembly's election system: corrections for Lijphart and Horowitz? Elections to the 108-member Assembly are required to be conducted under a proportional representation (PR) system, the single transferable vote (STV), in six-member constituencies— though the Assembly may choose, by cross-community consent procedures, to advocate change from this system that would be ratified

---

[20] One sage reporter describes the Mallon-Trimble relationship as 'poisonous', compounded by Trimble's character traits, 'unpredictable and mercurial, often bewildering, sometimes impossible', and by the nature of his career, 'a mixture of dashes and longeurs, alternatively crisis-ridden and becalmed, of tacks towards moderation interspersed with lurches to the confrontational' (McKittrick 2001: 27).

by Westminster. The Droop quota in each constituency is therefore 14.3 per cent of the vote, which squeezes the very small parties, or, alternatively, encourages them to form electoral alliances.[21] Thus the smaller of the two loyalist parties, the Ulster Democratic Party (UDP), won no seats in the first Assembly election. Conceivably, the two rival loyalist parties, the PUP and the UDP, may in the future see the need to coalesce to achieve better representation. Very small parties which can gather lower-order preferences from across the unionist and nationalist blocs, such as the Women's Coalition, have shown that the system need not preclude representation for small parties.

This system, STV-PR, is not what Lijphart recommends for consociational systems. He is an advocate of party-list PR systems, principally because he believes they help make party leaders more powerful and better able to sustain inter-ethnic consociational deals.[22] Those who would like to see David Trimble in greater control of the UUP might hanker after Lijphart's preferred form of PR. The Northern Ireland case, however, suggests that a modification of the consociational prescriptive canon is in order. Had a region-wide list system had been in operation in June 1998, the UUP would have ended up with fewer seats, and with fewer seats than the SDLP; and in consequence the implementation of the Agreement would have been even more problematic.

There is a further and less contingent argument against party-list systems in consociational systems, especially important where the relevant ethnic communities are internally democratic rather than sociologically and politically monolithic. A region-wide party-list election gives incentives for the formation of a wide variety of micro-parties. It would have fragmented and shredded the votes of the major parties which made the Agreement. Hardliners under party-list systems have every reason to form fresh parties knowing

---

[21] The Droop quota used in STV is $V/(N+1) +1$, where V = total valid votes, and N = number of Assembly members to be elected.

[22] Lijphart also argues for this system rather than STV because it (1) allows for a high district magnitude, making possible greater proportionality, (2) is less vulnerable to gerrymandering, and (3) is simpler for voters and organizers (Lijphart 1990*b*). In the text I argue implicitly for high thresholds to reduce fragmentation, as a trade-off against 'better' proportionality. Contra Lijphart, I maintain that STV, legislatively enacted with uniform district magnitudes and supervised by independent electoral commissions charged with creating uniform electorates, is not more vulnerable to gerrymandering than regional party-list PR. I concede that STV is suitable only for numerate electorates, but otherwise its complexities are not especially mysterious: no more so than the formulas used for achieving proportionality in party-list systems. Try discussing d'Hondt, Hare, and Sainte-Laguë in public bars!

that their disloyalty will penalize more moderate parties but without necessarily reducing the total vote and seat share of the relevant ethno-national bloc. This objection to Lijphart's favoured prescription is not merely speculative. The 1996 elections to the Northern Ireland Peace Forum used a mixture of a party-list system and 'reserved seats'. Party proliferation and the erosion of the UUP first-preference vote were among the more obvious consequences (Evans and O'Leary 1997*a*, *b*).[23]

STV, of course, does not guarantee party discipline, as multiple candidates for the same party in a given constituency may present, tacitly or otherwise, slightly different emphases on party commitments, as indeed happened in Northern Ireland in 1998. But, I suggest, the system, combined with higher effective thresholds than under most forms of party-list PR, makes it more likely that parties will remain formally unified and therefore able to make and maintain consociational deals. At the very least the prescriptive superiority of the party-list system for these purposes is unproven, and Lijphart's consistent counsel in this respect should be modified.[24]

As well as achieving proportionality, STV has the great merit of encouraging inter-ethnic 'vote-pooling' (Horowitz 1985: 628 ff): in principle, voters can use their lower-order preferences—'transfer papers'—to reward pro-Agreement candidates at the expense of anti-Agreement candidates.[25] In this respect, STV looks tailor-made to achieve the 'inter-ethnic' and 'cross-ethnic' voting favoured by Donald Horowitz, a critic of consociational thinking but a strong advocate of institutional and policy devices to facilitate conflict-reduction (Horowitz 1985; 1989*c*, *d*; 1991). Consistently, however, with his general premises Horowitz believes that STV damages the prospects for inter-ethnic cooperation because the relatively low quota required to win a seat in six-member constituencies—14.3 per cent—makes it too easy for hardline parties and their candidates to be successful.[26] He

[23] The nature of executive formation in the Agreement should act as one possible check on the possibilities of fragmentation under party-list PR, but that is true of any electoral system combined with this executive.

[24] My co-researcher John McGarry and I used to assume the prescriptive superiority of the party-list system (for example, McGarry and O'Leary 1990: 297). Facts and reflection have made me reconsider the merits of STV (O'Duffy and O'Leary 1995; O'Leary 1999*c*).

[25] This option is also open to anti-Agreement voters, but DUP and UKUP voters are unlikely to give their lower-order preferences to Republican Sinn Féin, an anti-Agreement nationalist party, should it ever to choose to stand for elections.

[26] Personal conversations with Donald Horowitz during his period as a Suntory-Toyota International Centre for Economics and Related Disciplines distinguished visiting professor at the London School of Economics, 1998–9.

also thinks that the Agreement's other institutions, biased towards the key consociational partners, nationalists and unionists, compound this effect by weakening the prospects of cross-ethnic parties, such as the Alliance, which he believes is likely to impair conflict-reduction.

The Northern Ireland case, in my view, suggests that normative and empirical challenges to Horowitz's reasoning are in order. Horowitz would generally prefer the use of the Alternative Vote (AV) in single-member constituencies in Northern Ireland, as he does elsewhere, because its quota—50 per cent plus one—would deliver strong support to moderate ethno-national and cross-ethnic candidates. The problems with this prescription are straightforward. First, the outcomes it would deliver would be majoritarian, disproportional, and unpredictably so, and they would be disproportional both within blocs and across blocs. They would, additionally, have much more indirectly 'inclusive' effects than STV. In some constituencies there would be unambiguous unionist and nationalist majorities[27]—and thus AV would lead to the under-representation of minority voters within these constituencies, and to local fiefdoms. Second, while candidates would often have to seek support for lower-order preferences under AV, it would not be obvious that their best strategy would be to seek lower-order preferences across the ethno-national divide because the imperative of staying in the count would dictate building as big an initial first and second preference vote tally as possible.[28] Third, AV would never be agreed to by hardline parties entering a consociational settlement if they believed it would be likely to undermine their electoral support. Since the Agreement was made possible by encouraging 'inclusivity', by facilitating negotiations which included Sinn Féin—the party that had supported the IRA—and the PUP and the UDP—the parties that had supported the loyalist Ulster Defence Association and Ulster Volunteer Force—it would have been perverse for their leaders to agree to an electoral system that minimized their future prospects.

Indeed, STV arguably worked both *before* and *after* the Agreement to consolidate the Agreement's prospects. To begin with, it helped to moderate the policy stance of Sinn Féin. After its first phase of electoral participation in elections in Northern Ireland in the 1980s

[27] One recent analysis concludes that only three of Northern Ireland's current 18 constituencies are marginal between nationalists and unionists (Mitchell, O'Leary, and Evans 2001), so it would be a major re-districting exercise to generate a high number of ethnically heterogeneous constituencies out of 108 districts.

[28] It may be that AV's presumptively Horowitzian moderating effects materialize better in multi-ethnic political systems with no actual or potentially dominant group in given districts—a situation that does not obtain in Northern Ireland.

and in the Irish Republic in the latter half of the 1980s, the party discovered that it was in a ghetto. Its candidates in some local government constituencies[29] would pile up large numbers of first-preference ballot papers and then sit unelected as a range of other parties' candidates passed them to achieve quotas on the basis of lower-order preferences. They received very few lower-order preferences from SDLP voters. However, once the party moderated its stance, promoted the IRA's ceasefire(s), and became the champion of a peace process and a negotiated settlement, it found that its first-preference vote, its transfer vote, and its seats won all increased.

The constitutional design argument that can be extracted from this story is this: once there has been party fragmentation within ethno-national blocs, then STV can assist accommodating postures and initiatives by parties and candidates, both intra-bloc and inter-bloc.[30] Horowitz's electoral integrationist prescriptions are most pertinent at the formation of a competitive party system. But once party formation and party pluralism within blocs have occurred, there will be few agents with the incentives to implement Horowitz's preferences; and if a third party or outside power did so it would be a provocation to the less moderate parties, and would therefore most likely re-ignite ethno-national tensions.[31] This argument is, of course, a qualified one: STV is not enough, and it may not be appropriate everywhere. But it can help promote accommodative moves and consolidate consociational deals in ways that the region-wide party-list systems and the AV in single-member district cannot.

---

[29] STV has been used in local government elections and European parliamentary elections in Northern Ireland since 1973 and 1979 respectively. Interestingly, the hardline unionist Ian Paisley has been most successful in the three-member district used to elect Northern Ireland's MEPs; in the more proportional five- or six-member local government constituencies the DUP has not fared as well.

[30] The corollary is that STV's positive effects apply to already polarized and pluralized party systems in ethno-nationally divided societies. If there has been no prior history of ethnicized party polarization within a state, or of pluralization of parties within ethno-national blocs, the merits of its implementation may be reasonably doubted on Horowitzian grounds. This consideration raises what may be the key problem with Horowitz's electoral integrationist prescriptions: they apply best to forestalling or inhibiting ethnic conflict and are less effective remedies for cases of developed, protracted, and intense ethnic and ethno-national conflict.

[31] The primary normative objection that can be levelled against Horowitz's position is that proportionality norms better match both parties' respective bargaining strengths and their conceptions of justice. Once party pluralism has already emerged some form of proportionality is more likely to be legitimate than a shift to strongly majoritarian systems, such as AV, or to systems with ad hoc distributive requirements that will always be—correctly—represented as gerrymanders, albeit well-intentioned.

There has been some empirical confirmation of the merits of STV since the Agreement was made. 'Vote pooling' occurred within the first Assembly elections, as we can surmise, to an extent, from actual counts (Sinnott 1998); and as Geoffrey Evans and I can confirm from a survey we helped design (Evans and O'Leary 2000). In short, *some* of the SDLP's and Sinn Féin's voters found it rational to reward David Trimble's UUP for making the Agreement by giving its candidates their lower-order preferences, and so helped them against Ian Paisley's DUP and Robert McCartney's United Kingdom Unionist Party (UKUP). Likewise, *some* of the UUP's and the PUP's voters transferred their lower-order preferences to pro-Agreement candidates within their own bloc, among the others and among nationalists. Of course, transfers also took place among the 'No' unionists and between 'Yes' unionists and 'No' unionists. In our survey, approximately 10 per cent of each bloc's first-preference supporters gave lower-order preference support to pro-Agreement candidates in the other bloc. Within-bloc rewards for moderation also occurred: Sinn Féin won lower-order preferences from SDLP voters, and the PUP had candidates elected on the basis of transfers from other candidates.

Tables 11.1 and 11.2 report the outcome of the June 1998 elections to the first Assembly. The proportionality of the results is evident with respect both to blocs and to parties. The deviations in seats won compared with the first preference vote primarily benefited the pro-Agreement parties. The UUP was the principal beneficiary of the transfer of lower-order preferences, which took its seat share— 25.9 per cent—significantly above its first-preference vote-share— 21.3 per cent—though these lower-order preferences came from voters who voted 'No' as well as those who voted 'Yes' to the Agreement, as was evident in ballot papers and in our survey (Evans and O'Leary 2000). The Women's Coalition was the most widespread beneficiary of lower-order preferences, winning two seats despite a very low first-preference vote. Its inclusive orientation towards both republicans and loyalists meant that the transfer process assisted it more than the Alliance, as its successful candidates won transfers from every party whereas the Alliance's appeal for lower-order preferences was confined more to middle-class SDLP and UUP voters. The net transfers by voters to the pro-Agreement candidates, though not as significant as had been hoped, performed one very important task. They converted a bare 'anti-Agreement' majority of the first preference vote—25.5 per cent— within the unionist bloc of voters into a bare 'pro-Agreement' majority—27.7 per cent—among seats won by unionists, a result

TABLE 11.2: *Party performances in the June 1998 elections to the Northern Ireland Assembly*

Party		First preference vote (%)	Seats No	%
SDLP	Social Democratic and Labour Party of Northern Ireland	22.0	24	22.2
SF	Sinn Féin	17.7	18	16.7
Other nationalists		0.1	–	–
UUP	Ulster Unionist Party	21.0	28	25.9
PUP	Progressive Unionist Party	2.5	2	1.8
UDP	Ulster Democratic Party	1.2	–	–
Other 'Yes' unionists		0.3	–	–
DUP	Democratic Unionist Party	18.0	20	18.5
UKUP	United Kingdom Unionist Party	4.5	5	4.6
Other 'No' unionists		3.0	3	2.8
APNI	Alliance Party of Northern Ireland	6.4	6	5.5
NIWC	Northern Ireland Women's Coalition	1.7	2	1.8
Others		1.3	–	–

Percentage figures for votes and seat shares rounded to one decimal place.
Source: O'Leary (1999*e*).

that may have been essential for the Agreement's (partial) stabilization.

The Northern Ireland Act 1998 and the Northern Ireland (Elections) Act 1998 opened one novelty in the practice of STV in Ireland. Both acts left it open to the Secretary of State to determine the method of filling vacancies: this may be done through by-elections, substitutes, or whichever method the Secretary of State deems fit. By-elections, used in the Republic of Ireland and hitherto in Northern Ireland, are anomalous in a PR system (Gallagher 1987). A candidate who wins the last seat in a six-member constituency and who subsequently resigns or dies is unlikely to be replaced by a candidate of the same party or persuasion in a by-election, which becomes the equivalent of the alternative vote in a single-member constituency. The Northern Ireland Assembly (Elections) Order of 1998 has provided for a system of alternates or of personally nominated substitutes with a provision for by-elections if the alternates system fails to provide a substitute. The disproportionality possibly induced by by-elections, with its consequent unpredictable ramifications for the numbers of registered nationalists and unionists and the cross-community rules, needed to be engineered out of the settlement, and it is a good sign that the parties cooperated with this concern in mind.

Recruitment and representativeness in the public sector Proportionality rules in the Agreement, combined with accommodative incentives, did not stop with the executive, the committee system in the Assembly, or the electoral system. The Agreement accepted past and future measures to promote fair employment and (weak) affirmative action in the public sector that will, one hopes, eventually ensure a representative and non-discriminatory civil service and judiciary. The civil service and the rest of the public sector have already been subjected to fair employment legislation, but in the entirety of important posts in the public sector the principles of representativeness or proportionality are to be applied, in the form either of party representatives holding others to account or of representative bureaucracies and public services. There is one exception: the judiciary.

Policing Most significantly, the Agreement envisaged a representative police force. Democratic consociation cannot exist where those of military age in one community are almost the sole recruitment pool for policing all of those in another community—a trait more characteristic of control systems (Lustick 1979). Policing had been so controversial that the parties to the Agreement could not concur on future arrangements, and it was not made a devolved function.[32] They did agree the terms of reference of a Commission, eventually chaired by Christopher Patten, a former UK minister in the region and now a European Commissioner. The Report of the Independent Commission—the 'Patten Report'—published in September 1999 was both an able expression of democratic thought on policing and the fulfilment of the Commission's mandate under the Agreement (Patten 1999; O'Leary 1999*b*).

To have effective police rooted in, and legitimate with, both major communities was vital. Eight criteria for policing arrangements were mandated in the Commission's terms of reference. They were to be impartial; representative; free from partisan political control; efficient and effective; infused with a human rights culture; decentralized; democratically accountable 'at all levels'; and consistent with the letter and the spirit of the Agreement. The Commission

[32] See McGarry and O'Leary (1999). A former Irish prime minister, Dr Garret FitzGerald, has described policing in Northern Ireland as having the status of Jerusalem in the Israeli-Palestinian peace process (FitzGerald 2000).

engaged in extensive research and interaction with the affected parties, interest groups, and citizens. It did not, and could not, meet the hopes or match the fears of all, but the Commissioners undoubtedly met their terms of reference.

The Patten Report was a thorough, careful, and imaginative compromise between unionists who maintained that the existing Royal Ulster Constabulary (RUC) already met the terms of reference of the Agreement and those nationalists, especially republicans, who maintained that the RUC's human rights record mandated its disbanding. However, the Police Bill presented to the Westminster Parliament in the spring of 2000 by Peter Mandelson was an evisceration of Patten, and condemned as such by the SDLP, Sinn Féin, the Women's Coalition, the Catholic Church, and non-governmental and human rights organizations such as the Committee on the Administration of Justice. It was also criticized by the Irish government, the US House of Representatives (H. Res 447, 106th Congress), and Irish Americans, including President Clinton.[33]

The veracity of the critics' complaints can be demonstrated by comparing some of Patten's recommendations with the original bill.

1. Patten recommended a neutral name, the 'Northern Ireland Police Service'. The Royal Ulster Constabulary's name was not neutral, so it was recommended to go. Patten recommended that the display of the Union flag and the portrait of the Queen at police stations should go. Symbols should be 'free from association with the British or Irish states'. These recommendations were a consequence of Patten's terms of reference, the Agreement's commitment to establishing 'parity of esteem' between the national traditions, and the UK's commitment to 'rigorous impartiality' in its administration. The original bill, by contrast, proposed that the Secretary of State have the power to decide on the issues of names and emblems.

2. Patten recommended affirmative action. Even critics of affirmative action recognized the need to correct the existing imbalance in which over 90 per cent of the police are local cultural Protestants. But the original bill reduced the period in which the police would be recruited on a 50:50 ratio of cultural Catholics and cultural Protestants from ten years to three, requiring the Secretary of State to make any extension, and was silent on 'aggregation', the proposed policy for shortfalls in recruitment of suitably qualified cultural Catholics.

[33] I described it as betraying Patten's 'substantive intentions in most of its thinly disguised legislative window-dressing' (O'Leary 2000).

3. Patten proposed a Policing Board consisting of ten representatives from political parties in proportion to their shares of seats on the Executive, and nine members nominated by the FM and DFM. These recommendations guaranteed a politically representative board in which no bloc would have partisan control. The original bill introduced a requirement that the Board should operate according to a weighted majority when recommending an inquiry, tantamount to giving unionist or unionist-nominated members partisan political control.

4. Patten avoided false economies but recommended downsizing the service, advocated a strong Board empowered to set performance targets, and proposed enabling local District Policing Partnership Boards to market-test police effectiveness. The original bill empowered the Secretary of State, not the Board, to set performance targets, made no statutory provision for disbanding the police reserve, and deflated the proposed District Policing Partnership Boards because of assertions that they would lead to paramilitaries being subsidized by taxpayers.

5. Patten proposed that new and serving officers should have human rights training and re-training, and codes of practice. In addition to the European Convention on Human Rights, due to become part of UK domestic law, the Commission held out international norms as benchmarks (Patten 1999: para 5.17). Patten's proposals for normalization—through merging the special branch into criminal investigations—and demilitarization met the Agreement's human rights objectives. The original bill, by contrast, was a parody. The new oath was to be confined to new officers. No standards of rights higher than those in the European Convention were to be incorporated into training and practice. Responsibility for a Code of Ethics was left with the Chief Constable. Patten's proposed requirement that the oath of service 'respect the traditions and beliefs of people' was excluded. Normalization and demilitarization were left unclear in the bill and the implementation plan.

6. Patten envisaged enabling local governments to influence the Policing Board through their own District Policing Partnership Boards and giving the latter powers 'to purchase additional services from the police or statutory agencies, or from the private sector', and matching police internal management units to local government districts. The original bill, by contrast, maintained or strengthened centralization: the Secretary of State obtained powers that Patten proposed for the FM and DFM and the Board, and powers to issue instructions to District Policing

Partnership Boards; and neither the bill nor the implementation plan implemented Patten's proposed experiment in community policing.

7. Patten envisaged a strong, independent and powerful Board to replace the discredited Police Authority (Patten 1999: para 6.23). The police would have 'operational responsibility' but be held to account and required to interact with the Human Rights Commission, the Ombudsman, and the Equality Commission. The Bill watered down Patten's proposals, empowering the Secretary of State to oversee and veto the Board, and the Chief Constable to refuse to respond to reasonable requests from the Board, and preventing the Board from making inquiries into past misconduct

8. Patten was consistent with the Agreement in letter and spirit. The original bill was not.

What explained the radical discrepancy between the Patten Report and the original bill? The short answer is that the Northern Ireland Office's officials under Mandelson's supervision drafted the Bill and took the views of the RUC and other security specialists more seriously than those of the Patten Commission. They treated the Patten Report as a nationalist report which they had to modify as benign mediators. They believed that they had the right to implement what they found acceptable, and to leave aside what they found unacceptable, premature, or likely to cause difficulties for pro-Agreement unionists or the RUC. The original bill suggested that the UK government was determined to avoid the police being subject to rigorous democratic accountability; deeply distrustful of the capacity of the local parties to manage policing at any level; and concerned to minimize the difficulties that the partial implementation of Patten would occasion for Trimble.

Under enraged nationalist pressure Mandelson beat a partial retreat, whether to a position prepared in advance only others can know. Some speculated that he designed an obviously defective bill so that nationalists would then be mollified by subsequent improvements, but all that the defective Bill achieved, according to Seamus Mallon, was to 'shatter already fragile faith in the Government's commitment to police reform'. Accusing his critics of 'hype', 'rhetoric', and 'hyperbole', Mandelson promised to 'listen'. He declared that he might have been too cautious in the powers granted to the Board. Indeed the Government was subsequently to accept over 60 SDLP-driven amendments to bring the bill more into line with Patten.

The bill was improved in the House of Commons and the House of Lords, but insufficiently. The quota for the recruitment of cultural Catholics became better protected. The Board was given power over the setting of short-run objectives, and final responsibility for the police's code of ethics. Consultation procedures involving the Ombudsman and the Equality Commission were strengthened, and the FM and DFM are to be consulted over the appointment of non-party members to the Board. The weighted majority provisions for an inquiry by the Board have gone.

Yet any honest appraisal of the act must report that it is still not the whole Patten; it rectifies some of the original bill's more overt deviations, but on the crucial issues of symbolic neutrality and police accountability, vital for a 'new beginning', it remains at odds with Patten's explicit recommendations.[34] Patten wanted a police rooted in both communities, not just one. That is why he recommended that the name of the service be *entirely* new: The Northern Ireland Police Service. The act, because of a government decision to accept an amendment tabled by the UUP, styles the service 'The Police Service of Northern Ireland (incorporating the Royal Ulster Constabulary)', which must be one of the longest names of a police service in the English-speaking world. The Secretary of State promised an amendment to define it 'for operational purposes' and to ensure that the full title would rarely be used and the parenthetic past generally be excluded. He broke this commitment at Report Stage. Mandelson declared he was merely following Patten's wishes that the new service be connected to the old and avoid suggestions of disbanding, but this was not true: Patten proposed an entirely new and fresh name, and proposed linkages between the old and new services through police memorials, and *not* the renaming adopted by the government. Critics fear there might develop a police force with two names—the Police Service and the RUC—just as Northern Ireland's second city has two names, Derry and Londonderry.

Patten unambiguously recommended that the police's new badge and emblems be free of association with the British or Irish states, and that the Union flag should not fly from police buildings. The act postpones these matters. Avoiding responsibility, the government passed the parcel to the local parties to reach agreement while providing reassuring but vague words in Hansard. Since Mandelson had already ruled that only the Union Jack, albeit just on specified

---

[34] For the defects in the bill and the accompanying implementation plan with regard to community policing, see Hillyard (2000).

days, should fly over the buildings of the devolved administration, nationalists lacked faith that he would deliver on cultural neutrality and impartiality.

Why have these symbolic issues mattered? Because they do in ethno-national conflicts, and because the best way to win widespread acceptance for police reform was to confirm Patten's strategy of symbolic neutrality.[35] Full renaming and symbolic neutrality would spell a double message: that the new police are to be everyone's, and the new police are no longer to be, as they were, primarily the unionists' police. Not following Patten's recommendations has spelled a double message: that the new police is the old RUC re-touched, and linked more to British than Irish identity: a recipe for the *status quo ante*.

To achieve effective accountability and follow-through, Patten recommended an Oversight Commissioner to 'supervise the implementation of our recommendations'. The UK government—under pressure—put the commissioner's office on a statutory basis, which it did not intend to do originally, but confined his role to overseeing changes 'decided by the Government'. Had Mandelson and his colleagues been fully committed to Patten they would have charged the Commissioner with recommending, now or in the future, any legislative and management changes necessary for the full and effective implementation of the Patten Report.

Patten recommended a Board that could initiate inquiries into police conduct and practices. The Police Act 2000 prevents the Board from inquiring into any act or omission arising before the eventual act applies. This was tantamount to an undeclared amnesty for past police misconduct, not proposed by Patten. Many have no objections to an open amnesty, especially as paramilitaries have received de facto amnesties (see below), but this method was dishonest and appeared driven by concern to avoid state officials being held to account for their responsibilities for the last 30 years of conflict (see Ní Aoláin (2000)).[36] The Secretary of State additionally has the authority to approve or veto the person appointed to

---

[35] An alternative path, legitimate under the Agreement, would have been to pursue a fully bi-national symbolic strategy (McGarry and O'Leary 1999). However even if the police were to have both an English and Irish title in each case the name should be neutral: Northern Ireland Police Service or Coras Siochana Thuaisceart Eireann.

[36] Over 300 police have been killed in the current conflict, for whom there is widespread sympathy, but nationalists do not forget that the outbreak of armed conflict in 1969 was partly caused by an unreformed, half-legitimate police service, responsible for seven of the first eight deaths.

conduct any present or future inquiry (clause 58(9)). Whereas Patten recommended that the Ombudsman should have significant powers (Patten 1999: para. 6.42) and should 'exercise the right to investigate and comment on police policies and practices', in the act the Ombudsman may make reports but not investigate—so it is not a crime to obstruct her work. The Ombudsman is additionally restricted in her retrospective powers (clause 62), again circumscribing the police's accountability for past misconduct.

Mandelson suggested his critics were petty, pointing out just how much he had done to implement Patten and how radical Patten was by comparison with elsewhere. This 'spin' was unconvincing. The proposed arrangements sealed off past, present, and future avenues through which the police might be held to account for misconduct— for example, in colluding with loyalist paramilitaries or covering up assassinations—and were recipes for leaving the police outside the effective ambit of the law. And Patten was not radical by the standards of North America: it is radical by the past standards of Northern Ireland.

Failure to deliver fully on police reform in the judgement of many was likely to herald disaster. The SDLP, Sinn Féin, and the Catholic Church were unlikely to recommend that their constituents consider joining the police, and may well have boycotted the Policing Board and District Policing Partnership Boards. In its strongest form disaster would decouple nationalists and republicans from the Agreement. The mismanagement of the Patten Report meant that in the course of 2000 the pressure eased on Sinn Féin within its constituency to get the IRA to go further in decommissioning than arrangements for international inspections of its arms dumps. The argument was made that the UK government had reneged on a fundamental commitment under the Agreement, so the IRA was under no obligation to disarm. In turn this led to a renewal of unionist calls for the exclusion of Sinn Féin from ministerial office, leading to Trimble's second resignation threat in the Spring of 2001.

Generously disposed analysts believe that Mandelson's conduct was motivated by the need to help Trimble and the UUP, who were in a precarious position and fearful of the DUP. It was, in part. 'Saving Trimble' may account for the tampering with Patten's proposals on symbolic matters, but it hardly accounts for the blocking of the efforts to have a more accountable service. Whatever his motivation, he forgot that it was not his role unilaterally to abandon or renegotiate the Agreement or the work of Commissions sent up under the Agreement, whether on his own initiative or at the behest of any party.

Patten's imagination   Patten's Report was a model of constitutional design for this aspect of the governance of a divided territory.
It articulated a fresh vision: policing should not be exclusively the
responsibility of the professionals, the police. Instead, responsibility for the security of persons and property should remain with
citizens and their representatives. This logic was apparent in the
title and composition of the recommended Policing Board—not
'Police Board'—bringing together ten elected politicians, drawn
according to the d'Hondt rule from the parties that comprise the
new Executive, with nine appointed members representative of civil
society, 'business, trade unions, voluntary organisations, community groups and the legal profession'. The elected members must not
be ministerial office-holders. The Board was to be representative
but at one remove from direct executive power.

The Report intended to let police managers manage, but to hold
them *ex post facto* accountable for their implementation of the
Board's general policing policy, and to enhance the audit and inves-
tigative capacities of the Board. It recommended rolling back the
centralization that had occurred in both the UK and Ireland
through giving directly elected local governments opportunities to
influence the policy formulation of the Board though their own
District Policing Partnership Boards. Decentralization of political
accountability was to be matched by the internal decentralization of
the police.[37]

The Report displayed philosophically coherent communitarian
but democratic and pluralist ideas, informed by economically efficient and rigorous management practices. Segmental policing, in
which each community would be policed by 'its own', was not considered and was not seriously proposed by any party. It would have
produced intractable problems. Instead, a representative but integrated service was advocated, appropriate for a region with a high
combination of both territorial segregation and mixing. Observing
that peace and the Agreement's implementation would increase the
likelihood of Catholics, nationalists, and republicans joining the
police, the Commission proposed recruiting Catholics and non-
Catholics in a 50:50 ratio from the pool of qualified candidates for
the next decade. This matches the population ratios in the younger

[37] The Report exhibited Machiavellian skill in handing some responsibility for
order to civil society organizations as well as to the police. It suggested that the
(mainly Orange) Loyal Orders be obliged to have their own trained marshals, and
their own policing plans, to accompany any requests to organize specific parades: a
nice example of combining a right—freedom of assembly—with a duty—the obligation to preserve the peace, law, and order in a democratic society.

age cohorts. Given early and scheduled retirements of serving officers, this policy would ensure that 30 per cent of the service would
be of Catholic origin after ten years and between 17 per cent and 19
per cent within four years—above the critical mass claimed essential to change the police's character. This is a slower pace of change
than some of us advocated (McGarry and O'Leary 1999) but by making each successive cohort representative now, and by ensuring that
the new service is impartial, the commissioners had an arguable
case.[38,39]

The Commission had to propose feasible policing arrangements
consistent with the internal and external spirit of the Agreement.
Patten delivered in this respect, including on recommendations for
better-structured cross-border cooperation with the Garda Síochana
in the Republic. Significantly, the Report's recommendations mostly
did not depend upon the Agreement's institutions for their implementation. The commissioners explicitly recommended most of their
changes, come what may.[40] The UK government's decision to dilute
both the content and the pace of Patten's recommendations meant
that policing reform, a core dimension of the Agreement in Irish
nationalist eyes, has become a serious source of continuing antagonism.

Communal autonomy and equality

Consociational settlements avoid the compulsory integration of peoples. Instead they seek, through bargaining, to manage differences
equally and justly. They do not, however, prevent voluntary integration or assimilation; and, to be liberal, such settlements must
protect those who wish to have their identities counted differently
or not as collective identities.

The Agreement left in place the arrangements for primary and secondary schooling in Northern Ireland in which Catholic, Protestant,

[38] The Commission also made recommendations to make the new service more
female-friendly and accommodating towards sexual and new ethnic minorities, but
without the same degree of rigour in legal and managerial prescription.

[39] Where the Report is deficient is in its tolerance of Orange Order, Ancient
Order of Hibernian, and Masonic membership by serving officers. One can be a fully
paid-up liberal but believe that certain public officials, such as electoral returning
officers, should be seen to be impartial. The Commissioners' counter-argument, that
'it is action or behaviour not attitude that matters', forgets that maintaining membership of a sectarian or secret organization is an action *and* behaviour.

[40] This analysis has benefited from detailed discussions with four members of
the Patten Commission and from the author's attendance at a conference at the
University of Limerick on 2 October 1999.

and integrated schools are to be equally funded—in the past Catholic schools received less capital funding, and before that also had to raise a significant proportion of their own staffing resources (McGrath 2000). In this respect Northern Ireland is now consociational but liberal: one can avoid Catholic and Protestant schools. Only the very small minorities of non-Christian religious believers, amounting to less than 1 per cent of the population, lack full and equal funding, and it would be generous and just to make such provisions for them where there is demand and numbers permit. The Agreement made new provisions for the educational use, protection, and public use of the Irish language, along the lines used for Welsh within Wales, thereby adding linguistic to educational protections of Irish nationalist culture. It made analogous provisions for 'Ulster Scots'.

Most significantly, the Agreement completes the equalization of both major communities as national communities, that is, as British and Irish communities, and not just, as is so misleadingly emphasized, as Protestants and Catholics. The European Convention on Human Rights, weak on the protection of collective rights and equality rights, will, it is promised, be supplemented by measures that give Northern Ireland its own tailor-made bill of rights, to protect both national groupings and individuals (O'Leary 2001*d*).

The worst illusion of parties to the conflict and some of its successive managers, based in London, Belfast, or Dublin, was that which held that Northern Ireland could be stable and democratic while being either British or Irish. The Agreement effectively makes Northern Ireland binational—and opens up the prospect of a fascinating and difficult jurisprudence, not least in the regulation of parades and marches.

The Agreement did not neglect the non-national dimensions of local politics, nor does it exclude the 'others' from effective political participation. All aspects of unjustified social equalities, as well as inequalities between the national communities, are recognized in the text of the Agreement and given some means of institutional redress and monitoring. The Agreement addresses national equality, the allegiances to the Irish and British nations, *and* social equality, that is, other dimensions that differentiate groups and individuals in Northern Ireland: religion, race, ethnic affiliation, sex, and sexuality. Equality issues, be they national or social, are not left exclusively to the local parties to manage and negotiate, which might be a recipe for stalemate. Instead, under the Agreement and section 75 of the Northern Ireland Act 1998, the UK government has created a new statutory obligation on public authorities: they must carry out all their functions with due regard to the need to promote equality of opportunity in relation to people's religious background and political opinions, and with respect to their gender, race, disabilities, age, marital status, and sexual orientation. This commitment is 'mainstreaming equality' (McCrudden 1999*a*, *b*; 2001). The UK government has established a new Human Rights Commission under the Agreement, charged with a role that is extended and enhanced compared with its predecessor, though still deficient in resources. Its role includes monitoring, the power to instigate litigation, and drafting a tailor-made local bill of rights.

Minority veto rights

The fourth and final dimension of an internal consociation is the protection of minorities through tacit or explicit veto rights. The Agreement achieves this through the Assembly's design, a new human rights regime, a Civic Forum, and through enabling political appeals to both the UK and the Irish governments.

The Assembly has procedures already described—parallel consent, weighted majority, and the petition—that protect nationalists from unionist dominance. Indeed, they do so in such a comprehensive manner that there are fears that the rules designed to protect the nationalist minority might be used by hardline unionist opponents of the Agreement to wreck it: what will happen if and when the DUP and 'No' unionists' become a majority within the unionists in the Assembly?

The 'others' are less well protected in the Assembly: they can be outvoted by a simple majority or any nationalist-unionist supermajority, and their numbers leave them well short of being able to trigger a petition on their own. However, since the 'others' have not been at the heart of the conflict, it is not surprising if they are not at the heart of its pacts—though it is not accurate to claim that they are excluded.

In the courts, the others, as well as disaffected nationalists and unionists, will have means to redress breaches of their human and collective rights. The content of the European Convention on Human Rights is well known. What is less clear is what package of collective rights the new independent Northern Ireland Human Rights Commission will recommend (see O'Leary 2001*d*). It is still possible that the new policing arrangements, if they follow the Patten Report, will be infused with a human rights culture, and that the absence of legal personnel within the RUC with expertise in human rights will be remedied.

What has not been addressed directly and immediately is the composition of the local judiciary who will supervise the new system(s) of rights protection. The Agreement provides for a review of the criminal justice system that includes 'arrangements for making appointments to the judiciary', and it will be a vital, though so far neglected, part of embedding the settlement that the judiciary reflects the different communities in Northern Ireland and is committed to the human and minority rights provisions that it will increasingly interpret.

Non-national minorities have not been forgotten. In the Civic Forum created in the north and inaugurated on 9 October 2000, with a prospective southern counterpart, and through the Inter-Governmental Conference of the British and Irish governments, mechanisms have been established to ensure that 'others', outside the blocs, will be able to express their voices and ensure that the new 'rights culture' does not exclude them.

The External Settlement: Confederal and Federal Elements of the Agreement

The Agreement is not, however, only internally consociational: it is also externally confederalizing, and federalizing. Its meshing of internal and external institutions marks it out as novel in comparative politics. Let me make it plain why the Agreement is both confederalizing and federalizing, though my emphasis is on the former. The argument rests on these stipulative definitions: confederal relations exist when political units voluntarily delegate powers and functions to bodies that can exercise power across their jurisdictions; and a federal relationship exists when (1) there are at least two separate tiers of government over the same territory and (2) neither tier can unilaterally alter the constitutional capacities of the other.[41]

The all-Ireland confederal relationship

The first confederal relationship is all-Ireland in nature: the North-South Ministerial Council (NSMC). Finally brought into being on

---

[41] My definition is a necessary element of a federal system. Whether it is sufficient is more controversial. Normally a federation has sub-central units that are co-sovereign with the centre throughout most of the territory of the state in question. My point is that any system of constitutionally entrenched autonomy for one region makes the relationship between that region and the centre functionally equivalent to a federal relationship.

the same day as power was devolved to the Northern Ireland Assembly and Executive, 2 December 1999, it brings together those with executive responsibilities in Northern Ireland and in the Republic. Its first plenary meeting was held in Armagh on 12 December 1999; the DUP Ministers did not attend.

What was intended by the Agreement is clear. Nationalists were concerned that if the Assembly could outlast the NSMC, it would provide incentives for unionists to undermine the latter. Unionists, by contrast, were worried that, if the NSMC could survive the destruction of the Assembly, nationalists would seek to bring this scenario about. The Agreement was therefore a tightly written contract with penalty clauses. Internal consociation and external confederalism were welded together: the Assembly and the NSMC were made 'mutually interdependent'; one cannot function without the other. Unionists were unable to destroy the NSMC while retaining the Assembly, and nationalists were not able to destroy the Assembly while keeping the NSMC.[42]

The NSMC linked northern nationalists to their preferred nation-state, and is one means through which nationalists hope to persuade unionists of the attractions of Irish unification. The Irish government successfully recommended a change to its constitution to ensure that the NSMC and its delegated implementation bodies would be able to exercise island-wide jurisdiction in those functional activities where unionists were willing to cooperate.

The NSMC functions much like the Council of Ministers in the European Union, with ministers having considerable discretion to reach decisions but remaining ultimately accountable to their respective legislatures. The NSMC meets in plenary format twice a year and in smaller groups to discuss specific sectors on a 'regular and frequent basis'. Provision was made for the Council to meet to discuss matters that cut across sectors and to resolve disagreements. In addition, the Agreement provided for cross-border or all-island 'implementation' bodies. The scope and powers of these institutions was somewhat open-ended. The Agreement, however, required a meaningful Council. It states that the Council '*will*'—not '*may*'—identify at least six matters where 'existing bodies' will be

[42] The Agreement does not mention what happens if both institutions, and therefore the Agreement itself, collapse. In my view what would happen is this: Northern Ireland would be governed, as at present, by the British government with input from Dublin through the British-Irish intergovernmental conference. The two governments would likely pursue those aspects of the Agreement that do not require the devolutionary arrangements. Intergovernmentalism, veering towards a British-Irish condominium, would be the dominant option.

the appropriate mechanisms for cooperation within each separate jurisdiction, and at least six matters where cooperation will take place through cross-border or all-island implementation bodies. The latter were subsequently agreed to be: inland waterways, food safety, trade and business development, special EU programmes, the Irish and Ulster Scots languages, and aquaculture and marine matters. The parties further agreed on six functional areas of cooperation, including some aspects of transport, agriculture, education, health, the environment, and tourism, where a joint North-South public company was established. These zones and modes of cooperation were to be decided during a transitional period between the Assembly elections and 31 October 1998, but were not in fact resolved until 18 December. The Agreement provided an annex that listed twelve possible areas for implementation[43] but left it open for others to be considered.

The NSMC differed from the previous attempt to establish a cross-border body of a confederal kind, namely, the Council of Ireland of 1974 which enraged many Ulster Unionists and contributed to the collapse of the Sunningdale settlement. The name change was significant: a concession to unionist sensibilities, even though the reference to the 'North' is more nationalist than unionist. Ireland is not in the title, the equality of North and South is implied. The NSMC, as its name suggests, is a ministerial rather than a parliamentary council. There was no provision in the Agreement to establish a North-South joint parliamentary forum as there was in the Sunningdale Agreement of 1973, but the Northern Ireland Assembly and the Irish *Oireachtas*[44] are asked 'to consider' one.

Nationalists wanted the NSMC to be established by legislation from Westminster and the *Oireachtas* to emphasize its autonomy from the Northern Ireland Assembly. Unionists preferred that the NSMC be established by the Northern Ireland Assembly and its counterpart in Dublin. The Agreement split these differences. The NSMC and the implementation bodies were brought into existence

---

[43] These were: Agriculture (animal and plant health); education (teacher qualifications and exchanges); transport (strategic planning); environment (protection, pollution, water quality, waste management); waterways; social security/social welfare (entitlements of cross-border workers and fraud control); tourism (promotion, marketing, research and product development); European Union programmes (such as SPPR, INTERREG, Leader II, and their successors); inland fisheries; aquaculture and marine matters; health (accident and emergency measures and related cross-border issues); and urban and rural development.

[44] This is the collective name in Gaelic for the two chambers of the Irish Parliament, *Dail Eireann* and *Seanad Eireann*.

by British and Irish legislation, but in the transitional period it was for the Northern executive and the Republic's government to decide, by agreement, how cooperation should take place and in what areas the North-South institutions should cooperate. Once these were agreed, the Assembly was unable to change these agreements except by cross-community consent.

The Agreement explicitly linked Ireland, North and South, to another confederation, the European Union (EU). It required the NSMC to consider the implementation of EU policies and programmes as well as proposals under way at the EU, and makes provisions for the Council's views to be 'taken into account' at relevant EU meetings.

The signatories to the Agreement promised to work 'in good faith' to bring the NSMC into being. There was not, however, sufficient good faith to prevent the first material break in the timetable scheduled in the Agreement occurring over the NSMC, though this was patently a by-product of the crisis over executive formation and decommissioning. The signatories are required to use 'best endeavours' to reach agreement and to make 'determined efforts' to overcome disagreements over functions where there is a 'mutual cross-border and all-island benefit'.[45]

Several economic and sociological developments may underpin this new constitutional confederalism. As the Republic's 'Celtic Tiger' economy continues to expand, Northern Ireland's ministers and citizens, of whatever background, should see increasing benefits from North-South cooperation. And, if the EU continues to integrate, there will be pressure for both parts of Ireland to enhance their cooperation, given their shared peripheral geographical position and similar interests in functional activities such as agriculture and tourism, and in having regions defined in ways that attract funds (Tannam 1999). Northern Ireland may even come to think that it would benefit from membership of the Eurozone, though the

[45] Participation in the NSMC has been made an 'essential' responsibility attaching to 'relevant' posts in the two Administrations; 'relevant' means, presumably, any portfolio a part of which is subject to North-South cooperation. This leaves open the possibility that a politician opposed to the NSMC may take a seat on it with a view to wrecking it. *But* ministers are required to establish the North-South institutions in 'good faith' and to use 'best endeavours' to reach agreement. Since these requirements are subject to judicial review it means it is unlikely that potential wreckers would be able to take part in the NSMC for long. One of the requirements for membership of the Executive is that ministers must 'support . . . all decisions of the Executive Committee' and they can be removed if they do not—though that presupposes decisions being made by the Executive Committee, and votes on exclusion by cross-community consent by the Assembly.

Northern Ireland 1998 Act, unlike the Agreement, made currency matters non-devolved.

The British-Irish confederal relationship

There is a second, weaker, confederal relationship established by the Agreement, affecting all the islands of Britain and Ireland. In the new British-Irish Council (BIC), the two governments of the sovereign states and all the devolved governments of the UK and neighbouring insular dependent territories of the UK can meet and agree to delegate functions, and may agree common policies. This proposal meets unionists' concerns for reciprocity in linkages and provides a mechanism through which they might in future be linked to the UK even if Northern Ireland becomes part of the Republic.

Unionists originally wanted the NSMC subordinated to a British-Irish, or East-West, Council. This did not happen. There is no hierarchical relationship between the two Councils. Indeed, there are two textual warrants for the thesis that the NSMC is more important and far-reaching than the BIC. The Agreement required the establishment of North-South implementation bodies while leaving the formation of East-West bodies a voluntary matter, and stated explicitly that the Assembly and NSMC were interdependent, making no equivalent provision for the BIC. The development of this confederal relationship may be stunted by an Irish governmental reluctance to engage in a forum where it may be outnumbered by at least seven other governments—of Westminster, Scotland, Wales, Northern Ireland, Jersey, Guernsey, and the Isle of Man—though rules may develop to ensure the joint dominance of the sovereign governments. The BIC may, however, flourish as a policy formulation forum if the devolved governments of the UK choose to exploit it as an opportunity for intergovernmental bargaining within the UK or to build alliances with the Irish government on European public policy—in which case it will give added impetus to other federalist or quasi-federalist processes.

A UK-Northern Irish federalizing process

The Agreement was a blow to unitary unionism in the UK, already dented by the 1997–8 referendums and legislative acts establishing a Scottish Parliament and a Welsh National Assembly (Hazell and O'Leary 1999).[46] But does the Agreement simply fall within the

---

[46] The formation of an English Parliament would be the last blow.

rubric of 'devolution within a decentralized unitary state'? Arguably not. Two unions make up the UK: the union of Great Britain and the union of Great Britain and Northern Ireland. The constitutional basis of the latter union is distinct from the former, at least in nationalist eyes

The Agreement, unlike Scottish and Welsh devolution, was embedded in a treaty between two states, based on the UK's recognition of Irish national self-determination as well as British constitutional convention. The UK officially acknowledged in the Agreement that Northern Ireland has the right to join the Republic, on the basis of a local referendum, and it recognized, in a treaty, the authority of Irish national self-determination throughout the island of Ireland. Moreover, the Agreement's institutions were being brought into being by the will of the people of Ireland, North and South, in concurrent referendums, and not just by the people of Northern Ireland: recall the referendums and the interdependence of the NSMC and the Assembly. In consequence, the UK's relationship to Northern Ireland, at least in international law, in my view, has an explicitly federal character: Northern Ireland had become what Elazar (1987) called a federacy. The Westminster parliament and executive could not, except through breaking its treaty obligations and except through denying Irish national self-determination, exercise power in any manner in Northern Ireland that is inconsistent with the Agreement.[47] Plainly the suspension of the Agreement in February 2000 shows that the UK's authorities did not feel constrained by its reasoning.

Federalizing processes will be enhanced if the UK and Northern Irish courts treat Northern Ireland's relationships to Westminster as akin to those of the former dominions, which had a federal character, as they did in the period of the Stormont Parliament, that is, 1921–72.[48] Moreover, the nature of devolution in Northern Ireland is not closed by the 1998 Act. The Act created an open-ended mechanism for Northern Ireland to expand its autonomy from the rest of the UK, albeit with the consent of the Secretary of State and the approval of Westminster. No such open-ended provision has been granted to the Scottish Parliament or the Welsh Assembly. In short, maximum feasible autonomy while remaining within the union is

[47] The author first composed this last sentence immediately after the Agreement was made, and had it confirmed by Irish governmental sources.

[48] Legal friends advise me that the UK's legislative enactment of the Agreement may have modified the pertinent precedents in this previous jurisprudence by changing the nature of the 'vires' test that the courts will use to deal with jurisdictional disputes.

feasible, provided there is agreement to that within the Northern Assembly. Legal Diceyans insist that Westminster's sovereignty in Northern Ireland remains ultimately intact, but if the Agreement beds down the political development of a quasi-federal relationship between the UK and Northern Ireland may be assured whatever is said in the dry recesses of the Constitution's ancient regime.

Irish federalizing processes

The Agreement also opened federalist avenues in the Republic of Ireland, one of the most centralized states in Europe. The NSMC is seen by nationalists, North and South, as the embryonic institution of a federal Ireland: first confederation, then federation, after trust has been built. This stepping-stone theory is most loudly articulated and feared by 'No' unionists', but they are not wrong in their calculation that many nationalists see the NSMC as 'transitional'. Sinn Féin says so. Fianna Fáil says so.

The Irish people did not abandon their aspiration for unification when they endorsed the Agreement. Instead, it became 'the firm will of the Irish nation, in harmony and friendship, to unite all the people who share the territory of the island of Ireland, in all the diversity of their identities and traditions, recognising that a united Ireland shall be brought about only by peaceful means with the consent of a majority of the people expressed in both jurisdictions in the island' (from the new Art. 3). The amended Irish Constitution therefore officially recognises *two* jurisdictions that jointly enjoy the right to participate in the Irish nation's exercise of self-determination. Unification is no longer linked to 'unitarism', and therefore is entirely compatible with either full confederation or federation.

Irish unification cannot be precluded because of present demographic and electoral trends, which have led to a steady rise in the nationalist share of the vote across different electoral systems (O'Leary 1990a, b; McGarry and O'Leary 1995a: Ch. 10; see also O'Leary and Evans 1997). The unification envisaged in the redrafted Irish Constitution is, however, now very different. It no longer has anything resembling a programme of assimilation. Respect for 'the diversity of . . . identities and traditions' in the new Art. 3 connects with both consociational and (con)federal logic. The Republic, I maintain, is bound by the Agreement to structure its laws and its protection of rights so as to prepare for the possibility of a (con)federal as well as a unitary Ireland. Northern Ireland is recognized as a legal entity within the Irish Constitution. So its eventual absorption or elimination as a political unit is no longer a programmatic feature of *Bunreacht na hEireann* (Constitution of Ireland 1937). The Agreement also envisaged the subjection of both jurisdictions in Ireland to the same regime for the protection of individual and group rights: a situation entirely compatible with a subsequent formal confederation or federation. And there is now an Irish Human Rights Commission tasked with cooperating with its Northern counterpart, and possibly developing a common Charter of Rights for the island.

What might happen if a majority emerged for Irish unification within Northern Ireland—a possibility that is not, of course, guaranteed? If nationalists acquired local majority support it would not necessarily be in their considered interests to promote the region's immediate administrative and legal assimilation into the Republic. They would then have a new interest in preserving Northern Ireland as a political entity within a federated Ireland: after all, they would be a local majority. So would the governing coalition in the Republic, whose calculations might be disturbed by the entry of northern participants. Conversely, some unionists faced with this prospect might prefer a unitary Ireland as the lesser evil, calculating that their chances of being key participants in government formation in a bigger arena might protect them better than being a minority in Northern Ireland. But that is simply one possible future.

Meanwhile, the (con)federal dimensions of the Agreement are not merely pan-Irish or pan-British. They will evolve within a European Union which has its own strong confederal relationships and many ambitious federalists. There will be no obvious organizational or policy-making contradictions—though multiple networking clashes will arise from this extra layer of (con)federalizing—and they might help to transfer some of the heat from binary considerations of whether a given issue is controlled by London or Dublin.

Double protection and co-sovereignty

The subtlest part of the Agreement goes well beyond standard consociational thinking. This is its tacit 'double protection model', laced with elements of co-sovereignty. It is an agreement designed to withstand major demographic and electoral change. The UK and Irish governments promised to develop functionally equivalent protections of rights, collective and individual, on both sides of the present border. In effect, Northern Irish nationalists are promised protection now on the same terms that will be given to British unionists if they ever become a minority in a unified Ireland.

National communities are protected whether they are majorities or minorities, irrespective of the sovereign stateholder—whence the expression 'double protection'.

The two governments not only promised reciprocity for the local protection of present and future minorities, possibly through establishing the functionally equivalent protection or tights on both sides of the border, but they have also created two intergovernmental devices to protect those communities. One is the successor to the Anglo-Irish Agreement, the British-Irish inter-governmental conference (B-IGC) that guarantees the Republic's government access to policy formulation on all matters not—or not yet—devolved to the Northern Ireland Assembly or the NSMC. The B-IGC, in the event of suspension or collapse of the Agreement, is likely to resume the all-encompassing role it had under the prior Anglo-Irish Agreement. The other is the British-Irish Council. If Irish unification ever occurs the Republic's government would find it politically impossible not to offer the British government reciprocal access in the same forums.

It is important to note what has *not* happened between the two sovereign governments. Formal co-sovereignty has not been established. Unionists claim that they have removed the 1985 Anglo-Irish Agreement in return for conceding the formation of the NSMC. This claim is, at best, exaggerated. Under the new Agreement, the Irish government retained a say in those Northern Irish matters that have not been devolved to the Northern Ireland Assembly, as was the case under Art. 4 of the Anglo-Irish Agreement. And, as with that agreement, there will continue to be an intergovernmental conference, that is, the B-IGC, chaired by the Irish Minister for Foreign Affairs and the Northern Ireland Secretary of State, to deal with non-devolved matters, and this conference will continue to be serviced by a standing secretariat—though the secretariat will no longer be located in Belfast. The new Agreement, moreover, promised to 'intensify cooperation' between the two governments on all-island or cross-border aspects of rights, justice, prison, and policing, unless and until these matters are devolved to the Northern Ireland executive. There is provision for representatives of the Northern Ireland Assembly to be involved in the inter-governmental conference—a welcome parliamentarization—but they do not have the same status as the representatives of the sovereign governments. The Anglo-Irish Agreement fully anticipated these arrangements (O'Leary and McGarry 1996: Chs 6–7), so it is more accurate to claim that the Anglo-Irish Agreement has been fulfilled rather than simply removed.

The Military and Political Nature of the Agreement

The constitutional and institutional nature of the Agreement is complex, but matches the conceptual categories I have deployed. There is no need to evolve new terms for what has been agreed, except, perhaps, for the 'double protection' model. The Agreement was wide-ranging and multilateral, and had something in it for everyone who signed it. Its institutions addressed the 'totality' of relationships between nationalists and unionists in Northern Ireland, between Northern Ireland and the Republic, and between Ireland and Britain.

Describing constitutional architecture is one thing; informal political reality is often different. What lies behind this Agreement? And can it hold together? Everyone asks, 'Is it a house of cards, vulnerable to the slightest pressures?' Is it vulnerable to the play of either Orange or Green cards by hardline loyalists or republicans, or to miscalculations by softer-line politicians? Will its successful implementation prove more difficult than its formulation? These are not foolish concerns: far from it. The annual fracas at Drumcree, when the Orange Order demands to march down the Garvaghy Road against the will of its predominantly nationalist residents; the massacre at Omagh in August 1998 carried out by the Real IRA; intermittent breakdowns in the loyalist ceasefires; continuing punishment beatings by all paramilitaries; and the continuing crisis over weapons decommissioning jointly reveal high levels of ethnonational antagonism. However, there are reasons to be cheerful about the robustness of these novel institutions if we analyse the military and political nature of the settlement. There are, equally, reasons to be cautious.

The agreement on ending the armed conflict

The Agreement was a political settlement that promised a path to unwind armed conflict and thereby create a peace settlement, although, formally speaking, no military or paramilitary organizations negotiated the Agreement. The Agreement encompassed decommissioning, demilitarization, police reform, and prisoner release. It addressed these issues in this textual order, and it is plain that although all these issues are inter-linked they were not explicitly tied to the construction or timing of the new political institutions—with one exception.

Weapons decommissioning

The Agreement was clear on decommissioning, despite the difficulties it occasioned. No paramilitaries that abide by the Agreement have had to engage in formal surrender to those they opposed in war. The Independent International Commission on Decommissioning (IICD), chaired by Canadian General John de Chastelain, is to assist the participants in achieving 'the total disarmament of all paramilitary organisations'. All parties, but impliedly especially those parties that—informally—represented paramilitary organizations in the negotiations, were required to 'use any influence they may have to achieve the decommissioning of all paramilitary arms *within two years* following endorsement in referendums North and South of the agreement and *in the context of the implementation of the overall settlement*' (Government of the United Kingdom n.d., 1998: 20; para. 3, emphasis added).

The italicized passages above clarified the termination point for decommissioning, but not the moment of commencement. They also made it clear that decommissioning is linked to the implementation of the overall settlement, including the establishment of the governance structures—North, North-South, and East-West—and to police reform. That is why Trimble's demand that Sinn Féin achieve a start to decommissioning by the IRA before executive formation in the North was regarded as a breach of any reasonable interpretation of the text of the Agreement. Without executive formation in the North none of the formal institutions of the Agreement that required the cooperation of the local parties could get under way.

Sinn Féin nominated a representative to the IICD, issued a statement to the effect that the war was over; and for the first time issued an outright condemnation of other republicans—of the 'Real IRA' whose members carried out the Omagh bombing. It even assisted the Basque organization ETA in its organization of a ceasefire and efforts to accomplish political negotiations in Spain. But until November 1999 Trimble and some of his senior colleagues were unprepared to regard this activity as sufficient evidence of good intentions. Each move on Sinn Féin's part merely led the UUP to request more, and we have discussed the problems occasioned by the suspension precipitated by Trimble. In response to suspension the IRA withdrew its nominee to the IICD. But in May 2000 a package deal to restore the Agreement's institutions and to avoid the decommissioning deadline of 22 May was agreed: the deadline was shifted for a year, the IRA agreed to organize confidence-building inspections of its arms dumps and to put its weapons verifiably and completely beyond use, and the UK government indicated it would honour the Patten Report in full.

Demilitarization, police reform, and prisoner release

The Agreement promised, and the UK government has begun, a series of phased developments to 'demilitarize' Northern Ireland. It has not, however, published any complete demilitarization plan. 'Normalization' is explicitly promised in the Agreement; reductions in army deployments and numbers, and the removal of security installations and emergency powers, were promised 'consistent with the level of overall threat'. There was also a commitment to address personal firearms regulation and control: an extraordinary proportion of Northern Ireland's citizens, mostly Protestants and unionists, have legally held lethal weapons (Government of the United Kingdom n.d., 1998: 21, paras: 1–4).

It was, as discussed above, decided to address police reform through an Independent Commission (McGarry and O'Leary 1999). It was to propose a police service that is 'representative', 'routinely unarmed', 'professional, effective and efficient, fair and impartial, free from partisan political control; accountable . . . [and] conforms with human rights norms' (Government of the United Kingdom n.d., 1998: 22, paras 1–2). It was to report, at the latest, some nine months before decommissioning was scheduled to finish. It is difficult to believe that the choice of this timing on the part of the makers of the Agreement was an accident. The public outline of police reform was to be available as a confidence-building measure for republicans and nationalists before the major part of republican decommissioning could be expected. It remains the case that some pro-Agreement unionists and some UK public officials publicly wish to prevent the full implementation of the Patten Report, despite their obligations under the Agreement to support the implementation of all its aspects—thus contributing to the current crisis.

The early release of paramilitary prisoners sentenced under scheduled offences, and of a small number of army personnel imprisoned for murders of civilians, has, by contrast with decommissioning, police reform, and demilitarization, been proceeding with less disruption than might have been anticipated. Measures to assist the victims of violence have helped ease the pain occasioned in some quarters by these early releases. The early-release scheme has even worked in creating incentives for some loyalist rejectionist paramilitary organizations—such as the Loyalist Volunteer Force (LVF) —to agree to establish a ceasefire in order to benefit their prisoners.

The political nature of the agreement

So there was a bargain on how to unwind the military and paramilitary conflict as well as on institutions. Movement has been taking place on some dimensions, much more slowly in some cases than others. But before examining the obstacles to a final resolution let me examine the political nature of the Agreement. The Agreement was based on multiple forms of recognition, including recognition of the balance of power; it was an act of statecraft, but it was also based on hard-headed calculations, not pious sentiments.

Recognition The Agreement was an act of recognition between states and national communities. The Republic of Ireland has recognized Northern Ireland's status as part of the United Kingdom, subject to the implementation of the Agreement. The sovereign governments of each state have recognized each other's full names for the first time, 'Ireland' and the 'United Kingdom of Great Britain and Northern Ireland' respectively. The United Kingdom has recognized the right of the people of Ireland, meaning the whole island, to exercise their national self-determination, albeit conjointly and severally as 'North' and 'South'. It has confirmed that Northern Ireland has the right to secede, by majority consent, to unify with Ireland. Ireland has recognized unionists' British political identity. The United Kingdom has recognized northern nationalists as a national minority, not simply as a cultural or religious minority, and as part of a possible future Irish national majority. The two states have, in effect, recognized the paramilitaries that have organized ceasefires as political agencies. They have not required them to surrender themselves or their weapons to their respective authorities, and have organized the release of their prisoners on the assurances of their organizations' ceasefires. The paramilitaries on ceasefires have, with some minor exceptions, recognized one another. Unionists have recognized nationalists as nationalists, not simply as Catholics or as the minority. Nationalists have recognized unionists as unionists, and not just as Protestants. Nationalists and unionists have recognized 'others', who are neither nationalists nor unionists. There is no shortage of recognition: contemporary Northern Ireland would warm the cockles of Hegel's heart.[49] If ethno-nationalist conflicts are rooted in identity politics then this one has at last moved to the stage of multilateral recognition of the identities at stake.

[49] For sophisticated discussions of recognition that are indebted to Hegel see *inter alia* Ringmar (1996) and Taylor (1992).

Balance of power   The Agreement also rested on recognition of a balance of power. The Anglo-Irish Agreement of 1985 led to a new but ultimately productive stalemate. Republicans were left with no immediate prospect of significant electoral growth and their military capacity 'to sicken the Brits' proved limited. Loyalists reorganized in the late 1980s, and by the early 1990s were able to raise the costs of sustaining violence within the republican constituency. Unionists discovered the limits of just saying 'no' as British or bi-governmental initiatives occurred over their heads. There was thus a military stalemate and a political stalemate. But there were also underground structural changes beneath the 'frozen surface', noted by the late John Whyte (Whyte 1993). These included greater equality of opportunity and self-confidence among nationalists, and a shift in the demographic—and therefore electoral—balance of power between the communities. Together these changes underlined the fact that any political settlement could not return nationalists to a subordinate status. The initiatives of John Hume of the SDLP and Gerry Adams of Sinn Féin in the late 1980s and early 1990s constructively responded to this new stalemate. Much work had to be done before their initiative bore fruit (Mallie and McKittrick 1996).

The bargain   There is a bargain at the heart of the Agreement. Nationalists endorsed it because it promised them political, legal, and economic equality now, plus institutions in which they have a strong stake, with the possibility of Irish unification later through simple majority consent in both jurisdictions. They get to co-govern Northern Ireland rather than being simply governed by either unionists or the British government. Moreover, they obtained this share of government with promises of further reforms to redress past legacies of direct and indirect discrimination. Republicans in Sinn Féin and the IRA have traded a long war that they could not win, and could not lose, for a long march through institutions in which they can reasonably claim that only their means have changed, not their end: the termination of partition. Sinn Fein has been extensively rewarded for this decision; its vote has consistently increased with the peace process, culminating in passing the SDLP as the largest nationalist party in the 2001 Westminster and local government elections (O'Leary and Evans 1997; Mitchell, O'Leary, and Evans 2001).

Nationalist support for the Agreement is not difficult to comprehend. For them it is a very good each-way bet. But why did the UUP and the loyalist parties make this consociational bargain, this pact with the nationalist devil? The charms and latent threats of Tony Blair and Bill Clinton, the diplomacy of American Senator George Mitchell (Mitchell 2000), and the process of multiparty inclusive negotiations are not enough to account for Trimble's decision to lead his party where it was most reluctant to go, nor do these factors allow for his intelligence.

The unionists who supported the making of the Agreement were concerned not so much to end the IRA's long war but rather to protect and safeguard the union. Their calculations suggested that only by being generous now could they reconcile nationalists to the union and protect themselves against possibly seismic shifts in the balance of demographic and electoral power. Their calculus was that unionists would get a share in self-government now, avoid the prospect of a British government making further deals over their heads with the Irish government, and have some prospect of persuading northern nationalists that a newly reconstructed union offered a secure home for them. They made the Agreement, in short, to stave off something worse. It is not surprising therefore that there has been greater 'rejectionism' within the unionist bloc: they are conceding more, and some maintain there is no need to concede anything, at least not yet (see also Evans and O'Leary 2000). Nevertheless, significant proportions of supporters of the 'No' unionist parties, especially in the DUP, tell pollsters they would like the Agreement to work—which implies they are convertible to its merits, especially if there is IRA decommissioning, and they are strongly in favour of the Assembly rather than direct rule.

Ideas   Recognizing identities and interests is a necessary but not sufficient condition of a constitutional settlement. Ideas, however loosely understood or flexibly deployed, were also important in the Agreement. Their development, dissemination, and impact are harder to trace, but that does not mean the task cannot be accomplished. Fresh language and policy learning were evident in the making of the Agreement, but so were policy obstinacy and recalcitrance within the highest echelons of the dying Major government (O'Leary 1997) and of the spreadeagled rainbow coalition in Dublin during 1995–7. The crafters of the ideas were many and varied, including politicians, public officials, and many unofficial advisers. Defining and understanding the sources of the conflict in national terms, rather than as issuing from religious extremism or terrorism, was vital. Without this shift the Anglo-Irish Agreement, the Framework Documents, and the Agreement itself would not have been possible. Intimations and imitations of changes elsewhere—

the end of the cold war and its repercussions, political change in South Africa and the Middle East—all had their local register. The traditional explanations of the causes of the conflict had increasingly ceased to move the local participants, and many were open to compromises and political institutions that would mark a shift from the limitations of either London's or Dublin's conceptions of good governance.

The beauty of the Agreement is that both nationalists and unionists have sound reasons for their respective assessments of its merits, that is, for believing that they are right about the long term. They cannot be certain they are right, and so they are willing to make this elaborate settlement now. But is it in Yeats's phrase 'a terrible beauty'? Will the Agreement wither and die once it has become apparent who is right about the long term? That possibility cannot be excluded, but that is why the Agreement's architecture repays careful inspection. It is not any consociational model, like that of Lebanon, vulnerable to the slightest demographic transformation in the composition of its constituent communities.

There are incentives for each bloc to accommodate the other precisely in order to make its vision of the future more likely: that is, both have reasons to act creatively on the basis of self-fulfilling prophecies. The treat of the double protection model is that it eases the pain for whoever gets it wrong about the future. The confederalizing and federalizing possibilities in the Agreement ensure that both national communities will remain linked, come what may, to their preferred nation-states. Moreover, the Agreement does not preclude the parties agreeing at some future juncture to a fully-fledged model of British and Irish co-sovereignty.

The politics of the transition: games of unlikely partners and the temptations of 'legalism'

In the first six months of 2001 it was difficult to avoid pessimism about the prospects for the Agreement. The passage of the Police (Northern Ireland) Act in November 2000 had left the SDLP, Sinn Féin, and the Irish government strongly dissatisfied. Even though the final act was better than the original bill, it was still 'Patten lite'. The IRA had not formally re-engaged with the IICD, partly, it seemed, to put pressure on Mandelson to deliver on Patten and demilitarization—though it did facilitate a second inspection of its arms dumps. The UK government was refusing to move fast on demilitarization because of its security concerns, especially about dissident republicans, who were strongest in areas which have historically been vigorously republican—and where there is the greatest demand for demilitarization. The discipline of loyalist paramilitaries was breaking down: there was internal feuding, and sections of the UDA were targeting vulnerable Catholics with pipe-bomb attacks in predominantly unionist towns. On top of all this Trimble decided to play executive hardball, using what was called 'proportionate action'. To compel Sinn Féin to coerce the IRA to start decommissioning its weapons, as it had appeared to promise in May 2000, he embarked on a series of political sanctions. First, he blocked the two Sinn Féin ministers in the power-sharing executive from participating in the NSMC. The Sinn Féin Ministers and the SDLP Deputy First Minister promptly took Trimble to court, and won: Justice Kerr ruled his action 'unlawful' in January 2001. Trimble immediately appealed the decision—pending at the time of writing, but likely to go against him. Then just before the UK general election and the Northern Ireland local government elections of June 2001, Trimble repeated the tactic he had deployed in 2000. He wrote a post-dated resignation letter, effective on 1 July 2001, which he declared he would make effective if the IRA failed to move on decommissioning. His long-run calculation was that if his resignation became effective then the UK government would have to choose between suspending the Agreement's institutions—Trimble's preferred default—and leaving the Assembly to trigger fresh elections, because of its failure to replace the First and Deputy First Ministers within six weeks, that is, by 12 August 2001. His short-run calculation was that the resignation threat would immunize him and his party's candidates from criticism from other unionists over their willingness to share government with Sinn Féin in the absence of IRA decommissioning. Neither calculation was especially shrewd.

The elections did not deliver Trimble's desires. The DUP did very well, making significant gains at the expenses of the UUP, and Sinn Féin for the first time surpassed the SDLP in the nationalist bloc, consolidating its mandate within its community (Mitchell, O'Leary, and Evans 2001). The IRA did not move on decommissioning and Trimble resigned as First Minister, though not as UUP party leader, on 1 July, thus triggering Mallon's departure from office. Under the rules fresh elections for these positions have to be held within six weeks, and if the Assembly fails to elect new premiers then there must be fresh Assembly elections. This scenario provoked the two sovereign governments into convening negotiations between pro-Agreement parties and themselves at Weston Park, Shropshire, England, in July 2001. A new blame or blame-avoidance game had begun.

External observers agreed that two parties and one government shared most of the blame for the impasses in implementing the Belfast Agreement and stabilizing its institutions: Sinn Féin, the UUP, and the UK government. The IRA had initiated decommissioning of its weapons, if one counts international inspections of its arms dumps, but it had not moved to implement its pledge of 2000 to put its weapons completely and verifiably beyond use. None of its complaints about the UK government's failures to deliver on its pledges absolved Sinn Féin from its obligations to build confidence amongst its governmental partners that they were not sharing power with a private army, and nothing in the Agreement warranted the republican line that actual decommissioning must be the very last act of implementation. Prevarication merely maximized distrust about the IRA's long-run intentions.

The UUP had broken several of its obligations under the Agreement, while demanding that others deliver on their promises ahead of time. It blocked rapid executive formation. It rejected the Patten Report on policing, though it met the Agreement's terms of reference. The First Minister blocked Sinn Féin ministers' legitimate participation in the NSMC. He has twice threatened resignation, and the collapse or suspension of the Agreement's institutions, to force Sinn Féin to deliver the IRA to his deadlines. He encouraged the UK government to make the first formal break with the Agreement, and international law, by passing the Suspension Act in 2000, which Mandelson used, and Trimble has continued to press for its use with Mandelson's successor, John Reid.

The UK government so far has dishonoured its pledge of 5 May 2000—which preceded the IRA's promise of 6 May to put its weapons completely and verifiably beyond use—repeated in March 2001, to produce legislation and implementation plans fully reflecting the letter and the spirit of the Patten Report on policing. None of its excuses exonerate it in nationalist eyes, and it also has work to do to fulfil its obligations on demilitarization, the review of the administration of justice, and the protection of human rights. To complicate matters, nationalists see the 5–6 May 2000 statements as bargains essentially between the UK and the IRA, whereas the unionists see them as essentially bargains between Trimble and Sinn Féin.

At Weston Park the two governments sought to put together a package linking police reform, demilitarization, decommissioning, and securing the Agreement's institutions. The talks were not successful, though they were not fruitless. The governments have currently agreed to organize and implement their own package, declaring there will be no further inter-party negotiations. These will presumably address the outstanding issues: decommissioning, demilitarization, police reform, and securing the institutions of the Agreement. Whatever the outcome of this package the two sovereign governments will then have three choices: to leave further negotiation to the parties; to suspend the Agreement's institutions; or to have fresh Assembly elections. The first option does not seem likely to work, yet. The second option must be rejected by the Irish government, which regards the Suspension Act as a unilateral breach of the treaty accompanying the Belfast Agreement. The third option is to have fresh Assembly elections, consequent upon the failure to re-elect successors to Trimble and Mallon. The argument put against elections is that they will help the DUP and Sinn Féin rather than the UUP and the SDLP. Perhaps that possibility will itself act as an incentive for the UUP to compromise.

But there is another possibility emerging: if in any fresh Assembly elections the DUP and Sinn Féin do very well, then they would do best on moderated platforms. In this scenario we might anticipate IRA initiatives on arms and DUP briefings on how they seek to 'renegotiate', rather than destroy, the Agreement. The emergence of both parties as the clear majority within their respective blocs would create a fascinating if dangerous spectacle. Sinn Féin and the DUP would have to choose: to accept their respective nominees for the posts of First and Deputy First Ministers, or accept moderate SDLP and UUP nominees for these posts, or have fresh elections. That is, they would have to choose between stealing their opponents' clothes and wearing them, or showing that they remain wolves in sheep's clothing.

The Agreement's political entrenchment required that some short-term advantage-maximizing and game-playing temptations be avoided. At the heart of this Agreement lie four internal political forces: the SDLP and the UUP among the historically moderate nationalists and unionists, and Sinn Féin and the PUP/UDP amongst the historically hardline republicans and loyalists.[50] The Agreement requires these political forces to evolve as informal coalition partners while preserving their bases. Considerations of brevity oblige me to focus on just two of these constellations.

The UUP has been the most vigorous short-term maximizer and game-player, because it is the most divided. The party split most under the impact of the making of the Agreement. It made very

[50] In the new dispensation there are now eight minorities. Five are for the Agreement: nationalists, republicans, 'Yes' unionists, 'Yes' loyalists, and 'others'. Three are against the Agreement: 'No' unionists, 'No' loyalists, and 'No' republicans. The latter are in 'objective alliance'.

significant concessions on internal power-sharing and on all-Ireland dimensions. It has lost votes to the 'No' unionists in three successive elections. The temptation of its leaders has been to renegotiate the Agreement during its implementation. This way they hoped to refortify the party and draw off support from the 'soft No' camp among unionists. The UUP would have preferred an Agreement which was largely internal to Northern Ireland, and which involved them co-governing Northern Ireland with the SDLP in a weaker Assembly, on the lines established in Wales, and without the dual premiership and inclusive executive. It would have strongly preferred to govern without Sinn Féin. In consequence, the UUP's most tempting game plan has been to use the decommissioning issue to split what it sees as a pan-nationalist bloc. The signs of this game have been a phoney 'legalism', adversarial and petty-minded interpretation of the Agreement, postponement and prevarication, and brinkmanship. One clear example of this was when Trimble, on poor legal advice, availed himself of a technical clause in the Northern Ireland Act 1998 and refused to nominate the two Sinn Féin Ministers to carry out their obligations under meetings of the NSMC.

The other constellation is republican. Republicans too have been tempted to engage in game-playing. Sinn Féin has been tempted by hard legalism: extracting the full literal implementation of its contract with the UK, at the risk of damaging the informal political coalition that made the Agreement. They have insisted on full delivery by others, while postponing decommissioning, even if this insistence created great difficulties for the UUP and the SDLP, their informal partners. They thought they had an each-way bet: if the UUP delivered on the Agreement, well and good; if the UUP did not, then Sinn Féin would position itself to ensure that unionists get the blame for its non-implementation. For some hardline republicans, non-implementation may yet provide a pretext for a return to war. In contrast, softer-liners could only sanction any return to violence if governmental or loyalist forces were responsible for the first military breach, and many softer-liners argue that republicans have more to gain electorally both within Northern Ireland and the Republic through becoming a wholly constitutional movement. Even if there is a defunct Agreement, time and demography, they reason, are on their side.

To survive, and to be implemented in full, this consociational and (con)federal agreement therefore requires six processes to occur:

1. There must be vigorous British and Irish oversight to encourage the Agreement's full implementation.

2. Greater recognition is necessary among the informal coalition partners, especially within the UUP and Sinn Féin, that they may benefit more from not seeking maximum advantage from one another's difficulties and from not exaggerating their own.
3. The two governments and the pro-Agreement parties must agree that the remaining items for implementation are resolved to their mutual satisfaction. This will require the unravelling of some of Mandelson's stances on policing reform.
4. Republicans will have to move from the inspection of the IRA's arms dumps to accomplish wholly credible disarmament.
5. Action and discipline is required from the loyalist parties and paramilitary organizations, whose obligations on decommissioning tend to be forgotten in UK circles.
6. The UUP must be satisfied with republican action on decommissioning, but accept that the UK government has obligations to deliver on demilitarization and the full-scale reform of criminal justice and policing—in ways that are against their preferences.

It is a tall order, though not impossible. We will know soon whether a final deal can happen. But what happens if there is failure ahead?

Conclusion: Alternative Scenarios and Interim Evaluation

It makes good political sense to argue that there is no alternative to the Agreement, especially by its supporters, but only in the mind of Margaret Thatcher is it ever a matter of ontological truth that 'there is no alternative'.

Let us imagine three scenarios in which unionists are held culpable for the breakdown through wrecking the workings of the executive. In scenario 1 the UK government would come under strong pressure to shut the Assembly because nationalists did not negotiate for a purely internal settlement, though it would naturally want to avoid antagonizing anyone too much. The pressure to deliver policing reform to calm nationalists would be strong, but probably resisted by 'securocrats'. The reforms embedded in the human rights and mainstreaming equality provisions in the Agreement would continue. Dimensions of the Agreement that do not involve the local parties would be delivered. The British-Irish intergovernmental conference would become an active site for policy formulation, and in time would encourage sensible functional cross-border cooperation. This is a feasible but unattractive scenario: a cold peace with traits

of a local cold war, reform without significant devolution, tempered
by atrocities from the breakaway Continuity IRA and Real IRA, and
the LVF and its kindred spirits. Any wrong moves would destabilize
the ceasefires. The review of the Agreement would increasingly
resemble the most famous play by an Irish Protestant, *Waiting for
Godot*. Party politics might become more polarized: 'Yes' unionists
would lose further electoral ground to 'No' unionists, and the SDLP
to Sinn Féin within a demographically growing nationalist bloc. The
Alliance Party and the Women's Coalition are unlikely to flourish.

In scenario 2, a default plan would tempt some: de facto co-
sovereignty in and over Northern Ireland by the UK and Irish governments. In the absence of agreed devolution the two governments
would increase their cooperation. The formal declaration of shared
sovereignty would not, and need not, be rushed. Its gradual emergence would act as a standing invitation to unionists to win some
control over their own destiny through meaningful devolution. Co-
sovereignty has many merits, especially when considered from the
perspective of justice; but having just presided over a major institutional failure the two governments are unlikely to move rapidly
to a formal settlement of this kind, though coherent models of how
it might operate have been sketched (O'Leary *et al.* 1993).

In scenario 3, co-sovereignty could be accompanied by a local government option. This strategy would abandon the Assembly, and
stop treating Northern Ireland in a uniform and unitary fashion.
Significant multi-functional competencies could be devolved to reorganized local governments willing to adopt institutions of the type
made in the Agreement: in 20 of the existing 26 local councils, political parties practise power-sharing or senior-office rotation, the
remaining six being dominated by unionists in areas where the
nationalist minority is electorally weak. The proposals in the Patten
Report to link local government boundaries to police organization
and accountability could be built on. Local governments on the border, dominated by nationalists, could develop significant cross-
border arrangements with their southern counterparts—and the
Irish government. This would isolate the heartlands of unreformed
unionism while giving nationalists significant incentives to participate in a reformed Northern Ireland. The danger in this option
is that its 'cantonization qualities' might encourage further segregation and promote re-partitionist thinking.

The moral of all these three scenarios is clear. Worlds in which
unionists are held culpable for breakdown would not improve their
lot. The Agreement offers them a better chance of preserving the
union with their meaningful participation than the alternatives.

What of scenario 4, in which republicans are held culpable for breakdown? What happens if the IRA has failed to cooperate on decommissioning, though everyone else has delivered on their obligations? In these circumstances the UUP could trigger the collapse of the institutions of the Agreement, while retaining the benefits occasioned by the changes to Arts 2 and 3 of the Irish Constitution. A review would be initiated. The UK government would come under strong pressure from unionists to reconsider the imprisonment of republican paramilitary prisoners. Every punishment beating would prompt calls to review the ceasefires. There would be demands from the UUP to halt police reform. The SDLP would be pressed to condemn Sinn Féin, Sinn Féin to condemn the IRA, the IRA to condemn its hardliners. The present world, which offers mostly improving prospects for nationalists, would start to look much messier and uncertain. The Agreement has the solid endorsement of nationalists. Reforms are in train, whether the Agreement is fully implemented or not, but these reforms, especially police reform, might be jeopardized by republican intransigence. In short, for most republicans plausible cost-benefit analyses on renewed militarism are clear: they stand to gain more, North and South, through electoral politics than they do from an IRA which does not cooperate in decommissioning or which resumes assassinations or bombings. For that reason I expect actual IRA decommissioning to occur, provided the UK government delivers fully on police reform. That is a clear and testable prediction, with, I hope, the minimum infusion of wishful thinking.

The normative political science in this analysis is, I hope, clear. Consociational and confederal devices provide excellent repertoires where a sovereign border has separated a national minority living in its homeland from its kin-state, and where an historically privileged settler colonial portion of a *Staatsvolk* cannot, or is refused permission to, control the disputed territory on its own. Such devices are capable of being constructed with and without guidance from constitutional designers, though plainly diffusion of institutional repertoires is one of the neglected dimensions of what some call 'globalization'.

Comprehensive settlements, after inclusive negotiations, that incorporate hardliners and that address the identities, interests, and ideological agendas of all parties are likely to produce complex and interlinked institutional ensembles that look very vulnerable. Referendums may, however, assist the legitimization of such agreements and the consolidation of the pre-agreement pacts. Preferential voting in the STV mode both makes possible cross-ethnic 'vote-pooling' and benefits hardliners willing to become less hard-line. Double protection models offer imaginative ways to make possible changes in sovereignty less threatening, both now and later. But where any bloc is divided over the merits of such a settle-ment, and where its leaders respond more to the threat of being out-flanked than they do to the imperative of making the new, tacit, cross-ethnic coalition work, it may prove impossible to implement the agreement. These agreements are precarious equilibria, but they are infinitely better than their alternatives: fighting to the fin-ish, or the panaceas proposed by partisan or naive integrationists. What is rational, or optimal, does not always become real; and what is morally better is not always politically correct. But in this case Hegel may yet have to eat his heart out if the rational becomes real, and the new millennium marks the beginning of the end of what was British-Irish history.

Annex: The Mysterious Work of Viktor d'Hondt in Belfast

> I had never heard of d'Hondt until I went into the talks process, but we hear of nothing else nowadays.
>
> Paul Murphy, Minister of State, Northern Ireland Office, House of Commons, *Official Report* (319, 18 November 1998).

Viktor d'Hondt is a good answer to the *Trivial Pursuit* challenge to name a famous Belgian. This lawyer devised a method of propor-tional representation that is used for many purposes, including allo-cating political offices in the European Parliament. The method works by iteration, using a simple series of divisors, $1, 2, 3, \ldots n$, that are divided into a party's share of votes or seats. The two tables below show how the allocation worked for the Northern Ireland Executive Committee. The seats won by political parties and the order in which ministries were obtained are displayed in Table 11.3.[51]

All parties entitled to seats were willing to take them up. The party with the largest number of seats, the UUP with 27, obtained the first ministry, and then its seat share was divided by two, leav-ing it with 13.5. The next largest remaining number of seats was held by the SDLP, with 24; it chose the second ministry, and its seat

[51] The principal change from Table 11.1 above is that the UUP had lost one mem-ber to the 'No' unionists, reducing the party's membership in the Assembly to 27, and the UKUP had split, the party leaving its leader—or vice versa, depending upon the source—reducing its seat-share from five to four.

TABLE 11.3: *The d'Hondt rule and the distribution of ministries*

Divisor	UKUP		DUP		PUP		UUP		APNI		NIWC		SDLP		SF	
	S	M	S	M	S	M	S	M	S	M	S	M	S	M	S	M
1	4	–	20	(3)	2	–	27	(1)	6		2	–	24	(2)	18	(4)
2			10	(7)			14	(5)					12	(6)	9	(9)
3			6.6				9	(8)					8	(10)	6	
4			5				7						6		4.5	
All			20	2	2		28	3					24	3	18	2

M stands for Ministerial portfolio choice; the numbers in brackets in the M columns indicate the order in which parties won ministries of their choice; S is the number of seats each party has during each stage of the allocation.

share was divided by two, leaving it with 12. The next largest remaining number of seats was held by the DUP, with 20; it chose the third ministry, and its seat share was divided by two, leaving it with 10. The next largest remaining number of seats was held by Sinn Féin, with 18; it chose the fourth ministry, and its seat share was divided by two, leaving it with 9. The next largest remaining number of seats was the UUP, with 13.5; it chose the fifth ministry, and its total seat share was divided by three, leaving it with 9. And so on. Great foresight was shown in the legislative enactment of this agreement: where there was a tie in the number of seats held by parties during any stage of the allocation, precedence was given to the party with the higher share of the first-preference vote. The tie-breaker was required at stage 8, when both the UUP—27[52] seats—and Sinn Féin—18 seats—had a remaining seat total of 9. In accordance with the rule the UUP was given precedence in portfolio choice.

Unionists therefore obtained five ministries—three UUP and two DUP—and nationalists obtained five—three SDLP and two SF—a mild disproportionality by bloc, but not by party. What was not fore-seen was that unionists would not fare as well as nationalists in strategic decision-making over portfolio allocation. Nationalists obtained almost the entire welfare state portfolio—education at all levels, health and social services, and agriculture—as well as finance and personnel. What happened? Table 11.4 below shows the actual portfolios chosen by parties at each stage in the allocation.

Table 11.4: *Party choices of ministerial portfolios, 1999*

	Portfolio	Nominee	Party
1.	Enterprise, Trade, and Investment	Empey	UUP
2.	Finance and Personnel	Durkan	SDLP
3.	Regional Development	Robinson	DUP
4.	Education	McGuinness	SF
5.	Environment	Foster	UUP
6.	Higher and Further Education, Training and Development	Farren	SDLP
7.	Social Development	Dodds	DUP
8.	Culture, Art, and Leisure	McGimpsey	UUP
9.	Health, Social Services, and Public Safety	de Brun	SF
10.	Agriculture	Rogers	SDLP

[52] See n. 51.

There was no coordination between the UUP and the DUP, or between the SDLP and Sinn Féin; but since the negotiation and making of the Agreement relations between the SDLP and Sinn Féin have been more amicable than those between the UUP and the DUP. The UUP did not, as expected, take the Finance and Personnel portfolio with its first choice. This decision may have been affected by Empey's own preferences—as Trimble's right-hand man during the negotiations he may have had a free hand—or by the fact that Enterprise, Trade and Investment will mesh well with the Economic Policy Unit in the First and Deputy First Ministers' Office. More likely, the UUP may have calculated that it would be best to give the SDLP the lead negotiation and arbitration role over the budget, knowing that the SDLP would be better able to face down Sinn Féin's suggestions. The SDLP's choice of Finance and Personnel was no surprise given that the post was available. The DUP then had the choice of the third ministry. The party had decided to take office while refusing to interact with Sinn Féin ministers. It appeared to be seeking to wreck the Agreement from within, while obtaining some of the perks of office to which it was entitled. Its leader, Ian Paisley, nominated his deputy leader, Robinson, to the Regional Development portfolio, consisting largely of transport. Whether this was to prevent vigorous cross-border initiatives in this area, or for some other reason, is not known. This choice did, however, leave Sinn Féin free to pick the Education portfolio, which plainly shocked many unionist Assembly members. Sinn Féin's choice made strategic sense for a radical nationalist party; the ministry gives it access to a high-profile, big-spending, potentially redistributive and socializing ministry. The UUP then chose Environment, and the party leader nominated a relative unknown, Foster, to the portfolio. The ministry contains Local Government within its remit and Foster is a local government councillor; he was being rewarded by his party leader for delivering him crucial support. The choice may partly have been motivated by a desire to block unwelcome changes that might be proposed for local government. Whatever its rationale, it left the SDLP free to pick the Higher and Further Education, Training and Development portfolio. The DUP then claimed that the UUP's decisions, both in making the Agreement and in its choice of portfolios, had left nationalists in full control of education throughout Northern Ireland—this was not true because of the checks and balances in the Assembly, but a rhetorically powerful claim; and in any case the DUP could have picked either education portfolio for itself, but did not do so. It is not known whether it wanted to benefit from

unionists' anxieties over nationalists' grip on the education portfolios—the Machiavellian view—or whether it prioritized other
matters. The DUP then chose the Social Development portfolio, a
choice that left the UUP with a major headache. If it took either of
Health, Social Services and Public Safety or Agriculture then it
would leave one nationalist in charge of the Ministry of Culture,
Arts and Leisure, with its potential agenda-setting control over
items such as parades and binational and bi-lingual matters. The
UUP chose to sacrifice access to a big-spending ministry for this
reason. Sinn Féin and the SDLP then took the remaining portfolios,
appointing women to the last two ministries in a display of progressive politics.

  This story is intrinsically interesting, but also suggests some
major political science questions for formal theorists and comparative analysts. How does the Northern Ireland story fit with theories
of coalition government? Is the d'Hondt rule—and variations on it,
such as a Saint-Laguë rule—an efficient way of solving coalition-
making problems, one that saves on the transactions' costs of bargaining? Should parties be prevented from forming post-election
coalition pacts for the purpose of improving on their total number of
portfolios and the pecking order in which they receive ministries? Is
the d'Hondt rule a more likely outcome and a more efficient rule in
complex bargaining than the fair division rules for dispute resolution suggested by game theorists? How do the formal and informal
rules of executive formation vary across past and present consociational executives in the world, and is there any evidence of cross-
national learning?

12

The Eritrean Experience in Constitution Making: The Dialectic of Process and Substance

Bereket Habte Selassie

Historical Background

Eritrea's constitution was ratified on 23 May 1997 by a constituent assembly formed for that purpose. This event occurred on the eve of the sixth liberation anniversary from Ethiopian occupation, following 30 years of war. With the end of Ethiopia's occupation, the Eritrean People's Liberation Front (EPLF) created a provisional government pending formal independence, which came two years later. The delay came at the insistence of the EPLF leadership, which wanted to hold an internationally observed referendum. The leadership was confident that the people would freely choose independence and thus show a hitherto sceptical or indifferent world that the independence struggle had full popular backing.

The result of the referendum of 23–5 April 1993 fully justified this confidence. In voting certified as fair by a UN observer mission, 99.8 per cent majority opted for full independence. Soon after, Eritrea became a UN member. Then there began a transition process that culminated in the ratification of the constitution, capping three years of intense public debate and consultation, as will be explained in more detail below.

Eritrea is a creation of colonial history, not unlike most African countries. In pre-colonial times, the territory was known by various names, experienced different systems of government, and was subject to expansion and contraction, as well as population migrations that led to the intermingling of different cultures, including influences from ancient Greece and Egypt. Orthodox Christianity, centred around the city of Axum, has been present since the fourth century. Three centuries later came the rise of Islam. Eritrea is thus a rich legatee of these great world religions that generally coexisted in remarkable harmony, though at times there was strife, often driven by outside powers such as the Ottoman Turks or nineteenth-century Egyptian rulers.

Italian rule, beginning in 1890, introduced a typical colonial system of government in which the indigenous populations had no say. After the failure of its early attempts to suppress native laws and institutions, the colonial state contented itself with simply superimposing its own laws particularly in the areas of criminal, administrative, and commercial law, leaving customary laws and traditional institutions intact.

Then came the Second World War, which cost Italy its African colonies. The victorious allies and the United Nations, which they established, decided on the future of Libya and Somalia with comparative ease. The territorial ambitions of Emperor Haile Selassie, however, made Eritrea's future more contentious, and the Eritrean people's right to self-determination was sacrificed on the altar of cold war politics. Haile Selassie's claim to Eritrea converged with US foreign policy, which strove to keep Soviet influence out of strategic regions like the Horn of Africa by cultivating local allies such as Haile Selassie.

In 1950, a US-sponsored UN resolution joined Eritrea and Ethiopia in a lopsided federal arrangement under which Eritrea was given local autonomy short of independence. Haile Selassie gradually destroyed even this limited autonomy. In November 1962 he abolished the federation, declared Eritrea the fourteenth province of Ethiopia, and sent an army of occupation. A year earlier, an Eritrean liberation group had begun an armed struggle that was to last 30 years. During its final phase, this war came to encompass a sweeping social revolution that would turn out to be perhaps its most important legacy, with notable achievements in such areas as women's equality, human rights, social justice, and democracy. These values, acquired during the long armed struggle, critically influenced the process of constitution-making. As public debate made clear, Eritreans see the Constitution as fulfilling the liberation struggle, and thus as helping vindicate the enormous sacrifices involved in the struggle.

The Context of Democratic Transition

The government of Eritrea passed several laws that expressed commitment to democracy. One such law charged the government, *inter alia*, with the responsibility of 'preparing and laying the foundation for a democratic system of government'.[1] The Constitutional Commission of Eritrea was established a year later in fulfilment of this responsibility.[2] Moreover, the governing party, which had renamed itself the Popular Front for Democracy and Justice (PFDJ), adopted a National Charter at its third congress in February 1994. The Charter expressed the vision of the governing party for the future of Eritrea, setting forth as the guiding principles or objectives democracy, human rights, and social justice, together with stability, national unity, and economic development. The Constitutional Commission thus used the Charter as a principal source of national consensus and point of departure for the national debate that was to follow.[3]

Democracy, which is the linchpin of the national objectives listed above, is a universally recognized paramount political value of our epoch, and even dictators pay lip-service to it because it is used as an indicator of progress, together with human rights, the rule of law, and judicial independence. It is worth mentioning, in passing, that some political systems take issue, at times, with the notion of universal values when their application runs counter to some of their policies and practices. Human rights, in particular, has become the subject of controversy in which governments that are accused of violating them respond by asserting that such principles are relative and that what are being posited as universal are Western values.[4] The controversy goes on, as yet unresolved, although the progress in human rights continues incrementally.

As with human rights, so with democracy. Even though democracy is the most basic political value, differences may occur on its definition and practical application. In one of his noted works, *The Third Wave* (1991), Samuel Huntington, for instance, places great emphasis on procedural democracy, contending that elections and the proper enforcement of election laws is the critical element in any evaluation of a country's claim to being democratic. In laying emphasis on procedure, this view of democracy does not seem to give due weight to the substantive aspects of democracy. The Constitutional Commission of Eritrea dwelt on this point in order to

---

[1] Proclamation Number 37/1993.   [2] Proclamation 55/1994.

[3] See keynote address of the Chairman of the Constitutional Commission of Eritrea delivered at the opening ceremony of the International Symposium on the Making of the Eritrean Constitution (1995).

[4] See Huntington (1991: 6). In his recent visit to the United States, China's President Jiang Zemin made such an assertion to which his host, President Clinton, retorted that he was on the wrong side of history.

highlight the hazards of neglecting substantive aspects of democracy, of people's participation in their affairs beyond the election period. In the opinion of the members of the Commission and of the government of Eritrea, procedural democracy is incomplete without social justice and equitable access to resources to all citizens.[5]

Models of Constitution Making

Constitution making is a process which brings people and their government together to shape their future political life; it is a meeting point between the past, the present, and the future. If a hyperbole may be forgiven, it can be regarded as an historic rendezvous between state and society. The history of the great charters of the world attests to this contention, and one common feature of these historic documents is the principle that there must be certain limits to governmental power, even though their nature and extent differ from place to place and from period to period. The conflicts between king and barons that produced the Magna Carta gave more power to the barons. The strife between king and his aristocratic allies and kinsmen on the one hand, and the commoners on the other, that broke out some five centuries after the Magna Carta was resolved in favour of the commoners represented by the ascendant English bourgeoisie. In our own time the struggle between autocracies and the common citizens demanding democracy is going on all the time.

All these struggles are concerned essentially with the limits to government. The concept of constitutionalism expresses rule with appropriate limits placed on governments by law. Such limits are placed by various devices, including the submission of governments to periodic popular judgements at general elections, term limits to elective office, separation of powers, and federalism or other forms of decentralization of central government power. This concept of limits to power lies at the heart of a democratic system of government, and since it is best guaranteed in the constitution making has been the subject of continued debates and theorizing.

Apart from constitutions imperially, or royally, imposed on subject peoples historically, three main approaches to constitution making can be identified in modern times. There is, first, what may be called the Philadelphia model. Then there is the Westminster model, which may also be called the 'parliamentary' method. Third, there is the constitutional commission approach, combining the two

---

[5] For further discussion the varying definitions of democracy, see Selassie (1999).

other approaches, which may be characterized as state of the art. The governing principle common to all three approaches is that of legitimacy: the requirement that the constitution must be ultimately approved by an entity or entities in which sovereignty resides.

The Philadelphia Convention of 1787 debated and drafted the US Constitution, and the legislatures of the then 13 States legitimized it in the act of ratification. In the Westminster model, a committee of parliament is designated by parliament to draft a constitution and the parliament in plenary session approves it. The critical difference between the new method and the other two lies in the fact that in the new approach the public is directly and actively involved in the process. Another difference lies in the use of a constituent assembly to ratify what parliament may have approved, as in the case of Eritrea, or the parliament itself acting as the constituent assembly, as in the case of Namibia. In the Philadelphia model, the ratifying entities were the State legislatures themselves that had been elected with a larger mandate to represent their constituents, whereas in the new approach a new entity is elected specifically to debate and approve the constitution. The constituent assembly is elected for the sole purpose of ratifying the constitution, the Namibian case being an exception.

In analysing these various approaches and their differences, the criterion for choice is based on a democratic principle: to what extent does the method achieve the desired end, which is optimal public participation? On this view, the new approach seems to be a better method on the face of it. Its validity will depend, however, on the quality of the participation and the extent to which the constitutional commission concerned takes public opinion into account in drafting the constitution.

With these considerations in mind, let us now focus on the Eritrean experience and inquire to what extent the new method has been of value and whether it has enabled Eritreans to respond adequately to the challenges of citizenship in establishing constitutional government.

The Eritrean Experience: The Process

The work of the Commission was guided by a ten-member Executive Committee, drawn from the larger membership. The 50-member Commission represented a cross section of Eritrean society, including 21 women, the majority of whom were veteran liberation fighters. Each of Eritrea's nine ethnic groups was represented, as were the business and professional communities. The Commission's mandate was to run for three years, and its work was divided into a logistical phase—which occupied 1994—to be followed by three substantive phases. The law called for the draft produced by the Commission to be subjected to parliamentary approval, after which there would be further public debate on the approved draft.[6] In the second phase, the Commission would prepare a final draft, taking into account public opinion where deemed necessary. In the third phase, the final draft was then to go to parliament and, through it, finally, to a Constituent Assembly representing the whole nation.[7]

Eritrea's decision to create a constitutional commission charged with organizing public debates as well as taking expert opinion into account placed an unusually heavy emphasis on the direct and active involvement of the public during the drafting phase.[8] In standard models of constitution making, this first phase has usually been dominated by a constitutional convention or conference—often held under conditions of secrecy or quasi-secrecy, as was the case with the 1787 convention that drafted the American Constitution—or else by a specially appointed committee of the legislature, as in the Westminster model.

For the new approach to succeed, three principal prerequisites must be satisfied:

(1) a government committed to the ideal of constitutional democracy;
(2) a public aware of this ideal and willing to play a role in its attainment; and
(3) an entity with a clear legal mandate freely to solicit public views through widely held debates and other forms of popular consultation, views which it must then seriously consider when drafting the constitution. Needless to say, the members of this body must be selected not only on grounds of religious, ethnic, or regional representative grounds, but also on those of professional competence.

In Eritrea's case, these requirements were in place and we will make reference to them as appropriate, not necessarily in the order of their appearance above.

---

[6] Proclamation No. 55/1994, Art. 4(4) [7] Ibid.

[8] See Art. 12(4) of the law which enjoins the Chairman of the Commission to 'encourage the participation and contributions of Eritrean and foreign experts and/organize ad hoc advisory boards of experts to help expedite the process of preparing the Draft Constitution'.

Question and Answer Method and Folkloric Communication

Organizing debate on the most fundamental political questions facing a nation is far more than a technical or logistical matter. It involves issues of substance concerning the most appropriate literature to be translated and distributed, and the best way of communicating essential ideas about democracy and constitutional rule. In Eritrea, much attention was paid to preparing the public to make the fullest and best-informed contribution possible. An equal emphasis was placed on the need to record, collate, and eventually analyse the views that emerged during the public debate. This step had a twofold importance, for not only might such views be used in drafting the constitution, but the very fact of keeping track of them gave people a sense of ownership of the constitution.

The Commission began its work by posing a series of questions, questions that it set itself the task of answering before launching the public debate and drafting the constitution. The essence of the questions may be summed up as follows:

- What lessons, if any, do historical experiences offer in this respect?
- Do such experiences yield helpful models or guidelines?
- Is it desirable, or practicable, to use models: are they transferable like some technology?
- What, after all, are the values and goals that a nation needs, most emphatically to promote, nurture, and protect? And how should these be incorporated in a constitution?
- Should such values and goals be so incorporated or should they be left to be determined in the crucibles of political action and social interaction, in the daily discourse of culture?
- What form of government would be best suited for Eritrea?
- What degree of decentralization should there be?
- Should there be an official language or languages? If so, which ones do we select and why?

It was apparent from the outset that some things could be left out of the constitution while others could not, which made the question susceptible to debate. There were questions of detail, including some pertaining to technicalities such as the size of the constitution: should it be long or short? In particular, how detailed should the chapter on human rights be—should we incorporate international covenants on human rights by reference or by detailed inclusion in the constitution? All in all, the Commission listed 23 questions for consideration.

There was consensus from the outset that there should be no reliance on ready-made models, whatever their source. Rather, it was thought better to take stock of the reality and paramount needs of the country. The Commission's research and consultation activities were designed with that objective in mind. The Commission thus attached critical importance to the process; in its estimation, the process was as important as the end. Put another way, the end—that is, the constitution—prescribes the means, but the means shape the end.

One of the main difficulties to be overcome in public participation in Eritrea's constitution making was the low literacy rate—about 20 per cent—which required the extensive use of non-printed means of communication. These included songs, poetry or short-story recitals, and plays in the various vernaculars. Artists and writers were invited to compete in such efforts. A great deal of money, skill, and other resources went towards this end, with generally satisfactory results. Radio was a huge help. Public seminars, debates, mobile theatres, and the like were employed to enhance popular awareness of the fundamentals of constitutional democracy, including citizens' rights and duties, and the scope and limits of government's responsibilities to citizens.

Civic Education, Seminars, and Working Committees

The Commission's substantive efforts began with a well-attended international symposium in January 1995 (International Symposium on the Making of the Eritrean Constitution 1995). This was followed by a civic education campaign in which Commission members and more than 400 specially trained teachers instructed the public in village and town meetings on constitutional issues and related political and social questions. In addition to the non-printed media mentioned above, the Commission prepared pamphlets and translated into local vernaculars several international legal instruments, including the Universal Declaration of Human Rights and the 1966 International Covenants on Civil and Political Rights and on Social, Economic, and Cultural Rights. The civic education campaign reached more than half a million people out of a total population of about 4.5 million, and proved crucial in rallying public opinion behind the constitution-making process.

By the summer of 1995, the Commission was ready to dissemin-
ate a set of proposals that served to focus attention on and to clarify the most important issues. From September to December of that
year, extensive public debates about these proposals went forward.
At the end of the year, the Commission collected and analysed the
questions raised and the opinions expressed, and sat down to write
the first draft of the constitution (Constitutional Commission of
Eritrea 1995). Parliament approved this draft with a few amendments, and further public debate ensued in late 1996 and early
1997. The final phase involved the presentation of the draft to the
Constituent Assembly and ratification which occurred in May 1997,
as noted earlier.[9]

At the outset, the Commission divided its research work among
four ad hoc committees, plus a standing committee on civic education and public debate, acting under the general guidance of the
Executive Committee. The research committees on Governmental
Institutions and Human Rights, Economics, Social and Cultural
Affairs, and Governance and Related Issues were mandated to
establish subcommittees and to solicit the views and research
assistance of experts in general and of Eritrean professionals in
particular.

At the end of the substantive phase, it was decided to combine the
four research committees into one and to concentrate on producing
issue papers on the basis of previous research, the results of the
civic education seminars, and the international symposium. Also
during this period the issue-by-issue discussion strategy was
replaced by an approach that aggregated the issues into major questions. Issue papers, however, still dealt with individual topics such
as legislative, executive and judicial powers; electoral systems;
decentralization; fundamental rights and freedoms; social, economic, and cultural rights; and equality guarantees.[10]

Among the goals of these efforts, which would prove crucial to the
success of the public debate, were those of distilling the vital issues
to their essentials and framing them in a way that the average citizen could readily grasp. The proposals prepared for discussion thus
reflected not only the research committee's sophisticated and careful work but also the larger Commission's overall focus on concision
and accessibility.

---

[9] The Constituent Assembly was established under Proclamation No. 92/1996.
[10] See n. 8.

Drafting the Constitution with Popular Consultation

As noted earlier, the logic of creating a Commission to draft a constitution implies that decisions about what constitutional principles to incorporate must, in the first instance, be left to the Commission to determine. Yet there are matters regarding which the legitimate political authorities may reasonably retain the last word, even if they must take the views of the public and of experts into account. For instance, whether or not a constitution designed to serve a multilingual society such as Eritrea's should declare an official language is a question that must ultimately be determined by political leaders. Even then, however, the Commission plays a critical role by sounding out the views of the public and of experts, as well as assessing the political and cultural implications of each of the various options. Here, an ethno-linguistically balanced Commission is obviously a political imperative.

As to the central principles concerning the rights and duties of citizens and the powers and responsibilities of government, the Commission's word should be respected by the political authorities of the day. Assuming that the Commission is adequately representative and has members who possess the requisite legal expertise, it should enjoy complete autonomy not only in the management of the process but also in, initially, determining the contents of the constitution. This is what happened in Eritrea.

As the Commission set about its task of constitution making, it found itself confronting two sets of related questions. The first concerned the values and goals that the Eritrean nation as a whole sought to promote and attain, and which, therefore, had to be incorporated in the constitution; the second concerned the issues that had to be debated and resolved before the constitution could be completed. The answer to the first set of questions could be found, as already mentioned, in the PFDJ Charter, which sets forth the five major national goals that the Commission took as a point of departure for the public debate that began in May 1994 and lasted until ratification.

No argument as to the validity of these fundamental goals and values was needed, as the course of the debate both at home and among Eritreans living abroad readily confirmed the initial assumption that there was already a national consensus behind them. Clearly, a civil order cannot be viable without a broadly agreed-upon framework of goals and values, and the constitution is the principal instrument for expressing them. Without a reasonable degree of stability and national unity, moreover, there can be no civil order—as the tragic recent history of Somalia, Liberia, and Rwanda attest. Nor can there be serious dispute about the critical links among democracy, economic development, human rights, and social justice.

As for particular constitutional issues, the Commission started its work, as noted before, by selecting some twelve issues for special attention. It then prepared papers, eventually turning these into concrete proposals for public debate. The topics covered included the form and structure of government, separation of powers, structure and functioning the judiciary, issues of national languages, the electoral system, regional government, the armed and security forces, and fundamental rights (International Symposium on the Making of the Eritrean Constitution 1995).

The public's initial diffidence gradually gave way to more vigorous and candid involvement. The distribution of the Commission's proposals enabled the public to be more focused, to raise questions, and to express concerns on a range of issues. The most controversial issues centred on language, the election and powers of the president, form of government, regional government—decentralization—political pluralism, and aspects of human rights, notably 'procedural' human rights. The question of land and land rights had been settled by a law enacted early in 1994 which settled some controversial issues related to land. The Constitution codified the main principles of that law.[11]

Throughout the process, the Commission preached the gospel of constitutionalism unabashedly, explaining that the concept implies the reign of reason and the rule of law, according to which people are not mere objects but rather active subjects with rights and duties. The Commission did not have any problems in exhorting citizens to have faith in themselves as agents of history and not merely passive recipients of commands: it did not have problems because it was addressing a citizenry that had fought hard for its rights against overwhelming odds, with enormous sacrifice. The sacrifice included the loss and exodus of thousands of educated citizens. All branches of government, as well as society at large, are still facing, and will continue to face for several years, the impact of this loss. Thus the Commission augmented the trained and experienced manpower at its disposal by tapping into all available national human resources. The establishment of ad hoc subcommittees and two Boards of

---

[11] See Proclamation No. 59/1994.

Advisors, one national and the other foreign, helped in meeting the challenge.[12]

With regard to the collection and analysis of data, the main concern was to make full and accurate records of all meetings. The outcome of these efforts is the mass of documents now housed in the National Centre for Research and Documentation in Asmara, which will be of great interest to future researchers.

Some Salient Features of the Constitution

The first point to be made about the Eritrean constitution concerns its size: it is concise and flexible. In deciding to make the Constitution short and flexible rather than long and detailed, the Commission was aware that it was imposing a heavy burden on the judiciary as well as on the legislature. An important avenue of constitutional development will be through judicial interpretation, while another avenue will be through parliamentary legislation. Under Art. 49(a) of the Eritrean Constitution as ratified by the Constituent Assembly on 23 May 1997, the Supreme Court, in particular, is vested with the power to declare laws and administrative acts unconstitutional, which is a feature adopted from the American system, whereas under the Westminster system the supremacy of parliament precludes the courts from challenging laws passed by parliament. Eritrean constitution makers deliberately made the Constitution eclectic, particularly in terms of the structure and functions of the principal institutions of government. On the face of it, it is a parliamentary system. But an executive presidential feature is grafted on it. For, under Art. 41(1), although the president is an elected member of parliament, and is elected to the presidency by parliament, he performs the function of an executive president, *à la américaine.*

In this respect, concern was expressed and questions frequently raised during the public debate as to the wisdom of separating the president from the parliamentary base. One concern was that such separation might insulate him from public accountability, whereas, under the Westminster model, the prime minister and his cabinet colleagues sit in parliament and are thus subject to direct public

---

[12] The External Board of Advisors met twice formally, but informal contacts continued from he beginning to the end through the good offices of the Commission's Chairman and the Chairman of the Board of Advisors. The Board on Eritrean Customary law also met twice formally, and many of its members stayed engaged throughout the constitution making process.

scrutiny. This concern was met by the provision of various devices of accountability, including the following:

First, under Art. 47(2), parliament has the right to summon ministers to appear before it or any one of its committees—a presidential feature.

Second, under Art. 47(1)(b), parliament has the power to hold the cabinet ministers collectively responsible for their work as a government, although a vote of censure is not provided for. The omission of a vote of censure, with the associated requirement for a government losing the vote to resign, is made for fear that it would create institutional instability.

Third, under Art. 39(6), parliament has the power to impeach and remove the president from office for violation of the constitution or 'grave violation of the law'.

Another question is related to the election of the president. Some members of the Commission and of the public expressed concern that with the advent of multiparty politics a situation may arise in which the presidential candidate's party may not command the requisite majority to elect a president, thus creating an impasse. The answer is that this would be conducive to a healthy politics of consensus under which a party not enjoying an absolute majority would be forced to seek alliances. It is an aspect of democracy that may appear to be negative, but is in fact one of the mainstays of democratic politics.

The 'architecture' of the Constitution rests on the five pillars mentioned before, the fundamental goals and values: national unity and stability, democracy, sustainable economic development, human rights, and social justice. A glance at the chapter headings gives an idea of this and of the related principles enshrined in the Constitution. Chapter One, titled 'General Provisions', deals with the name and territory of the state, the supremacy of the Constitution, citizenship, and national symbols and languages. Chapter Two, 'National Objectives and Directive Principles', is self-explanatory, as are the following four chapters: 'Fundamental Rights, Freedoms and Duties' (Three), 'The National Assembly' (Four), 'The Executive' (Five), and 'The Administration of Justice' (Six). The Seventh and last chapter, 'Miscellaneous Provisions', deals with the Auditor-General, the National Bank, the civil service, the Electoral Commission, and procedures on amending the constitution.

Central constitutional principles such as the rule of law, popular sovereignty, and judicial independence are enshrined in the Constitution. Fundamental human rights and freedoms are amply provided for in Chapter Three, which is the longest chapter, with 16 out of 59 articles. Even this chapter is not as detailed as the constitution of South Africa, for example, which is one of the longest constitutions, if not the longest, in the world. Every care was taken, however, to include the essence of the universally recognized principles of human rights, leaving their application to be determined by legislation. The example of the rights of the child will serve to illustrate the point. Eritrea is signatory to the Convention on the Rights of the Child, with an obligation to abide by the requirements of the Convention. The Constitution's provision with respect to children is concise but pithy, recognizing as it does the importance of the family and national culture regarding the family. Article 22(3) of the Constitution thus simply provides: 'Parents have the right and duty to bring up their children with proper care and affection; and, in turn, children have the right and the duty to respect their parents and to sustain them in their old age.' In the view of the Constitutional Commission and of the Parliament and Constituent Assembly that approved of the Commission's draft, this formulation reflects modern, universal attitudes as well as national attitudes with regard to the family, including the respective roles of parents and children. The rest is a matter of legislation and implementation of laws.

Another example of detailed application of constitutional principles left to legislation is electoral law. Given the complexity of election politics, the Constitutional Commission decided to leave detailed provisions on the subject to legislation. Thus, Article 30(2) provides that the National Assembly (Parliament) shall enact an electoral law which shall prescribe for and ensure the representation and participation of the Eritrean people. It is also worth noting that Art. 7, titled 'Democratic Principles' provides, *inter alia*, 'Pursuant to this constitution and the laws enacted pursuant thereto all Eritreans without distinction are guaranteed equal opportunity to participate in any positions of leadership in the country'.

In sum, the flexibility principle with the concomitant requirement of concision is mainly designed to avoid frequent resort to amendment of the Constitution. Furthermore, detailed constitutional provisions hamstring government authorities, making effective action difficult. The British reliance on unwritten conventions, which makes for flexibility, is often cited as the best example of the importance of flexibility. The downside to flexibility is that it may be abused: in the absence of clearly laid down rules, people in authority may exercise discretionary power that may trample other people's rights.

But a carefully crafted constitution, however concise, should anticipate such an eventuality and provide for remedies. And in this respect, the courts of law are the last line of defence. Staffing the judiciary and maintaining a culture of respect for the judiciary is thus a categorical imperative.

Conclusion

It is one thing to write a good constitution; it is a quite another to secure the future of constitutional rule. Looking ahead, what are the prospects for successful application of Eritrea's new constitution? How close to the promise will the performance be?

In the view of the Constitutional Commission of Eritrea, in order to be effective, a constitution must reflect present realities as well as anticipate future development. And it must provide for the institutions that give it life and force, and for groups with the will and the ability to defend and enforce it. The Constitution of Eritrea does all this. But a constitution is only a framework, however crucial. Great challenges lie ahead. It will be necessary to nurture the growth of the institutions needed to put meat to the bare bones of the Constitution and make it a living force. Needless to say, vibrant civic institutions will also prove crucial to this process.

The recent history of Africa shows the crying need for balance between state construction and nation building, between the state and civil society. Ideally, the two should go hand in hand, with neither being allowed to wax great while the other wanes. Constitution makers must recognize and act on this need for balance, realizing that each nation must work out its own formula even as it gleans the experience of other nations for helpful lessons. The work does not end with the adoption of a constitution, of course, and much of the future responsibility falls upon the shoulders of legislators and judges.

A final note. What is the status of the Constitution of Eritrea, and what are the prospects? The Constitution was ratified but its effective date was left open in order to enable the government to clear the deck, so to speak, to make existing laws compatible with the Constitution, and also to create institutions that will facilitate the transition to a constitutional government. A committee was established to draft an electoral law. It was expected that an electoral commission would be established under the law and commence its work by the summer of 1998, to oversee the election of a new government on the basis of the Constitution. Unfortunately war broke out between Ethiopia and Eritrea in early summer of 1998. The war came to an end with the signing of a ceasefire agreement by the warring parties in July 2000. Then in following September the Transitional National Assembly of Eritrea passed a Resolution requiring for elections to be held in accordance with the constitution, before the end of 2001.[13]

Eritrea had begun with a good deal of promise. The foundation for a democratic system of government was laid. Two points need to be stressed in this connection. First, democracy needs time to take root and flourish. Second, democracy is a worldwide phenomenon, and thoughtful people everywhere are convinced that there is no better alternative to democracy. Nonetheless, no nation can afford to throw caution to the wind and push blindly for overnight democratization at any cost. Churchill's remark that 'democracy is the worst form of government, except for all the others', cynical as it may seem, forces us to consider the alternatives seriously and also be aware of the problems of democracy. History has shown that 'all the others' have ultimately failed humanity. I will end with Reinhold Niebuhr's apt aphorism: 'Man's capacity for justice makes democracy possible; but man's inclination to injustice makes democracy necessary.'

---

[13] The Eritrean government's delay in implementing the Constitution raised a storm of protests epitomized in what has come to be known as the Berlin Manifesto. It is a letter addressed to the president by 13 Eritrean academics and professionals; before it reached the president, however, it was leaked and caused a great deal of controversy. The letter is severely critical of President Isaias Afwerki for his undemocratic style of governance during several of the previous few years.

Many believe that the Berlin letter provoked an open challenge to the President's style of leadership in war and peace, that he was acting in a dictatorial and irresponsible manner. Matters came to a head when 15 members of the governing party's central committee and of the transitional parliament demanded that he convene a meeting of the party's congress as well as of the parliament. He refused to do this, whereupon the group published an open letter, first to the members of the parliament, then to all members of the party, and finally to the Eritrean people, stating their case clearly and comprehensively. It was a letter that has galvanized the people. On September 18, the president ordered the arrest of eleven of these people, closed the private newspapers, and arrested the editors of the said papers. The demand for the implementation of the constitution and, through it, for transition to a democratic government has thus been shelved. A very promising beginning has thus been halted, one hopes, temporarily.

Indonesia's Democratic Transition: Playing by the Rules

R. William Liddle

Introduction

In a process that began in July 1997, Indonesians have created but not yet consolidated a democracy. The turning point or defining moment of the transition was 7 June 1999 election for Parliament (Dewan Perwakilan Rakyat, People's Representative Council), the first democratic general election in Indonesia in nearly half a century. Subsequently, on 21 and 22 October 1999 a new president and vice-president, Abdurrahman Wahid and Megawati Sukarnoputri, were elected by the 695-member People's Consultative Assembly (Majelis Permusyawaratan Rakyat), a body comprising 462 elected and 38 appointed members of parliament from the armed forces plus 130 indirectly elected regional delegates and 65 appointed representatives of a variety of social groups.

The presence of appointed Parliament and Assembly members, particularly the 38 armed forces' delegates, means according to most scholarly definitions that Indonesia is not yet a full democracy.[1] However, the genuinely democratic quality of the parliamentary election, in which 91 per cent of registered voters chose among 48 political parties after a well-publicized campaign free of authoritarian constraints (International Election Observation

---

[1] See, for example, Linz, Stepan, and Gunther (1995). In the Indonesian case, the regional delegates, five per province for each of the 26 provinces—excluding East Timor, which voted on 30 August 1999 for independence—qualify as democratically elected members of the Assembly. They were selected by members of the provincial legislatures, who had themselves just been chosen in a provincial election held at the same time as the national parliamentary election. Continuing a format established in the New Order period, voters were given three ballots, one each for parliament, their provincial legislature, and their district or municipal (*kabupaten* or *kotamadya*) legislature.

Mission 1999), together with almost complete acceptance of the rules of the presidential/vice-presidential selection process, indicate that the threshold from authoritarianism to democracy has been crossed.

The transition was marked by three successive moments of decision, crises, or challenges that were faced by elite actors, including civilian and military government officials plus party and societal leaders, that will be discussed in the third section of this chapter. These were: (1) the challenge to President Suharto's personal leadership created by the economic crisis that began in July 1997; (2) the regime legitimacy crisis following Suharto's resignation on 21 May 1998; and (3) the challenge to elect a president in the People's Consultative Assembly after the June 1999 general parliamentary election.

In 1997 the principal actors were President Suharto, top military officers, and the leaders of forces in society opposed to Suharto's military authoritarian New Order, which had then been in power for more than three decades. In 1998 the actors were B. J. Habibie, Suharto's vice-president who became president when Suharto stepped down, military officers, and leaders of the opposition forces that had just succeeded in overthrowing Suharto. In 1999 they were the leaders of the five electorally most successful political parties—three from the New Order, two newly created—and military officers.

The resolution of each of these crises had a positive impact, in the sense that Indonesia moved step by step toward democratization. Several factors undoubtedly played a role in resolving each of the crises and in determining the final democratic outcome. These included the democratic predisposition of many members of the elite—both inside and outside the government—and mass actors, the manifold weaknesses and tactical mistakes of Suharto, Habibie and their allies, and the actions of the United States and other foreign governments and international institutions.

In this chapter, however, I want to focus on just one exceptional factor: the acceptance of and use made by elite actors of the Constitution of 1945, which has been in effect since 1959 and was skilfully employed by both Presidents Sukarno and Suharto to structure and legitimize their authoritarian regimes. The current elite's use of the Constitution served two positive transition-related ends, one more or less consciously in the minds of many of the actors and the other an unintended outcome of their interaction within its procedural and institutional framework.

The conscious goal was manageability or reduction of uncertainty and fear through providing institutionalized 'mutual guarantees' to government and opposition forces (Dahl 1971: 217–18). By maintaining a set of familiar rules in a time of great turmoil, the contestants for power could more easily predict and therefore respond appropriately to each other's behaviour during the successive crises. Staying within this frame also reassured players on both sides that they would not be arrested or killed, as hundreds of thousands of communists and communist sympathizers had been during the last transition in 1965–6.

The unintended outcome was the heightened probability of a powerful democratic executive, that is, an elite and popular acceptance of the presidency as the central governmental decision-making institution plus sufficient political support for the newly elected president to enable him or her to govern the country effectively. A strong political centre is a necessity for a huge archipelagic country as divided along as many lines—ethnic/regional, religious, and social class—as is Indonesia.

The 1950–7 parliamentary system, the country's one previous attempt at democracy, provided representation across virtually the whole range of Indonesian political diversity, but was unable to create a strong and stable centre. Prime ministers and cabinets rose and fell at the rate of more than one a year during this period. During 1959–65, President Sukarno's personalistic authoritarian Guided Democracy promised but did not deliver a strong centre. President Suharto's military authoritarian New Order regime, in power from 1966 to 1998, was the mirror image of the parliamentary democracy of the 1950s: a powerful and stable centre capable of formulating and implementing policy but without democracy and with only limited and controlled representation of group interests outside the state.

In 1999, a new foundation for a strong but democratic centre may have been laid. This was accomplished by a political elite acting through the mechanism of indirect election of the president by the Assembly, the great majority of whose members had been elected in Indonesia's first genuinely democratic parliamentary election since 1955. This outcome increases the probability that the new government will be relatively more democratic, effective, and stable than its predecessors. It does not, however, by itself resolve several other daunting challenges, including the threat of national disintegration, religious conflict, economic stagnation, official corruption, a possibly resurgent military, and, ironically, the post-transition need for constitutional reform.

The Constitution of 1945 under Sukarno and Suharto

The Constitution of 1945 is the predecessor and successor to the democratic Constitution of 1950, under which Indonesia was governed as a parliamentary democracy for most of the 1950s.[2] The 1945 Constitution was written in the last few weeks of the 1942–5 Japanese occupation by the Preparatory Committee for Indonesian Independence, a Japanese-sponsored body consisting mostly of older Indonesian nationalist leaders who were also collaborators (Cribb and Brown 1995: 17–18, 47–9).

Though promulgated on August 18 1945, one day after the declaration of independence, it was never fully implemented during the 1945–9 revolutionary period. Its original purpose was to provide Sukarno, Indonesia's pre-eminent nationalist leader and about-to-become first president, with sufficient authority and flexibility to defend the new nation-state against its enemies, particularly the returning Dutch colonial ruler. Within a few months, however, pressure from leftists and revolutionary youth groups forced its replacement by a de facto parliamentary system that constrained the powers of the president and allowed for more broadly-based power sharing.

Because of the haste with which it was composed, and the intention to create a strong presidency, the 1945 Constitution is incomplete and vague. There is no mention of how members of Parliament or the Assembly are to be chosen. The article on the Assembly says only that it 'shall consist of members of [Parliament] augmented by delegates from the regions and groups in accordance with regulations prescribed by statute'. Indeed, 17 articles or sub-articles out of a total of 65, including that on 'freedom of association and assembly, of expressing thoughts and of issuing writing and the like' say only that the subject 'will be prescribed by statute' (Department of Information, Republic of Indonesia n.d.).

The Constitution of 1950, modelled on the Netherlands' parliamentary constitution but with a president instead of a monarch as head of state, was intended to be temporary until a constitutional convention, elected in 1955, could write a new one.[3] Despite the formal change, there was considerable continuity in practice between

---

[2] There was briefly a third constitution, that of the federal Republic of the United States of Indonesia, in force from December 1949 to August 1950. Nationalist leaders considered the federal state a Dutch imposition and dismantled it soon after the transfer of sovereignty.

[3] On the politics of the 1950s, see Feith (1962).

the new constitution and the de facto arrangement that had evolved after 1945. Parliamentarism, first de facto and then de jure, meant a multi-party system, cabinet government under a prime minister, and a ceremonial president.

In 1959, President Sukarno, with support from the armed forces, unceremoniously dissolved the constitutional convention, whose members had stalemated over the issue of whether Indonesia should be an Islamic state, and decreed a return to the Constitution of 1945. He argued that Indonesia needed a strong executive, democracy with leadership or 'guided democracy' (*demokrasi terpimpin*), to resolve deep conflicts of religion, ethnicity/regionalism, and social class that had immobilized Parliament and the convention and were threatening to break up the country (Feith 1963).

The 1945 Constitution does in fact place predominant authority in the hands of the president, who is elected for a five-year term by the Assembly and is eligible for re-election. Although the president must obtain the agreement of Parliament to proposed legislation, he or she is not responsible to that body as is a prime minister in a parliamentary system. The president, again with the agreement of Parliament, 'declares war, makes peace, and concludes treaties'. The president has the sole right to appoint ministers, who are not responsible to Parliament, and 'holds the highest authority over the Army, the Navy, and the Air Force.' He or she also appoints diplomatic representatives, grants titles, decorations, amnesty, and restoration of rights, and may declare a state of emergency (Department of Information, Republic of Indonesia n.d.).

A contemporary official *penjelasan* (explication or elucidation) of the Constitution stresses at some length, and in a defensive or apologetic tone, that the president is not all-powerful but is instead checked by Parliament and the Assembly and even by his or her own ministers. Parliament cannot be dissolved by the president. Its members are all concurrently members of the Assembly, which 'exercises in full the sovereignty of the people'. All laws, including the annual state budget, must be approved by Parliament. While the president has the right to make government regulations on an emergency basis, these must be approved by Parliament at its next session. Ministers are 'not ordinary high-ranking civil servants . . . [but rather] Leaders of the State' (Department of Information, Republic of Indonesia n.d.).

Whatever the intention of the framers, the use to which Sukarno put the 1945 Constitution was as a scaffold for constructing a regime of personal authoritarianism. In fact, Sukarno did not succeed in becoming a full-fledged dictator. For the six years in which he ruled under the 1945 Constitution, 1959–65, he was dependent for political support first on the national armed forces leadership and then on the Communist Party. The generals' backing was crucial for dissolving the constitutional convention and for combating regional rebels in the late 1950s; in the 1960s the Communist Party mobilized the masses in support of Sukarno's campaigns against continued Dutch control of the western half of the island of New Guinea—subsequently called Irian Jaya by the victorious Indonesians and in January 2000 renamed Papua—and against the formation of Malaysia out of the former British colonies of Malaya, Singapore, Sabah, and Sarawak.

Under General Suharto, who took power in March 1966, many things changed, but not the way in which the Constitution was used.[4] The armed forces, dominated by the army, became the principal base of political power in Suharto's authoritarian New Order regime, which was at its peak of monolithic, hierarchical control from the mid-1970s to the mid-1990s. Sukarno was deposed and the Communist Party was banned. Other parties were shunted to the margins and ultimately forced to fuse into two new parties, the Partai Demokrasi Indonesia (PDI, Indonesian Democracy Party) for Muslim syncretists, secularists, and non-Muslims and the Partai Persatuan Pembangunan (PPP, Development Unity Party) for modernist and traditionalist Muslims.[5]

---

[4] On the political structure of the New Order, see Liddle (1996, esp. Ch. 1).

[5] Eighty-six per cent of Indonesia's 210 million people are Sunni Muslims; there are no Syi'a. They are divided politically into modernists, traditionalists, Javanese syncretists, and secularists. Modernists, a new group in the early twentieth century with roots in the Middle Eastern reformism of Mohammad Abduh, look directly to the Qur'an for their understanding of their religious obligations. Sociologically they tend to be urban traders, professionals such as school teachers, or—increasingly today—civil servants. Traditionalist Muslims adhere to the classical Syafi'i school of Qur'anic jurisprudence. They have tended historically to be small farmers or rural landlords, although today younger traditionalists can be found everywhere in urban middle-class Indonesia. For hundreds of years a majority of ethnic Javanese, who make up about half of the total population and live mainly in the eastern two-thirds of the island of Java, have been syncretists, mixing ancient animistic and Hindu beliefs and practices with Muslim ones. There is evidence that for the last half-century or so the syncretists have been becoming more orthodox, either as traditionalists or modernists. Finally, the tiny group of urbane secularists tend to be better educated and to live in Jakarta and a few other large cities.

Politically, modernists tend to see themselves as the only true Muslims and regard both traditionalists and syncretists as misguided or weak Muslims. In the 1955 parliamentary election, Indonesia's only genuinely democratic election before 1999, they supported the Masyumi political party, which received 21% of the vote and favoured an Islamic state. Traditionalists, especially on Java, are mostly affiliated with the social and educational organization Nahdlatul Ulama (NU, the

A tightly controlled general election was held every five years. A new corporatist-style state party, Golkar (Golongan Karya, Functional Groups), backed by the civilian bureaucracy and the military establishment, won more than 60 per cent of the vote in each of the six New Order elections. Suharto became a friend, both politically and economically, of the West and Japan, and Indonesia enjoyed an East Asian-style growth rate of over 6 per cent a year for nearly three decades.

The legitimacy of Suharto's New Order rested on many claimed achievements. These included saving the country from communism, developing the economy, providing stability against separatists and enemies—in the president's vocabulary—of the left (underground communists), right (militant Muslims) and centre (supporters of representative democracy), and—not least—upholding the 1945 Constitution.

The Constitution provided an institutional and procedural framework for Suharto's highly centralized and personal style of rule. At the same time it linked him to the almost sacred 1945–9 revolution for independence, when he had been a second-echelon player as a young army officer, and even to the deposed Sukarno as national founding father and restorer of the Constitution. Sacralization of the Constitution itself began under Sukarno in the 1960s, and was deepened by Suharto, who required all school children to learn his version of national history.

Under Suharto, the Assembly met every five years as required by the constitution to choose the president and vice-president and 'set the broad outlines of state policy' for the coming term. The elected Parliament met annually, again as specified in the Constitution, to pass the budget and other bills sent to it by the government. Under Sukarno, a poorly organized authoritarian and an economic illiterate, the government had operated for the most part without a formal budget and a general election for Parliament had never been held. Government policies, especially those relating to the 'development trilogy' of growth, equality, and stability, were also typically justified in terms of their fidelity

---

Awakening of the Traditional Religious Teachers/Scholars). In 1955 NU was also a political party that received 18% of the vote. Its leaders were lukewarm toward the Islamic state idea. Javanese syncretists are fearful of political Islam, especially as represented by the modernists. In 1955 they divided their vote between Partai Nasional Indonesia (PNI, Indonesian National Party), at 23% the largest party in the country, and Partai Komunis Indonesia (PKI, Indonesian Communist Party), the fourth largest party with 16%.

to the Constitution, especially to the famous Five Principles (*Pancasila*) articulated in its preamble.[6]

For most of the New Order period, public discussion of constitutional change was taboo, outside the 'national consensus' on rules of the game imposed by the regime. Most educated Indonesians seemed to recognize that pro-government propagandists made the Constitution mean whatever Suharto wanted it to mean. At the same time they appeared to accord legitimacy, even revolutionary sacredness, to the document itself. Only a few brave souls, such as the human rights lawyer Adnan Buyung Nasution, a perennial thorn in Suharto's side, dared to suggest that the emperor had no clothes. Writing in 1992, he argued that the 1945 Constitution should be seen as 'provisional, as a constitution not yet complete, with clear defects' (Nasution 1992: 432).

With the growing challenge to Suharto's power beginning in early 1998, support for the Constitution deteriorated rapidly. Nasution's fringe view became the norm. Many pro-democracy politicians and commentators pointed to the Constitution's weaknesses, including its lack of a bill of rights, its failure to specify general elections as the means for choosing members of Parliament and the Assembly, the odd relationship between Parliament and the Assembly as a kind of super-Parliament or permanent constitutional assembly consisting in part of members of Parliament,[7] and the excessive and unchecked power given to the president. Most foreign observers and consultants agreed with these criticisms.

Among Indonesian elite actors a new consensus quickly emerged that only the preamble to the Constitution, which contains a statement of the most basic national values, including Pancasila, must be preserved intact. Everything else could in principle be replaced. No serious attempt was made, however, by the pro-democracy political

---

[6] The principles were conceived by Sukarno in June 1945, before the declaration of independence on August 17 at the end of the Pacific War, as a way of resolving ideological tensions among Indonesian nationalists, especially between proponents of a secular and of an Islamic state. They are, as inscribed in the preamble to the 1945 Constitution: 'Belief in the One, Supreme God, just and civilized Humanity, the unity of Indonesia, and democracy which is guided by the inner wisdom in the unanimity arising out of deliberation amongst representatives, meanwhile creating a condition of social justice for the whole of the People of Indonesia.' The formulation of the first principle, monotheism but no Islamic law, was a compromise designed to keep both pious Muslims and others in the polity.

[7] The origins of this arrangement were apparently in the Dutch colonial Volksraad (People's Council), a quasi-legislative body like the Assembly 'whose day to day business was handled by a smaller representative College of Delegates' like the Parliament (Cribb and Brown 1995: 49, n. 2).

elite either to amend or to replace the Constitution. Instead, as I have asserted above and will document in the next section, it became the institutional and procedural framework within which the transition took place.

Three Moments of Decision: 1997, 1998, and 1999

1997

The first moment of decision was the challenge to Suharto's leadership and ultimately to the political role of the armed forces, the organizational core of the New Order regime, produced by the East Asian economic crisis of 1997. The fall of the rupiah against the dollar and other foreign currencies, beginning slowly in July, was serious enough by October to bring an International Monetary Fund (IMF) team to Jakarta to offer President Suharto's government a package of economic assistance in return for policy reforms.

To Indonesia watchers, specifically to New Order watchers, this was a familiar scenario (Liddle 1991). Since the mid-1960s, when he took power in the midst of a massive political and economic crisis, Suharto had repeatedly faced and overcome economic crises, usually with the assistance of international financial institutions and foreign governments. Some of the crises were of his and his cronies' own making, like the $10 billion unpayable debt incurred by the national petroleum company Pertamina in the early 1970s.

Others were a consequence of openness to foreign commodity markets, such as the collapse of the world oil price in the early 1980s at a time when more than half of Indonesia's foreign exchange earnings and budgetary revenues were derived from the sale of petroleum products. In each instance, after some initial hesitation, Suharto listened to the advice of foreign bankers, economists, governments, and his own economic advisers—professional economists mostly trained in the United States—and implemented required reforms.

The result was political longevity, because Suharto's personal legitimacy and that of his regime were heavily dependent upon successful economic development. Development meant a high growth rate, based upon selling to foreign markets, which created the wealth that could be distributed to individuals and groups whose support he sought.

Rice farmers, agricultural labourers, urban consumers of subsidized petroleum and foodstuffs, traders who used the new roads and bridges constructed by the government, children across the archipelago for whom schools and universities were built, all had reason to be grateful to the Father of Development, a title bestowed mid-career on Suharto by the People's Consultative Assembly. So did most business people, who could operate in a predictable market, and civil servants and military personnel, who enjoyed steady employment and rising incomes. Top bureaucrats and armed forces' officers, the most loyal and valuable regime supporters, were given many additional opportunities to enrich themselves at the expense of the state and domestic or foreign business.

In 1997, however, Suharto was unable to repeat his earlier successes in overcoming economic crises. He signed agreements with the IMF in October 1997 and again in January 1998, but failed to implement them to the satisfaction either of economists or the international currency market. For several months, while the economy continued to erode, he toyed with the idea of creating a currency board, promoted by his daughter Tutut, a prominent businesswoman, but opposed by most knowledgeable professionals at home and abroad.

By March 1998 Suharto's economic performance-based legitimacy had vanished. The rupiah was trading at more than Rp. 10,000 to the US dollar compared with Rp. 2,400 in July 1997; most banks and many modern sector businesses were technically insolvent if not actually shut down; millions of people had lost their jobs; inflation was running at an annual rate of 150 per cent; and there were shortages of basic commodities, including medical supplies as well as foodstuffs and common household items.

Despite the gravity of the economic situation, it was by no means clear even as late as March that the president would soon step down. The legitimacy of the New Order, and of Suharto's personal leadership, was heavily but not entirely dependent on economic performance. Over many decades Suharto had carefully constructed a set of institutions and procedures, based on the 1945 Constitution, designed to provide democratic legitimacy for his regime. A parliamentary election—the last of the New Order, as it turned out—had been held in May 1997, producing a massive Golkar victory. Golkar received 74 per cent of the vote, while the Muslim PPP won 23 per cent and the syncretist, secular, plus non-Muslim PDI only 3 per cent.[8]

---

[8] PDI had received 15% in the 1992 election, and had been expected to increase its vote as the premier party of the opposition in 1997. But PDI voters left in droves after President Suharto's forced expulsion in 1996 of PDI national chair Megawati Sukarnoputri.

The 1997 parliamentary election was the first event in a standard sequence, repeated six times over the course of the New Order, that culminated in a session of the People's Consultative Assembly in March 1998, at the point when the economy had reached its nadir. Suharto gave his quinquennial 'accountability' speech, accounting for his implementation of the 'broad outlines of state policy' adopted by the last Assembly session in March 1993.[9] Suharto and his choice for vice-president, B. J. Habibie, were elected by acclamation for the 1998–2003 term, and the new 'broad outlines' were also passed without debate. In accepting the new term, Suharto said pointedly that he expected to be back in March 2003 to make his next accountability speech.

Although the New Order at its peak had been accorded considerable legitimacy both in economic performance and in democratic terms, it was in the final analysis a military authoritarian regime, dependent upon the willingness of its armed forces' leaders, headed by General (retired) Suharto, to use coercion against its opponents. The regime was born in an anti-communist pogrom that resulted in at least half a million deaths and the incarceration for decades of tens of thousands of leftists (Cribb 1990). On many occasions thereafter Muslim, student, and other protesters were arrested and jailed, after unfair trials, for long periods. An urban crime wave in the 1980s was countered by special army units who tracked down and killed, vigilante-style, several thousand criminals.

From the mid-1990s religious- and ethnic-based violence escalated in many parts of the country, and so did the use of armed forces' repression as the principal means of resolving conflict (Liddle 1997). In 1996, Suharto's army forcibly ousted Megawati

---

[9] Article 3 of the 1945 Constitution states that the Assembly 'shall determine the Constitution and the guidelines of the policy of the State'. The official explication adds that 'the President must execute the policy of the State according to the guidelines which have been determined by the [Assembly]. The President, who is appointed by the [Assembly], is subordinate to and responsible to the [Assembly]. He is the "mandatary" of the [Assembly], he is obliged to execute the decisions of the [Assembly]'. In March 1967, President Sukarno was called to account, under Article 3, to the Assembly for his stewardship as president by the Suharto forces, who were already in de facto control of the government. His speech was rejected by an Assembly whose pro-Sukarno members had been expelled and replaced with Suharto supporters. Suharto was elected president by the Assembly in March 1968, and subsequently gave accountability speeches to the Assembly in March of 1973, 1978, 1983, 1988, 1993, and 1998. Parliamentary elections were held in 1971, 1977, 1982, 1987, and 1997. The 500 elected members of Parliament constituted half of the 1,000 members of the New Order era Assembly. The other 500 members were appointed from the regions and social groups in processes tightly controlled by Suharto himself.

Sukarnoputri from her position as national chair of PDI, to which she had been elected in 1993. The party's national headquarters in Jakarta was stormed by soldiers in mufti, resulting in several deaths and producing a counter-reaction in the form of rioting and looting in central Jakarta that lasted for several days. The 1997 parliamentary election campaign was also marked by considerable local-level violence among contestants that necessarily brought in the security forces, both police and army.

In 1997 and early 1998, after the economic crisis began, student demonstrators at dozens of universities across the country were met initially with a combination of negotiation and force. As the demonstrations escalated, however, force became the principal response. Several student activists were kidnapped and tortured, and some were apparently killed—that is, they had not reappeared by the end of 1999—by army special forces. The shooting—probably by police—of unarmed students in Jakarta precipitated the worst mass rioting in modern Indonesian history. During three terrible days, 13–15 May, hundreds of buildings burned and more than a thousand people were killed in the capital.

For most of the period I have been describing, from July 1997 to May 1998, the opposition did not have strong leaders. Activist student organizations proliferated, mostly along religious lines between self-consciously Islamic groups, themselves divided into modernist and traditional camps, and all others, including Javanist or syncretist Muslims, secularists, Christians, Hindu Balinese, and other non-Muslim religious groups.[10] These organizations did not throw up new leaders; their members instead deliberately chose to act collectively so that individual leaders would not be co-opted by the government as had frequently happened in the past.

Senior opposition figures also did not play prominent roles at this stage in the transition. PDI's Megawati Sukarnoputri, the main hope for anti-Suharto leadership since 1993 among most non-Muslim groups and even among many traditionalist Muslims, did virtually nothing to hasten or otherwise help effect Suharto's departure. At the time other PDI leaders offered a variety of rationalizations for her behaviour, but she seems in retrospect to have had neither a goal nor a plan of action.[11] Abdurrahman Wahid, the head of Nahdlatul Ulama (NU), with more than 30 million claimed members the largest traditional Muslim organization in Indonesia, was

[10] See n. 5 for a discussion of different kinds of Indonesian Muslims.
[11] Interviews, Kwik Kian Gie, PDI leader, August 1998; Sabam Sirait, PDI leader, August 1999.

incapacitated with a stroke in January 1998 and did not recover sufficiently to play a major role until well after Suharto's resignation.

The one partial exception to the general rule was Amien Rais, head of Muhammadiyah, with more than 20 million claimed members the largest organization of modernist Muslims in Indonesia, and a professor of international relations at Gadjah Mada University in Yogyakarta.[12] Amien had been an irritant to Suharto since his rise to national prominence in the early 1990s. He called earlier and more loudly than any other national politician for genuine democratization—prior to the 1997 parliamentary election—and for Suharto to step down—between the election and the Assembly session of March 1998. During the last weeks of Suharto's presidency he was the most prominent elite amplifier of the students' demand that Suharto resign. At the very end, however, as the conflict escalated nearly out of control, Amien shifted gear, persuading the students to call off a major anti-Suharto demonstration that would almost certainly have led to great bloodshed.

At this point in the transition, adhering to or opposing the 1945 Constitution was not on the agenda of the students or of the opposition leaders. Their first and in most cases only priority was forcing Suharto to resign. Some of the more radical student leaders also called for Habibie to resign, the armed forces to go back to the barracks, and a revolutionary committee or triumvirate of opposition leaders to take power temporarily until elections could be held. Few members of the governing or opposition elite supported these demands.

Suharto resigned on 21 May 1998 in a brief ceremony at the presidential palace. He was succeeded by Vice-President Habibie, who had served as vice-president for a little more than two months. Armed Forces Commander General Wiranto, a former Suharto adjutant, like Habibie newly appointed to his post, participated in the ceremony. Wiranto appealed to the nation to support the new president and added that 'the armed forces will continue to protect the safety and honor of former presidents, including Father Suharto and his family' (*Kompas* 1998: 5).

In terms of the 1945 Constitution, this event set a pattern for the subsequent moments of decision to be discussed below. To foreign and domestic detractors concerned about a possible succession crisis, President Suharto had claimed repeatedly that there would be

---

[12] Amien has an M.A. from the University of Notre Dame and a Ph.D. from the University of Chicago, where he wrote a dissertation on the Egyptian Islamic Brotherhood.

no crisis because Article 8 of the 1945 Constitution provided for an orderly succession.[13] In his resignation speech he referred explicitly to the constitutional procedure. General Wiranto, as leader of the armed forces, also underlined that his institution was acting within the Constitution by accepting Suharto's resignation and Habibie's accession.

Before we move on to the second moment of decision, it is important to point out that neither President Suharto nor General Wiranto had to act as he did on 21 May. Suharto, perhaps for the first time befuddled by age—he was 76 on 6 June 1997—wavered and vacillated for months and either allowed or ordered the kidnapping of activist students by army special forces officers allied with his son-in-law, Lieutenant General Prabowo Subianto, commander of the army's strategic reserve. After the riots of 13–15 May, Suharto is reported to have seriously considered declaring martial law.

General Wiranto's actions throughout this period suggest that he saw himself and the armed forces as implementers of President Suharto's policies, not as independent decision-makers. In a confidential interview, an assistant to General Wiranto stated unambiguously that 'if the president had declared martial law, we would have implemented his command'.[14] On the other hand, the armed forces have since the 1950s regarded themselves as the saviours of the country, which implies an independent role. The same assistant admitted that he had asked General Wiranto, two days before Suharto resigned, if the armed forces should prevent a Habibie presidency.[15] Wiranto answered no, 'as I hoped he would', but the very fact that the question was asked suggests that the generals believed that they had options.

1998

After 21 May, President Habibie continued to act within the framework of the 1945 Constitution while making new choices designed

[13] 'Should the President die, cease from executing or be unable to execute his duties during his term of office, his office shall be taken by the Vice-President until the expiry of that term.'

[14] Confidential interview, Jakarta, July 1998.

[15] Habibie was generally disliked by officers largely because strategic industries such as munitions, aircraft manufacturing, and ship repair, that had once been sources of armed forces patronage, were given by Suharto to Habibie when he served as minister of research and industry from the 1970s to the 1990s. For this reason it was widely believed for many years that the armed forces would never accept a Habibie presidency.

to keep himself in power.[16] Opposition groups, now beginning to move on to centre stage after decades in the wings, responded positively to Habibie's initiatives because they accorded with their own goals and offered hope of taking power and of democratization by peaceful means. The armed forces, still under the leadership of General Wiranto, reacted passively, allowing Habibie to set the policy and political agenda as long as he stayed, in their lights, within the Constitution.

Habibie began as an extremely weak president, disliked personally and disdained politically by nearly every important group in Indonesian society, including significant elements of his own Golkar party. He inherited a regime whose strength and stability had depended primarily upon its economic development success and its capacity to coerce its opponents with armed force. Moreover, the New Order had been led since its inception by its founder, who had seemed to grow in political strength over the decades until cumulative familism and cronyism and finally old age took their toll. In the 1990s Habibie had managed, with Suharto's help, to build a political base among modernist Muslims within the state bureaucracy, but had not been able to turn this base into a major personal power resource.

Perhaps because he recognized that his initial position was so weak, Habibie almost immediately announced two surprising initiatives: he declared his full acceptance of IMF discipline; and he promised genuinely democratic elections within a year. Moreover, he backed up his words with deeds. In the economy, for example, he continued the appointment of the incumbent coordinating minister for the economy, an old political enemy but one of the few Suharto officials trusted by the IMF at the time, and enlisted the services of the most respected Indonesian economists as his policy advisers.

In the polity, he directly freed the press and the party system by stating that his government would not ban publications or prohibit the formation of new parties as Suharto had done. He also promised to implement a four-step process that was procedurally within the frame of the 1945 Constitution, and thus familiar to all elite players, but substantively new in that it would be genuinely instead of cosmetically democratic. The four steps were: calling a special session of the Assembly at the end of 1998 to set a new date for parliamentary and regional elections; passage by Parliament, sometime in early 1999, of new laws to enable free and fair elections and open party competition; holding elections in the middle of 1999; and

---

[16] For more detailed analysis of this period, see Liddle (1999).

calling a regular session of the Assembly at the end of 1999 to elect a new president and vice-president.

Habibie's economic policy initiative was surprising because for a quarter century, as state enterprise head and Suharto's research and technology tsar, he had been a principal opponent of the economists who guided the government's macroeconomic policy. 'They are the brake and I am the gas', he often claimed in the 1970s and 1980s. In the 1990s he began to portray the economists' pro-market approach as the policy of the past and his own state protectionism as the policy of the future. Politically, Habibie had never given any indication as minister or vice-president that he favoured genuine democratization. 'In politics, Suharto is my professor', he had said many times, perhaps sycophantically but also indicating that he genuinely approved of the regime that Suharto had created and in which he had prospered.

Habibie's economic and political rebirth was the direct result of a calculation that with these initiatives he had a chance to stay in power at least until the promised regular session of the Assembly at the end of 1999 and perhaps, if he played his cards well, for a five-year term after that. Radical student groups and even a few senior elite politicians were arguing on a variety of grounds, including the unsuitability of the 1945 Constitution as an instrument of democratization, that Habibie should step down immediately. All opposition forces wanted genuinely democratic elections as soon as possible.

By framing his elections offer within the Constitution, Habibie was staking the claim that his own succession from the vice-presidency to the presidency was legitimate. He should therefore be given at least a year and a half until elections and an Assembly session could be held. If by that time he could claim a double success—democratization plus restoring economic growth—then he might be able to secure his own five-year term. Restoring growth would of course require persuading the Sino-Indonesian and foreign investors who had fled in 1997–8 to return. Acceptance of the IMF's reform package, Habibie's other major policy initiative, was, he believed, the key to achieving this goal.

Habibie's calculation was accurate, at least in terms of achieving his short-term goal of staying in office until democratic elections and an Assembly session to elect a new president and vice-president could be held. The mainstream opposition accepted his offer and shifted its focus from overthrowing Habibie through street politics to rewriting the election and related laws and then mobilizing for the elections. The opposition included Megawati's PDI, now called PDI-P

(Partai Demokrasi Indonesia-Perjuangan, Indonesian Democracy Party-Struggle) to differentiate it from the Suharto-era PDI, which still had legal possession of party offices but little mass support, and PPP, the government-approved Muslim party of the New Order, plus dozens of new parties.

The most important of the new parties were: Partai Kebangkitan Bangsa (PKB, National Awakening Party), created by Abdurrahman Wahid as the official party of the traditional Muslim organization NU but in principle open to all Indonesian citizens; and Partai Amanat Nasional (PAN, National Message Party), founded by Amien Rais, the head of the modernist organization Muhammadiyah, but with explicitly nationalist and populist rather than religious goals. Many nationally prominent non-Muslim intellectuals, political activists, and non-governmental organization leaders joined PAN, although its mass base was largely provided by Muhammadiyah. On the Islamic right, modernists founded several other parties, two of which gained modest support: Partai Bulan Bintang (PBB, Moon and Star Party); and Partai Keadilan (PK, Justice Party).

General Wiranto's armed forces were minor players throughout the election period. Initially, however, their actions were a cause of some concern to democratizers. After accepting the legitimacy of the Habibie succession, they then helped Habibie and his national Golkar chair, Akbar Tanjung, to gain control of the party organization by applying pressure to provincial-level party officials, many of them retired officers, in a crucial party congress in July 1998. Habibie in turn allowed Wiranto to consolidate his personal control over the armed forces through a series of changes in key personnel, a process that had already begun with the reassignment in late May of Suharto's son-in-law Lieutenant General Prabowo Subianto and several of his allies.

The intervention in Golkar was reminiscent of the New Order, when Suharto repeatedly ordered the high command or individual officers to interfere in the internal affairs of parties—as, most spectacularly, with Megawati's PDI in 1996—and social organizations of all kinds, from churches and Muslim organizations to youth and women's groups, labour unions, and sports associations. The military had been active in each of the six New Order elections when its territorial command structure, which reaches—in principle, but not always in practice—into every village in the country, was mobilized together with the civilian government bureaucracy to persuade or pressure voters to choose Golkar.

Despite initial fears, however, the armed forces stayed out of the 1999 election, except perhaps in some remote areas where old habits are hardest to change. Habibie's and Wiranto's instructions to the territorial commanders and their subordinates in the districts, subdistricts, and villages not to support any party were clear. This included the former state party Golkar, which was now billing itself modestly as just one party, albeit the party with the greatest governmental experience, in a multiparty system. The new party leaders, foreign and domestic poll watchers, and newly unchained journalists made sure that the policy was enforced. At the local level, many individual officers felt relieved that they no longer had to side with one political group against others.

The armed forces' principal political effort between the Golkar intervention in July 1998 and the parliamentary and regional elections in June 1999 had a more narrow focus. It was directed to ensuring that they would retain some representation in the new Parliament and Assembly. For most of the Suharto years the military held 100 appointed seats, of a total of 500, in Parliament, and were given a small number of additional seats in the 1,000-member Assembly: 500 members of Parliament plus 500 additional appointed members, most from the provinces. Suharto, for reasons he never made clear, had reduced their representation in the 1992–7 Parliament to 75.

In the post-Suharto era, most civilian politicians want in principle to end armed forces representation entirely, in Parliament if not in the Assembly. In practice, however, many argue that in the short run it might be better to have the still politically powerful military inside the reformers' tent rather than outside it. In 1998, the armed forces proposed a reduction to 55, and finally accepted a figure of 38, but with the apparent understanding that the 2004–9 Parliament will consist entirely of elected representatives.

What accounts for the low-key, almost diffident, political behaviour of the armed forces in 1998–9? The question is particularly puzzling when we recall that they have accumulated since the 1950s political, economic, and status interests that are now threatened by civilianization and democratization. For three decades under the leadership of Suharto they claimed a permanent right to intervene—the so-called 'twin-functions' doctrine—and exercised this right on many occasions up to the mid-1990s.

Perhaps the most accurate proximate answer is that when Suharto resigned on 21 May 1998 General Wiranto and other senior generals chose to adhere to the 1945 Constitution, as they understand that document, and have seen no reason to change course since then. On 21 May they were faced with a simple question: should they accept a transfer of power from Suharto to Habibie?

They answered 'yes', explaining their choice to others and partly to themselves on constitutional grounds. Subsequent political decisions have flowed naturally from this initial choice and been justified in the same way.

Behind the proximate answer are of course several factors shaping the initial decision to accept the Habibie presidency. One is the political inexperience of Wiranto's generation of officers, none of whom was given significant opportunities to make decisions on their own as long as Suharto was in power (Said 1998). While the armed forces were certainly the main base of Suharto's support, they were also the instrument of his power. In the 1990s, no individual officer was given much room to manoeuvre either inside the military or in its relations with society. When faced with Suharto's departure, they were confused, unsure of what to do next.

Second, today's officers are more sensitive to international opinion than were their predecessors as recently as the 1980s. During the cold war, many sins of Third World authoritarians—like the murder of hundreds of thousands of Communists in Indonesia in 1965–6 or Suharto's 1975 invasion of Portuguese East Timor—were overlooked by First World governments, but this is no longer the case. In part, too, it is the result of globalization, especially the revolution in telecommunications, which has made it much more difficult for governments to hide their misdeeds.

In the Indonesian case, the turning point in sensitivity came in November 1991 when Indonesian troops massacred more than 200 student protesters in Dili, East Timor (Asia Watch 1991). International reporting of this event—British television cameras and American reporters happened to be on the scene—led to the creation of a military honour commission and to trials of several lower-ranking officers. The impact of this trauma can be seen in the subsequent reluctance of the military to use excessive force in the many outbreaks of local-level violence that began in the mid-1990s and continued through the transition.[17] Officers today are also

---

[17] A powerful counter example, however, is the brutal treatment of pro-independence East Timorese in 1999, which was not stopped by the outside world until well after the independence referendum on August 30. For a careful analysis, see Col. (ret.) John B. Haseman (1999).General Wiranto and other high-ranking officers deny mobilizing the anti-independence East Timor militia groups, who were responsible for much of the violence, but United States and Australian government officials claim to have clear evidence that they did. It is also not clear to what extent President Habibie knew and/or approved of the officers' actions. The principal explanation offered for the lack of sensitivity to international opinion of the Indonesian armed forces in this instance is that they had too much at stake, in two senses. First, the top brass feared that letting East Timor become independent

aware of the worldwide trend to democratization and the difficulties that a military government would face in convincing Sino-Indonesian and foreign business to reinvest in the Indonesian economy.[18]

The combination of leadership inexperience and sensitivity to international political and economic opinion has made Wiranto and his fellow generals timid and conservative political actors who have swallowed whole much of Suharto's and their own political rhetoric. Suharto the master politician sacralized the 1945 Constitution partly for his personal political interests, but his words can be heard expressed much more straightforwardly and naively by his former adjutants and palace guard commanders. Similarly, the belief that one military coup will inevitably beget others has long been an unexamined cliché among officers, and almost certainly influenced their actions in the last days of Suharto. As these officers acquire more political experience, this behaviour may change, but so far it has not.

1999

The principals in the final moment of decision were the leaders of the five parties with the largest number of seats in the Assembly plus the armed forces high command and Assembly delegation members. The focus of their political activity was the election of a president and vice-president by the Assembly, as specified in the 1945 Constitution. All of the actors, even those whose interests might have dictated otherwise, agreed that the Assembly process was legitimate. The party leaders—particularly Abdurrahman Wahid of PKB, Amien Rais of PAN, and Akbar Tanjung of Golkar— played the most important role in determining the outcome, which

might start a chain reaction that would end in national disintegration. Second, many individual officers, including senior officers in Jakarta, had served long tours in East Timor. They therefore had personal ties there and an emotional commitment to keeping the region part of Indonesia. General Wiranto himself referred publicly to this problem in explaining his difficulties in controlling the militia after 30 August. It is also true that what happens in East Timor is not of great concern to most Indonesians, for whom it is a small, distant, and backward region. Because its population is almost entirely Catholic, many Indonesian Muslims care even less about what happens there. The officers may have therefore felt freer to act autonomously in East Timor than in Jakarta, where an attempt to influence the parliamentary election in the old New Order way would have ignited a fire storm of popular protest.

[18] For the current views of armed forces reformers, see Wirahadikusumah (1999).

was the selection of Abdurrahman as president, Megawati as vice-president, Amien as chair of the Assembly, and Akbar as chair of Parliament for the 1999–2004 term. The armed forces officers' goals were again modest: they did not try to shape the outcome but rather merely to ensure that when final votes were cast for each of the key positions they were on the winning side.

This decision period began with the successful conclusion of the parliamentary and regional elections on 7 June. Five large and medium-sized parties emerged from the elections as significant players in democratic Indonesia: PDI-P, with 34 per cent of the national vote and 153 seats in Parliament; Golkar, 22 per cent and 120 seats; PKB, 12 per cent and 51 seats; PPP, 10 per cent and 58 seats; and PAN, with 7 per cent of the vote and 34 seats. PBB received 2 per cent and 13 seats and PK 1 per cent and 6 seats. Fourteen additional parties won at least one seat each for a total of 21. The armed forces were given 38 seats, for a grand total of 500.[19] Because of discrepancies in the proportion of population to seats among provinces, which constituted electoral districts, Golkar and PPP received slightly more seats and PDI-P and PKB slightly fewer than would have been the case if the whole country had been a single district.

The percentage of seats held by each party in the Assembly, which elected the president and vice-president, was similar to the distribution in Parliament, except that Golkar became relatively stronger. The 195 additional Assembly seats were occupied by 130 regional delegates—five per province times 26 provinces—and 65 representatives of a range of social groups, as mandated by the Constitution. The regional delegates were picked by the newly elected members of the provincial legislatures, and followed the distribution by party of the provincial vote. This gave an advantage to Golkar, whose vote was more widely distributed in the less populous provinces outside Java than that of other parties. Golkar won 62 of the 130 seats allotted to regional delegates.

The non-partisan group representatives were picked by the General Election Commission (Komisi Pemilihan Umum), comprising mostly delegates of the parties plus a few government representatives chosen for their autonomy. In the end, the group delegation was also reported to have a Golkar bias, largely due to the corporatist pattern of interest representation in the New Order rather than to deliberate government or Commission policy. From the mid-1960s to the late 1990s, most prominent social organizations were

---

[19] Data from National Democratic Institute (1999).

either created by the government, forced to affiliate with Golkar, or had their leaders approved by the government.

Why did all of the players so readily accept the Assembly process as the frame for the post-election continuation of their struggle for power? Several could have claimed with some justification that a different system, either straight parliamentary or presidential, would have been fairer. For example, Abdurrahman's PKB, because of its concentration of voters in east and central Java, received fewer Parliament and Assembly seats per vote than any other party. Because of its better distribution, PPP, with only 10 per cent of the vote, won 58 seats in Parliament while PKB, with 12 per cent, won only 51.

All of the parties could have claimed that Golkar had an unfair advantage due both to characteristics of the electoral system, especially its greater strength in less populous districts, and to the legacy of the New Order. In addition to the corporatism described above, Golkar was widely believed to have superior access to financial resources, including Sino-Indonesian business interests, state enterprise profits, and political slush funds once controlled by Suharto and other prominent New Order figures. The major concern of both players and observers for much of the period between June and October was that Habibie's group in Golkar would buy enough Assembly votes to win the presidency.[20]

Megawati's PDI-P was the most obviously disadvantaged of the major parties by the Assembly process, but raised no objections either before or after the October session. It was the clear parliamentary election winner, with a vote margin 12 per cent above Golkar, its nearest competitor. Megawati expected to be the next president, an outcome also fervently desired by many millions of Indonesians who had voted for her.[21] 'The president should be the candidate of the party that won the election', became her and the PDI-P's mantra between June and October. In a straight popular election, or one based on districts and municipalities rather than

[20] A bank scandal involving close associates of President Habibie, including the Golkar treasurer, who were alleged to have skimmed about $80 million from a central bank loan repayment to a private bank convinced observers that they were right to be concerned. The IMF froze its relations with Indonesia until after the Assembly session in October, which probably ended whatever chance Habibie had had to be elected. Habibie was also widely condemned at home for his January 1999 decision to allow the East Timorese to choose independence.

[21] A nationwide survey of nearly 2,500 citizens conducted one month after the elections asked respondents if they had a favourite party leader. The 1,694 who said 'yes' were further asked: 'Which of the party leaders do you like most?' By far the largest percentage, 38%, chose Megawati (Liddle and Mujani 2000).

provinces as the electoral units, she almost certainly would have won the presidency outright. To win in the Assembly, however, she had to put together a coalition of several parties, which required the use of negotiating skills that, as it turned out, were a scarce resource in PDI-P.

Prior commitment to a planned and familiar course of events was perhaps the most important reason why all the principals, including the military, accepted the Assembly process of electing the president and vice-president. This was after all the last stage in the four-stage process that Habibie had offered shortly after becoming president more than a year before, and that they had accepted at that time. All parties had been able to make their calculations at each stage, with the stages yet to come clear in their minds because they had experienced the Suharto version of these same events many times before.

With the exception of Megawati, who naively expected to the end to become president simply because her party had won the parliamentary election, all of the leaders seem to have worked out fairly complex strategies well before the Assembly session. These strategies, like the more general commitment to the Assembly process and to the 1945 Constitution, relied heavily on precedent, on making use of old procedures and institutions for new purposes.

For example, it was realized early on by anti-Habibie politicians that if Habibie could be required to deliver an accountability speech, as Suharto had done at each New Order Assembly session, there was a good chance that a majority of the Assembly would vote to reject his stewardship of the previous year. The precedent they had in mind was the Sukarno accountability speech staged by Suharto 32 years earlier.[22] In that event, Habibie would have to withdraw from the presidential election, which is in fact what happened.

A second reason why the principal players, again with the possible and partial exception of Megawati and other PDI-P leaders, accepted the discipline of the Assembly process so readily in this third moment of decision was that from the beginning of the transition they had seen their commitment to the institutions and procedures of the 1945 Constitution as temporary and provisional. They were pragmatic politicians who saw the 1945 Constitution not as sacral, as both Sukarno and Suharto had done, but as a human creation containing flaws that needed correction. But they made a conscious decision to postpone consideration of those flaws and

[22] Confidential interviews, national Golkar leaders, August 1999.

corrections to the post-transition period, after the Constitution had served as a bridge between the authoritarian past and the democratic future. I will return to the implications of this strategic decision in the conclusion.

Finally, it is in watching the unfolding of this third moment of decision that one can see most clearly the positive impact of the 1945 Constitution in producing a heightened probability of a powerful democratic executive. The five major, two minor, and 14 tiny parties represented in the Assembly, plus the armed forces, were required by the rules of the game to produce a majority of at least 348 votes to choose a president to serve for a five-year term. They did so, electing Abdurrahman president by a vote of 373 to 313 for Megawati, the only other candidate.

President Abdurrahman moved quickly to take up the reins of power, choosing his vice-president, appointing his cabinet, and setting out a bold domestic and foreign policy agenda. If he was in some respects reminiscent of Suharto at his confident peak in the 1970s and 1980s, this time it was a democratic Suharto, with the uncoerced, authentic support of a majority of the members of the Assembly, themselves chosen—except for the armed forces and group members—in a democratic general election.

Of course there is a downside to Abdurrahman's government, the possibility of immobilism or fragmentation because his net has been cast so broad. His presidential bid was supported by the large majority of Golkar, PPP, PKB, PAN, PBB, PK, and tiny party members, plus the armed forces delegation. To win those votes, as he frankly admitted soon afterwards, he made promises of cabinet seats. Megawati's acceptance of the vice-presidency meant that his governing coalition expanded to include virtually the whole of the Assembly. His cabinet formation team—General Wiranto (armed forces), Megawati (PDI-P), Akbar Tanjung (Golkar), Amien Rais (PAN), and himself (PKB)—reflected that diversity. So did the actual cabinet, which contains representatives of all seven major and minor parties and the military, and is also balanced in terms of religion and region.

Optimists dubbed the cabinet, following the New Order practice of naming each new cabinet, the Kabinet Persatuan Nasional (National Unity Cabinet) while pessimistic observers wondered if there was a policy centre and how long the government could hold together. Indeed, within weeks a PPP cabinet member, the coordinating minister for social welfare, was forced to resign under a cloud of accusations of corruption. His party then threatened to withdraw its 58 seats from the coalition and form a shadow government.

The Abdurrahman government is likely to fare better, however, than the parliamentary governments of the 1950s, the last time Indonesia was a democracy. One reason for this is formal-institutional, that is, that the 1945 Constitution is more like a presidential system than it is like a parliamentary one. Simply put, the president and vice-president, and the chairs of Parliament and the Assembly as well, were elected for five year terms, 1999–2004.

Of course it is also true that a determined Assembly majority could at any time demand an accountability speech from the president. Article 7 of the Constitution says that 'The President and Vice-President shall hold office for a term of five years and shall be eligible for reelection'. The official explication, however, adds that if Parliament 'considers that the President has in fact transgressed against the policy of the State determined by the Constitution or by [the Assembly] . . . [the Assembly] can be called for a special sitting to ask the President to account for his responsibility'.

A second reason to expect the Abdurrahman government to endure is more political. Between June and October 1999, the party leaders of democratic Indonesia—with the military playing only a passive role—following the rules of the constitutional game, forged a governing coalition. At the outset, each party had goals and priorities and something of a plan for achieving them. In the ensuing struggle for power, some of each party's goals were achieved, some were not, and still others emerged out of the negotiating process. The result—the Abdurrahman government, together with the independently elected leadership of Parliament and the Assembly—is of course a human creation and thus subject to change. But it has already undergone a tempering process, a working out of relative positions and relations among its key constituent members, that now constitutes a source of internal unity and a political resource in meeting the challenges ahead.

Challenges to Consolidation

The positive role played by the 1945 Constitution in Indonesia's democratic transition is an extraordinary irony of history, a striking instance of the way in which authoritarian institutions and ideologies can be turned against politicians who have spent decades fashioning them as instruments of autocratic power. But, in a further irony, it now looms as a major obstacle to democratic consolidation.

The new power holders—President Abdurrahman Wahid, Assembly Chair Amien Rais, and Parliament Chair Akbar Tanjung in particular—appear to believe that for Indonesia to become a full democracy the Constitution must be substantially amended, if not virtually replaced. In other words, they believe that they no longer have the luxury of 'muddling through' with incremental or 'strategic' changes to a well-established framework of rules, to borrow the terminology of Charles E. Lindblom.[23]

Indonesia's new leaders have in fact already embarked on the course of large-scale or 'synoptic' constitutional reform. An Assembly session to approve a package of major constitutional changes, probably including direct election of the president and a shift to single-member parliamentary districts, is scheduled for late 2000. Early evidence from the debate suggests that few Indonesians have a clear understanding of the relationship between these proposed changes and their possibly negative impact on democracy, political stability, and national unity.[24]

There are several reasons for this, including the country's lack of experience with alternative democratic institutions and procedures, the leaders' own diverse political interests and lack of cause-and-effect knowledge, and deficiencies in democratization theory. The

[23] Lindblom and Braybrooke (1963) elaborate a distinction between two methods of policy-making—strategic and synoptic—that is similar to the contrast I am drawing between the behaviour of Indonesian politicians during (strategic) and after (synoptic) the transition. Strategic policy-making is incremental, trial and error, based on incomplete analysis, makes use of rules of thumb and habitual responses, and is concerned more with making an advance than solving a problem. Synoptic policy-making has larger aspirations, is concerned with developing broad-gauge analytical tools and identifying and solving problems 'correctly'. The two methods derive from a more fundamental distinction between two models of human intellectual capacity, one which stresses fallibility and the other competence. See also Lindblom (1977).

[24] In the event, increasing conflict between the president on the one hand and the Parliament and Assembly on the other overshadowed the 2000 Assembly session, which did not tackle the large questions of direct election of the president and a shift to single-member parliamentary districts. By June 2001 the Assembly was preparing to meet in two months to demand that the president account for actions alleged to be in violation of the broad outline of state policy passed by the Assembly in October 1999. Most observers expected that he would be dismissed from office and replaced by Vice-President Megawati. These developments could be interpreted to argue that the presidency as a governmental institution is now weaker than I have claimed in this chapter. In my view, the fault has been not with the institution but with the incumbent, who has made an extraordinary number of poor political choices in 2000 and 2001. He has virtually abandoned the coalition that he had formed in 1999, alienating all of the parties that had supported him and making no effort to build a new coalition. The issue of constitutional reform is now on hold until President Abdurrahman is either reaffirmed in office or dismissed and replaced by Megawati.

most fundamental reason, however, is the ubiquity of unexpected consequences of political and social action, the dangers of which—as Lindblom argues persuasively—are increased by larger, more complete, and comprehensive synoptic changes and decreased by smaller, partial, and more incremental strategic ones.

Moreover, constitutional reform is not taking place in a vacuum. President Abdurrahman and his team confront several daunting challenges, some of which could derail the democratization process and indeed destroy the country. There is a powerful separatist movement in Aceh, Indonesia's westernmost province, which if successful could set off a chain reaction ending in the breakup of the country. Religious tension continues, especially between modernist Muslims and all others, including traditionalist, syncretist, and secular Muslims and non-Muslims like Christians and Hindu Balinese. Within weeks of the Assembly session that created a new modus vivendi among these groups, a civil war between Christians and Muslims broke out in the Moluccas in eastern Indonesia.

Economic growth, despite former President Habibie's best efforts, has not yet restarted.[25] If it does not, Indonesian democracy will soon take the lion's share of the blame. President Abdurrahman has promised to tackle the massive problem of official corruption, including the case of former President Suharto. If he does not—and he has been ambivalent on this issue—campus and street politics may once again distract the nation's attention and destabilize its politics.

Finally, the principal beneficiary of civil unrest caused by conflicts among ethnic, religious, and economic interest groups might well be the armed forces, particularly the army. Since the 1950s, most army officers have believed that in a crisis it is they who have the duty and the right to save the country. If social conflict worsens, and if their individual and collective interests are seriously threatened by the new government, the officers may move once again to establish their control of the polity. The threat is not immediate, but it is certainly real.

---

[25] In 2000, the economy grew by 5%, compared with no growth in 1999 and negative 14% growth in 1998, but most economists believed as of June 2001 that the surge was temporary and not the result of policies of the Abdurrahman government.

14

Institutional Design, Ethnic Conflict Management, and Democracy in Nigeria

Rotimi T. Suberu and Larry Diamond

Introduction

Nigeria, Africa's most populous country and one of the world's most deeply divided societies, has trodden a complex, turbulent, and contradictory political trajectory since gaining independence from Britain in 1960. In four decades of independent statehood, Nigeria has fashioned six separate federal constitutions, witnessed the rise and replacement of eleven different national administrations, and straddled the political poles between democratic pluralism and military authoritarianism, between pseudo-federalism and institutionally balanced federalism, between Westminster-style parliamentary government and American-type presidentialism, and between inter-ethnic reconciliation and fierce, often violent, ethnic conflicts. This dizzying political odyssey offers a compelling canvas for illustrating some of the dramas and dilemmas of institutional politics in deeply divided societies. In particular, the Nigerian experience offers rich material for reflection on a number of crucial institutional themes:

(1) The relative impact of democratic constitutionalism and military authoritarianism on inter-ethnic outcomes.
(2) The relationship between the form and the character of federalism on the one hand, and success or failure in ethnic conflict-management on the other.
(3) The relative auspiciousness of presidentialism and parliamentarism for deeply divided developing countries.
(4) The latent tensions between integrative and accommodative—consociational—solutions to the dilemmas of national unity (Sisk 1996).

(5) The duality and complementarity of formal and informal ethnic conflict-management practices. The severe constraints on both democratic development and inter-ethnic accommodation in societies where the state is overweening rather than self-restraining, and where virtually the whole gamut of social existence is 'open to political determination . . .' (Mackintosh 1966: 619).

(6) The possible elements of a reform agenda for promoting or enhancing stable, peaceful, and democratic ethnic conflict-management.

Briefly stated, these are the seven themes we intend to sketch in the following discussion of institutional design, ethnic conflict management, and democracy in Nigeria.

Political Cycles and Inter-ethnic Outcomes in Nigeria's Post-independence History

Nigeria's post-independence political history may be demarcated into five broad moments. The initial phase, often referred to as the First Nigerian Republic, spanned the five-year period beginning with Nigeria's independence in October 1960 up until the time the military violently overthrew the Republic in January 1966. The second phase involved the 13-year era of military rule from January 1966 to September 1979. The next phase was the Second Republic; a brief interregnum of civilian rule between October 1979 and December 1983. The fourth phase began with the second coming of the military on the eve of 1984 and ended with the restoration of civilian democratic rule in May 1999. That restitution ushered Nigeria into the fifth, and ongoing, moment of its post-independence political history.

The First Republic laboured under immense structural strains largely induced by the British colonial legacy. This legacy, which began with the annexation of the port city of Lagos in 1861, involved three major elements. The first was the arbitrary consolidation of three major ethnic nationalities, accounting for some two-thirds of the country's 100 million people, and about 200 smaller ethnicities into a single state in 1914. The second was the differential administration and modernization of the northern and southern sections of this colonial state. This differentiation engendered a huge historic geopolitical fissure between the political hegemony of the north and the socio-economic ascendancy of the south, which has continued to haunt Nigerian politics to this day. The third element of the British legacy was the establishment in 1954 of a three-unit federal structure that secured political autonomy and hegemony for the principal ethnicities of Hausa-Fulani, Yoruba, and Igbo in the northern, western, and eastern regions respectively. This ethno-regional federal structure, along with the abuse of the liberal political game by competing sectional political coalitions, engendered the series of conflicts and crises that culminated in the fatal military coup of January 1966 and the demise of parliamentary government in Nigeria.

The immediate impact of military rule was the militarization and exacerbation of ethno-regional conflict. This led to the gradual isolation of the Igbo-dominated eastern region from the federation. Amidst the looming spectre of eastern secession and national disintegration, however, the military moved decisively in May 1967 to transform the country's regionalized federation into a more integrated structure of twelve states, six each in the north and south. Although this initiative could not avert—and, in fact, actually precipitated—the tragic 30-month civil war, it contributed decisively both to the defeat of the secessionists and to the long-term stability of the federation. Specifically, the new multi-state federalism diluted the widely resented hegemony of the geographically and demographically preponderant northern region, fragmented the regional bastions of domineering ethnic majority chauvinism and separatism, satisfied the longstanding constituent statehood aspirations of key ethnic minority groups—including non-Igbo groups in the secessionist east—and broadly promoted a more institutionally balanced, structurally integrated, and ethnically decentralized system of federalism. The phenomenal expansion in centrally collected oil revenues as from the 1970s, and the creation of seven new states in 1976, consolidated the integration of the federation. This era of remarkable institutional engineering by the military climaxed with the inauguration of the Second Nigerian Republic in October 1979. It was also to heavily influence the context for subsequent constitutional planning in Nigeria, a 'constrained' setting in which the military would initiate and supervise future 'transition' or re-democratization programmes in general and exercise the prerogative to dictate, reject, alter, modify, or approve the recommendations of constitutional review bodies and/or constituent assemblies in particular (Linz and Stepan 1996: 82–3; Joseph 1987: 70).

The new democratic dispensation reflected both structural change and attitudinal continuity vis-à-vis the First Nigerian Republic. Institutionally, the key element of change involved the shift from the parliamentary system of the First Republic to a presidential system. The choice of a relatively strong executive presidency was promoted by the military and their civilian associates— mainly bureaucrats, intellectuals, and elements of a 'politico-commercial' class—as an integrative antidote to the relentless sectionalism of the First Republic. The anticipated shift from the centrifugal politics of the First Republic, it was hoped, would be facilitated by such other institutional changes as the multi-state federalism, stringent constitutional prescriptions for federation-wide parties, and the substantial expansion in the legislative powers of the federal government in areas like local government, land use, the police, revenue collection, and electoral processes. Although condemned by many as unduly overcentralizing, these integrative reforms helped significantly to mitigate ethno-regional polarization.

Continuity between the First and Second Republics was tragically reflected in the corruption, economic mismanagement, violence, intolerance, and electoral fraud that the politicians unleashed on the polity. Although ethno-regional conflict was not a manifest source of the Second Republic's collapse, the massive rigging of the 1983 elections, mainly by the northern-dominated ruling party, all but destroyed the delicate institutional balance of partisan and ethnic interests that had underpinned Nigerian federalism since the inception of the Republic in 1979.

The Nigerian military self-righteously resumed governance of the country on 1 January 1984. However, by the time of its disengagement from the polity on 29 May 1999, the military had been denuded of all moral, institutional, or professional integrity. Egregious abuses typified the second phase of military rule in Nigeria. These transgressions included breathtaking corruption and financial mismanagement, the repeated manipulation and trivialization of political transition programmes, the ultimate abortion of the Third Nigerian Republic—even before its formal inauguration—following the annulment of the June 1993 presidential election, the monopolization of power by an ethno-military oligarchy, the centre's emasculation and immiseration of subnational governments, the wanton violation of civil and communal rights, and the attendant intensification and mobilization of disintegrative ethno-regional resentments. The election of 12 June 1993 marked a watershed event in the political life of Nigeria because it was the first time that a southern candidate won the chief executive office of the country in a democratic process, and yet that candidate, Moshood K. O. Abiola, did so by capturing extensive support in the north, including the home state—Kano—of the opposing candidate. Its annulment accelerated Nigeria's descent into the abyss of authoritarianism and ethnic turmoil.

Essentially, the 1984–99 era represented the degeneration of military rule from the regime of hegemonic exchange that was institutionalized for much of the post-civil war period to a system of severe hegemonic repression (Rothchild 1991: 190–215). Although both are systems of non-democratic—military or one-party—rule, hegemonic *exchange* involves practices designed to ensure some equitable stabilization or accommodation in state-ethnic and inter-ethnic relations, while hegemonic *repression* is characterized by ethnic exclusion, domination, and coercion. To cite the most obvious evidence, while the four military governments of the 1966–79 era were headed by a southern Igbo Christian, northern minority Christian, northern Hausa-Fulani Muslim, and southern Yoruba Christian, respectively, all four military governments in the 1984–99 era were headed by northern Muslims.

In general, the worst sectarian upheavals in Nigeria's history, and the greatest threats to the country's corporate existence, have occurred under military rather than civilian rule. Examples include the bloody ethno-military coups of January and July 1966, the 1966–7 anti-Igbo pogroms in northern Nigeria, the ghastly three-year civil war, and the controversy during 1975–8 over shariah (Muslim) law, all of which took place during the first phase of military rule. During the second phase, Nigeria was buffeted by such sectarian crises as the controversy over General Babangida's surreptitious enlistment of Nigeria into the Organization of Islamic Conference (OIC) in 1986, the attempted expulsion of the Muslim north from the federation by military putschists in 1990, southern Yoruba mobilization against the annulment of M. K. O. Abiola's 1993 presidential election victory, the executions in 1995 of the 'Ogoni nine'—ethnic minority activists in the long-suffering but oil-rich Nigeria Delta area, led by famed novelist Ken Saro-Wiwa, who was among those hanged by the military—the general upsurge of violent separatist nationalism in the oil-rich Delta region, and the broad clamour in southern Nigeria for a Sovereign National Conference that would reconsider the desirability or modalities of Nigeria's continued survival as one country.

Although ethnic, regional, and—more recently—religious mobilization and conflict have been extensive in politics under civilian rule, civilian constitutional rule has generally seen less violent and convulsive sectional conflict because a civilian multiparty constitutional regime provides a framework—and if structured properly, certain incentives—for building multi-ethnic political coalitions and expressing ethnic interests and grievances through peaceful means.

Quite obviously, the constitutional institutions and competitive processes of a truly democratic system assure some voice or representation for diverse ethnic views and interests, preclude the systematic transgression of basic group rights, provide for an iterative bargaining process among ethnic elites, and consequently reduce the likelihood of violent ethnic confrontation and polarization. Military regimes are rarely subject to these institutional restraints and incentives. Thus, although the military has been consistently sanctimonious in proclaiming its commitment to the unity or survival of the Nigerian state, and although it has been able to implement swift and decisive action to enforce that commitment, it has also tended to be ethnically exclusive and provocative in composition and conduct.

Nevertheless, the capacity of Nigerian democracy effectively to promote inter-group equity and stability has often been undermined by flawed political institutions or by abusive or repressive behaviour on the part of dominant partisan interests. What is more, prolonged abusive rule by the military has piled up political contradictions and stakes that make the post-military regime distinctly more vulnerable to sectarian turmoil. Nigeria's Fourth Republic now bears the burden of multiple debilitating legacies of military rule: a flawed and contested constitutional framework, arising from an undemocratic process of constitution-making that lacks legitimacy; a culture of militant ethnic agitation and mobilization, especially in Niger Delta region; the persistence and resurgence of inter-communal violence, which claimed more than one thousand lives within the first seven months of the Fourth Republic; the politicization of religion; and, most important, a federal system that has been centralized, battered, and bloated by successive military administrations concerned primarily with concentrating control over resources while shoring up their sagging legitimacy by creating ever more States and local government areas.

The Federal System: From Crisis to Reform to Decay

Nigeria is Africa's most consistently federal polity (Adamolekun and Kincaid 1991). At the same time, the Nigerian system of federalism has been characterized variously as 'peculiar', 'bizarre', 'irregular', 'misleading', 'purely distributive' or 'failed', and as representing a 'hollow federation' or 'a unitary state in federal guise'.[1] These characterizations point to certain specificities and pathologies in the evolution and operation of the Nigerian federation.

Leaving aside the centrifugalism inherent in the character of Nigeria as a 'holding together' or disaggregative—as opposed to 'coming together' or aggregative—federation (Stepan 1997: 4), the three-unit federal arrangement established by the British in 1954 was a recipe for ethno-regional friction and convulsion. Specifically, by institutionalizing the hegemony of one constituent unit—the north, which official census figures since 1954 have given a slight population majority—over the rest of the federation, by constructing the internal boundaries of the federation around the country's three principal rival cultural segments, by denying the country's ethnic minority communities the security of their own constituent States or regions, and by providing for just three—four, after 1963— units in the federation, the federal system of the First Republic served not to moderate but to exacerbate ethnic and regional conflicts (Diamond 1988: 155).

The transformation of this unwieldy federal structure into a system of twelve, later 19, States during the 1967–79 era has been mentioned. However, the enormous ameliorative achievement and promise of this multi-state federation became only truly visible after the reintroduction of competitive party politics in the Second Republic (Horowitz 1985: 604).

In the first place, the constitution of the 19 States as units that cut across the country's principal ethnic and regional divisions reduced the politicization and polarization of ethno-regional identities. Thus, for instance, the ten States of the old monolithic northern region, and particularly the former region's four core Muslim Hausa-Fulani States, were no longer submerged under the one-party regional rule that obtained in the First Republic. Instead, they divided their partisan loyalties effectively between two or more parties in the Second Republic. Although bloc ethnic voting took place in the two Igbo States and four Yoruba States in 1979, this outcome had begun to dissolve into a more fragmented and decentralized ethno-political configuration by the time of the 1983 elections.

Second, the 19-State system endowed the ethnic minorities—now constituted into approximately nine largely heterogeneous States—

---

[1] See Mackintosh (1962: 2330; Diamond (1988: 155); Osaghae (1992: 182); Welch (1995: 635); Bach (1997: 346); Soyinka (1999: 27); *AM News* (1996: 14); Williams (1980: 100).

with an effective independent or mediatory role in the overall system. Their electoral support, which was vigorously courted by ethnic majority politicians, was critical in the victory of the National Party of Nigeria (NPN) in the 1979 and 1983 elections.

Third, the 19-State system spawned a robust system of intergovernmental relations. This showed that Nigerian politics could be re-channelled creatively along institutional rather than purely ethno-patrimonial lines. Specifically, a multi-ethnic, multipartisan, and multi-regional intergovernmental coalition of opposition-controlled States emerged to defend States' rights against encroachment by the NPN-controlled federal government. Unfortunately, a major source of the abuses that characterized the 1983 elections and delegitimized the Second Republic involved the attempts by elements in the NPN to use the centre's relatively superior institutional and fiscal resources to 'uproot' this intergovernmental opposition coalition (Suberu 1990: 283).

Fourth, the existence of the States as alternative and substantive arenas of governance helped significantly to moderate the intensity or the potential destructiveness of the competition for power at the federal level. Following the 1979 elections, the NPN, the party in power at the centre, controlled only seven of the 19 States in the federation. The Unity Party of Nigeria (UPN) was in control of five States, the Nigerian People's Party (NPP) three, and the Great Nigerian Peoples Party (GNPP) and the Peoples Redemption Party (PRP) two each. Thus, although embittered by its legally controversial loss of the federal presidency to the NPN, the UPN could take solace in the relatively substantial power it enjoyed at the sub-federal level. Again, this critical element of federalist accommodation was undermined during the 1983 elections when the NPN fraudulently seized control of 12 States, thereby reducing the number of opposition-controlled States to seven—four, two, one, and none for the UPN, NPP, PRP, and GNPP, respectively.

Finally, and related to the preceding point, the 19-State system functioned as an important vehicle for the decentralization and dissemination of resources, developmental undertakings, and welfare delivery to diverse local constituencies. The States increased their share of the joint 'Federation Account' and total government expenditures from about 20 per cent and 28 per cent, respectively, under military rule to 30.5 per cent and 48 per cent by the end of the Second Republic (Mbanefoh 1986: 18). In essence, the States were not only important sources of patronage and positions for their indigenes but also critical centres of policy innovation and experimentation. Several of the States, especially those controlled by the welfarist PRP and UPN, embarked on ambitious social programmes, including housing delivery and mass literacy or 'free education' programmes, that were significantly more successful or effective than comparable initiatives at the federal level.

Sadly, these federalist achievements were undermined by contradictions arising from the operation of the centrist 1979 constitution, by the overwhelming economic reliance of virtually all the States on statutory distribution of declining centrally collected oil revenues, by political corruption and intolerance, and by the predictable return of the military at the end of 1983. Thereafter, the decline of Nigerian federalism was dramatic and consequential. Apart from the sheer centralism arising from renewed military rule, this institutional attrition was induced and underscored by four factors.

The first involved the extravagant proliferation, by military fiat, of new States and local government areas, under the pressure of incessant mobilization from various communities that have felt themselves 'marginalized'. The 19-State structure instituted in 1976 was reorganized into 21 States in 1987, 30 States in 1991, and 36 States after 1996. Similarly, the localities increased from the 301 areas that were first established in 1976 and then reinstated in 1984, to 449 in 1989, 589 in 1991, and 774 in 1996. These reorganizations were ostensibly designed to respond to local agitation for political and economic decentralization, which pressures were largely fuelled by the considerable official reliance on the principle of inter-unit equality as the basis for the devolution of central revenues and related developmental patronage. Yet, instead of satisfying the pressures for decentralization in any meaningful way, the reorganizations served to weaken the size and resource base of individual sub-federal units, to augment the hegemony and visibility of the central government, to increase administrative costs, and to provoke often violent inter-communal rivalries and conflicts over the administrative location, ethnic configuration, and distributive disposition of the new units of government (Suberu 1997).

The second element of Nigeria's federal decline during the 1984–99 era involved the systematic and self-serving centralization and manipulation of the revenue allocation system by the 'Federal Military Government'. Basically, this involved the gross underpayment of centrally collected revenues into the Federation Account, the direct appropriation by the centre of all special funds—that is, monies not directly allocated to any of the three tiers of government—in the Account, the reduction of the States' statutory share of the Account from 30.5 per cent in 1981 to 24 per cent since 1992, and the centre's usurpation or restriction of States' jurisdictions over such taxes as the value added tax and personal income tax. As a result of these and related fiscal manipulations, the federal government's share of public expenditures expanded dramatically from 52 per cent in 1983 to 74 per cent in 1995, while the State governments' share declined from over 40 per cent to about 20 per cent during the same period (Adedotun 1997: 33). Yet, given the effective assimilation of State administrations into the military command structure, it was impossible—indeed, unthinkable—for these administrations, headed by middle-ranking or relatively junior officers typically concerned more with personal enrichment than governance, to challenge the abuses of the federal government.

Sectional domination of the central state apparatus was the third feature of Nigeria's federal decline during the 1984–99 era. As already indicated, northern Muslims headed all four military governments of this period. For much of the period following General Abacha's rise to power in 1993, in particular, the positions of head of state, chief of defence staff, Inspector-General of Police, Secretary to the Government of the Federation, Minister of Internal Affairs, National Security Adviser, Chief Justice of the federation, and several other strategic or sensitive offices were occupied by northern Muslims. In a country that is not only almost equally demographically divided between north and south, Muslim and Christian, but also long committed to reflecting its 'federal character' or cultural plurality in the composition of government agencies, this sectionalism provoked much alarm, alienation, and even paranoia.

The final feature of Nigeria's federalist crisis during the second phase of military rule was the official campaign of overt ethnic repression that was conducted under the Abacha Government, the single most venal and abusive in the country's history. This repression, which was emblematic of the pervasive climate of human rights violations that prevailed throughout the federation during Abacha's rule, was 'particularly severe' in the oil-rich, ethnic minority-populated, Niger Delta region (Human Rights Watch/Africa 1995: 2). In this region, nearly three decades of developmental and ecological neglect by the Nigerian state and oil multinational corporations, as well as unfulfilled communal demands for the reallocation of centrally collected oil revenues on a derivation basis, produced a militant indigenous movement for ecological rehabilitation, economic restitution, and political self-determination. In 1995, Abacha approved, but did not implement, a constitutional body's recommendation for an expansion from 3 per cent to 13 per cent of the proportion of mineral revenues to be allocated on a derivation basis. In fact, the primary response of the military to the agitation of the oil-bearing communities involved the proscription of ethnic minority associations, the promulgation of a treasonable offences decree for minority group activists, the military invasion and suppression of restive oil-producing villages or areas, and the harassment, detention, arbitrary prosecution, and quasi-judicial—or extra-judicial—execution of ethnic minority activists.

Much of the euphoria that accompanied the inauguration of civilian rule in Nigeria in May 1999 reflected the popular expectation that the restoration of democratic governance would end, and perhaps reverse, the systematic vandalization and desecration of federal structures and processes by the military. Yet the new post-military dispensation will be challenged by at least two fundamental obstacles to genuine federalism. The first is Nigeria's array of structurally and fiscally weak sub-federal administrations, which depend, on the average, on the Federation Account and other external sources of revenue for some 70 per cent of their expenditures. Indeed, for some of the States created in the 1990s, like Kebbi and Yobe, the level of dependence on external funding is as high as 99 per cent (Federal Office of Statistics 1996: 21). As noted by a group of Nigerian scholars, 'what to do with these military-created states, some of which may be unable to perform the normal functions of states in a full-fledged federal system, will be one of the thorniest issues in a post-military reform of Nigerian federalism' (Ekeh 1997: 16). The second onerous challenge of post-military federalism involves the division of powers in the 1999 Constitution, which has restored the highly centralized and contentious construction of the 1979 constitution. In essence, under the new Constitution, there 'are few, if any . . . areas in which state governments can act independently of the Federal Government' (Joye and Igweike 1982: 94).

The significant continuity between the 1979 and 1999 constitutions has also meant the preservation of Nigeria's break with the parliamentary system of its First Republic. It is to this theme that we now turn.

From Parliamentarism to Presidentialism: A Flawed Transition?

It was the declared intention of the military managers of Nigeria's transition to the Second Republic that the parliamentary system of the 1960 (Independence) and 1963 (Republican) constitutions should be abandoned for a presidential system under the 1979 constitution. This preference was subsequently endorsed, 'after a prolonged and heated debate', by two separate constitutional bodies instituted by the military during the 1975–9 transition process (Nwuabuenze 1987: 11). These were the 49-member Constitution Drafting committee (CDC) and the 232-member Constituent Assembly, which prepared and debated the draft of the 1979 constitution before it was finally amended, ratified, and promulgated by the Supreme Military Council (SMC). Both then and now, proponents of presidentialism have cited several advantages of the system in the Nigerian milieu. These include: presidentialism's presumed compatibility with African indigenous kingship or chieftiancy traditions; the system's capacity to overcome the First Republic's conflicts of authority, personality, and ethno-political interest between the (ceremonial) president and the prime minister; the role that the president could play as a 'symbol' of 'national unity' by virtue both of his pre-eminent constitutional status as the chief executive of the federation and his direct election by the whole nation voting as one constituency; the presidential system's capacity to lend relatively greater energy, stability, initiative, and direction—in short, effective leadership—to the process of government; presidentialism's greater institutional consistency with Nigeria's federalist commitments; and the system's greater structural elegance and 'democraticness' in imposing a strict separation of powers between the executive and the legislature, in specifying fixed terms of office for the chief executive, and in providing for regular rather than unstable electoral cycles that could minimize the advantages of incumbency in the Nigerian setting (Federal Republic of Nigeria 1976: i. xxix–xxi). Of these asserted advantages, presidentialism's capacity to foster greater inter-ethnic unity was the factor that was most consistently stressed officially. According to former military head of state and now civilian president, Olusegun Obasanjo, 'the greatest advantage of the presidential system is that the country is the constituency of the president. He is obliged to know the country and seek support across the country. Even if he is a tribal baron, his horizon and outlook will be broadened by the end of a nationwide campaign' (Obasanjo 1994: 24). For this reason, and despite the purely self-serving promotion of the idea of a presidential-parliamentary system under the Babangida and Abacha administrations, the military has regularly projected presidentialism as an 'agreed' or immutable 'ingredient' of Nigeria's 'political order' (Babangida 1989: 48). What is more, because both parliamentarism and presidentialism have collapsed in Nigeria, broad scepticism has often greeted any suggestions for a further change in the country's governmental system. The primary source of contemporary Nigerian instability, it is argued, is not presidentialism but the misdemeanours of the political class (Federal Republic of Nigeria 1987: 71).

Yet, as reflected in the growing passionate criticisms of presidentialism by some sections of the Nigerian political class, there is a sense in which the presidential system may have exacerbated some of the pathologies of Nigerian politics. In the first place, the huge financial costs associated with a federation-wide presidential campaign seem to constitute an invitation for the further 'monetization' and corruption of politics, the very bane of Nigerian public life. As things stand, the presidential race in Nigeria has become an exclusive turf war for the so-called 'money bags' or wealthy barons and their 'fronts'.

Second, one may question the wisdom of instituting an executive presidency with very wide powers in Nigeria given the fragile and faltering nature of the country's federalism, the already relatively strong traditions of executive political domination and development, the weakness of legislative institutions and formal party structures, the fledgling nature of civil society, the general vulnerability of horizontal and vertical institutions of accountability, and the overwhelming socio-economic position of government in general and the central state apparatus in particular. Under these conditions, a presidential system could promote personal rule at the expense of 'shared rule' and 'limited rule', further immerse the political system in a statist and monolithic mould, and engender destructive competition for the pre-eminent position of the presidency. At a minimum, there is a compelling case for constraining presidential power by strengthening such institutions of horizontal accountability as the legislature, judiciary, and counter-corruption apparatus and by largely removing the president from the appointment of judges and members of various regulatory bodies.

Third, and most important, presidentialism has exacerbated the politics of ethno-regional anxiety in Nigeria. Much inter-ethnic suspicion, contention, and recrimination have been generated in Nigeria by the perception that such a singularly important position is in, or could fall into, the hands of a politician from a rival ethnic group. The problem is exacerbated by the fixed four-year term of the president and by the ability of an incumbent president under the constitutions of the Second, Third, and Fourth Republics to win a second term. The CDC's subcommittee on the executive recommended an antidote to this problem. This involved an elaborate scheme for the rotation of nominations to the presidency and vice-presidency among four geopolitical zones—two each in the north and the south—in the country. Each zone, in turn, was to comprise between four and six of the country's then 19 constituent State units. The subcommittee recommended the rotation of the presidency 'until there has been a president from each zone', and ultimately, from each State (Federal Republic of Nigeria 1976: ii. 68–9). This rotational scheme was, however, rejected by the whole committee of the CDC. According to a prominent academic member of the CDC, the scheme would have been adopted but for the realization that it would take some States 'no less than 144 years' to produce the president, even as some ethnic groups in the States would still 'stand no chance of their members ever becoming the president . . .' (Dudley 1982: 162). Moreover, a scheme to rotate the presidency on a geopolitical basis would appear to contradict the objective of projecting the office as a unifying symbol. Consequently, opinion in the CDC 'swung to the more realistic position of ensuring that whoever became the president had the widest possible acceptability among the electorate' (Dudley 1982: 162). The result is Nigeria's widely acclaimed presidential election formula, which has been variously and controversially reinterpreted and adjusted since it was first formulated by the CDC in the draft 1979 constitution. Under the current 1999 Constitution, similar to that in the 1979 constitution, this formula requires a successful presidential candidate to obtain a nationwide majority or plurality—depending on whether there are two or more candidates—plus 'not less than one-quarter of the votes cast . . . in each of at least two-thirds of all the states in the federation and the federal capital Territory, Abuja' (Federal Republic of Nigeria 1999: 55).

Apart from its potential capacity to generate an electoral deadlock, as was graphically underscored by the 1979 presidential election controversy, it is dubious whether the presidential election formula has 'de-ethnicized' the presidency in the perceptions of Nigerians. As president in the Second Republic, Shehu Shagari never passed the test of ethno-regional neutrality or escaped insinuations that he worked 'to preserve the strategic position of his own northern culture and society' (Sylvester 1991: 266, 271). Babangida's annulment of M. K. O. Abiola's presidential election victory in 1993 prevailed because several northern military officers and politicians would not tolerate a 'southern president'. And after Obasanjo assumed the presidency in May 1999, he was accused of implementing a 'Yoruba agenda' by dismissing predominantly northern Muslim functionaries from the military and bureaucracy, and assigning 'plum' federal positions to persons from 'some states of the South-West' (O. Adeniyi 1999; Ekpu 1999). Thus, notwithstanding Obansanjo's previous

reputation as a 'detribalized' Nigerian, and his overwhelming political rejection by the Yoruba electorate in the 1999 elections, in favour
of a different Yoruba candidate, the perception is strong that he has
become beholden to his own section of the country as president. All of
this can be taken as support for Arend Lijphart's counsel that 'a
broadly supported presidency' is still an inferior mechanism of ethnic
accommodation to a parliamentary-type, 'broadly representative', or
inclusive collegial executive (Lijphart 1990*d*: 266 n. 8).

Yet there would be serious problems with a parliamentary system
in Nigeria as well, as there were in the First Republic. In particular, the dependence of a government on a parliamentary majority in
the context of endemic corruption in Nigeria would probably lead to
even more expensive ethnic logrolling to form and maintain governments, and possibly the frequent holding of governments
hostage to expensive 'side-payments' and sheer gross bribery in
exchange for fending off votes of no confidence. A requirement for a
'constructive vote of no confidence' might pre-empt the most opportunistic efforts in this regard, but the possibility of recurrent
regional, ethnic, partisan, and political blackmail would remain.
The frequent resort to impeachment and removal of legislative officials in the first few months of the Fourth Republic does not inspire
confidence about the prospects of parliamentary government in
Nigeria.

Nonetheless, since the 1979–83 experiment Nigerian politicians
have continued to promote constitutional reform proposals for
reducing the zero-sum ethno-political outcomes associated with
presidentialism. Apart from the resuscitation and popularization of
formulas for zoning and rotating the presidency, these reform proposals have included suggestions for the limitation of the tenure of
the president to a single term of between four and six years, partly
in order to facilitate or accelerate the geo-ethnic rotation of the
presidency; the introduction of multiple vice-presidents in order to
broaden the ethno-regional base of federal executive power; and the
selection of the presidential cabinet from elected members of the
national legislature who would, therefore, owe their loyalty not only
to the president but also to specific local or regional constituencies
(Federal Republic of Nigeria 1995). Nevertheless, these proposals
have been not only condemned by several critics as inherently
unworkable and undesirable but also disallowed by the military
promulgators and supervisors of the Nigerian constitutions and
political transitions.

All of this is not to conclude, however, that presidentialism has
been foisted by the military on the Nigerian people 'against their

legitimate yearnings and aspirations', as claimed by the Nigerian National Democratic Coalition (*Guardian* 1999*b*). Although no referendum has been held on the issue or on any of the Nigerian constitutions, recent constitutional discussions and conferences suggest that a presidential system, with or without significant modifications, still remains the preference of a majority of Nigerians (Federal Republic of Nigeria 1987: 73). However, the growing opposition to this preference underscores a wider and deeper tension in the country between integrative and accommodative solutions to the problems of unity.

Between Integration and Accommodation: A Perennial Dilemma

This global institutional dilemma was succinctly formulated in the Nigerian setting over three decades ago by the editors of the magazine *West Africa* (1966) in the following words:

The great question remains: If tribal feeling is still as strong in Nigeria as recent events suggest, is the best course to create constitutional and administrative machinery that allows this feeling full expression or, is it, as we think, better, while avoiding any kind of provocation, to create machinery which encourages development of national feeling and, above all, national political parties?

Like the editors of *West Africa*, the military architects of Nigeria's four post-civil war constitutions—1979, 1989, 1995, and 1999— leaned towards a nationally integrative rather than ethnically accommodative approach to the country's problems of unity. In other words, faced with the dilemma of sustaining Nigerian unity amid the pressures of ethnic fragmentation and competition, the military sought to rein in, rather than give free rein to, ethnic group interests. Thus, as already indicated, federalism was used to cut across the identities of the country's three major groups, while presidentialism was deployed as an instrument for inducing an integrated electoral process and for providing a potential pan-ethnic symbol of national unity. While subsequent military governments avoided General Aguiyi-Ironsi's fatal misadventure in 1966 in abolishing federalism altogether, they all nevertheless ruled the country as a 'unitary state in federal disguise' and maintained the ban he imposed on ethnic political associations (Suberu 1999: 76–9).

Indeed, no issue better illustrates the ultra-integrative bias of political engineering under military tutelage in Nigeria than the constitutional provisions for national parties. Since General Mohammed's charge to the CDC in 1975 to engineer 'genuine and truly national parties', successive Nigerian constitutions have required political associations to fulfil a number of stringent conditions before they could be registered by the national electoral agency and function legally as political parties. The most important of these conditions include: the absence of any sectional—ethnic, regional, or religious—connotation in the name, emblem, or motto of the association; a membership that is open to every Nigerian citizen 'irrespective of religion or ethnic grouping'; the maintenance of functional branches in, or a governing body that includes members from at least, two-thirds of the States in the federation; and the location of the headquarters of the association in the federal capital territory.[2] Beyond these common constitutional requirements, the governments of Babangida, Abacha, and Abubakar, all in the name of ensuring genuinely national parties, imposed additional conditions for party formation. The most bizarre condition was imposed by the Babangida Government which, under the 1989 constitution for the still-born Third Republic, restricted electoral competition to only two government-designated and state-funded political parties (Constitution of the Federal Republic of Nigeria (Promulgation) Decree No. 12 of May 1989: A140). While avoiding the democratic aberration of a mandatory two-party system, both the Abacha and Abubakar administrations imposed novel statutory—not constitutionalized—conditions of their own. The Abacha Government required prospective parties to establish offices in two-thirds of the local government areas in each State of the federation, and to enlist at least 40,000 members in each State, plus 10,000 members in the Federal Capital Territory (FCT)—over a million members total! (Human Rights Watch 1996: 13). To qualify for permanent registration under General Abubakar's transition programme, political associations were required to win at least 10 per cent—later reduced to 5 per cent—of national local government election votes in two-thirds of the States, and in the FCT.

Predictably, the various stipulations for integrating the Nigerian party system have provoked criticisms. They have been denounced as anti-democratic and anti-federalist because they restrict the freedom of individuals to associate freely in partisan formations and deny effective autonomous political expression to legitimize

---

[2] See New Nigerian Newspapers (1981: 64); Constitution of the Federal Republic of Nigeria (Promulgation) Decree No. 12 of May 1989 (1989: A141); Federal Republic of Nigeria (1995: i. 95; 1999: 86).

ethno-territorial interests. Because they are directed at the institutional expression and not the underlying structural conditions of ethno-political affiliations, the provisions may also be dismissed as largely superficial. More concretely, implementation of the provisions has almost always provoked criticisms regarding the partisan manipulation of the party registration process by the electoral agency. In addition, the regulations have tended to promote the emergence of weak, faction-ridden, crisis-prone, clientelistic parties, and to 'muscle . . . out . . . parties of deep philosophical expression . . . of conscience . . . belonging to the deep political tradition . . .' (*Guardian* 1999a).

The choice of a directly and explicitly regulated and integrated party system in Nigeria partially accounts for the almost complete lack of attention to electoral system design or reform in the country. From the commencement of national electoral politics in the pre-independence era up to the present time, Nigeria has maintained the first-past-the-post, single-member constituency electoral system.

However, in 1975 the subcommittee of the CDC on electoral systems recommended a proportional representation (PR) party list system for the upcoming Second Republic. In making this recommendation, the subcommittee claimed it had considered such criteria of a desirable electoral system as 'representativity', equitability, intelligibility, ease of implementation and capacity to promote governmental stability, free and fair elections, and a positive-sum 'conception of the political process' (Federal Republic of Nigeria 1976: ii. 181). The subcommittee surmised that, 'on balance', the party list system was more representative and equitable, and less prone to electoral corruption and zero-sum outcomes, than the simple plurality system. It also argued that the party list system was as intelligible and easy to operate as the single-member constituency system. The other major forms of PR—that is, the alternative vote and single transferable vote—the subcommittee argued, were better than the party list system only with respect to the criterion of representativity; evidence for the potential relative impact of the various electoral systems on governmental stability, according to the subcommittee, was inconclusive 'in our circumstances'. In essence, 'PR based on a list system' was the 'best . . . [and] also the least objectionable of the different systems we could have adopted'. Finally, the subcommittee acknowledged such potential disadvantages of the use of the PR as 'possible remoteness of representatives from the electorate, likelihood of skewness in spatial representation [and] party proliferation' (Federal Republic of Nigeria 1976: ii. 182). It argued, however, that these disadvantages could be mitigated in the Nigerian setting through appropriate civic education programmes, the establishment of equivalent moderate-sized constituencies, and the constitutional provisions for federation-wide parties.

Yet the plenary committee of the CDC, and subsequently the Constituent Assembly and the military, opted to continue with the 'single-member constituency system' (Federal Republic of Nigeria 1976: ii. 212). Ten years later, as Nigeria embarked on the ill-fated transition to the Third Republic, a separate constitutional body simply dismissed PR as 'an inappropriate electoral system' for Nigeria (Federal Republic of Nigeria 1987: 134).

The principal, if not sole, proponent of the party list system in the CDC's subcommittee on electoral systems was the late Billy Dudley, the country's leading political-science professor at that time. Dudley's characteristically ponderous simulations of the workings of the PR system in the report of the subcommittee belied the argument that the PR would be easy to understand and operate in Nigeria's still largely illiterate society. What is more, the report of the subcommittee also included such unfamiliar, or complex and potentially contentious, ideas as a recommendation for the declaration of the runner-up in a presidential race as the vice-president of the federation, and another for the resolution of an inconclusive presidential contest through an electoral college using the alternative vote system (Federal Republic of Nigeria 1976: ii. 186). In essence, the 'academic' nature of the subcommittee's recommendations, coupled with the broad suspicion that a PR system would simply give vent to narrow partisan and sectional interests, undermined the case for the party list system (Oyediran 1996: xii). Paradoxically, however, the use of the first-past-the-post system for electing legislators from predominantly ethnically homogeneous, single-member districts in Nigeria has simply served to reinforce parochial legislative politics, and to marginalize dissident sentiments and fissures within various tribal bastions (Diamond and Plattner 1994: xxv). Indeed, contrary to the largely integrative aspirations of the Nigerian constitutions, informal political exchanges in the country have tended to promote freewheeling ethnic representation and accommodation.

Ethnic Conflict Management: 'The Informal Sector'

In conducting informal ethno-political exchanges in Nigeria, the country's politicians have derived enormous inspiration and encouragement from the 'federal character' provisions of Nigeria's post-civil war constitutions. However, while the 'federal character' principle explicitly mandates only the effective or equal representation of the States in national bodies, the politicians have reinvented it to incorporate principles and strategies for regional, geopolitical, religious, ethnic, and sub-ethnic 'balancing' at both federal and sub-federal levels. The most popular of these informal ethnic balancing or bargaining practices has remained the ethnoregional allocation and rotation of political offices and party posts: that is, the constitutionally unrecognized principle of zoning and rotation. The relatively rigorous implementation of zoning was a crucial factor in the electoral success of the NPN in the Second Republic. The party implemented a zoning scheme that effectively assigned the presidency of the federation to the far—predominantly Muslim Hausa-Fulani—north, the vice-presidency to the Igbo south-east, the party chairmanship to the Yoruba south-west, the Senate presidency to the south-south—southern minorities—and, effective from the 1983 elections, the office of the Speaker of the House of Representatives to the lower north or northern minorities, otherwise known as the 'Middle-Belt' or north-central zone. Had the Second Republic survived into 1987, the presidential nomination of the party would have rotated south, with consequential adjustments in the zonal allocation of other key offices.

The two parties of the unfulfilled Third Republic adopted even more elaborate zoning procedures. In the Social Democratic Party (SDP), the presidential candidacy went to the south-west, the vice-presidency to the north-east, the national chairmanship of the party and the deputy Senate presidency to the south-south, the Senate presidency and the post of party publicity secretary to the north-central zone, the offices of the Speaker of the House of Representatives and party treasurer to the south east, and the posts of party secretary and Deputy Speaker of the House of Representatives to the north-west. The rival NRC, for its part, zoned its presidential nomination to the Muslim far north, the vice-presidential candidacy to the former eastern region, the party chairmanship to the old western region, and the post of party secretary to the north-central zone.

Of Nigeria's four post-civil war, military-sponsored, constitutions, the 1995 constitution of the Abacha dispensation was exceptional in having sought explicitly to formalize or constitutionalize the principle of zoning and rotation. Reflecting southern disenchantment with the 1993 presidential election annulment, and a broader national anxiety over real or perceived sectional political marginalization, the constitution provided for the rotation of the presidency between the north and south, a tripartite vice-presidency, the establishment of a 'Federal Character' commission, and the proportional representation in the federal executive of all parties winning up to 10 per cent of national legislative seats (Federal Republic of Nigeria 1995: i. 65, 69, 71, 98). Indeed, the national electoral agency asked all prospective parties under the Abacha transition project to 'accept the principle of power sharing and rotation of political offices as enshrined in Chapter VI of the Constitution of the Federal Republic of Nigeria 1995' (Human Rights Watch/Africa 1996: 13). Finally, in October 1995, General Abacha himself announced an entirely novel scheme for rotational zoning. This was expected to involve the rotation, over an experimental 30-year period, of the six offices of president, vice-president, prime minister, deputy prime minister, Senate president, and Speaker of the House of Representatives among the six geo-political zones of north-west, north-east, north-central, south-west, south-east, and south-south. However the duplicity of this scheme became apparent when all the five parties registered by the government went on to nominate General Abacha as their joint presidential candidate. The scheme collapsed, along with the five parties, with Abacha's demise in June 1998.

Rotational zoning resurfaced as an autonomous convention of party politics, rather than an explicit principle of constitutional stipulation, with the emergence of the Peoples Democratic Party (PDP), the All Peoples Party (APP), and the Alliance for Democracy (AD) under the transition programme of Abacha's successor, General Abubakar. Reflecting continuing southern agitation for a genuine regional 'power-shift', all three parties zoned their presidential nomination and party chairmanship to the south and north, respectively. In the event, the two candidates for president in the February 1999 election were both Yorubas from the south-west, Obasanjo of the PDP and Olu Falae of the APP/AD Alliance, who paired with vice-presidential candidates Abubakar Atiku (north-east) and Umaru Shinkafi (north-west), respectively. Following its triumph in the presidential and national assembly elections, the PDP zoned the Senate presidency to the south-east, the post of Speaker of House of Representatives to the north-west, the Deputy Senate presidency to the north-east, and the posts of Deputy Speaker of the House of Representatives and Secretary to the Government of the Federation to the south-south.

The PDP also asked president Obasanjo 'to ensure that . . . key ministries [read federal cabinet appointments] are not concentrated in one geographical region' (*Guardian* 1999c). Although Obasanjo's cabinet appointments of June–July 1999 did observe the formal constitutional requirement to include at least one minister from each State, and also incorporated elements from the APP and AD, they were generally perceived to have been insufficiently faithful to the informal principle of equitable geopolitical sharing of strategic ministries. To cite one revealingly blunt newspaper analysis of the appointments:

. . . the northwest is in control of foreign affairs and communications . . . while finance, defense and FCT . . . have gone to a particular zone—northeast. North-central has industries, while southwest has internal affairs, power/steel, education and aviation as portfolios of consequence . . . southeast has transport, while south-south has works/housing. In summary northwest has two good ones, northeast three, north-central one, southwest four, southeast one, and south-south one. (A. Adeniyi 1999)

In essence, principles and strategies of ethno-regional power sharing, outside of the formal constitutional framework, have developed in Nigeria. They provide a consociational or accommodative complement to the integrative emphasis of formal constitutional rules, and could compensate for real or perceived weaknesses in those rules. As flexible conventions, these informal practices lend some degree of creativity to ethnic conflict management in Nigeria. Indeed, they legitimize and institutionalize accommodative and bargaining practices that would be impossible or unwise to codify constitutionally. Above all, they reflect and reinforce Nigeria's 'multiple ethnic balance of power' and the broad desire to preserve the Nigerian state on an equitable inter-segmental basis, given the apparent unavailability of more peaceable or stable alternatives to the country's federal union (Lijphart 1977; 16; Suberu 1997). When they are respected, these informal practices could enhance significantly the stability of the entire system. When ignored, they could fuel a corrosive current of ethnic discontent. Such discontent could be particularly potent in the Nigerian setting because of the mammoth resources and powers of the state, and the pervasive apprehension regarding the possible use of the state apparatus to promote the interests of particular groups to the detriment of the welfare or security of other sections.

Restraining the Multi-ethnic State

The roots of democratic instability and ethnic anxiety in Nigeria lie not so much in cultural diversity as in the destructive competition, the polarization, and the repression that have come to be associated with the political struggles for control of the enormous socio-economic powers and resources of the state. Given the country's relative economic underdevelopment, cultural artificiality, and pervasive ethno-clientelistic ties, such competition, polarization, and repression have crystallized along communal, ethnic, regional, and, to a lesser extent, religious lines. Had Nigeria been a more ethnically homogeneous or culturally consolidated state, the destructively intense socio-economic premium on political power would still have undermined democracy, but perhaps without threatening the territorial disintegration of the state.

Institutional engineering to manage ethnic differentiation could compensate for the cultural artificiality of the state, or help to cement the basic 'political community' essential to democratic coexistence, without necessarily yielding a viable democratic order. However, repeated transgressions of the rules of the political game in the desperate competition to win or maintain power inevitably inflame the fissures inherent in a plural society, thereby jeopardizing not only democracy but also the very survival of the state. Thus, along with institutions explicitly directed at managing its ethnic diversity, a critical goal of constitutional design in Nigeria must 'be to check, balance, and decentralize political power as extensively and innovatively as possible, and hence to reduce both the stakes in any electoral contest and the scope for behavioral abuses' (Diamond 1987: 210).

Nigeria has several fledgling or potential institutions of restraint, but perhaps the three most crucial are the judiciary, the electoral commission, and the counter-corruption apparatus. Although blessed with some outstanding judges, the Nigerian judiciary has been enfeebled, particularly under military rule, by considerable executive control of its appointment and funding, extra-judicial military decrees, blunt authoritarian intimidation, corrupt inducement, ethno-political manipulations, and financial starvation. A key and novel achievement of the 1999 Nigerian Constitution is its attempt to strengthen the judicial branch through the establishment of a National Judicial Council. This 21-member council of jurists is to be headed, and largely appointed, by the Chief Justice of the Federation. It is empowered to make virtually binding recommendations, based on the advice of federal and State judicial service commissions, to the president and State governors regarding the appointments of persons to judicial positions at the federal and State levels, which appointments may also be subject to confirmation by the relevant legislative authorities. Quite significantly, the National Judicial Council is also empowered to 'collect, control and disburse all moneys, capital and recurrent, for the judiciary' (Federal Republic of Nigeria 1999: 145).

These provisions represent an important departure from past constitutional practice, when the judiciary lacked financial autonomy and the judicial service commissions merely advised the executive on judicial appointments. To be sure, the new provisions have been criticized for not being explicit or far-reaching enough, and for somewhat centralizing control of the entire judiciary, at both federal and State levels, in the office of the Chief Justice of the Federation. Yet it appears the real challenge is for the judiciary to rise from the legacy of its perversion in the recent past to the demands of its now significantly enhanced status as 'umpire' in the federal democratic political process.

Unfortunately, the wise pragmatism that informed the establishment of the National Judicial Council has been absent in the design of the electoral administration. As in the past, members of the federal electoral agency, now rhetorically designated the 'Independent' National Electoral Commission (INEC), will be appointed by the president, acting on the advice of the Council of State, and subject to confirmation by the Senate. State governors would exercise similar powers of appointment over the State electoral commissions, which conduct local government elections only. In the absence of the mitigating effects that could have come from the adoption of proposals for single or non-successive terms for elected office holders, the self-serving manipulation of the electoral machinery by incumbents will continue, and Nigerian elections are likely to remain violent, fraudulent, and contentious. The only potential restraining influences on the electoral process would be the 'horizontal' oversight that may be exercised by the judiciary, and the 'vertical accountability' that could be enforced through the evolving tradition of local and international election monitoring (Diamond, Plattner, and Schedler 1999: 11). Similarly, the design of the institutional apparatus to control corruption, the Code of Conduct Bureau and Tribunal, has failed historically to produce bodies with sufficient political autonomy, will, professionalism, and resources to enforce seriously the laws and the code of conduct, which is on paper quite rigorous. President Obasanjo has submitted a bill to the National Assembly for creation of a Independent Commission Against Corruption, but human rights groups have expressed concern over its considerable abridgement of due process and the concentration of appointment and removal powers solely in the office of the president. If the premium on political power is to be reduced so that the ethnic stakes in winning office can be attenuated at least somewhat, Nigeria must have a counter-corruption apparatus that is imaginatively insulated from partisan politics, amply funded and staffed, and vigorously led.

Nigeria's federal institutional structure also represents a potential instrument for restraining, balancing, and dispersing the powers of the state. To date, this potential has been heavily constrained by the centralizing legacies of military rule and the pathologies of the monolithic, oil-centric, political economy. A constitutional review process to consider modalities for restructuring or energizing the States, the permanent exclusion of the military from politics, and the shrewd use of revenue allocation arrangements to stimulate sub-federal fiscal capacity and autonomy, is imperative for the revitalization of Nigeria's weak federalism.

Astute observers recognize 'federalism as an analogue to the market'. The distribution of governmental functions among several competitive or cooperative jurisdictions is analogous with the economic relegation of 'allocative and distributive choices . . . to the workings of markets' (Buchanan 1995: 19–20). By restraining, constraining or delimiting the domain of state power, both devices—federalism and the market—help to reduce the vulnerability of individuals and groups, including identity groups, to political manipulation, domination, coercion, exploitation, or alienation. While the Nigerian state must play a key, and as yet largely unrealized, role in the stimulation and direction of broad-based socio-economic development, the attainment of the country's long-standing goals of national unity, democratic stability, and material progress would require the reduction of state control over economic resources and rewards.

An Agenda for Institutional Reform

No institutional design, however imaginative and fitting, can ensure the survival of democracy and the peaceful management of ethnic and regional conflict. The future of democracy in Nigeria, and of Nigeria itself, lies in the hands of politicians who have at virtually every critical juncture to date been driven by the quest for personal enrichment and ethnic and regional advantage over any commitment to the Constitution, the democratic process, or the nation itself. Yet institutions do structure incentives, and they can also restructure them. The challenge for Nigeria's Fourth Republic is to craft institutions that will restructure or at least constrain the pathological incentives that now prevail in politics.

We have placed considerable emphasis on strengthening and restructuring institutions of horizontal accountability that can gradually generate key elements that have been grossly deficient in Nigeria's three previous attempts at democracy: fairness, transparency, probity, and a rule of law. No one would dispute the importance of these principles for the legitimacy, and hence viability and ultimately consolidation, of democracy. Yet students of ethnic conflict might understandably question the emphasis we give to them here for addressing the specific challenge of managing ethnic and regional conflict. Our priority stems from the grotesque distortion of the incentive structure in Nigerian public life today. The premium on political power is simply too great to sustain democracy and to manage peacefully and democratically the ethnic and regional—as well as factional and individual—competition for it. Since the First Republic, there has been little, if any, effective check on the power of office holders. They have been free to use their power virtually at will to enrich and aggrandize themselves and their communities, to return themselves to office, and to punish and disadvantage the political opposition. In those circumstances, where political power means so much to the life chances of individuals and groups, and where there is no perception of neutrality, autonomy, and fairness on the part of institutions that are charged to manage, supervise, and arbitrate the competition for power and resources, it is almost inevitable that electoral and political competition will be ruleless, abusive, and violent, whether it is polarized into grand ethnic and regional cleavages or fragmented along lower-scale lines of communal and sub-ethnic conflict and grievance. The latter do not threaten national disintegration and civil war in the same way that highly aggregated ethnic conflict does, particularly between north and south, Muslim and Christian, and the three largest ethnic groups, Hausa-Fulani, Yoruba, and Igbo. However, more fragmented and dispersed ethnic conflicts can also destabilize democracy and the nation itself. If democracy, development, and good governance are to be viable in Nigeria, the root causes of chronic political instability must be addressed.

We have mentioned three crucial agencies of horizontal accountability: the judiciary, whose management is now entrusted substantially to the National Judicial Council, the electoral commission, and the code of conduct or counter-corruption institutions. But there are other crucial functions of horizontal accountability and refereeing of political and ethnic conflict. The census has been a recurrent bone of bitter, explosive ethnic and regional conflict, for from the census figures flows the allocation of political power and financial resources, as most States and local governments derive the overwhelming bulk of their revenue from federal revenue allocations. Like the National Judicial Council, the Independent National Electoral Commission, and the anti-corruption commission, the national census or population commission must be appointed and managed in a way that is insulated from partisan politics. This goes as well for the commissions and boards that oversee the civil service, the auditing of government agencies, the police, and the allocation of revenue.

All of these bodies which restrain, oversee, monitor, or referee the competition among communities and parties must be seen as neutral and fair if conflict is to be managed and contained. No formula can ensure that these sensitive functions are insulated from partisan conflict and ethnic or regional dominance and managed professionally and fairly. But imaginative constitutional provisions can be deployed to improve the image of neutrality and the prospects of insulation from partisan and ethnic politics. Currently, it is the president, subject to the advice of the Council of State and/or the confirmation of the Senate, who is entrusted with the appointment of many of these bodies. In the case of the counter-corruption commission proposed by the Obasanjo administration, the situation is potentially even worse: it is the president unilaterally who is to appoint the members of the commission and who can remove them for any cause. We think a new way must be found to appoint and oversee the agencies of restraint and refereeing in Nigeria. A Council of State is a valuable constitutional concept for this purpose; and, charged with this function, it can become the pinnacle of a virtual fourth branch of government, separated from and checking the other three. But to do so, the Council must be autonomous of partisan politics. Currently it is composed primarily of serving politicians: the president, vice-president, Senate president, the Speaker of the House of Representatives, the federal attorney-general, the State governors, former presidents—including former military heads of state who came to power through coups! The only potentially non-partisan members of the Council are the former Chief Justices of the Federation. Nigeria needs to find a new way to constitute this Council of State so that its members come from civil society and are not serving politicians. Ironically, President Obasanjo himself, writing in the late 1980s as a retired head of state, proposed that the Council of State become a non-partisan independent body, whose members would be required to relinquish any party membership or affiliation (Obasanjo 1989: 90–1). He proposed then that the president of Nigeria be the only partisan member of the Council, and not its chairman. Other Nigerians have pondered whether it might be possible to draw membership of the Council from among respected organizations in civil society, like the Nigerian Bar Association, the Nigerian Medical Association, the Nigeria Labour Congress, the National Association of Nigerian Students, women's and human rights organizations, and so on. Many of these human rights and good government groups came together in a coalition, the Transition Monitoring Group, to ensure the fair completion of the Abubakar transition to democracy during 1998–9. We think it is now time for these participants in civil society to turn their attention to this crucial challenge of how best to constitute and insulate the agencies of accountability.

There are, of course, many other institutional changes of a more conventional nature for managing ethnic conflict that could be proposed. But the scope to implement them is quite limited. Nigeria is too wedded to constituency representation to render feasible the kind of system of PR in small to moderately sized multi-member districts that Reynolds (1999a) has proposed for African countries. However, as a federal system, Nigeria has the advantage of having two houses of parliament. The lower house of the National Assembly, the House of Representatives, must be elected on the basis of single-member territorial districts. We think no other system of election would be accepted in Nigeria. However, it is quite conceivable that the Senate, which is now composed of three representatives from each of the 36 States plus one from the FCT of Abuja, could be elected by some other means. It would be feasible, for example, to make each of the States a three-member electoral district for the election of senators on the basis of PR. Such a small district would offer only modest scope for a party with a base and an identity from a different ethnic group or region to gain a foothold in a 'foreign' area. But it would begin to generate some possibility for such trans-ethnic alignments and linkages to emerge, and some greater incentive for parties to campaign and invest resources in States where they have historically been weak. Particularly in a two- or three-party system, lowering the effective threshold for election of a representative from the range of 40–50 per cent to 25–30 per cent might well create a much more complex picture of electoral competition.

A system of PR for election of the Senate would work far better with larger States and hence larger electoral districts. But this would require fewer States. If the current 36 States could be consolidated down to 21 or even 24, and the number of senators were increased to five per State, the Senate would be roughly the same size as today: in the range of 106–121 members, adding one for

Aubja, compared with the current 109. Consolidation of States would thus serve the principle of ethnic conflict management, while making State government a more viable level of governance again and restoring some of the complexity to politics at the State level. Consolidation is thus a worthy and, we think, almost necessary goal for the effective functioning of federalism in Nigeria. However, it is one that would surely set off intense ethnic and regional mobilization and violence, as the communities that would be losing States and State capitals would also see themselves to be losing governors, civil services, and various types of resources. The Nigerian military has done a grave disservice to federalism and governance in Nigeria by creating so many States, but it is not a change that will be easily reversible any time soon. Institutional redesign must proceed with a sense of realism about what is possible in the near term.

Conclusions

Nigeria has demonstrated a capacity creatively to nurture 'unity in diversity'. It has also betrayed a vulnerability to disintegrative sectarian conflicts. The Nigerian experience shows that the establishment of a vertically and horizontally balanced system of federalism, and the implementation of both formal and informal strategies for national integration and ethnic accommodation, can help to contain the threats to institutional stability inherent in a multi-ethnic developing state. The same experience instructs that the distortion or decline of federalism, the transgression or abortion of basic democratic processes, and the general underdevelopment of institutions of political restraint could inflame the fissures of a plural society, and precipitate the disintegration of an otherwise reasonably manageable multi-ethnic state. The fortunes of Nigeria's Fourth Republic, launched with as much optimism as pessimism in May 1999, may determine which of the two historic tendencies finally prevails in the country.

····················
15
····················

Ethnic Diversities, Constitutional Designs, and Public Policies in India

David Stuligross and Ashutosh Varshney

Introduction

This[1] chapter deals with how India's constitutional provisions and public policies have dealt with the nation's ethnic diversities.[2] We concentrate on four such diversities, viewed as critical to nation building in India: religion, language, caste, and tribe. Nearly 40 per cent of the country speaks Hindi as its 'mother tongue', but 15 other languages are spoken as a 'mother tongue' by at least ten million people each (Table 15.1). Though having a Hindu majority, India has several other religions (Table 15.2). There are three meta-categories of caste: upper, middle, and ex-untouchables (Table 15.3).[3] Although the last two, viewed as historically deprived, constitute a majority by a huge margin, the upper castes have on the whole dominated the nation's political, social, and economic landscape. Tribes, constituting 8.1 per cent of the population, are the least known but an increasingly important category. Culturally quite distinct from the mainstream, they are mostly concentrated in the middle and north-eastern part of the nation (Fig. 15.1). On the whole, language and tribe tend to be geographically concentrated, whereas religion and caste are more evenly spread throughout the country.

---

[1] Following the recent shifts in social science discourse, we will use the term 'institutions' for both constitutional designs as well as public policies. By 'institutions' we mean a *formal* set of rules and norms in a polity. These can consist of constitutional rules, laws, or public policies.

[2] We use the term 'ethnic' in its broader sense, by which we mean any group-based *ascriptive* identity, actual or imagined. Why we should have this larger view is persuasively argued by Donald Horowitz (1985).

[3] Caste is essentially a local category, and there are thousands of castes in India. With some qualification they can, however, be grouped together in larger, meta-categories. The meta-classification is also known as *varna* classification.

TABLE 15.1: India's principal languages

Language	Spoken by % of India's population
Hindi	40.0
Bengali	8.3
Telugu	7.9
Marathi	7.5
Tamil	6.3
Urdu	5.1
Gujarati	4.9
Kannada	3.9
Malayalam	3.6
Oriya	3.4
Punjabi	2.8
Assamese	1.6
Other	4.7

Source: Census of India (2001: Table 25). Accessed 22 April 2001.

We ask the following three questions: (1) how did India's constitution-makers and founding fathers propose to deal with the problems of each category, as they went about building a nation?; (2) what has been the impact of such constitutional provisions, institutional frames, and public policies?; and (3) could constitutional and public policy engineering have achieved its objectives, or have some other factors crucially intervened in the processes that generate the outcomes we observe?

Our argument is that on linguistic diversity India's institutional design has been a great success, but on all other ethnic categories the record is mixed. We define 'success' as the realization of outcomes that the institutional designs set out to achieve. We would also like to argue that it could not but have been otherwise. While institutional designs are important, they do not entirely determine the outcomes we observe, at least in India. Political and social contexts have a great deal to do with the actual consequences of institutional designs. To resolve political problems associated with ethnic diversity, we should indeed seriously consider the appropriate institutional designs as we step into the next millennium, but we should see them one of several important variables determining the outcome we seek to achieve.

We start with a necessary background. In the first section, we outline the various models that India's politicians have employed concerning the relationship between ethnic diversities and nation-building, indicating which ones dominated constitution-making and

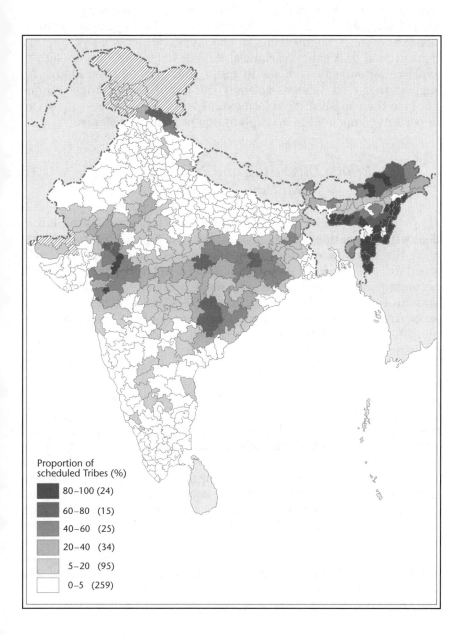

FIGURE 15.1: *Distribution of India's scheduled tribes*

whether the political context is changing. In the second section, we outline the constitutional and policy provisions concerning each ethnic category. In the third section, we assess the impact of constitutional and policy engineering. In the fourth section we ask whether institutional and policy variables, though important, are enough to explain the outcomes we see in India, and arguably elsewhere. We suggest that civil society—not only the number of civic institutions but also their qualitative relationships with one another—is also an important component to an explanation of political violence.

Ethnic Diversities and Nation-building: Multiple Narratives

How did India's founding fathers and constitution-makers plan to deal with the nation's many diversities? The answer has much to do with the ideology of India's freedom movement, the principles it stood for, and the kind of nation it sought to build. The movement, becoming mass-based under the leadership of Mahatma Gandhi and later Jawaharlal Nehru during 1920–47, recognized diversities as central to India as a nation. The leaders of the freedom movement had what is now known as the 'salad bowl' as opposed to the 'melting pot' view of the nation.[4]

In India, the master narrative of nation building came to be called 'composite nationalism'. It guided the national movement under Gandhi and Nehru and was legitimized by the country's constitution after independence. This narrative evokes the image of nation as a family. According to this narrative, all religions, as well as languages and ethnic groups, would have an equal place in the national family and, in principle, none would dominate the functioning of the state. This narrative emphasizes that one's religious faith or one's linguistic, caste, or social background would not determine citizenship in the country and the rights that go with it. Birth in India and naturalization would be the sole legal criteria.

The rationale for this narrative came from a reading of Indian culture and history explicitly articulated by the leaders of the national movement. Ideas of tolerance, pluralism, and syncretism, they contended, have historically defined Indian society and

[4] For a longer treatment, see Varshney (1993), on which the discussion below heavily relies.

culture.[5] India is not only the birthplace of several religions—Hinduism, Buddhism, Jainism, and Sikhism—but in its history it has also repeatedly received, accommodated, and absorbed 'outsiders': Muslims, Parsis, Jews, and 'Syrian Christians'—followers of St Thomas, arriving as early as the second century, thus reaching India before Christians reached Europe—and, even earlier, waves of migrants from south-east Asia and central Europe that arrived so long ago that they are sometimes described as India's original peoples.

In the process, and partly as a consequence, the founding fathers argued that syncretistic forms of culture have become part of India.[6] Apart from syncretism, which means a 'coming together' and merging of cultures, pluralism and tolerance have been the other features: different communities always found their niche in India by developing principles of interaction with others while keeping their identity intact. India's constitution, as we will see later, is in large part a formal and institutional expression of this narrative.

Within this narrative, however, the focus of Indian nationalism has been directed clearly at the individual. India's early national leaders were keenly sensitive to the fact that, strong though each may be, the lines of social and cultural division do not cumulatively reinforce each other; they tend rather to cut across one another. Depending on need or situation, the same individual can choose from a shelf of markers for political purposes. She may highlight her regional identity (say, Bengali) or religious marker (say, Muslim) or a caste (Brahmin) or some other label to serve her purpose. Just as one may say that India is multicultural, individual Indians also either are, or prospectively can be, multicultural (Das Gupta 1988: 147). India's nation-builders sought to provide each citizen, whether as an individual or as a member of a politicized ethnic or social community, equal access to the offices of state. Such an ideology does not deny the

[5] The best source for the secular nationalist construction is Nehru's *The Discovery of India*. Syncretism, pluralism and tolerance are the main themes of Nehru's recalling of India's history: 'Ancient India, like ancient China, was a world in itself, a culture and a civilization which gave shape to all things. Foreign influences poured in and often influenced that culture and were absorbed. Disruptive tendencies gave rise immediately to an attempt to find a synthesis. Some kind of a dream of unity has occupied the mind of India since the dawn of civilization. That unity was not conceived as something imposed from outside, a standardization . . . of beliefs. It was something deeper and, within its fold, the widest tolerance of belief and custom was practised and very variety acknowledged and even encouraged' (Nehru 1989: 62).

[6] Urdu—a language combining Persian and Hindi, written in Arabic script—is a prototypical syncretistic language, developed under Muslim rule in medieval times.

existence of social communities; it denies the primacy of any one over the others and creates incentives for the development of political communities that cut across social boundaries.

Though the Congress Party, which led the national movement, has been the prime representative of this narrative in Indian politics, most political parties and currents have on the whole subscribed to this view of diversities and the nation. The main challenges to this narrative have clear implications for how India deals with ethnic diversity.

The first challenge came from what may be called 'religious nationalism'. It has primarily taken two forms: Muslim and Hindu.[7] Muslim nationalism emerged in the first half of the twentieth century. It led to the birth of Pakistan in 1947. The argument for Pakistan was simply that Hindus and Muslims were not two different religious communities but two separate nations. Hindu nationalism, which became quite powerful in India during the 1990s, is the mirror image of the Muslim nationalism that led to creation of Pakistan. Its view of the nation is embedded in a 'melting pot' model. Hinduism, according to this narrative, gives India its distinctive national identity, and other religions must *assimilate* to the Hindu centre. India, according to this narrative, is originally the land of the Hindus and it is the only land which the Hindus can call their own. Most of India's population is, and has been,[8] Hindu by religion—anywhere between 65 per cent and 70 per cent in early twentieth-century India and 82 per cent today.[9] A common faith in Hinduism brings India's diversity together. India thus viewed is a Hindu nation (Golwalkar 1939). Whether or not Hindus can enjoy legal primacy, they must, according to Hindu nationalists, have cultural and political primacy in shaping India's destiny.

As a conception of nation, religious nationalism has been the chief competitor of composite nationalism in the twentieth century. Muslim nationalism was the *bête noire* of composite nationalists during the national movement. Once Muslim nationalists left India for Pakistan, Hindu nationalists became composite nationalism's

---

[7] In the 1980s, Sikh nationalism, a third type of religious nationalism, led to a decade-long insurgency in the State of Punjab. Sikh nationalism is currently quiet. It seems to have settled for a place in the federal system as opposed to outright independence.

[8] Some historians disagree. They argue that a Hindu identity is at best a creation of the last 200–300 years. Before that there were different sects, but no Hindu identity as such. See Romila Thapar (1989).

[9] Most of the percentage change is accounted for by the creation of Pakistan. Two-thirds of the Muslim population of British India either lived in or migrated to Pakistan shortly after independence in 1947.

principal ideological adversaries. Within months after independence, in a highly symbolic act, a Hindu nationalist killed Mahatma Gandhi, the father of the nation, for practising tolerance especially towards the Muslims. Since 1947, the Bharatiya Janata Party (BJP), until 1977 known as the Bharatiya Jan Sangh (BJS), has been the principal patron of religious nationalism in politics.

The aim of Hindu nationalists, one should also note, is not only to emphasize the centrality of Hinduism to India but also to build Hindu political unity. The Hindus, after all, are a religious majority only in a manner of speaking. They are divided internally by multiple caste cleavages. As an ideology, Hindu nationalism is thus opposed to both composite nationalism and the other principal Indian ideology based on caste, as described below. On language, its position is not clear-cut. The reason simply is that its main concern is the relationship between religion and nation, not language and nation.

A second challenge to the master narrative of secular nationalism has come from a caste-based narrative.[10] This narrative is not directly opposed to secular nationalism; rather, it challenges the composite premises of which diversity are politically important and which should be central to nation-making. Instead of talking about the nation in general and the placement of religious or linguistic groups therein, the caste narrative speaks of the deeply hierarchical and unjust nature of the Hindu social order, where the lower the caste has historically been in the ritual hierarchy, the weaker have also been its political rights and the greater its oppression. An egalitarian restructuring of Hindu society is the chief goz`al of the caste narrative: caste should not determine whether an individual is treated as an inferior or superior human being.

This narrative thus, concentrates on India's religious majority, the Hindus. When it speaks of non-Hindu groups, it does so by arguing that both religious minorities as well as lower Hindu castes suffer from discrimination by the higher castes. An alliance of lower castes and religious minorities, therefore, is natural. Moreover, according to this narrative, to make up for centuries of caste oppression, affirmative action favouring the lower castes in government jobs and education should be the primary vehicle of achieving social justice. On linguistic diversity, this narrative takes no position. Its main concern, with respect to Hinduism, is intra-religious, not inter-religious or linguistic.

The 'lower caste narrative' has, by and large, risen to all-India prominence of late. It was a south Indian narrative to begin with,

---

[10] For an account by one of the founders of the narrative, see Lohia (1964).

used as it was to mobilize the masses in the first half of the twentieth century in south India (Ross Barnet 1967; Hardgrave 1969).
Capitalizing on their numbers in a democracy, the lower castes of
south India ended the political and social dominance of the
Brahmins in the 1960s and 1970s. In the 1980s and 1990s, this narrative of politics finally spread to the north and the west. By now,
relying heaving on the opportunity given by democracy to organize
and express their interests, the lower castes have come of political
age in much of India, pressing the polity in new directions and
achieving significant public policy successes. The changes in, and
the broadening of, India's affirmative action programme, as it was
originally conceived in the 1950s, has a great deal to do with the rise
of lower castes in politics.

The third challenge focused on how India's tribal communities
ought to be incorporated into the new Indian nation. Both composite
nationalists and religious nationalists, whether of Hindu or Muslim
stripes, acknowledged that tribal communities occupied, at best,
awkward places in India's dominant social networks. Composite
nationalists saw tribes people as yet another ingredient for its salad
bowl; Hindu nationalists sought to emphasize the somewhat uncomfortable place Vedic Hinduism granted to practitioners of indigenous
animist religions;[11] Muslim nationalists sought to generate a parallel separatist movement by tribal communities that adopted their
'separate religion, separate state' narrative. Unlike the other narratives, however, the 'tribal narrative' was conducted almost exclusively 'from above'. Although tribal concerns were an important
topic of many political discussions, very few tribal leaders themselves were directly engaged in these debates.

For the purposes of this chapter, the discussion above not only
provides the necessary background of ideas underlying constitution-making in India but also suggests how some shifts in politics
and political power, if achieved, may produce very different pressures, as public policies are re-engineered in changing political contexts. The first narrative, composite nationalism, continues to be
the bedrock of the Indian Constitution. Its biggest opponents, the
Hindu nationalists, have come to power in India, but only in a coalition. They have substantially, though not totally, changed India's

---

[11] This place has two sources of inspiration. First, the Hindu epic *Mahabharata*
includes one story about tribal assimilation into the Hindu fold: a Hindu archery
guru agrees to accept a tribesperson named Eklavya as his student, but only after
Eklavya agrees to cut off his thumb. Second, Hindu nationalist philosophy that
evolved in the late nineteenth century included in the definition of Hinduism all
religions that are indigenous to India, including tribal religions.

political culture, but they do not yet have the electoral or legislative numbers to alter the basic properties of the Constitution, nor does it appear that they will be able to do so.

Constitutional amendments require a two-thirds parliamentary vote in India and support from half of the States. The Congress Party had the ability to deliver these at one point. During the 1990s, the political space became highly pluralized and is likely to remain so for the foreseeable future. No party is likely to replace the Congress both at the centre *and* in the States, making constitutional amendments aimed at changing India's official view of diversities rather difficult. Many of the BJP's coalition partners are supporters of composite nationalism. If the BJP were to press its assimilationist view of the nation, the coalition would break and the party would be thrown out of power. The compulsions of ruling India, thus, have pushed the BJP to put its melting-pot view of the nation on the back burner.

Constitutional Provisions and Public Policies

Language

When India gained independence in 1947—indeed, during the half-century preceding independence—its political institution-builders faced a pair of now familiar challenges. First, they had to make political sense of a population divided by social, religious, political, and linguistic traditions. Nehru and other senior Congress Party leaders were firmly committed to crafting state institutions that would enable all Indians to be represented equitably, regardless of social background. Second, they had to make administrative sense of more than 600 semi-sovereign units within the subcontinent, including largely autonomous frontier areas and princely States, in addition to the provinces governed directly by the British rulers.[12] The two challenges were addressed in part by creating federal States whose boundaries correspond to populations with important cultural similarities.

But which federating logic was to be used? The founding fathers faced this question immediately after independence. As it turned out, language in most of India and tribe in the seven small north-eastern States became the key principles. Because language was

---

[12] Despite the common perception of a subcontinent wholly united by the British, in fact the Raj had no direct administration and limited influence in nearly one-quarter of the subcontinent's landmass.

the rationale for statehood for most parts of India, the federal scheme came to be called 'linguistically based'. Each State has its own official language; central government business is conducted either in Hindi or in English.[13]

An overwhelming majority of people in their speak one of 15 languages in their respective States. These 15 'state languages' are included on the Eighth Schedule of the Indian Constitution and are the basis of most Indian State boundaries.[14] With the exceptions of Hindi, which is the main language in six States, and Bengali, which is the main language in two, each of the 15 languages is both the main language in a single State and is rarely spoken outside that State.[15]

Language was chosen as a boundary arbiter for several reasons. Although initially critical of language-based States, Nehru used a four-step argument to explain how such States could help people to bridge cultural differences: language is a prerequisite to communication; communication makes interaction possible; broader and deeper interaction leads to greater understanding; greater understanding leads to peace in modern times (Brass 1974). Major language groups were simultaneously given a direct stake in the Indian system and separated from one another. Their stake came in the form of politically legitimized regional subnationalism, but such subnationalisms, by institutional design, cut across religions and social diversity *within* the regions.

[13] The choice of the term 'official language' implied that it was not to be confused with the much wider implication carried by the term 'national' language. An official language in India refers to a designated language approved for official transactions of the State mainly at the administrative levels and for formal political communication. A national language implies a much wider range of communication.

[14] English, Sanskrit, and Sindhi are also included in the Eighth Schedule for political or historical reasons. Beyond the 15 official languages, an additional seven languages are spoken by more than one million people (Breton 1997: 192–6).

[15] *Ex post facto*, 15 looks natural. *Ex ante*, it was not so. The 1951 census reported 845 languages and dialects in India, but the designation of a language or dialect is both subjective and political. The 1961 census mentioned 1,642 'mother tongues' as reported by Indian citizens, but did not clarify the meaning of 'mother tongue'. Citizens sensitive to the political meaning of language enumeration have used the census strategically. During the 1950s and beyond, upper-caste Sikhs pressed for a revision of the Punjab State boundary such that a majority of the population spoke Gurumukhi— rather, they claimed to write it, for script is the main difference between Gurumukhi and Hindi. In response, Hindus and lower-caste Sikhs who were opposed to the proposed State reported in the 1961 census that they spoke Hindi. The central government has also made political choices regarding linguistic categories: in 1981, the Census Bureau arbitrarily decided not to enumerate languages spoken by fewer than 10,000 citizens. The number of languages reported dropped to 106.

A political party in Tamil Nadu, or in Gujarat, or in Karnataka would be hard pressed to come to power in that State without invoking commonly held notions of Tamil, Gujarati, or Kannada cultural pride. But language groups are also separated because claims supporting Tamil heritage, for example, are meaningless outside the State of Tamil Nadu. Hindus, Muslims, Christians, and castes can be found in most States, but not speakers of Tamil, Gujarati, or Kannada. Political power is gained one region—indeed, one legislative seat—at a time. Linguistic federal logic added a hurdle to politicization according to other logics, such as caste or religion.

Language made great sense from a regional perspective, but what about language communities that do not speak the State's official language? Such groups are protected under the Constitution in two ways. First, Arts 29 and 30 guarantee that all children may receive primary education in their mother tongue and that the State government may not discriminate against educational institutions on the basis of the language of instruction. Second, Art. 351 mandates a Special Officer for linguistic minorities who will serve as a watchdog over these communities' social and cultural rights. Despite these cultural protections, great pressure for regional assimilation remains.

From an all-India perspective, too, multiple languages as a basis of State communication seemed problematic to begin with. For greater national cohesion, Art. 351 directs the central government to promote Hindi 'so that it may serve as a medium of expression for all the elements of the composite culture of India', and Art. 343 provides for the English language only for a period of 15 years (Government of India 1994). In practice, however, the challenge of several official languages was not as intense as the challenge of quelling social mobilization that followed attempts to delegitimize regional language groups. To date, the central government has limited its efforts at Hindi evangelism and, every 15 years, Parliament reinstates English as an official language. Basically, a multilingual India has been accepted as a reality, especially after it became clear that the linguistic formation of States led to a decline in language-based violence. Arguably, the choice to demarcate linguistic States also reduced the political relevance of other social categories, thereby reducing other politically motivated social violence as well.

The choice of linguistic identities as a basis for statehood in the federation has had an overwhelmingly positive effect on the ability of Delhi to peacefully mediate many political conflicts, but, as is clear from the description above, the choice was not simply an act of far-sighted statesmanship. Many of India's most violent social mobilizations in the pre- and post-independence periods were organized along linguistic lines. Regional language guarantees, for both education and government service, were implemented only in response to major riots, particularly in the southern States. The first linguistic State, Andhra, was created in 1953 following riots inspired by a 'fast unto death' by a linguistic promoter.[16] Fuel was added to the fire of statehood demands by several current northeastern States in 1966, when Assam declared an 'Assamese only' language policy. In Assam at the time, language and religion overlapped: Hindus overwhelmingly spoke Assamese, Muslims generally spoke Bengali, and the sizeable tribal population spoke a variety of languages. For reasons discussed below, the tribal groups successfully lobbied the central government to redraw State boundaries around themselves, thus limiting both the linguistic and religious influence of Assamese Hindus.

In short, as it finally emerged, the linguistic basis of federalism was a synthesis of principles, pragmatism, and learning through experimentation. Though the Congress Party had agreed in theory that language would be the federal principle as far back as the 1920s, this principle was given concrete institutional and administrative form only following linguistically based social mobilization in the 1940s and 1950s. And the first round of successful linguistic organization generated support for additional linguistic States.

Religion

Though India is a land of multiple religions (Table 15.2), Hindu-Muslim relations dominated the thinking of its founders and constitution-makers. The reasons were historical and political, rooted in the most traumatic period of India's twentieth-century history. In 1947, as the British left, India was partitioned and Pakistan was born as a Muslim homeland in the subcontinent. Partition was accompanied by between 250,000 and a million deaths—no one knows exactly how many. Moreover, anywhere between 12 million and 15 million people migrated across either side of the border. Not all Muslims, however, became citizens of Pakistan. Of the 100 million Muslims in the undivided India of 1947, 65 million acquired the

[16] Andhra was comprised of the Andhra-speaking portion of Madras province. It evolved into Andhra Pradesh in 1956, when the Andhra-speaking portion of neighbouring Hyderabad was added. That portion, known also as Telengana, was the site first of a violent communist secessionist struggle and then of a violent Muslim secessionist one. Linguistic statehood effectively reduced the Telengana problem to a simmering level, where it has remained—unresolved but by and large non-violent.

citizenship of Pakistan. About 35 million Muslims stayed behind, becoming citizens of India, whether because they wished to or because they were too poor to migrate. Numbering 110 million today, constituting 12 per cent of the population, and scattered over most of India,[17] the Muslims are India's largest religious minority.

Table 15.2: *India's religious profile*

Religious group	% of population
Hindus	82.0
of whom	
a) Caste Hindus	67.2
b) Scheduled castes	14.8
Muslims	12.1
Christians	2.3
Sikhs	2.0
Buddhists and Jains	1.2
Others	0.4

Source: Census of India (2001: Table 23). Accessed 22 April 2001.

On religion, India's constitution-makers were faced with four big issues: (1) what the relationship should be between religion and the state; (2) whether religious communities should continue to have 'separate electorates' and reservations in government posts, as they did under the British; (3) whether they should have their religiously given personal laws or a unified body of civil code for marriage, divorce, property inheritance, and so forth; and (4) whether religious minorities should continue to have educational institutions.

Looking at the relationship between religion and nation-building in post-independence India through the prism of the movement for Pakistan in the pre-independence period, the constitution-makers struck a middle ground between what they called the 'divide and rule' policies of the British and a genuine concern for the protection of the religious identity of minorities. Their aim was to give minorities a stake in the new nation, allay their fears of identity loss, and end the communal, Hindu-Muslim, violence that had so rocked India before independence. Constitution-makers saw a response was necessary especially to Muslim anxieties, but they did not want to craft a response that would end up deepening the Hindu-Muslim divide instead of bridging it. This principle led to the following answers to the questions above:

[17] For how the Muslims are geographically spread, see Weiner (1989: Ch. 2).

1. The state would not have an official religion and would allow religious freedom, including freedom to propagate religion,[18] but the state would not be secular in the French-American sense. The state would reserve the right to interfere in religious matters, but it would do so with equidistance. Instead of a radical separation between the state and church, the state would practice neutral involvement, that is, interfering if necessary but not displaying favouritism towards any religion.[19]

2. The British system of separate constituencies for religious communities would be abolished altogether, to be replaced by joint constituencies where all citizens would vote and all could contest for power. The only exception was made with respect to the ex-untouchables and tribes, for whom the Constitution created 'reserved', though not 'separate', constituencies. In these reserved constituencies, all would vote but only the ex-untouchable and tribal people could run for office. Separate constituencies, the constitution-makers argued, were an expression of the divide-and-rule policy. They were the primary reason that, according to them, a separate Pakistan emerged, for in separate constituencies only the Muslims could vote and contest for office. Such constituencies created institutional incentives for Muslim politicians not to appeal to Hindus, created Hindu-Muslim divisions, obstructed the evolution of common and composite nationhood, and led thereby to the frequent Hindu-Muslim riots and the eventual vivisection of the country. Similarly, religiously based quotas in government jobs, another British practice, were also disbanded. These decisions stemmed from the belief that religiously driven politics, called 'communalism' in India, was the biggest enemy of nationalism, or nation-building. All attempts were to be made to undermine electoral incentives for the use of religion in electoral politics and public policy.

3. Religiously prescribed personal laws would be allowed so long as the communities themselves wished to keep them.[20] Such a posture was, however, seen as a second-best policy, the first-best being the evolution of a common civil code for the entire country regardless of religious differences. The first-best ideal was presented as a 'directive principle of state policy' (Art. 44), normatively prescribed for the future but not legally required. The second-best was given the status of a legally enforceable fundamental right.

[18] This principle is enshrined in Art. 25(1) of the Constitution.
[19] The best guide to the constitutional debates over this matter is Smith (1963).
[20] For a fuller discussion, see Verma (1997).

4. Minority educational institutions would survive if religious minorities thought they were necessary for the protection of religious or cultural identity. The state, moreover, would provide financial assistance to such institutions.

The objective of these provisions was both to create a deeper sense of common nationhood and to allay minority fears of a loss of identity. It was also expected that this approach would promote peace and end communal rioting, a big concern after the carnage at the time of India's partition.

Caste

Of all Indian social categories, caste has befuddled the observers most. A brief description of what caste has historically meant would therefore be in order.

Caste, simply put, has been a defining principle of Hindu social order. In its pristine purity going back centuries, the Hindus developed a hierarchy based on birth, and birth also became the basis of professional specialization. Born to a particular caste, a person had little choice but to practise the profession assigned to that caste. The Hindu social order was, thus, an ascriptive division of labour, to which notions of pollution and purity were also added. Some professions—cleaning, working with hides, alcohol-making, and so on—were considered 'polluting' and the castes assigned to them also deemed 'polluting'. Other professions—scholarship, priesthood, business, war-making—were deemed superior and reserved for the higher castes.

The social order was, broadly speaking, tripartite. At the top were the priests and scholars, the *Brahmins*; the warriors, the *Kshatriyas*; and the businessmen, the *Vaishyas*. Peasants, artisans, and servicemen constituted the middle, the *Sudras*.[21] And the third category, the untouchables, stood at the bottom and their jobs, according to tradition, consisted of cleaning all forms of waste, crafts based on hides and other 'polluting' materials, and production of crude forms of alcohol. Each caste, needless to add, had different social and economic rights and privileges: the lower the caste, the fewer the privileges. In addition to the untouchables, the middle castes were also subjected to social condescension and discrimination by the upper castes.

---

[21] Over time, some rich landed castes, initially viewed as peasants, achieved a higher caste status because their landholdings gave them considerable social and political power. They were called 'dominant castes': not ritually high but powerful due to landholdings.

The description of some of these caste categories has changed by now. The term 'upper caste' has more or less always covered the first category: *Brahmins*, *Kshatriyas*, and *Vaishyas*. At independence, untouchability was outlawed, and the third category—the ex-untouchables—came to be known as 'scheduled castes'. There was political consensus among the constitution-makers that the scheduled castes had been victims of centuries of prejudice and discrimination. The middle category was also given a new name after independence: the 'other backward castes' (OBCs). While it was recognized that the OBCs had suffered at the hands of the upper castes, there was no consensus on whether the discrimination practised against them by the upper castes was as vicious and debilitating as that against the scheduled castes.

It was also believed that the OBCs, a large meta-category, had numbers on their side. The upper castes at this point are estimated to be about 16 per cent of India's population, the scheduled castes about 15 per cent, and the OBCs 44 per cent (Table 15.3). The OBCs could clearly use their numbers to influence the distribution of political power in a democracy. Finally, since the case that the OBCs had suffered historically from upper-caster discrimination was ambiguous, it was left to the States to formulate affirmative action programmes for them. The central government did not believe that the rationale for a nationwide affirmative action policy was strong.

The first States to respond to the discretionary provisions were all south Indian. Benefiting from a history of mobilization, the OBCs had already organized themselves in the south prior to independence. As a consequence, they could apply strong pressure on

Table 15.3: *India's caste composition*

Religious group	% of population
Upper castes	16.1
'Other backward castes'	43.7
Scheduled castes	14.9
Scheduled tribes	8.1
Non-Hindu minorities	17.2

Since no caste census has been taken since 1931, these figures can be seen as best guesses, not exact estimates. They are, however, sufficient to show the overall magnitudes. Also, the upper castes in this calculation include the dominant castes that are no longer considered deprived, even though they were ritually not placed in the upper category (see n. 21).

Source: Government of India (1980: 56).

southern State governments. Since the 1960s, close to 50 per cent of State government jobs have been reserved for OBCs in the State of Karnataka; in Tamil Nadu, OBC reservation was 25 per cent to begin with and was increased to over 50 per cent later; in Kerala, the OBC quota has been 40 per cent; and in Andhra Pradesh, 25 per cent.

In the early 1990s, the OBCs were finally added to the *federal* list of beneficiaries of affirmative action as well. Reserved today are 27 per cent of public sector jobs and seats in government-funded institutions of education, a policy initiative the Supreme Court has upheld as consistent with the spirit of the Constitution.[22]

The rise of the caste-based narrative in north Indian politics propelled the change in policy. Political parties based among the lower castes rose to prominence in the 1980s and 1990s. In a pattern roughly similar to what happened in south India between the 1920s and 1960s, the OBCs in north India used their electoral clout to organize themselves horizontally, breaking their vertical dependence on upper castes.[23] Once having achieved electoral weight, they successfully pushed for an enlargement of affirmative action programmes beyond the scheduled castes—and tribes. About 50 per cent of federal jobs and seats in government-funded educational institutions are thus reserved now on the grounds that past discrimination undermines the ability of some castes to compete. Only the remaining half is fully competitive.

Tribe

Scholars and policy-makers have never agreed on a definition of a 'tribal person' or 'tribe', let alone the appropriate relationship between such communities and the Indian state. Most commonly, the 'tribal' category has been conceived as an amalgam of otherness: the tribespeople traditionally do not practice high-tradition Vedic Hinduism, they are not Muslim, not economically or ritually stratified, and not integrated into the 'modern economy or civilization' that surrounds them. Each of these attributes is contested (Beteille 1997). Indeed, in 1991, as many scheduled tribes people reported their religion as Hindu, Muslim, or Christian as reported their traditional religion; and more reported their state's official language

---

[22] For an overview of the issues involved, see Beteille (1992). For a comparison of affirmative action programmes in the US and India, see Weiner (1989: Ch. 6).

[23] For how horizontal and vertical caste mobilizations differ, see Rudolph and Rudolph (1967).

as their mother-tongue as reported their customary language.[24] The Commission for Scheduled Tribes and Scheduled Castes has, on occasion, expressed frustration at the futility of such definitional exercises.

The Commission's basic approach, like that of the central and State governments and the British Raj before them, has been to devise lists rather than definitions. Those communities whose names appear on the schedule of tribes, which varies by State, are scheduled tribes; those whose names do not appear are not. The lists are only occasionally contested and, with the exception of a substantial amendment in 1976, have remained quite stable (Galanter 1984: 135).[25] From a political perspective, once a tribe is placed on the schedule, that tribe's particular social and cultural attributes become politically irrelevant. Scheduled tribespeople are set in competition with one another for concrete governmental resources designated to benefit 'the scheduled tribes' in general.

Some features of the institutional relationships devised for the tribes are worth noting. First, six 'tribal' states, all in north-east India, are drawn around territories that include 'tribal' majority populations.[26] This means simply that a majority of citizens in these states is tribal, but it should be noted that no single tribe comprises the majority in any Indian State.

Second, in some north-eastern States,[27] constitutionally mandated Autonomous District Councils (ADCs) ensure numerically small but geographically concentrated tribal populations a voice in both developmental choices and legal protections. ADCs have limited rights of taxation and legislation as well as rights to judicial and developmental administration. They make their own laws, run

[24] Census of India (1991: Schedule D). A fascinating example is the Rabha tribe, whose population was divided first by a cartographer's pen between Assam and Meghalaya and later by migration to West Bengal. In the 1991 census, those who identified themselves as Rabha tribespeople in Assam, Meghalaya, and West Bengal respectively returned Assamese, Bodo, and Bengali languages as their mother tongues (Singh 1993: 12).

[25] Today, 4,635 tribes are included on the schedule. This number overstates the number of tribal communities because the list is a composite of 25 State lists and several tribes have populations that cross State boundaries *and are recognized* as scheduled tribes in several States (Singh 1994: 4).

[26] Nagaland (1963), Manipur (1972), Meghalaya (1972), Tripura (1972), Mizoram (1987), and Arunachal Pradesh (1987). Language also—differently— unites a majority of the populations in Manipur and Tripura. While Tripura was a tribal-majority State when it was created in 1972, emigration, mainly of Bangladeshi Muslims, has reduced the tribal population to minority status (Census of India 1991: Table SC/ST-1(F)).

[27] Meghalaya, Tripura, Mizoram, Arunachal Pradesh, and Assam.

their own courts, and use money they collect on developmental projects designed by them. ADCs established in 1952 evolved into the present States of Meghalaya, Mizoram, and Arunachal Pradesh; each of these States, as well as Assam and Tripura, contains ADCs within its boundaries today (Stuligross 1999: Ch. 3). The north-east ADC experience has shaped political actions elsewhere in India. In recent years, autonomous areas based on the ADC model have been created for the Nepali portion of West Bengal, the tribal portion of Bihar, and the Buddhist area of Kashmir.[28]

In addition to the federal arrangements for tribes, the Indian Constitution allows for several other means of tribal incorporation. The most important consociational device is the reservation system. Tribespeople comprise 8.1 per cent of India's population; they are guaranteed 8.1 per cent of higher education admissions, 8.1 per cent of government jobs at all levels, and 8.1 per cent of Parliament and State assembly seats. Central positions are guaranteed on a national basis, while State positions are guaranteed in proportion to the tribal population in each State.

The Constitution also mandates three direct institutional linkages of tribes to the State and central governments. The Fifth Schedule of the Constitution mandates a Tribal Advisory Council (TAC) in every State outside north east India. The TAC was designed to advise both the governor and the chief minister regarding tribal and regional developmental issues. Moreover, Article 339 mandates a commission that would regularly report on the welfare and administration of policies affecting the scheduled tribes. Third, Article 164 mandates a State ministry of tribal welfare for Madhya Pradesh, Orissa, and Bihar, the central Indian States with the largest tribal populations.[29]

Thus, the institutional arrangements for the incorporation of India's tribal population into the polity are comprehensive. Where tribespeople comprise a majority of a State's population, parties

[28] These councils are called the Darjeeling Autonomous Area Council, the Jharkhand Autonomous Area Council, and the Ladakh Autonomous Council, respectively. These councils in turn, like their north-eastern predecessors, have provided political legitimacy to previously unrecognized cultural groups and a political forum through which statehood demands can be voiced. In August 2000 the central government redemarked India's state boundaries to create three new states: Jharkhand (formerly southern Bihar), Chhattisgarh (eastern Madhya Pradesh), and Uttaranchal (northwestern Uttar Pradesh). The rest of this section draws heavily from Stuligross (1999: Ch. 5).

[29] All States with more than 3% tribal populations added a tribal component to their administrative structures following the 1967 central government introduction of a 'Tribal Sub-Plan' to the national budget.

that appeal directly to tribal sentiments can and do win election to the State assembly and directly influence their own social and economic development. Where tribes are a minority, they are guaranteed not only limited representation and economic opportunity but also a direct lobbying link to the State government and constitutionally mandated device—the commissioner's reports—with which to press their case. As we shall see below, the plan has been implemented imperfectly.

What Have Been the Consequences?

Language

Linguistic federalism is one of India's great successes in its experiments with multicultural nationalism. Language riots, endemic in India in the 1950s and 1960s, have for all practical purposes disappeared from the political scene after the formation of linguistic States. Regional, linguistically based cultures have gained legitimacy in the Indian state *as regional cultures*. Indeed, they have been thriving and no significant political force favours any longer the imposition of a single language—it used to be Hindi—all over the country.

This has led to pressures for assimilation within States, which have been countered by constitutional and other institutional structures designed to safeguard India's multicultural heritage. It has also inhibited political action on the basis of groups whose populations cross State boundaries. Religion and tribe are the most notable among such prospective political groupings; caste, on the other hand, is at its most meaningful both socially and politically in relatively small territories. Political entrepreneurs have used each of these three categories to mobilize their constituencies, yet they have for the most part had to work within the institutional incentives and constraints inherent in federal states.

Religion

On religion, the results are mixed. Religious minorities have maintained their religious identity in India; minority educational institutions continue to flourish; and their personal laws have not been disturbed by the state.[30] Moreover, especially for the Muslims, no

---

[30] In the famous Shah Bano case in the mid-1980s, the state had an opportunity to intervene in Muslim personal laws. The Supreme Court did intervene, but the executive, after some vacillation, restored the status quo ante. See Verma (1997); Varshney (1993).

separatist political party, paralleling the pre-partition Muslim League, has re-emerged. Most Muslims have voted for multi-religious parties or, in States where Muslim parties have been successful, they have been on the whole moderate and involved in the give and take of democratic politics. This was an important objective of the decision to go for joint constituencies and, conversely, a reason the British-style separate constituencies were abolished.

However, riots have continued to erupt. On the whole, Hindu-Muslim riots may be concentrated only in some cities, but, even though locally concentrated, the overall level of violence has been quite high, especially in the 1980s and 1990s. If ending communal riots was one of the key objectives of abolishing separate electorates for Muslims, that objective of institutional engineering remains unrealized. We return to this theme in the fourth section.

Caste

On caste, too, the record is mixed. Affirmative action was originally envisioned as a temporary measure, necessary only for a decade, perhaps two. It has, however, become deeply embedded in politics and has often been highly contentious. Nearly five decades after the promulgation of the Constitution, affirmative action programmes are not only alive and well but have also been enlarged to include more and more castes.

The success story has to do with the empowerment of lower castes. A substantive objective of affirmative action programmes was to empower the weak by giving them state protection to begin with, while hoping they would come into their own eventually. Remarkable progress towards that goal has been made, though there remains considerable room for the greater empowerment of the ex-untouchables and the lower castes.

How this has happened makes for an interesting story. The indirect effects of affirmative action have been most important. India's affirmative action concerns only government jobs, not the private sector. In 1992, of the nearly 300 million people in the workforce, only 20 million were in the public sector. Affirmative action in the public sector could directly have benefited only a small proportion of the deprived.

How does one assess the impact, direct and indirect, of reservations in government jobs and educational institutions? This question can be split into two parts: (1) affirmative action for the OBCs—in addition to the scheduled castes—which has taken the form of quotas in much of south India since the 1950s; and (2) affirmative action for the *scheduled castes*, implemented all over India since the 1950s, to which the OBCs have been added outside the south only after 1990. Clearly, it is far too early to evaluate the impact of affirmative action for the OBCs beyond southern India. For the scheduled castes, however, our empirical judgements can be national in scope.

No detailed caste-wise breakdown of State bureaucracies in the South is available, but the reason partly is that there is no mystery left about the results. It is widely known that Brahmins simply migrated out of south India as the OBC quotas were instituted. Once access to government jobs, their traditional stronghold, was substantially reduced, some Brahmins went into the private sector, becoming businessmen for the first time, but a large number migrated to Delhi, Bombay, the United Kingdom, and the United States. Indeed, so large was the flight and so capable were the Brahmins of getting jobs that their migration to, and rise in, Bombay led to a serious anti-southern movement in the late 1960s and early 1970s (Katzenstein 1979). By now, bureaucracies of southern states have become remarkably, though not entirely, non-Brahmin.[31] Moreover, though systematic empirical studies have not been undertaken, it is also widely recognized that southern States are governed better than north Indian States like Bihar and Uttar Pradesh. Large-scale affirmative action in bureaucratic recruitment does not appear to have undermined governance in the south. The confidence all of this has given to southern OBCs is demonstrated by the fact that it is possible today for OBC parties to have Brahmin leaders once again, for the lower castes know they have arrived politically and socially.

Let us now turn to the impact of reservations for the scheduled castes. Kanshi Ram, the leading scheduled-caste politician of India today, argues that affirmative action has 'now done enough for the scheduled castes', noting that in the state of Uttar Pradesh, of the 500 officers in the elite Indian Administrative Service, 137 are from the scheduled castes. However, affirmative action, Kanshi Ram adds, is 'useful for a cripple but a positive handicap for someone who wants to run on his own two feet'. The scheduled castes should now focus on winning power through elections, for 'the capture of political power will automatically transform the composition of the bureaucratic elite' (Mendelsohn and Vicziany 1998: 224). Thus, in a new sign of political confidence, he says that it is time now to play the game of democratic politics more equally. His politics are

---

[31] And the faculties of science and engineering in many American universities, as well as software companies, have a lot of south Indian Brahmins!

premised upon the assumption that non-elected institutions do not trump the elected institutions; rather, capturing elected institutions will transform the bureaucracy and police much more fundamentally.

Between independence and the 1980s, the scheduled castes had primarily supported the Congress Party in India. Though the leaders of the Congress Party typically came from the upper castes, they were able to garner scheduled caste support partly because the Congress Party was the first architect of the affirmative action programme and partly because traditional patron-client relationships in villages were on the whole alive and robust.

In 1984, a new political party of the scheduled castes—the Bahujan Samaj Party (BSP)—was launched. Receiving 4.0 per cent, 4.7 per cent, and 4.3 per cent of India's vote in the 1996, 1998, and 1999 national elections respectively, the BSP may not yet be a powerful force in national Parliament but, viewed in terms of share of the national vote, it has become the fourth largest party in India, following the Congress, the BJP, and the Communist Party Marxist (CPM).[32] More importantly, the BSP has developed a substantial political presence in almost all north Indian states. In Uttar Pradesh, India's largest State, the party has been twice in power, though each time briefly and with the support of other parties. By 1996, the BSP had started receiving as much as 20 per cent of the Uttar Pradesh vote, crippling the once-mighty Congress in its citadel of great historic strength. In the 1996, 1998, and 1999 national elections, the Congress polled less than BSP's vote in Uttar Pradesh. Well until the mid-1980s, such scenarios for the Congress in Uttar Pradesh were altogether inconceivable.

How did the BSP break the dependence of the scheduled castes on the Congress? New research shows that the BSP's success was built upon two factors. [33] First, affirmative action for the scheduled castes has led to the emergence of a middle class among them. *The new middle class is almost entirely made up of government officers and clerks.* Despite experiencing upward mobility, these officers have continued to face social discrimination. Endured silently earlier, such discrimination has by now led to a firm resolve to fight for respect and dignity.

[32] However, the number of seats the BSP wins is not as high as some smaller parties, such as the Samajwadi Party and Telegu Desam Party, for its vote is not as geographically concentrated.

[33] The analysis here is based on new research conducted by Kanchan Chandra for her doctoral dissertation at Harvard University. The first publication based on that research is Chandra (2000). The analysis below relies heavily on Chandra's methodologically well-grounded and empirically thorough research.

Second, the scheduled castes within the Congress experienced a 'representational blockage'. Upper caste politicians dominated most district committees of the Congress. Scheduled caste leaders were mere tokens and symbols in the party structure. Since the early 1990s, such meagre rewards of clientelism have been considered largely insufficient by the newly mobile scheduled castes.

The new middle class eventually took over as local BSP leaders. Their strategy was to argue that *humiliation*, rather than economic deprivation, was the main problem of the scheduled castes; and greater political representation, instead of material advantage, was the principal solution. The scheduled castes had to be horizontally mobilized, had to have a party of their own, and win assembly seats. Financed by the new middle class, the BSP took off in much of north India and developed a large group of cadres.

In short, the most telling evidence of the impact of affirmative action on the scheduled castes is *indirect*, not direct. Only a small proportion of the scheduled castes has, and could have, benefited from the quotas in government jobs, given how small the proportion of public sector jobs in India's labour market is. But the small middle class created by affirmative action led to the birth of new community leaders and a new political awakening, both in tandem producing a vibrant and strong political presence of scheduled castes in Indian electoral politics.

Tribe

North-east India, where India's tribes have a big concentration, continues to be a political 'hot spot'. Reports of ethnic violence of every stripe—Hindu-Muslim, Hindu-Tribal, Tribal-Tribal—appear regularly in the newspaper headlines. However, two positive notes must be made about political development in north-east India. First, since the 1947–71 period, the level of violence has subsided tremendously; notable pauses occurred at each stage of statehood formation. Second, violence in the first 25 years of India's independent history was directed toward secession; violence in the second 25 years has been directed toward inclusion. Virtually all groups in the north-east buy into the idea of India; their violent competition is over the terms of incorporation.

In central India, the other region of tribal concentration, the tribal population has failed to receive developmental benefits from linguistic States; or perhaps it only seems to be so because, unlike other groups that have faced representational and developmental challenges within India's federal system, tribal communities are relatively concentrated geographically. Cartographers might have drawn a State boundary around a central Indian region that contained a majority tribal population at the time of Independence; such a State would have been of comparable size to many existing States. This region was instead divided among West Bengal, Bihar, Uttar Pradesh, Madhya Pradesh, and Orissa.[34] Meaningful participation of the central Indian tribal population in Indian governance continues to be elusive, but the scattering of this population among five States has hampered tribal mobilization for either institutional or concrete developmental benefits.[35]

Further, the non-federal aspects of tribal incorporation have been less than fully implemented.[36] Tribal Advisory Councils have failed to aggressively promote tribal issues, for two reasons. First, chief ministers—the elected heads of government at the State level—took advantage of an ambiguity in the Constitution's language to make themselves chairpersons of the TAC in their State. The chief ministers, then, set the agenda of the council. Thus, a council that was designed to be a check on the chief minister's authority has come to reinforce that authority. Second, the council is comprised of elected scheduled tribespeople. Such representation is guaranteed under the tribal reservations system, and, to be sure, tribespeople are elected to national Parliament and State assembly in proportion to their population. Every citizen who lives in a 'scheduled tribe constituency' may vote for his or her preferred candidate, but only members of the scheduled tribes may run for office from that constituency. Thus, several tribespeople are competing for votes and appeals to non-tribal populations often tip the electoral balance. This had led to considerable non-radicalization of tribal leaders.

Other aspects of institutional incorporation of tribespeople into the Indian polity have been incompletely implemented. Employment and education reservations have been severely under-filled and, to the extent that the employment quota is filled, it is filled overwhelmingly at the lowest wage levels. The national Commissioner for Scheduled Castes and Scheduled Tribes produced reports on nearly an annual

[34] Once again, Census politics come into play. Bihar's tribal population reported in the 1941 census was 53%; the proportion in 1951 was 41%. Quoted in Stuligross (1999: 505).

[35] It is hampered also by a strategic dilemma: a demand for a new State requires an argument that the existing State does not—cannot—represent sub-state interests; a demand for greater developmental benefits requires working with that same State. Factionalization along this strategic line weakens the abilities to mobilize of both institutionalists and developmentalists.

[36] The rest of this section draws heavily from David Stuligross (1999), especially Ch. 4, 'Jharkhand I: The Making of a Politicized Region'.

basis from 1957 to 1986, and these reports provided a wealth of statistical and qualitative data that criticized government policies vis-à-vis the tribal population. Since 1986, however, no report has been published. The Commission still exists and reports have been prepared, but a series of short-lived governments over the course of the 1990s has made it possible for the formal presentation of the report to be stalled repeatedly. Finally, tribal ministries are up and running in most States and both central and State governments include 'tribal sub-plans' in their budget calculations. However, a strongly held perception persists that, although the tribal budget is spent in tribal areas, non-tribal populations benefit disproportionately from such expenditures.[37]

In central India, as peaceful, institutionalized political discourse continues to fail to generate developmental benefits, tribal communities sporadically engage in violent political expressions directed against the institutions that were designed, but failed, to serve them. Violence against bureaucratic headquarters, police stations, railways, and transportation infrastructure is a means of expressing their demand for genuine political inclusion. In parts of Bihar, Orissa, and Madhya Pradesh, the concrete demand is for redrawing State boundaries in a way that will ensure a greater proportion of tribal representatives.

On the other hand, many individual tribespeople are forsaking their tribal identities in favour of alternative identity markers; a majority now report their State language as their mother tongue, substantial minorities have converted to another religion, generally either Hinduism or Christianity. Indeed, much of the 'tribal' violence of recent years has been perpetrated by 'traditional' tribal communities against those who, for developmental or other reasons, have rejected aspects of their tribal past. Similarly, much 'anti-Christian' violence has been perpetrated against recent tribal converts to Christianity by other tribals who have also converted—to Hinduism.

In short, institutional designs for India's tribes, though comprehensive and wide-ranging, have not been entirely successful. The extent to which institutional objectives have been realized has depended, in significant part, on the quality of tribal political mobilization. Yet we must keep in mind that the institutions themselves

---

[37] The perception came through clearly through extensive interviews in tribal regions of Bihar, Orissa, and Madhya Pradesh in 1996. Hard data is much more difficult to come by. The only study to address the issue, conducted in 1984, strongly supported the continuing perception. See Singh and Singh (1984).

were compromises among proponents of three competing national narratives. A 'failure' to retain a politically autonomous tribal culture and psyche—to the extent that such ever existed—is simultaneously a 'success' at generating institutional incentives toward assimilation and national cohesion.

Institutional Designs in Perspective

That political institutions and public policies matter is beyond doubt. But can they explain the outcomes we observe? Let us show how other factors intervene by concentrating on Hindu-Muslim riots. We will argue that the whole panoply of institutional interventions—joint constituencies, separate personal laws, Muslim educational institutions—has failed to achieve an important objective, namely, stemming communal violence by encouraging greater integration. As argued at length elsewhere, the rhythms and concentrations of Hindu-Muslim riots have depended on civic, not institutional, factors.[38] Moreover, the relationship between civil society and political institutions is on the whole indeterminate.

By 'civil society', we refer to that space which (1) exists between the family on the one hand and the state on the other, (2) makes interconnections between individuals or families possible, and (3) is independent of the state. Business associations, professional organizations, reading clubs, film clubs, sports clubs, festival organizations, NGOs, trade unions, and cadre-based political parties are some of the examples of civil society organizations. Unlike institutional designs—electoral rules, personal laws, and public policies— that tend to be national or at the very least State-based in their coverage, civic factors tend to have locally varying texture and intensity. In specific cities and towns, Hindus and Muslims may be integrated in civic life, but that may not be true of the entire state or the nation. Where they are integrated, riots do not on the whole take place; where they are not, riots erupt.

Generally speaking—and this is true beyond India—communal or ethnic violence tends to be locally concentrated. Short of nation-wide civil wars, it tends not to be evenly spread across a country. Pockets of violence and stretches of peace often coexist.

Consider the patterns of Hindu-Muslim violence in India. First, the share of villages in communal rioting has been remarkably small. During 1950–95, rural India accounted for a mere 3.6 per cent of

---

[38] This entire section is based on Ashutosh Varshney (2000).

the country's deaths in communal violence. Hindu-Muslim violence is, primarily, an urban phenomenon. Second, within urban India, Hindu-Muslim riots are highly locally concentrated. Eight cities account for a hugely disproportionate share of communal violence in the country: a little over half of all urban deaths, and 49 per cent of all deaths, in Hindu-Muslim violence. As a group, however, they represent a mere 18 per cent of India's urban population and about 5 per cent of the country's total population, both urban and rural. Eighty-two per cent of urban population has not been 'riot-prone'.

Thus, *India's Hindu-Muslim violence is city-specific, not State-specific. State—and national—politics or institutions provide the context within which the local mechanisms linked with violence get activated.* To understand the causes of communal violence, we must investigate these local mechanisms.

Civic linkages across communities constitute these mechanisms. The key lies in realizing that such links tend to differ locally or regionally. Electoral institutions—joint constituencies, first past the post—or public policies with respect to Muslims—personal laws, minority educational institutions—do not differ locally. Such institutions or policies thus cannot explain the patterns of peace and violence. National factors are, by definition, constant across local settings. To explain variation with what is constant would be methodologically fallacious. National-level factors may provide a *context* for the violence, but unless they are joined with local variables they cannot constitute the *cause* of locally concentrated violence.

Of course, one should not overstate the importance of civic links and dismiss the existing institutional arguments as entirely irrelevant. The level of analysis is a key issue here. Because political or electoral institutions are typically system-wide—an entire polity is either federal or unitary, consociational or liberal, parliamentary or presidential—institutional factors can explain why violence in a given country on the whole goes up or down once the new institutions are introduced, or older ones abrogated. If the comparison is at a *national* level, such system-wide institutions can be a helpful tool in our understanding.

Reconsider an example already given. Despite early anxieties, a linguistic reorganization of Indian federalism in the 1950s and 1960s significantly reduced the level of violence between linguistic groups in India (Weiner 1989). Each linguistic group got a State of its own in the federal polity, which in turn diminished the anxieties and fears of most language groups. Compared with the political passion and rioting associated with it in the 1950s and 1960s, language has by now become a minor issue in Indian politics.

In contrast, triggered by language issues, Tamil-Sinhalese relations in Sri Lanka moved from bad to worse after the late 1950s (for a brief overview, see Daniel 1997: Ch. 2). It is suggested that, unlike India, the absence of federalism made Sri Lankan conflict more and increasingly violent.[39] Much of the Tamil minority is concentrated in the northern part of the country and could therefore have found a limited measure of self-governance, provided by federalism, a moderating force. However, the political elite of the Sinhalese majority continued to insist on a unitary political system, offering federalism far too late as a solution to the political aspirations of the Tamil minority.

In other words, when we compare national-level aggregation of ethnic violence in India and Sri Lanka,[40] a hypothesis based on the effects of a federal versus unitary polity is likely to go very far. But if we were to move from national-level variation in violence to one *within* a nation, an explanation that invoked system-wide institutional factors would be quite inadequate. Such a hypothesis would not be able to explain, for example, why ethnic riots in Sri Lanka were concentrated repeatedly in some parts of the island, when they did erupt. To explain the latter, we have to rely on factors that vary locally or regionally.

Being highly local in its intensity and texture, civil society begins to explain how connections between groups provide a city, town, or region with, as it were, an immune system that can take exogenous shocks—or 'viruses'—emerging from outside. Conversely, the absence of such links makes a city or town highly vulnerable to such shocks. Local-level factors can not be read off the system-wide institutions. They have a life of their own, and may, depending on what is at issue, be more decisive.

If civic factors were not so spatially differentiated and were also constant through time, they would play roughly the same role as system-wide political institutions. That is why in societies where civic organizations are repressed by the state and no autonomous public space for human organization and deliberation exists, almost the entire society can go up in flames when the state begins to weaken. Alternatively, the entire society may look very peaceful when the state is strong. A totalitarian polity, opposed to autonomous non-state spaces, is thus typically a clay-footed colossus, as so many states of the former Soviet bloc discovered after the

[39] Tamil activists in Sri Lanka have often made this argument.
[40] This is not to say that language was the only issue in Tamil-Sinhalese conflict, only that it was very important and could have been handled through federalism.

late 1980s. Civil society, if present and especially if vibrant, can provide self-regulating mechanisms, even when the state runs into a crisis.

India's repeated encounters with ethnic violence of all kinds— religious, linguistic, caste—and its equally frequent return from the brink have a great deal to do with the self-regulation that its largely integrated and cross-cutting civil society provides. Local structures of resistance and recuperation, as well as local knowledge about how to fix ethnic relations, have ensured that even the worst moments—1947–8 and 1992–3—do not degenerate into an all-out collapse of the country into ethnic warfare. A Rwanda, a Burundi, a Yugoslavia are not possible in India unless the state, for an exogenous reason such as a long-protracted war, kills all autonomous spaces of citizen activity and organization.

To conclude, constitutional or policy engineering undoubtedly has partial validity in explaining outcomes of peace and violence in India, but a large part of the explanation for what we observe has to come from the character and pattern of civil society, which tends to be locally or regionally differentiated, whereas institutional or policy factors have been common across States or the whole nation.

References

Adamolekun, Ladipo and Kincaid, John (1991). 'The Federal Solution: Assessment and Prognosis for Nigeria and Africa'. *Publius: The Journal of Federalism*, 21/4: 178–88.

Adeniyi, Olusegun (1999). 'The Plot to Hijack PDP'. *This Day*. Lagos. 11 July: 16.

Adeniyi, Abiodun (1999). 'Long Nights of Politics of Appointments.' *The Guardian*. Lagos. 4 July: 8.

Agranoff, Robert (1994). 'Asymmetrical and Symmetrical federalism in Spain: An Examination of Intergovernmental Policy', in Bertus de Villiers (ed.), *Evaluating Federal Systems*. Cape Town: Juta.

Albaugh, Ericka A. (1999). 'Electoral Change in West Africa' (unpublished manuscript). Durham, NC: Duke University.

Altman-Olin, David (1999). 'The Politics of Coalition Formation and Survival in Multiparty Presidential Democracies: The Case of Uruguay (1989–1999)' (unpublished manuscript). Notre Dame: Department of Government, University of Notre Dame.

Alvarez, Mike, Cheibub, José Antonio, Limongi, Fernando, and Przeworski, Adam (1996). 'Classifying Political Regimes'. *Studies in Comparative International Development*, 31/2: 3–36

AM News (1996). Lagos: 7 January.

Amorin Neto, Octavio (1998). 'Of Presidents, Parties and Ministers: Cabinet Formation and Legislative Decision-Making Under Separation of Powers' (Ph.D. thesis). San Diego: Department of Political Science, University of California.

——and Cox, Gary W. (1997) 'Electoral Institutions, Cleavage Structures and the Number of Parties'. *American Journal of Political Science*, 41: 149–74.

Anderson, Benedict (1996). *Imagined Communities: Reflections on the Origin and Spread of Nationalism*. London: Verso.

Anderson, Christopher J. and Guillory, Christine A. (1997). 'Political Institutions and Satisfaction With Democracy'. *American Political Science Review*, 91: 66–81.

Anderson, John (1990). *Cognitive Psychology and Its Implications* (3rd edn). New York: W. H. Freeman.

Anderson, Jon (1999). *Kyrgyzstan: Central Asia's Island of Democracy?* Amsterdam: Harwood Academic Publishers.

Asia Watch (1991). 'East Timor: The November 12 Massacre and its Aftermath'. *Indonesia Issues*, 17–18: December.

Austin, Granville (1972). *The Indian Constitution: Cornerstone of a Nation*. Bombay: Oxford University Press.

Babangida, Ibrahim (1989). *Portrait of a New Nigeria: Selected Speeches of Ibrahim Badamosi Babangida*. Marlow: Precision Press.

Bach, Daniel (1997). 'Indigeneity, Ethnicity and Federalism', in Larry Diamond, Anthony Kirk-Greene, and Oye Oyediran (eds), *Transition Without End: Nigerian Politics and Civil Society Under Babangida*. Boulder, CO: Lynne Rienner.

Banducci, Susan A, Todd, Donovan, and Karp, Jeffrey A. (1999). 'Proportional Representation and Attitudes about Politics: Results from New Zealand.' *Electoral Studies*, 18: 533–55.

Banks, Arthur S. (1993). *Cross-National Time-Series Data Archive* (magnetic tape). Binghamton, NY: Center for Social Analysis, State University of New York.

——, Day, Alan J., and Muller, Thomas C. (eds). *Political Handbook of the World, 1997*. Binghamton, NY: CSA Publications.

Banlaoi, Rommel C. and Carlos, Clarita R. (1996). *Political Parties in the Philippines: From 1900 to the Present*. Makati City, Philippines: Konrad Adenauer Foundation.

Barkan, Joel (1998). 'Rethinking the Applicability of Proportional Representation for Africa', in Timothy D. Sisk and Andrew Reynolds (eds), *Electoral Systems and Conflict Management in Africa*. Washington, DC: US Institute of Peace Press.

Barkey, Karen (1994). *Bandits and Bureaucrats the Ottoman Route to State Centralization*. Ithaca, NY: Cornell University Press.

—— and von Hagen, Mark (1997). *After Empire: Multiethnic Societies and Nation-Building—The Soviet Union and Russian, Ottoman, and Habsburg Empires*. Boulder, CO: Westview Press.

Ross Barnet, Marguerite (1967). *The Politics of Cultural Nationalism in South India* Princeton, NJ: Princeton University Press.

Barry, Brian (1975a). 'Political Accommodation and Consociational Democracy'. *British Journal of Political Science*, 5: 477–505.

—— (1975b). 'The Consociational Model and Its Dangers'. *European Journal of Political Research*, 3: 393–412.

Bartolini, Stephano and Mair, Peter (1990). *Identity, Competition and Electoral Availability*. Cambridge: Cambridge University Press.

Bean, Clive (1997). 'Australia's Experience with the Alternative Vote'. *Representation*, 34/2: 103–10.

——, Bennett, Scott, Simms, Marian, and Warhurst, John (eds) (1997). *The Politics of Retribution: The 1996 Australian Federal Election*. Sydney: Allen and Unwin.

Bednar, Jenna. (1998). 'An Institutional Theory of Federal Stability'. Paper presented at the annual meeting of the American Political Science Association. Boston, MA: 3–6 September.

—— (1999). 'Federalism: Unstable by Design'. Paper presented at the annual meeting of the American Political Science Association. Atlanta, GA: August.

Beteille, André (1992). *The Backward Classes in Contemporary India.* Delhi: Oxford University Press.

—— (1997). 'The Concept of Tribe with Special Reference to India', in André Beteille (ed.), *Society and Politics in India: Essays in a Comparative Perspective.* Delhi: Oxford University Press.

Billig, Michael (1995). *Banal Nationalism.* London: Sage.

Birch, Sarah. (1997). 'Ukraine: The Perils of Majoritarianism in a New Democracy', in Andrew Reynolds and Ben Reilly (eds), *The International IDEA Handbook of Electoral System Design.* Stockholm: International Institute for Democracy and Electoral Assistance.

—— (1998). 'Electoral Reform in Ukraine: The 1988 Parliamentary Elections'. *Representation*, 35/2/3: 146–54.

—— and Wilson, Andrew (1999). 'The Ukrainian Parliamentary Elections of 1998'. *Electoral Studies*, 18: 276–82.

Blais, André and Carty, Ken (1990). 'Does Proportional Representation Foster Voting Turnout?'. *European Journal of Political Research*, 18: 167–81.

Blaustein, Albert P. and Flanz, Gisbert H. (eds) (1971). *Constitutions of the Countries of the World.* Dobbs Ferry, NY: Oceana.

Bogaards, Matthijs (2000). 'The Uneasy Relationship Between Empirical and Normative Types in Consociational Theory'. *Journal of Theoretical Politics*, 12: 395–423.

Bogdanor, Vernon and Butler, David (eds) (1983). *Democracy and Elections.* Cambridge: Cambridge University Press.

Borisova, Y. (1999). 'Court Rules Against Secret Budget'. *Moscow Times*, 11 November.

Bose, Sumantra (1999). 'Kashmir: Sources of Conflict, Dimensions of Peace'. *Survival*, 41/3:149–71.

Boston, Jonathan, Levine, Stephen, McLeay, Elizabeth, and Roberts, Nigel S. (1996). *New Zealand Under MMP: A New Politics?* Auckland: Auckland University Press.

Brams, Steven J. (1990). *Negotiation Games: Applying Game Theory to Bargaining and Negotiation.* New York: Routledge.

—— and Taylor, Alan D. (1996). *Fair Division: From Cake-Cutting to Dispute Resolution.* Cambridge: Cambridge University Press.

Brass, Paul (1974). *Language, Religion, and Politics in North India.* London: Cambridge University Press.

Bratton, Michael, and Van de Walle, Nicolas (1996). *Political Regimes and Regime Transitions in Africa: A Comparative Handbook* East Lansing: Department of Political Science, Michigan State University.

Breton, Roland (1997). *Atlas of the Languages and Ethnic Communities in South Asia.* New Delhi: Sage Publications.

Brown, J. (1994). *Hopes and Shadows: Eastern Europe After Communism.* Durham, NC: Duke University Press.

Brown, Michael, Cote, Owen, Lynn-Jones, Sean M., and Miller, Steven E. (1997). *Nationalism and Ethnic Conflict.* Cambridge, MA: The MIT Press.

Brown-John, Lloyd (1994). 'Asymmetrical Federalism: Keeping Canada Together?', in Bertus de Villiers (ed.), *Evaluating Federal Systems*. Cape Town: Juta.

Boase, Joan Price (1994). 'Faces of Asymmetry: German and Canadian Federalism', in Bertus de Villiers (ed.), *Evaluating Federal Systems*. Cape Town: Juta.

Buchanan, James (1995). 'Federalism as an Ideal Political Order and an Objective for Constitutional Reform,' *Publius: The Journal of Federalism*, 25/2: 19–27.

Budge, Ian, Newton, Kenneth, McKinley, R. D., and Kirchner, Emil. (1997). *The Politics of the New Europe*. London: Longmans.

Bullain, Inigo (1998). 'Autonomy and the European Union', in Markku Suksi (ed.), *Autonomy: Applications and Implications*. The Hague: Kluwer.

Bulmer, Martin (1986). 'Race and Ethnicity', in Robert G. Burgess (ed.), *Key Variables in Social Investigation*. London: Routledge and Kegan Paul.

Carey, John M. (1997). 'Institutional Design and Party Systems', in Larry Diamond, M. F. Platter, Y.-H. Chu, and H.-M. Tien (eds), *Consolidating the Third Wave Democracies: Themes and Perspectives*. Baltimore, MD: The Johns Hopkins University Press.

——, Amorin Neto, Octavio, and Shugart, Matthew S. (1997). 'Appendix: Outlines of Constitutional Powers in Latin America', in Scott Mainwaring and Matthew S. Shugart (eds), *Presidentialism and Democracy in Latin America*. Cambridge: Cambridge University Press.

Carlos, Clarita R., and Banlaoi, Rommel C. (1996). *Elections in the Philippines: From Pre-Colonial Period to the Present*. Makati City: Konrad Adenauer Foundation.

Carvalho, Jose M. (1982). 'Political Elites and Statebuilding: The Case of Nineteenth Century Brazil'. *Comparative Studies in Society and History*, 24: 378–99.

Census of India (1991). http://www.censusindia.net/cendat
—— (2001). http://www.censusindia.net/

Chandra, Kanchan (2000). 'The Transformation of Ethnic Politics in India: The Decline of Congress and the Rise of the Bahujan Samaj Party in Hoshiarpur'. *Journal of Asian Studies*, 59/1: 26–61.

Cheibub, José Antonio (1998). 'Elections and Alternation in Power in Democratic Regimes'. Paper prepared for delivery at the 1998 annual meeting of the American Political Science association, Boston, MA, 3–6 September.

—— (1999). *Divided Government, Deadlock, and the Survival of Presidents and Presidential Regimes*. Princeton: Political Economy Workshop, Princeton University.

—— and Przeworski, Adam (1999). 'Democracy, Elections, and Accountability for Economic Outcomes', in Adam Przeworski, S. Stokes, and B. Manin (eds), *Democracy and Accountability*. Cambridge: Cambridge University Press.

Choe, Yonhyok (1997). *How to Manage Free and Fair Elections: A Comparison of Korea, Sweden and the United Kingdom*. Göteburg: Göteburg University.

Constitution of Ireland (1937). Dublin: Government Stationery Office (as amended.

Constitution of the Federal Republic of Nigeria (Promulgation) Decree No. 12 of May 1989 (1989). *Supplement of the Official Gazette of the Federal Republic of Nigeria*, 76/29: A61–214.

Constitutional Commission of Eritrea (1995). *Information on Strategy, Plan and Activities*. Asmara: Constitutional Commission of Eritrea.

Conversi, Daniele (2000). 'Autonomous Communities and the Ethnic Settlement in Spain', in Yash Ghai (ed.), *Autonomy and Ethnicity: Negotiating Claims in Multi-ethnic States*. Cambridge: Cambridge University Press.

Copland, Ian (1997). *The Princes of India in the Endgame of Empire, 1917–1947*. Cambridge and New York: Cambridge University Press.

Cox, Gary W. (1997). *Making Votes Count: Strategic Coordination in the World's Electoral Systems*. Cambridge: Cambridge University Press.

Cribb, Robert (ed.) (1990). *The Indonesian Killings of 1965–1966: Studies from Java and Bali*. Melbourne: Centre of Southeast Asian Studies, Monash University.

—— and Brown, Colin (1995). *Modern Indonesia: A History Since 1945*. London and New York: Longman.

Dahl, Robert A. (1971). *Polyarchy*. New Haven: Yale University Press.

Daniel, E. Valentine (1997). *Charred Lullabies*. Princeton, NJ: Princeton University Press.

Das Gupta, Jyotirindra (1988). 'Ethnicity, Democracy and Development in India: Assam in a General Perspective', in Atul Kohli (ed.), *India's Democracy*. Princeton, NJ: Princeton University Press.

Dawisha, Karen and Parrott, Bruce (1997). *The End of Empire? The Transformation of the USSR in Comparative Perspective: The International Politics of Eurasia*. Armonk, NY: M. E. Sharpe.

de Silva, K. M. (1998). 'Electoral Systems', in Crawford Young (ed.), *Ethnic Diversity and Public Policy*. Basingstoke: Macmillan.

de Smith, Stanley (1964). *The New Commonwealth and Its Constitutions*. London: Stevens.

Dehesa, Grace Ivana (1997). 'Goviernos de Coalici n en el Sistema Presidencial: America del Sur' (Ph.D. thesis). Florence, European University Institute.

Deletant, Dennis and Saini-Davies, Peter (1998). 'The Romanian Elections of November 1996'. *Representation*, 35/2/3: 155–67.

Department of Information, Republic of Indonesia (n.d.). *The 1945 Constitution of the Republic of Indonesia*. Jakarta: Department of Information, Republic of Indonesia.

Diamond, Larry (1987). 'Issues in the Constitutional Design of a Third Nigerian Republic'. *African Affairs*, 86: 343. 209–26.

Diamond, Larry (1988). *Class, Ethnicity and Democracy in Nigeria: The Failure of the First Republic*. London: Macmillan.

Diamond, Larry (1996). 'Is the Third Wave Over?'. *Journal of Democracy*, 7: 20–37.

——(2000). *Developing Democracy Toward Consolidation*. Baltimore, MD: The Johns Hopkins University Press.

——and Plattner, Marc (1994). 'Introduction', in Larry Diamond and Marc Plattner (eds), *Nationalism, Ethnic Conflict and Democracy*. Baltimore, MD: The Johns Hopkins University Press.

——— and Schedler, Andreas, 'Introduction', in A. Schedler, L. Diamond, and M. Plattner (eds), *The Self-Restraining State: Power and Accountability in New Democracies*. Boulder, CO: Lynne Rienner.

Dixon, Paul (1997). 'Consociationalism and the Northern Ireland Peace Process: The Glass Half Full or Half Empty?'. *Nationalism and Ethnic Politics*, 3/3: 20–36.

Douglas, Amy (1993). *Real Choices, New Voices: The Case for PR Elections in the United States*. New York: Columbia University Press.

Dudley, Billy (1982). *An Introduction to Nigerian Government and Politics*. London: Macmillan.

Duverger, Maurice (1954/1964). Political Parties: Their Organization and Activity in the Modern State. New York: Wiley.

——(1980). 'A New Political System Model: Semi-Presidential Government'. *European Journal of Political Research*, 8: 165–87.

EBRD (European Bank for Reconstruction and Development) (1999). *Transition Report 1999*. London: EBRD.

Eckstein, Harry (1966). *Division and Cohesion in Democracy: A Study of Norway*. Princeton, NJ: Princeton University Press.

——(1998). 'Congruence Theory Explained', in Harry Eckstein, Frederic J. Fleron, Erik P. Hoffmann, and William M. Reisinger (eds), *Can Democracy Take Root in Post-Soviet Russia?* Lanham, MD: Rowman and Littlefield.

Edelman, Martin (1994). *Courts, Politics and Culture in Israel*. Charlottesville: University of Virginia.

Eesti (1992). *Eesti Vabariigi põhiseadus* [The Constitution of the Republic of Estonia]. Tallinn: Olion and Eesti Entsüklopeediakirjastus.

Eide, Asbjorn (1998). 'Cultural Autonomy: Concept, Content, History and Role in the World Order', in Markku Suski (ed.), *Autonomy: Applications and Implications*. The Hague: Kluwer.

Ekeh, Peter (ed.) (1997). *Wilberforce Conference on Nigerian Federalism*. Buffalo: Association of Nigerian Scholars for Dialogue.

Ekpu, Ray (1999). 'For Love of Title'. *Newswatch*. Lagos. 26 July: 6.

Elazar, Daniel (1987). *Exploring Federalism*. Tuscaloosa: University of Alabama Press.

Elster, Jon (1989). *The Cement of Society: A Study of Social Order*. Cambridge and New York: Cambridge University Press.

——(1998). 'A Plea for Mechanisms', in Peter Hedström and Richard Swedberg (eds), *Social Mechanisms: An Analytical Approach to Social Theory*. New York: Cambridge University Press.

——, Offe, Claus, and Preuss, Ulrike (1998). *Institutional Design in the Post-Communist World: Building Ships at Sea*. New York: Cambridge University Press.

Evans, Geoffrey and Norris, Pippa (eds) (1999). *Critical Elections: British Parties and Voters in Long-term Perspective*. London: Sage.

—— and O'Leary, Brendan (1997*a*). 'Frameworked Futures: Intransigence and Flexibility in the Northern Ireland Elections of May 30 1996'. *Irish Political Studies*, 12: 23–47.

—— —— (1997*b*). 'Intransigence and Flexibility on the Way to Two Forums: The Northern Ireland Elections of 30 May 1996 and Public Opinion'. *Representation*, 34/3–4: 208–18.

—— —— (2000). 'Northern Irish Voters and the British-Irish: Foundations of a Stable Consociational Settlement?' *Political Quarterly*, 71/1: 78–101.

Farrand, Max (1913). *The Framing of the Constitution of the United States*. New Haven: Yale University Press.

Farrell, David (1997). *Comparing Electoral Systems*. London: Prentice Hall/Harvester Wheatsheaf.

FCRC (Fiji Constitution Review Commission, 'Reeves Commission') (1996). *Towards A United Future: Report of the Fiji Constitution Review Commission* (Parliamentary Paper 13). Suva: FCRC.

Federal Office of Statistics (1996). *Socio-economic Profile of Nigeria*. Lagos: Federal Office of Statistics.

Federal Republic of Nigeria (1976). *Report of the Constitution Drafting Committee, Volumes 1 and 2*. Lagos: Federal Ministry of Information.

—— (1987). *Report of the Political Bureau*. Lagos: Federal Government Printer.

—— (1995). *Report of the Constitutional Conference, Volumes 1 and 2*. Abuja: National Assembly Press.

—— (1999). *Constitution of the Federal Republic of Nigeria 1999*. Lagos: Federal Government Press.

Feith, Herbert (1962). *The Decline of Constitutional Democracy in Indonesia*. Ithaca, NY: Cornell University Press.

—— (1963). 'The Dynamics of Guided Democracy', in Ruth T. McVey (ed.), *Indonesia*. New Haven: HRAF Press.

Fentress, J. and Wickham, C. (1992). *Social Memory*. Oxford: Blackwell.

Figueiredo, Argelina and Limongi, Fernando (2000). 'Presidential Power, Legislative Organization, and Party Behavior in the Legislature'. *Comparative Politics*, 32/2: 151–70.

Figueiredo, Rui de, and Weingast, Barry R. (1997). 'Self-Enforcing Federalism: Solving the Two Fundamental Dilemmas'. Manuscript.

Fiji Parliamentary Paper 24/1975

Fiji Parliamentary Paper 17/1997.

Filippov, Mikhail and Shvetsova, Olga (1999). 'Asymmetric Bilateral Bargaining in the New Russian Federation: A Path-dependence Explanation'. *Communist and Post-Communist Studies*, 32: 61–76.

Filippov, Mikhail, Ordeshook, Peter, and Shvetsova, Olga (1999). 'Party Fragmentation and Presidential Elections in Post-Communist Democracies'. *Constitutional Political Economy*, 10: 3–26.

FitzGerald, Garret (2000). 'Watering Down of Patten Unnecessary'. *Irish Times*, 12 August.

Flemming, John and Micklewright, John (1999). *Income Distribution, Economic Systems, and Transition* (Innocenti Occasional Papers, Economic and Social Policy Series #70). Florence: UNICEF.

Foweraker, Joe (1998). 'Review Article: Institutional Design, Party Systems and Governability—Differentiating the Presidential Regimes of Latin America'. *British Journal of Political Science*, 28: 651–77.

Frankel, Jon (2000). 'The Triumph of the Non-Idealist Intellectuals? An Investigation of Fiji's 1999 Election Results' (unpublished manuscript).

—— (2001). 'The Alternative Vote System in Fiji: Electoral Engineering or Ballot-Rigging?' *Journal of Commonwealth and Comparative Politics* 39(2): 1–31.

Freedom House (1998). *Freedom in the World 1996–1997*. New York: Freedom House.

Frye, Timothy (1997). 'A Politics of Institutional Choice: Post-Communist Presidencies'. *Comparative Political Studies*, 30/5: 523–52.

—— (1999). 'Cashing In: The Dynamics of Presidential Power in the Post-Communist World'. Manuscript. Columbus: Ohio State University.

—— and Commander, Simon (1999). 'The Politics of Economic Reform'. *Transition Report, 1999*. London: EBRD

——, Hellman, Joel, and Tucker, Joshua (2000). 'Data Base on Political Institutions in the Post-Communist World' (unpublished). Ohio State University, The World Bank, and Princeton University.

Galanter, Marc (1984). *Competing Equalities: Law and the Backward Classes in India*. Delhi: Oxford University Press.

Gallagher, Michael (1987). 'Does Ireland Need a New Electoral System?' *Irish Political Studies*, 2: 27–48.

Ganev, Venelin I. (1997). 'Bulgaria's Symphony of Hope'. *Journal of Democracy*, 8/4: 125–39.

Gasiorowski, Mark and Power, Timothy J. (1998). 'The Structural Determinants of Democratic Consolidation'. *Comparative Political Studies*, 31/6: 740–70.

Geddes, Barbara (1995). 'A Comparative Perspective on the Leninist Legacy in Eastern Europe'. *Comparative Political Studies*, 28/2: 239–74.

Gellner, Ernest (1983). *Nations and Nationalism*. Oxford: Blackwell.

Ghai, Yash. (1997). 'The Recommendations on the Electoral System: The Contribution of the Fiji Constitution Review', in Brij V. Lal and Peter Larmour (eds), *Electoral Systems in Ethnically Divided Societies: The Fiji Constitution Review*. Canberra: National Centre for Development Studies, The Australian National University.

—— (2000a). 'Universalism and Relativism: Human Rights as a Framework for Negotiating Interethnic Claims'. *Cardozo Law Review*, 21/4: 1095–140.

—— (2000*b*). 'The Implementation of the Fiji Islands Constitution', in A Haroon Akram-Lodhi (ed.), *Confronting Fiji Futures*. Canberra: Asia Pacific Press.

—— (2000*c*). 'Ethnicity and Autonomy: A Framework for Analysis', in Yash Ghai (ed.), *Autonomy and Ethnicity: Negotiating Claims in Multi-ethnic States*. Cambridge: Cambridge University Press.

—— (2000*d*). 'Autonomy Regimes in China: Coping with Ethnic and Economic Diversity', in Yash Ghai (ed.), *Autonomy and Ethnicity: Negotiating Claims in Multi-ethnic States*. Cambridge: Cambridge University Press.

—— (2001). *Minorities and the Right to Political Participation*. London: Minority Rights Group.

—— and McAuslan, Patrick (1970). *Public Law and Political Change in Kenya*. Nairobi: Oxford University Press.

—— and Regan, Anthony (1992). *The Law, Politics and Administration of Decentralisation in Papua New Guinea*. Waigani: The National Research Institute.

Given, James B. (1990). *State and Society in Medieval Europe: Gwynedd and Languedoc Under Outside Rule*. Ithaca, NY: Cornell University Press.

Glazer, Nathan (1977). 'Federalism and Ethnicity: The Experience of the United States', *Publius: The Journal of Federalism* 7/4.

Glezer, Olga (1992). 'Russian Republic: No Longer Soviet Socialist Federative'. *Moscow News*, 7 (12 February).

Golwalkar, M. S. (1939). *We or Our Nationhood Defined*. Nagpur: Bharat Publications.

Government of India (1980). *Report of the Backward Classes Commission* (The Mandal Commission Report), First Part, Vol. 1. Delhi: Government of India.

—— (1994). *Constitution of India* (13th edn). Lucknow: Eastern Book Company.

Government of the United Kingdom (n.d., 1998). *The Agreement: Agreement Reached in the Multi-Party Negotiations*.

Grofman, Bernard (1997). 'SNTV, STV, and Single-Member District Systems: Theoretical Comparisons and Contrasts', in Bernard Grofman, Sung-Chull Lee, Edwin A. Winckler, and Brian Woodall (eds), *Elections in Japan, Korea and Taiwan under the Single Non-Transferable Vote: The Comparative Study of an Embedded Institution*. Ann Arbor: University of Michigan Press.

—— and Davidson, Chandler (eds) (1992). *Controversies in Minority Voting*. Washington, DC: Brookings Institution.

—— and Lijphart, Arend (eds) (1986). *Electoral Laws and their Political Consequences*. New York: Agathon Press.

——, Mikkel, Evald, and Taagepera, Rein (1999). 'Electoral Systems Change in Estonia, 1989–1993'. *Journal of Baltic Studies*, 30: 227–49.

Guardian (1999*a*). Lagos. 1 May: 48.

—— (1999*b*). Lagos. 20 May: 15.

—— (1999*c*). Lagos. 2 July: 7.

Guelke, Adrian (1999). 'Deeply Divided Societies and Their Shared Experience of Conflict Transformation: The Cases of South Africa and Northern Ireland' (unpublished manuscript). Belfast: Queen's University.

Gurr, Ted Robert (1993). *Minorities at Risk: A Global View of Ethnopolitical Conflicts*. Washington, DC: United States Institute of Peace Press.

Haggard, Stephan and Kaufmann, Robert R. (1995). *The Political Economy of Democratic Institutions*. Princeton, NJ: Princeton University Press.

Hall, Peter (1986). *Governing the Economy*. New York: Oxford University Press.

Halpern, Sue (1986). 'The Disorderly Universe of Consociational Democracy'. *West European Politics*, 9/2: 181–97.

Hannum, Hurst (1990). *Autonomy, Sovereignty, and Self-Determination: The Accommodation of Conflicting Rights*. Philadelphia: University of Philadelphia Press.

Hardgrave, Robert (1969). *The Nadars of Tamil Nadu*. Berkeley: University of California Press.

Hardin, Russell (1989). 'Why a Constitution?', in Bernard Grofman and Donald Wittmanz (eds), *The Federalist Papers and the New Institutionalism*. New York: Agathon Press.

Haseman, John B. (1999). 'Interview: A Deliberately Planned Covert Operation'. *Van Zorge Report on Indonesia*, 24: 18–19 (9 October). http:www.vanzorgereport.com.

Hazan, Reuven Y. (1996a). 'Presidential Parliamentarism: Direct Popular Election of the Prime Minister, Israeli's New Electoral and Political System'. *Electoral Studies*, 15/1: 21–37.

——(1996b). 'Three Levels of Election in Israel: The 1996 Party, Parliamentary and Prime Ministerial Elections'. *Representation*, 34: 240–9.

Hazell, Robert and O'Leary, Brendan (1999). 'A Rolling Programme of Devolution: Slippery Slope or Safeguard of the Union?', in R. Hazell (ed.), *Constitutional Futures: A History of the Next Ten Years*. Oxford: Oxford University Press.

Hearl, Derek J., Budge, Ian, and Pearson, Bernard (1996). 'Distinctiveness of Regional Voting: A Comparative Analysis Across the European Community (1979–1993)'. *Electoral Studies*, 15/2: 167–82.

Hedström, Peter and Swedberg, Richard (1998). *Social Mechanisms: An Analytical Approach to Social Theory*. New York: Cambridge University Press.

Heintze, Hans-Joachim (1998). 'On the Legal Understanding of Autonomy', in Markku Suksi (ed.), *Autonomy: Applications and Implications*. The Hague: Kluwer.

Hellman, Joel (1997). 'Constitutions and Economic Reform in the Post-Communist Transitions', in Jeffrey Sachs and Katharina Pistor (eds), *The Rule of Law and Economic Reform in Russia*. Boulder, CO: Westview Press.

——(1998). 'Winners Take All: The Politics of Partial Reform'. *World Politics*, 50/2: 203–34.

Hideo, Otake (ed.) (1998). *How Electoral Reform Boomeranged: Continuity in Japanese Campaigning Style*. Tokyo: Japan Center for International Exchange.

Hillyard, Paddy (2000). 'Police Bill is Not Faithful Reflection of Patten'. *Irish Times*, 2 August.

Holmes, Stephen (1995). 'Conceptions of Democracy in the Draft Constitutions of Post-Communist Countries', in Beverly Crawford (ed.), *Markets, States and Democracy: The Political Economy of Post-Communist Transformation*. Boulder, CO: Westview Press.

Horowitz, Donald L. (1979). 'About-Face in Africa: The Return of Civilian Rule in Nigeria'. *Yale Review*, 68/2: 192–206.

——(1985). *Ethnic Groups in Conflict*. Berkeley: University of California Press.

——(1987). 'Is the Presidency Failing?'. *The Public Interest*, 88/Summer: 3–27.

——(1989*a*). 'Incentives and Behaviour in the Ethnic Politics of Sri Lanka and Malaysia'. *Third World Quarterly*, 11/4: 18–35.

——(1989*b*). 'Is There a Third-World Policy Process?'. *Policy Sciences*, 22/3–4: 197–212.

——(1989*c*). 'Ethnic Conflict Management for Policymakers', in J. P. Montville (ed.), *Conflict and Peacemaking in Multiethnic Societies*. Lexington, MA: Heath.

——(1989*d*). 'Making Moderation Pay: The Comparative Politics of Ethnic Conflict Management', in J. P. Montville (ed.), *Conflict and Peacemaking in Multiethnic Societies*. Lexington, MA: Heath.

——(1990). 'Debate: Presidents v. Parliaments'. *Journal of Democracy*, 1: 730–91.

——(1991). *A Democratic South Africa? Constitutional Engineering in a Divided Society*. Berkeley: University of California Press.

——(1993). 'Democracy in Divided Societies'. *Journal of Democracy*, 4: 18–38.

——(1996). 'Comparing Democratic Systems', in Larry Diamond and Marc F. Plattner (eds), *A The Global Resurgence of Democracy*. Baltimore, MD: The Johns Hopkins University Press.

——(1997*a*). 'Self-Determination: Politics, Philosophy, and Law'. *NOMOS*, 39: 421–63.

——(1997*b*): 'Encouraging electoral accommodation in divided societies', in Brij V. Lal and Peter Larmour (eds), *Electoral Systems in Ethnically Divided Societies: The Fiji Constitution Review*. Canberra: National Centre for Development Studies, The Australian National University.

——(1999). 'The Draft Laws on Indonesian Political Parties, Elections, and Legislative Bodies: An Analysis' (unpublished manuscript). Washington, DC: National Democratic Institute.

——(2000). 'Constitutional Design: An Oxymoron?'. *NOMOS*, 42: 253–84.

——(2002). 'Explaining the Northern Ireland Agreement: The Sources of an Unlikely Constitutional Consensus'. *British Journal of Political Science*, 32/2: 57–84.

Hsieh, John Fuh-sheng (1997). 'Electoral Politics in New Democracies in the Asia-Pacific Region'. *Representation*, 34/3/4: 157–65.

——and Niou, Emerson M. S. (1996). 'Taiwan's March 1996 Elections'. *Electoral Studies*, 15: 545–50.

Human Rights Watch/Africa (1995). *Nigeria: The Ogoni Crisis; A Case-Study of Military Repression in Southeastern Nigeria*. New York: Human Rights Watch.

——(1996). *Nigeria: Permanent Transition; Current Violations of Human Rights in Nigeria*. New York: Human Rights Watch.

Huntington, Samuel P. (1991). *The Third Wave: Democratization in the Late Twentieth Century*. Norman: University of Oklahoma Press.

Huskey, Eugene (1997). 'Kyrgyzstan: The Fate of Political Liberalization', in Karen Dawisha and Bruce Parrott (eds), *Conflict, Cleavage and Change in Central Asia and the Caucasus*. Cambridge: Cambridge University Press.

Inman, Robert P. and Rubinfeld, Daniel L. (1997). 'The Political Economy of Federalism', in Dennis Mueller (ed.), *Perspectives on Public Choice*. New York: Cambridge University Press.

International Crisis Group (1998). 'Changing the Logic of Bosnian Politics: Discussion Paper on Electoral Reform'. Brussels (10 March).

——(1999). 'Breaking the Mould: Electoral Reform in Bosnia and Herzegovina'. Brussels (4 March).

International Election Observation Mission (1999). *Post Election Statement No. 3*. Washington, DC: National Democratic Institute (July).

International Symposium on the Making of the Eritrean Constitution (1995). *A Summary Report*. Asmara: International Symposium on the Making of the Eritrean Constitution (7–12 January).

Ishiyama, John (1997). 'Transitional Electoral Systems in Post-Communist Eastern Europe'. *Political Science Quarterly*, 112/1: 95–115.

Jacobsohn, J. (1993). *Apple of Gold: Constitutionalism in Israel and the US*. Princeton, NJ: Princeton University Press.

Jasiewiecz, Krzysztof (1994). 'Poland'. *European Journal of Political Research*, 26: 130–67.

——(1997). 'Poland: Walesa's Legacy to the Presidency', in Ray Taras (ed.), *Post-Communist Presidents*. Cambridge: Cambridge University Press.

Jenkins, Roy (Lord Jenkins) (1998). *The Report of the Independent Commission on the Voting System* (Cm 4090-1). London: Stationery Office.

Jervis, Robert (1976). *Perception and Misperception in International Politics*. Princeton, NJ: Princeton University Press.

Jones, Mark P. (1994). 'Presidential Election Laws and Multipartyism in Latin America'. *Political Research Quarterly*, 47: 41–57.

——(1995a). *Electoral Laws and the Survival of Presidential Democracies*. Notre Dame: University of Notre Dame Press.

——(1995b). 'A Guide to the Electoral Systems of the Americas'. *Electoral Studies*, 14/1: 5–22.

——(1997). 'A Guide to the Electoral Systems of the Americas: An Update'. *Electoral Studies*, 16/1: 13–15.

Joseph, Richard (1987). 'Principles and Practices of Nigerian Military Government', in John Harbeson (ed.), *The Military in African Politics*. New York: Praeger.

Jowitt, Kenneth (1992). *New World Disorder*. Berkeley: University of California Press.

Joye, Michael and Igweike, Kingsley (1982). *Introduction to the 1979 Nigerian Constitution*. London: Macmillan.

Jung, Courtney and Shapiro, Ian (1995). 'South Africa's Negotiated Transition: Democracy, Opposition, and the New Constitutional Order'. *Politics and Society*, 3: 269–308.

Kashyap, Anirban (1990). *Disintegration and Constitution*. New Delhi: Lancer Books.

Katz, Richard (1997). *Democracy and Elections*. Oxford: Oxford University Press.

Katzenstein, Mary (1979). *Ethnicity and Equality*. Ithaca, NY: Cornell University Press.

Kavanagh, Dennis (1992). 'David Butler and the Study of Elections', in Dennis Kavanagh (ed.), *Electoral Politics*. Oxford: Clarendon Press.

Kaviraj, Sudipta (1997). 'The Modern State in India', in Martin Doornbos and Sudipta Kaviraj (eds), *Dynamics of State Formation*. New Delhi: Sage Publications.

Keeler, John T. S. and Schain, Martin A. (1997). 'Institutions, Political Poker, and Regime Evolution in France', in Kurt von Mettenheim (ed.), *Presidential Institutions and Democratic Politics: Comparing Regional and National Contexts*. Baltimore, MD: The Johns Hopkins University Press.

Khmelko, Valeri and Wilson, Andrew (1998). 'Regionalism and Ethnic and Linguistic Cleavage in Ukraine', in Taras Kuzio (ed.), *Contemporary Ukraine*. Armonk, NY: M. E. Sharpe.

Kingdon, John W. (1984). *Agendas, Alternatives, and Public Policies*. Boston: Little, Brown.

Kitschelt, Herbert (1992). 'The Formation of Party Systems in East Central Europe'. *Politics and Society*, 20/1: 7–50.

——, Mansfeldova, Zdenka, Markowski, Radek, and Toka, Gabor (1999). *Post-communist Party Systems: Competition, Representation, and Interparty Cooperation*. Cambridge: Cambridge University Press.

Klug, Heinz (2000). 'How the Centre Holds: Managing Claims for Regional and Ethnic Autonomy in a Democratic South Africa', in Yash Ghai (ed.), *Autonomy and Ethnicity: Negotiating Claims in Multi-ethnic States*. Cambridge: Cambridge University Press.

Krasner, Stephen (1999). *Sovereignty: Organized Hypocrisy*. Princeton, NJ: Princeton University Press.

Kompas (1998). 22 May.

Komsomol'skaia pravda (1991). 14 March.

Krupavicius, A. (1997). 'The Lithuanian Parliamentary Elections of 1996'. *Electoral Studies*, 16: 541–75.

Kurian, George Thomas (ed.) (1998). *World Encyclopedia of Parliaments and Legislatures* (2 vols). Washington, DC: Congressional Quarterly, Inc.

Kymlicka, Will (1998*a*). 'Is Federalism a Viable Alternative to Secession?', in Percy Lehning (ed.), *Theories of Secession*. London: Routledge.

——(1998*b*). *Finding our Way: Rethinking Ethnocultural Relations in Canada*. Toronto: Oxford University Press.

Laakso, Markku and Taagepera, Rein (1979). 'Effective Number of Parties: A Measure with Application to West Europe'. *Comparative Political Studies*, 12: 3–27.

Lakeman, Enid (1974). *How Democracies Vote*. London: Faber and Faber.

Lal, Brij (1993). 'Chiefs and Indians: Elections and Politics in Contemporary Fiji'. *The Contemporary Pacific: A Journal of Island Affairs*, 5: 275–301.

——(1995). 'Rabuka's Republic: The Fiji Snap Elections of 1994,' in *Pacific Studies*, 18: 47–77.

——(1998). *Another Way: The Politics of Constitutional Reform in Post-Coup Fiji*. Canberra: Asia Pacific Press.

——(1999*a*). 'Towards a United Future: Report of the Fiji Constitution Review Commission'. *Journal of Pacific History*, 32: 71–84.

——(1999*b*). 'The Voice of the People: Ethnic Identity and Nation Building in Fiji'. *Journal of the Pacific Society*, 22/3/4: 1–12.

——(1999*c*). *A Time to Change: The Fiji General Elections of 1999* (Discussion Paper 23). Canberra: Department of Political and Social Change, The Australian National University.

——(ed.) (2000). *Fiji Before the Storm: Elections and the Politics of Development*. Canberra: Asia Pacific Press.

——and Larmour, Peter (eds) (1997). *Electoral Systems in Ethnically Divided Societies: The Fiji Constitution Review*. Canberra: National Centre for Development Studies, The Australian National University.

Lamounier, Bolivar (1994). Brazil: Toward Parliamentarism?', in Juan J. Linz and A. Valenzuela (eds), *The Failure of Presidential Democracy: The Case of Latin America*. Baltimore, MD: The Johns Hopkins University Press.

Lande, Carl (1989). 'Social Cleavage and Political Party Division in Post-Marcos Philippines'. Paper read at Third International Philippine Studies Conference, 1989, Manila.

Laver, Michael and Schofield, Norman (1998). *Multiparty Government: The Politics of Coalition in Europe*. Ann Arbor: University of Michigan Press.

Lavrov, A. (1996). 'Mify i rify Rossiiskogo biudzhetnogo federalizma' [Myths and Reefs of Russian Budgetary Federalism]. Manuscript for 'Open Society' Institute, Higher Education Programme, Moscow (December).

——(1997). 'Donory i izhdiventsy' [Donors and Dependants]. *Rossiiskie vesti*, 6 August.

Lawson, Stephanie (1993). 'Conceptual Issues in the Comparative Study of Regime Change and Democratization'. *Comparative Politics*, 25: 183–205.

Lewis, W. Arthur (1965). *Politics in West Africa*. London: Allen and Unwin.

Liddle, R. William (1991). 'The Relative Autonomy of the Third World Politician: Suharto and Indonesian Economic Development in Comparative Perspective'. *International Studies Quarterly*, 35: 403–27.

——(1996). *Leadership and Culture in Indonesian Politics*. Sydney: Allen and Unwin.

——(1997). 'Coercion, Co-optation, and the Management of Ethnic Relations in Indonesia', in Michael E. Brown and Sumit Ganguly (eds), *Government Policies and Ethnic Relations in Asia and the Pacific*. Cambridge, MA: The MIT Press.

——(1999). 'Indonesia's Democratic Opening'. *Government and Opposition*, 34: 94–116.

—— and Mujani, Saiful (2000). 'The Triumph of Leadership: Indonesian Voters and the 1999 Legislative Election'. Paper presented at the annual meeting of the American Political Science Association, Washington (September).

Lijphart, Arend (1969). 'Consociational Democracy'. *World Politics*, 21: 207–25.

——(1977). *Democracy in Plural Societies: A Comparative Exploration*. New Haven: Yale University Press..

——(1984). *Democracies: Patterns of Majoritarian and Consensus Government in Twenty-One Countries*. New Haven: Yale University Press.

——(1985). *Power-Sharing in South Africa*. Berkeley: Institute of International Affairs, University of California.

——(1986). 'Degrees of Proportionality of Proportional Representation Formulas', in Bernard Grofman and Arend Lijphart (eds), *Electoral Laws and Their Political Consequences*. New York: Agathon Press.

——(1990*a*). 'Size, Pluralism, and the Westminster Model of Democracy: Implications for the Eastern Caribbean', in Jorge Heine (ed.), *A Revolution Aborted: The Lessons of Grenada*. Pittsburgh: Pittsburgh University Press.

——(1990*b*). 'Electoral Systems, Party Systems and Conflict Management in Divided Societies', in R. Schirer (ed.), *Critical Choices for South Africa*. Cape Town: Oxford University Press.

——(1990*c*). 'Foreword: One Basic Problem, Many Theoretical Options— And a Practical Solution?', in J. McGarry and B. O'Leary (eds), *The Future of Northern Ireland*. Oxford: Clarendon Press.

——(1990*d*). 'The Puzzle of Indian Democracy: A Consociational Interpretation'. *American Political Science Review*, 90/2.

——(1991*a*). 'Constitutional Choices for New Democracies'. *Journal of Democracy*, 2: 72–84.

——(1991*b*). 'Proportional Representation: Double Checking the Evidence'. *Journal of Democracy*, 2: 42–8.

——(ed.) (1992). *Parliamentary versus Presidential Government*. Oxford: Oxford University Press.

Lijphart, Arend (1993). 'Constitutional Choices for New Democracies', in L. Diamond and M. F. Plattner (eds), *The Global Resurgence of Democracy*. Baltimore, MD: Johns Hopkins University Press.

——(1994*a*). *Electoral Systems and Party Systems: A Study of Twenty-Seven Democracies, 1945–1990*. New York: Oxford University Press.

——(1994*b*). 'Prospects for Power-Sharing in the New South Africa', in Andrew Reynolds (ed.), *Election '94 South Africa*. London: James Currey.

——(1994*c*). 'Presidentialism and Majoritarian Democracy', in Juan J. Linz and Arturo Valenzuala (eds), *The Failure of Presidential Democracy*. Baltimore, MD: Johns Hopkins University Press.

——(1995*a*). 'Multiethnic Democracy', in Seymour Martin Lipset *et al.* (eds), *The Encyclopedia of Democracy*. Washington, DC: Congressional Quarterly.

——(1995*b*). 'Electoral Systems', in Seymour Martin Lipset *et al.* (eds), *The Encyclopedia of Democracy*. Washington, DC: Congressional Quarterly.

——(1999). *Patterns of Democracy: Government Forms and Performance in 36 Countries*. New Haven: Yale University Press.

—— and Grofman, Bernard (eds) (1984). *Choosing an Electoral System: Issues and Alternatives*. New York: Praeger.

—— and Waisman, Carlos (1996). *Institutional Design in New Democracies*. Boulder, CO: Westview Press.

Lim, Hong Hai (1997). 'The Malayan Electoral System: Its Formulation and Change' (Ph.D. thesis). Kuala Lumpur: University of Malaya.

Limongi, Fernando and Figueiredo, Argelina (1995). 'Partidos Pol ticos na mara dos Deputados, 1989–94'. *Dados*, 38: 497–525.

Lindblom, Charles E. (1977). *Politics and Markets*. New York: Basic Books.

—— and Braybrooke, David (1963). *A Strategy of Decision*. New York: Free Press.

Linz, Juan J. (1990*a*). 'The Perils of Presidentialism'. *Journal of Democracy*, 1/1: 51–69.

——(1990*b*). 'The Virtues of Parliamentarism'. *Journal of Democracy*, 1/4: 73–91.

——(1994). 'Presidential or Parliamentary Democracy: Does it Make a Difference?', in Juan J. Linz and Arturo Valenzuela (eds), *The Failure of Presidential Democracy*. Baltimore, MD: The Johns Hopkins University Press.

——(1997). 'Democracy, Multinationalism, and Federalism'. Paper delivered at the conference on Democracy, Nationalism, and Federalism, Oxford University. 5–8 June.

—— and Stepan, Alfred (1996). *Problems of Democratic Transition and Consolidation: Southern Europe, South America and Eastern Europe*. Baltimore, MD: The Johns Hopkins University Press.

—— and Valenzuela, Arturo (eds) (1994). *The Failure of Presidential Democracy*. Baltimore, MD: The Johns Hopkins University Press, 1994.

Linz, Juan J., Stepan, Alfred, and Gunther, Richard (1995). 'Democratic Transition and Consolidation in Southern Europe, with Reflections on Latin America and Eastern Europe', in Richard Gunther, Nikiforos Diamandouros, and Hans-Jurgen Puhle (eds), *The Politics of Democratic Consolidation*. Baltimore, MD: The Johns Hopkins University Press.

Lipset, Seymour Martin (1963). *Political Man: The Social Bases of Politics*. Garden City, NY: Anchor Books.

Lohia, Rammanohar (1964). *The Caste System*. Hyderabad: Lohia Samata Vidyalaya Nyas.

Lovenduski, Joni and Norris, Pippa (eds) (1993). *Gender and Party Politics*. London: Sage.

Lucky, Christian (1994). 'Tables of Presidential Power'. *East European Constitutional Review*, 2/4: 81–94.

Lustick, Ian S. (1979). 'Stability in Deeply Divided Societies: Consociationalism versus Control'. *World Politics*, 31: 325–44.

——(1997). 'Lijphart, Lakatos, and Consociationalism'. *World Politics*, 50: 81–17.

MacKenzie, W. J. M. (1957). 'The Export of Electoral Systems'. *Political Studies*, 5: 240–57.

——(1958). *Free Elections: An Elementary Textbook*. London: Allen and Unwin.

Mackintosh, John (1962). 'Federalism in Nigeria'. *Political Studies*, 10/3: 223–47.

——(1966). *Nigerian Government and Politics*. Evanston: Northwestern University Press.

Madden, A. F. (1980). '"Not for Export": The Westminster Model of Government and British Colonial Practice', in N. Hillmer and P. Wigley (eds), *The First British Commonwealth: Essays in Honour of Nicolas Mansergh*. London: Frank Cass.

Mainwaring, Scott (1993). 'Presidentialism, Multipartism, and Democracy: The Difficult Combination'. *Comparative Political Studies*, 26/2: 198–228.

——and Scully, Timothy (eds) (1995). *Building Democratic Institutions: Party Systems in Latin America*. Stanford: Stanford University Press.

——and Shugart, Matthew S. (1997a). 'Presidentialism and Democracy in Latin America: Rethinking the Terms of the Debate', in Scott Mainwaring and Matthew Shugart (eds), *Presidentialism and Democracy in Latin America*. New York: Cambridge University Press.

—— ——(1997b). 'Conclusion: Presidentialism and the Party System', in Scott Mainwaring and Matthew Shugart (eds), *Presidentialism and Democracy in Latin America*. New York: Cambridge University Press.

Mallie, Eamonn and McKittrick, David (1996). *The Fight for Peace: The Secret Story Behind the Irish Peace Process*. London: Heinemann.

Manglapus, Raul S. (1987). *Will of the People: Original Democracy in Non-Western Societies*. New York: Greenwood.

Maphai, Vincent T. (1996). 'The New South Africa: A Season for Power-Sharing'. *Journal of Democracy*, 7: 67–81.

Massicotte, Louise and Blais, André (1999). 'Mixed Electoral Systems: A Conceptual and Empirical Survey'. *Electoral Studies*, 18: 341–66.

Mattes, Robert B. and Gouws, Amanda (1999). 'Race, Ethnicity and Voting Behavior: Lessons from South Africa', in Timothy Sisk and Andrew Reynolds (eds), *Electoral Systems and Conflict in Divided Societies*. Washington, DC: USIP Press.

Mbanefoh, Gini (1986). *Military Presence and the Future of Nigerian Fiscal Federalism*. Ibadan: Faculty of Social Sciences, University of Ibadan.

McCrudden, Christopher (1999*a*). 'Equality and the Good Friday Agreement', in J. Ruane and J. Todd (eds), *After the Good Friday Agreement: Analysing Political Change in Northern Ireland*. Dublin: University College Dublin Press.

—— (1999*b*). 'Mainstreaming Equality in the Governance of Northern Ireland'. *Fordham International Law Journal*, 22/April: 1696–775.

—— (2001). 'Equality', in C. Harvey (ed.), *Human Rights, Equality and Democratic Renewal in Northern Ireland*. Oxford: Hart Publishing.

McGarry, John and O'Leary, Brendan (eds) (1990). *The Future of Northern Ireland*. Oxford: Oxford University Press.

—— —— (1995*a*). *Explaining Northern Ireland: Broken Images*. Oxford, UK, Cambridge, MA: Basil Blackwell.

—— —— (1995*b*). 'Five Fallacies: Northern Ireland and the Liabilities of Liberalism'. *Ethnic and Racial Studies*, 18: 837–61.

—— —— (1999). *Policing Northern Ireland: Proposals for a New Start*. Belfast: Blackstaff.

McGrath, Michael (2000). *The Catholic Church and Catholic Schools in Northern Ireland: The Price of Faith*. Dublin: Irish Academic Press.

McGregor, James (1994). *The Presidency in East Central Europe* (RFE/RL Research Report, 3/2). Prague (14 January).

McGuire, James W (1995). 'Political Parties and Democracy in Argentina', in Scott Mainwaring and Timothy Scully (eds), *Building Democratic Institutions: Party Systems in Latin America*. Stanford: Stanford University Press.

McKittrick, David (2001). 'The Running Man of Drumcree'. *Independent on Sunday*, 1 July.

Mendelsohn, O. and Vicziany, M. (1994). 'The Untouchables', in O. Mendelsohn and U. Baxi (eds), *The Rights of Subordinated Peoples*. Delhi: Oxford University Press.

—— —— (1998). *The Untouchables*. Cambridge: Cambridge University Press.

Menon, V. P. (1956). *The Story of the Integration of the Indian States*. Calcutta: Orient-Longmans.

Mihailisko, Kathleen (1997). 'Belarus: Retreat to Authoritarianism', in Karen Dawisha and Bruce Parott (eds), *Democratic Changes and Authoritarian Reactions in Ukraine, Belarus, and Moldova*. Cambridge: Cambridge University Press.

Milanovich, Branko (1998). *Income, Inequality, and Poverty during the Transition from Planned to Market Economy*. Washington, DC: World Bank.

Mill, John Stuart (1861 [1958]). *Considerations on Representative Government*. New York: Liberal Arts Press.

Milne, David (1994). 'Exposed to the Glare: Constitutional Camouflage and the Fate of Canada's Federation', in Leslie Seidle (ed.), *Seeking a New Partnership: Asymmetrical and Confederal Options*. Ottawa: Institute of Public Policy.

Mitchell, George C. (2000). *Making Peace*. Berkeley: University of California Press.

Mitchell, Paul, O'Leary, Brendan, and Evans, Geoffrey (2001). 'Northern Ireland: Flanking Extremists Bite the Moderates and Emerge in Their Clothes'. *Parliamentary Affairs* (forthcoming).

Moraski, Bryonand and Loewenberg, Gerhard (1999). 'The Effect of Legal Thresholds on the Revival of Former Communist Parties in East-Central Europe'. *Journal of Politics*, 61/1: 151–70.

Morrison, Donald George, Mitchell, Robert Cameron, and Paden, John Naber (1989). *Black Africa: A Comparative Handbook* (2nd edn). New York: Paragon House.

Moser, Robert (1999). 'Electoral Laws and the Number of Parties in Post-communist States'. *World Politics*, 51: 359–84.

Motyl, Alexander and Krawchenko, Bohdan (1997). 'Ukraine: From Empire to Statehood', in Ian Bremmer (ed.), *New States, New Politics: Building the Post-Soviet Nations*. New York: Cambridge University Press.

Mozaffar, Shaheen (1997). 'Electoral Systems and their Political Effects in Africa: A Preliminary Analysis'. *Representation*, 34/3/4: 148–56

Murphy, Alexander (1995). 'Belgium's Regional Divergence: Along the Road to Federation', in Graham Smith (ed.), *Federalism: The Multiethnic Challenge*. London: Longman.

Nachmias, David and Sened, Itai (1998). 'The Bias of Pluralism: The Redistributional Effects of the New Electoral Law in Israel's 1996 Election', in Asher Arian and Michal Shamir (eds), *Election in Israel—1996*. Albany: SUNY Press.

Nasution, Adnan Buyung (1992). *The Aspiration for Constitutional Government in Indonesia*. Jakarta: Sinar Harapan.

National Democratic Institute (1999). *The 1999 Presidential Election, MPR General Session and Post-Election Developments in Indonesia: A Post-Election Assessment Report*. Washington, DC: National Democratic Institute (28 November).

Nehru, Jawaharlal (1989). *The Discovery of India*. Delhi: Oxford University Press.

New Nigerian Newspapers (1981). *The Constitution of the Federal Republic of Nigeria 1979*. Kaduna: New Nigerian Newspapers.

Ní Aoláin, Fionnuala (2000). *The Politics of Force: Conflict Management and State Violence in Northern Ireland*. Belfast: Blackstaff Press.

Nohlen, Dieter (ed.) (1993). *Enciclopedia Electoral Latinoamericana y del Caribe*. San Jose, Costa Rica: Instituto Interamericana de Derechos Humanos.

Nohlen, Dieter (ed.) (1996). *Elections and Electoral Systems*. Delhi: Macmillan.

Nordlinger, Eric A. (1972). *Conflict Regulation in Divided Societies*. Cambridge, MA: Harvard University Center for International Affairs

Norris, Pippa (1985). 'Women in European Legislative Elites'. *West European Politics*, 8/4: 90–101.

——(1995). 'The Politics of Electoral Reform'. *International Political Science Review* (Special Issue on Electoral Reform), 16: 65–78.

——(1997a). 'Choosing Electoral Systems: Proportional, Majoritarian and Mixed Systems'. *International Political Science Review*, 18: 297–312.

——(1997b). *Electoral Change Since 1945*. Oxford: Blackwell.

——(1997c). 'Equality Strategies in the UK', in Frances Gardiner (ed.), *Sex Equality Policy in Western Europe*. London: Routledge.

——(ed.) (1997d). *Passages To Power: Legislative Recruitment In Advanced Democracies*. Cambridge: Cambridge University Press.

——(1997e). 'Anatomy of a Labour Landslide', in Pippa Norris and Neil Gavin (eds), *Britain Votes 1997*. Oxford: Oxford University Press.

——(1998a). 'Institutional Explanations for Political Support', in Pippa Norris (ed.), *Critical Citizens: Global Support For Democratic Governance*. Oxford: Oxford University Press.

——(1998b). *Critical Citizens: Global Support For Democratic Governance*. Oxford: Oxford University Press.

——(2000). 'Women's Representation and Electoral Systems', in Richard Rose (ed.), *The International Encyclopedia of Elections*. Washington, DC: CQ Press.

—— and Crewe, Ivor (1994). 'Did the British Marginals Vanish? Proportionality and Exaggeration in the British Electoral System Revisited'. *Electoral Studies*, 13: 201–21.

—— and Lovenduski, Joni (1995). *Political Recruitment: Gender, Race and Class in the British Parliament*. Cambridge: Cambridge University Press.

North, Douglass C. (1990). *Institutions, Institutional Change and Economic Performance*. Cambridge: Cambridge University Press.

Northern Ireland Assembly (1999). *Official Report* (Hansard). http:www.ni-assembly.gov.uk/hansard.htm

Norton, Robert (1990). *Race and Politics in Fiji* (revised edn). Brisbane: University of Queensland Press.

Nwabueze, Ben (1987). 'Nigerian Constitution–2'. *Guardian* (Lagos),18 June.

Obasanjo, Olusegun (1989). *Constitution for National Integration*. Lagos: Friends Foundation Publishers.

——(1994). 'Keynote Address', in A. Mahadi, G. Kwanashie, and A. Yakubu (eds), *Nigeria: the State of the Nation*. Kaduna: Arewa House.

O'Brien, Patrick K. (1999). *Oxford Atlas of World History*. Oxford: Oxford University Press.

O'Donnell, Guillermo (1994). 'Delegative Democracy'. *Journal of Democracy*, 1: 55–69.

—— (1996). 'Illusions About Consolidation'. *Journal of Democracy*, 7: 34–51.

O'Duffy, Brendan and O'Leary, Brendan (1995). 'Tales from Elsewhere and an Hibernian Sermon', in H. M. Smith (ed.), *Turning Japanese? Britain with a Permanent Party of Government*. London: Lawrence and Wishart.

O'Leary, Brendan (1990). 'Appendix 4. Party Support in Northern Ireland, 1969–89', in J. McGarry and B. O'Leary (eds), *The Future of Northern Ireland*. Oxford: Oxford University Press.

—— (1990). 'More Green, Fewer Orange'. *Fortnight*, 281:12–15; 282: 16–17.

—— (1995). 'Afterword: What is Framed in the Framework Documents?'. *Ethnic and Racial Studies*, 18: 862–72.

—— (1997). 'The Conservative Stewardship of Northern Ireland 1979–97: Sound-Bottomed Contradictions or Slow Learning?' *Political Studies*, 45: 663–76.

—— (1999*a*). 'The 1998 British-Irish Agreement: Consociation Plus'. *Scottish Affairs*, 26/Winter: 1–22.

—— (1999*b*). 'A Bright Future and Less Orange' (Review of the Independent Commission on Policing for Northern Ireland). *Times Higher Education Supplement*, 19 November.

—— (1999*c*). 'The Implications for Political Accommodation in Northern Ireland of Reforming the Electoral System for the Westminster Parliament'. *Representation*, 35/2–3: 106–13.

—— (1999*d*). 'The Nature of the Agreement'. *Fordham Journal of International Law*, 22: 1628–67.

—— (1999*e*). 'The Nature of the British-Irish Agreement'. *New Left Review*, 233: 66–96.

—— (2000). 'What a Travesty: Police Bill is Just a Parody of Patten'. *Sunday Business Post*, 30 April.

—— (2001*a*). 'The Belfast Agreement and the Labour Government: How to Handle and Mishandle History's Hand', in A. Seldon (ed.), *The Blair Effect: The Blair Government 1997–2001*. London: Little, Brown & Company.

—— (2001*b*). 'The Character of the 1998 Agreement: Results and Prospects', in R. Wilford (ed.), *Aspects of the Belfast Agreement*. Oxford: Oxford University Press.

—— (2001*c*). 'Comparative Political Science and the British-Irish Agreement', in J. McGarry (ed.), *Northern Ireland in a Divided World*. Oxford: Oxford University Press.

—— (2001*d*). 'The Protection of Human Rights under the Belfast Agreement'. *Political Quarterly*, 72: 353–65.

—— and Evans, Geoffrey (1997). 'Northern Ireland: La Fin de Siècle, The Twilight of the Second Protestant Ascendancy and Sinn Féin's Second Coming'. *Parliamentary Affairs*, 50: 672–80.

——, Grofman, Bernard, and Elklit, Jorgen (2001). 'Divisor Methods to Facilitate and Sequence Portfolio Allocation in a Multi-Party Cabinet Coalition: Evidence from Northern Ireland.' Paper delivered at the European Public Choice Conference, Paris, 19 April.

O'Leary, Brendan and McGarry, John (1996). *The Politics of Antagonism: Understanding Northern Ireland* (2nd edn). London and Atlantic Heights, NJ: Athlone.

——, Lyne, Tom, Marshall, Jim, and Rowthorn, Bob (1993). *Northern Ireland: Sharing Authority*. London: Institute of Public Policy Research.

Olson, David (1998). 'The Parliaments of New Democracies and the Politics of Representation', in S. White, J. Batt, and P. G. Lewis (eds), *Developments in Central and East European Politics 2*. Durham, NC: Duke University Press.

O'Neil, Patrick (1997). 'Political Transition and Executive Conflict: The Balance or Fragmentation of Power?', in Ray Taras (ed.), *Post-Communist Presidents*. Cambridge: Cambridge University Press.

Onuf, Peter S. (1983). *The Origins of the Federal Republic*. Philadelphia: University of Pennsylvania Press.

Ordeshook, Peter C. and Olga Shvetsova (1994). 'Ethnic Heterogeneity, District Magnitude and the Number of Parties'. *American Journal of Political Science*, 38: 100–23.

—— —— (1996). 'Whither Russian Federalism?' (manuscript). Pasadena: California Institute of Technology (November).

Osaghae, Eghosa (1992). 'The Status of State Governments in Nigeria's Federalism'. *Publius: The Journal of Federalism*, 22/3: 181–200.

Oyediran, Oyeleye (1996). 'Introduction', in Oyeleye Oyediran (ed.), *Governance and Development in Nigeria: Essays in Honor of Billy Dudley*. Ibadan: Agbo Areo Publishers.

Pajić, Zoran (1999). 'A Critical Appraisal of the Dayton Constitution of Bosnia and Herzegovina', in Wolfgang Benedek (ed.), *Human Rights in Bosnia and Herzegovina after Dayton: From Theory to Practice*. The Hague: Martinus Nijhoff.

Pammett, Jon H. and DeBardeleben, Joan (eds) (1988). 'Special Issue: Voting and Elections in Post-Communist States'. *Electoral Studies*, 17/2.

Parekh, Bhiku (1997). 'Cultural Diversity and the Modern State', in Martin Doornbos and Sudipta Kaviraj (eds), *Dynamics of State Formation*. New Delhi: Sage Publications.

Patten, Christopher (1999). *A New Beginning: The Report of the Independent Commission on Policing for Northern Ireland*. Belfast: Independent Commission on Policing for Northern Ireland.

Paul, James (2000). 'Ethnicity and the New Constitutional Orders of Ethiopia and Eritrea', in Yash Ghai (ed.), *Autonomy and Ethnicity: Negotiating Claims in Multi-ethnic States*. Cambridge: Cambridge University Press.

Peaslee, Amos J. (1970). *Constitutions of Nations*. The Hague: Nijhoff.

Peeters, Patrick (1994). 'Federalism: A Comparative Perspective—Belgium Transforms from a Unitary to a Federal State', in Bertus de Villiers (ed.), *Evaluating Federal Systems*. Cape Town: Juta.

Peled, Yaiv (1992). 'Ethnic Democracy and the Legal Construction of Citizenship: Arab Citizens of the Jewish State', *American Political Science Review*, 86: 432–44.

Petrov, Nikolai (1999). 'Sovet federatsii i predstavitel'stvo interesov regionov v Tsentre' [The Federation Council and the representation of regional interests in the Center], in Nikolai Petrov (ed.), *Regiony Rossii v 1998 G.* Moscow: Moscow Tsentr Carnegie.

Phadnis, Urmila (1968). *Towards the Integration of Indian States, 1919–1947.* Bombay: Asia Publishing House.

Philips, Adedotun (1997). *Nigeria's Fiscal Policy, 1998–2010* (Monograph Series No. 17). Ibadan: Nigerian Institute of Social and Economic Research.

Pomper, Gerald (1997). *The Election of 1996.* Chatham, NJ: Chatham House.

Posen, Barry R. (1993). 'The Security Dilemma and Ethnic Conflict'. *Survival*, 35/1: 27–47.

Powell, G. Bingham, Jr (1989). 'Constitutional Design and Citizen Electoral Control'. *Journal of Theoretical Politics*, 1/2: 107–30.

—— and Whitten, Guy D. (1993). 'A Cross-National Analysis of Economic Voting: Taking Account of the Political Context'. *American Journal of Political Science*, 37: 391–414.

Power, Timothy J. and Gasiorowski, Mark J. (1997). 'Institutional and Democratic Consolidation in the Third World'. *Comparative Political Studies*, 30/2: 123–55.

Prasad, Satendra (2000). 'Fiji's 1999 General Elections: Outcomes and Prospects', in A. Haroon Akram-Lodhi (ed.), *Confronting Fiji Futures.* Canberra: Asia Pacific Press.

Przeworski, Adam (1991). *Democracy and the Market: Political and Economic Reforms in Latin America and Europe.* New York: Cambridge University Press.

——, Alvarez, Michael, Cheibub, José Antonio, and Limongi, Fernando (1996). 'What Makes Democracies Endure'. *Journal of Democracy*, 7/1: 39–55.

—— —— —— ——(2000). *Democracy and Development: Political Institutions and Well-Being in the World, 1950–1990.* Cambridge: Cambridge University Press.

Rabinovic, Itamar (1985). *The War for the Lebanon 1970–85.* Ithaca, NY: Cornell University Press.

Rae, Douglas (1971). *The Political Consequences of Electoral Laws.* New Haven: Yale University Press.

Reeve, Andrew and Ware, Alan (1992). *Electoral Systems: A Comparative and Theoretical Introduction.* London and New York: Routledge.

Reilly, Ben (1997). 'Preferential Voting and Political Engineering: A Comparative Study'. *Journal of Commonwealth and Comparative Politics*, 35/1: 1–19.

—— and Reynolds, Andrew (1999). *Electoral Systems and Conflict in Divided Societies.* Washington, DC: National Academy Press.

Reynolds, Andrew (1993). *Voting for a New South Africa.* Cape Town: Maskew Miller Longman.

——(1994). *Election '94 South Africa: The Campaign, Results and Future Prospects.* New York: St Martin's Press.

Reynolds, Andrew (1995). 'The Case for Proportionality'. *Journal of Democracy*, 6/2: 117–24.

——(1999*a*). *Electoral Systems and Democratization in Southern Africa*. Oxford: Oxford University Press.

——(1999*b*). 'Majoritarian or Power-Sharing Government'. Paper presented at the Conference on Constitutional Design 2000, Kellogg Institute, Notre Dame University, 9–11 December.

——, Reilly, Ben, *et al.* (1997). *The International IDEA Handbook of Electoral System Design*. Stockholm: International Institute for Democracy and Electoral Assistance.

Riker, William H. (1962). *The Theory of Political Coalitions*. New Haven: Yale University Press.

——(1964). *Federalism: Origin, Operation, Significance*. Boston: Little, Brown and Co.

——(1975). 'Federalism', in Fred Greenstein and Nelson Polsby (eds), *Handbook of Political Science*. New York: Harcourt Brace.

——(1990). 'Political Science and Rational Choice', in J. Alt and K. Shepsle (eds), *Perspectives on Positive Political Economy*. Cambridge: Cambridge University Press.

Ringmar, Erik (1996). *Identity, Interest and Action: A Cultural Explanation of Sweden's Intervention in the Thirty Years War*. Cambridge: Cambridge University Press.

Roberts, Nigel S. (1997),' "A Period of Enhanced Surprise, Disappointment, and Frustration"? The Introduction of a New Electoral System in New Zealand', in Jørgen Elklit (ed.), *Electoral Systems for Emerging Democracies: Experiences and Suggestions*. Copenhagen: Danida.

Rokkan, Stein (1970). *Citizens, Elections, Parties: Approaches to the Comparative Study of the Processes of Development*. Oslo: Universitetsforlaget.

Rose, Richard (1995). 'Beware the Opinion Polls—There are Too Many Parties to Pick One Winner'. *Transitions*, 22: 6–13.

——, Munro, Neil, and Mackie, Tom (1998). *Elections in Central and Eastern Europe Since 1990*. Strathclyde: Centre for the Study of Public Policy.

Rothchild, Donald (1991). 'An Interactive Model for State-Ethnic Relations', in Francis Deng and William Zartman (eds), *Conflict Resolution in Africa*. Washington, DC: Brookings Institution.

Rudolph, Lloyd and Rudolph, Susanne (1967). *The Modernity of Tradition*. Chicago: University of Chicago Press.

Rule, Wilma (1994). 'Women's Underrepresentation and Electoral Systems'. *PS: Political Science and Politics*, 4: 689–92.

——and Zimmerman, Joseph (eds) (1994). *Electoral Systems in Comparative Perspective: Their Impact on Women and Minorities*. Westport, CT: Greenwood.

Said, Salim (1998). 'Suharto's Armed Forces: Building a Power Base in New Order Indonesia, 1966–1998'. *Asian Survey*, 38: 535–52.

Sakamoto, Takayuki (1999). 'Explaining Electoral Reform: Japan versus Italy and New Zealand'. *Party Politics*, 5: 419–38.

Sartori, Giovanni (1970). 'Concept Misformation in Comparative Politics'. *American Political Science Review*, 64: 1033–53.

—— (1976). *Parties and Party Systems: A Framework for Analysis*. Cambridge: Cambridge University Press.

—— (1986). 'The Influence of Electoral Systems: Faulty Laws or Faulty Methods?', in Bernard Grofman and Arend Lijphart (eds), *Electoral Laws and Their Political Consequences*. New York: Agathon Press.

—— (1997). *Comparative Constitutional Engineering: An Inquiry Into Structures, Incentives, and Outcomes* (2nd edn). New York: New York University Press.

Schelling, Thomas C. (1960). *The Strategy of Conflict*. Cambridge, MA: Harvard University Press.

Schiemann, John (1999). 'Risk, Radicalism, and Regime Change: Institutional Choice in Hungary, 1989' (Ph.D. thesis). New York: Department of Political Science, Columbia University.

Selassie, Bereket Habte (1999), 'Democracy and the Role of Parliament Under the Eritrean Constitution'. *North Carolina Journal of International Law and Commercial Regulation*, 24: 221–61.

Shafir, Michael (1992). 'Romania's Election Campaign: The Main Issues', *RFE/RL Research Report*, 36: 29–31.

—— (1995). 'Agony and Death of An Opposition Alliance' *Transition*, 8: 23–8.

Shlapentokh, Vladimir (1994). 'Public Opinion Polls and December 1993 Elections in Russia'. *Public Opinion Quarterly*, 58: 579–602.

Shugart, Matthew (1995). 'The Electoral Cycle and Institutional Sources of Divided Presidential Government'. *American Political Science Review*, 89: 327–43.

—— (1996). 'Executive-Legislative Relations in Post-Communist Europe'. *Transition*, 9: 6–11 (13 December).

—— (1998). 'The Inverse Relationship Between Party Strength and Executive Strength: A Theory of Politicians' Constitutional Choices'. *British Journal of Political Science*, 28: 1–29.

—— and Carey, John (1992). *Presidents and Assemblies: Constitutional Design and Electoral Dynamics*. Cambridge: Cambridge University Press.

Shvetsova, Olga (1999). 'A Survey of Post-Communist Electoral Institutions: 1990–1998'. *Electoral Studies*, 18: 397–409.

Simon, Janos (1997). 'Electoral Systems and Democracy in Central Europe, 1990–1994'. *International Political Science Review*, 18: 361–79.

Singh, K. S. (1993). *Languages and Scripts* (People of India, ix). Delhi: Oxford University Press.

—— (1994). *The Scheduled Tribes* (People of India, iii). New Delhi: Oxford University Press (for the Anthropological Survey of India),

Singh, Kashi and Singh, Rama (1984). 'Levels of Regional and Tribal Development in Tribal Areas: Are They Identical?'. *National Geographical Journal of India*, 30: 1–12.

Sinnott, Richard (1998). 'Centrist Politics Makes Modest but Significant Progress: Cross-Community Transfers were Low'. *Irish Times*, 29 June.

Sisk, Timothy D. (1996). *Power Sharing and International Mediation in Ethnic Conflicts*. Washington, DC: US Institute of Peace Press.

——and Reynolds, Andrew (1998). *Electoral Systems and Conflict Management in Africa*. Washington, DC: US Institute of Peace Press.

Smith, Donald E. (1963). *India as a Secular State*. Princeton, NJ: Princeton University Press.

Smith, Graham (ed.) (1995). *Federalism: The Multiethnic Challenge*. London: Longman.

Solchanyk, Roman (1994). 'The Politics of State Building: Centre-Periphery Relations in Post-Soviet Ukraine'. *Europe-Asia Studies*, 46/1: 47–68.

Solnick, Steven L. (1998). 'Hanging Separately: Cooperation, Cooptation and Cheating in Developing Federations'. Paper presented at Annual Meeting of the American Political Science Association, Boston, MA, 3–6 September.

Soyinka, Wole (1999). 'The Federal Quest'. *Daily Champion*. Lagos: 22 March.

Spruyt, Hendrik (1994). *The Sovereign State and Its Competitors: An Analysis of Systems Change*. Princeton, NJ: Princeton University Press.

——(1998). 'Rebellion in the Ranks: Incentives for Loyalty, Secession and Bids for Power among Imperial Agents'. Manuscript.

Stepan, Alfred (1997). 'Towards a New Comparative Analysis of Democracy and Federalism'. Background paper for the Conference on Democracy and Federalism, Oxford University, June.

——(1999). 'Federalism and Democracy: Beyond the US Model'. *Journal of Democracy* 10/4: 19–34.

——and Skach, Cindy (1993). 'Constitutional Frameworks and Democratic Consolidation: Parliamentarism Versus Presidentialism'. *World Politics*, 46/1: 1–22.

Stevens, R. Michael (1977). 'Asymmetrical Federalism: The Federal Principle and the Survival of the Small Republic'. *Publius: The Journal of Federalism*, 7/4: 171–203.

Strom, Kaare (1990). *Minority Government and Majority Rule*. Cambridge: Cambridge University Press.

Stuligross, David (1999). 'A Piece of Land to Call One's Own: Ethnic Federalism and Institutional Innovation in India' (Ph.D. thesis). Berkeley: Department of Political Science, University of California.

Suberu, Rotimi (1990). 'Political Opposition and Intergovernmental Relations in the Second Nigerian Republic'. *Journal of Commonwealth and Comparative Politics*, 28/3: 269–87.

——(1993). 'The Travails of Federalism in Nigeria'. *Journal of Democracy*, 4/4: 39–53.

——(1997). 'Federalism, Ethnicity and Regionalism', in Paul Beckett and Crawford Young (eds), *Dilemmas of Democracy in Nigeria*. Rochester: University of Rochester Press.

—— (1999). *Public Policies and National Unity in Nigeria* (Research Report No. 19). Ibadan: Development Policy Center.

Taagepera, Rein (1994). 'Beating the Law of Minority Attrition', in Wilma Rule and Joseph Zimmerman (eds), *Electoral Systems in Comparative Perspective*. Westport, CT: Greenwood.

—— (1997). 'The Tailor of Marrakesh: Western Electoral System Advice to Emerging Democracies', in Jørgen Elklit (ed), *Electoral Systems for Emerging Democracies: Experiences and Suggestions*. Copenhagen: Danida.

—— (1998). 'How Electoral Systems Matter for Democratization'. *Democratization*, 5/3: 68–91.

—— and Shugart, Matthew S. (1989). *Seats and Votes: The Effects and Determinants of Electoral Systems*. New Haven: Yale University Press.

Tambiah, Stanley (1992). *Buddhism Betrayed? Religion, Politics, and Violence in Sri Lanka*. Chicago: University of Chicago Press.

Tannam, Etain (1999). *Cross-Border Cooperation in the Republic of Ireland and Northern Ireland*. Basingstoke: Macmillan.

Taras, Raymond and Ganguly, Rajat (1998). *Understanding Ethnic Conflict*. New York: Longman.

TASS (1990). 7 August.

Taylor, Charles (1992). *Multiculturalism and the Politics of Recognition*. Princeton, NJ: Princeton University Press.

Taylor, Michael (1987). *Fiji: Future Imperfect*. Sydney: Allen and Unwin.

Thach, Charles C., Jr (1969). *Creation of the Presidency, 1773–1789* (2nd edn). Baltimore, MD: The Johns Hopkins University Press.

Thapar, Romila (1989). 'Imagined Religious Communities? Ancient History and the Modern Search for Hindu Identity'. *Modern Asian Studies*, 23/2: 209–31.

Thelen, Kathleen, and Steinmo, Sven (1992). 'Historical Institutionalism in Corporate Perspective', in Sven Steinmo, Kathleen Thelen, and Frank Longstreth (eds), *Structuring Politics: Historical Institutionalism in Comparative Politics*. New York and Cambridge: Cambridge University Press.

Thio, Li-am (1997). 'The Elected President and the Legal Control of Government', in Kevin Tan and Lam Peng Er (eds), *Managing Political Change in Singapore*. London: Routledge.

Thomson, Janice E. (1994). *Mercenaries, Pirates, and Sovereigns: State-Building and Extraterritorial Violence in Early Modern Europe*. Princeton, NJ: Princeton University Press.

Tilly, Charles (1990). *Coercion, Capital, and European States, AD 990–1990*. Cambridge, MA: Blackwell.

Treisman, Daniel (1998). 'Dollars and Democratization: The Role and Power of Money in Russia's Transitional Elections'. *Comparative Politics*, 31/1: 1–21.

—— (1999a). 'Political Decentralization and Economic Reform: A Game-theoretic Analysis'. *American Journal of Political Science*, 43: 488–517.

—— (1999b). *After the Deluge: Regional Crises and Political Consolidation in Russia*. Ann Arbor: University of Michigan Press.

Tsebelis, George (1990). 'Elite Interaction and Constitution Building in Consociational Democracies'. *Journal of Theoretical Politics*, 2: 5–29.

——(1995). 'Decision Making in Political Systems: Veto Players in Presidentialism, Parliamentarism, Multicameralism, and Multipartyism'. *British Journal of Political Science*, 25: 289–325.

Tully, James (1995). *Strange Multiplicity: Constitutionalism in an Age of Diversity*. Cambridge: Cambridge University Press.

Turner, Ralph H. (1956).'Role-Taking, Role Standpoint, and Reference-Group Behavior'. *American Journal of Sociology*, 61/4: 316–28.

van Schendelen, M. P. C. M. (1984). 'The Views of Arend Lijphart and Collected Criticisms'. *Acta Politica*, 19: 19–55.

Vakatora, Tomasi (1998). *From the Mangrove Swamps*. Suva: author's publication.

Varshney, Ashutosh (1993). 'Contested Meanings'. *Daedalus*, 3/Summer: 227–61.

——(2000). *Ethnic Conflict and Civic Life: Hindus and Muslims in India*. New Haven: Yale University Press.

Vengroff, Richard (1994). 'The Impact of Electoral System on the Transition to Democracy in Africa: The Case of Mali'. *Electoral Studies*,13: 29–37.

Verma, Rina (1997). 'Politics and Personal Laws in India' (Ph.D. thesis). Cambridge, MA: Department of Government, Harvard University.

Vowles, Jack, Aimer, Peter, Banducci, Susan, and Karp, Jeffrey (1998). *Voters' Victory? New Zealand's First Election under Proportional Representation*. Auckland: Auckland University Press.

Walzer, Michael (1997). *On Toleration*. New Haven: Yale University Press.

Watson, Alan (1985). *The Evolution of Law*. Baltimore, MD: The Johns Hopkins University Press.

Watts, Ronald (1994). 'Contemporary Views on Federalism', in Bertus de Villiers (ed.), *Evaluating Federal Systems*. Cape Town. Juta.

——(2000). 'Federalism and Diversity in Canada', in Yash Ghai (ed.), *Autonomy and Ethnicity: Negotiating Claims in Multi-ethnic States*. Cambridge: Cambridge University Press.

Weiner, Myron (1989). *The Indian Paradox*. Delhi and Newbury Park, CA: Sage Publications.

Weingast, Barry R. (1993). 'Constitutions as Governance Structures: The Political Foundations of Secure Markets'. *Journal of Institutional and Theoretical Economics*, 149/1: 286–320.

——(1995). 'The Economic Role of Political Institutions: Market-Preserving Federalism and Economic Development'. *Journal of Law, Economics and Organization*, 11: 1–31.

——(1997). 'The Political Foundations of Democracy and the Rule of Law'. *American Political Science Review*, 91: 245–63.

Welch, Claude (1995). 'The Ogoni and Self-Determination: Increasing Violence in Nigeria'. *Journal of Modern African Studies*, 33: 635–50.

West Africa (1966). London. 11 June: 647.

Whitaker, Sylvester (1991). 'The Unfinished State of Nigeria', in Richard Sklar and Sylvester Whitaker (eds), *African Politics and Problems in Development*. Boulder, CO: Lynne Rienner Publishers.

White, Stephen (1995). 'Public Opinion and Political Science in Postcommunist Russia'. *European Journal of Political Research*, 27: 507–26.

Whitten, Guy D., and Palmer, Harvey D. (1996). 'Cross-National Analyses of Economic Voting'. Paper delivered at the American Political Science Association Annual Meeting, San Francisco, 1996.

Whyte, John (1993). 'Dynamics of Social and Political Change in Northern Ireland', in D. Keogh and M. Haltzel (eds), *Northern Ireland and the Politics of Reconciliation*. Cambridge: Cambridge University Press.

Wilford, Rick (2001). 'The Assembly and the Executive', in R. Wilford (ed.), *Aspects of the Belfast Agreement*. Oxford: Oxford University Press.

Williams, Gavin (1980). *State and Society in Nigeria*. Idanre: Afrografika Publishers.

Williamson, Oliver (1985). *The Economic Institutions of Capitalism*. New York: The Free Press.

Wilson, Andrew (1997). 'Ukraine: Two Presidents and Their Powers', in Ray Taras (ed.), *Post-Communist Presidents*. Cambridge: Cambridge University Press.

Wimmer, Andreas (1997). 'Who Owns the State? Understanding Ethnic Conflict'. *Nations and Nationalism: Journal of the Association for the Study of Ethnic Conflict*, 3: 631–65.

Wirahadikusumah, Agus (ed.) (1999). *Indonesia Baru dan Tantangan TNI: Pemikiran Masa Depan*. Jakarta: Sinar Harapan.

Wolchik, Sharon (1997). 'Democratization and Political Participation in Slovakia', in Karen Dawisha and Bruce Parrott (eds), *The Consolidation of Democracy in East-Central Europe: Authoritarianism and Democratization in Postcommunist Societies 1*. Cambridge: Cambridge University Press.

World Bank (1997). *World Development Indicators 1997*. Washington, DC: World Bank (CD-Rom).

Zartman, I. William (1991). 'Conflict and Resolution: Contest, Cost, and Change'. *Annals of the American Academy of Political and Social Science*, 518 (November): 11–23.

Index